Robert Southey

❧ A LIFE ❧

Mark Storey

Oxford · New York

OXFORD UNIVERSITY PRESS

1997

Oxford University Press, Great Clarendon Street, Oxford OX2 6DP

Oxford New York

Athens Auckland Bangkok Bogota Bombay Buenos Aires
Calcutta Cape Town Dar es Salaam Delhi Florence Hong Kong
Istanbul Karachi Kuala Lumpur Madras Madrid Melbourne
Mexico City Nairobi Paris Singapore Taipei Tokyo Toronto

and associated companies in
Berlin Ibadan

Oxford is a trade mark of Oxford University Press

Published in the United States by
Oxford University Press Inc., New York

British Library Cataloguing in Publication Data
Data available

Library of Congress Cataloging in Publication Data
Storey, Mark.
Robert Southey: a life / Mark Storey.
p. cm.
1. Southey, Robert, 1774–1843—Biography.   2. Authors,
English—19th century—Biography.   I. Title.
PR5466.S76 1997   821'.7—dc20   96–38250
ISBN 0–19–811246–7

1 3 5 7 9 10 8 6 4 2

Typeset by Pure Tech India Ltd., Pondicherry
Printed in Great Britain by
Biddles Ltd.
Guildford and King's Lynn

FOR MY MOTHER
AND IN MEMORY OF
MY FATHER

PREFACE

WHEN it was said of Edward Dowden that he looked like a man born to write a life of Southey, the hit in both directions was deemed a palpable one. The Poet Laureate vilified by Byron and by Hazlitt could be appropriately and safely entombed in the English Men of Letters series; honourable burial would be preferable to misguided praise. That was a hundred years ago, and it is only recently that Southey has begun to emerge from the shadow of his detractors, to be taken seriously by scholars and critics. But, apart from some valuable facsimiles of first editions, there are no texts available; old copies of the *Life of Nelson* can be picked up in the odd second-hand bookshop, and anthologies of the Romantic period might rise to a few extracts, but that is the extent of it. The writer who in his lifetime was on a par with Wordsworth and Coleridge—and not just because they were friends and neighbours—is now less well known than the unknown writer he himself did not acknowledge—John Clare—in his account of 'Uneducated Poets' in 1831. This is a very strange state of affairs, and less an endorsement of Southey's faith in his 'hold upon posterity' than an index of the whirligig of time's cruel revenges.

The flame has been kept alight, but only just: soon after his death, his son Cuthbert and son-in-law John Warter produced valuable, if far from reliable, editions of much of his correspondence, ten volumes in all; Warter edited Southey's Common-place Books in four volumes, and *The Doctor*; M. H. FitzGerald produced the standard *Poetical Works* in 1909; some of Southey's Journals have been edited with due care. But when Jack Simmons wrote his Life of Southey in 1945, much material still remained unpublished; Simmons's work, brief and perceptive, has been the most reliable study of the man and his writings for fifty years. He absorbed the details of William Haller's 1917 study of Southey's early years (up to 1803), and managed to give a sense of the range and extent of Southey's achievement; he also pointed out that Southey, as Byron joked, rhymed with 'mouthey', but this has not stopped most people calling him, as the Lakers tended to, Suthey. Geoffrey Carnall produced, in 1960, an excellent account of *Southey and His Age*, again, like Simmons, having to resort to unpublished manuscript sources, and in the process giving a full account of Southey's complex political and literary allegiances. The publication of Kenneth Curry's two volumes of *New Letters* (1965) provided an undoubted boost to Southey's flagging reputation, as did Curry's other bibliographical work—less so his brief study of the life and work of 1975.

Southey's importance has begun to emerge, biographically, in Richard Holmes's wonderful book on Coleridge and Stephen Gill's masterly account of Wordsworth's life (both 1989). Marilyn Butler's Cambridge Inaugural Lecture of 1988 had provided an intimation of further work to come, from her and from other scholars of Romanticism, on Southey's place in the canon. But, since Simmons, no one, apart from Jean Raimond in France (1968), has tried to look at Southey whole. The material is available, in massive quantities, in libraries and repositories, but it is highly unlikely that the 2,000-odd unpublished letters (scattered here, there, and everywhere between Keswick and Kentucky) will ever be published; part of my task has been to sift through this mass of evidence, in an attempt to build up a portrait of Southey at least as true as his favourite portrait of himself, by Samuel Lane, which now hangs in his Alma Mater, Balliol College, Oxford.

In Trollope's *Lady Anna* (1874), a novel about radical politics in the first decades of the nineteenth century, a chapter is devoted to the 'Keswick Poet': every reader would have recognized the portrait:

There was then still living in that neighbourhood a great man, a poet, who had nearly carried to its close a life of great honour and of many afflictions... The poet was hardly yet an old man, but he had all the characteristics of age. His shoulders were bent, and his eyes were deep set in his head, and his lips were thin and fast closed. But the beautiful oval of his face was still there, in spite of the ravages of years, of labour, and of sorrow, and the special brightness of his eye had not yet been dimmed.

Many visitors to the beautiful house, Greta Hall, in Keswick, with its magnificent views across the Lakes, had recorded, with similar reverence and devotion, their impressions of the man who had settled there in 1803, virtually withdrawn from the world, nestling at the foot of Skiddaw, far from the madding crowd, until his death forty years later. A German, Philip Kempferhausen, made a visit to the Lakes in summer 1818, and sent some letters about the landscape, Wordsworth, and Southey, to *Blackwood's Edinburgh Magazine*, where they appeared the following year:

I found myself sitting in an elegant little parlour, with my unknown host, a lady, who I saw was his wife, and two very beautiful children. I know not how it was, but all at once I felt assured that I was in the house of Robert Southey. There reigned in the mansion so still, and yet so cheerful, an air of serenity—there was such a total absence of any professional air about its master, and, at the same time, something so much more elegant and scholar-like in his demeanour than I had ever seen in any English country-gentleman merely, that before I perceived in him any of the distinctive traits of the poet, or heard him say anything at all extraordinary, I ventured to hint, that I suspected the intellectual rank of the man in whose presence I had the honour to sit...I soon felt myself perfectly at ease; for there was no affectation in this lively and happy carelessness of mind, evidently unbending itself with pleasure in the bosom of a beautiful family, from those severe and higher studies which have raised his name among the immortals...His hair is black, and bushy, and strong, and gives him a bold, free, and even dignified look—his face is sharp—his nose high—and his eyes, without having that piercing look which is often felt to be disagreeable, because too searching, in the eyes of men of genius, are, without exception, the most acute and intelligent I ever beheld...

'I am not afraid of the judgment of the people of England on my character, either moral or intellectual,' said Southey to me that evening, with a confidence inspired by the consciousness of having deserved well of his country. He had no cause to fear. Even amid all the violence of faction—all the bitterness of party—all the prejudices of sectarian spleen—all the levity and indifference, real or affected, of mere worldly men to the character and pursuits of a recluse poet and philosopher like Southey;—how splendid and noble a reputation is his,—and with what authority his very name comes upon the ear when pronounced in any company of enlightened and good men, citizens, and Christians...

More is at stake here than the whims of critical fashion. It is certainly true that long narrative poems, with improbable plots and implausible characters, have lost their appeal; if it is not for *Balder Dead* that Matthew Arnold is now remembered, still less is Southey for *Roderick, The Last of the Goths* (however much admired by Byron, who, with his mockery of Southey's *Vision of Judgement*, perhaps did more than most, single-handedly, to destroy Southey's reputation). Those who know the story of the Three Bears (and who does not?) are surprised to hear that its first printed version comes from the poet they have been taught to mock. Partly it is a matter of the sheer amount and range of what Southey wrote: his collected poems filled ten volumes in 1838, his prose writings ranged from a mammoth *History of Brazil*, through a *History of the Peninsular War*, to his *Book of the Church*; Lives of *Wesley* and *Nelson* jostle with the *Life and Works of Cowper*, his last major undertaking. As Byron put it, admiringly, he was England's 'first existing entire man of letters'; but to be so prolific can lead, paradoxically, to writing yourself out of the history books. We cannot bear too much literariness.

There is an added dimension to Southey's decline and fall from favour; not only was he Poet Laureate (and that can be a neutral honour), he was regarded as the arch apostate of the Romantic period. The attacks from his contemporaries were as much to do with his politics, as he moved from the eager embrace of Revolutionary ideals as a young student at Oxford in the 1790s to something much more cautious within the decade, and then to his position as unofficial Tory establishment spokesman, writing for a *Quarterly Review* that supported an anti-Reform Government, whilst also writing poems which sang the praises of royalty, dead or alive. We can retort that Wordsworth and Coleridge—even Blake—traced similar arcs across the political firmament; but Southey was deemed to be more persistent, more consistent, as it were, in his inconsistency, readier to feign surprise that anyone should question his right to change his mind, or his right, as Hazlitt suggested, to insist that he was right, whatever anyone else might say, think, or do.

And yet, in *The Spirit of the Age* (1825), Hazlitt devoted twenty pages to Southey, an acknowledgement, apart from anything else, of his importance in any assessment of the period. Even Hazlitt, who let loose the full coruscating brilliance of his prose upon Southey's tergiversations, had good, kind things to say about him—as did many—for he recognized the central paradox, that Southey was a man well-loved and also well-hated, a reflection, perhaps, of his ability to love and also to hate others. Here is Hazlitt trying to sum up this weird man:

With a tall, loose figure, a peaked austerity of countenance, and no inclination to *embonpoint*, you would say he has something puritanical, something ascetic in his appearance. He answers to Mandeville's description of Addison, 'a parson in a tye-wig.' He is not a boon companion, nor does he indulge in the pleasures of the table, nor in any other vice; nor are we aware that Mr. Southey is chargeable with any human frailty but—*want of charity*! Having fewer errors to plead guilty to, he is less lenient to those of others. He was born an age too late. Had he lived a century or two ago, he would have been a happy as well as blameless character. But the distraction of the time has unsettled him, and the multiplicity of his pretensions have jostled with each other. No man in our day (at least no man of genius) has led so uniformly and entirely the life of a scholar from boyhood to the present hour, devoting himself to learning with the enthusiasm of an early love, with the severity and constancy of a religious vow—and well would it have been for him if he had confined himself to this, and not undertaken to pull down or to patch up the State! . . . In all the relations and charities of private life, he is correct, exemplary, generous, just. We never heard a single impropriety laid to his charge; and if he has many enemies, few men can boast more numerous or stauncher friends.—The variety and piquancy of his writings form a striking contrast to the mode in which they are produced. . . . He passes from verse to prose, from history to poetry, from reading to writing, by a stop-watch . . . His mind is after all rather the recipient and transmitter of knowledge, than the originator of it. He has hardly grasp of thought enough to arrive at any great leading truth. His passions do not amount to more than irritability. With some gall in his pen, and coldness in his manner, he has a great deal of kindness in his heart. Rash in his opinions, he is steady in his attachments—and is a man, in many particulars admirable, in all respectable—his political inconsistency alone excepted!

That, in its way, is fair, and strangely touching. Critics have more recently begun to acknowledge that Southey was a central figure from the mid-1790s until the 1830s; not only was he producing those epics Byron found tiresome and repetitive, he was engaged in all the political debates of the time. He did not always enjoy having to write to order, but necessity for him did, much of the time, prove the mother of invention. If we want to know about the complex relations between literature and politics, then we have to read Southey, whether it be to do with the French Revolution, the Napoleonic Wars, the Reform Bill, the industrial age, or the question of slavery. His strong sense of duty impelled him towards an engagement with those forces which he thought were operating to his country's detriment; that these forces changed over the years can be held against him, but that they did so is in itself a comment on more than just Southey, it is a comment on the turbulence of the age. When Hazlitt spoke of Southey's 'fierce extremes', he could have been speaking of the first thirty years of the century. For this reason, much of the narrative of this biography concerns Southey's varied life as a writer, trying to trace the growth and shifts in his ideas, placing them in as detailed a context as is possible, whilst recognizing that in his clockwork-like existence he is, one minute, writing a romance, like *The Curse of Kehama*, and, the next, writing a review of some minor Portuguese verse, and, the next, considering the problems of the Corn Laws. Writers as diverse as Coleridge, Lamb, Byron, Hazlitt, and Landor all acknowledged Southey's stature as a writer, both of poetry and of prose.

But Southey was not just a 'man of letters'. For all his self-confessed cold exterior, he led a life that was both exemplary and deeply moving: the following pages chart the many aspects of his life—his rebellious early years at Westminster and Oxford, his deep friendship with Coleridge, his strangely mysterious marriage (in that it is hard to know, quite, the force of the bond between him and the self-effacing Edith), his friendships with a range of interesting people (from William Wilberforce to John Rickman the census-taker, from the civil servant Grosvenor Bedford to the vivacious artist and writer Mary Barker), his family life at Greta Hall in Keswick. It is true that he was essentially a private man, and much of his happiness derived from the comfort that for him, only a wife and children could give. But the family was also the source of his greatest sorrows, and there would be no point in minimizing his life's tragedies. This biography explores as many facets as possible of a life that had its own nobility and heroism. Southey lived with the past, with the dead writers of the books that lined his study; but, for him, to write was a matter of breathing life into the dead, of asserting their importance. It would be a just reward if, by dwelling on his own life, readers were encouraged to see not only the purposeful shape and value of that life but the life represented in his own writings. He drew life and sustenance from those dead authors; we can do the same from him.

ACKNOWLEDGEMENTS

To devote a fair part of one's life to the life and work of another is a strange experience, intimidating, exhilarating, and at times solitary. I could not have completed this biography without the help and support of many people: although it is, relatively, a handful of years since I actively started to work on him, Southey has been in my mind, on and off, for very much longer. On the bicentenary of his birth, in August 1974, I gave a talk about him on Radio 3: the BBC producer was a young poet called Paul Muldoon, who, twenty years later, published a remarkable poem, *Madoc: A Mystery*, based on the premiss that Southey and Coleridge did indeed emigrate to their ideal colony in America. I would like to think that we both benefited from those few hours in the studio. From that point onwards I knew that Southey mattered, and that he deserved the kind of concentrated attention that very few had given him this century. It then became a question of persuading myself that, at some point in the future, I would be able to approach the task. Firm foundations were provided by a few scholars of a previous generation, by libraries across the world, and by colleagues and friends (not, happily, mutually exclusive).

William Haller, Jack Simmons, Kenneth Curry, and Jean Raimond have, in their different ways, contributed towards a better understanding of Southey: Curry, in particular with his bibliographical and editorial work, showed the extent of the materials, and thereby that of the problem. His edition of *New Letters* (1965) revealed just how much archival material remained unpublished and, incidentally, how unreliable were the nineteenth-century editions of Southey's correspondence. I could not have got very far without the generous help of librarians and archivists, whom I pestered with queries, requests for photocopies, and often with lengthy visits. There is a list, in the Select Bibliography, of where most of the Southey manuscripts are held, but I would particularly like to thank the following institutions and all their willing helpers for their hospitality, their co-operation, and their interest: the Beinecke Rare Book and Manuscript Library at Yale, the Berg Collection at the New York Public Library, the Bodleian Library in Oxford, Boston Public Library, the British Library, the Brotherton Library at Leeds, Cornell University Library, the Huntington Library in California, Keswick Museum and Art Gallery, the National Library of Scotland, the National Library of Wales, the Library of the University of Rochester, NY, and the Wordsworth Trust at Dove Cottage, Grasmere. For generous funds to visit these institutions I am particularly indebted to the British Academy, and to the Faculty of Arts at the University of Birmingham; study leave from the School of English at Birmingham gave me time to make such visits, and then to finish the writing. For help with illustrations I owe thanks to Dr John Jones of Balliol College Oxford, Jeff Cowton and the Trustees of Dove Cottage, and the National Portrait Gallery.

I would like to use the term 'colleagues'—not, I hope, presumptuously—to embrace not just those at Birmingham, but those from the wider community of scholars who have advised and encouraged at various times: in particular, in the early stages, Stephen Gill, Robert Woof, and, later, Marilyn Butler. The late and much-missed Edward Thompson gave me some valuable information about John Thelwall, and he and Dorothy Thompson provided much more than hospitality. Closer to home, a clutch of Birmingham colleagues lent invaluable support (and sometimes crucial help with technology ranging from the humble pencil to the more advanced word-processor); this list is, I fear, incomplete: Maureen Bell, Ben Benedikz, J. T. Boulton, Valerie Edden, Steve Ellis, Andrzej Gąsiorek, Wendy Gillespie, Anne McDermott, Suzanne Reynolds, Ian Small, Kelsey Thornton, Marcus Walsh, and Nigel Wood. I apologize for any omissions, and hope these people all know the particular extent of my gratitude. At Oxford University Press I had the encouragement of Kim Scott Walwyn, the wise and prompt advice of Judith Luna, and the benefit of a meticulous copy-editor.

Friends and relations as far apart as Birmingham and New Hampshire have kept me going. I could recite (but won't) the names of nearly half the inhabitants of Hillsborough, New Hampshire (where some of the book was written, and talked about—occasionally with a mirth that would have surprised Southey—in the most delightful of surroundings); thanks to Olivia Storey I had what became known as 'the Southey room' in which to work. Here, I have been fortunate in having friends and neighbours who have shown interest and knowledge: Pat Conaty (the first person to point out to me that a quotation from Southey rather incongruously adorns part of the Bull Ring) and Rosemary Foggit gave me food and drink, shared cats, lent books; Charles and Sharon Wall, appearing not to mind if I mentioned Southey, provided light relief, music, and more good food. Without the ministrations of many members of the National Health Service it is unlikely that I would have got much done at all: my profound thanks to them all. Tom, Jonathan, Hetty, and Hannah Storey, as so often, provided the best reasons, when things seemed particularly difficult, for carrying on; Becky Storey continued to be interested in my doings. I was deeply saddened that Bruce and Jo Perry, good Bristolians both, and for long such good friends, died before they could see this tangible result of their encouragement. No one could have been more loyal and supportive than my parents: would that my father were here to receive, with my mother, this inadequate token of my gratitude.

CONTENTS

LIST OF ILLUSTRATIONS

1

EARLY YEARS

1774–1792

T H E Southey family had established itself in the West Country, especially around Wellington and Taunton, from the sixteenth century onwards; the Hill family, into which Southey's father Robert married in 1772, was also from Somerset.[1] Robert Southey senior had moved from London to Bristol, as an apprentice to William Britton, a draper, in Wine Street: after a dozen years he had a shop of his own, in the same street, but in spite of the fact that Bristol was a thriving port, and with a potentially wealthy clientele—the other side of the radical politics for which the city was soon to become famous—business in the linen shop was never very brisk. By contrast, his brother John developed a prosperous lawyer's practice in Taunton, and when he died he was to leave his fortune to another brother, Thomas: both of them seemed determined that none of the Southey nephews should inherit any of the family wealth.

On the other side of the family, the Hills were better placed in the social order, with more money to confirm their higher station. Margaret Hill, Southey's mother by his maternal grandmother's second husband—a lawyer with ample means—was a sprightly 20-year-old when she married; Southey loved her dearly:

Never was any human being blessed with a sweeter temper or a happier disposition. She had an excellent understanding, and a readiness of apprehension which I have rarely known surpassed. In quickness of capacity, in the kindness of her nature, and in that kind of moral magnetism which wins the affection of all within its sphere, I never knew her equal.[2]

When Southey was born in Wine Street, on 12 August 1774, just before half-past eight in the morning (an astrologer later predicted, accurately enough, on the strength of this, that he would suffer from a pain in the bowels when he was 30),[3] it was the start of a life that, appropriately enough in the Bristol context, would always have its political resonances; he was also born into a home that was, because of financial circumstances, hardly home. The two facts could well be connected.

By the time he was 2 years old, he had been packed off to stay with his Aunt Elizabeth Tyler, a forceful, rather frightening figure who lived in Bath, in some jaded splendour—just the sort of life that could be expected of a flamboyant woman with at least some means; she was much older than his mother—her half-sister—wealthier, more profligate, more domineering, an adventurous woman who had spent a brief spell in Portugal, where she had found her half-brother Herbert Hill a post as chaplain at Oporto. There is a veiled portrait in Southey's work, *The Doctor*, which suggests something of her character:

Miss Trewbody was a maiden lady of forty-seven, in the highest state of preservation. The whole business of her life had been to take care of a fine person, and in this she had succeeded admirably. Her library consisted of two books; Nelson's Festivals and Fasts was one, the other was 'the Queen's Cabinet unlocked;' and there was not a cosmetic in the latter which she had not faithfully prepared. Thus by means, as she believed, of distilled waters of various kinds, May-dew and butter-milk, her skin retained its beautiful texture still, and much of its smoothness; and she knew at times how to give it the appearance of that brilliancy which it had lost... Her other great business was to observe with the utmost precision all the punctilios of her situation in life; and the time which was not devoted to one or other of these worthy occupations, was employed in scolding her servants, and tormenting her niece...[4]

Aunt Tyler led quite a high social life, especially among the cultured clique of Bath: through her close friend, a Miss Palmer, whose father owned theatres in Bristol and Bath, she knew all the leading lights of the stage, both actors and writers; the novelist Sophia Lee was among this self-regarding group. Gainsborough had painted her portrait, and in her exotically furnished house in Bath, like some kind of oriental museum, a curtain was carefully drawn over the picture, to keep it from the attentions of the sun and of flies. Aunt Tyler had a pathological fear of dirt, which she passed on to her nephew in his adult years. As a child, he observed his mother's obeisance to this domineering woman:

My mother was one of the few persons (for a few such there are) who think too humbly of themselves. Her only fault (I verily believe she had no other), was that of yielding submissively to this imperious sister, to the sacrifice of her own inclination and judgment and sense of what was right. She had grown up in awe and admiration of her, as one who moved in a superior rank, and who, with the advantage of a fine form and beautiful person, possessed that also of a superior and cultivated understanding... never did I know one person so entirely subjected by another, and never have I regretted anything more deeply than that subjection, which most certainly in its consequences shortened her life.[5]

It is small wonder that Southey was always to rail against such subjection: his life would provide him with several opportunities.

Until he was about 6 years old, Southey spent most of his time in Bath, leading a solitary life without friends, and getting whatever comfort he might from sharing his aunt's bed. He learnt to be quiet, endlessly patient, and to respect the peculiar virtues of cleanliness; unlike Tom Kitten, he could not afford even to risk affronting his surrogate mother by soiling his new clothes in the garden. The sole consolations were children's books and the local theatre (where he saw Mrs Siddons in her prime, and where most of Shakespeare and of Beaumont and Fletcher became part of his inner, imaginative world). His father would visit, occasionally, but he saw little of his young sister Eliza, who died in her third year, in 1779. Thus early was Southey introduced to the fact of child mortality. (Out of a family of nine children, only four boys survived into adulthood: Thomas was to become a naval captain, Henry Herbert a doctor, and Edward, at best, no more than a strolling player, and a continual thorn in his older brother's side.)

Ironically, Southey's favourite flower, the evening primrose, was called 'mortality' by the maternal grandmother he worshipped. She lived in a large Georgian house in Bedminster, where there was all the comfort inside that Aunt Tyler did not offer, and all the delights outside of a well-stocked garden, in which he was free to get as dirty as he wished. With an almost Proustian sense of smell (unlike Wordsworth, who could apparently smell and taste practically nothing), he would recall in later life the scents of the Bedminster garden and remember that at least parts of his childhood were idyllic. But the dark side of these few years was the dame's school he had to attend, run by another frightening woman, a Miss Powell, who had no eyelashes—something calculated to terrify most children aged 3. As if this were not bad enough, he had to dress up in a rather absurd costume 'of nankeen for highdays and holydays, trimmed with green fringe; it was called a *jam*.'[6] Perhaps we should not be surprised that he engaged in daydreams, including a plan to escape to an island where he could be free of all this petty tyranny.

But escape was not to be immediate. In 1780 one school was exchanged for another, Bath for Bristol, as he went to William Foot's establishment on St Michael's Hill. He was to learn that schools, even when run by a God-fearing Baptist, could be rough, savage places, where the violence of the staff was reflected in the bullying of the pupils. A good pair of fists, and a readiness to use them, was handy, long before the brutalities of Tom Brown's Rugby. The school at Corston, a few miles outside Bath, was less unpleasant, and Southey recalled a year there, after his year with Mr Foot, with some pleasure: he did not learn much, but he got to know his vegetables and to enjoy the scenery. 'The Retrospect', written in 1795, gives some account of his life at Corston. The master, Thomas Flower, did not keep a particularly tight ship, but there was something rather melancholy about the place:

There were vestiges of former respectability and comfort...walled gardens, summer-houses, gate-pillars, surmounted with huge stone balls, a paddock, a large orchard, walnut trees, yards, outhouses upon an opulent scale. I felt how mournful all this was in its fallen state, when the great walled garden was converted into a playground for the boys, the gateways broken, the summer-houses falling to ruin, and grass growing in the interstices of the lozenged pavement of the fore-court...[7]

Although he came to enjoy the school, 'When two small acres bounded all my fears', the whole experience was framed by gloom. The arrival was inauspicious, with Southey only too conscious, even then, of a glorified, manorial past replaced by the drab realities of the present:

> There now in petty empire o'er the school
> The mighty master held despotic rule;
> Trembling in silence all his deeds we saw,
> His look a mandate, and his word a law;
> Severe his voice, severe and stern his mien,
> And wondrous strict he was, and wondrous wise I ween.
>
> Even now through many a long long year I trace
> The hour when first with awe I view'd his face;
> Even now recall my entrance at the dome,..
> 'T was the first day I ever left my home!
> Years intervening have not worn away
> The deep remembrance of that wretched day,
> Nor taught me to forget my earliest fears,
> A mother's fondness, and a mother's tears;
> When close she prest me to her sorrowing heart,
> As loth as even I myself to part;
> And I, as I beheld her sorrows flow,
> With painful effort hid my inward woe...[8]

Leaving home had been traumatic: in a letter of 1797 he recorded the day he left for Corston, when he went upstairs and found his mother sitting on her bed in tears. 'I have sometimes since wondered', he wrote, 'at the resolution with which I then suppressed my own feelings—leapd about the shop as if to overpower agitation of mind by exercise of body—& when some person asked me if I liked going to school, replied "I don't care where I go—so I can have my own way"—& then my heart came up into my mouth & with a great gulp I choakd the rising tumult.'[9] This sad anecdote seems to tell us as much about Southey as any other revelation: the child is indeed the father of the man. In his 'Hymn to the Penates' (1796), he was to put these feelings into verse:

> When a child... (for still I love
> To dwell with fondness on my childish years,)
> When first, a little one, I left my home,
> I can remember the first grief I felt,
> And the first painful smile that clothed my front
> With feelings not its own: sadly at night
> I sat me down beside a stranger's hearth;
> And when the lingering hour of rest was come,
> First wet with tears my pillow...[10]

After this there were four years spent back at Bristol, at a school known as 'The Fort', and run by a congenial enough Welshman, William Williams. Southey's home life became rather migratory: when his maternal grandmother died in 1782, he went to stay with his aunt in the house at Bedminster, until such time as it was sold. He loved the house, partly because of its associations with his grandmother:

[The] porch was in great part lined, as well as covered, with white jessamine; and many a time have I sat there with my poor sisters, threading the fallen blossoms upon grass stalks. It opened into a little hall, paved with diamond-shaped flags. On the right was the parlour, which had a brown or black boarded floor, covered with a Lisbon mat, and a handsome timepiece over the fireplace; on the left was the best kitchen, where the family lived.... a cheerful room, with an air of such country comfort about it, that my little heart was always gladdened when I entered it during my grandmother's life. It had a stone floor, which I believe was the chief distinction between a best kitchen and a parlour... The room was wainscotted and ornamented with some old maps, and with a long looking glass over the chimney-piece, and a tall one between the windows, both in white frames. The windows opened into the fore-court, and were as cheerful and fragrant in the season of flowers as roses and jessamine, which grew luxuriantly without, could make them...[11]

But he also enjoyed being there because of the company of his two uncles, especially William, full of fun and yarns. Southey memorialized him, again in *The Doctor*, as William Dove:

He was born with one of those heads in which the thin partition that divides great wits from folly is wanting. Had he come into the world a century sooner, he would have been taken *nolens volens* into some Baron's household, to wear motley, make sport for the guests and domestics, and live in fear of the rod. But it was his better fortune to live in an age when this calamity rendered him liable to no such oppression, and to be precisely in that station which secured for him all the enjoyments of which he was capable, and all the care he needed... Whatever event occurred, whatever tale was current, whatever traditions were preserved, whatever superstitions were believed, William knew them all; and all that his insatiable ear took in, his memory hoarded...[12]

There was something of Uncle William in Southey, that love of the absurd, of particularities, of details for their own sake; when Southey grew up, he discovered he had inherited his uncle's gift for imitating all the animals and birds in God's kingdom, and he was able to delight his children just as he had been delighted.

When the house in Bedminster was sold, Southey moved to be with his parents back in the house in Wine Street, whilst his aunt moved to Bath, where he would spend his holidays. Then in 1785 she moved into a house on the edge of Bristol, and Southey was happier than he had been, in spite of everything, to be under the same same roof, once again, as her and Uncle William. There were more books to read; he came under the spell of Spenser, Milton, the classical writers, Pope, Sidney, Chatterton, Gray, Chaucer, the Bible, whatever he could lay his hands on. He began to write, launching himself into ambitious epic themes, and relying on Bysshe's *Art of Poetry* for the rudiments of verse composition. Even at this tender age, Southey was prepared to tackle anything, without any apparent sense of its possible absurdity. He and his friend Shadrach Weeks, brother of Miss Tyler's maid, built a little puppet theatre which provided endless delight for both boys. When they were not inside, the pair wandered around the countryside, looking for flowers:

Perhaps I have never had a keener enjoyment of natural scenery than when roaming about the rocks and woods on the side of the Avon with Shad and our poor spaniel Phillis. Indeed, there are few scenes in the island finer of their kind; and no other where merchant vessels of the largest size may be seen sailing between such rocks and woods.[13]

Even in this tranquil Eden, the commercial activities of Bristol reminded Southey that there was indeed a world elsewhere, and one he seemed happy to embrace.

One world in particular had its special fascination for him, that of the Fricker family.[14] The paterfamilias, Stephen Fricker, had tried his hand at various commercial ventures, including a pottery at Westbury and a coalyard at Bath. He liked to live in style, and his wife Martha was anxious for her daughters to have a decent education. But any plans were thrown into confusion when Stephen Fricker died in 1786, aged 48, a bankrupt. Mrs Fricker found lodgings on Redcliff Hill, in Bristol, where she opened a small school. Sara, Mary, and Edith, three of the five daughters, were sent out to earn what they could with their needlework; one of the women

drinker and consequently less of a disciplinarian than was expected in a school prone to local acts of rebellion (as indeed were most of the English public schools—and Oxbridge colleges, come to that). Most of the unpleasantness came from Southey's fellow-pupils, in the time-honoured tradition of such places, including a bully with whom he had to share a room. Southey endured various torments: being held out of a first-floor window by one leg, having water poured into his ear as he slept, being assaulted by his persecutor clad in a ghost-like white sheet. He rose to such taunts, almost revelling in the strength with which he could clasp his fingers around his attacker's throat. If his later poems of violence—in which the moral struggle between good and evil is acted out repeatedly in grotesquely physical form—have their roots in his youth, we need look no further than his first years at Westminster. He was careful to distinguish between two bullies: Brice, with no redeeming features, and Forrester, 'a great brute', but at least prepared to stand up to Brice: '[Forrester] would have made a good prize-fighter, a good buccaneer, or, in the days of Coeur de Lion or of my Cid, a good knight, to have cut down the misbelievers with a strong arm and a hearty good will.'[17]

As compensation, Southey made some good, lasting friendships: his 'substance', to whom he was the 'shadow', was George Strachey, who ended up as Chief Secretary to the Government in India, and 'one of the best-hearted men I ever knew'; it was possibly through Strachey that he had access to the library in Dean's Yard, Westminster, where he read Picart's *Religious Ceremonies* (1723), which first set him off on the long haul through all the world's mythologies: 'The book impressed my imagination strongly; and before I left school, I had formed the intention of exhibiting all the more prominent and poetical forms of mythology which have at any time obtained among mankind, by making each the groundwork of an heroic poem.'[18] Although there might be times when we catch a hint of George Eliot's Casaubon, even in the young Southey, by and large he steers clear of that dessicated scholarship which freezes the blood of the young Dorothea on her honeymoon in Rome; after all, Casaubon gives no thought to poetry. Charles Watkin Williams Wynn, the son of a Welsh baronet, was perhaps Southey's most important friend, a rather serious fellow but with Southey's interests always at heart, who would do what he could for his older friend from the time he became MP for Old Sarum at the age of 21 until he became, on and off, a Cabinet Minister: Southey later said that he owed everything to Wynn. Grosvenor Bedford was another intimate (and another possible source of access to books in Dean's Yard) with whom he kept in touch all his life: they even wrote poems together. Bedford became a civil servant, and therefore

thus obliged was Southey's mother. The girls got to know the formi
Aunt Tyler ('elegant, handsome and fashionable'), who did wha
could for them: Mary was steered towards the theatrical world of
and Bristol; Sara's society accomplishments were fostered by Miss T
own social aspirations. Although Miss Tyler thought the Fricker gir
than ideal companions for her nephew, when she was back at B
Southey was able to cultivate his friendship with Sara: and there see
have been a family understanding that it was the vivacious and bea
Sara to whom Southey was first attracted ('He had a friendship
mama first', recalled the young Sara Coleridge years later).[15] Edith,
ever, was beautiful too, his own age, and of a mild disposition. At
time in 1793 he would transfer his affections to Edith, who fitted in
rather tortuous plans remarkably conveniently. But we know little ;
Edith Fricker, compared to the sister who was one day to marry Cole
Sara's daughter commented fifty years later that Edith was 'an exceec
fine girl but very unanimated'. This helps to explain the intimate, r
joshing relationship that developed between Southey and his s
in-law Sara, when the strange turn of their lives brought them tog
again, ten years later.

An end to this quietly idyllic life was in sight, as his Uncle Herberl
in Lisbon, urged the family to put Southey in for Westminster Scho
his expense), which would lead naturally to Christ Church, anc
doubt, the Church as a profession. Like uncle, like nephew. To this
Southey had to undergo cramming, four hours a day, with a not
lively tutor —a clergyman called Lewis—and some equally unprepc
sing fellow-students. But, most importantly, he continued to
voraciously—and, as so often with precocious children, reading I
writing, if only in the form of imitation. He was to say, years later, 'I d
remember in any part of my life to have been so conscious of intelle
improvement as I was during the year and a half before I was plac
Westminster.'[16] In April 1788 he entered the famous London school, w
had a roll-call of distinguished former pupils—Dryden, Prior, Chur
Vincent Bourne, William Cowper, and a host of politicians. Miss
and Miss Palmer basked in the reflected glory of the young schol
London, about to enter this prestigious school.

Westminster might have seen better days; but it was still regard
second only to Eton in terms of what an English school could
William Vincent, a scholar if not a gentleman, became Headm
soon after Southey's arrival there: a geographer, a controversialist, r
lazy, with an erratic temper. 'Botch' Hayes, the usher of Ottley's Hou
which Southey belonged, was a decent enough classicist, but a h

useful to Southey because of his connections, as well as because of his innate friendliness and affection; there was a younger brother, Horace Bedford, whom Southey got to know a little later. Peter Elmsley, who later became a distinguished classicist, and famous for his rotundity, was another valuable friend who went up with him to Oxford in the fullness of time. When Wynn left Westminster in 1791 to enter Christ Church, the son of Johnson's biographer James Boswell moved in to share a room with Southey; another friend was Thomas Lamb, of Sussex, with whom he spent several enjoyable holidays at his rather grand house at Mountsfield, near Rye, getting to know the father and enjoying the company of the sister.

Before that, though, there was the traditional classical grind, relieved by the time in which Southey could pursue his own reading, particularly in exotic myths and legends, and the obvious books of the age—Goethe's *Werther*, Voltaire, Rousseau, Gibbon. Paradoxically, this apparently quiet, bookish young man found in his reading the very fuel his rebellious streak required; he, too, could assert himself, but in a cause that was just. There was talk of several episodes in which he had acted against the school authorities: there was a rebellion of sorts, of the kind fairly common in English public schools; he might have been involved in an incident in which a statue of Major André (one of the American heroes in their War of Independence) in Westminster Abbey was mutilated; he wrote a prose romance, *Harold*, in which Richard Cœur de Lion is praised as a democratic monarch, as against the present rulers of Britain;[19] he wrote an essay against Edmund Burke, the author of *Reflections on the Revolution in France*. This is the strongest reminder we have of the political circumstances in which Southey's final school years were played out.

Thirty years later Southey was to write: 'Few persons but those who have lived in it can conceive or comprehend what the memory of the French Revolution was, nor what a visionary world seemed to open upon those who were just entering it. Old things seemed passing away, and nothing was dreamt of but the regeneration of the human race.'[20] It would be wrong to dismiss this as middle-aged idealization; if some of his friends, like Wynn, were to take a more cool-headed attitude to events in France, it was perfectly natural for a young man of Southey's temper to be swept up in the fervour of the Revolution. After all, much of Britain had, in 1788, been celebrating the centenary of the Glorious Revolution of 1688; Southey's reading of Voltaire and Rousseau would naturally, as it did for many in France, feed into a general distrust of the *ancien régime*. Economic unrest and constitutional turmoil led, in 1789, to a crucial meeting in June, at which the gauntlet was thrown down to Louis XVI:

the so-called Third Estate declared itself, in effect, the National Assembly, and the King's right-hand man, Necker, was dismissed. On 14 July the Bastille was stormed; this symbolic act, against the King, his troops, and his hitherto inviolable sovereignty, set everything else in motion. By the end of August a Declaration of the Rights of Man and of the Citizen (modelled on the American Declaration of 1776) seemed to mark the beginning of the end for the French monarchy. Within a year it was clear that the Revolutionary momentum could not be halted by half-measures aimed at keeping the proletariat pacified. An attempt by the King and Queen to escape across the Rhine, whence they would return with their supporters and restore the monarchy, was foiled, and the royal family became prisoners of the Paris Commune. The Revolutionaries fought among themselves, the less extreme Girondins against the more eagerly republican Jacobins, represented by the charismatic Danton (who inaugurated the Committee of Public Safety) and later by Robespierre and Saint-Just.

The British looked across the Channel, and held their breath. In 1789 Richard Price produced his *Discourse on the Love of our Country* in which he welcomed the prospect of revolution sweeping across Europe. Edmund Burke, the Irish Whig who up till this point was best known for his *Philosophical Enquiry into the Origin of Our Ideas of the Sublime and Beautiful* of 1757, knew that Price spoke for a large part of the population, and immediately responded with his *Reflections on the Revolution in France* (1790). As we shall see, the 'pamphlet war' had begun, all the more urgent because everyone knew that more than mere pamphlets was at stake. Britain's freedom and constitution were to be held up to the kind of scrutiny that was soon to lead, in France, to chaos.[21]

At Westminster School rebellion took less savage forms: the rebellious streak that had occasionally showed itself in Southey's younger years came to the surface when in 1792 he founded, with his friends but very largely with Bedford, a school magazine called the *Flagellant*, published as a proper book by the London bookseller Egerton; the idea was that this would replace an earlier Westminster journal, the *Trifler*, and act as a rival to Eton's satirical *Microcosm*. Under the pseudonym of 'Gualbertus', Southey penned on 29 March for the fifth number a savage attack on corporal punishment. This was like an attack on the very foundations of the educational system: up and down the country, public schools depended upon flogging for the maintenance of law and order. Southey was having none of it:

It is utterly inconsistent with the character of a school master... thus by making use of so beastly, so idolatrous a custom to follow the abominations of the children

of Moab, of the Hittites and the Shittites and the Gergusites and other idolators
whose names alone remain an awful instance of divine justice ... Now, since there
is but one God, whosoever flog, that is, performeth the will of Satan, committeth
an abomination: to whom therefore and to all the consumers of birch as to priests
of Lucifer,
    Anathema, Anathema ...[22]

For the publicity-conscious Vincent, to find himself equated, rather like
Louis XVI, with Satan was the final straw; he could not sit back and quietly
admire the cheeky rhetoric. Southey, once his identity was revealed, had
to go and in April he went. Vincent promptly preached a sermon on 13
May at St Margaret's, Westminster (subsequently published as *A Discourse addressed to the People of Great Britain*), in which he urged the
importance of education in the fight against dangerous ideas.

Not surprisingly, Southey did not know quite where he belonged, or
what the future held. He had dreamt, all those years ago, of an island to
which he could escape to create his own home with a few close friends.
When he had gone up to Westminster, the dream—the logical future—lay
ahead, as it was to for Hardy's Jude, amongst the spires of Oxford, with a
comfortable living at the end of it. But when he left Westminster under
that rather enormous cloud, the future was completely uncertain. All he
could do was to give it the same wide-eyed stare as the schoolmistress with
no eyelashes.

2

OXFORD

1792–1793

SOUTHEY'S response to Dr Vincent's decision to expel him, and the consequent rejection by Oxford, was defiant: that almost violent self-righteousness for which he was to be praised and reviled in later life asserted itself in his avowed determination to kill his headmaster and to continue with the *Flagellant* (in fact, and rather disappointingly, we might think, he did neither). He announced, 'The paper must succeed for it has enemies.' This relish for conflict might have made him unduly optimistic at this moment of crisis, but there was an element of truth in his apparently curious logic. He was also determined that there should be no distinction drawn between the principle of the thing and the person-alities of those involved: 'expulsion is a bitter pill & will not go down unless I sweeten it over, but for every pill I swallow Vincent shall have a bolus—"thus by myself I swear".' At the same time Southey was sensible enough to acknowledge the need to be careful; he realized (and again this is significant for his later development) that he could turn the tables on his accusers. 'Our last [number] was extremely correct & I hope & have vanity enough to believe will acquire us some credit . . . Conceal the names & it will improve the sale at Cambridge. At Oxford I hope one day to see a strong party in its favor.'[1] There is a canny eye here for the future, a determination not to give in lightly. Rather typically, Southey is abso-lutely certain he has done nothing wrong, and he is not going to trim his sails, whatever the consequences: 'I will never submit.' He can afford to make the youthful grand gesture ('should I be rejected at Oxford the grave is always open—there at least I shall not be molested'), whilst at the same time contemplating a future publication of the *Flagellant* in one volume, with about 250 subscribers.[2]

However, there is another side to this episode, demonstrating the complexities of Southey's character; once again, the formative years foreshadow his later career. In one of the many letters he writes to Bedford around this time, he moves, in one sentence, from that self-confident virtuousness to something rather less complacent. 'I am not conscious of

having acted wrong—my future welfare may or may not be affected by
malicious envy but the firm assurance of rectitude cannot—your last
[letter] waked me from a pleasant dream & I believe all my pleasant
dreams are doomd to be disturbd—.'[3] ('Rectitude' was to be a word often
applied to Southey, not always admiringly.) At this stage in his career
(although that is hardly the right word when the very idea of a career
seems in jeopardy), he has to come to terms with some harsh realities. It is
all very well taking on the enemy, but the personal cost might well be too
high. In any case, it is not simply a matter of fighting back. There are
family councils to consider, the advice of wiser, cooler heads such as the
old family friend Mrs Dolignon, who takes him under her roof when
Westminster has had enough (she 'had been to me almost as a mother', he
was to say later in life).[4] And so, although it is 'like parting with a limb'
(one of his favourite phrases), he withdraws from the *Flagellant* . 'I can
resist & even despise reproach or persecution—entreaties I cannot. I have
suffered much since I saw you—a very little more will overset the balance
of reason—drop the *Flagellant* I must!'[5] He might have derived some
comfort from the prospect of a general rebellion at Westminster (as he
confided to his erstwhile schoolfellow Tom Lamb), but resignation creeps
upon him.[6] He can write a poem in which he places himself in a long line
of illustrious writers who have suffered in the face of ignorance (including
Homer and Ovid—Southey, even now, is ready to raise the stakes):

> Ah Bedford—not alone do we complain
> Our laurels blasted & our labours vain—
> Like us full many a hapless victim led
> Before fell Ignorance has bowd & bled—

but he is well aware of the inglorious end of most newspapers:

> Tis night—alone & pensive thro the air
> I see the dismal taper's dreary glare—
> Ha—hollow murmurs all my spirits daunt
> The Ghost arises of the Flagellant!
> Not bound & gilt as once I hoped to see
> The ornament of all the library
> No—a vile grocers hand the paper handles
> To wrap up butter or a pound of candles—[7]

This is skittish enough, but there is something much more desperate in
his declaration to Bedford: 'I look upon myself with contempt & fly from
the hideous retrospect.' He has written to Vincent, admitting his errors: 'I
deserve to be despised, I deserve to be shunned but I do not think you will
despise me.' In spite of the notion of revenge (quite what form it would

take, apart from the murder of Vincent, is never quite clear) he has 'more than once . . . approachd the very brink of destruction'. Still only 17, Southey feels an old man: 'I am not quite eighteen & few men of eighty have been more persecuted.' Such self-dramatization is partly explained by his sense of having to carry his family's misfortunes on his shoulders. This again becomes a recurrent refrain. But there is also a curious sense, as so often when reading Southey's letters, of watching someone watching himself from a great height; it is hard always to believe that he believes what he says.[8] (The same might be said of Coleridge.)

A visit in early spring to Mountsfield, near Rye, in Sussex helped Southey to bounce back. This was where his Westminster friend Tom Lamb lived, and Southey got on famously with Lamb's father; much later in life he told his daughter Edith May that 'the sunniest days of my youth were those which I passed at Mountsfield'.[9] Southey suggested to Bedford that they revive some of their earlier journalistic plans, 'the Medley—the Hodge Podge—the What do you call it', or perhaps their 'old plan—Monastic lucubrations'. Perhaps Charles Wynn could be brought in, and other Westminsters like Charles Collins, even William Rough. The old school ties were still asserting their pull.[10] Down in Sussex, meanwhile, Southey enjoyed himself: there were a couple of days of heavy drinking in Brighton at the end of May, but there was also time for reading and writing. *Tristram Shandy* occupied him, and set off in his mind the strange, internal 'lucubrations' that were to surface forty years later in his own monument to inconsequentiality, *The Doctor*. He read Richard Watson's *Chemical Essays* (1781–7), saying airily that he hoped 'to practise a little chemistry at Oxford when I get there'.

Just as important, he was writing verse. Not surprisingly, he was drawn to imitations—Watts, Shenstone, and, more modishly, 'Della Crusca' (Robert Merry). Southey was aware of the charges of affectation levelled at the Della Cruscans, but he was undeterred: 'I think him [Merry] often beautiful.' So far as Southey was concerned, it was all grist to the mill. He wrote a paper on wigs (in itself a further sign of rebellion, in that for him wigs represented the old guard, the traditional, the conventional), which he thought might get an airing 'in the fag end of the *Flagellant* when we reprint it'. When, not if. Southey was already beginning to enjoy the sheer range and variety that writing could bring him, and to recognize his own peculiar virtues as a writer. 'I have observed every man I saw with the eye of a periodical writer and noted him in my pocket book.' Although in years to come he would curse the position such talents landed him in—the eternal reviewer unable to escape the monthly drudge of another book to write about—his keen eye, allied to his ability to find the right phrase to catch the image, was to make him one of the best prose writers of his age. (Some critics thought his pocket-book was the greatest enemy to his own powers as a poet, but that is another matter.) The letter to Bedford, in which he comments on his own powers of observation, ends with a nice example of his sharpness and fluidity of style: 'breakfast is ready the tea making Tom Lamb tying up his boots and his mother pouring out the tea so quicks the word'.[11]

Southey's spirits continued to soar. In early June he planned to return to London, but to take his time about it. He would walk to Bath, drinking in the sights and sounds along the way. There might be something patronizing in his tone here, but there is also a jaunty combination of the potential journalist and the light-hearted poet. He is not really taking himself too seriously: 'equipped in my oldest cloaths to sally on with a great stick in search of adventures & eat at the country alehouses so that I may see a country life & manners in its grossest view—do not object to the scheme. When I am tired upon the way I will sit down & write an ode.'[12] Odes were becoming something of an obsession with him; they allowed him the freedom he was enjoying away from the confines of Westminster. 'All my Odes are irregular except Ignorance which you have. Grays Spring & drownd cat are pretty I think—but I am not regular myself & detest regularity.'[13] In the Preface to his 1797 volume he was to declare: 'I now think the Ode the most worthless species of composition as well as the most difficult, and should never again attempt it, even if my future pursuits were such as allowed leisure for poetry.' He could not, of course, at this stage in his life anticipate just how many odes he would find himself writing, whether he wanted to or not.

The light-heartedness could not be sustained for long. Southey was aware that something had to be sorted out. From Bath in late June, where he had been amusing himself by hunting for wild flowers, he told Bedford: 'This is a damnd world & the sooner I quit it the better. God gave me the happiest disposition ever mortal was blessd with had he not I must have sunk long ago . . .' He had still not forgiven Vincent, but more urgent was his own future. He fancied some kind of appointment in the East Indies, but it was all very vague. The traditional professions offered little hope: 'the church is a hypocritical line of life—the law a dishonest one—my friends the Doctors have no interest at Calcutta.'[14] Oxford beckoned, in spite of Dr Vincent's efforts, but Southey could not wax enthusiastic at the prospect of five years of further study. 'I am ready to run mad over the mathematics! which I have just begun & wish I had just concluded.' He envied Lamb: 'all your drudgery is over.' In the mean time, he consoled himself with the delights of the countryside around Bath and Bristol:

Wokey Hole was admired, and Wells Cathedral, 'one of the finest Gothic buildings in England'.[15]

Southey was still in Bristol, at his Aunt Tyler's, at the end of the summer. As a result of Dr Vincent's words to the Dean of Christ Church, Cyril Jackson, he had to settle for Balliol, which did not seem to bother him unduly (until he got there).[16] There were other things to worry about. On the one hand, there were the family finances; on the other, events in France. Southey's own expulsion and subsequent anxiety about his future have to be set in this broader context. He soon learnt that he was acting out his life on a much larger stage (and that was the image he came to use). European turmoil took the place of the upheavals at his old school, and there was a necessary reordering of priorities. There was the prospect of years 'poring over Euclid & the Fathers, &...laying out plans for the future, which probably will never be put in execution.' But as he told Bedford on 6 October, he was engaged in 'a most arduous & important task. Euclid I lay aside & have began to look seriously into myself.'[17] This introspection was all the more painful and necessary in view of the turn of the Revolution in France. It was as though another of his dreams had been shattered. Like so many of his contemporaries, Southey had to come to terms with the full implications of the Revolution, both politically, and also for himself. The charge of apostasy has been frequently levelled, but Southey's political development is actually very complex.[18] There is certainly a tendency for Southey to be excoriated not only for his own perceived changes of mind, but for those of Wordsworth and Coleridge as well. In October 1792, whilst waiting to go up to Oxford, Southey mulls over what has been happening in Europe. We should not be surprised that there is confusion in his reactions, nor should we blame him for attempting to draw a distinction between his republican ideals and the reality of what has happened.

In early October Southey wrote, in significantly apocalyptic terms, to Lamb, acknowledging that Lamb's misgivings had been warranted. 'Time has justified all your prophecies with regard to my French friends. The Jacobins, the Sans Culottes, and the fishwomen carry everything before them. Every thing that is respectable, every barrier that is sacred, is swept away by the ungovernable torrent.' It is interesting that, two months earlier, Southey had sent to Lamb a curiously comic verse about the need to keep things 'within bounds'.[19] This is precisely what he had not done at Westminster. It is also instructive that, at this stage, the image of the torrent is the one he resorts to; again, it is a commonplace Romantic image with its own inherent contradictions. (There is certainly an irony in the fact that, even in 1822, when he has become an established Tory figure, embracing and extolling the virtues of control and order, his most famous anthology piece should be 'The Cataract of Lodore', written for his children in one of his many outbursts of childish exuberance.[20]) Southey continues, in his letter to Lamb, with a resolute honesty:

The people have changed tyrants, &, for the mild irresolute Louis, bow to the savage, the unrelenting Petion. After so open a declaration of abhorrence, you may perhaps expect that all the sanguine dreams of liberty are gone for ever. It is true, I have seen the difficulty of saying to the mob, 'thus far, no farther.' I have seen a structure raised by the hand of wisdom, & defended by the sword of liberty, undermined by innovation, hurled from its basis by faction, & insulted by the proud abuse of despotism. Is it less respectable for its misfortunes? These horrid barbarities, however, have rendered me totally indifferent to the fate of France, & I have only to hope that Fayette will be safe. . . . Before I quit the French, let me remark that that very National Assembly, which you have stigmatised as a rabble of pettifogging attorneys & illiterate barbarians, has furnished men who had the courage to preserve their duty at the expense of their lives.[21]

It is quite clear that Southey is doing more than merely answering Lamb's gloomy prognostications; he is confronting his own doubts and uncertainties, his own allegiances when it is no longer the case that 'to be young was very heaven'. The French, he says, have always had a 'national ferocity'. '"They order these things better in England". Peg Nicolson is only in Bedlam; Tom Paine is treated with lenity.' But his own experiences tell him that even this distinction is not that simple: 'but woe be to him who dares attack the divine will of schoolmasters to flog, or who presumes to think that boys should neither be treated absurdly or indecently.' He is conscious of the underlying hypocrisy of English society; the rebel in him, as well as the republican, sees the logic of the French Revolution, but cannot accept where that logic has led the French. As he says in some perplexity, 'before they appeared as protectors of revolution (you see I use an ambiguous term)'; it is important for us to see his own ambiguity here. The only way he can cope (not having access to Wordsworth's revivifying spots of time, nor anything like the same belief in the powers of the imagination) is to build up his own defences. He will use his own private problems, and his reactions to them, as a model of how to confront political events: 'I have undergone enough to break a dozen hearts; but mine is made of tough stuff, & the last misfortune serves to blunt the edge of the next. One day it will, I hope, be impenetrable. 'Tis well I can speak with levity.' Fortunate too, we might think, that he can apparently have his cake and eat it.[22]

Britain was itself increasingly in ferment. Riots spread across the country, as republican sympathizers with the French cause clashed with those in Britain anxious to quell any unrest. The *Gentleman's Magazine* announced in its preface to 1793, with appropriate portentousness, 'Europe, since the period when it was overrun by the Goths and Vandals, has never experienced more alarm and danger than at the present moment—Religion, Manners, Literature, and the Arts, are all equally menaced by a foe, whose characteristic is a compound of impetuosity, ignorance, and crime.'[23] There had seemed something unusually significant in the curiously stormy weather that afflicted Britain in July 1792. Meanwhile, the King of Prussia was leading 5,000 men towards France. In the midst of all this Southey had his own professional and financial concerns. His sense of isolation at the prospect of going up to Oxford, away from his friends, was deepened by his failure to get money off his Uncle John, the lawyer at Taunton (there was considerable toing and froing between Bristol, Bath, Taunton, and Rye). Southey's father had fallen on hard times, through 'the treachery of his relations & injustice of his friends'; ironically, in view of subsequent events, the day was momentarily saved by Southey's Bristol aunt. So far as Southey was concerned, this might have been a mixed blessing, but family honour meant that his father must not languish in prison because of debt. Southey persuaded himself that his wealthy uncle, with property amounting to £100,000 and with no child, would one day be passing on a large chunk of this wealth to his nephew—'it will I hope enable me to despise the world & feel myself independant.' This was a dream he clung on to for many years, a sign perhaps of his sublime innocence in these matters, and perhaps more disturbingly of his inability to see what the true state of affairs might be.

National and international events pressed upon him; but his own role in these events puzzled him. He might scoff at his friend Collins's eye-rolling worldly wisdom about such things ('like a wise man who is doubtful of the event & wishes to be thought in the secret'), but his own response is far from clear-cut:

I can pity Louis *the last* as one who is unfortunate—the man deserves not pity—the King less—the abject prisoner certainly claims it. Perhaps they may canonise him alamode Charles 1st. I hope not. Now I am upon the republic system I must tell you that Bristol seems preparing for it. A pamphlet proposes the abolition of the corporation as unconstitutional & arbitrary & hints the same to all other corporate towns. It is very well written. These little attacks upon the outworks sap the foundations of the citadel. If France models a republic & enjoys tranquillity who knows but Europe may become one great republic & Man be free of the whole. You see I use Paines words, but politics must not make us quarrel. You know the fable of the oak & the reed. I have been the oak & was pulled up by the roots & cast up. Let me try to be the reed.[24]

Southey sometimes allows himself to be swept away by enthusiasm. Although he likes the idea of being a Fellow at Balliol, he is conscious of the futility of studying ('the prime of my life is to pass in acquiring knowledge') when the world is in ferment, 'when Europe is on fire with freedom—when man & monarch are contending'. He would like to be a philosopher, but has his doubts about its usefulness, especially when confronted with the reminders of mortality when he visits the family tomb. He laments, in a letter to Bedford, the rawness of the present: at least his ancestors had 'an independent patrimony', and 'lay hid from the world too obscure to be noticed by it, too elevated to fear its insult'. This, he realizes, is the true value of philosophy—'it teaches us to search for applause from within & to despise the flattery or the abuse of the world alike'—and it is precisely this kind of sentiment he was to have urged upon him when he met Edmund Seward at Oxford. Southey was already open to the blandishments of stoicism, even as he denounced its 'unfeeling dictates'.[25]

As the year came to its end, Europe's future seemed increasingly precarious, whatever that of the young Robert Southey. He was fascinated by the prospect of the new French constitution, but appalled by rumours of a secret treaty between France and Prussia; he could see that the French, having 'rid themselves for awhile of foreign enemies', would 'now quarrel among themselves'.[26] A letter to Bedford in early December contained the full range of this confusion. He was fascinated, when he went to the theatre in Bristol, to see the anti-Royalist Citizen Bailey refusing to take his hat off for the national anthem; and yet he could see that 'these are perilous times. Give me three lines of any mans writing said Richlieu & I will extract treason from them.' It had been in May 1792 that the decree was passed against the writing, printing, and publishing of seditious material (and of which Thomas Paine had fallen foul); it is easy to see how Southey related this to his own sedition at Westminster, and how he would feel sympathy with the English radicals who fell victim to such a decree. He knew he was on dangerous ground, as was the country: civil war could lead to 'seas of blood'. Revealingly, he told Bedford to scratch out anything in his letter that he might find 'offensive', and then resorted to one of his favourite images: 'it is a horrid subject—like a current you no sooner touch it than it carries you away.'

Literature offered one way out. He had sent the odd bit of verse in his letters to Bedford, but reading Juvenal's 8th Satire led him to see that there was another possible form of response, a mixture of retreat and bravado. He might express a determination (partly bolstered by Juvenal, and Johnson's imitations of him) to be 'political only in private', but there is something much grander, Keatsian even, in this posture: 'Nature never intended me for a soldier—when I am agitated every nerve trembles but at those moments when a bystander would think me palsied with some fear I could leap to pluck bright honor from the palefaced moon. I could write an ode & stand to be shot at.' Keats does indeed seem to be the appropriate reference point here: Southey anticipates that central debate on the role of the artist as opposed to the man of action, the debate that runs through all Romantic writing. What is surprising is that Southey's confusions here emerge as distinctively different from the Words-worthian or Coleridgean forms of the dilemma (and of course he has yet to meet either); he has that disturbing honesty that we associate with Keats (as yet, of course, unborn, and hence our surprise at this conjunction), and his recognition of his contrary impulses is worth emphasizing: 'intolerable Indolence & impatient Curiosity—what I am curious for no human being can divine.'[27]

As he prepared, in his reluctant way, for Oxford, Southey took stock, determinedly placing himself in the historic stream of events. '1792 is expiring—good god how many events have transpired—from the fall of Gualbertus to that of Louis! from my libel upon rod to Paines upon sceptres...' It is hard to know quite how much self-mockery there is here: Southey is not always the best person to understand himself, or see the possible irony of some of his claims. (He asks Bedford, in the same letter, whether he is 'in any of these tremendous associations', but he must have known it highly unlikely that the aristocratic Bedford would have joined any of the London Corresponding Societies.) But, just as importantly, there is a sense of the world, and his own life, somehow taking shape. He takes leave of the year as though it were the end of the first act in an unfolding drama. He was about to leave the world he had known, to enter the strange world of Oxford, which did not immediately fill him with optimism: 'I expect to meet with pedantry prejudice & aristocracy from all which Good Lord deliver poor Robert Southey.' He missed his old schoolfriends, and wondered what would become of them all: 'must [Basil] follow Gualbertus? or turn timeserver? or go to France? Ah ca ira ca ira ca ira.' There he summed up the choices, and curiously anticipated some of his own future behaviour. But when he himself eventually went to France, it was to be very much as a tourist.[28]

The sense of an ending, rather than of a new beginning, was made worse by the news of his father's death at the end of December. Southey had stayed with him when he last travelled through Bath to Oxford, and saw him lying in bed. It is a touching vignette, foreshadowing the sad sequence of deaths that were to haunt his life: 'he prest my hand with affection & for the only time in his life blest me. Why it was I know not but it struck me that I never should see him more. I never did. In a better world I shall.' The importance of father figures in Southey's poetry is worth touching on at this point; especially in *Thalaba* and *The Curse of Kehama*, it is as though Southey is pursuing, in his narratives, a search for the father, mirroring his own sense of loss, and lost opportunities, when his father died. His own affection for his children later in life is the other side of the same coin. For all his still smouldering republicanism Southey makes, on his father's death, one of his early declarations of the importance of religion: 'The man who destroys religion deprives us of the only substantial happiness.' As we have already seen, Southey prided himself on his ability to cling on to happiness in all circumstances, but it is worth registering the tenuousness with which he does it.[29]

He tells Bedford that he finds comfort in books, reading voraciously, and in thought. 'I take the pen for relaxation [he sends a verse epistle, 'Titus to Berenice'] & at least possess negative happiness.' It is also a lonely state, made worse by not hearing from his friend: 'I remain like a solitary oyster feeding upon thought.' He consoles himself with the thought that Bedford might at least visit him in Oxford: he already has created in his mind's eye the domesticity for which he had always yearned, a domesticity intimately bound up with his close friends. He promises Bedford 'a great chair & a good fire & a bottle', and the chance of meeting Charles Wynn, 'the only man upon earth whom I at once love & respect' (we might wonder, not for the last time, what the recipient would make of such a comment). He adds, rather desperately, as if to show how 'negative' his happiness really is: 'the opportunities of happiness are so rare that we ought to snatch them eagerly ere they disappear.' Some lines he writes on 30 December manage to capture the range of his concerns (the quality of the verse is another matter):

> Since bleeding Memory still her way will force
> Brood oer a lifeless Fathers claycold corse
> Let Contemplation come in solemn state
> For ah what Time more fit to contemplate!
>
> .   .   .   .   .   .
>
> Nor I alone in this eventful year
> Of wicked libels & sedition hear
> To hope that Truth would shelter me how vain
> When Truth & Eloquence both faild for Paine![30]

Once arrived at Balliol in January 1793 Southey was struck above all by the folly of the place, the petty regulations—no boots allowed, powdered wigs the order of the day, bread and cheese the only food allowed in one's rooms—and the stupidity of his masters. It was not an auspicious beginning. As he wrote to Bedford soon after his arrival: 'behold me now my friend entered under the banners of science or stupidity which you please & like a recruit got sober looking back to the days that are past & feeling something like regret... solitude I do not dislike for I fear it not—but there is a certain Daemon named Reflection that accompanies [it] whose arrows though they rankle not with the poison of guilt are yet pointed by Melancholy.' This might seem like literary posturing; but it reveals something of Southey's *Angst*.

Nor did Oxford seem to afford him much chance to assert the rather self-conscious awkwardness that had got him expelled from Westminster. Resigned, it seems, to being called into orders in four years' time, he laments the necessary reining in of his Bucephalus. 'I must learn to break a rebellious spirit which neither Authority or Oppression could bow ever—it would be easier to break my neck. I must learn to work a problem instead of writing an ode... I must learn to cringe to those whom I despise & to pay respect to men only remarkable for great wigs & little wisdom.' He did in fact start writing odes (such as 'Poetry' and 'Contemplation'), and thought them rather better than George Richards' ode, *Aboriginal Britons, a Prize Poem*, which had been published in Oxford in 1791. In his lack of recognition, he was already comparing himself to the Chatterton whose works he would one day edit. He enclosed in this same letter one of his early ballads, 'The Wedding Day', remarking in passing that 'regular lyrics are like despotic monarchies—they look stately but lose all the energy of freedom.' Typically, and importantly, writing and politics are intertwined. Southey was intent on using 'plain language': 'Truth came naked out of the well—with me she shall be only simplex munditiis—Mr Burke has so bedizend out Falshood that it takes much trouble & tears to get a sight of the real form.'[31] At this stage of Southey's life, Burke represents everything he abhorred: with his *Reflections on the Revolution in France* (1790), Edmund Burke had become the representative of the old order, and whilst William Pitt and Charles James Fox had praised in Parliament the ideals of the French Revolution, and the Revolution Society (formed in 1788, in commemoration of the Glorious Revolution of 1688) sent congratulations to the French National Assembly, Burke feared that what had happened in France could well happen in Britain. Richard Price's *Discourse on the Love of our Country* (1789), with its embrace of possible universal liberation from monarchy, provided the chance for Burke to attack; ironically, not only were his *Reflections* immensely popular (30,000 copies sold) with those who might have been tempted to look to France for a change of course, they became the sounding board for the whole revolutionary debate in England. Burke's rhetoric led to the radical outcries of Thomas Paine, William Godwin, and Mary Wollstonecraft.

For Southey at this point, writing means prose as much as poetry—another pointer to the future. At the same time, whilst resorting to the Horatian principle of simple truth, he cannot find much pleasure in actually translating Horace: 'there is something in the character of the little fat parasite which sullies it very much.' Southey is expressing something more than his lifelong thin man's contempt for the portly; he is anxious to assert his distaste for playing the patronage game. As he says of Dr Vincent in the same letter, he cannot bring himself to speak well of him: 'quid Romae faciam? mentire nescio!' By the same token, when he first met his peers he presented them with his unadorned locks—no wig for him; and by marching into hall for dinner with his glorious curly hair down to his shoulders, he soon set a fashion for the college.

The absurdities of Balliol led him to contemplate the unequal luxuries of Oxford, and the dangers of wealth. He was not going to stop thinking about society just because he was cloistered in Balliol; in some ways that very imprisonment (as it seemed to him) forced him to think, if confusedly, even more intently about the state of the nation. The radicalism of Bristol had already rubbed off on him, but his reading of Paine especially had had a salutary effect. Thomas Paine's *Rights of Man* (1791, 1792) led to his arrest for sedition, and his escape to France, where he actually held a seat in the Revolutionary National Convention; he had already been involved in the American Revolution, recorded in *Common Sense* (1776): the Declaration of Independence was clearly influenced by Paine. If Burke was popular, Paine could claim sales of 200,000: his radicalism appealed to more than the middle classes, as cheap, readily available editions showed, and it was precisely this availability of such dangerous ideas that made him a threat to the Government. Paine would have none of the divine rights of kings or governments: he promulgated the kind of democracy that was beginning to seem so attractive to the younger generation in Britain. Southey accordingly wrote at some length to Bedford about the idea of the monarchy, questioning that it had the support of the majority, and putting forward an argument based on Paine: 'I only ask the exercise of reason. Truth never shuns investigation. Falshood only fears the spear of Ithuriel. The objections to monarchy... are such, that even its adherents are obliged to own a republic best in theory. Experience tells us it is possible in practice. Thebes Sparta Athens & Carthage have been. America is.' He believed that all troubles derived from the monarchy, and the associated abuse of power. But this was not just a theoretical debate.

look at the hundreds of aged & infirm mendicants who throng your streets—& then ask your own heart if all is right—that Bedford will answer with justice. The labourer toils during the years of vigor & earns his scanty morsel with the sweat of his brow—yet this man even in the vilest beer he drinks pays to support a set of pensioned courtiers who drink their wines heedless of his wants & cry out—all is right—like Dr Pangloss when every thing belies them.

Southey was acutely conscious of the sufferings of the poor, the iniquities of the press-gang, sinecures, and imprisonment for debt. Not all this outrage was merely a matter of personal circumstances; he could see that Burke had been answered by Paine and James Mackintosh. The 'first duty' of the peerage 'where Liberty & Equality flourish is to regard the education of the people'. Southey consistently pursues this quarry throughout his writing life; but the following cry could only come from him when he was young: 'good god are we to hear again of the divine right of Kings & the impiety of the unanointed republic?'[32]

As he settled into Oxford life he found a few kindred spirits. There was Charles Collins, with whom he had corresponded regularly in his final year at Westminster and before going up to Oxford, and of whom he grew increasingly fond, before disillusion set in; another old Westminster friend at Christ Church was Edward Combe, along with Henry 'Horse' Campell (so called not because of any oddity of feature but because he was allowed, for a brief period, actually to keep a horse). Charles Wynn was an important friend, of course, and Nicholas Lightfoot at Balliol made an impression on the young Southey. Most important in terms of Southey's development was Edmund Seward, 'a man of sterling virtue', whom he called '*Talus* for his unbending morals & iron rectitude'; Southey later said that Seward was one of the best reasons for being at Balliol. He soon realized that Christ Church would not have suited him anyway: 'I should have been a grave owl amongst a set of chattering jays.' Seward had apparently been something of a young tearaway, indulging in wine, and allowing himself the delights of butter and sugar; but now, a reformed character, he drank water and had only tea and bread for breakfast.[33] His stoic philosophy of duty appealed to Southey as he tried to find his bearings in this unfamiliar new world. 'This I take to be true philosophy of that species which tends to make mankind happy because it first makes them good.' On the severely practical level this led Southey to start rising at 5.00 a.m.; there just was not enough time to do—or read, or write—all he wanted (on the other hand, as one of his doggerel pieces tells us, he also managed to oversleep on at least one occasion, and, by getting to chapel just in time, avoided an ignominiously early sending down). On the metaphysical level, he was able to write to Bedford, rather more optimistically than a month or so earlier, 'remember that a mind disposed to be happy will find happiness everywhere & why we should not be happy is beyond my philosophy to account for.' There is no doubting Seward's influence here, the combination of discipline and religious faith. Southey had his own doubts about what kind of religion he might subscribe to (he had already wondered and worried about the Athanasian Creed, for example), but he declared to Bedford, 'no human character [is] so truly enviable as that [of] a true Xian. Morose austerity & stern enthusiasm are the characteristics of Superstition, but what is in reality more chearful or happy than Religion?'[34]

Louis XVI's death at the guillotine on 21 January 1793 drew forth an uneasy response from a Southey who had just congratulated himself on his happiness: 'in pitying the man I drew a viel over the faults of the monarch. With respect to the illfated Louis you cannot feel more repugnant to his death than I do but [quoting the fat little parasite, Horace] "non civium ardor prava jubentium mente quatet solida"'. Rather more flippantly, but just as typically, the same letter could say, 'To me it must matter little which way the balance of power incline so my money & life be not thrown into the scales.' This disturbing selfishness, this Panglossian view that all is for the best (in spite of what he had himself said, only recently, about Pangloss), casts some shadows over Southey's integrity of vision and philosophy in these early months at Oxford. Reading about the mutiny on the *Bounty* led him to imagine some kind of ideal community, anticipating the Pantisocratic ideal that was still a year hence. It is important to register his apparent optimism, bolstered no doubt by Seward's stoicism, but also his genuine confusion, his acknowledgement of the fragility of the dream.

Is humanity so very vicious that society cannot exist without so many artificial distinctions linked together as we are in the great chain? Why should the extremity of that great chain be neglected? At this moment I could form the most delightful theory of an island peopled by men who should be Xtians not Philosophers & where Vice only should be contemptible, Virtue only honourable where all should be convenient without luxury all satisfied without profusion.[35]

This is all very well, but when he wondered what life might be like twenty years on, his demands were less high-flown: 'Let me have 200 a year & the comforts of domestic life & my ambition aspires no further.' He hoped that his life would be of use to his family, and provide himself with some happiness. He was already beginning to think of himself as a writer, but typically discounting his own claims as 'one who can boast of no other recommendation than that of composition'. One of his favourite pieces was an 'Ode to Contemplation', which interestingly does not reach beyond a mixture of mid-eighteenth-century gloom and the autobiographical:

> Faint gleams the evening radiance thro' the sky,
> The sober twilight dimly darkens round;
> In short quick circles the shrill bat flits by,
>   And the slow vapour curls along the ground.
>
>   ·   ·   ·   ·   ·   ·   ·
>
> Thus wandering silent on and slow
> I'll nurse Reflection's sacred woe,
>   And muse upon the perish'd day
> When Hope would weave her visions gay,
> Ere FANCY chilled by adverse fate
> Left sad REALITY my mate.[36]

Happiness, as it turned out, was not to be all high-minded. Southey enjoyed rowing on the Cherwell in early March, going up as far as Godstow with his friends Collins and Richard Lewis, dining on 'crawfish', mutton chops, eggs and bacon. His fascination with the tale of Rosamund and the ruins of Godstow nunnery allowed him to dwell on the mournfulness of the place, but also on the significance of women ('think of her I Young Man! and learn to reverence Womankind!'[37]), which in turn led him to start thinking of an old plan for Protestant nunneries. This led him, some years later, in conjunction with his friend John Rickman, to explore the possibility of an English equivalent of the Belgian *béguinages*. Oxford college life, with its claustrophobic maleness, pushed him further in this direction. Southey's resolve not to drink alcohol had left him by mid-March, judging by his description of a wine party starting at 5.00 p.m., and ending in a scuffle in town. He might have felt ashamed when he compared himself with Rousseau's strict discipline (no child of his, he told Bedford, would go either to public school or to university), but in some doggerel he set out his own rather ambiguous stall:

> No Bedford no longer oer classics Ill pore
> Till Fancy & Nature are ready to snore
> The gifts that she gave, I with gratitude take
> Nor what Nature has made shall Oxford unmake.
>
>   ·   ·   ·   ·   ·   ·   ·
>
> What is life but a dream both of sorrow & joy
> But a dream which the first breath of wind may destroy—

Tis a soft placid stream gliding gently its way
Tis a torrent that sweeps every barrier away...

Those last two lines tell us a lot about Southey's internal contradictions. In this rebellious and confused mood he is going to 'sing & despise' (not quite Seward's approach): 'and surely Bedford the resolution is founded upon Philosophy & common Sense. This season of life undoubtedly is of all others the most qualified for rendering us happy but those collegiate scholars have no idea of rendering study agreable.' For Southey, it was as though the place itself provided more of an education: the sense of history, which he increasingly felt as he began to walk around Oxford and the surrounding countryside, was to become the foundation for much of his work.

When I walk over these streets what various recollections throng upon me, what scenes Fancy delineates from the hour when Alfred first marked it as the seat of learning... I have walked over the ruins of Godstow nunnery with sensations such as the site of Troy or Carthage would inspire, a spot so famed by our Minstrel so celebrated by tradition & so memorable in the Annals of legendary, yet romantic truth cannot fail at once to sadden & to please.[38]

There might be an element of the picturesque here, but there is a distinctive Southeian sense of literary, historical, and personal possibilities. He was distressed that Bacon's study had been demolished, and that whilst his windows looked on to the spot where Latimer and Ridley had been burnt at the stake, 'there is not even a stone to mark the place where a monument should be erected to religious Liberty'. In 1797, whilst in Bath, Southey penned a less than completely successful inscription 'For a Monument at Oxford':

> Here Latimer and Ridley in the flames
> Bore witness to the truth. If thou hast walk'd
> Uprightly through the world, just thoughts of joy
> May fill thy breast in contemplating here
> Congenial virtue. But if thou hast swerved
> From the straight path of even rectitude...[39]

Like so many of these poems, this tells us more about Southey than about his heroes.

It was in this context that Southey decided to spend the Easter vacation walking around Worcestershire with Seward. It was partly a matter of making a virtue out of necessity (something he was rather good at): he could not prise Collins away from his books, Wynn was 'too genteel to visit Balliol often', Combe had gone home with a 'scrofulous eruption'. He was also anxious not to return to Bristol, where mercantile failures lay behind civil disturbance. Southey felt that he had been right: 'these are the first fruits of war'.[40] Like Wordsworth and Coleridge later, he discovered the sheer delight of walking, as opposed to being 'stewed in a leathern box', and he gave, in a chatty letter to Collins, a lengthy account of their trip to Woodstock, Evesham, Kidderminster, Bewdley, and Ledbury (where Seward's brother lived).[41] Part of the trip took them to Enstone, and its famous water-works, about which Southey wrote many years later in his *Espriella* letters; in a marginal note in his own interleaved copy he wrote, 'Having made no memoranda upon the spot a vague & melancholy impression is all that I have left.—& yet this impression is so strong that I have more than once since dreamt of the decaying water-works & forlorn garden at Enstone.'[42] This is typical of the way in which aspects of the past could haunt him. Whatever the attractions of the past, he could not bring himself, as 'a democratic philosopher', to go to Blenheim. We should note that he let the cat out of the bag in a letter to Tom Lamb: 'Of this stoicism I fear I should not have been guilty, but for the remembrance that Combe intended to go with me early in the summer.' So much for fine principles.

Southey succumbed to the delights of the natural world: 'What scenes can be more calculated to expand the soul than the sight of nature, in all her loveliest works?' Moreton-in-Marsh was less pleasing: 'a vile, unhealthy, horrible town [Southey was to harp on his hatred of towns throughout his life] ... we slept together. He took all the bed & I took all the clothes; but we did not need rocking.' Matters in France must have seemed far away. As he wrote to Lamb, 'the state of French affairs pleases *you* I hope. Peace! Peace! is all I wish for... Nor does it become a young mad-headed enthusiast to judge of these matters.' And then, an ambiguous conclusion: 'Time may alter my opinions: I do not much think it will. Let those opinions be what they will, you will not despise me for them.' And just to compound the veiled ambiguity: 'I had some more lines to have sent, but as they might not exactly have accorded with what is politically good, they are suppressed.'[43] As he grew older, Southey increasingly cared less whether or not anyone would approve of what he said.

Even with a sprained ankle, Southey carried on walking, about twenty miles a day, reading (Henry Mackenzie's popular paean to sensibility, *The Man of Feeling*, modishly enough), writing. He smilingly called himself 'a peripatetic philosopher', and confided to Bedford what he might not have admitted to Seward, that 'my sentiments will be found more enlivened by the brilliant colours of Fancy Nature & Rousseau than the positive dogmas of the Stagyrite [sc. Aristotle] or the metaphysical refinements of his antagonist.' In a revealing passage in the same letter, he described an almost Coleridgean form of associationism: 'ideas spring up with the scenes I view—some pass away with the momentary glance—some are engraved upon the tablet of memory & some impressed upon the heart.' He was clearer in his own mind about the nature of philosophy, even if this meant some recanting of his own earlier snook-cocking at Oxford conventions: it was

not reading Johannes Secundus because he may have some poetical lines—it is not wearing the hair undressd in opposition to custom perhaps—this I feel the severity of & blush for—it is not rejecting Lucan lest he should vitiate the taste & reading without fear what may corrupt the heart, it is not clapt on with a wig, or communicated by the fashionable hand of the barber—it had nothing to do with Watson when he burnt his books—it does not sit upon a woolsack—honor cannot bestow it—persecution cannot take it away... it has no particular love for colleges—in crowds it is alone, in solitude most engaged—it renders life agreeable & death enviable.[44]

Again, that curiously Keatsian tone creeps in when we least expect it.

When Southey got back to Oxford in April he had to endure Wynn's scoffing at his walking habits; but he knew that the three-week trek had been formative ('three ages in this sink of science could not erase the ideas resulting from it'). He was frustrated by his inability to describe fully all that he had seen and experienced, that strange combination of pain and pleasure (which Wordsworth was to celebrate much more astutely in *Lyrical Ballads*)—'a certain tinge of melancholy heightens every shade around & disposes the mind more fully to enjoy the awful grandeur of the scene'. He had wanted to finish his letter to Bedford in a 'spot the most romantic I ever recollect to have seen', but he had to rely on memory. Southey is already placing himself in a particular and specific Romantic tradition:

a spring dropping over a rock which it had made amid the wood—thro a narrow opening in the wood a cascade caused by the dissolving snow—a brook between so clear so broken by stones! the opposite side a hill almost perpendicular with excellent timbers & on the summit as far as sight would reach (here a very small space) such a house as brings to remembrance Switzerland & St Preux.[45]

Southey had been invigorated by his expedition, and looked forward to Bedford's coming up to Oxford for the installation as Chancellor of the Duke of Portland in the first week of July. Wynn, no doubt less than pleased by the fact that Southey stole his clothes whilst he was swimming ('leaving him to sport fresco like a young satyr with the game keeper at the cool evening hour'), charged Southey with lack of ambition. Southey did not mind; he was more interested in writing as much as possible: poems on the death of Odin, Mortality, Romance, even an Ode to Exercise. 'The young Egalites deserve the tribute I have paid them & as (since then) they have forsaken the enthusiasm of Republicanism you may perhaps be more likely to believe it. The ode led me upon this and I drop it if possible for ever. Peace be to all men!' What particularly concerned him was any prospect of idleness: 'I am resolved if possible never to suffer one moments vacancy of mind—fly from one employment to another but never permit that fatal vacuum which lies open to every thing that is evil.' This was a resolution that would dictate the whole of his career as a writer. At the same time, even at this early stage in his life, Southey was beginning to think along more domestic lines. In a poem to Bedford in the same letter, he wrote:

> And if by Fate decreed a Wife
> Should crown the comforts of my Life
> Ah let not Fashions tempting throng
> Seduce the heedless steps along...[46]

There was a short, two-week break at the end of May, and then Southey set off again with a couple of friends, this time to visit Seward's brother at Cambridge: a walk of eighty miles in three days (setting out at 4.00 in the morning as the nightingale sang). They went through Kidlington, Bicester, Stowe ('the gardens are well worth seeing & the buildings though very ridiculously situated are beautiful when abstractedly considered'), then on to Buckingham (where they stayed the night), Wolverton ('where I observed many walls covered with cow dung dried & stuck on'), Newport Pagnell, Bedford, Eaton, Buckden ('a most capital breakfast'), Huntingdon, Godmanchester, Fenstanton. Cambridgeshire he disliked for its flatness, and Cambridge city had only King's Chapel to compare with Oxford. Apart from Seward's brother at St John's he met some of his old school chums, before the return trip; they were back at Balliol in time for tea on the third day.[47]

If all this seems something of a mad rush, they still found time whilst in Cambridge to attend the famous trial of William Frend in the Senate House. Frend, a mathematics Fellow at Jesus College, and a Unitarian, was at the centre of radical activities in Cambridge. His pamphlet, *Peace and Union* (1793), had as its targets not just the Anglican Church and its doctrines but the declaration of war against France and the oppression of the Midlands poor. The young Samuel Taylor Coleridge was only too happy to allow his rooms at Jesus to become a focal point for the friends of 'Frend and Liberty'. As Charles le Grice later recalled, 'pamphlets swarmed from the press. Coleridge had read them all; and in the evenings, with our *negus*, we had them *viva voce* gloriously.' The trial itself, on a charge of 'sedition and defamation of the Church of England', became a *cause célèbre*, a tussle between the Establishment and the youthful radicals who jeered and shouted and clapped throughout. The political signi-ficance of Frend's trial was viewed, in retrospect, by the Vice-Chancellor: 'I don't believe Pitt was ever aware of how much consequence the expul-sion of Frend was: it was the ruin of the Jacobinical party as a *University thing...*'[48]

Although Southey did not know it, Coleridge too was at the trial, listening raptly to what Southey called 'a most capital piece of oratory' (by Frend in his own defence). When Southey actually got round to reading Frend's pamphlet, at the end of July, he changed his tune. 'Frend's conduct I despise—that of his persecutors I execrate ... [the] pamphlet [was] too contemptible to deserve notice.'[49] But it is important to acknowledge that the visit to Cambridge had revived his political sensi-bilities. His old Westminster friend, the printer William Rough, had even suggested a periodical paper, to be produced in Cambridge; Southey was certainly interested in the idea, provided he did not have to run it himself. It is perhaps significant that as soon as he got back, he wrote a 64–line poem on 'The First of June':

> Hail merry month, beneath whose smile
> Expanding, Nature spreads her charms
> On every tree, in every flow'r
> That decks the varied field ...

He also wrote an allegory about Ambition, and the way in which 'Reason has clipped the wings of Imagination'. It is almost as though he is providing his own answer to Wynn's chidings about his lack of ambition.

Tho I have still some little cacoethes remaining, I hope I have lost much of those sanguine expectations with which Vanity had once so inflated me, not that the failure of the *Flagellant* damped them for of that I still am proud, but to my ideas the pleasure of gratifying a few friends with those productions which partiality will make them esteem is infinitely more delightful than the applause of critics or the echo of popular praise.[50]

It was perhaps the more necessary for him to lower his sights in view of the more pressing concerns that beset him in midsummer. Family, and therefore financial, problems would take him from Oxford very soon, and he did not intend to come back for the Michaelmas term. His heart was not really in it: Oxford had not offered him much. Southey certainly felt he had not changed, or grown intellectually, as much as he would have liked. On the other hand, home life offered little respite: 'home', he told

Bedford rather pathetically, 'is far from being to me the comfortable retreat you enjoy. I have been so long enured to misery there that the idea of it when it comes across happier scenes clouds them.' He was also conscious of the confinement of Oxford, the lack of female company, the sense that he did not fit into the expected pattern: 'I am as visionary & childish, or indeed more so, than ever as noisy as wild & sometimes as melancholy.' Furthermore, writing was taking an increasing hold on him—he aimed at an essay a fortnight; and he preferred (as no doubt many students would) to write a poem about going to a logic tutorial than actually going to the tutorial.[51]

There was another reason for getting back to Bristol. He had, earlier in the year, spoken to Bedford about his desire for domestic bliss, based on a loving relationship. The particular object of his affections was Edith Fricker of Bath, with whom, as we have seen, he had established a close bond based on a family friendship going back a long way.[52] But his return to Bristol did not mean immediate bliss: for a start, Bristol, for all its charms, was not Bath, and it was teeming with soldiers. 'Here I am, the most insulated being existing with the most unbounded *continental* views.' He still could not reconcile his European aspirations with what was actually happening: 'the red robes of slaughter militate very strongly against my ideas. When I see men at least negatively good & certainly useful, taken from the plough to learn the trade of murder I wonder where the thunder sleeps.'

Southey's views were made more complex by the long poem he was working on. He had been collecting materials for *Joan of Arc*, and was now looking forward to getting down to the writing. He gave Bedford a sketch of the poem, questioning the notion that an epic should be national, or that it should follow the rules of Aristotle. 'The blank verse flows easily from the pen' (perhaps too easily), and he did not care about posterity's verdict; as he had said in a similar vein, earlier in the year, 'the approbation of a few friends contents me'. (At the same time, he began to imagine, once he had suspected Milton of being a 'republican as well as a poet', that he might be a second Milton, before modestly realizing the absurdity of the comparison.) *Joan of Arc* is an important poem, crucial to Southey's development both as writer and as public figure, and we shall return to it later. What needs to be said here is that he clearly sees it as a political statement, however ambiguous that might seem: 'I hope soon to hear of the fall of Marat Robespierre Thuriot & David . . . Vive La Republique! my Joan is a great democrat, or rather will be.'

Southey began to feel frustrated by the sheer quantity of things that passed through his mind, the range of interests that occupied him. Again, it is something of a Coleridgean problem (although, of course, they had not yet met), his recognition of the impossibility of keeping all these ideas in his head at once:

> What would not that man deserve who should invent a camera obscura to retain every idea as it is formed—you would have had a quire of letters from me had I been possessed of it before now. I had so much to say upon the lower classes of life lost to society by the total neglect of society—upon hope & disappointment—authors—travelling, *Tristram Shandy* etc; but this world of ideas is dissolved.

Fortunately, not totally so: the rest of his life can be seen as an attempt to recapture these lost thoughts and impressions. *Tristram Shandy* would lead to *The Doctor*, the ideas on poverty and education would find their outlet in lengthy articles in the *Quarterly Review* twenty years later. As if he sensed the possibilities of the future, he looked ahead to the time when he would be 'sailing with every wind along the ocean of life without helm pilot victualling or port'.[53]

In the mean time he would travel—Hereford, Worcester, the Wye valley, Brixton (where at Bedford's, in the garden, he finished *Joan of Arc*). He visited his uncle; he heard from Seward, and was glad to get his approval for democracy. He wrote furiously, 'moralizing & essayizing upon all—forming a letter upon different subjects every hour'; one moment it was an Ode on Gooseberry Pie:

> Roast beef and plumb pudding
> I find not much good in
>   Nor care for them one fig do I.
> For venison & turtle
> Let aldermen hurtle
>   But give me a gooseberry pie...[54]

('A most Horatian ode', he declared it. Six years later he was to return to the subject, in Pindaric mode, in 'Gooseberry pie is best...'.[55]) The next moment it was serious reflections on religion. He could not approve the Established Church (at Oxford he had seen its 'pillars...wallowing in all the filth of debauchery'—a disturbing early example of the hysteria that was to characterize at least some of his later political writings); he expresses the 1790s radical abhorrence of the establishment: 'church & state produce but a mulish kind of barren religion.' But he was perfectly ready to subscribe to a creed of 'God is one, Christ is the saviour of Mankind'. He denied any apostasy (again, an ironic anticipation of the very charge that would be levelled at him later in life): 'my principles & practice are equally democratic.' Just to prove the point, he emphasized his domestic activities, 'washing mending & marking, cleaning leather breeches, repairing shoes & getting together linen which has mouldered for six months.'

Southey was certainly in a strange mood during these late summer months: he can be witty, mock-solemn, and melancholy within a paragraph. No doubt much of this had to do with his own confusions as to his future, his finances, his beliefs. He had finished *Joan of Arc*, and now wanted to write an Ode to Paine, but not so far in the back of his mind were Seward's warnings about the dangers of indulging in literature 'merely for self-amusement'. He had to admit to a selfishness that was 'deeply implanted', recognizing that behind this lay a serious problem: concern with self could lead to lack of usefulness to society. For a man in turmoil, trying to come to terms with a Europe in turmoil, this presented difficulties. His very travels became a symbol and symptom of his own uncertainty of direction (Smollett's *Humphry Clinker*, a novel based on the hero's wanderings around Britain, was an appropriate book to be reading at the time). To leave Bedford and Brixton was itself a cause for immediate pain, but also a reminder of the links between the public and the private. 'I know nothing so unpleasant', he wrote on 14 October, 'as leaving the friends we love & yet such is the state of society that life is hardly anything than continual parting.'[56]

It is small wonder that so many of his poems in these early years are about home, and about the ambiguities of that very concept. He saw himself as someone dreaming up various schemes—'theories of happiness'—which he would never be able to put into practice. Significantly, whilst at Brixton, he had some kind of plaster cast made of himself, and wrote a poem, 'To the Me at Brixton', which sums up his confusions:

> O thou Myself who now
>   At Brixton rear'st aloft my pretty head
> Perchance sad emblem what I once may be
>   When I am dead.
> O thou other Me,
>   Thou with white face & Paris plaister brains
>   Attend to this Me's salutary strains.

This latter-day Hamlet cannot even get his tenses straight.

There was a further problem: whenever Southey railed against Oxford and the education system, he soon ended up talking about the absurdity of celibacy. It is quite clear that this is no abstract concern. As we have seen, there was Edith Fricker (or perhaps we should say, the Fricker sisters, and their communal allure). But other women caught his eye. Between June 1792 and February 1793 he had written what he quite rightly called

'An Improbable Tale', in which the hero, Robert, has to confront his despair at the loss of a loved one. 'Matilda is the wife of Edgar but she is still my friend & I will love her as a sister.'[57] Just what lies behind this it is hard to determine, but it seems quite clear that it reflects something of his own turbulent love-life at this period of his life. He had told Bedford at the end of July about an Ellen Shepherd he had met at Uley; out of a typically (for Southey) grotesque incident—the killing of a stoat by two dogs, the stoat then eaten by a kite—he constructed a literary conceit, and presented Ellen with these lines: 'Lifeless within this breast the victim lies, I Slain by the fatal power of Ellen's eyes'. He went on to describe her as 'a most agreable lively girl' (perhaps registering that no one ever described Edith Fricker as lively), but was anxious not to idealize her: 'with that face which a critic would call ugly, but of which a Physiognomist would pronounce more favourably, a pair of eyes well illuminated by sense & the same nose that made such havoc in the seraglio of Soliman.' He imagined himself thinking of her 'often... with pleasure'. (She was to crop up again in his life, a respectable married woman, forty years later.) He starts to talk openly about marriage, and rather typically manages to have it both ways: he has the necessary requisites to remain a bachelor ('I can smoke tobacco & play backgammon'), but contemplates a future wife who would be 'a companion in my studies & knew how to make a good pudding.'[58]

On the way back to Bristol, he made a twenty-mile literary detour on foot to Dunnington (taking only one break for a biscuit and some blackberries), and went into appropriate literary raptures: '[I] threw myself on the bank & contemplated the walls where Chaucer wore out the evening of his days.' His reward was a slap-up dinner at Newbury. But there was also another bright-eyed woman to engage his attention. In a jaunty set of verses he describes his tending, with more than disinterest, a Miss Colburne, laid up in bed with a broken thigh.[59] There is not much that we know about this woman, and Southey seems not to refer to her in any other letters. But exactly ten years later, to the very day, he published a poem to 'Mary', in the *Morning Post* for 20 October 1803, and there is some reason to believe that Southey's intervening silence is eloquent. He was never one to say much about his feelings, certainly not amorous ones: if we know very little about Edith Fricker, it is as much due to his reticence as to her notorious reluctance to put pen to paper. If the poem published ten years later does indeed refer to Miss Colburne, then she clearly played a significant part in his emotional development, precisely because they went their separate ways:

MARY! ten chequer'd years have past
Since we beheld each other last;
Yet, Mary, I remember thee,
Nor canst thou have forgotten me.

The bloom was then upon thy face,
Thy form had every youthful grace;
I too had then the warmth of youth,
And in our hearts was all its truth.

. . . . . .

At our last meeting sure thy heart
Was even as loth as mine to part;
And yet we little thought that then
We parted...not to meet again.

Long, Mary! after that adieu,
My dearest day-dreams were of you;
In sleep I saw you still, and long
Made you the theme of secret song.[60]

There was yet another romance nipped in the bud, when he visited Edmund Seward at Sapey. In the same house was Augusta Roberts, with whom he became infatuated, only to discover after he had gone that Seward's brother John was attached to her. Although Edmund was not going to sue on his brother's behalf, Southey followed the dictates of duty imbibed from Seward. 'At the expense of my happiness I preservd that of two persons more deserving. I directed him to burn my letter, desird him to forget it & promisd what never can be performed, to forget Augusta.'[61] Southey says no more about the matter; but we need not be surprised that, in December, he writes an ode on Grief. Nor, for that matter, that on 22 December he warns Horace Bedford against love: it 'must ultimately mellow into friendship'. Clearly he speaks feelingly about the dangers of speaking too feelingly.[62]

Southey headed back to Bristol, getting there on 19 October. He had missed the latest riots of September, in which twelve people died and fifty were wounded, because of a dispute over a toll bridge. (A year earlier, he had registered how Bristol, in its radical fervour, had seemed on the verge of eruption.) Southey saw and heard about the effects, the lost lives, the revolutionary graffiti. 'Damn to Bateman—&—Daubeny dies—are writ-ten upon every watch box & corner. It is melancholy that all these lives are lost thro the imprudence of the commissioners in taking off the toll & then imposing it again: the people have carried their point...'[63] He was exhausted after all his travels, and sought solace in philosophy, but found himself resorting to facetiousness when he tried to explain himself to

Bedford. 'Dont think me drunk for if I am tis with sobriety—& I certainly feel most seriously disposed to be soberly nonsensical.' Bedford would certainly have been surprised by Southey's apparently sudden enthusiasm, not for Epictetus (Seward's favourite book), but for Epicurus. Southey would not, of course, countenance Epicurus' denial of the Deity. But mention of Epicurus led him to think of Plotinus' desire to build an ideal city based on Plato's teaching, and this in turn led him to remember his earlier dream sparked off by the mutiny on the *Bounty*, and to start imagining his own ideal city, far removed from the carnage and turmoil of Bristol, and perhaps embracing at least some of the tenets of Epicurus. There, in Southeyopolis, would be Southey with his clique of Plato, Alcaeus, Lucan and Milton, and Bedford, 'dreaming of Utopian things possessed of the virtues of the Antonines—regulated by peers every one of whom should be a Falkland—& by a popular assembly where every man should unite the integrity of a Cato—the eloquence of a Demosthenes—& the loyalty of a Jacobite'. Southey knew that he was moving away from Seward's teachings, just as he was irked by Bedford's supposition that he would be pleased at the death of the Queen of France. As he pointed out rather curtly, 'I can condemn the crimes of the French & yet be a Republican nor am I as you have stiled me a theoretical one.' The trouble with Bedford, felt Southey, was to do with the blindness of prejudice; his description of his own Southeyopolis scheme was certainly not the result of prejudice. He was actively pursuing different possibilities, different ideals which would accommodate his shifting views. It would be wrong to think that all this talk was mere escapism, even if we might have to acknowledge that Southey's awareness of the difference between theory and practice was not always as acute as he implies here. Within a year, none the less, all this talk would be fleshed out in the grand scheme of Pantisocracy.[64]

Southey became acquainted with William Godwin's writings, especially *An Enquiry Concerning Political Justice* (1793) in October 1793. Godwin's rationalism and atheism, allied to a deep-seated republicanism, provided just the kind of intellectual support Southey needed. For a few years, no Romantic radical could avoid Godwin's influence: Coleridge, Wordsworth, and, later, Shelley—all came under his spell. Within a year Coleridge was able to contribute a sonnet on Godwin to the *Morning Post*, alongside one to Pitt (portrayed as Judas Iscariot). Wordsworth and Godwin saw each other regularly in 1794–5. Coleridge and Wordsworth both changed their minds, especially about Godwin's extreme rationality, and in April 1796 Coleridge dismissed Godwin's principles as 'vicious . . . his book is a Pandar to Sensuality'. Southey held faith a little longer. For the moment, in the autumn of 1793, Godwinism enabled Southey to believe in an ideal of perfection and in the benevolence of humankind ('this is real Philosophy'); it also enabled him, ironically—in view of his own dreams and fancies—to see the dangers of the Imagination: 'when Fancy thrusts herself into the throne of Reason & boldly heads into the regions of abstraction metaphysics & absurdity—instead of admiring the ingenuity we should rather lament abilities so perverted.' At this distance we can see Southey's own blurring of distinctions, which helps to account for his own confusions; but we can also see how such a view was to lead him, ere long, to find fault with Coleridge's metaphysics. By the end of the year Southey's internal contradictions could scarcely be denied: on the one hand, he could write in verse to Horace Bedford that Reason was the only solace open to those 'doomd to taste of woe' (for Reason led to a belief in Heaven, and therefore eternal consolation); on the other hand, as he strolled around the streets of Bristol he found himself 'commenting & rhapsodizing aloud!' Before he knew what he was doing, he was using the word Romance, and equating it with goodness.[65]

By November 1793 Southey felt no more optimistic than he had a year before; he had achieved nothing. He was the archetypal wanderer: 'still pushing for the Fortunate Islands, I discovered that they existed not for me, & that, like other wiser & better than myself, I must be content to wander about & never gain the port!'[66] His self-loathing was made worse by his sense of the world's falling apart: tyranny and oppression were everywhere, and there was no place for virtue. 'Here are you & I', he told Bedford, 'theorising upon principles we can never practise & wasting our time & youth—you in scribbling parchments & I in spoiling quires with poetry.' It would have been preferable for his friends to have encouraged him to be a carpenter. Then, in a rather poignant turn in this letter, he looks back to the apparent idyll of his childhood, to the bond with his grandmother (who had died when he was 8 years old). It is a reminder of how, at 19, Southey was still not much more than an over-grown child, looking for security but aware that it lay behind him, out of time and out of reach. 'Oh if life were all one agreable dream—or rather if death were— would there be crime in taking laudanum as an opiate?' 'I have no object of pursuit in life', he told Horace Bedford, 'but to fill the passing hour—& fit myself for death: beyond these views I have nothing.'[67]

The idea of an alternative community, far away, began to have renewed appeal. On the one hand, there was the ideal of Greece ('what a republic! what a province!'); but there was also the comfortingly literary example of the desire of the seventeenth-century poet Abraham Cowley to settle in

America. Southey, however, was interested in more than solitude: 'I should be pleased to reside in [a] country where mere abilities would ensure respect, where society was upon a proper footing & Man was considered as more valuable than money—& where I could till the earth & provide by honest industry the meal which my wife would dress with pleasing care—redeunt spectacula mane...'[68] The motives change: they are not all high-minded. World-weariness led him to make his will at the end of November 1793 (witnessed by his servant and friend Shadrach Weeks and his dear cousin Margaret Hill); 'when the worms are honey-combing my carcase', he writes, with that ghoulish relish that was to surface in his ballads, 'what signifies the fly blows upon fame? I am tired of politics—I am tired of this place...'[69]

Things were not improved by his total lack of conviction over the Church as his future career. As he confided to Horace Bedford, in a letter underlining the way his doubts reinforced his lack of orthodoxy (his favourite put-down of his friend Lightfoot was that he was too 'ortho-dogs'), 'to obtain future support—to return the benefits I have received— I must become contemptible infamous & perjured.'[70] In November and December he kept returning to Godwin's idea of the perfectibility of the human race; he exchanged ideas with Seward, who talked of the immutable laws of Religion, whereas he, Southey, spoke of the immutable laws of Justice. The difference, Southey averred, existed 'only in terms'. Sin, he tried to persuade Horace Bedford, was not innate, but artificial, 'the monstrous offspring of government & property. The origin of both was injustice.' To Grosvenor Bedford he cried, Blake-like, 'priestcraft has chained down the human mind—& I can neither get rid of the chains or feel their necessity'.[71] Not surprisingly, he felt he could only grit his teeth and keep on going: he was conscious of a family, including two young brothers, to support. There was still the hope of getting at least something from the estate of Lord John Somerville, his father's elder brother—but that was more self-delusion than realistic.

What began to emerge as a possibility was that he might actually make some money by his pen; he had written reams and reams, and began 'to wish publication'. This would at least be preferable to the bottle, which was a passing temptation. His meeting with another young writer, Robert Lovell, was no doubt instrumental in encouraging his belief in writing as one way out of the mess. Lovell, from a Bristol Quaker family, was at Balliol, and a promising poet, with whom Southey would publish his first volume in 1794; he was also to marry Mary Fricker, Edith's sister. Southey told Horace Bedford that Lovell was 'very moderate in democracy, & no politician in poetry. So you two must curb me.' Ironically, in view of his

frequent assertions that the European stage was something upon which
he no longer wished to walk, he now found that events in France provided
a welcome distraction from his own wretched, despairing solitude, in
which he felt on the verge of madness: 'how much happier should I feel
were I on the frontiers of France every hour expos'd to death in a cause I
must feel to be just.'[72]

As if to give the spur to his growing recognition of himself as a writer, he
finished copying out his long poem, *Joan of Arc*, bound in marble paper
and tied with a green ribbon. He was working on a poem on Memory, and
Joan, he declared, would be followed by a string of other epics. In this he
was not far wrong. And yet he still did not know what view to take of
himself; he knew he was a bag of contradictions, and he shifted from one
mood to another with disconcerting ease: 'I must be either too trifling or
too serious, the first can do no harm; & I know the last does no good.'
Announcing to Bedford that he now felt able to look upon the whole
world as his country, and reiterating his horror at the prospect of the
Church, he asked him to imagine him in America:

imagine my ground uncultivated since the creation & see me wielding the axe now
to cut down the tree & now the snakes that nestled in it. Then see me grubbing up
the roots & building a nice snug little dairy with them. Three rooms in my cottage,
& my only companion some poor negro whom I have bought on purpose to
emancipate. After a hard days toil see me sleep upon rushes &, in very bad weather
take out my casette & write to you, for you shall positively write to me in America.
Do not imagine I shall leave rhyming or philosophising, so that your friend will
realise the romance of Cowley & even outdo the seclusion of Rousseau, till at last
comes an ill-looking Indian with a tomahawk & scalps me—a most melancholy
proof that society is very bad & that I shall have done very little to improve it! So
Vanity Vanity will come from my lips—& poor Southey will either be cooked for a
Cherokee or oysterised by a tyger.[73]

Much of this is light banter: and yet a few days earlier he had been
talking in all seriousness about the nature of society and evil, and the
importance of Godwin in the argument. It seems entirely appropriate
that he should, in the same letter, foresee his own epitaph: 'Here lies an
odd mortal whose life only benefited the paper manufacturers & whose
death will only hurt the post-office.' Once again the levity conceals an
uneasy truth, one regarded with some ruefulness by a posterity worn
down by the sheer amount of paper he covered. As though preparing for
the end, he went through all the verses he had written, burning about
10,000 lines, and keeping the same number in fair copies, neatly made.

Southey knew he was trying to escape. Society required 'desperate
remedies' which he felt unable to supply. But America could only be

another dream, because of his lack of money, his family commitments, and his conviction that he was chained to the Church. So that constant self-employment he had spoken of the previous year became at least a safety valve, as he flitted from one activity to another. 'You see I must fly from thought. Today I begin Cowper's Homer & write an ode—tomorrow read & write something else.'[74] One poem was his 'To my Great Coat' (that bear-like garment he cherished for its warmth and companionship, as though it were another person)—a typically light-hearted piece to Bedford.[75] Another, more serious, was a poem to the parting year, sanctioned, because of its metre, by Milton, Collins, Mrs Barbauld, and Sayers. A third poem anticipated, with rather more sobriety than his 'epitaph', his own death:

> Then when the inexorable hour shall come
>   To tell my death let no deep requiem toll
> No hireling sexton dig the venal tomb
>   Or priest be paid to hymn my parted soul
> No let my children near their little cot
>   Lay my old bones beneath the turf to rot
> So let me live unknown—so let me die forgot.[76]

But as the year turned, and he prepared for the return to Balliol, Southey was ready to put behind him such literary despair. He had decided to switch to medicine.

COLERIDGE AND PANTISOCRACY

1794–1795

'ONCE more am I settled in Balliol', Southey wrote to Horace Bedford in January 1794, 'once more among my friends, alternately studying & philosophizing, railing at collegiate folly, & enjoying rational society. My prospects in life totally altered, waiting eagerly to cut up human flesh & resolved to come out Asculepius secundus.' Southey had conveniently forgotten his earlier revulsion when 'Horse' Campbell had shown him the half-dissected body of a woman on the anatomy table; Campbell, for his part, was delighted that his friend was doing medicine (it partly made up for his having had to part with his horse), delighted, too, that his horse had been replaced by a dog given him by Dr Pegg, with which he happily slept. As Southey commented, 'The Doctors room may be smelt at Woodstock whiffing the accumulated stinks of the dead bodies, the Dog & the Doctor himself.' Tom Lamb was up at Christ Church; Southey was less keen now on Collins, with his 'overbearing manner in conversation & front of adamant', and preferred the friends of Elmsley and Wynn, especially some Corpus men, including John Horseman. He did not approve of their shooting parties, but took pleasure in their music-making (he had what he describes as a 'discordant' voice, but all his life enjoyed singing): George Burnett of Balliol (another friend who was to crop up in his life in various guises) had a harpsichord, Lightfoot a flute, '& if I had but a Jews-harp the concert would be complete'.

On the literary front, he was reading and writing more than ever. Rising to Horace Bedford's comments on *Werther*, Southey declared it one of his favourite books (along with those of Milton, Collins, Frank Sayers, and Beattie), even though suicide was a crime; it clearly appealed to his burgeoning Romantic sensibilities, and had the kind of effect on him that Schiller's *Robbers* would have, before long, on Coleridge. He was also taken with Glover's poems: *Boadiciea, Medea,* and especially *Leonidas,* which had the sanction of no less an authority than Joseph Warton; Southey admired the simplicity, as he saw it, of Glover's style, as opposed to the 'vitiated taste' of the present, with its 'awkward imagery &

cumbrous metaphor. Into this meretricious stile I know myself frequently to have fallen,—& am pleased to see myself daily reclaiming. Simplicity is all in all...' Southey's alertness to stylistic problems and possibilities is instructive, in that he was going through a similar education to that described by Coleridge in his *Biographia Literaria*. But he never fully resolved the problem of what the appropriate style was, certainly for his poetry: he seems to have been clearer in his mind about what he could do in prose. But he was starting to write a series of Botany Bay Eclogues, in which he began to see how social issues could—in fact should—be confronted in verse that had no particular ambitions of its own.

Like his sonnets on the slave trade, these poems explore the pathos of the wronged exile, whilst anticipating something of what we might equate with Byronic egotism. For example, 'Frederic' begins:

> Where shall I turn me? whither shall I bend
> My weary way? thus worn with toil and faint
> How thro' the thorny mazes of this wood
> Attain my distant dwelling? that deep cry
> That rings along the forest seems to sound
> My parting knell: it is the midnight howl
> Of hungry monsters prowling for their prey!
> Again! oh save me—save me gracious Heaven!
> I am not fit to die!

There is a persistent desire to recall the lost domesticity of England, idealized no doubt, in the context of Botany Bay, but understandable precisely because of that context, as in 'Humphrey and William':

> Ah Humphrey! now upon old England's shore
> The weary labourer's morning work is o'er:
> The woodman now rests from his measur'd stroke,
> Flings down his axe and sits beneath the oak,
> Savour'd with hunger there he eats his food,
> There drinks the cooling streamlet of the wood.
> To us no cooling streamlet winds its way,
> No joys domestic crown for us the day,
> The felon's name, the outcast's garb we wear,
> Toil all the day, and all the night despair...

These poems, for all their faults, were to take up considerable space in the 1797 volume of his poems; Southey knew that he was touching a raw nerve, and that a certain rustic simplicity was appropriate for his purposes. His 'English Eclogues' would carry the process a stage further; but by then, Wordsworth and Coleridge's *Lyrical Ballads* of 1798 had extended the terms of the debate in a way that Southey had not quite foreseen, and perhaps did not fully understand.[1]

Given all this activity, it is perhaps not surprising that he complained of bad eyes; he could neither read nor write by candlelight. This was to be a recurrent problem, and not ideal for a budding writer, if that in fact was what he was. The question of a career was still a vexed one; whatever his declarations about 'Asculepius secundus' he soon lost his interest in medicine. There seemed to be only three possibilities: the Church, the army, and the law. He never considered the army, the oaths for the Church were for him a major stumbling block, and law did not have much to do with justice. This was brought home to Southey by an event at Christ Church, where a female servant of 15 had strangled her new-born baby. Southey was deeply disturbed by the human aspects of this tragedy, but also by the implications for woman's position in society: 'Nothing is more astonishing to me than that a virtue so rigidly demanded from woman should be so despised among men.' This led him to question the essentially parasitic nature of the legal system: 'The lawyer lives by the vices & follies of his neighbours, blows up the coals of discord, & when the fire is spent, is paid for quenching it.' He wanted to believe that there were some 'immutable' laws of justice, but he found it increasingly difficult to hold on to the concept. This was another side to the coin, reflecting the 'natural ardor of his temper'; he was, he told Horseman, 'romantic & eccentric', and this was no doubt as true a description of him as any at this time.[2] Godwin did not have all the best tunes. Southey was, after all, a poet, or at least a versifier, and it was hard to be that whilst also being a strict Godwinite. But, as if to prove his radical credentials, he grew a beard (surprisingly, apparently surprised that it was black), and then painfully cut and scraped it off. Interestingly, his poem to the Chapel bell played down the importance of religion when it was at the expense of poetry.

> 'Lo I—the man who erst the Muse did ask
>   Her deepest notes to swell the Patriot's meeds,
> Am now enforst a far unfitter task
>   For cap and gown to leave my minstrel weeds,'
> For yon dull noise that tinkles on the air
> Bids me lay by the lyre and go to morning prayer...[3]

In April, Southey set off for Bristol, with Combe and a handful of other Oxonians whose 'folly...taciturnified me'. He was never one to suffer fools gladly. He was glad to leave Oxford and its lack of liberality; his friend Robert Allen—'a man of extraordinary ability...an excellent republican'—was the only one he knew who 'searches after truth with all the boldness the search requires'. (Leigh Hunt, in his *Autobiography* (1850) described Allen as 'so handsome ... that running one day against a barrow-woman in the street, and turning round to appease her in the midst of her abuse, she said "Where are you driving to, you great hulking, good-for-nothing,—beautiful fellow, God bless you!"'[4]) Horseman had left a few days earlier, and Southey and Allen spent a lot of time 'in all the luxury of democratic converse'. As they drove down to Bristol, Southey allowed his thoughts to wander, pondering on the awfulness of London, 'an overgrown monster devouring its own children ... a large sink of folly dissipation & iniquity'. Whereas 'large cities are inevitably destructive to morality', he found comfort and strength in recollecting childhood scenes from his Bristol days, even as he reprimanded himself for indulging in these 'dreams of fancy' that render the mind 'totally unfit for serious contemplation & abstract reasoning'.[5] He decided to walk the last part of the journey, and paused by a brook within a mile of one of his old schools. 'The lapse of twelve years have not obliterated one image from my memory—& I have seldom past half an hour more agreably in solitude than the one yesterday morning.' This 'pleasing melancholy' we might well associate with William Lisle Bowles, and sure enough Southey quotes at this point one of Bowles's sonnets, 'To the River Itchen near Winton'. But lest Bedford think he was becoming too maudlin and melancholy, Southey enclosed his comic 'Ode to my Stick yclept the Sans Culottes'.[6]

Back in Oxford after a fortnight, Southey looked forward to a visit from Lovell: the plan was to publish their joint volume, under the pseudonyms of Valentine and Orson, at Oxford. It should be said that, however precious this might seem now (and the impression is not, nor was, helped by the appearance of 'Bion' and 'Moschus' in the book itself), Valentine and Orson crop up, in passing, in Godwin's radical *Caleb Williams* (1794), and would therefore be an indication of the political motivations of the volume. In the mean time Southey had started writing a play, based none too promisingly, but typically, on Tacitus, *Annales* 14, centring on the death of Pedanius Secundus and the execution of 400 slaves. More promising was 'The Miser's Mansion', which he sent to Bedford on 11 May, a combination of Gothic gloom, pity for the poor, and a rather cloyingly religious sentimentality, at odds, we might think, with Southey's general views at the time.[7] He was also advising Wynn and Bedford on their respective love lives (Wynn was separated from his beloved; the more cavalier Bedford was getting over a brief fling with a gypsy), at a time when he was thinking increasingly of his own emotional life. But there were still the practical problems of a career and finance. He had both

Wynn and Bedford looking up wills at Doctors' Commons, in the hope that something could be retrieved from the family coffers, in particular those of John Cannon Southey, who had died in 1760. It is clear from what he says to Bedford in May that his own hopes of domestic happiness depend upon getting his finances sorted out.

If my reversion can be sold for any comfortable independance I am sure you would rather advise me to seize happiness with mediocrity than lose it in waiting for affluence...Every day do I repine at the education that taught me to handle a lexicon instead of a hammer—& destined me for one of the drones of society... twenty is young for a Stoic you will say—but they have been years of experience & observation...oh! for emancipation from these useless forms, this useless life, these haunts of intolerance vice & folly!...Had I a sufficiency in independance, I have every reason to expect happiness. The most pleasing visions of domestic life would be realized. Knowing this I may be allowed sometimes to repine at the situation which debars me. Do not show this to anyone.[8]

The cautious, circumspect Bedford was discouraging: he thought Southey was unwise to resist the Church, so Southey had to spell it out. He would not entertain a 'prospect which leads to starving in creditable celibacy upon 40 pounds a year... There is no alternative I will not prefer to taking orders. I may forfeit happiness but God forbid that I should ever cease to deserve it.' Southey knew how much all this would distress his friend, but he was determined to insist on his own integrity. And, as his mention of celibacy indicates, he was now driven by more than financial desperation. Fortunately, he had Wynn's support: and Wynn's mother happened to be the sister of the Foreign Secretary, Lord Grenville. In spite of all he had thought and said about law as a profession, it was the legal profession that he saw as a solution to his problems. 'I want an obvious reason for abandoning Oxford & a certainty of existence till my own ability allow me to marry.' He could not marry without 'a competency' and he was determined to get one. As he warmed to his theme, he sensed that he had at least a fair chance: he was not completely useless, and he was (again, perhaps, ominously) adaptable.

My abilities are only fixd in the principal of Justice—In application they are versatile. I can turn them from one species of composition to another & experience tells me that my success is the same in all. I am above vanity—but I despise the affectation of modest Falshood...[9]

It seems of some personal significance that he should, at this stage in his life, this turning-point, meditate upon the nature of free will: man, he thought, acted from necessity, which was not the same as predestination; mixed up in all this was the sense of duty to which he felt both Bedford and he could turn, as explanation for most things.[10] Meanwhile, his poems continued to pour forth, reflecting his own concerns: a monodrama, a poem about Aristodemus visiting the tomb of the daughter he had killed in rage (Southey's sense of guilt was clearly as strong as Wordsworth's), and 'The Retrospect' ('One of the prettiest pieces I have written'), which stated with greater eloquence than he had yet managed the importance of the past in his view of things, even whilst he upbraided himself for dwelling on that very past. It is not a particularly remarkable piece, but worth noting for its Bowlesian influence.

> On as I journey through the vale of years,
> By hopes enliven'd, or deprest by fears,
> Allow me, Memory, in thy treasured store,
> To view the days that will return no more...[11]

Southey's body was as sensitive as his mind. Whilst he waited in Oxford to hear what success Wynn would have on his behalf, his bowels, not for the first nor the last time, erupted. 'My poor trullibubs are empty', he declared on 12 June to Bedford. 'A dose of salts yesterday & another this morning has been scouring out my tripes. This may possibly remove indisposition for a little while, but I am not fool enough to hope it will remove the cause. Continual anxiety will wear out a stronger frame than mine—oh, that gripe.' His 'trullibubs' were not helped by Wynn's pointing out that Southey's republicanism—so publicly declared—would work against any legal position. Southey, perversely we might think, rejoiced at this: it meant he did not have to forfeit his integrity. Or, at any rate, if he did, it would be on his own terms. He was certainly not going to deny his republicanism: 'The false hopes which deceived me are gone, & it is but turning adventurer at last, or be villain enough to take orders & grow fat in ease indolence & iniquity.' As if to drive the point home, he urged Bedford not to add 'Esquire' when he wrote to him. He was more determined than ever to leave Oxford. Again anticipating what was to become a common Romantic resort to Milton's famous line, he wrote ' "The world is all before me" ', and then went on, '& a wide & wearying world it is when I cast my eyes around & see no haven of shelter!'[12] But as his bowels were exploding, and the brief dream of a legal position faded, Southey's life was about to be altered by a new acquaintance (who also had trouble with his bowels: when Coleridge produced his journal, the *Watchman*, he must have enjoyed using the quotation from Isaiah as an epigraph, 'Wherefore my Bowels shall sound like an Harp'). His reaffirmation of his republican ideals owed much to the fact that his democratic friend Allen had turned up at his Balliol rooms with the wild-haired, visionary-eyed, adenoidal Samuel Taylor Coleridge.[13]

Not only was Coleridge already established as a rallying figure for Cambridge Jacobins; he was also something of a character, rejoicing in his flamboyance, boating on the Cam with rather more self-conscious hilarity and swagger than Southey on the Isis or the Cherwell. He was writing furiously, too, countering the tedium of lectures, but with more success than had hitherto come Southey's way. In June 1792 his highly topical Greek 'Ode on the Slave Trade' had won the Browne Gold Medal; in July he recited the poem at the Encaenia. But Coleridge was no more enamoured of university life than was Southey. Not many months earlier he had, thanks to family manœuvrings, returned to Cambridge with his tail between his legs, after a brief and bizarre episode as a private in the army, under the improbable name of Silas Tomkyn Comberbache. He had shown, however dramatically and foolishly, that he could actually escape. Southey had so far only dreamt of escape. Even at 22, and with no great achievements behind him (though his scholarly record was certainly more impressive than Southey's)—and no clear sense of a future—Coleridge had already established a charismatic reputation.

Southey might well have thought that the stop-over in Oxford (Coleridge was off on one of his walking expeditions to Wales with his old friend Joseph Hucks) was part of the necessitarian plan he had spoken of to Bedford. The two men immediately took to each other, no doubt recognizing just how much they had in common: personal and financial anxieties, doubts about their role in life, a passion for literature, and, above all, an eager, optimistic republicanism. Southey saw straightaway that he had found a kindred spirit, 'one whom I very much esteem & admire tho two thirds of our conversation be spent in disputing on metaphysical subjects'. Southey was not really a metaphysician, but it was as though Coleridge supplied this deficiency in himself, and was the more valuable (it was not to be always thus). Southey had celebrated other new friends before, but never so ecstatically: 'He is of most uncommon merit—of the strongest genius, the clearest judgment, the best heart.' As Coleridge and Hucks continued on their tour, Southey remained behind, more than ever convinced that he was right not to renounce his republican sympathies just to become a civil servant ('Nature never intended me for a negative character'), and equally determined to leave Oxford in July. Southey later told the poet James Montgomery that his first meeting with Coleridge 'fixed the future fortunes of us both . . . I reformed his life, & he disposed me towards Christianity . . . For this dream [a republic of 'Reason and Virtue'] I gave up every other prospect.'[14] We have to remember that Southey's later recollections, like Coleridge's, are not always entirely reliable, and it is hard to credit entirely the claim that until that point in his life, Coleridge had not given politics much thought.

At the end of June Southey quoted, defiantly, in a letter to Bedford, the final stanzas of his own poem, 'The Exiled Patriots', which Coleridge was to quote in his contentious lecture of 1795, *Conciones ad Populum*:

> Tho cankering cares corrode the sinking frame
> Tho Sickness rankle in the shallow breast
> Tho Death himself should quench the vital flame
> Think but for what ye suffer and be blest.

> So shall your great examples fire each soul
> So in each freeborn heart for ever dwell
> 'Til' Man shall rise above the unjust controul
> Stand where ye stood—& triumph where ye fell.

As he added poignantly, 'You will like the poetry better than the sentiment, but the man who wrote & felt those lines must never be guilty of silence.'[15]

On 6 July Coleridge wrote from Gloucester: 'S. T. Coleridge to R. Southey—Health & Republicanism!' Southey had been used to the down-to-earth, seriously sensible correspondence of a Bedford or a Wynn. Nothing could have prepared him for Coleridge's wonderfully inspired flights of fancy:

Verily, Southey—I like not Oxford nor the inhabitants of it—I would say, thou art a Nightingale among Owls—but thou art so songless and heavy towards night, that I will rather liken thee to the Matin Lark—thy *Nest* is in a blighted Cornfield, where the sleepy Poppy nods it's red-cowled head, and the weak-eyed Mole plies his dark work—but thy soaring is even unto heaven.—Or let me add . . . that as the Italian Nobles their newfashioned Doors, so thou dost make the adamantine Gate of Democracy turn on it's golden Hinges to most sweet Music.

But Coleridge was not just interested in flattering Southey; behind the exuberance lay the newly conceived plan of Pantisocracy. Coleridge had enabled what seemed at the time like the fulfilment of Southey's dream, not just of escape, but of a new republic based on a principled rejection of all the old, royalist ways. No doubt referring back to the fate of Louis XVI, and Southey's own confused response to that cataclysmic event, Coleridge pointed out that it was necessary to kill kings: 'When Serpents *sting*, the only Remedy is—to *kill* the Serpent, and *besmear* the *Wound* with the *Fat.*'

Although much later in life Coleridge was to play down the significance of Pantisocracy (as he was to disown much of his radical youth), it would be wrong to accept his later view as the truth. Several commentators have been content to take his word for it, in the *Friend* in 1809, that Pantisocracy was 'a plan as harmless as it was extravagant'—in other words, little more, as many have argued, than an undergraduate piece of pipe-dreaming. But the scheme was not an isolated phenomenon: it was part of the complex debate sparked off by the American War of Independence, by the French Revolution, and by a wide range of writers who were addressing, in different ways, the problematical relationship between the individual and society at a time of social upheaval, the connection between 'civilized' society and the natural world, and the extent to which humanity could be regarded as essentially good. There are many strands here, and it is virtually impossible to separate them all. But there can be little doubt that Coleridge's metaphysical bent gave the whole scheme a philosophical structure it might otherwise have lacked. He certainly helped to provide some of the vocabulary. In the same letter of 6 July he wrote to Southey, apologizing for some rather un-humanitarian sentiments (Coleridge, too, was confused):

When the pure System of Pantocracy shall have aspheterized the Bounties of Nature, these things will not be so—! I trust, you admire the word 'aspheterized' from α non $\sigma\phi\acute{\epsilon}\tau\epsilon\rho o\varsigma$ proprius ! We really *wanted* such a word—instead of travelling along the circuitous dusty, beaten high-Road of Diction you thus cut across the soft, green, pathless Field of Novelty—Similies forever! Hurra![16]

There are two contemporary accounts of Pantisocracy which need to be quoted.[17] First, Thomas Poole, Coleridge's tanner friend from Somerset, wrote on 22 September 1794:

Twelve gentlemen of good education and liberal principles are to embark with twelve ladies in April next. Previous to their leaving this country they are to have as much intercourse as possible, in order to ascertain each other's dispositions, and firmly to settle every regulation for the government of their future conduct. Their opinion was that they should fix themselves at—I do not recollect the place, but somewhere in a delightful part of the new back settlements; that each man should labour two or three hours in a day, the produce of which labour would, they imagine, be more than sufficient to support the colony. As Adam Smith observes that there is not above one productive man in twenty, they argue that if each laboured the twentieth part of time, it would produce enough to satisfy their wants. The produce of their industry is to be laid up in common for the use of all; and a good library of books is to be collected, and their leisure hours to be spent in study, liberal discussions, and the education of their children . . . The regulations relating to the females strike them as the most difficult; whether the marriage contract shall be dissolved if agreeable to one or both parties, are not yet determined. The employments of the women are to be the care of infant children, and other occupations suited to their strength; at the same time the greatest attention is to be paid to the cultivation of their minds. Every one is to enjoy his own religious and political opinions, provided they do not encroach on the rules previously made, which rules, it is unnecessary to add, must in some measure be regulated by the laws of the state which includes the district in which they settle.[18]

The more he thought about it, the less enthusiastic Poole felt about the scheme; what worried him especially were the practicalities. But, as George Burnett pointed out two years later, the initial scheme had not been fully thought through by the time Coleridge left Oxford that June. The plan had apparently been mooted at a friend's rooms in Worcester College, but they were 'mere outlines', to be fleshed out later. Whilst Coleridge and Hucks went on their way to Wales, Burnett and Southey walked to Bristol, talking all the journey about this new scheme, and deciding that it was only in America that it would be practicable. Burnett, in his letter to Lightfoot, gives the basis of the scheme; interestingly, he concentrates on the theory:

Our grand object then was, the Abolition of Property; at least of individual property. Conceiving the present unequal distribution of property, to be the source of by far the greater part of the moral evil that prevails in the world; by the removal of the *cause*, we thought, & as it appears to me justly thought, that the *effect* must also cease. In the present state of society, the love of distinction, the strongest motive to action, has for its gratification, the accumulation of wealth. In such a state as I am describing this passion would be diverted into a more proper channel. Here no man could gain applause or distinction from his fellow-men, unless by superiority of genius and virtue. The field would be sown and the harvest reaped by community of toil, and the fruits enjoyed in tranquillity and peace.[19]

There was a general interest in America at the end of the eighteenth century. Southey, Coleridge, and Wordsworth all had access to a range of travel books, such as William Bartram's *Travels through the Carolinas* (1791), Gilbert Imlay's *Topographical Description of North America* (1792), J. P. Brissot de Warville's *Travels in the United States* (translated 1792), and Hector St John de Crèvecœur's *Letters from an American Farmer* (1782). But as these titles and authors suggest, such books were not merely topographical accounts; there were forceful political implications. Brissot, for example, quoted by Coleridge in his *Conciones ad Populum*, was a dominant figure in the French Revolution who fell foul of the Jacobins late in 1792 ('Happy had it been for France', lamented Thomas Poole, 'had all her leaders been like Brissot')[20]. By June 1795 the *Gentleman's Magazine* was reporting that a group of Girondon *émigrés*, followers of Brissot, had settled, appropriately, in Frenchtown, near the Susquehanna. Several English radicals not only looked to America for salvation, but went there to embrace it. Thomas Cooper had settled, with his father-in-law, the Dissenter Joseph Priestley, by the Susquehanna, and produced *Some Information Concerning America* in 1794; it was as though the radical Dissenters felt, perhaps aptly as it turned out, that there was no place for them in England, especially when the favoured version of Girondon republicanism collapsed in 1793 with the September massacres.

Richard Price (the initial butt of Burke's *Reflections*) believed that 'the independence of the English colonies in America is one step ordained by Providence to introduce [the millennium]'. The Revolution and its aftermath naturally led to millenarianism and ideas of the Apocalypse. There was some irony in the fact that Price and Priestley, both opposed to Robespierre and the excesses of the Jacobins, should be called traitors and French sympathisers. Coleridge 'and other radical Dissenters found themselves in an ideological cul-de-sac from which emigration seemed to be the most plausible escape'.[21] Coleridge later claimed, in that famous piece in the *Friend*, that Pantisocracy had actually saved him from Jacobinism; Southey was outraged by such an apparent recantation, but one of the problems was that the nice discriminations between Jacobin, republican, and democrat were often too nice to be nicely observed: in the end everyone could use the most convenient term, and, more than twenty years later, when Southey's past came back to haunt him, the game could be played with all the benefit not only of hindsight but also of distance. It is important to emphasize that the desire to go to America was not merely a matter of escape. The impassioned feelings aroused by the trial of Frend (let alone the trial of all the others) indicated the significance and complexity of the argument: there were genuine reasons for wanting to set up an alternative community, and if Cambridge hardly seemed the place, neither did Oxford; if Priestley had found it necessary to emigrate in 1791, then others might want to follow.

Priestley believed in the perfectibility of mankind, in necessitarianism, in the equality of rights; vice was a product of circumstance. If this sounds familiar, then that is because, to us, it is. All the Romantic poets had to come to terms with William Godwin, and his *Enquiry Concerning Political Justice* was a key statement for those not content with the status quo. Southey's cry of delight in October 1793—'I am studying such a book'— found an echo in Coleridge and Wordsworth, and later Shelley.[22] Again, it is easy to trivialize Godwin's beliefs, to make him seem an arid advocate of reason at the expense of all else; it is certainly true that Coleridge and Wordsworth and eventually Southey, too, reacted in their different ways against Godwin. Here he is in typically rigid mode: 'A consequence of the doctrine of necessity is its tendency to make us survey all events with a tranquil and placid temper... to be superior to the tumult of passion... to reflect upon the moral concerns of mankind with the same clearness of perception, the same unalterable firmness of judgment and the same tranquillity as we are accustomed to do upon the truths of geometry.'[23] Thus abstracted, such a view can indeed seem cold and heartless, the very antithesis of what we normally associate with the Romantic writers. We might well want to suggest that Southey indeed clung on to at least part of this creed, that belief in the fundamental rightness of a particular course of action, a belief that can become dangerously self-deceiving in its Panglossian view. And, of course, radicals and revolutionaries can find such appeals to reason heady in their transparency: some of this emerges in *Joan of Arc* and *Wat Tyler*.

But *Joan of Arc* also declares its hand in favour of that other major concept of the time, benevolence. Coleridge himself frequently turned to the philosopher David Hartley for support: his *Observations on Man, his Frame, his Duty, and his Expectations* (1749) had so impressed Coleridge that he named his first son after him. Hartley's influence can be seen in these comments from Coleridge: 'The search after Truth must love and be beloved; for general Benevolence is begotten and rendered permanent by social and domestic affections.... The paternal and filial duties discipline the Heart and prepare it for the Love of all Mankind. The intensity of private attachments encourages, not prevents, universal Benevolence.'[24] Another advocate of benevolence, closer to home, and a crucial influence on Coleridge, Southey, and Wordsworth was George Dyer, Charles Lamb's old schoolfriend from Christ's Hospital, and immortalized in a couple of Lamb's famous essays.[25] As Lamb wrote to Coleridge in 1800, 'The oftener I see him, the more deeply I admire him. He is goodness itself.'[26] Dyer wrote three major prose works, each of them demonstrating his radical compassion: the *Inquiry into the Nature of Subscription* (1792) led naturally to *The Complaints of the Poor People of England* of the following year; and, in 1795, *A Dissertation on the Theory and Practice of Benevolence*. Dyer was not only a theorist (a charge Southey was to level at Godwin); he had a strong sense of practicalities, of the evils of poverty: a government that allows such things 'is defective in wisdom, in justice, in mercy'.

Thomas Paine's *Rights of Man* (1791–2) lies behind much of this, and that of course was no mere theoretical work. Dyer had his own answer ready to those like Burke, who had, in May 1792, attacked Dissenters, especially against the repeal of the Test Acts, as revolutionaries:

the dissent on their part is fundamental, goes to the very root: and it is at issue not upon this rite or that ceremony, on this or that school opinion, but upon this one question of an establishment, as unchristian, unlawful, contrary to the Gospel, and to natural right, popish and idolatrous. These are the principles violently and fanatically held and pursued—taught to their children, who are sworn at the altar like Hannibal. The war is with the establishment itself, no quarter, no compromise. As a party, they are infinitely mischievous: see the declarations of Priestley and Price—declarations, you will say, of hot men . . .

Dyer remained defiant:

Yes! . . . I approved, and still approve, the doctrine of the Rights of Man; and the french revolution I contemplated, and still contemplate, as the most important aera in the history of NATIONS.—But because men rejoiced to see so many millions of people enslaved struggling for liberty, does it follow, that they are enemies to her country?[27]

This was the question many of Dyer's younger contemporaries were to address, in their own perplexed ways, in the years ahead. There is no need to rehearse here the classic instance of Wordsworth, whose self-lacerations mark so much of *The Prelude* (nor should we forget that *Salisbury Plain*, from the summer of 1793, can be seen as a working-out, much closer to the event, of the confusions he felt). What is instructive, for our present purposes, is that Southey could well have echoed Dyer: but within twenty years both he and Coleridge were to sound much more like Burke. In the 1790s Southey and Dyer both shared the militancy of Paine, and it was natural for them both to support the defendants in the 1794 treason trials. Once again, it is the interweaving of theoretical and practical politics which is particularly germane.

Dyer's account of the *Complaints of the Poor People of England* is important as a sociological document. In its concern for the poor it anticipates, amongst other things, Wordsworth's poems on poverty and deprivation in *Lyrical Ballads*; it anticipates the concerns of Coleridge's lectures of 1795; it anticipates Southey's poems of 1797. Once again, though, the practicalities cannot be divorced from a belief in the restorative powers of the natural world. To read Wordsworth's Preface to *Lyrical Ballads* is rather like reading Rousseau mediated through Dyer. In his *Dissertation on Benevolence* Dyer was in no doubt about the connection between the natural world and moral behaviour; both Coleridge and Wordsworth took this up, in their poetry and their political writings. This might not, in itself, seem a particularly radical departure: after all, it was not only Bowles from the eighteenth century who had in his *Sonnets* explored the influence of the natural world on human growth. But it led in two important directions (leaving on one side the whole theory of the

Imagination, which is another question): first, to the belief in a sense of commonality between all living creatures, which could in turn lead to absurdity and therefore ridicule. Coleridge's address to a Young Jackass (published in the *Morning Chronicle* on 30 December 1794, and 'the first public allusion to Pantisocracy in print') led to his own portrayal as a jackass in one of Gillray's cartoons in the *Anti-Jacobin*, the notorious 'New Morality' of July 1798;[28] when Wordsworth's *Peter Bell* (dedicated to Southey) appeared in 1819, twenty-one years after it was actually written, few of its mockers could appreciate what all the fuss was about—a poem about a donkey beaten to death by its frustrated rider. 'The Ancient Mariner'—to us, perhaps, one of the classic statements of Coleridge's idea of the 'One Life'—drew its fair share of guffaws in 1798, including a handful from Southey himself. The second direction this relation between nature and humanity took was perhaps more radical. Pantisocracy, as Burnett told Lightfoot in his 1796 letter, had to do with property. The cumulative logic of Paine, Priestley, Godwin, and Dyer led to this conclusion: property was in itself a contradiction, and therefore no one should own anything.

In practice, of course, such a communist view of things was impractical, and it soon became for Coleridge a matter of the equalization of property. In his 1795 lectures he pronounced: 'Property is Power and equal Property equal Power. A Poor Man is necessarily more or less a Slave. Poverty is the Death of Public Freedom.'[29] To say this in 1795 was an index of radicalism. To argue that Pantisocracy was 'at once republican, equalitarian and anti-Jacobin' is a moot point, though the radical Dissenter John Aikin, writing in 1823, can be quoted in support: '*Republicanism*, the spirit of which is, in fact, the very essence of every thing free in political constitutionl, is not *Jacobinism*, but the very reverse.' But whether that is how Southey saw it in 1794 is open to question.[30]

There were, of course, and as always, ambiguities. It is easy to scoff at the speculative, exploitative aspects of Priestley's American activities, and there is no doubt that there is a colonizing aspect that creeps into Pantisocracy.[31] This comes out most dramatically in Southey's long poem *Madoc*, which germinated during these crucial years, even though it took him ten years to finish it. His friend William Taylor wrote to him in 1803, asking half-facetiously, 'Do you still think of his [Madoc's] imitating the Carthaginian students whom Augustine mentions in his *Confessions*, and who were to have gone into the back settlements, beyond the blue mountains of Africa, to found a Christian platonical pantisocratical republic, and to become the Mango Capado and Madocs of the paulo-post-future Timbuctoos?'[32] Southey most assuredly did, and *Madoc* appeared in 1805. But the original plan gets altered. The Welsh bardic 'Unitarians' were to have gone to Peru to escape the Saxon Catholic tyranny at home; by 1805 Peru had become North America, and the religious cruelties of the Aztecs form the focal point. The white colonists rescue the natives.

Southey could not share Coleridge's apparently boundless enthusiasm for the Pantisocratic scheme, if only because he was by temperament a less headstrong and impulsive person. In a letter of 13 July Coleridge chid him for his melancholy, urged him not to enter the Church (surely he could get a clerical job with an accountant?) and reminded him of his 'high advantages'—'Health, Strength of Mind, and confirmed *Habits* of strict Morality. Beyond all doubt, by the creative powers of your Genius you might supply whatever the stern Simplicity of Republican Wants could require...' But Coleridge, too, for all his apparent bravado ('I have positively done nothing but dream of the System of no Property every step of the Way since I left you'), was confronting an emotional trauma that was to get entangled with the scheme, and with Southey's own emotional life, in ways neither could have dreamt of. Coleridge had been deeply in love with one Mary Evans, but had allowed her to slip through his fingers. On his travels in Wales, whom should he bump into but Mary and her sister, who were visiting their grandmother. His equanimity vanished at a stroke; Coleridge knew how much he still loved her: 'her Image is in the sanctuary of my Heart, and never can it be torn away but with the strings that grapple it to Life.——Southey! There are few men of whose delicacy I think so highly as to have written all this...'[33]

Southey was less unbuttoned in his correspondence of the time, more secretive about his own sexual desires. But he was also doing his best to get things done. He went to Bath in mid-July, planning to join Coleridge and Hucks in Aberystwyth, before going off to Seward's in Worcestershire to finalize the American scheme. And if Bedford thought he was mad, he said, 'surely you will not think Edmund Seward likely to be led away by fairy visions'.[34] He was disillusioned with his erstwhile friend Collins, who, increasingly cold, scoffed at the whole republican ideal, but he derived comfort from his tutor, Thomas Howe ('half a democrat'), who had not only wisely told him not to bother with lectures, but, more importantly, 'surprized me much by declaiming against the war, praising America & asserting the right of every country to model its own form of government'. His poetic schemes went on apace, as though Coleridge's bursting on the scene injected fresh urgency into his idea of himself as a writer. On 19 July he took the proposal for *Joan of Arc* to the printers, in the belief that if the poem was successful, it would 'carry me over & get some few acres a spade & a plough'. (He told Bedford that he was having a linen coat made for himself in Bristol.) Southey had begun to believe that publication would bring in some money, whilst also 'preserving his memory' in the country that he was about to leave. Bedford, he thought optimistically, might accept a dedication at the front of *Joan of Arc*, just as he might, 'when the storm bursts on England...perhaps follow us to America'. Bedford declined the dedication, and as it transpired, even if he had wanted to, there was to be no following the others to America, for the simple reason that none of them went. As summer wore on into autumn, the early enthusiasm gave way to increasingly intractable complications and disagreements.

On 21 July Southey set off from Bath to Bristol, to persuade Robert Lovell and Mary Fricker to join the Pantisocrats; after some effort, he seems to have succeeded. To cap his triumph, whilst he was dining with the Lovells, who should arrive but Coleridge himself, the man Southey described as 'of most uncommon merit—of the strongest genius, the clearest judgement, the best heart'. He was, according to 'Mrs Codian', as 'brown as a berry'; according to Sara Fricker, he was 'plain, but eloquent & clever'. But he was unkempt, in ragged clothes and with long hair, as opposed to the dapper Southey, 'very neat, gay and smart'. Within two weeks Coleridge and Sara Fricker were engaged to be married, on a somewhat frail acquaintance; this was to be a costly instance of Coleridge's impulsive nature, and much of the next few months was to be spent regretting this commitment. It was hardly the basis for a happy marriage.[35]

At the beginning of August, Southey sent a poem to Horace Bedford about the impending voyage to America.

> Horace if ought my verse may boast of Truth,
>   If ought to Freedom friendly it convey
>   To Peace or Justice, haply the Bards lay
> May not have flowd in vain.
>
>   .   .   .   .
>
>   To the distant shore
> Where Freedom spurns Oppressions iron reign
>   I go: not vainly sorrowing to deplore
>   The long-loved friends I leave to meet no more,
> But the high call of Justice to obey.
> Sometimes recall the Minstrel in his lay.[36]

Although they would not now be going before next summer, Southey's excitement and determination were clear; his apocalyptic view of the

likely turn of political events made him the keener to get as many of his
friends out there as possible: 'you must all come when the fire & brim-
stone descend'. Even his mother planned to come with them, much to his
delight, as did his brother Tom (only too ready to leave the navy, especially
after two weeks at home trying to get rid of chilblains and scurvy), and of
course Lovell. But it was still something of a secret: of his other friends,
only Wynn was to be told. Southey hugged to himself (or at least himself
and Bedford) the delight he felt:

Never did so delightful a prospect of happiness open upon my view before. To go
with all I love—to go with all my friends except your family & Wynn! to live with
them in the most agreable & most honorable employment, to eat the fruits I have
raised, & see every happy face around me, my Mother sheltered in her declining
years from the anxieties which have pursued her, my brothers educated to be
useful & virtuous.

To cap everything, *Joan of Arc* (still wanting thirty-six subscribers to make
up the necessary fifty) was to be one of the handsomest volumes ever
published, 'wove paper, hot pressd, frontispiece, vignette, dedication...
preface & notes'. But for all his talk of republicanism to Bedford, his
closing comments on his new young epic suggest a prevarication that was
to cause Coleridge some perturbation: 'You know it breathes freedom,
but a piece ending with a coronation can hardly be stiled republican.'[37]

Coleridge was flitting about the place, from Bristol to Bath to Cambridge and back again. In mid-August he and Southey set off from Bath to
visit Thomas Poole in Nether Stowey. Poole was himself a democrat, but
regarded as something rather worse by the Government, who began to
open his correspondence; in his bluff no-nonsense manner, and his
eagerness for reform (as opposed to revolution), he was an obvious
person to visit, and a good foil for the younger undergraduates. Poole
has provided an instructive portrait of both men. Coleridge

speaks with much elegance and energy, and with uncommon facility, but he, as it
generally happens to men of his class, feels the justice of Providence in the want of
those inferiour abilities which are necessary to the rational discharge of the
common duties of life. His aberrations from prudence, to use his own expression,
have been great; but he now promises to be as sober and rational as his most sober
friends could wish.

Southey made less of an impression, as was usually the case with
people accompanying the young Coleridge. But he struck Poole with
the amount of information he had, and with the violence of his principles.
These are two characteristics that are to be associated with Southey
throughout his long life. Furthermore, Poole concludes: 'In Religion,

shocking to say in a mere Boy as he is, I fear he wavers between Deism and Atheism'.[38]

Towards the end of August Coleridge and Southey made a long and delightful expedition to the Cheddar Gorge. This tour clearly cemented their friendship (partly perforce, in that they were obliged to share a bed in an inn, and awoke to find themselves locked in, on suspicion of being footpads), and allowed them to think through the implications of their scheme: Southey assured Horace Bedford that it was the 'effect of much deliberation & deep inquiry'. If they could invoke Cowley, Godwin, Priestley, Cooper, and others, there was also Adam Smith to support their belief that property led to all the vices and misfortunes of mankind: in America they would establish a system 'where every motive for vice should be annihilated & every motive for virtue strengthened'. He could also see himself as another Adam, in a new Eden, significantly freed from any past; and to make this Eden that much more desirable, 'our females are beautiful amiable & accomplished'. One small cloud on the horizon was his beloved Edith's growing reluctance to leave her mother behind.[39]

A bigger cloud was represented by the death of Robespierre: 'I had rather have heard of the death of my own father', Southey is reported, famously, to have cried, perhaps a bit too easily to escape the censure of a posterity eager to point out that, since his father was already dead, this was not an option. Thomas Poole, interestingly, did his best to absolve Southey of any calculated coolness, or even of merely wild rhetoric.[40] But the point was that Robespierre's death, along with the turbulent events surrounding it—all reported in the English newspapers in August— brought Coleridge and Southey up against the need to see their own plans in that wider European sphere which was partly the model, partly the cause for, their behaviour, but also, paradoxically, partly responsible for the need to escape. For Coleridge and Southey, Robespierre's death was a tragedy: not so for Wordsworth, who received the news with 'joy | In vengeance, and eternal justice'.[41] But the two Pantisocrats believed that Robespierre

was the benefactor of mankind & that we should lament his death as the greatest misfortune Europe could have sustained—the situation of Europe is surely most melancholy—it presents to the eye of humanity a prospect of carnage from which it shrinks with horror. The coalesced tyrants are obstinate in pursuing the war. The French tho actuated at home by mean & selfish motives, act abroad with a steadiness & energy which at once delight & astonish me.[42]

It took the two men two days to write their drama *The Fall of Robespierre*; Lovell was originally to have been involved, but when he dropped out

Southey took over his share as well, which meant that Coleridge contributed no more than the first act. Coleridge was persuaded that his
name alone on the title-page would help sales (and there was a mercenary
motive behind this grand political gesture, in that Southey had learned
that he was not old enough to benefit from any reversion of any relative's
will)—'at least a hundred Copies at Cambridge. It would appear ridiculous to put two names to *such* a Work...' Southey apparently did not
object, nor did he question Coleridge's logic. Accordingly the volume
appeared from the press of the radical Cambridge printer Benjamin
Flower, at one shilling, with Coleridge's name on the title-page, and just
as significantly his college: as we have seen, Jesus was notorious for its
Jacobin sympathies.[43]

Coleridge's apologia, addressed as a Preface to H. Martin, also of Jesus,
is interesting, not only for his claim to sole authorship, but for his
ambivalence as to the significance of the work. Southey would have
been less equivocal. Coleridge wrote: 'I have endeavoured to detail, in
an interesting form, the fall of a man, whose great bad actions have cast a
disastrous lustre on his name.' The more we address the meaning of this
sentence, the more elusive it becomes. Rather similarly, his defence, in
aesthetic terms, is curiously two-edged. 'In the execution of the work, as
intricacy of plot could not have been attempted without a gross violation
of recent facts, it has been my sole aim to imitate the empassioned and
highly figurative language of the French Orators, and to develope the
characters of the chief actors on a vast stage of horrors.' On the one hand,
Coleridge is able to see the whole work as some kind of rhetorical exercise;
on the other hand, he is only too conscious of the horror of events. What
his prefatory comments cannot conceal, however, is the underlying ten-
sion between the two authors as to the full significance of this terrible
drama.

It is no surprise, in view of the rhetoric of Southey and Coleridge
elsewhere, that the opening, all-consuming image of the drama should
be that of the tempest, and with it a sense of betrayal, of morality turned
upside down. Because of the brevity and compression of the piece, there is
not much in the way of psychology (whatever Coleridge might have
hoped), apart from fear and vengeance. It is the dark world of Marlowe,
of the Shakespeare History plays, but without their depth or range—a
version of Machiavellian policy, as it were, in shorthand:[44]

> The tempest gathers—be it mine to seek
> A friendly shelter, ere it bursts upon him.
> But when? and how? I fear the Tyrant's *soul*—
> Sudden in action, fertile in resource,

And rising awful 'mid impending ruins;
In splendour gloomy, as the midnight meteor,
That fearless thwarts the elemental war.

In the scene in which Robespierre appears with his allies, two things emerge which deserve some comment: first, St Just's comments on the rebel Tallien:

A calm is fatal to him—then he feels
The dire upboilings of the storm within him.
A tyger mad with inward wounds!—I dread
The fierce and restless turbulence of guilt.

Tallien is presented as a Richard II figure, luxuriating in the pomp of splendour; but beneath this surface is that inner tumult. If the tiger makes us think of Blake (and the date is surely significant, in that *Songs of Innocence and of Experience* appeared in 1794), perhaps it should also make us think of Coleridge's fellow-writer, the less than completely stable young Southey. The second point is that when Robespierre is asked what remains if everyone were to forsake him he replies, in tones only too reminiscent of the self-righteous Southey (both in youth and age):

Myself! the steel-strong Rectitude of soul
And Poverty sublime 'mid circling virtues!
The giant Victories, my counsels form'd,
Shall stand around me with sun-glittering plumes,
Bidding the darts of calumny fall pointless.

Couthon, alone, has an observation that can, from our vantage point, be seen as Coleridge's comment on Southey's too upright virtue:

So we deceive ourselves! What goodly virtues
Bloom with poisonous branches of ambition!
Still, Robespierre! thou'l't guard thy country's freedom
To despotize in all the patriot's pomp.

Robespierre—again, we might think, Blake-like—scoffs at the idea of 'Mercy'. His position is, in essence, quite simple: there is a remorseless logic to revolution, which has to work itself out. This is the aspect that Coleridge finds terrifying, whereas Southey, in his part of the drama, is gripped by its warped inevitability. A year later, Coleridge was to say in a letter to Southey that 'Domestic Happiness is the greatest of things sublunary', and refer to Adelaide's song in *The Fall of Robespierre* as an exemplification of this; he printed the song separately as 'Domestic Peace'.[45] For his part, Southey, in Acts 2 and 3, assumes the mantle of his hero. With his appeals for truth, justice, and vengeance we hear the voices of Paine and Godwin; we also hear the voice of Gualbertus, protesting his righteousness against the tyrant Vincent:

> Once more befits it that the voice of truth
> Fearless in innocence, though leagerd round
> By envy and her hateful brood of hell,
> Be heard amid this hall; once more befits
> The patriot, whose prophetic eye so oft
> Has pierced thro' faction's veil, to flash on crimes
> Of deadliest import.

If, earlier in the play, Coleridge might have been pointing, none too subtly, at Southey's cold virtue, Southey embraces that very virtue against any sloppy, sentimental, fraternal feeling (almost undermining the 'yours fraternally' of Coleridge's Preface):

> Brother, by my soul
> More dear I hold thee to my heart, that thus
> With me thou dar'st to tread the dangerous path
> Of virtues, than that nature twined the cords
> Of kindred round us . . .

Southey's brothers might in later life have read these lines with a certain degree of ruefulness: brotherly love only went so far.

Of course, the historical facts cannot be avoided: Robespierre must fall, and fall he does. But not without dignity, and not without a brief apologia from St Just. Furthermore, Tallien himself resorts to the very ideas of justice and vengeance that Robespierre had found so convenient. Southey is too astute a writer, and political thinker even in his muddled way, not to see the irony of this. And there is something poignantly empty about the final act, in which Robespierre is a notable absentee, unable, in fact, to die, even by his own hand. Barrere's final speech, in celebration of Freedom, is spattered with blood. That is one of several ironies. Another is that France (lest we forget, now at war with Britain) survives at the end of the drama as the image and symbol of freedom against 'the despot yoke'; by implication that belongs to Britain. Southey has the last laugh:

> though the leagued despots
> Depopulate all Europe, so to pour
> The accumulated mass upon our coasts,
> Sublime amid the storm shall France arise,
> And like the rock amid the surrounding waves
> Repel the rushing ocean.—She shall wield
> The thunder-bolt of vengeance—she shall blast
> The despot's pride, and liberate the world!

He would no doubt have been gratified by the *Critical Review*'s comment that the third act 'closes beautifully'; this would have compensated for the same organ's preference for the first act.[46]

Coleridge hoped that if he printed the plans for Pantisocracy, some funds might be forthcoming; but nothing came of this plan of the plan. He had worked out that £2,000 was needed, and the money had to be got from somewhere. He met, through some of his Cambridge friends, the Unitarian George Dyer, who in turn knew Joseph Priestley. Dyer was 'enraptured' by the idea of Pantisocracy, and 'pronounced it impregnable' (not surprisingly, since it echoed many of his own ideas); he also liked what he had seen of *Robespierre*. Coleridge spent much of his time in London, at the Salutation and Cat in Newgate Street, mixing with friends old and new; by chance he met a former pupil of Christ's Hospital who was now a land agent, and who had spent five years in America. This man assured Coleridge that land would be cheaper there than elsewhere, and recommended somewhere along the Susquehanna 'from its excessive Beauty, & it's security from hostile Indians'; there was a good chance for literary people of making money there.[47]

While Coleridge did what he could in London, Southey in Bath drew up the growing list of fellow-travellers—apart from himself and Coleridge there would be Lovell and his wife, the two remaining Fricker sisters and their mother; his mother, his cousin Margaret; Burnett and Allen. (Ideally, Burnett would have married Martha Fricker, but his overtures were rebuffed.) His brother Tom would be relied on for navigation. Southey still had time to give some careful thought to his wardrobe, in spite of lack of money.[48]

The difficulties and the delays were beginning to affect Coleridge: as Southey a few months earlier, he was 'turbulent of Bowell, and inappetent'. He dreamt, prophetically, that Mrs Southey refused to go to America; and he became morose about his dead sister. He wrote, revealingly, to Edith Fricker:

There is no attachment under heaven so pure, so endearing ... My Sister, like you, was beautiful and accomplished—like you, she was lowly of Heart. Her Eye beamed with meekest Sensibility. I know, and *feel*, that am *your Brother*—I would, that you would say to me—'I *will* be your Sister—your *favorite* Sister in the family of Soul. [']⁴⁹

This might sound spiritual and high-minded, but what had happened was both simple and immensely confusing: Coleridge had fallen in love with Edith's sister, Sara, the woman to whom he had become engaged so precipitately. This was not, as it has often been portrayed, the result of some cold calculation on Southey's part, whereby the three friends should each be married to one of the Fricker sisters; but it certainly kept things in the family. For Coleridge, the resulting tumult was almost too much:

America! Southey! Miss Fricker!—Yes—Southey—you are right—Even Love is the creature of strong Motive—I certainly love her ... Pantisocracy—O I shall have such a scheme of it! My head, my heart are all alive ... we shall be frendotatoi meta frendous. Most friendly where all are friends.[50]

But all was not quite so friendly. Southey and Coleridge were starting, ominously, to quarrel with each other, both over details and over the larger plan. Coleridge found Southey's 'undeviating Simplicity of Rectitude' a bit too much at times.[51] Southey sent a poem to Bedford on 10 September in which he depicted himself as an exile, 'Driven by Misfortunes ruthless hand | To sojourn in some foreign land'.[52] He was torn between a desire to be gone and his regret and sorrow at leaving his friends and his mother behind: 'my mind is full of Futurity—& lovely is the prospect. I am now like a Traveller, crossing precipices to get home, but my foot shall not slip.'[53] There were still good reasons for going, as the world seemed to be falling around Europe's ears, and Britain full of treason trials: Downie and Watt were executed in Edinburgh on 19 October, and Southey feared, now that 'the sword of iniquity is drawn', that the same fate awaited the radicals John Thelwall, John Horne Tooke, Thomas Holcroft, and a host of others who had dared challenge authority. Things were made more complicated, ironically, when the defendants were acquitted, to such popular acclaim that Southey began to fear for the consequences. As he wrote in November, 'There are bad men & mistaken men in England who do not know that revolutions should take place in mind. Let the violence of either party prevail & the moderate will be equally proscribed.' It was more important than ever, he thought, to be in America. (He did not seem to see the contradiction that if 'the cause of Liberty everywhere was gaining ground' it was being firmly suppressed in Britain.) 'This Pantisocratic scheme has given me new life new hope new energy. All the faculties of my mind are dilated. I am weeding out the few lurking prejudices of habit & looking forward to happiness.'[54]

An unforeseen complication arose. His fearful Aunt Tyler learnt of the scheme, as she was bound to do, and immediately booted Southey out of her house on College Green. She was even less pleased to hear of his intended marriage to Edith Fricker. Southey carried on regardless, happy that Coleridge's young friends from Christ's Hospital—Robert Favell and Charles le Grice—were likely to join them, and hiding, somewhat unrealistically, behind a façade of injured innocence: 'my conduct', he told

Tom, 'has been open, sincere, & just; & though the world were to scorn
& neglect me, I should bear their contempt with calm'.[55] Southey had an
almost infinite capacity for contempt, if he thought himself in the right.
This certainty, once he felt he had got things sorted out, was of no use to
Coleridge, now struggling with his revived feelings for Mary Evans, who
had been prompted by George Coleridge to write to Samuel urging him to
forget the Pantisocratic scheme; there was even family talk of getting
Coleridge into an asylum, so irrational did his behaviour seem. 'I loved
her, Southey! almost to madness . . . My Resolution has not faltered—but
I want a Comforter.' There is little evidence that Southey was disposed to
offer comfort. In his despair, Coleridge sought some relief in a brief
flirtation with the actress Elizabeth Brunton; but he was soon announcing
that he had 'restored my affections to her, whom I do not love—but
whom by every tie of Reason & Honor I ought to love. I am resolved,—but
wretched!'

As if this were not enough to dampen both men's ardour, there were
disagreements over the role of servants in the scheme. Shadrach Weeks,
the friend of Southey's youth and a family servant in Bath, was to come
with them, but Coleridge regretted that Southey still felt the need for a
servant—as opposed to a friend. The women would fulfil their proper
functions, the younger ones producing and looking after babies, the older
ones cooking. Coleridge's state of mind can be gauged by his comment on
a sonnet he sends ('Thou bleedest, my poor Heart!'): 'When a Man is
unhappy, he writes damned bad Poetry, I find.'[56]

Coleridge still had his moments of renewed enthusiasm, as when he
spent six hours talking about Pantisocracy with two Cambridge Fellows.
But he was beginning to worry about the details: were women sufficiently
'saturated with the Divinity of Truth?' Were children desirable companions? 'Are they not already *deeply* tinged with the prejudices and errors of
Society?' He even acknowledged the imperfection of the system, but '*must
it be?*' He could not write his 'Book of Pantisocracy' until these questions
were ironed out. 'Is it not a pity, that a System so impregnable in itself
should be thus blasted?' He asked Southey if he had forgotten the principle of Justice (presumably with reference to the servant issue), and told
him to be 'on your Guard against [*Feelings*]'.[57] This curiously Godwinian
injunction sits a little uneasily with Coleridge's own fevered sensibilities:
he said to Southey that he had hoped to comprise, in the Pantisocratic
scheme, 'all that is good in Godwin', but then added that he thought less
highly of Godwin than did Southey. It is hard for a dispassionate observer
to gauge Coleridge's mood: he tells Francis Wrangham rather grandly (as
though remembering his injunction to Southey), 'where Justice leads,

I will follow', but then resorts to the kind of comedy which so easily opened up the idealists to ridicule: 'I call even my Cat Sister in the Fraternity of universal Nature'.[58] (This would have pleased Southey, a great lover of cats, but he was not one to rise to such heights of fancy, and tended to give his cats rather silly names.[59])

Southey grew more inward, priding himself on the calm disdain with which he had responded to his aunt's invective, but worried about the effect the episode was having on his mother. It was unlikely, he thought, after all this hubbub, that he could contemplate marriage in England. He confessed to a heavy heart, and could only hope that Edith would save him. Once again, he had to confront his own apparent weakness, in his confessions to others, the weakness of the 'stern serious philosophic Robert Southey'. But the truth was, confusingly if conveniently, that 'mine is the philosophy of the heart'. As he told Bedford, in his under-stated way when it came to private emotions, 'her face expresses the mildness of her disposition—& if her calm affection cannot render me happy I deserve to be wretched. She is mild & affectionate. You know me.'[60] In a rare letter to Sara Fricker, he even regretted Edith's low opinion of herself: 'Your sister is like the lilly of the valley lovely in humility but like that delicate & lowly flower she would bend before the storm of pride. If error can be amiable the error of too much humility is so'. She was not even a very good letter writer. 'I am lonely and dull', he told Sara.[61]

Coleridge returned to the attack on the subject of servants: 'a *willing* Slave is the worst of Slaves'. He was so enfeebled he could hardly bring himself to care any more; but he was still worried about the presence of women. In particular he fought shy of the two mothers coming, with their children: 'Are you wounded by my want of feeling? No! how highly must I think of your rectitude of Soul, that I should dare to say this to so affectionate a Son! *That* Mrs Fricker—we shall have her teaching the Infants *Christianity*.' Coleridge's 'want of feeling' was balanced by his discovery of Schiller's *Robbers* : 'Who is this Schiller? This Convulser of the Heart?'[62] So much for the cool reason he advocated. And within a few days he was denying to his brother that he was a democrat, even though he was one. 'Talk not of Politics—*Preach the Gospel!*'[63] There is a strong sense of Coleridge's completely losing his grip on things. He even wrote to Mary Evans, as though Pantisocracy had never been thought of, 'In a few months I shall enter at the Temple & there seek forgetful Calmness—where only it can be found—in incessant & useful Activity'.[64]

Southey, at the other end, as it were, of this emotional see-saw, was happy to be seen, in his aunt's eyes, as a 'great monster, a bad man, & an ugly Xian'. The treason trials had not fulfilled his worst expectations;

acquittals had come thick and fast, and Gerrald, Holcroft, and Godwin ('the three first men in England, perhaps in the world') even lent their blessing to the Pantisocratic scheme (this was not Coleridge's impression of Holcroft's view). So fired up was Southey that he started to write a poem about the rebel Wat Tyler; he claimed some kinship with this poll-tax rebel, and it was as though this provided another way of getting back at his conservative Aunt Tyler.[65] In addition, there was the added authority of Paine, who declared that Tyler's 'fame will outlive' the barons' 'falsehood. If the Barons merit a monument to be erected at Runnymede, Tyler merits one in Smithfield.'[66] On 6 November Southey raised the toast: 'May there never be wanting a Wat Tyler whilst there is a Tax-gatherer.' Little could he know that this dramatic poem, not published at the time, would come back to haunt him over twenty years later.

The personal echo was no doubt pertinent, but the political impetus was just as strong: if the death of Robespierre had presented him with some unwanted complications, at least this English drama had a simpler moral, and also the benefit of distance. A call to rebellion based on the fourteenth-century rebel would at least have indirection in its favour. Not that Southey cared too much; in fact he almost went out of his way to court publicity. When in London in January 1795, he made a point of visiting, in Newgate, two of the recently imprisoned rebels—Joseph Gerrald, who was soon to be sent off to Botany Bay and to an early death, and the printer Ridgeway, to whom Robert Lovell had passed on a copy of *Wat Tyler*. As Southey told Edith Fricker on 12 January, 'I am to send them [Ridgeway and Symonds] more sedition to make a 2 shilling pamphlet. They will print it immediately, give me 12 copies & allow me a sum proportionate to the sale if it sells well. All the risk is their own.'[67] That might, purely in financial terms, have been true at the time. Southey claimed, many years later, to have assumed that the poem was not worth publishing, and gave it no more thought, 'thinking in fact no more of it than of a college or school exercise'. But, as we shall see, the risk proved to be greater than he could have imagined with something he was so prepared to forget.

It is now impossible for us to disentangle the poem from its subsequent reception in 1817, when publishers Sherwood, Neely, and Jones somehow got hold of the manuscript and published it.[68] However, it is important, if we are to begin to understand Southey's frame of mind in late 1794, to register something of the force and character of this strange work. As with *The Fall of Robespierre*, *Wat Tyler* confronts the spectacle of public disorder, but this time from a different perspective: Southey is concerned not with the cruel logic of rebellion but with the need of the poor to rebel against their masters. There might seem something cloying and absurdly patronizing about the merry youngsters dancing around the maypole at the start (until we remember the deliberate simplicities of Blake's world of innocence); but against this is the tempest that dominated the earlier drama. As Tyler says,

> Aye, we were young;
> No cares had quelled the hey-day of the blood:
> We sported deftly in the April morning,
> Nor mark'd the black clouds gathering o'er our noon;
> Nor fear'd the storm of night.

Furthermore, this present storm is ominously linked to another war with France; had the poem been published when written, the contemporary reference could not have been clearer. The poem is anti-Royalist, but also anti-war. The sole purpose of the tax is to appease 'Our ministers—panders of a king's will ... to fill their armies | And feed the crows of France! year follows year, | And still we madly prosecute the war...' The cry from Parliament is '*more money* | *The service of the state demands more money*'.

Hob despairs, anticipating in his question a theme that is to run through so much of Southey's political writings, 'Just heaven! of what service is the state?' Tyler's ironic answer echoes parts of *The Fall of Robespierre* : 'Oh! 'tis of vast importance! who should pay for | The luxuries and riots of the court?' Power is itself corrupting: not in itself a remarkable insight, but important for Southey to spell out in a way that sets up what we might now think of as a Romantic opposition between the natural world and the human.

> Nature gives enough
> For all; but Man, with arrogant selfishness,
> Proud of his heaps, hoards up superfluous stores
> Robb'd from his weaker fellows, starves the poor,
> Or gives to pity what he owes to justice!

Once again, Blake and Godwin rub shoulders here, as when the saintly John Ball is decried for heresy because he actually puts into practice the Christian doctrine of love, and, for his pains, is imprisoned. Whereas the young, idealistic Piers equates virtue with happiness, the embittered Tyler can see that virtue is no proof against the ravages of poverty. It is worth underlining the complexity of the argument, not only because Southey is going several stages further than Wordsworth was to go, four years later, in *Lyrical Ballads*, but also because he is anticipating some of his later, prose arguments about the nature of poverty and popular disaffection. It is also, of course, an implicit defence of the French Revolution.

At the same time, as Tyler acknowledges, honest reason is not enough —if it were, then Piers's simple argument would be unanswerable. There is passion in Tyler's speech, but also resignation: I have done my duty, | I have punish'd the brute insolence of lust | And here will wait my doom.' If we hear Southey's voice behind Tyler's, his sense of righteous indignation that has found its outlet in duty, then we should also recognize that, in his final speech in Act 1, Tyler appeals to everyone to rise up on their own accounts, rather than his. He has fulfilled his dramatic function, and his role is passed, as it were, to John Ball, who has also done his duty.

The central moment in the poem is John Ball's long speech, in which he asserts his credentials as a Christian rebel.

> Friends! Brethren! for ye are my brethren all;
> Englishmen met in arms to advocate
> The cause of freedom! hear me! pause awhile
> In the career of vengeance; it is true
> I am a priest; but, as these rags may speak,
> Not one who riots in the poor man's spoil,
> Or trades with his religion . . .
>   oh, my honest friends!
> Have ye not felt the strong indignant throb
> Of justice in your bosoms, to behold
> The lordly baron feasting on your spoils?
> Have you not in your hearts arraign'd the lot
> That gave him on the couch of luxury
> To pillow his head, and pass the festive day
> In sportive feasts, and ease, and revelry?
> Have you not often in your conscience ask'd
> Why is the difference, wherefore should that man
> No worthier than myself, thus lord it over me,
> And bid me labour, and enjoy the fruits?

Ball is anxious to make a distinction between revenge and justice; if justice is what the mob seeks, then it must be tempered with mercy. Interestingly, when Tyler speaks to the King he talks of justice, but reverts to the Godwinian, Blakean scorn for pity, and even the hitherto docile Piers cries out for vengeance.

In Act 3 it is John Ball who has to engage in more than metaphysical debate with Piers. However we might have been swept along by the rhetoric of *The Fall of Robespierre*, the arguments here are subtler, more humane. And, significantly, when Tyler has been killed, Ball does not want to mourn him 'for himself': 'severe in virtue, | He awed the ruder people whom he led | By his stern rectitude'. The danger is that, without him, the people will have no one to control them. It is hard not to remember that similar cold aloofness of Robespierre; Coleridge had been less ambiguous about it there, but here it is Southey having to confront an aspect of his own character.

The ambiguities are compounded by John Ball's growing realization that perhaps he has failed in his quest for equality:

> now, perhaps,
> The seemly voice of pity has deceiv'd me,
> And all this mighty movement ends in ruin!
> I fear me, I have been like the weak leech,
> Who, sparing to cut deep, with cruel mercy
> Mangles his patient without curing him.

There is a bitter irony in the conclusion: the Royalist troops win, precisely because 'there is not a man of them will lend an ear | To pity'. And yet, as with *The Fall of Robespierre*, so here, in spite of defeat and death, it is the rebels who win. For the King, appropriately, the 'law will take vengeance on the rebels', and in saying this he condemns himself out of his own mouth. John Ball's final speech is defiant, even heroic: he has the 'rectitude of soul' earlier ascribed to Wat Tyler. Behind them both lurks the figure of Southey himself, happy in his own rightness, and happy to believe in the eternal light, the eternal sun, of truth. Such certainties would appear less certain as he got older. For Wordsworth the evening clouds were to take a sober colouring from the setting sun; for Southey, too, but perhaps more damagingly, the rising sun of revolution would reach its zenith at midday, and then sink, none too slowly, in the west.

> Why be it so. I can smile at your vengeance,
> For I am arm'd with rectitude of soul.
> The truth, which all my life I have divulg'd,
> And am now doom'd in torment to expire for,
> Shall still survive—the destin'd hour must come,
> When it shall blaze with sun-surpassing splendor,
> And the dark mists of prejudice and falsehood
> Fade in its strong effulgence. Flattery's incense
> No more shall shadow round the gore-dyed throne;
> That altar of oppression, fed with rites,
> More savage than the Priests of Moloch taught,
> Shall be consumed amid the fire of Justice;
> The ray of truth shall emanate around,
> And the whole world be lighted!

The Pantisocratic scheme was beginning to crumble, even whilst Southey still contemplated leaving England: he felt he had been through a storm. But his mother was no longer prepared to go, nor was his beloved Edith. He derived comfort, once again, from Bowles, and sent his own poem, 'Corston', to Horace Bedford, as an index of his feelings.

> As thus I stand beside the murmuring stream
> And watch its current, memory here pourtrays
> Scenes faintly form'd of half-forgotten days,
> Like far-off woodlands by the moon's bright beam
> Dimly descried, but lovely. I have worn
> Amid these haunts the heavy hours away,
> When childhood idled through the Sabbath-day;
> Risen to my tasks at winter's earliest morn;
> And when the summer twilight darken'd here,
> Thinking of home, and all of heart forlorn,
> Have sigh'd and shed in secret many a tear.
> Dream-like and indistinct those days appear,
> As the faint sounds of this low brooklet, borne
> Upon the breeze, reach fitfully the ear.

Southey clung on to an ideal of domesticity, but there seemed less likelihood of this being realized across the sea. 'Linen drying at the fire! one person clean starching—one ironing—& one reading aloud in the room—blessed scene to write in! Oh for my transatlantic log house!'[69] The next person to drop out was his brother Tom: their mother thought it imprudent of him to leave the navy for what increasingly looked like a hair-brained scheme. But the coming 'storm' still persuaded Southey that the plan could, indeed must, be carried out; as calamities hedged them in, he told Bedford that 'I shall be soon beyond the sphere of their destruction'.[70]

But not so far beyond as he had hoped. He announced on 4 December that the furthest they were likely to get, because of finances, was Wales. He puffed himself in a letter to Bedford, no doubt conscious that he must seem to have lost some of the wind from his sails: 'I shall be the Leader of a sect—which you will esteem fanatical & seditious. Well well. You will pity & love me—& I must pity & love you.'[71] Coleridge was furious at the Welsh scheme, though he seemed to have no idea how they would get the money for anything else. It was not as though *The Fall of Robespierre* had made much money.[72] In his deep gloom, Coleridge turned to addressing the details of Southey's poems, and gave some good advice: 'Before you write a Poem, you should say to yourself—What do I intend to be the *Character* of this Poem—Which *Feature* is to be predominant in it?—So you may make it a Unique.'[73] He also wrote a poem addressed to Southey, which was published in the *Morning Chronicle* on 14 January 1795, and showed his anti-Government feelings with a savage attack on Pitt. The poem to Southey touches on the particular importance to Coleridge of Southey's sensibilities, his capacity for comforting and reviving:

> Southey! thy melodies steal o'er mine ear
> > Like far-off joyance, or the murmuring
> > Of wild bees in the sunny showers of Spring—
> Sounds of such mingled import as may cheer
>
> The lonely breast, yet nurse a mindful tear:
> > Wak'd by the Song doth Hope-born FANCY fling
> > Rich showers of dewy fragrance from her wing,
> Till sickly PASSION's drooping Myrtles rear
>
> Blossom anew! But O! more thrill'd, I prize
> > Thy sadder strains, that bid in MEMORY's Dream
> > The faded forms of past Delight arise...[74]

But as the year petered out, both men were coming to a full realization of what had happened: the great scheme of Pantisocracy was not to be. Coleridge declared himself 'calm ... as an Autumnal Day, when the Sky is covered with grey moveless Clouds'.[75] He could not forget his love for Mary Evans, but marriage to Sara Fricker beckoned: '*I will do my Duty*'. Yet another year came to an end in resignation. Only this time Southey's gloom had its echoes in that of the person on whom he had pinned all his hopes; and the same could no doubt be said of Coleridge. To some extent, they had failed each other.

Southey was increasingly insistent that Coleridge return to Bristol, but when he and Lovell walked, in the New Year, to Marlborough, in order to meet Coleridge as arranged, he was not there; even by 9 January there was no sign of him, and Southey was increasingly befuddled. His patience could hold out no longer, and he decided to go up to London to find Coleridge, who was living it up with another Bluecoat, Charles Lamb, at the Salutation and Cat. The pleasure of meeting the gentle, droll Lamb was offset by Coleridge's reluctance to contemplate Wales as any kind of satisfactory alternative to America. Southey was utterly depressed by the suggestion that they both find some kind of job in London until they had enough money (Coleridge declared to Southey in mid-January that 'It was total Want of Cash that prevented my Expedition').[76] Southey 'went to bed in dirty sheets—& tost & turned, cold, weary & heart sick till seven in the morning'. He turned rather helplessly to Edith Fricker, beseeching her love: he seemed genuinely to fear losing her, the fear all the greater because she was his only source of comfort. In these circumstances, the London printer Ridgeway's decision to print *Wat Tyler* as a two-shilling pamphlet hardly seemed sufficient to lift the spirits; nothing came of this, in any case.[77]

Relations with Coleridge cooled, as the two bickered over the future of their scheme. Coleridge felt that Southey was blaming him for inexplicably abandoning the principles of Pantisocracy, and responded with an attack on Southey's own world-weariness. It is only fair to point out that Coleridge was clearly as muddled as Southey:

your sentiments look like the sickly offspring of disgusted Pride. *Love* is an active and humble Principle—It flies not away from the Couches of Imperfection, because the Patients are fretful or loathsome.

Why, my dear very dear Southey! do you wrap yourself up in the Mantle of self-centering *Resolve* and refuse to us your bounden Quota of Intellect? Why do you say, I—I—I—will do so and so—instead of saying as you were wont to do—It is all *our Duty* to do so and so—for such & such Reasons—[78]

Perhaps Coleridge felt too keenly how much his own heightened sense of duty was driving him into the arms of Sara Fricker. However that may be, by the end of this same letter, and persuaded by Lovell rather than by Southey, he was ready to agree to the Welsh scheme, given a three-month interval, and on the assumption that £300 would be enough to cover all the costs.

This was enough for the two men to make things up, and within a few weeks Southey, Coleridge, and Burnett were installed in 25, College Street, Bristol, planning the 'Provincial Magazine' (which never materialized), and embracing a new kind of future. Southey declared to Bedford on 8 February that 'Coleridge is writing at the same table. Our names are written in the book of destiny on the same page.' This was to cry up, rather, their prospects. But Southey rejoiced in the stir occasioned, especially in Bristol, by the Pantisocrats; he was happy to be 'at once the object of hatred & admiration: wondered at by all—hated by the aristocrats—the very oracle of my own party.' In speaking as he does here, Southey anticipates the relish of his later years in his combative role; to be the centre of attention seemed to him cause for self-congratulation, and it did not matter whether he was loved or hated.[79]

Although Southey contributed a pseudonymous piece of prose, in the form of a letter to Canning, to the *Telegraph*, he could not take up a regular post as a reporter, because he did not want to work in the evenings. Coleridge had higher hopes in that line, whereas Southey felt he was not fitted to be a journalist. He none the less tried to offer Bedford some reassurance as to his own condition:

there is the strangest mixture of cloud & sunshine! an outcast in the world! an adventurer! living by his wits! yet happy in the full conviction of rectitude— in integrity & in the affections of a mild & lovely woman...—Bedford Bedford mine are the principles of peace—of non-resistance—you cannot burst our bands of affection—do not grieve that circumstances have made me thus. You ought to rejoice that your friend acts up to his principles even tho you think them wrong.[80]

At least there was a greater sense of purpose now, helped no doubt by Coleridge's falling wildly and unexpectedly in love with Sara Fricker. The Bristol political climate was ripe for what otherwise might have seemed little more than student presumption. Southey and Coleridge decided to give a series of lectures. Coleridge's were the more spectacular, the more political, the more inflammatory.[81] His very first one, 'A Moral and Political Lecture', was published soon after he had delivered it, and he was thought to be treading dangerously close to treason. Southey's lectures, on the other hand (which started in March), were more obviously historical, 'unconnected with', as Coleridge told Dyer, 'at least not *immediately* relative to the politics of the Day'.[82] But Southey was to tell Horace Bedford a year later that, although his lectures masqueraded as history, they were 'to all intents political' (to this end he kept the secret from Wynn); he claimed that he was 'treading in the steps of Thelwall with more boldness & more ability!', a claim that would have surprised Thelwall. John Thelwall (known as 'Citizen John') became a standard-bearer for the radicals after his trial for high treason—along with Thomas Hardy, Horne Tooke, and Holcroft—in 1794 (they were all famously acquitted). Thelwall was renowned for his political lectures in London, in which his revolutionary ideas were given their full head. Coleridge corresponded with him in the final months of 1799, by which time Thelwall seemed an almost irredeemable atheistical radical, but when he came to stay at Nether Stowey in 1797, Coleridge wrote about him:

[he] is a very warm hearted honest man ... He is a great favorite with Sara ... he is intrepid, eloquent, and—honest.—Perhaps the only *acting* Democrat that *is* honest for the *Patriots* are ragged cattle—a most execrable herd—arrogant because they are ignorant, and boastful of the strength of reason, because they have never tried it enough to know its *weakness*.

Ironically Thelwall, perhaps seduced by the peace and quiet of Nether Stowey, was erelong to find his own retreat in Wales, not far from Tintern Abbey.

Meanwhile, Coleridge assured Dyer that he would like Southey, but in one of those ambiguously veiled tributes that have haunted Southey's reputation ever since: 'His Genius and acquirements are uncommonly great—yet they bear no proportion to his moral Excellence—He is truly a man of *perpendicular Virtue*—a *downright upright Republican!* He is *Christianizing* apace.'[83]

Coleridge's lectures, with all their bravura, survive. Southey never intended to publish his, and all we have is the prospectus, for a 'Course of Historical Lectures . . . (Unconnected with the Politics of the Day)'.[84] It is sufficiently daunting to be worth quoting, if only to demonstrate his confidence at tackling what would now be called 'big issues':

1795.–MARCH
Sat. 14–Introductory—On the Origin and Progress of Society.
Tues. 17–Legislations of Solon and Lycurgus.
Fri. 20–State of Greece from the Persian War to the Dissolution of the Achaean League.
Tues. 24–Rise, Progress, and Decline, of the Roman Government.
Fri. 27–Progress of Christianity.
Tues. 31–Manners and Irruption of the Northern Nations; Growth of the European States; Feudal Systems.

APRIL
Fri. 3–State of the Eastern Empire to the Capture of Constantinople by the Turks; including the Rise and Progress of the Mohammedan Religion and the Crusades.
Tues. 7–History of Europe to the Abdication of the Emperor Charles the Fifth.
Fri. 10–History of Europe till the establishment of the Independence of Holland.
Tues. 14–State of Europe, and more particularly of England, from the Accession of Charles the First to the Revolution in 1688.
Fri. 17–Progress of the Northern States; History of Europe to the American War.
Tues. 21–The American War.

All this for half a guinea. Even if it were true, as Coleridge was to claim, that it was he who had written at least half of these lectures, the sheer range and scope is impressive for someone barely past 20. We might also think it hubristic, but then both these young men would have thought that a virtue. Southey claimed to think of his lectures as 'only splendid declamation', but he was not, even then, an inspired orator in the Coleridge mould, and confessed to awkwardness when he first began the two-lectures-per-week course, 'teaching', as he put it, in that morally upright fashion Coleridge had more than once hinted at, 'what is right by showing what is wrong'.[85] The Bristol *Observer* commented of Southey's lectures that the 'language was that of truth, it was the language of Liberty!' On the other hand, 'his gesticulation and attitude when he is speaking in Public is not the most pleasing, his body is always too stiff, his features are apt to be distorted...'[86] Southey was sufficiently alert to his own deficiencies to acknowledge the truth of such comments; whereas Coleridge went on to make a name for himself as a lecturer, Southey was much happier with a pen in his hand. (The *Observer* did, however, disapprove of Coleridge's shabby appearance and unkempt locks.) Two years later Southey confessed to Wynn his lack of fluency in public speaking, which would obviously work against a career as a lawyer (and Wynn must have wondered where Southey had learnt of his shortcomings). Even in conversation, apparently, 'I express myself with difficulty & awkwardness.'[87] What kept them both going was the hope that, between them, they might earn £150 a year, just enough for them to marry their respective Fricker sisters, retire into the country, and get to grips with the basic problems of agriculture, prior to setting off for America—'still the grand object in view'.

On the literary front, the Bristol publisher Joseph Cottle had become deeply embroiled in their concerns: *Joan of Arc* would go to press in April, and there was the possibility of another volume of poems coming out even before then. Southey was also signed up by John Scott to write for a new journal, the *Citizen*, at a guinea and a half per week. This was to turn out to be another forlorn venture. Cottle was more than just a publisher: he took a keen interest in his young authors, and when there was a heated argument between Coleridge and Southey, he took it upon himself to help sort things out. Coleridge had failed to turn up to deliver one of his lectures, one on the Roman Empire which he had claimed he was particularly anxious to give. Southey had nobly, but resentfully, stepped in at the last moment. The tensions between the two had never really settled, and when it became clear that Coleridge was succumbing to the waywardness and 'indolence' of the opium-addict, Southey was not amused. But even in his own lectures on 'Revealed Religion' we can see some of their disagreements emerging, in that Coleridge was anxious to express his reservations about Godwin; he had revelled in the sight of the classicist, Richard Porson '*crushing*' Godwin, Holcroft and other Jacobins—'they absolutely tremble before him.'[88] On the other hand, Coleridge's lecture on the slave trade was very much in line with Southey's sympathies: he addressed the argument that 'the plantation slaves are at least as well off as the peasantry in England. Now I must appeal to common sense, whether to affirm that slaves are as well off as our peasantry, be not the same as to assert that our peasantry are as bad off as negro-slaves? And whether, if our peasantry believed it, they would not be inclined to rebel?' Many years later, Southey was to place himself in a position where he could be attacked on similar grounds; he would have done well to remember Coleridge (but, then, so too would Coleridge: these young radical writers often found their pasts catching up with them). In any case, given the growing unpleasantness between the two of them, Cottle invited them, along with the Fricker sisters, on an excursion to the Wye valley, most of which was spent trying to patch up the quarrel. Symbolically, they all got lost as night fell, and went round and round in circles before eventually finding an inn at Tintern. After such an episode, it was only Southey and Cottle who were ready, after supper, to do to their duty by the Picturesque, and admire the nearby foundry.[89]

In spite of such hiccups, when the lectures were over Southey was jubilant. He had put his head in the political lion's den, and felt the exhilaration that came with that engagement. He boasted to his brother Tom that he

said bolder truths than any other man in this country has yet ventured. Speaking of my friend Tom I cried O Paine! hireless Priest of Liberty!—unbought teacher of the poor! Chearing to me is the reflection that my heart hath ever acknowledged—that my tongue hath proudly proclaimed—the truth & Divinity of thy Doctrines![90]

But, typically, he almost immediately drew in his horns. It was as though, having got all that off his chest, he could settle back into reading, writing, and solitude. He was certainly writing furiously: another Botany Bay eclogue, 'Elinor', a couple of poems written with Coleridge ('The Outcast', 'The Soldier's Wife'), the comic 'Ode to a Frog'.[91] His desire for domesticity ('I have almost insulated myself from mankind') was reflected in the sonnet he wrote to Edith ('Fair is the rising morn'); much more ambitiously, he had got to the end of the first book of his new poem *Madoc*, which would occupy him, on and off, for the next ten years. He would have, he told Bedford, to study the Bible, Homer, and Ossian before he could get much further with it, but he was convinced, even at this stage, that the poem was so far the best thing he had done; the task of correcting *Joan* (whose plan, he felt, was faulty) perhaps made him feel this even more strongly.[92] That *Madoc* is devoted to the exiled Welsh hero's establishment of a Christian colony in America is of obvious autobiographical as well as political significance.

Southey became increasingly reluctant to mingle with other people, and he knew this was not entirely a virtue. On the one hand, he expressed himself 'indifferent to society yet I feel my private attachments growing more & more powerful & weep like a child when I think of an absent friend' (perhaps this was because, as he said, 'Poetry softens the heart'); he relished sitting at home, either with Edith or alone, in a big chair by the fire. But, on the other hand, he half-glimpsed that such a fire was perhaps a means of providing the warmth he himself lacked. In talking of his difficulty with invitations, he touches on his own raw nerve: 'if you knew the fearful anxiety with which I sometimes hide myself to avoid an invitation, you would perhaps pity—perhaps despise me.' He caused great offence by not calling on a local family that Coleridge visited, with apparent ease, three or four times a week. Southey was not a conversationalist; as he told Bedford (who probably did not need being told), 'the torpido coldness of my *phizmahogany* has no right to chill the circle'. He thought he looked like a bandit: 'I have put on the look at the glass so as sometimes to frighten myself.' At least he could laugh at this aspect of his character—and it would never change. He even knew that his dreams of married life with Edith might get a jolt from reality: 'brown bread & wild Welch raspberries—heigh ho! this school boy anticipation follows us thro life & Enjoyment uniformly disappoints expectation.' But he could at least anticipate such things: news of battles, of the loss and waste of young lives, left him cold.[93] Coleridge tried desperately to cure him of this 'misanthropical system of indifference', but Southey was unpersuaded. 'Timon respected mankind enough to hate them. I don't think them worth hating . . . a strange dreaminess of mind has seized me.' For his part, Coleridge remained determined to marry Sara. Against a whispering campaign in Bath and Bristol about the unseemly haste of the forthcoming marriage (not only were the Fricker sisters regarded as unconventional, the whole Pantisocratic scheme was viewed as one that 'dispensed with the marriage-tie'—after all, Godwin was accused of just such a crime), Coleridge and Sara began looking for somewhere to live; it was not long before they discovered a little cottage in Clevedon, for £5 a year.

News of the death of Edmund Seward reached Southey on 15 June: Southey was awakened from his reveries.

Bedford—he is dead, my dear Edmund Seward, after 6 weeks suffering. These Grosvenor are the losses that gradually wean us from life. May that man want consolation in his last hour who would rob the survivor of the belief that he shall again behold his friend.

You know not Grosvenor how I loved poor Edmund, he taught me all that I have of good.

When I went with him into Worcestershire I was astonished at the general joy his return occasioned. The very dogs ran out to him . . .

It is like a dream, the idea that he is dead, that his heart is cold—that he whom but yesterday morning I thought & talked of—as alive—as the friend I knew & loved—dead—when these things come home to the heart they palsy it. I am sick at heart, & if I feel this acutely what must his sisters feel—what his poor old mother—whose life was wrapped up in Edmund. Good God I have seen her look at him till the tears ran down her cheek.

There is a strange vacancy in my heart, the sun shines as usual—but there is a blank in existence to me...

Grosvenor I am a child & all are children who fix their happiness on such a reptile as man, this great this self-ennobled being called man! The next change of weather may blast him.

There is another world, where these things will be emended...[94]

Although he was able to occupy himself with arrangements for printing *Joan of Arc*, getting his artist friend Richard Duppa (whom he had met at Balliol in 1794) to provide not just a frontispiece but an illustration for some lines; although he sought some relief in teaching Edith Greek, and found some comfort in a recently acquired dog—Cupid;[95] in spite of all this, Southey was very conscious of how he had changed in the last two years. Life was like a journey, and already evening was coming on. In a letter to Bedford, whom he was soon to visit in London, he recalled what seemed to him now the happier times of his youth, and drew a rather sad conclusion:

perhaps I never spent three months happier than at Brixton—tis a period I love to think of. The wasps—Mr Coyte & the imminent danger from my republican neighbours—the ditch, where I wrote Joan of Arc.—Therefore Grosvenor is it a misfortune to love—because he who loves is restless in every company but that of one.[96]

In August Southey's uncle, Herbert Hill, returned to England from Lisbon and began to put pressure on Southey to enter the Church. Southey, who felt more strongly than ever that he was totally unsuited for it, was distressed: 'the gate is perjury—& I am little disposed to pay so heavy a price at the turnpike of orthodoxy.'[97] He sought advice from Coleridge, who spoke precisely in the same terms of perjury. But Coleridge also warned against the 'perilous Temptation' of domesticity: 'Domestic Happiness is the greatest of things sublunary', but this was not the time to be thinking of such a thing, at least not as a solution to everything else.[98] No doubt Coleridge had his own reasons for putting it like this; in any case, relations between them were still cool. Coleridge thanked God when he heard that Southey was defying his uncle, but there was something distant and perfunctory about his comment: 'he leaves our Party however, & means, he thinks, to study the Law.'

During the late summer a young poet called William Wordsworth was staying with some friends, the Pinneys, at Bristol, before he went to take up residency as a tenant of Racedown Lodge in Dorset; some time in late August or early September he met his two young contemporaries. None of them at this stage was an established writer, but perhaps Wordsworth was the least known of the three: his *Evening Walk* and *Descriptive Sketches* had both appeared in 1793, but they could hardly be said to have made a great splash in the literary world. Wordsworth did not even have the radical credentials of Coleridge or Southey. The meeting with Coleridge was to have far-reaching consequences, leading to the *Lyrical Ballads* of 1798, and to one of the most fruitful friendships in literary history. Southey impressed Wordsworth with his 'manners ... and I have every reason to think very highly of his powers of mind'.[99] There was even some interchange over Wordsworth's attempt at a satire, to which Southey contributed a couple of lines; but at this stage the two men did not seem to have much in common, and Southey appears to have made no mention of the meeting. It is really only later in life, when the two men are living near each other in the Lake District, that they get to know each other: there is then a growing warmth between them, but never anything like the closeness between Wordsworth and Coleridge.

Southey spent as much time as possible in Bristol, with Edith and Cottle, who even offered him the use of his house (publishers were more genial in those days). He kept on with *Madoc*, still believing it would be the making of him as a writer. He was pleased with a laudatory letter from Wynn's cousin, Lord Carysfort, to whom he had sent his poem, 'The Retrospect', even though he resented Wynn's suggestions that he should curry the favour of such a 'great man': 'the very idea ... disgusts me';[100] the pragmatism for which Hazlitt was later to berate Southey emerges early in his life. But there was something less sure-footed in his communications to his friend Bedford. It is strange, in view of the moral rectitude Coleridge had pinpointed, to find Southey confessing to a scepticism based on a realization of his own frequent mistakes of judgement. He spoke of Godwin with some ambivalence, disliking the man whilst acknowledging his influence. And yet he saw through Godwin's fundamental error, one to which he had subscribed only too readily in his student days: 'he theorizes for another state—not for the rule of conduct in the present.' Such scepticism led him to cry out, as though this solved the problem, 'Hang all wars!' He ended with an acknowledgement of a more than poetic debt to Coleridge. As he said with the sang-froid of someone not knowing what the postman would bring in a month's time, 'he did me much good—I him more'.[101]

Coleridge certainly did not see things quite like that. All the simmering resentments and disagreements of the past year finally exploded in a dreadful argument. Southey thought that Coleridge had behaved 'wickedly towards me ... Altogether my mind has been upon the continual stretch'. Coleridge, for his part, fired off a 5,000-word broadside attack in November questioning the very basis of their relationship.

After all this, it was probably a relief to visit Hannah More at Cowslip Green, near Bristol, where the middle-aged bluestocking was organizing a group of schools to promote the Evangelical spirit she so valued. Hannah More was part of the reaction against what were seen as the seditious writings of the radicals: her cheap repository tracts (so cheap that they sold up to two million copies in monthly instalments) were aimed specifically at the 'lower orders', and were as 'improving' as her attempts at poetry and, later, her novel *Coelebs in Search of a Wife* (1809). Not for nothing was she known by Cobbett as the 'Bishop in Petticoats'. In spite of their political differences, neither Southey nor Hannah More allowed the occasion of their first meeting to be soured. Southey derived further pleasure from reading an old translation of Montaigne's essays, liking what he called his 'honest egotism'; he was again reading *Tristram Shandy*, and also Cottle's 'Monody on John Henderson', in his *Poems* of 1795. He prudishly advised Bedford against getting his translation of Musaeus published: it was 'too immoral'. But Bedford, undeterred, went ahead, no doubt mildly surprised that his radical friend had such scruples.

Southey's plans, such as they were, received a sharp jolt from his uncle. Herbert Hill, displeased at his nephew's refusal to enter the Church, felt that at least he could save him from the other two evils in his life: radical politics and the impending marriage to Edith Fricker. If he could get Southey to Lisbon, Hill was sure the distance would solve both problems. Southey knew he had little choice, and resigned himself to his uncle's plan. As he wrote on 24 October to Bedford, 'my heart is very heavy—I would have refused but I was wearied of everlastingly refusing all my mothers wishes—& it is only one mode of wearing out a period that must be unpleasant to me anywhere. Edith is to be with my Mother during my absence. On this condition only would I go.' Edith wept, but urged him to go. Typically, he consoled himself with the thought that he could learn Portuguese and translate the choicest parts of the literature; the climate might be good for him, and he might actually put on some weight; he could even—though this seems less of a benefit to someone not obsessed with the finer details of native fashion—learn about Spanish costume. The embryonic antiquarian in Southey could, it seems, find a blessing in everything. He might even be captured by the French, or end up being circumcised in Algiers; looking on what he called 'the white side of the shield', if 'they [the damned Algerians] should take me—it might make a very pretty subject for a chapter in my memoirs, but of this I am very sure that my Biographer would like it better than I should.'[102] That might well be true, but since it did not happen, his speculation cannot be put to the test. It is none the less interesting that even at this time of anxiety he could both laugh at what might happen, but also entertain the possibility of a biography. Working on the final changes to *Joan of Arc* no doubt encouraged his sense of posterity; but Cottle's request that he sit for a portrait before his departure must also have boosted his ego, and his sense of a future in which at least someone would be interested in him.

During these last hectic days before his departure for Lisbon, Southey seems to have forgotten about Coleridge. But in fact, even before that awful letter of recrimination, Coleridge had married Sara Fricker on 4 October at St Mary Redcliffe in Bristol, and then gone off to their Clevedon cottage for their honeymoon. 'On Sunday Morning', Coleridge wrote to his friend Poole, 'I was *married* . . . united to the woman, whom I love best of all created Beings . . . Mrs Coleridge—MRS COLERIDGE!!— I like to *write* the name'. Poole endorsed the relationship in his generous way: 'He has united himself to her he loves, regardless of every other consideration. It is thus that, lifted above the cupidity almost interwoven in the hearts of all who live in a society such as ours, he presents himself an object which awakens every tender and noble sensation of the soul.'[103] A rather more private, even secretive wedding took place in mid-November, between Southey and Edith Fricker. Southey reported the event to Bedford, almost as though there was nothing much to be said about it. Although he gave some convoluted explanation to Cottle as to why he had married then, he could but state the fact to Bedford. 'On Saturday morning the ceremony was performed with the utmost privacy—the day was very melancholy. My Edith returned home at night, & I slept as usual at Cottles. The next day we parted.' Edith was to keep her maiden name— mainly to stop tongues wagging, although of course once the news was out (and how could it not be?), it had the opposite effect. Southey was not even sure that when he returned he would be able to live with his new bride. 'The moment I had left her I burst into tears.'[104]

He set off with his uncle towards Falmouth. They stayed at Nan Swithin, on the way, with a Mr Hoblyn, one of his uncle's friends. Southey was miserable enough, and the dreadful journey made matters worse. He hated Cornwall, and received little comfort from his uncle's lack of knowledge of his poems; even Mr Hoblyn had seen them in the *British Critic*. Southey wrote with feeling and good cause: 'never had man so many relations so little calculated to inspire confidence.' He could at least turn to Bedford, and confess to his emotions at the altar: 'never before did man stand at the altar with such strange feelings as I did.' It had been more like a funeral than a wedding; it was certainly not the happy culmination of those months of eager anticipation. It was as though Southey had had a rather terrifying insight into the peculiar workings of human beings; things did not make the kind of sense he had led himself to expect. Although he was writing to Bedford, he felt the gaps and silences between them: 'Grosvenor! what should that necromancer deserve who would transpose our souls for half an hour, & make each the inhabitant of the others tenement? there are so many curious avenues in mine, & so many closets in yours of which you have never sent me the key.' This bemusement was no doubt heightened by that long letter he had received from Coleridge, the very day after he had got married. If anything was calculated to upset a man about to enter a not so brave new world, that was it. If Coleridge and Bedford were both far less known to him than he might have thought, what about Edith? As he said with pained simplicity, 'Edith did not shed a tear when I left her. She returned the pressure of my hand— & we parted in silence.'[105]

It is striking that, at this extreme moment, he should mention Godwin, and Godwin's vanity, the 'bane of virtue'. Partly it is because he is half thinking about his own *Joan of Arc* (out next month), and puzzled that his 'mind is now compleatly disengaged' from it, although when he was writing it he was totally absorbed; in his confusion, he is anxious to deny that he was driven, when writing it, by the kind of vanity he attributes to Godwin. But there is another point, and that is the apparent divorce between a person and his writings: Godwin's work was valuable, but '*he* is contemptable'. Southey seems to be making a connection with himself: 'I am afraid that most public characters will ill endure examination in their private lives.'

At the beginning of December they set sail. Bedford had Southey's will (such as it was); he left his papers with his mother and Edith. The Cottle sisters ('they make even bigotry amiable') would look after Edith. Southey told Bedford, 'Edith you will see & know & love. But her virtues are of the domestic order & you will love her in proportion as you know her. I hate your daffedown dilly women—aye & men too.'[106]

4

PROSPECTS

1796–1799

SOUTHEY did not greatly enjoy his first visit to Portugal; the voyage had been dreadful: 'I can now form a tolerable idea of what a man feels at the point of death.'[1] They stayed five days at Corunna with the English consul, Sir Alexander Jardine, and then spent nearly three weeks on the road to Madrid, than which 'no situation can be worse', then another fifteen days to Lisbon, only to be greeted by an earthquake. Southey had been so thrown by the events of the last few years that he no longer knew where he was. As he wrote to Wynn on 26 January, 'My prospects in life have varied so often that I almost doubt the stability of any one.'[2] (Coleridge, meanwhile, back in England, was expressing, rather more dramatically, a similar sense of disorientation: 'My past life seems to me like a dream, a feverish dream! all one gloomy huddle of strange actions, and dim-discovered motives! Friendships lost by indolence, and happiness murdered by mismanaged sensibility!'[3]) He really just wanted to get back home. When he heard from the *London Chronicle* that, whatever his state of mind, Coleridge was in Birmingham, drumming up support for a newly projected journal, The *Watchman*, Southey was resolved, not for the first time, to keep out of politics. Drink, rather ominously, just about made things tolerable.[4] However, we should not be surprised to see that Southey was developing his skills for sharp observation. Cottle had engaged him, before leaving, to produce a series of *Letters* about Portugal, and Southey accordingly tried out his hand at descriptive writing in some of his letters home.[5]

His uncle's plan to wean him away from Edith was doomed to failure. A poem Southey wrote on 'Christmas Day, 1795' was all about Christmas as a child, and how he missed his bride ('How many a heart is happy at this hour in England!'). He was particularly vexed when Herbert Hill deliberately tried to get him interested in one of the Tonkin daughters (local expatriates); given his exasperation at this, he cared little when his marriage was in all the papers, and Edith was now known as Mrs Southey. One of his few consolations was that he met the painter Mary Barker, who was to be a lifelong friend, someone in whom he felt able to confide. She proved a sympathetic listener, and did not need to defend him against his uncle's ploys: 'Edith is mine—& all the relations of the world weigh nothing when opposed to her.'[6] In advising Bedford about some emotional problem, Southey made a rather touching and revealing—almost frightening—comment about the difference between Edith and other women he had known: 'I never found it difficult to become intimate with any woman except Edith—& in her company I experienced always that unquiet state of delight which made me embarrassed & sometimes made me wish myself away.'[7] This simply serves to underline something of the mystery of Southey's personal relations. Not that his uncle was too worried about such complexities; he simply blundered on, assuming that his nephew would enter the Church, and on one occasion even showing him on the map the living that was in his gift, which would bring in £500 a year. But Southey had no cause to trust his uncle, expecially when the 46-year-old bachelor fell in love with the very woman (half his age) he had hoped Southey would fall for: the fact that she was very like Edith made things even worse.

Southey's three and a half months at Lisbon ('this foul place...from which God grant me a speedy deliverance!') hardly tempted him to like it; it was dirty, smelly beyond endurance, ridden with vermin, and inhabited by people with whom he felt little sympathy. (He did, however, meet a number of people who were to crop up later in his life as good friends, including the wine merchant John May). The Catholic Church showed itself in the colours in which Southey was to see it for the rest of his life; he attributed what he saw as the squalor of Spain and Portugal to the Catholic King Carlos in Spain, and the corrupt clergy in Portugal. It seemed symbolic that for part of their journey from Madrid to Lisbon Southey should find himself trailing behind the 7,000-strong retinue of the pillaging royals. Southey never recovered from his revulsion at the combination of superstition, worship of images, and the pomp and ceremony that he associated with the Catholic Church. At least he had the opportunity, encouraged by his uncle, to read and speak Spanish and Portuguese. One of the redeeming features of his stay was a trip to Cintra: 'I shall always love to think of the lonely house, & the stream that runs beside it, whose murmurs were the last sounds I heard at night, & the first that awoke my attention in the morning.'[8] Rather like a Wordsworthian spot of time, this memory—like that of his childhood haunts in Bristol—would remain with him all his life.

He began to think more about his writing. As so often, he wished he had the *Flagellant* with him, almost as though that represented the starting-point of all his endeavours. He urged Bedford to celebrate 1 March 1792, when they first took up their schoolboy pens; he recalled the time at Brixton when Bedford was working on the third article, and how 'we dined on mutton chops and eggs'. One day, perhaps, Bedford would show the whole collection to Edith: it was an important part of his life that he wanted her to know about. In the mean time, he fretted about *Joan of Arc*, especially the Preface, which, because of the rush in which it was written, was 'a hodge podge of inanity'. He had still not seen the whole poem in print, but was convinced it would need further alteration. He quite rightly thought there was too much fighting in it. He also wanted Bedford's help with 'The Retrospect'; *Madoc* was a better prospect: 'there is a fine ocean of ideas floating about my brain pan for Madoc—& a high delight do I feel sometimes indulging them till selfforgetfulness follows.'[9]

His doubts about *Joan* were, certainly in terms of its reception, unnecessary. Towards the end of April he told Wynn that 'the accounts are more favourable than I expected; the aristocrats are as much pleased as the democrats, & some of the most intolerant order have even thanked me by proxy for the pleasure they derived from it.'[10] This led him to anticipate, quite correctly, a call for a second edition. This was his first literary success, and although it might be argued that most of the reviews were from the republican stable, it is worth dwelling on the poem and its reception.

When *Joan of Arc* appeared, Wordsworth scoffed at Southey ('a coxcomb') and his '*epic*' pretensions. 'This preface is indeed a very conceited performance and the poem though in some passages of first-rate excellence is on the whole of very inferior execution.'[11] The speed with which the poem was written—six weeks in all—and then corrected as it went through the press has become legendary, and was one of the chief causes of criticism at the time; Coleridge had contributed the opening section of Book II, but the poem, unlike *The Fall of Robespierre*, was otherwise Southey's work. Southey, in his Preface, was almost boastful about all this, as though speed were in itself some kind of virtue; alongside this youthful innocence were his remarks on the nature of epic (a form he was later to reject altogether), ranging grandly from Homer, through the 'favourite of his childhood', Spenser, to Glover, a more recent favourite of his Oxford days. He sets out his stall with a vengeance: 'It has been established as a necessary rule for the epic, that the subject be national. To this rule I have acted in direct opposition, and chose for the subject of my poem the defeat of my country. If among my readers there be one who can wish success to injustice, because his countrymen supported it, I desire not that man's approbation.' Whatever the distance of events, then, there can be no mistaking the underlying political thrust of the poem. It might not, indeed, be strictly allegorical, but it is appropriate that it was the Jacobin journals which welcomed it most warmly; the poem, even with Coleridge's lofty metaphysical flights of Book II, fits into the revolutionary sequence of *The Fall of Robespierre* and *Wat Tyler*.

As its length and scope suggest, *Joan of Arc* is much more ambitious than the other two works; furthermore, Southey worked at it much more diligently than his rather throwaway prefatory remarks would suggest. (Even in 1837, when he prepared all his works for publication, he made numerous changes, both local and structural.[12]) The second edition of 1798 was itself carefully reworked, and had all those additional footnotes which Southey increasingly believed were a necessary part of any long poem worth its salt. But even though the poem is rooted in historical events, the main impression is not one of a fixed time and place, let alone a coherent sequence of episodes; it anticipates, rather, the extravagances of *Thalaba* and *The Curse of Kehama*, in particular, in its wild career. There are battles which rage on, page after page; but for all their action-packed bravura, these are not, perhaps, the scenes most readers would dwell on. What matters far more is Southey's attempt to create a climate of feeling, 'breathing', as John Aikin put it in the *Monthly Review*, 'the purest spirit of general benevolence and regard to the rights and claims of human kind'.[13] As Coleridge recognized, there could be too much of a good thing: 'I *think* too much for a *Poet*; he too little for a *great* Poet. But he abjures *thinking*—& lays the whole stress of excellence—on *feeling*.—Now (as you [Thelwall] say), they must go together'. Coleridge agreed with Thelwall that 'he who thinks & *feels* will be virtuous: & he who is absorbed in self will be vicious—whatever may be his speculative opinions';[14] this could well be applied to what he thought of Southey. Coleridge's impractical solution was an amalgamation of them both, some kind of monstrous pair of Siamese twins. But it is possible to see what he means; his own contribution to the poem, whilst too cerebral for its own good, anticipates the crucial shift, by Coleridge and Wordsworth, towards the One Life, and all the complexities of that teasingly simple notion. Southey's verse, in spite of its frequent felicities, never reaches such heights.

Of course, this is slightly unfair to Southey, who is having to cope with the whole poem, and does not have the sort of luxury allowed to, or claimed by, Coleridge. He told Horace Bedford that whilst he was writing the poem, 'I was tempest-tost on the ocean of life—but at the moment of composition—I soard eaglelike into the regions of tranquillity above the storm.' Epictetus had been one of his comforts.

I often walked the streets at dinnertime for want of a dinner. When I had not eighteen pence for the ordinary, ate bread & cheese at my lodgings, but do not suppose that I thought of my dinner when I was walking—my head was full of what I was composing—when I lay down at night I was planning my poem—& when I rose up in the morning the poem was the first thought to which I was awake.[15]

None the less, there is a sense in which Southey is almost overwhelmed by the importance and magnitude of his subject. Joan is at the centre, representing Freedom; but it is spiritual, as much as political, freedom, 'the high command of Duty' that must be obeyed. We are reminded of the 'stern rectitude' of his other heroes, only this time there is more than the complicating factor of a historical parallel. What is striking is the recognition of a loss of Eden:

> how man
> Fell from perfection, from angelic state,
> Plung'd deep in sin, and pluck'd the fruit of woe,
> And bow'd the knee to fiends, and mock'd at God,
> 'Till Christ expiring on the sacred cross
> Pour'd forth the atoning life ...

Much later in the poem, Conrade remembers a comparable Eden,

> when all the family of man
> Freely enjoyed the goodly earth he gave,
> And only bow'd the knee in prayer to God.

Behind this conjunction of two paradises lies the dream of Pantisocracy, but with the darker colouring that derives from the realization that it is in the past.

There is a marvellous phrase in Book IV, 'the fearful features of futurity', and it is this which rings through much of the poem, a sense that the storms we have seen elsewhere are necessary and unavoidable. As we are reminded early on, in a confrontation between Joan and Conrade,

> Such mingled passions charactered his face
> Of fierce and terrible benevolence,
> That I did tremble as I listened to him.
> Then in mine heart tumultuous thoughts arose
> Of high atchievements, indistinct, and wild,
> And vast, yet such they were that I did part
> As tho' by some divinity possess'd.

Benevolence, then, is a difficult concept, and we can see Southey anticipating here the complexities Wordsworth would draw out of his own reading of Godwin and Dyer in 'Lines Written a Few Miles above

Tintern Abbey'.[16] In the debate between Joan and the Priest in Book III, Southey helps Wordsworth, as it were, towards his own working-out of the problem, by having Joan argue strenuously against the idea of sinful nature.

> It is not Nature that can teach to sin:
> Nature is all Benevolence—all Love,
> All Beauty! In the greenwood's simple shade,
> There is no vice that to the indignant cheek
> Bids the red current rush.

There can be little doubt that Wordsworth's 'Ruined Cottage' owes its origins, at least in part, to the kind of vignette we get in Book VII of *Joan of Arc*, where Southey anticipates what he himself was to do within a couple of years in his 'English Eclogues':

> At her cottage door
> The wretched one shall sit, and with dim eye
> Gaze o'er the plain whereon his parting steps
> Her last look hung. Nor ever shall she know
> Her husband dead, but tortur'd with vain hope,
> Gaze on—then heart-sick turn to the poor babe,
> And weep him fatherless!

There is more than mere sentiment at play here: Southey is adapting his own supple blank verse to the necessary suppleness of thought and feeling. It is not a tone he can always sustain; but it is significant that he achieves it at precisely the point where benevolence and exile are conjoined. For one of the poem's main themes is exactly that, of people driven from their homes. We think of the poems on the slave trade, the Botany Bay Eclogues, the English Eclogues, the exile of Thalaba and of Madoc. Joan's retrospective glance over the lost scenes of childhood recall Southey's own 'Retrospect' ('I, far away, remember the past years, | And weep'). It is at this level of personal loss and suffering that the poem works best, as Joan is vouchsafed some kind of Dantesque vision of hell, in which we find those

> Bards
> Whose loose lascivious lays perpetuate
> Their own corruption. Soul-polluted slaves,
> Who sat them down, deliberately lewd,
> So to awake and pamper lust in mind,
> Unborn...;

these wretched bards rub shoulders with the 'Murderers of Mankind! | Monarch, the great! the glorious! the august!' Henry V acknowledges his guilt, and foresees a time when the 'whole human race ... | shall form one brotherhood. | One universal Family of Love'.

Southey's basic problem is to balance these grand gestures with the less exalted manifestations of suffering; it is not a problem he solves here. But, for all its faults, the poem deserved quite a lot of its contemporary credit. It was a bold effort, and a brave one. We could argue that the white heat at which Southey worked at it became an advantage, in that the torrent of verse was appropriate to the theme. He was conscious, too, of the central paradox. Joan's famous fate forms no part of the poem: it lurks off the page, in the future. Southey joked that a poem which ended with a coronation could hardly be considered republican; but there is a wryness about the conclusion—or lack of conclusion—that cannot be lost on us. Joan has the last word, instructing the king in kingship, urging upon him the very benevolence that historically has not been the lot of kings— 'Protect the lowly, feed the hungry ones, | And be the Orphan's father!' Joan speaks for Southey here. Even forty years later, in his reworking of the poem, Southey might have altered the words; but the sentiment remained.

Coleridge quoted with approval several lines from *Joan of Arc* in the *Watchman*, which prompted Lamb to exclaim, 'Why, he is a very Leviathan of Bards—the small minnow I—', whilst at the same time protesting at the size and cost of the volume, and the lack of modesty implied by such a production. But then, whatever internal doubts Southey might harbour about his talents as a poet, he seldom gave voice to them; and Lamb's perception was accurate when he semi-ironically looked forward to the day when 'Southey becomes as modest as his predecessor Milton'. However, when he got a chance to see the whole poem, he had to admit to his own delight, particularly in the 'exquisite combination of the ludicrous and the terrible [in Book IX] ... such as I conceive to be the manner of Dante and Ariosto'; he was even prepared to see the day when Southey would rival Milton, and not just in modesty. 'I already deem him equal to Cowper, and superior to all living Poets Besides.'[17]

Southey announced his arrival in Portsmouth, in a letter to Bedford of 15 May 1796. After six months away, and a loathsome sea voyage of ten days, he was ecstatic: whilst his uncle lamented his nephew's lack of 'common sense or prudence', and feared a waste of talents, Southey indulged in that devil-may-care attitude that reminds us of his youthfulness (he was, after all, still only 22 years old). He felt he now knew of things, both pleasurable and painful, which were beyond the ken of most mortals. He did not know how things

would turn out, but he presented a more than sanguine face to his beloved
England:

I shall soon have enough to place me above want—& till that arrives shall support
myself in ease & comfort like a silkwork by spinning his own brains [within two
years, he had turned this image, in his poem 'The Spider', into a touching account
of his role as a writer] . . . Lord Somerville [his relative] is dead—no matter to me I
believe for the estates were chiefly copyhold, & Canon Southey minded wine &
women too much to think of renewing for the sake of his heirs.[18]

He urged Bedford to come to Bristol, where he could meet his old friend,
the admirable Charles Danvers, and Cottle 'with his oddities & his
excellent heart'. Cottle received a note from Coleridge on 17 May: 'I
sincerely rejoice at Southey's safe arrival—May the literary Republic
rejoice!'[19]

Whatever sourness or sarcasm was contained in that brief line, Southey's ebullience was cruelly punctured when he got to Bristol. His brother-
in-law Robert Lovell had died of putrid fever; although the two men
were not as close as they had once been, the shock to Southey was still
great. 'It has been seldom my lot', he wrote, 'to meet a man so naturally
urbane, so close & clear in reasoning & yet in argument so gentle &
unassuming. The tidings of his death was the most sudden check I have
experienced.' Edith and Coleridge had both sat through the nights with
the dying Lovell, in spite of the obvious dangers of infection. Coleridge
rather perversely tried to offer the atheistical Lovell in his dying agonies
some kind of Christian comfort; but the most useful thing he could do on
the practical level was to bring Mary Lovell into his own house, as she
herself was on the verge of hysteria. Coleridge later recalled the horror of
the situation: 'It was, you know, a very windy night—but his loud, deep,
unintermitted groans mingled audibly with the wind, & whenever the
wind dropt, they were very horrible to hear, & drove my poor young
Sister-in-law frantic.'[20]

Whereas Edmund Seward's death had signalled the loss of a formative
figure from his Oxford days, Lovell's death brought home to him forcibly
that poets, too, were not immortal. Southey hoped that Wynn and Bedford would both come down to Bristol, to help restore his equilibrium.
The loss of Lovell reminded him, not just of happier times in Oxford with
Wynn, where they had parted two years ago, but of the more distant past
of his childhood. Recognizing how different they all were from those days,
he wanted to recall their youthful visits as schoolboys to Bristol, 'our early
walk among the rocks here, & the ships goings out'. More than ever he felt
the need of his small circle of friends, now that, as he put it, so 'little of that

ardent enthusiasm which so lately feverd my whole character remains'. More than ever he wanted to have little to do with politics, little to do with people; 'how does time mellow down our opinions!', he cried to Bedford, perhaps forgetting just how much his had fluctuated over the last few years.[21] There had never really been a core of stability to his views; only now, in his desire to be settled, to become, as a lawyer, part of the establishment, he felt able to resort to Horatian disdain and detachment: 'Odi profanum vulgus!' It might not be the whole truth, but it was certainly an important part of it. When he learnt that the aristocrats had been kind to *Joan of Arc*, he could say, making one think that perhaps Coleridge was being sarcastic, after all, 'if they favour me by forgetting that I ever meddled too much with public concerns, I will take care not to awaken their memories.'[22]

In their lodgings on Kingsdown, near Bristol, Southey took pleasure from the flattering reviews of *Joan of Arc*, from his newly acquired taste in porter, and, of course, from being at last under the same roof as his beloved Edith: they could now, openly, be man and wife. He proceeded apace with his *Letters* from Portugal, hoping to pass them on for publication to Cottle in September. The local Bristol elections brought little comfort (for however quiet a life Southey wanted he still held to his principles): he had no good opinion of either Charles Bragge or 'that rascal Sheffield', who had resolutely failed to vote against the slave trade, and he knew that both of the new MPs would vote for a continuance of the war. Coleridge was not surprised, as he had less regard for the citizens of Southey's favourite place: 'the Bristolians rank very low in the orders of intellect; and form, I suspect, that subtle link, which (in the great chain of things) connects Man with the Brute Creation.'[23]

Much nearer to home Southey was having to think about the future of his younger brother Edward, who was to be a thorn in his flesh for years to come; he hoped he might get him into St Paul's School, and in a fit of optimism persuaded himself that, even if nothing was forthcoming from the Somerville estate, he would somehow become rich. A note to Horace Bedford a week later suggests that he has, in spite of, or perhaps because of, the turmoil of the last few years, arrived at some new level of stoic acceptance. He talks here (misleadingly, we might think, knowing all his oscillations) like the apostle of whom Seward would have been proud:

I have experienced much of the villainy of mankind—but I have discovered virtues enough to set the balance even, & if the falshood of a bosom friend sometimes induced a passing thought of misanthropy, the benevolence of others soon reconciled me to human nature. After all the trash of metaphysics our characters are born with us. For if they were totally formed by circumstances—how is it that mine has remained the same thro so many a vicissitude?[24]

Even Horace Bedford might have seen through this self-deception. He could not, though, have anticipated just how much of a hostage to fortune Southey was offering up; at least at this stage Southey had the benefit of privacy.

He repeated to Horace's brother Grosvenor Bedford his renunciation of metaphysics in favour of 'common sense', as opposed to nature, the 'French Goddess' of liberty ('for whom I profess veneration') and truth. This is a curiously sudden, and it seems half-reluctant change of tune. Maybe it has to do with the way he and Coleridge had so dreadfully fallen out; maybe it genuinely reflects his belief that it was his innate character that had carried him through. Certainly Charles Lamb was regretting, at the end of May, the serious difference between Coleridge and Southey, and quoted Milton at them: 'Between you two there should be peace.' But Coleridge had compared Southey unfavourably with their old Bristol friend Charles Danvers, cursing him as 'a specious rascal who deserted me in the hour of distress', and Pantisocracy as 'a scheme of Virtue impracticable and romantic'.[25] Perhaps Coleridge would have agreed with Southey that it all boiled down to the matter of his character; but philosophy played its part, too. Southey might have thought he was echoing Godwin, whom he still upheld against the snarls of his friend Richard Duppa; Mary Wollstonecraft, and the *Rights of Woman* (1792), made a deep impression on him. But, crucially, he was less impressed by Godwin's *Caleb Williams* (1794), precisely because he thought Godwin 'little acquainted with human characters. I have planned a work', he went on, 'to delineate existing systems & their consequent vices & misery, & hope to do some good by it if I have ever leisure to fill up the outlines.' Southey seems to have arrived at an unnerving truth: 'our opinions seldom regulate our conduct. Half the democrats I know would be despots if they could ... the affections of the heart form the man. Hence the fatal consequences of existing systems ...' He referred, as so often before, to the public-school system which led to tyranny and vice; the turn of events in France must also have been uppermost in his mind. As he said to Horace Bedford in June, 'when I left you in London my hopes were centred in the wilds of America. I had devoted myself to the establishment of a system to be the panacea of all human calamities, & in the future completion of which I expect a promised millennium. But in the ardent perception of the end—I glanced rapidly over the means.'[26] Grosvenor Bedford received a more confused statement of the nature of things: 'this is a ridiculous world—& a beastly world & a worthless world—notwith-standing it is the best of all possible worlds, & I don't know how the Devil you & I & half a dozen more dropt into it—but such as it is we must make the best of it.'[27]

In this frame of mind, with domesticity his main desire, Southey found refuge in his writing: 'I have a Helicon-kind of dropsy upon me, & crescit indulgens sibi'. He would write more verses than Lope de Vega, more tragedies than Dryden, more epics than Blackmore (he was not entirely joking, as his collected works were to testify). When he was not thinking about the *Letters*, *Madoc* occupied his mind. He had already rewritten a book and a half: even at the tender age of 22 he saw it as, at least potentially, his last will and testament; with that finished, 'I shall have done enough'. Typically, he saw the poem as a challenge to acknowledged literary tastes and expectations; he challenged Warburton's view that the epic had reached such a state of perfection that there was no room for improvement; he scorned the Homeric age, and thought *Paradise Lost*, for reasons not explained, 'the fatal source of all the corruptions of Christianity'. One thing that had not changed was his belief in himself.

Southey none the less felt the need to justify himself. 'This is indeed a change', he admitted to Bedford, with reference to his increasing domesticity, and resorted to the image of a liquor that, once it has stopped fermenting, does not become flat: 'the beer then becomes fine—& continues so till it is dead.' As if to reinforce the point, he drew a distinction between himself, even as a schoolboy, and his friends Tom Lamb and Combe. Again, this might seem, from what we know, like a severe distortion of the truth, but it is important for Southey to be able to justify his claim that 'the less we think of the world the better':

I had enthusiasm of character—& a highly cultivated taste for the το πρεπον—they—little more than great good humour. While at school the ascendancy of my mind—kept them within the bounds of regularity, & even gave them some love for study, but the seed fell among thorns—at Oxford they mixt with other society—Lamb was drunk every night—& Combe was agreable in all company because he adapted himself to all. I love to remember Westminster—how little can (in general) be judged of the man by the boy!

Although he claimed to have 'tamed Bucephalus', Southey was still throwing himself into *Madoc* with almost unnatural eagerness (partly because it was so much more preferable than the law), still rejoicing in the success of *Joan of Arc* (it 'has secured my reputation'), still ready to send off to the *Courier* and the *Telegraph* what he called 'a seditious Ode in the ludicrous stile addressed to the Cannibals'. That he signed it C. Gracchus was not without significance, since this was the pseudonym of a piece, supporting Godwin, that had appeared in the *Watchman*, to the provocation of Coleridge; it is also of significance that the French revolutionary Babœuf, so admired by Southey, was known as 'Caius Gracchus'. There is good reason to believe that Southey was the author of the piece in the *Watchman*. 'I do hunger & thirst for sedition', he declared on 25 July. 'Yet a little while & I must change that study for Law!' It is certainly interesting that Southey was, at the same time, questioning some of his cherished notions, such as that of universal benevolence.[28] He told Bedford that there were two classes of society, the oppressors and the oppressed: 'I hate the one class for active evil—I despise the other for *patient* suffering.' He derived some comfort from being able to describe himself and Bedford as 'Nondescripts'. Within a month he had become more virulent, talking of the 'Beast' and telling Horace Bedford that he had 'learnt heartily to despise the reptile race that pollute the world'. For Southey the only way out of this impasse was the 'total reorganization of society'; his Christianity allowed him to believe that this must take place.[29] Otherwise he would have turned to the atheism of his old Oxford friend Robert Allen; but Allen's political solution was too Guy Fawkes-like for a Southey wondering just how much change might be effected without revolution. This helps to explain Southey's increasing desire to retreat from society— he imagined himself and Grosvenor Bedford living somewhere near the sea, with dogs and cats, and cabbages and potatoes, and cider and wine.[30]

The *Letters* would be out in October; his *Poems* by Christmas. He was then to enter Lincoln's Inn; once qualified, he would leave London for the country. He was becoming increasingly introverted, wanting to stay at home with Edith. 'Besides I am a very reserved man, never unbending except to those whom I love. Consequently to any but my friends I am not an agreable companion ... Grosvenor I despise the world. I hate the mob ... I shall mingle in the world, but it will be only with the view of enabling myself to get out of it.'[31] His literary schemes were enough to occupy him for life: a list of possible dramas; the epic *Madoc* in twenty books; a novel *Edmund Oliver*, in three volumes; a Norwegian Tale; an Oriental poem of 'The Destruction of Dom Daniel'; and, 'in case I adopt Rousseau's system', the Pains of Imagination. As we shall see, not all of this was idle dreaming, by any means: *Madoc* was indeed to appear, after *Thalaba*, which grew out of the Dom Daniel saga. In order to encompass all this, Southey was settling down to the clockwork regularity that was to become his hallmark: working from 5.00 to 8.00 in the morning, then from 9.00 to 12 noon, then again from 1.00 to 4.00 p.m. This enabled him to fit in articles about Spanish literature for the *Monthly Magazine* at five guineas per sheet. He was also reading William Taylor's translations, in the *Monthly*, of some of Bürger's ballads. Before long, he would be meeting and corresponding with Taylor, and contributing his own poems to the flood of balladry that spilt across Europe at the turn of the century, including of course the volume he would review, with something less than total acclamation, in 1798, Wordsworth and Coleridge's *Lyrical Ballads*.[32]

What Southey also intended to embark upon ('Life is but a bad voyage at the best—particularly if we be seasick upon it') was an autobiographical work. It is our loss that he never got further with this than the letters he wrote to his friend John May between 1820 and 1826, which provide the basis for any account of his early years, up until the expulsion from Westminster. He was very clear about his powers of recall: 'no man ever retained a more perfect knowledge of the history of his own mind than I have done. I can trace the *developement* of my character from infancy— for *developed* it has been, not changed. I look forward to the writing of this history as the most pleasing & most useful employment I shall ever undertake.' This is an important qualification to what he had been saying in previous weeks; it could act as some kind of text for Southey's whole life, and his attitude towards it. He himself, in the same letter, suggested a rather different, more teasing image. 'A little taper will lighten a room, but place it to illuminate the street—it will do no good, & the wind will speedily extinguish it. There is the text which my life is to illustrate. They who do not like the maxim may amuse themselves with the metaphor.'[33]

In spite of all these plans, Southey was in August preparing for the legal profession, and feeling that his days as a poet were over. *Joan of Arc*, he had said in July, had secured his reputation, but by late August he was less sure: '[it] may give pleasure, & cannot do harm.'[34] Coleridge, too, by the end of the year could not see literature as his primary occupation any more: if a choice had to be made, he would rather be a gardener than a Milton. Southey had seen or heard from a number of his friends: Burnett was off to Manchester, to study rather improbably for the Church for two years; Robert Allen's future was bleak, in that his wife was dying of consumption. She had been a widow with two children when they got married, and in spite of her fortune Allen had, as part of the agreement, to support himself. Southey's sympathy on this point might help to explain his apparently cold account of Mrs Allen's impending demise: 'she is a woman of accomplishments—but I hear of dissipation—her physiognomy is bad, & tho he will of course severely feel her loss—I do not think it can be deemd a severe misfortune.' His former friend Charles Collins, due to be married at Christmas, might have deemed this a bit rich, if he had known about it, coming from the man who had described *him* as 'equally vain impertinent cold-hearted & selfish'. More pleasing had been a visit from Wynn—the first time they had met since leaving Oxford; Peter Elmsley, with £20,000 of his own, could perhaps afford to be 'as fat & as happy & as studious as usual', a 'walking Encyclopedia' to Wynn and all. Southey sold the copyright of *Joan of Arc* to Cottle, for a profit of about 80 guineas; with such financial security, he could say with some feeling, 'how infinitely more interesting now do the revolutions in the little circle of my own friends appear to me than all the changes that are now convulsing Europe.'[35]

There was still time to attend to the volume of poems. He told Bedford at the end of August that he had begun a 'Hymn to the Penates', which would—and did—conclude the volume. This 'Hymn' might seem a rather trite poem about domestic affections; but for Southey it represents one of his central beliefs, that home is where the hearth is.

> As on the height of some huge eminence,
> Reach'd with long labour, the way-faring man
> Pauses awhile, and gazing o'er the plain
> With many a sore step travelled, turns him then
> Serious to contemplate the onward road,
> And calls to mind the comforts of his home,
> And sighs that he has left them, and resolves
> To stray no more: I on my way of life
> Muse thus PENATES, and with firmest faith
> Devote myself to you. I will not quit
> To mingle with the mob your calm abodes,
> Where, by the evening hearth CONTENTMENT sits
> And hears the cricket chirp; where LOVE delights
> To dwell, and on your altars lays his torch
> That burns with no extinguishable flame...

Many of his longer poems explore the relation of child to parent, of home and exile; here he idealizes, in many respects, a childhood he had never had. But in the year that *Joan of Arc* appeared—a great trumpet-blast of a political poem, as we have seen—he was anxious to represent himself as the man 'unfit... | To mingle with the world', the Stoic philosopher modelling himself upon his dear dead friend Edmund Seward.[36]

Southey still planned a tragedy, in the hope that this would bring in enough money to furnish a house, as opposed to lodgings; he also planned a volume consisting of specimens of the early English poets: these would be less well-known writers, represented by hitherto unanthologized selections. The whole volume would, he imagined, take less than a month to prepare. (This was something he was to rue ever telling Bedford about.) But, as Bristol filled up for the annual fair ('the Beast has got a holyday', he writes, outGissing Gissing a hundred years *avant la lettre*): 'I do not know anything more delightful than to lie on the beach in the sun & watch the rising waves, while a thousand vague ideas—pass over the mind—like the summer clouds over the water. Then it is a noble situation to Shandeize.' It was to be one of his pleasures later in life to take his children to the seaside, or to swim in one of the lakes around Keswick, just as he remembered his own childhood escapades with Bedford. Southey was not at all wrong to see the continuity and coherence of his life.[37]

In the state of mental torpor that he found he could enjoy, even in Bristol, Southey even found himself wanting children. In that oddly Coleridgean (or Shandean) form of associationism that he had celebrated more than once, it perhaps seemed natural for him to realize that perfect domesticity must include the children he and Edith would eventually have. But he was glad to meet Wordsworth's revolutionary friend, James Losh, 'one of the most open manly democratic faces I ever saw'.[38] In the mean time, as though to fend off the prospective awfulness of having to be in London, he read Saint-Pierre's *Études de la nature* and thought them wonderful. Whatever their differences, Southey and Coleridge were having rather similar thoughts: Coleridge was 'anxious that my children should be bred up from earliest infancy in the simplicity of peasants, their food, dress, and habits completely rustic'. Furthermore, perhaps more definitively than Southey, he declared 'I have . . . snapped my squeaking baby-trumpet of sedition'.[39] In November, Coleridge was telling his Cambridge publisher, Benjamin Flower—who had published *The Fall of Robespierre*, and started the *Cambridge Intelligencer*, where many of Coleridge's and Southey's works first appeared—that in the second edition of his poems he would leave out 'all the political allusions'.[40] The *Watchman* had folded, and Coleridge, much more than Southey, was anxious to begin that process of covering his tracks which would end with the revised version of his own life, *Biographia Literaria* (1817). But there was certainly something paradoxical in Southey's telling the aristocratic Bedford in the New Year that 'your mind is set in a revolutionary state—mine is calm & settled. I have a belief in politics & religion, both of which I apprehend you want.'[41] Coleridge was to ask Thelwall, in November, about his 'Corresponding Society Magazine' (the *Tribune*), saying that Southey was a benefactor: this led him to place Southey in some sort of context. 'Homer is the Poet for the Warrior—Milton for the Religionist—Tasso for Women—Robert Southey for the Patriot.' Since he was basing this comment on *Joan of Arc*, it has an odd ring to it.[42]

Charles Lamb, at the end of October, realized that it was absurd for the two former friends to have fallen out 'like boarding-school misses'; and he was aware of this because he knew just how much they had in common. He told Coleridge to 'kiss, shake hands, & make it up'. Southey did his best to make amends, and there was some kind of patching-up in the autumn of 1796. But Coleridge reported on New Year's Eve, 'We are now reconciled; but the cause of the Difference was solemn,—& "the blasted oak puts not forth it's buds anew"—we are *acquaintances*—& feel *kindliness* towards each other; but I do not *esteem* or LOVE Southey, as I must esteem & love the man whom I dared call by the holy name of FRIEND!— and vice versa Southey of me—I say no more—it is a painful subject.'[43]

Southey approached the move to London with dread ('the noise the smoke the filth the Beast—oh'). His only way of coping would be to creep into his shell like a snail, or 'roll myself up like a hedgehog in my rough outside'.[44] This exterior gets a more candid appraisal in another letter: 'the repellent coldness of my manners will protect me from any acquaintance, for I cover the milk of human kindness with as rough an outside as the Cocoanut.'[45] He would certainly not be joining Bedford's gregarious gentlemen's literary club. As the New Year began, he once again took stock, prompted perhaps by his friend Bedford's doing likewise. Southey saw the similarities between the two of them: 'we think equally ill of mankind, & ... I believe you think as badly as I do of their rulers. I fancy you are mounted above the freezing point of aristocracy to the temperate degree where I have fallen.' Southey recalled how once he had been talkative and enthusiastic, whereas now he was 'again as silent, as *self-centering* as in early youth'. He spoke of how he planned some kind of closet-drama based on the tragedy of *Joan of Arc*, and this led him to think, yet again, of his own life in dramatic terms. 'John Doe & Richard Roe must however form the chief personages in the last act of my life. Grosvenor will it be a tragedy or a comedy?'[46] The extent to which his life was comedy or tragedy has been much debated, and it is significant that Southey should raise the question himself. A dispassionate observer would have said, even at this point, that he had moved from the sublime to the ridiculous and back again. In a letter to Wynn in January 1797 he wrote, with typical self-contradiction, 'I do not think the *Monk* can be praised too highly, or blamed too severely'.[47] (Matthew Lewis's *The Monk, a Romance* appeared anonymously in 1796: it leant upon Ann Radcliffe's *Mysteries of Udolpho* (1794), and helped to further the tradition of Gothic horror and apparent immorality; it was the latter to which Southey objected so severely.) That sentence could be said to reflect the wide-ranging absurdity of much of his own life; not even Polonius could have come up with an appropriate definition for the drama of Southey's life.

Southey left for London on the last day of January 1797, and on Saturday, 4 February wrote the following lines to the city of his birth, 'the first day of my residence in London':

> BRISTOL! I did not on thy well-known towers
> Turn my last look without one natural pang:—
> My heart remembered all the peaceful years
> Of childhood, & was sad ...
> There as a stranger in my father's house:-
> And where my evil fortunes found a home
> From this hard world, the gate has closed upon me:
> And the poor spaniel, that did love me, lies
> Deep in the whelming waters.—fare thee well
> Oh pleasant place! 'I had been well content
> 'To seek no other earthly home beside!'[48]

In many respects, this departure from what George Eliot in *The Mill on the Floss* was to call the 'golden gates' of childhood, what Dickens was to refer to allusively as the Eden of Pip's life at the forge in *Great Expectations*, was much more a break with the past than going up to Oxford: he had, after all, spent much time away from home when at Westminster School. But now he was entering the adult world, represented on one level by the admission fee of £12. 15s. he had to pay to Gray's Inn, on another by the lodgings he found (a mere couple of rooms, but clean, and with the necessary bookcase) at Mr Peacock's, 20 Prospect Place, Newington Butts. He awaited Edith's arrival with eagerness. In the mean time he struggled through from day to day: 'I rise in the morning without expecting pleasure from the day, & I lie down at night without one wish for the morning.'[49] (He was, all the same, able, like a good boy scout, to whistle cheerfully and loudly enough to annoy Bedford when he visited.) By the end of February Edith was installed, and this gave him another welcome excuse for not joining Bedford's literary society: a man should stay with his wife in the evening. Or, as he put it, rather more dauntingly, 'duty & happiness [are] inseparable'.[50]

There is more talk, in his letters of the early months of 1797, of writing than there is of the law. He was embarking on a translation of the second volume of Jacques Necker's account of the French Revolution, for twenty-five guineas: this was very much along the lines of Burke, and Necker's argument for the status quo ante the revolution was not likely to have found much favour with Southey, whatever his desire to escape from the world. It is rather a surprise to find him undertaking this translation at all, except for the money. More congenial, one imagines, were the articles he was writing on Spanish and Portuguese poetry for the *Monthly Magazine*, thereby getting his foot in the door of journalism, where it would remain, for better or worse, firmly stuck for many a long year. He planned some poems on his travels in Spain and Portugal. By the beginning of May he had two books of *Madoc* ready for Danvers to pass on to Cottle in Bristol. He was no doubt encouraged by his new landlord's quite extraordinary zeal in buying and distributing copies of both his Portuguese *Letters* and the *Poems*; and Cottle was calling for a new edition of both *Poems* and *Joan of Arc* (which Southey wanted in two volumes). 'Mary Maid of the Inn', one of his most popular ballads, appeared in the *Oracle*; there were sonnets in the *Telegraph*, 'with outrageous commendation'.[51]

In the nature of things, Southey met in London a wide range of people, many of them Jacobin writers introduced to him by George Dyer: Mary Imlay (Mary Wollstonecraft's daughter) he liked, apart from a touch of superiority that reminded him of Horne Tooke; Mary Hays, author of *Emma Courtney*, was 'agreeable ... & a Godwinite' (a mixed blessing, since he was now making fun not only of Godwin's nose, but also of the 'nonsense' he talked 'about the collision of mind'); he met and approved the poet, Ann Cristall, whose *Poetical Sketches* of 1795 had been published by Joseph Johnson—'a fine, artless, sensible girl!'—and reported that Gilbert Wakefield, once a hero, 'has a most critic-like voice, as if he had snarled himself hoarse'.[52] George Dyer ('that man is all benevolence'[53]) gave Southey a copy of his poems, but Southey was not much impressed, in spite of the fact that 'The Poet's Fate' made direct reference to the abandoned Pantisocratic scheme: Dyer had written of the various options open to a budding poet—

> Or plough, in learned pride, the Atlantic main,
> Join Pantisocracy's harmonious train;
> Haste, where young Love shall spread his brooding wings,
> And freedom digs, and ploughs, and laughs, and sings.

A note singled out Southey and Coleridge: 'These two young poets are equally distinguished for their ardent love of liberty; the former more remarkable for his powers of description, and for exciting the softer feelings of benevolence; the latter for a rich and powerful imagination.'[54] Dyer's judgement was perceptive. Southey saw quite a lot of the medical man Anthony Carlisle; he met Thomas Holloway and William Westall, the artists, but it was John Opie who made a strong impression, even though there was a strange contrast, disturbing to the fastidious Southey, between his 'genius ... & the vulgarity of his appearance—of his manners

& language sometimes'. On a less exalted note he met Dr George Gregory, the evening preacher at the Foundling Hospital, and did not relish having to dine with someone so fat, solemn, and intolerant: 'a very brawn looking man—of most episcopal pinguitude—& full moon cheeks. There is much tallow in him.'[55] At times like this, it is not too fanciful to see something of the novelist in Southey, an almost Dickensian ability to capture the full extent of someone's absurdity. (This was presumably the very same Gregory who had written a life of Chatterton in 1789, the life which would appear at the front of Southey's edition of Chatterton in 1803.)

The translation of Necker was finished on 26 April, and he told Cottle rather regretfully that he could now get back to his regular occupations: 'Would that digging potatoes were among them!'[56] But there was a plan to move out of London, and just a month later he arrived at Southampton, on the evening of 24 May. En route he dined with Mary Wollstonecraft, 'of all the literary characters the one I most admire...she is a first-rate woman, sensible of her own worth, but without arrogance or affectation'. The belief that Southey was more than half in love with her is without foundation; but there is no doubt about his admiration, which led him to preface his 'Triumph of Woman' (1797) with a poem to her. And he told Mary Barker that 'as for panegyric, I never praised living being yet, except Mary Wollstonecraft, not even Bonaparte in his honest days'.[57] He looked forward to being by the sea, where he could 'pickle [himself] in that grand brine tub.' Edith was unwell, which meant he would have to set off on his reconnoitring trip without her. He was reluctant to do so. On the other hand, he wanted somewhere for them to settle, and Southampton held few attractions: 'its inhabitants are people connected with shipping—& sharking shopkeepers—its visitors the very top scum of aristocracy, the carrion that these vultures feed upon.' Bristol was a possibility: he would be near some of his good friends, especially Danvers and Cottle, and he would have the woods and rocks of Avon as companions. As he had written of the New Forest,

the feelings that fill me when I lie under one tree & contemplate another in all the majesty of years—are neither to be defined or expressed. & these undefinable inexpressible feelings are those of the highest delight. They pass over the mind like the clouds of the summer evening—too fine & too fleeting for Memory to retain.[58]

Within a week they had settled in Christchurch, Hampshire, and Southey was already jotting down regularly the kind of observations he had made in his letters to Cottle (to be used subsequently in his poems, he told Wynn). They planned to stay about six to seven weeks, before moving off westwards. But even here, amidst the kind of scenery he had yearned for, he could not forget his legal obligations. He wondered aloud to Wynn whether he might not be better suited to Chancery, rather than criminal law; it was partly a matter of moral responsibility—he did not want to send a man to the gallows—but he did not think he would be very good at cross-examination. 'No man is more easily disconcerted than myself': a blockhead with rhetorical bravura would soon put him off his stride.[59] He was also reworking *Joan of Arc*, deciding that he would remove Coleridge's lines from the beginning of Book II, and the whole of Book IX (this was to form a separate poem, and Coleridge would use his own lines elsewhere). Life in the countryside also allowed him to think out more deeply some of his ideas about society. He confessed his disappointment in the way things had turned out in France: 'if it be true that Babœuf be put to death—she has now no man left whom we may compare with the Gracchi.' He was, as he had always been, still opposed to poverty and its attendant misery: it was at least necessary to 'destroy Greatness & Wealth' as a start, but he was not clear how this could be achieved. He told Horace Bedford, rather enigmatically, 'I think I know the solution': the alternative was to follow Rousseau and go back to the safe state of nature. This must have had its appeal as he indulged his 'delight in a clear stream—there is such a world of business going on in it'—and such a different world of business from that of the loathsome city.[60] The issue of slavery was also at the front of his mind, and he liked to think that his poetry was a reflection of these concerns: he was not just amusing himself with verses. 'I may not live to do good to mankind personally; but I will at least leave something behind me to strengthen those feelings & excite those reflections in others from whence virtue must spring.'[61]

But Southey's apparent optimism here is tempered in the same letter by an acknowledgement that we cannot in fact change people. Since this is a rather crucial moment in Southey's development of his ideas about society, it requires quotation in full:

The ablest physician can do little in the great lazar house of society; it is a pest-house that infects all within its atmosphere. He acts the wisest part who retires from the contagion; nor is that part either a selfish or a cowardly one; it is ascending the ark, like Noah, to preserve a remnant which may become the whole... The rich are strangely ignorant of the miseries to which the lower & largest part of mankind are abandoned.—& even of those who see & pity & relieve their distresses, you will scarcely find one who has ever felt shocked at the reflection that God has given to the poor mental capabilities that might have infinitely benefited mankind—& given them in vain—only to be stifled by society. There is not one spot on this earth where man enjoys 'The unfettered use of all the powers which God for use hath given.' The savage & civilized states are alike unnatural, alike unworthy of the origin & end of man. Hence the prevalence of scepticism & atheism, which from being the effect became the cause of vice; & the civilized world sunk into a depravity dreadful as that which characterised the last ages of Rome seems again about to be renovated by a total revolution. It is covered by pestilential fogs which nothing but tempests can scatter & those tempests are begun.

What this passage demonstrates is Southey's growing ability and desire to write about society in a way that is at least approaching the analytical, whilst at the same time still not quite able to reconcile this discernment with, on the one hand, a desire to escape, to leave it all behind him, and, on the other, that apocalyptic tone which in fact blurs the very analysis on which he wants to embark.

In the summer months of 1797, Southey's day to day life to some extent reflected these contradictions. The house at Burton, near Christchurch, became quite busy, with his mother and his naval brother Tom coming to stay. The presence there of Charles Lloyd, a writer and friend of Coleridge who was slightly unbalanced and prone to epileptic fits, proved a mixed blessing: his untidiness and his rather chaotic love-life were the two most obvious bones of contention at this point. Cottle came over to visit; there was a pleasant neighbour in Charles Biddlecombe, 'rich enough to buy books, & very friendly'. Most importantly, Southey got to know John Rickman.[62]

Rickman became Secretary to the Speaker of the House of Commons, Charles Abbot, from 1802 until 1816; in 1814 he was made second clerk assistant, and then clerk assistant, in the Commons, where he remained for all his working life. His main claim to political and historical fame lies in his preparation of the first population Census in 1801, followed by three more in 1811, 1821, and 1831. He compiled many government reports, most notably the annual abstracts of the poor-law returns, which enabled him to provide Southey in later years with the necessary statistics for his many essays on poverty and parliamentary reform. Rickman became one of Southey's closest friends, and his house in London was a frequent port of call, not only for Southey, but for Southey's children. The two men corresponded frequently, in a rather formal, friendly way, each skirting around the embarrassments of too intimate an acquaintance. But at this stage of his life Rickman was not quite sure what he wanted to do: after leaving Lincoln College, Oxford, in 1792, he seems to have decided that he did not want to enter the Church, and he was living in Christchurch, waiting for something to turn up. Southey turned up in June, and told Cottle, in Bristol, that Rickman was 'a sensible young man, of rough but mild manners, and very seditious'. With much in common, they were almost mirror-images of each other, except that Rickman was no poet, and Southey had no head for figures. In 1809 Southey spoke of his friend to Walter Savage Landor: 'His manners are stoical; they are like the husk of the cocoa nut,—his inner nature is like the milk within its kernel . . . He gives me but half his hand when he welcomes me at the door, but I have his whole heart . . .'[63] (If Rickman seems to us like Southey, to Southey he seemed like Thomas Poole.) When Rickman contemplated marriage at the end of 1802, he commented with all the pragmatism of a Southey: 'I shall be forced to find out a wife, and though I am rather past falling in love, I daresay I should not chuse the more unwisely for that.'[64] Even the gentle-hearted Charles Lamb thought highly of Rickman: 'He is a most pleasant hand; a fine *rattling* fellow, has gone through Life laughing at solemn apes; himself hugely literate, oppressively full of information . . . a new Class. An exotic . . . The clearest headed fellow. Fullest of matter with least verbosity.'[65]

The bad weather made Southey still less enchanted with England, and yet he derived pleasure (in spite of stiff knees, swollen feet, and blisters) from a walk of eight miles, during which he had called on Lady Strathmore, a woman with a good library and therefore useful to know, but not as clever as rumour had it, and over-insistent with her invitations.[66] On another walk, when Joseph and Amos Cottle came over, Southey got stuck in a bog (which could be seen retrospectively as something more than literal). Southey was excited by the Polish General Kosciusko's reception in Bristol (envying Danvers's chance actually to meet him), and he stored this event in his mind for later use in the *Letters from England*, by the fictitious Spaniard Espriella, in 1807. He concerned himself with the fate of a French Captain Boutet, who had saved Tom when his ship went down; Southey wanted to repay the debt by getting Boutet freed. This is a typical act of kindness on Southey's part, similar to many he performs unobtrusively throughout his life, using what contacts he has when he can.[67]

On the literary front there was still *Joan*; his uncle had sent some views of Portugal, which he hoped would get into the second edition of the *Letters* (but cost prevented it). Southey was going to edit, mainly out of charity towards the family, the works of Chatterton; Cottle would publish the volume without any eye to profit. Coleridge was not entirely enthusiastic about this venture when Southey approached him for help; he certainly did not want his early *Monody* on the death of Chatterton reprinted. He made an interesting comment, self-revealing but also no doubt meant partly as a criticism of Southey: 'It appears to me, that strong feeling is not *so* requisite to an Author's being profoundly pathetic, as taste & good sense.' As if to prove the point, he sent 'This Lime-tree Bower My Prison', one of his extraordinary 'conversation' poems that were to enable Wordsworth's writing of the 'Lines Written a Few Miles above Tintern Abbey'. By this stage Coleridge and Wordsworth were installed in the rather grand house at Alfoxden in Somerset, and Coleridge extended Wordsworth's invitation to come and stay there: 'so divine and wild is the country that I am sure it would increase your stock of images.'[68]

Both Southey and Coleridge were deeply perturbed by the way the war with France was going; Southey was horrified at the prospect of a peace made by Pitt, and managed to kill two birds with one stone in defence of his position: 'my bones shall never rot in a soil that nourishes slaves.'[69] Coleridge was railing against the Patriots—'a most execrable herd'—partly because of their perverted form of Godwinism: 'arrogant because they are ignorant, and boastful of the strength of reason, because they have never tried it enough to know its *weakness*—O my poor Country! The Clouds cover thee—there is not one spot of clear blue in the whole heaven.'[70] One of the great ironies of the situation was that Coleridge and Wordsworth were already suspected of treacherous behaviour; for Thelwall to join them in Somerset would be asking for trouble (after all, even the mild-mannered Thomas Poole was thought to be a spy). At such a time there was something appropriate about Anna Seward's 'Philippic on a Modern Epic', which appeared in the *Morning Chronicle*.

> Base is the purpose of this Epic song,
> Baneful its powers:—but, oh, the Poesy
> ('What can it less when Sun-born GENIUS sings?')
> Wraps in reluctant ecstasy the soul
> Where Poesy is felt!
>
> .   .   .   .
>
>   Oh, unnat'ral Boy;
> Oh beardless Parricide!—thy treach'rous Muse
> In Comet splendour, in MEDUSA'S beauty
> Balefully deck'd, an impious task essays...

Joan of Arc was a work of potentially explosive political import.[71]

Southey did not take up the invitation to go to Alfoxden. He was anxious about his mother's failing health; he was also trying to placate his uncle, none too pleased by the book on Spain and Portugal. Bedford offered a London roof over their heads; but Southey, although tempted, felt uneasy. For a start, there was the problem of furnishing their own apartment on their return; he was also keen (shades of the quarrel with Coleridge here) to keep a servant on, as he put it, 'for various oeconomical reasons'. At the same time Bedford had decided that he, too, was not suited to the law, and Southey, in a couple of letters to Wynn, displayed what can only be called hypocrisy in view of his own prevarications. He had told Bedford in an apparently understanding way, 'As for the Law I am less surprised at your laying it down than at your taking it up'. But to Wynn he lamented Bedford's lack of 'steadiness', condemned his 'general fickleness', and pronounced, 'I believe his irresolution will never leave him & that he will never be useful to others or happy in himself... there is a very excellent fellow spoilt.'[72] No doubt Southey saw in Bedford someone rather too like himself (he had said as much in an earlier letter). He confessed to Bedford at the beginning of September that he did not really understand him, and then in fact urged him to give up the law—'my *best* opinion you know you possess' (not quite what Wynn would have told him); and he added what was to become his own creed for every ensuing personal calamity: 'I think it is of high importance to be careless of applause or censure of any existing being, & to act wholly in reference to our own judgement.' Here we see that self-righteous, hard coconut exterior which was to carry him through the turbulent waters that lay ahead.[73]

Something of a nomadic period began. Tom Southey and Charles Lloyd went off to the Isle of Wight, and on their return, Southey and Lloyd set off from Burton to walk via Stonehenge to Bath and Bristol. Edith would travel separately with Southey's mother and Tom. Southey enjoyed this combination of exercise and work (which mainly consisted of yet more alterations to *Joan*). He sent back to Wynn a description of a 33-mile walk, 'in which I have been pickled with sea spray, washed fresh with the rain— half buried in a sand shower which would not have disgraced Arabia.'[74] They arrived at Bath on 22 September, where news of Mary Wollstone-craft's death unsettled Southey; he wondered how Godwin could bear the loss, and registered his belief that if it were not for faith in the afterlife, half of us would commit suicide. He also asked Bedford if he would act as his 'confessor', as recipient of a series of letters in which Southey would give an account of his own life.[75] True to his word, he sent off the first letter at the end of the month, with the sobering comment, 'A man may know himself—but it may be doubted if he can know any one else.'[76]

By early November Southey's mother had found a buyer for her Bristol house; he could then contemplate going up to London, to keep term, on 21 November, and looked forward to dining with Bedford and with the estate-agent William Thomas; London itself was less enticing: 'almost could I prefer a snow-proof hovel in Siberia.'[77] The artist Robert Hancock had made what Southey thought a 'fine drawing' of him, although failing to catch '*the Sedition of my countenance*'; the drawings of his mother were also welcome, if not true to life: having them in London would allow him to 'growl' at her.[78] Things became slightly more complicated than they need have been, in that Southey turned down Bedford's offer of hospitality, in favour of one from John May, to whom Southey apparently felt more obligation than to his old schoolfriend; he had known the wine merchant May since his Lisbon days, and when May moved to Richmond they developed a long and fruitful friendship, much of it conducted, as so often with Southey, by correspondence. It seems as though there was more to the disagreement with Bedford than just a matter of accommodation; Bedford had been challenging Southey's apparent lack of sympathy, his apparent—or actual—coldness, and this gave Southey the opportunity to get on his high horse: 'Why not trust the settled quietness to which my mind has arrived? it is wisdom to avoid all violent emotions. I would not annihilate my feelings—but I would have them under a most Spartan despotism.' It is as though Southey has remembered Coleridge's advice about the dangers of excessive emotion in poetry, and applied it to every aspect of life: he finds sanction in Boethius' urgings to banish all joy, hope, fear, and sorrow.[79] When Southey arrived in London in early December, he wrote to the wounded Bedford a brief note that is both touching and strangely chilling: 'As our intimacy seems to be in proportion to our distance from each other, I pray you think that I am a thousand miles off. R. S.'[80]

Southey was, in fact, more or less round the corner. Wordsworth, with Dorothy, was also in London, hoping to get a staging of *The Borderers*, a work that Southey had read and been deeply impressed by (more so than by *Osorio*, Coleridge's drama that was rejected around now by the London theatre, and which Coleridge had read to Southey earlier in the year at Bath). Southey's old friend Burnett, now a Unitarian minister at Yarmouth, was lined up to take on the education of Southey's younger brother Henry Herbert (known as Harry), then 14—less of a problem than Edward, but requiring some schooling in all senses before he was to come out quite as Southey wished.[81] Southey regarded Burnett, at this point in his life, as 'the only man whom I should wish to live with, & that constant gentleness & evenness of mind which make him ever desirable as an inmate give him great advantages as a tutor'.[82] Poor Burnett was not to live up to this encomium, and both Southey and Rickman were soon wringing their hands in despair at the waywardness of this former paragon (Rickman was inclined to blame it all on Southey's baleful influence at Oxford: all that Pantisocratic talk had quite turned the young man's head). In the mean time, advice had to be given to Southey's naval brother Tom, who was less than happy with life. The elder brother pronounced: 'It is almost as foolish for a man to quarrel with his profession as with his wife. A man is an ass if he is enraged with an ill which he cannot remedy, or if he endures one that he can.'[83] There is a *non sequitur* here; we can also hear the pot calling the kettle black. But, then, Southey was rather good at that.

Almost immediately, Southey started to write for the *Critical Review*: his first task was to review Amos Cottle's *Edda*, and the fact that he had contributed a lengthy prefatory poem did not ruffle any scruples; he was still working on Book IX of *Joan of Arc*, now to be called 'The Maid of Orleans'. His work was helped by gaining access to the famous Dr Williams's Library, in Redcross Street. Of the large 1,000 edition of his poems, 750 copies had been sold: he might still need the occasional £10 from Cottle to tide him over, but things were looking up. So much so that he allowed himself to be diverted into a practical scheme to help the sick. John May and Carlisle called round one night, and, spurred on by the sight of a dying woman they had come across, they talked about planning a convalescent asylum for about forty people, with a vegetable garden which, within three years, would enable it to be self-sufficient. Here was a chance to put at least the philanthropic aspect of the Pantisocratic scheme into action. Whatever his earlier bouts of pessimism, he had told May a month or so earlier that 'the full belief of universal regeneration is become a feeling in me'. But his brother Tom could well have laughed his head off when he received the literal-minded description of how things might work: 'a man with one leg may make holes for cabbages with his wooden leg, & a fellow with one arm follow & put in the plants...'[84] Southey seems to have derived a curious satisfaction from his contemplation of the halt and the maimed: several such examples feed into his weird ballads. But the surviving plans indicate that they all meant business: it was no mere madcap idea. The asylum would be within five miles of Covent Garden market, there would be two cows, two horses, and pigs; labour would be limited to six hours a day (four for those without one limb); the estimate for the building came to £1,685. 5s. 8d., a curiously precise figure which was raised to £3,000, to get the scheme up and running. Even Wynn, serious at all times, approved.[85]

In January 1798 Southey explained to May that there was still some delay: Wynn had been out of town, and was now in Wales; they were still awaiting Carlisle's papers. But Saxon, the architect, had come to town with plans, drawings, and estimates. Southey heard that Coleridge, too, was beginning to get to grips with the demands of the world, on the verge of taking up the post of Unitarian minister at Shrewsbury, for £140 a year plus a house. But writing and publishing remained Southey's main preoccupations. The new edition of his poems had been stalled at the printers, and for the second volume another firm was to be brought in; Book IX of *Joan* still proved a problem, and Southey was beginning to feel the pressure of time, in that he wanted to get on with other things, including a second edition of his *Letters Written During a Short Residence in Spain and Portugal*. Part of the impetus came from his dissatisfaction with the lodgings in Lamb's Conduit Street: if he could earn about £100 from his writings, he thought he would be able to furnish a house— always his ambition. He could not settle for Charles Lloyd's life in a boarding-house, 'a vast number of new acquaintances, a false tail, a barber to powder him every morning... & as happy as he wishes to be'. He wanted to correct and reprint his favourite poem 'The Retrospect', and planned some metrical letters, reminding himself that his early verse epistles 'taught me to rhyme'.[86] One of the best of these was to be his verse letter to his beloved cousin Margaret Hill at Bath, written in January. It is a poignant and revealing poem, liked, significantly, by Charles Lamb, and not to be lost in Lamb's general comment about the 1799 volume that Southey was 'too apt to conclude *faintly*, with some cold moral'.[87]

> MARGARET! my Cousin, ... nay, you must not smile,
> I love the homely and familiar phrase:
> And I will call thee Cousin Margaret,
> However quaint amid the measured line
> The good old term appears...
>
> .   .   .   .
>
> Loth indeed were I
> That for a moment you should lay to me
> Unkind neglect; mine, Margaret, is a heart
> That smokes not, yet methinks there should be some
> Who know its genuine warmth...
>
> .   .   .   .
>
> In a narrow sphere,
> The little circle of domestic life,
> I would be known and loved; the world beyond
> Is not for me...
>
> .   .   .   .
>
> And often, Margaret,
> I gaze at night into the boundless sky,
> And think that I shall there be born again,
> The exalted native of some better star;
> And, like the untaught American, I look
> To find in Heaven the things I loved on earth.[88]

When Charles Lloyd produced his novel *Edmund Oliver*, the frictions between the two of them were exposed. This had been the title of a work Southey had listed as one of his plans in 1796; there was no doubt that Lloyd incorporated into his book things that Southey, in moments of indiscretion (there were several of them), had said about Coleridge. Southey can be seen behind the figure of Maurice, a 'co-operator with infinite benevolence', someone who believes, or seems to believe, in something more like a Wordsworthian 'wise passiveness' than active revolt. This in itself is important, as it is further evidence of Southey's being suspended between two positions; he is still a radical, sending poems to the *Morning Post*, but not wedded to the violence of the Revolution: as he had said, what mattered was 'revolution in mind'. Although many of his newspaper poems followed the democratic line, several celebrated that very retirement he and Coleridge and Thelwall had so often lauded. But the immediate response to the novel was on a personal level: once again, and perhaps with good reason, Coleridge felt let down by his erstwhile fellow Pantisocrat, and brother-in-law. But Southey, too, felt betrayed. The time Lloyd had spent as Southey's lodger had not been a great success, and he had in fact moved out after a while. Southey told Tom that the problem was Lloyd's lack of 'a steady & consistent character'; he was prone to 'little contemptible frivolities... those ficklenesses that I despise... I do not respect him, & I cannot love where I cannot respect'. Lloyd's brother in Birmingham was unwell, and at the end of January he went up to see him. Southey could not resist a jibe at Lloyd's father: 'too civil—too fawning—too oily'. Not charges often levelled against Southey.[89]

After a week or two of socializing—even going to Drury Lane, to see George Colman's *Bluebeard*, and to Covent Garden, where there was, appropriately enough, a ballet of 'Joan of Arc, or the Maid of Orleans'— Southey decided that they had to leave London for a while. Edith was again unwell, and by 18 February they were in the Westgate buildings in Bath on their way to Bristol for the spring and summer. Whether or not Edith's newly acquired wig did anything for her spirits we cannot know; certainly by 7 March Southey was reporting to his brother Harry that she was better.[90] He could therefore start to contemplate a visit to Yarmouth in May, to see Harry and George Burnett, and perhaps take in Cambridge on the way, to see Amos Cottle. Of Burnett he said, less than tactfully, to the still miffed Bedford, 'there are few persons whom I love so entirely' (this was the very same man of whom he and Rickman were so frequently to despair, as his life lurched from one disaster to another).[91] For the moment, however, Kingsdown suited them—'the Buenos Ayres of Bristol exactly'—largely because Southey felt so much happier in the countryside; he was happy, too, to be with Charles Danvers and his mother. As he explained to Bedford:

my intercourse with men teaches me nothing worth learning.—An evening walk gives me some new image for poetry. In the country I have no feeling but what delights me—fills me—makes me better. I should be very religious Grosvenor had I a home in the country, where I could always see the sun set, where I could lie down & watch the running water, or sun myself on a prime-rose bank . . . [In town, by contrast] I am another being, my soul seems annihilated.[92]

Southey was rather anxious about Tom, who was wounded in a fight between his ship *Mars* and the French *Hercules*, but who was made a Lieutenant for his bravery. Southey was relieved to hear that he would be going to Lisbon with Wynn's cousin, Lord Proby (otherwise known as Lord Carysfort): Uncle Herbert Hill, whatever his failings, would be there to offer some kind of help, in that he had money and connections. Tom's own uncertain future seemed to mirror his own. 'I feel life is like a journey—we are never satisfied until we arrive at the end of it. We must always be looking on, & surely this proves a hereafter, or we might sleep away existence like a beast.' Whatever the logic of this (and Southey was later to admit, revealingly, that logic was not one of his strong points), we can see why, as he moved back and forth, from London to Bath and Bristol, the image of the journey should be such a potent one.[93]

Edith's health faltered again, and she seemed to be approaching what Southey said of himself, 'the true skeleton proportion'.[94] They were back in Bath at the start of April, and the combination of Edith's extreme sickness and his mother's ill health made Southey 'apprehensive about the future'. He was still not certain about the chances of getting a house; perhaps the best thing would be to get his mother to Lisbon. He wrote to his uncle accordingly. As he told Wynn, 'A few months will determine all these uncertainties,—& perhaps change my views in life—or rather destroy them. This is the first time that I have expressed the feelings that often will rise.'[95] Rather remarkably, amidst all this confusion, Southey managed to continue with the convalescent scheme, encouraged by the news from Wynn that an appropriate house might be found. Southey was conscious of the iniquities in the distribution of charitable funds, and hoped that Wynn might get something through the House of Commons; but the way the slave-trade issue was going did little to raise his hopes. In fact Southey, whilst curiously glad that Wynn had not spoken in Parliament about the slave trade, was anxious lest he ended up swimming with the stream. Southey felt much more could be done; on the practical level, he urged Bedford to buy sugar beet, rather than cane:

this was a fairly common radical solution to the moral dilemma of sweet-toothed opponents of slavery, but it was more than moral self-indulgence; there was a genuine belief that the economic effects on the West Indies plantations would be enough to bring down the whole system. Similarly on the question of the poor, it was simply a matter of 'only restoring to them what is pilfered'. Southey still had a lot to learn about the complexities of the social issues he wanted to tackle.[96]

Southey began to send unsigned poems to the *Morning Chronicle*, for a guinea a week. Many of these were ballads, whose importance he was anxious to downplay, but which did, in fact, represent a major aspect of his writing character. When Charles Lamb read part of the *Jew of Malta*, he was reminded of Southey's lines about Hell in *Joan*, 'in the true Hogarthian style'. 'There is', he said of Marlowe, 'a mixture of the ludicrous and the terrible in these lines, brimful of genius and antique invention.' He could have said the same of many of Southey's ballads; when he read Southey's 'Spider' he likened it to a 'compound of Burns and Old Quarles . . . a terseness, a jocular pathos, which makes one feel in laughter'.[97] When 'Monk' Lewis decided to print a collection of Gothic poems in May 1798, Southey was only slightly anxious about the possible unveiling of his anonymity: what concerned him more was accuracy: 'alter a word he must not'. However slight some of these poems might have seemed, they mattered greatly to Southey.[98]

On 1 May Southey wrote to John May, saying that he had reluctantly moved back from Bristol to Bath, for the sake of his mother. He had been attending the lectures of Thomas Beddoes, the radical writer and physician ('I had a ticket from him', he announced proudly), but could not stay for the whole course. Southey would come up to London on 18 May, and leave four days later for Yarmouth; he started to pack up his books, ready for sending off. But it was hard to remain optimistic for long, as Edith's health continued to fluctuate: she 'makes me think that she is slowly—but certainly declining'. Southey presented his stoical face to May: 'My dear friend I am prepared for the future—& it is well therefore as much as possible to lose myself in the present.' He felt exhausted: 'the machine was not made to last too long—but it will last as long as I shall wish it.'[99] To make matters worse, Tom suffered rather more dramatically when he fell between two ships, and was only saved by catching hold of a convenient rope. He came to Bristol to convalesce: there were three large pike wounds to heal. It is hardly surprising that Southey should have felt irritated by Charles Lloyd's erratic behaviour towards his beloved Sophia Pemberton: a rather wayward courtship, with Lloyd, now at Caius College, Cambridge, at one point suggesting a runaway marriage at Gretna Green, eventually ended with a formal marriage ceremony in April 1799. Once again, Southey sees the simple, clear view—as applied to someone else—which had so often eluded his own introspective moments (of which there had been plenty): 'I believe we must never trust a fluctuating mind. Surely the right road is always very plain & very straight & a man need not be loitering backward & forward to find it out.'[100]

Southey's sense of what was right on this occasion took him to London, from where, on 21 May, he wrote to his ailing wife, telling her that he was taking 'abundant extracts' from Sir John Mandeville's Travels, for use in his next poem. After a good breakfast, he continued, he left with Grosvenor Bedford to see Charles Lamb, and Benjamin Flower of Cambridge; he had already seen Anthony Carlisle at Brixton, and Horace Bedford, Grosvenor's brother ('a wonderful lad'). This led him to one of his anti-London diatribes: 'I always as you know gape about me in London streets & read the Advertisements like a Loon just come from the country—among these I see a child advertised as lost, a boy as absconded from school—a gentleman as having left his family, & a young woman as stolen—& by her own account in a letter "confined & not permitted to say where or by whom." Now these things seem improbable in novels.' Whatever Edith might have felt about being left behind, she could console herself with the thought that her young husband still had a sense of social outrage. There is no record of her saying or thinking that charity begins at home.[101]

Even in Yarmouth Southey did not escape other people's ill health. Burnett, with whom he stayed, had had lumbago, and was now laid up with sciatica; but even in this state Burnett's affections were laid siege to by some young woman who 'bombards him during his confinement with blamonge'. News came of Uncle Herbert's not being well in Lisbon, which explained the delay in correspondence, and therefore in money being sent for Southey's mother. Southey wrote with some excitement about a new acquaintance, the writer and translator William Taylor—'a young man of fortune, much diffidence, much genius, & very uncommon acquirements'.[102] He later told John May that Taylor's 'attainments are infinitely beyond those of any young man whom I ever knew, & he has no parade, no ostentation of knowledge'.[103] Southey had already come across Taylor's translations of German ballads, but this was more than a merely literary friendship. He went to stay with him in Norwich, happy to confirm his view of him in his home surroundings: 'when you see a man at home, you see him most fairly'.[104] Southey liked the radical set at Norwich, including Dr Frank Sayers, whose poetical works on Northern mythologies had already made an impression on him at Oxford; he told Bedford that

'Sedition there is in plenty in the circle to which I have been introduced'.[105] He was also comforted that Harry was not only 'a great favourite' there, but was actually growing up to be an amiable, healthy young man.

Although Norfolk seemed like a foreign country, and the sea was so cold that even the inveterate swimmer could not take it more than once, Southey liked the countryside, and wrote home about it; ideally, he said, he would write about it in blank verse: 'You know I love descriptive poetry, tho a species that blends with the domestic feelings,—that I connect with all those associations that soften & amend & elevate the heart.'

By the end of the week, Southey was reluctant to be leaving this new world. Taylor, apart from being good company, had introduced him to the delights of Klopstock's Odes, which seem to have opened Southey's eyes to lyric poetry. 'All that I had previously seen were the efforts of imagination. These are the bursts of feeling from one who has fed upon the scriptures till he thinks & feels & writes with the holy enthusiasm of Isaiah.' This religious streak was encouraged by a picture he saw, by Carlo Dolce, of St Cecilia: 'the countenance is raised toward heaven & expresses everything that is resigned & holy, mingled with the anguish of human feelings.'[106] We can see here that move towards the sentimental and the religiose that was to mar so much of Southey's later writing.

When he was back in Bath (having passed through London and upset Bedford yet again by not calling on him), Southey sent off to his old schoolfriend Tom Lamb a large copy of the second edition of *Joan*. As he announced, with more honesty than some might have given him credit for, 'since last I saw you, all my views in life, and many of my opinions, have been changed more than once during that period'. Lloyd and Bedford would both have liked to hear this. Southey even told Lamb that his difficulties were over, and he was now, not a burgeoning lawyer, but a writer: 'necessity joined with inclination to make me an author, & now only the pleasant motive remains.'[107] But a letter to Wynn the next day contains a reminder of his legal obligations: he was going to go through Blackstone again, in an effort to 'methodize Coke' (both legal textbooks). Practical matters were moving fast: his mother was moving out of her house—the sale of her furniture cleared all the debts—and Southey was looking for somewhere with quiet country air. His rather accident-prone brother Tom was back from a visit to Taunton, where his uncle had, rather misleadingly as it turned out, talked of 'fixing the family name' in a large house and estate in Wales. This must momentarily have lifted Southey's heart, as he had always dreamt of some such familial boost to his fortunes. Tom was having to rest on the sofa, to recover from a fall whilst riding.[108]

The search for suitable accommodation ended triumphantly: Martin Hall, in Westbury on Trym, outside Bristol, proved ideal. The house had wonderful views, there was plenty of room, a large well-stocked garden: as he told Tom on 27 June, 'we cut our own cabbages, live upon currant puddings, & shall soon be comfortably settled'.[109] Both Edith and his mother were better, and he was for the first time in what seemed like at least semi-permanent accommodation in the country: things were looking up. Certainly he regarded Martin Hall as home: as he told John May in July, he knew it well enough to go around the house in the dark, and that was the real test. His cousin Margaret was also there, 'disabled ... by an intermitting eruption almost as dreadful as the leprosy'.[110] There is little doubt but that this is the psoriasis from which Southey and some of his own children were to suffer; Coleridge too had severe skin complaints that were most probably psoriatic in nature, judging by his descriptions of the symptoms. Southey was putting up shelves in the recesses where the windows had been blocked up; this was all the more urgent as his books—a considerable library already—had started to arrive. The large sitting-room was 'papered with cartridge paper, bordered with yellow vandykes edged with black'. But even as he was describing this apparent idyll to Harry a week later he was rather perversely looking forward to being settled in London, 'where I may collect all my chattels together, & move on contentedly for some dozen years in my profession'.[111] It is tempting to wonder just what kind of domestic discussions took place about whether they were, or were not, settled. Southey's restlessness eventually worked itself out of his system, but until it did, there was always the likelihood of another upheaval. He told Wynn that he had burnt a lot of his papers, 'all that did not accord with my present poetical creed like a good Catholic'. This is another strange thing for him to have said, given his view of Catholics. At least he did not say 'political'.[112]

There was still much to attend to. The 'Vision of the Maid of Orleans' (originally Book IX of *Joan of Arc*) was to go to press soon; the *Letters* would be printed as soon as a new stock of paper arrived. The second edition of *Joan* had been sold by Cottle to Longman. He was able, at last, to think again about *Madoc*, his long-cherished project. Wynn was advising him to read Milton, and he had himself read, whilst in Norwich, ten volumes of Trissino's *Italia Liberata*, which at least taught him the dangers of imitation. His pride, even in what he had done so far in *Madoc*, lay in its complete originality. So keen was he to keep to his schedule that he began getting up at 5.15 in the morning, just like the old Oxford days. By September the plan at least was complete, and he thought it 'very fine'.

Events in Ireland began to worry Southey, as well they might. The Irish rebellion of 1798 was, after all, nearer to home than the French Revolution had been, and made more complex by French involvement. Sure enough, within two years the Act of Union was passed, to Southey's evident approval; but it did not solve the problem. Southey was clearly reminded of the turmoil of the French Revolution, the confusions both international, national, and personal. He might hide behind the occasional (rather feeble) Irish joke, but he knew that was a defence mechanism. Wynn, for his part, was inclined to come down heavily on the Irish insurrectionists. Harvey, the leader of the Wexford rising, had been hanged on 26 June, and Southey observed tartly that it was wrong to infringe 'a general principle for a particular good . . . Bad as the Irish are—& God knows I have a most evil opinion of the half-christened herd—I cannot but think the ruling party in Ireland worse.' As he put it in a letter to Wynn of 27 June, the British soldiers were as brutal as the Irish rebels: 'one may certainly be easily reconciled to the slaughter of either or both.' Southey believed that Union would be the best solution, in spite of the inevitable opposition to it; but he confessed to Wynn that 'I do not understand the pro & con of the Union enough to have an opinion'.[113] The Irish question was an extension of the problems of England: 'Violent men there undoubtedly are among the Democrats as they are always called. But is there any one among them whom the Ministerialists will allow to be moderate?' This was a decent point. But the conundrum was not something he could dwell on for long; far safer to think about reforming the poor laws, something practical and possibly manageable. 'The old systems of government must fall; but in this country the immediate danger is on the other hand, from our unconstitutional & unlimited power.'[114] Southey had not lost his sense of what democracy should be; he was particularly annoyed by the attempts of the Anti-Jacobin, which he rightly saw as a spokespiece for the Government, to stir things up, 'inflaming the animosities of the country'. Wynn had suggested that Southey might produce a pamphlet about the political state of the nation; but Southey knew, first, that he would not produce quite what Wynn wanted (they differed 'at root'), and secondly, and perhaps more damningly, 'I do not feel myself at all calculated for anything that requires methodical reasoning'. This was a verdict many of his enemies in later life would have been happy to concur in.

As if to get away from all this political confusion, he continued his travels around Herefordshire, visiting the old Tyler family haunts, 'where the old mansion house is now untenanted & in ruins, & where I am visiting a stranger among strangers'.[115] His poem of 23 July, 'The Old Mansion House', gave him particular pleasure, as one of 'these poems which will be calculated to do as much good as poems can do, by exciting good feelings, that are the germs of good actions'. This poem was the first of a group of poems, published in his volume of 1799, as 'English Eclogues', with a prefatory comment claiming that they bore 'no resemblance to any poems in our language'. Those who had read the first edition of Lyrical Ballads might have raised an eyebrow, especially as Southey went on to say: 'How far poems requiring a colloquial plainness of language may accord with the public taste I am doubtful. They have been subjected to able criticism and revised with care. I have endeavoured to make them true to nature.' This raises many of the questions provoked by Wordsworth and Coleridge's anonymous volume of 1798, which Southey reviewed, anonymously, in the Critical Review. It has to be said that Southey is being more than a little disingenuous here. There is no doubt that some of his poems from this period are extremely effective dramatizations of scenes of rural poverty and hardship. But a few lines from 'The Old Mansion House' will soon show that Southey is treading in Wordsworth's footsteps:

> Why yes! for one with such a weight of years
> Upon his back. I've lived here, man and boy,
> In this same parish, near the age of man,
> For I am hard upon three score and ten.

Wordsworth's 'Simon Lee' had the lines:

> Of years he has upon his back
> No doubt, a burthen weighty;
> He says he is threescore and ten,
> But others say he's eighty.

Rather similarly, Southey's 'Sailor's Mother' has the lines:

> Sir I am going
> To see my son at Plymouth, sadly hurt
> In the late action, and in the hospital
> Dying, I fear me, now.

The reader of Lyrical Ballads would hear the echo of 'Old Man Travelling':

> 'Sir! I am going many miles to take
> A last leave of my son, a mariner,
> Who from a sea-fight has been brought to Falmouth,
> And there is dying in an hospital.'[116]

On the other hand, it can be said that sometimes, as with *Madoc*, Southey got there first, and was himself echoed. The problem with these earlier poems is that Southey later reviewed *Lyrical Ballads*, some of which he had 'copied', claiming originality for what he had done. He then went on and, in some instances, 'rewrote' Wordsworth's poems, to accord with his own view of how feeling should be portrayed in poetry. Eight such examples of 'borrowing' have been identified; but there is a 'puzzling lack of contemporary comment on Southey's borrowings'.[117] Even Wordsworth seems not to have said anything.

Southey, then, was writing a lot, and reading, but not much to do with law. The Hereford Cathedral library merely served to whet his appetite for the life of the gentleman scholar. 'I love to write at my own desk—to see my books by me, & to look every evening from the same window at the setting sun.' Within five years, he would be able to indulge in just such a dream. For the moment, he could take wry pleasure in being mistaken in Wales for a spy.[118] But then, we might ask, who was not?

He was writing several ballads, including one of his most famous, 'The Old Woman of Berkeley'; he had started the long poem which would appear in 1801 as *Thalaba*, and had written 1,400 lines of something planned as the 'Kalendar', modelled on Ovid's *Fasti*, and consisting of a selection of other people's writings, which would be 'popular & useful'.[119] Southey had to have an eye for the market, as he increasingly realized that he would have to live or die by the pen. When he found himself carica-tured in the *Anti-Jacobin*, he must have felt with some gratification that he was no longer an insignificant, struggling writer: there he was, mocked alongside Coleridge, Lloyd, Lamb, Fox, the Duke of Bedford, company he was proud, and amused, to be in.[120] Perhaps it was this sense of impor-tance, among other things, that allowed him to confide to John May, on 26 September, that the *Lyrical Ballads*, which had just appeared, were 'of very unequal merit'.[121] That was one thing. But it was something else for Southey to review the volume, without telling the authors, in the *Critical Review*. Southey was not persuaded by this 'experiment': he was as little inclined to applaud 'The Idiot Boy' ('no tale less deserved the labour that appears to have been bestowed upon this') as 'The Ancient Mariner' ('Genius has here been employed in producing a poem of little merit'). On the other hand, 'Tintern Abbey' received high praise, and, 'ill as the author has frequently employed his talents, they certainly rank him with the best of living poets'. Later in his life, Southey declared that the 1800 Preface to *Lyrical Ballads* contained his own poetic creed. But in 1798 neither Coleridge nor Wordsworth (who had not even been pilloried in the *Anti-Jacobin*) was amused. Wordsworth had commented earlier in the

year on Southey's 'most rigidly virtuous habits... [he] is, I believe,
exemplary in the discharge of all Domestic Duties'. After Southey's review,
Wordsworth's testimonial to Southey's virtues would have been even less
enthusiastic. As he spluttered to Cottle in the summer of 1799, perhaps
conscious that he ought to have offered a better defence, 'He knew that I
published these poems for money and money alone.'[122]

Southey set off with Danvers to walk to Wales, hoping to sort out his
miscreant brother Edward. He sent the plan of 'Dom Daniel' to Taylor:
this was to become *Thalaba*. He boasted that 'it will have all the pomp of
Mohammedan fable, relieved by scenes of Arabian life, & then contrasted
again by the voluptuousness of Persian scenery & manners'.[123] Southey
was clearly seduced by the very material that half of him found repellent: this emerges in the finished poem, as we shall see. He wrote back
affectionately to Edith, giving her a marvellously detailed account of his
travels.

By 22 October Southey was back in Westbury, reporting rather sourly
to John May on his mother's readiness to lend her sister money, and
therefore remain in debt herself; his aunt was becoming increasingly
violent and irrational in her behaviour. He planned to return to London
by mid-November, even though Edith was again unwell. She had enjoyed
the country air, and had learnt to ride; but her exuberance, such as it was,
had not lasted long. Nor was his own health all that good: Beddoes had
told him that his sedentary existence was bad for his heart, and he must
walk eight miles each day.[124] Generally, the outlook was not auspicious: he
had his mother with him, his cousin too, 'poor girl'; Harry needed more
financial help, and the obvious source, Uncle Herbert, was so far unforth-
coming. When May offered financial help, Southey's pride would not
allow him to accept. He began to wonder just how Harry's education in
Yarmouth could continue, especially since Burnett was on the move
again.[125]

In December he wrote to Nicholas Lightfoot, recalling the days
they spent together at Abberley (near Hereford), where Seward's
brother-in-law lived. He went through a roll-call of common friends:
Parsons had taken over from John Davy as Master of Balliol; Wynn 'is
still my most particular friend' out of the Christ Church set; Martin
Butt was a curate at Witley; Charles Collins was worse than ever,
and had 'forced me to dine with him'. Southey wondered—and this
was the real point of the letter—if there was any chance of Lightfoot, an
usher at Kingsbridge School, taking on Harry as a pupil. Despite such
anxieties, Southey was still able to declare, 'the world & I however agree
well together. I have as much enjoyment as a man ought to expect or

desire, & as for labouring for it, there is something pleasant in not being one of the drones of society.'[126]

The medicine for Southey's indisposition was a mixed blessing, as he told Wynn: 'You do not know the comfort of slipping eight miles thro the mire for the mere purpose of exercise, with no other end or object, and in all weathers.' He could see the funny side of it, fortunately, as he went about in his huge greatcoat against the bitterly cold weather, 'almost like a dancing bear in hirsute appearance'.[127] At least it seems to have worked, helped along, no doubt, by the ether he took every night. One of the advantages of having Beddoes as his physician was that he had access to the various gases Beddoes and Humphry Davy were experimenting with at the Bristol Pneumatic Institution; one of the disadvantages was that these gases, like Coleridge's opium, could be addictive. They could also induce indolence, which was the very charge levelled at Southey by Charles Lamb when he could not get Southey to take up the offer of a job at the East India House. 'For Gods sake, Southey, if it does not go against you to ask favors, do it now,—ask it as for me.'[128] But this fell on deaf ears. At least one of the pressing problems—Harry's education—had been solved. A Dissenting minister at Lowestoft, Mr Maurice, had taken Harry on as one of his ten pupils; he would only charge thirty—as opposed to sixty—guineas for the year. Since the same terms would have applied at Kingsbridge, Southey was content to keep his brother in the East Anglia he was familiar with.[129] As 1799 began, he felt considerably relieved.

'POETRY IS MY PROVINCE'

1799–1803

SOUTHEY, prompted by William Taylor, started to set his mind to another literary scheme, something along the lines of the French and German almanacs: this was to become, very quickly, the *Annual Anthology*, which he edited for a couple of years, and to which many of his contemporaries contributed. *Madoc* and 'Dom Daniel' also occupied him, and Amos Cottle's *Edda* had prompted the possibility that he too might produce 'a Runic song'. He was still prepared to try anything, and an interest in the plays of Joanna Baillie led him to outline a few possible dramatic plots of his own, including (a particular favourite) one on Queen Mary: 'its main tendency will be to occasion charity towards each others opinions'.[1] (When he later met Joanna Baillie, he gave no indication of surprise that the presumed male author of the *Plays*, published anonymously in 1798, was in fact a woman.[2]) It is interesting to find him saying to John May that there was perhaps too much indifference on such matters, and that 'the feelings activating my leading characters will be coldly comprehended & thought unnatural or ridiculous'. This was certainly true of many of his other works: 'Queen Mary' was never finished. At the same time, he was conscious that he might have over-reached himself in some of his longer poems: 'my mind', he wrote, 'has been turned too much to the epic, which admits a larger action, & passes over the uninteresting parts.'[3] This was not advice he actually kept to; as so often, he was rather uncertain as to where his talents lay. He had doubts, now, about his eclogues ('monotonous'), thought perhaps drama would be a waste of time, could not give much thought to the correction of his ballads, and yet clearly wanted to carry on writing such things. He disclosed to Wynn one idea for such a ballad: 'a grotesque being—a little man who can extend his limbs to any length—put up his hands to count the eagles eggs—crane up his neck to the top-tower window—open his mouth & swallow anybody, which is to be the conclusion . . . I shall hardly be satisfied till I have got a ballad as good as Lenore.'[4] William Taylor had quite a lot to answer for. At least all this work, including regular contributions to the *Morning Post*, provided a distraction from the cold weather: the bread froze, and Southey resorted to a Welsh wig to keep him warm in the evenings.[5]

The ballads Southey wrote at Westbury are among his most remarkable poems, and it is tempting to quote from much of his work of this period, because it shows him in complete control of his material. Apart from the ballads, there are more meditative poems like 'To a Spider', 'The Holly Tree', and 'The Ebb Tide', and a cluster of fairly impressive sonnets. But two poems in particular call for special notice: 'The Battle of Blenheim' and 'God's Judgement on a Wicked Bishop'. The first combines Southey's love of the ballad form with his humanitarian concerns to produce one of the most powerful anti-war poems that we have:

> 'It was the English', Kaspar cried,
>   'Who put the French to rout;
> But what they fought each other for,
>   I could not well make out;
> But every body said', quoth he,
> 'That 't was a famous victory.
>
> 'My father lived at Blenheim then,
>   Yon little stream hard by;
> They burnt his dwelling to the ground,
>   And he was forced to fly;
> So with his wife and child he fled,
> Nor had he where to rest his head.
>
> 'With fire and sword the country round,
>   Was wasted far and wide,
> And many a childing mother then,
>   And new-born baby died;
> But things like that, you know, must be,
> At every famous victory.
>
> 'They say it was a shocking sight,
>   After the field was won;
> For many thousand bodies here
>   Lay rotting in the sun;
> But things like that, you know, must be
> After a famous victory.'

Such lines require no commentary. The other poem is more Gothically gruesome, based on Bishop Hatto's starving of the poor, whilst his granaries are full; he burns the villagers alive as they are locked in his barn:

> So then to the palace returned he,
> And he sat down to his supper merrily,

> And he slept that night like an innocent man;
> But Bishop Hatto never slept again.
>
> In the morning as he enter'd the hall
> Where his picture hung against the wall,
> A sweat like death all over him came,
> For the Rats had eaten it out of the frame . . .

The rats have their inevitable revenge:

> And in at the windows and in at the door,
> And through the walls helter-skelter they pour,
> And down from the ceiling and up through the floor,
> From the right and the left, from behind and before,
> From within and without, from above and below,
> And all at once to the Bishop they go.
>
> They have whetted their teeth against the stones,
> And now they pick the Bishop's bones;
> They gnaw'd the flesh from every limb,
> For they were sent to do judgement on him!

This might seem little more than conventional, blood-curdling ballad-verse, the very thing Wordsworth was setting his face against in *Lyrical Ballads*. But it is clearly more than that: the writing has a striking direct-ness and intensity, and once again there is a strong social and political element to the poem. Southey is addressing the abuse of power. Now, this was to become an increasingly important concern of his, both in poetry and in his prose writings. There are several occasions when the ghost of Bishop Hatto rises to the surface, to haunt him; similarly, the rats return in various guises throughout his writing life. His whole career could almost be seen in terms of how far his sympathies are with the Bishop or with the vermin.

In fact, apart from such wonderful poems, things were not looking so good after all. Both his own health and Edith's were cause for concern. Southey felt increasingly unwell, his 'nerves in a vile state', not quite the 'Scotch fir' he had blithely imagined himself to be; he could not sleep (rare for him). He thought perhaps he should, after all, be in an office job, although he would not be able to bear the confinement.[6] He decided to go up to London at the beginning of February, telling John May that 'with [his] habit' if he did not get better now, he had been told he never would: this is presumably a reference to the wonder-working ether.[7] But even by 10 February, a bad cough kept him cooped up at home. In his rather gloomy way, he told Bedford he would like him to have all his papers, should Bedford survive him. He thought more about the proposed almanac—perhaps it should be called 'Poetical Gleanings'?—hoped to finish *Madoc* by the summer, and then keep it, like a good wine, for ten years. He continued doggedly with his exercise: 'I am setting off thro a fine snow-soup for my walk.'[8] And then in that extraordinary way Southey had of getting things done once he got down to it, he was telling John May on 26 February that the almanac would be going off soon to press, in spite of the fact that he had been trying to sort out his mother's affairs with the estate agent, keeping an eye on Harry, who was doing well with Maurice in Lowestoft, and returning to his play, but without too many hopes for it.[9]

Far more serious than any of this, one of Coleridge's children had died suddenly in February, and Sara had been with the Southeys for a couple of weeks. This was yet another extraordinary episode in Coleridge's tangled life. He was in Germany at the time, and there was much debate between Sara and Thomas Poole as to how and when the news of Berkeley's death should be broken to his father. Poole wished to protect Coleridge, Coleridge wished to protect himself; he did not return from Germany until August. Sara in her anguish had been supported by Southey and Edith; but even they could not stop her hair falling out. She resorted, as Edith had and would, to a wig. Southey wanted to get away, to London if necessary, but preferably to the sea: 'I sadly want bracing.'[10]

The Southeys were still at Bristol at the end of March. If Aunt Tyler's affairs were a problem (she must 'resolutely determine to live within her income'), his brother Edward was proving more of a headache. Southey could not stand having him in the house for much longer: 'I never saw a lad with a better capacity or with habits more compleatly bad.'[11] Edward was to prove a problem for many years to come, yet another reminder of Southey's views on the difficulties of his own family life. However, he consoled himself with the fact that twelve books of *Madoc* were now finished, and Wynn's suggestion that Southey might visit Wales, where Wynn resided as MP for Merionethshire, was welcome, as he needed as much detailed local historical and antiquarian knowledge as possible. There was sad news from his friend Charles Biddlecombe, of Burton in Hampshire: he too had a sick child, and Southey's attempt at comfort, especially in view of the Coleridge tragedy, is revealing: 'These things make one tremble... Your little girl—I hope she will be spared—but the life of an infant is even more uncertain than our own, it is dangerous to fix our affections on earth & yet unless we do what is existence!'[12]

Southey's response to such tragedies, such reminders of life's frailties, was to forge ahead with 'Dom Daniel', exploring the possibilities of

irregular stanzas, eschewing simplicity ('I must build a Saracenic mos-
que—not a Quaker meeting house'). His brother Tom called in on his way
to London, where he was due to pass out as Lieutenant; Mary Barker was
painting a picture for 'Mary Maid of the Inn'; Southey was getting to
know more of Humphry Davy, Beddoes' brilliant young assistant: Davy
'possesses the most miraculous talents I ever met with or heard of, & will I
think do more for medicine than any person who has ever gone before
him'. Southey, of course, had his own reasons for saying that they 'were
doing wonders at the Pneumatic Institution'.[13]

By the beginning of May Southey was indeed in London, but finding it
dirty and exhausting; he felt lonely, and wrote back to Edith saying how
much he missed her, and pining 'for a draft of good Westbury air... I
cannot walk a street without wanting to wash my hands—the air is so
thick that my very lungs feel dirty. Nothing but noise & nastiness'. Apart
from eating his law dinners (the food not as good as at home), he was busy
socializing, in a rather reluctant way. He was glad to see Burnett and
Taylor again, and also Wynn, Charles Lamb, and George Dyer; he was also
happy to see Kotzebue's plays being performed, and rejoiced in their
'thoroughly Jacobinical' tendency. But he soon tired of the social round:
'one never enjoys the company of a friend till we have been long enough
together to be silent.' Friends were one thing; social calls were something
else. He visited 'monkey' Lewis, and was tickled that the great novelist had
his servant put his sugar in his coffee for him. Less comic was a dreadful
dinner party, where someone proposed a toast to the Russian General
Suwarrow ('Who loved blood as an alderman loves marrow', according to
Byron in *Don Juan*), and there was some rather heated and unpleasant
debate. At least Southey's books seemed to be selling well, and his epic
ambitions were encouraged by the fact that Dyer, Thelwall, and Samuel
Rogers were all engaged in writing epics; Taylor sent him Bodmer's *Noah*,
which provided further stimulus.[14]

Southey was, with due lack of modesty, tempted to vie with Milton and
Klopstock: he had 'the Deluge floating in my brain with the Dom Daniel
& the rest of my unborn family'. Interestingly, in view of later developments, he was already talking of a possible version of the Noah story in
hexameters. A new enterprise was the learning and reading of Dutch; but
against such seriousness, mercifully, was his tossing off a poem about a
pig, 'the best of all my quaint pieces':[15]

> Jacob! I do not like to see thy nose
> Turn'd up in scornful curve at yonder Pig,
> It would be well, my friend, if we, like him,
> Were perfect in our kind!...

It is scarcely surprising that another letter to Edith, on 13 May, emphasized the sheer hectic nature of life in London. He saw the Opies, Mrs
Inchbald, Mary Hays, Carlisle; there was also, of course, Bedford, and it
was not long before they were talking politics. Bedford apparently said
that 'we had the essence of liberty in England', to which Southey replied,
in his sternly witty way, 'Then it was the *volatile* essence, for it had all fled
away.' To visit the radical Gilbert Wakefield and Benjamin Flower in
prison (for libel against the Bishop of Llandaff) was to be reminded of
the troubled times they lived in: 'these are evil times & I believe I may write
the epitaph of English liberty! Well well Buonaparte is making a home for
us in Syria, & we may perhaps enjoy freedom under the suns of the East, &
a land flowing with milk & honey.' A more realistic prospect was a return
to Bristol and Edith, who seems to have made up an entirely self-
contained world for him. However, he did say that Wynn had suggested
that, if Southey was no better by the end of the year, it might be a good
idea to spend the winter in Portugal.[16]

Southey was troubled that he did not hear from Edith, whom he missed
painfully ('I count the days like a school-boy'), and his dependence upon
her showed in the tetchiness with which he upbraided her for her apparent neglect.[17] In such circumstances he found Charles Lamb's love for a
certain Ann Simmons rather irksome, in that Lamb was only too ready to
show his feelings, and laugh at everything in a way which Southey could
not grasp. 'My opinions are for the world but my feelings are to myself.'
He met some of Bedford's Quaker friends, and was tempted to like them;
but typically he said of Quakers that 'there is a profession of kindness, an
affected meekness & amiability... they are so plaguey civil that they must
be insincere.'[18] He was indeed a hard man to please. But he felt slightly
better (attributing this to the wine he had been drinking, and no doubt
making Seward turn in his grave), and suggested a summer trip to
Devonshire with Edith and his mother. In the mean time the social round
continued. His fastidiousness was offended by Joseph Towers the librar-
ian ('I wish he would wash his hands for they dirted my cotton gloves
which happened to be clean on'[19]); but his spirits were revived when he
met the famous radical Major Cartwright. Southey's paean to Cartwright
is an unambiguous reminder of his own still firmly held belief in freedom:
'when the Pantheon of British Liberty shall be erected [there is] no man
whose name will more deserve to be inscribed on the columns of glory.'[20]
Taylor had left London, which was a loss, and Bedford he felt less inclined
to see these days: 'He does not improve nor is he likely to. He has no
opinion of his own, no principles of his own, no knowledge on which to
erect any... As for mending him, it would not be worth while—twould be

like putting claret in a crackd bottle.'[21] Southey's own principles were challenged by Mary Hays, with reference to Coleridge's 'Ode' on France, published as 'Recantation': she asked if he, Southey, had changed his principles in the manner of Coleridge. 'Had she known more of me I should have been hurt at the question.'[22]

Coleridge's poem had appeared in the *Morning Post* at a time when even that newspaper was showing what were thought of as 'anti-Gallican' sentiments. In 'France' and in 'Fears in Solitude' (with the subtitle, 'Written in April 1798, during the Alarm of an Invasion'), Coleridge charted his move from 'exultation' at the start of the French Revolution, that hope that France would recover from its 'blasphemies and horrors' as from a 'transient storm', to the French conquest of Switzerland ('Helvetia'), and his realization that France mocked the liberty he worshipped, a liberty that had nothing to do with government, everything to do with the individual and with 'God in Nature'.[23] This is all very well, but sidesteps the crucial point that it is governments who are at the centre of the argument. Importantly, Southey held his ground, and certainly did not think that Switzerland should be seen as a turning-point, any more than should the possible French invasion of England: as he wrote to Humphry Davy in October 1799, using the appropriate metaphor: 'Massena, Buonaparte, Switzerland, Italy, Holland, Egypt, all at once! the very springtide of fortune! It was a dose of gaseous oxide to me, whose powerful delight still endures!'[24] In September, Coleridge had urged Wordsworth to write a long blank-verse poem to those who, 'in consequence of the complete failure of the French Revolution, have thrown up all hopes of the amelioration of mankind, and are sinking into an almost epicurean selfishness, disguising the same under the soft titles of domestic attachment and contempt for visionary *philosophes*'.[25] This is an important statement of Coleridge's complex response to events; although the Revolution had 'failed', it was necessary to avoid escapism; he had, of course, embraced the very domesticity he seems here to want to challenge.

What seemed like a long sojourn in London was soon to end, and Southey looked forward to being back home. As he wrote to Edith, 'it often occurs to me what widely different beings we are from what a single life would have rendered us.' In the same letter, he told her that 'the duty of marriage is for two persons to render each other happy'.[26] Once again, there is a strangely touching combination of the stern and the affectionate. When he heard of the death of Burnett's father, he suddenly panicked at the thought of losing Edith: 'I must not lose you thro eternity my Edith—at least if I thought it a thing probable it would deaden all earthly enjoyment.' This is both moving and alarming. Southey had a tendency to boast of his independence, of his ability to soldier on against all the odds; but underneath that rather cold stoic exterior was a striking insecurity.[27]

His delight at being back in Bristol by the end of May was tempered by his mother's ill health, unseasonably cold weather ('a March wind howling & a March fire burning'), the delays at the printers, and the prospect of having to move house yet again, 'after taking root here for 25 years'. As we have seen, this is not actually a true account of his first quarter-century, but Bristol was the place he regarded as home, and he found it hard to contemplate leaving the area for good. His new friend Davy had the very thing to cheer him up, the nitrous oxide which was designed for the relief of pain, but which, like opium, had its own pleasures: 'the wonder-working gas which excites all possible mental & muscular energy & induces almost a delirium of pleasurable sensation without any subsequent dejection'. He was going to try it on Edith. Southey can become almost Keatsian in his delight at this new gas: 'laughter, a delightful sensation in every limb—in every part of the body—to the very teeth; & increased strength with no after relaxation. It is a high pleasure for which language has no name, & which can be estimated by no known feeling.'[28] He later told Taylor that 'I can conceive this gas to be the atmosphere of Mohammed's Paradise'.[29] By the second week in June he was certainly feeling better, eating and sleeping as he had not done in the winter months. His friend Biddlecombe was trying to get them a house back in Burton, near Christchurch at £8 a year; this plan he confirmed to Wynn on Midsummer Day. The only snag was that they would not be able to take possession until Michaelmas, so they would travel for a bit. Off they went to Somerset.

Southey announced to his brother Tom that he finished *Madoc* on 11 July, and that he was going to start immediately on *Thalaba*. He fondly hoped that *Madoc*, when it was eventually published, would provide necessary income for his family in the event of his untimely death. It was to prove a very poor insurance policy. But the problem now was not his health but Edith's: 'extreme debility, pains in the back & bowels, & a wasting away, with sleeplessness, & total want of appetite, these are her complaints.' Southey found it impossible to keep to his usual routine, and began to sink into his own form of despair: 'restless & uneasy I turn from one thing to another & find myself unfitted for all...I fall into gloomy daydreams, & dread the future while I wish the present were past...the weather is cold & stormy, & I carry with me no chearful thoughts.' As if this were not enough, he went on to ponder his own death, preferably alone, 'to crawl like a dog into some corner & expire unseen. I would neither give nor receive unavailing pain.'³⁰ Amidst such terrible gloom and despondency, there was a serious attempt on Coleridge's part to mend the fences between them both. He wrote a couple of beseeching letters, and with Tom Poole's help managed to persuade Southey to come to Stowey to stay with his wife and sister-in-law. Southey was duly able to write from Stowey on 21 August, before they all set off to Ottery and then on to Sidmouth: 'The reconciliation between Coleridge & myself . . . has restored me one source of enjoyment.' Coleridge wrote to Poole from Exeter: 'We arrived safely, & were received with all love & attention— Southey & his wife sojourned at Ottery a few Days & went to Exeter from whence & from whose Room I now write—to morrow I set off for a little Tour of 3 or 4 days with Southey.'³¹

Southey enjoyed some of the walks they took, for example to Lynmouth. 'I never felt the sublimity of solitude before.'³² It was almost as though renewed friendship with Coleridge opened his eyes to the wonders of the landscape, taking him out of his introspective self. Devon, after Somerset, seemed 'flat & uninteresting', but he kept his spirits up by plotting, with Coleridge, a rather improbable hexameter poem about Muhammad. As he said to May, Muhammadanism 'has been miserably perverted & fatally successful.—it is now a system of degradation & depopulation, whose overthrow is to be desired as one great step to universal amelioration'.³³ As the Preface to *Thalaba* was soon to show, Southey's threshold of religious tolerance was low. (The poem 'Mohammed' survives in a fragment that was not published until 1845.³⁴) There were other grand schemes, almost as though Exeter's awfulness demanded some kind of creative counterweight. The presence of George Dyer, 'a thinking, extraordinary man', was soothing.³⁵ More electrifying was the effect of Landor's *Gebir*, just published, and reviewed by Southey in the *Critical Review*—'the miraculous work of a madman', he told John May, 'its intelligible passages are flashes of lightning at midnight'.³⁶ Landor's wildly extravagant verse appealed to Southey's own Oriental streak, and helped to shape the tone and texture of *Thalaba*. Southey told Cottle that *Gebir* contained 'some of the most exquisite poetry in the language'. The one exotic appealed to the other. Charles Lamb was less impressed: he wrote in October, 'I have seen Gebor! Gebor aptly so denominated for Geborish, *quasi* Gibberish. But Gebor hath some lucid intervals.'³⁷ Just to keep his feet on the ground, Southey announced that his next large project was to be a History of Portugal.

The move to Hampshire took place at the beginning of October: they had to stay in lodgings in Christchurch, whilst the Burton house was 'revolutionized'; furthermore, the tenant of the house Biddlecombe had found for them was reluctant to move out. Southey was unperturbed, and wrote to Coleridge:

This is a business that suits me, & I have not to pay for it. Nothing like a thorough reformation! radical improvements! the waters are abating & the country losing its dreariness and sublimity. The night of our arrival it was magnificent. I stood on the bridge—you have heard me describe it. The water washes the walls of a small but striking ruin. Above stands the keep with a huge rift in its side thro which the sky is seen. Behind, the church, one of the finest in the kingdom. To the right & left the flats were inundated. The night was wild, the moon rolling among driven clouds, & the rush of the flood, now mingled with the roar of the wind, & now was heard in its pauses. Every object was distinct & solemn—I cannot remember it without emotion.

A letter from John May with some domestic news led Southey, in his reply, to conclude teasingly, 'it is wonderful how we use words & understand them not—or not below the surface of their meaning'. Ironically, in the same letter, he showed just how powerfuly he could use words. Again, it is as if the spirit of Coleridge imbued his vision, enabling him not only to see the complexities of the landscape, but to capture them, in all their 'visionary dreariness', in a prose remarkably spare and precise, reworking what he had said to Coleridge:

Today the sun shines & I am in hopes that the flood gates are shut & the deluge abating. The country exhibits a sad appearance. Here the marshes are flooded of course. This does no harm & makes by moonlight a scheme of magnificent dreariness. It impressed me much on my arrival—the ruins & church by moon-light & the waterspout—& the sky stormy & wild, the moon rolling among scattered clouds, & the rush of the waters now mingling with the wind, now heard alone.[38]

His own poetry, especially *Thalaba*, was going well. Southey could not contain his confidence in a note to Cottle: 'from the success of its metre, its publication may probably make an era in the history of English poetry'.[39] The *Annual Anthology* was coming on apace, and Coleridge had promised 'Christabel' to open the volume. Southey's editorial labours on Chatterton would be finished as soon as he was settled. *Madoc* was still on the stocks, and Coleridge was heaping praise on Southey's head, urging him to publish this poem 'quam citissime—not hastily, but yet speedily.—I will instantly publish an Essay on Epic Poetry in reference to it...there are other faults in the construction of your poem, but nothing compared to those in the Aeneid.'[40] Southey told Coleridge that he was 'convinced that the best of way of writing is to write rapidly, & correct at leisure'.[41] A policy certainly better aimed at writing than at marriage; but some of his critics were to say he wrote too rapidly, and did not correct sufficiently.

His new neighbours made Hampshire especially attractive. Apart from Biddlecombe, and his old friends the Tonkins from Portugal, there was John Rickman, of course, 'rough, coarse, well informed on all subjects, believing nothing, jacobinical, & watching every little opportunity of showing attention & supplying your want'.[42] With Coleridge Southey had visited several others; he now called in to see Gilbert Wakefield, now imprisoned at Dorchester, 'in a comfortable room, peeping at green fields thro iron bars & over a prison wall'. Southey was luckier, and relished the prospect of his new abode and garden:

the garden is a large piece of ground, & quite empty, so that I may please myself in filling it, & have already in my head allotted out its various divisions of potatoes, peas, cabbages, artichokes, currant & gooseberry bushes, & the near turf plot where a few larger fruit trees may be ornamentally planted—planting is a trifling expense, & I shall at least have the pleasure of seeing the trees grow—tho perhaps the changes of life may prevent me from enjoying any other advantage. A spring rises close by the garden & fills a fishpond at the bottom. I mean to take much of my due exercise in the useful employment of gardening, which will be putting out time upon good interest.[43]

But his political opinions were still important enough to be spelt out to his friend May. Christianity was his bedrock, sustaining his view of society: 'hence the love of equality which is rooted in my heart & blended with all my associations. I see evil produced by existing establishments & know that it might be better & am with all the ardour & sincerity of my soul a Republican.' It is only fair to Southey to register this insistence, at a time when Coleridge was being much more pessimistic about the state of the nation, and the future of democracy, let alone republicanism.

Just as Southey was settling in, enjoying his new domesticity, replying to Bedford's (fairly justified) critical attacks on the *Annual Anthology* with a jaunty insouciance, looking forward to Harry's coming home for Christmas, rejoicing at the news that Tom, after a false alarm, was safe after all, his body began to let him down. In mid-November he wrote to Bedford: 'I am miserably unwell—in pain in every possible part—from my head to the very termination of the rectum, sore all the way. A bowel-complaint has in three days reduced me to almost a palsied debility...'[44] Southey was alarmed: if the immediate solution would be to return to Bristol, where he could get proper medical treatment, there was the possibility of going to Lisbon, which would be good for his health, and also enable him to get on with the History of Portugal. In fact, he was back in Bristol in the first week of December. Beddoes, in whom he had 'perfect faith', thought the problems were nervous, the 'effect of excessive irritability'.[45] Southey needed rest, and must not write. Southey, ever the amateur doctor, was convinced he suffered from what he called 'an organic affection'; the pain was at its worst after eating. The remedy, strangely and prophetically enough, was to lean to the right. How Hazlitt, who saw the significance of Coleridge's inability to walk in a straight line, would have liked to know this personal detail, especially when they faced up to each other in the sparring match of 1817.[46]

This bout persuaded Southey, whatever the financial consequences, to stop writing verses for Daniel Stuart's *Morning Post*, and to pour all his efforts into *Thalaba*. He thought that if he kept the copyright, and printed it like the small octavo edition of *Joan of Arc*, he could still sell the whole edition to a London bookseller, and make enough money to allow him to get abroad for a while. Coleridge did not want Southey to sell his rights in his works; Longman had paid £370 to Cottle for the copyright of *Joan of Arc* and the first volume of Southey's poems. Coleridge resorted to one of Southey's favourite images: 'You are a strong Swimmer & have borne up poor Joey with all his leaden weights about him, his own & other people's.' He was generously disturbed by what he heard of Southey's condition, and assured him that money would not be a problem. If Southey were to come to London ('your name is prodigiously high among the London Publishers'), he could stay with the Coleridges. He told Southey about the general admiration for their joint effort, 'The Devil's Thoughts' (a light-hearted enough squib, sufficiently dry to anticipate, ironically, some of Shelley's more savage political ballads), which had appeared, anonymously, in the *Morning Post* on 6 September, and oddly attributed to the classical scholar Dr Porson, of Trinity College, Cambridge. Southey wrote the first three stanzas, Coleridge the remaining fourteen; in 1830 a much lengthier version was published, as *The Devil's Walk*, with Coleridge's and Southey's names on the title-page:

> From his brimstone bed at break of day
>   A walking the Devil is gone,
> To look at his little snug farm of the World,
>   And see how his stock went on.
>
> Over the hill and over the dale,
>   And he went over the plain;
> And backward and forward he swish'd his tail,
>   As a gentleman swishes his cane.
>
> How then was the Devil drest?
> Oh, he was in his Sunday's best

His coat was red and his breeches were blue,
And there was a hole where his tail came through...

An Apothecary on a white horse
    Rode by on his vocation;
And the Devil thought of his old friend
    Death in the Revelation...

He saw a pig rapidly
    Down a river float;
The pig swam well, but every stroke
    Was cutting his own throat;

And Satan gave thereat his tail
    A twirl of admiration;
For he thought of his daughter War
    And her suckling babe Taxation...

Quite clearly, the two writers were able to egg each other on to flights of fancy that were more than mere whimsy.[47]

Importantly, Coleridge suggested that Southey should go abroad. It is almost as though he had a brief flickering of remembrance for the grand schemes of yesteryear: he wanted to be near Southey, to form a small community. 'I think it not impossible', he wrote, slightly disingenuously, 'that a number might be found to go with you & settle in a warmer Climate.' Certainly Southey was telling Bedford on 21 December that he planned to go abroad, preferably to Italy.[48] He was, in effect, taking his leave of the law, which would hardly have been a surprise to anyone, as he seemed to have taken his leave long ago. He hoped that Harry would come with them, and Coleridge too. With £150 from *Thalaba*, as he hoped, the finances would be taken care of. Coleridge encouraged the idea of 'a pleasant little Colony' in Italy or the South of France. 'Peace will soon come', he announced, with some confidence. If Southey wanted to write, he might think about a paper on 'Levellers and the Levelling Principle'.

Coleridge, as the year ended, was writing inflammatory pieces for the *Morning Post*, urging the hanging of Sieyès and Bonaparte: 'Guillotining is too *republican* a death for such Reptiles!'[49] Ironically the *Anti-Jacobin* was at the same time charging Coleridge with deserting his wife and children, and with being a 'citizen of the world'.[50] Southey's views fluctuated, as we might expect; he still clung on to the Jacobin ideal, even whilst having to acknowledge that republicanism was finished: on 10 November Napoleon had effected his own *coup d'état*, which left him in firmer control than ever of the reins of power. Southey speculated on what might have happened if, after Robespierre, there had been a law-giver, a Lycurgus, 'a man loved for his virtue, & bold & inflexible, & who should have levelled the property of France, & then would the Republic have been immortal, & the world must have been revolutionized by example'.[51] But he had to admit that he now had the 'cynic growl', and on New Year's Day 1800 wrote to Bedford: 'Damn the French!—that came heartily from the depths of a Jacobine heart.'[52] Coleridge felt like Southey, and reviewed the constitution of the Abbé Sieyès in the *Morning Post* at the end of December. Both men saw that, from now on, it would be difficult to lend support to the French republican cause. On the other hand, Southey could still hold Napoleon in some regard, as a comment a year or so later suggests: 'Why had not the man perished before the walls of Acre in his greatness and his glory? I *was* asked to write a poem upon that defeat, & half-tempted to do it because it went to my very heart.' He recollected in January that Mary Wollstonecraft had told him that the French revolutionary Babœuf had been 'the most extraordinary [man] she had ever seen, & in the orgasm of the Revolution the system of total equalisation would have been wise'. But Babœuf had come too late. Southey, like so many of his contemporaries, now wanted to make the crucial national distinction. Sieyès and Bonaparte 'have trod upon my Jacobine corns—& I am a thorough English republican'.[53] But even this was too radical for Coleridge, who was telling Taylor on 25 January that the 'Jacobins as men are heroes in virtue, compared with Mr. Fox and his party. I know enough of them to know, that more profligate and unprincipled men never disgraced an honest cause.'[54]

Whatever his encouragement of Southey as a poet, Coleridge seemed anxious to wash his hands of this difficult case.

Poor Southey, from over great Industry, as I suspect, the Industry too of solitary Composition, has reduced himself to a terrible state of weakness—& is determined to leave this Country as soon as he has finished the Poem on which he is now employed. 'Tis a melancholy thing—so young a man & one whose Life has ever been so simple and self-denying![55]

It was certainly true that Southey's industry seemed unabated. Apart from transcribing *Thalaba* to send up to Coleridge, he was ready to undertake the essay on the Levellers, provided it could be done anonymously: he was by now only too conscious of the dangers of being charged with republicanism, at a time when the principle of Jacobinism 'now lies with little hope of a joyful resurrection'.

His friend Rickman was also suggesting that Southey put pen to paper on social matters, this time on the place of women in society. There was again talk between them of the Belgian *béguinages*, a system of women's co-operatives that appealed to them both; Southey said there was a comparable establishment operating in Bristol when he was a child, and his father used to supply them with linen. But he felt that he did not have the right mental powers for the kind of work Rickman was suggesting: 'the compositions in which I have indulged have encouraged rapidity of feeling, a sudden combination of ideas,—but they have been unfavorable to regular deduction & methodical arrangement... poetry is my province... a good mental manure'. Consequently he was glad to use the excuse of going abroad, and made the point that Rickman would no doubt write a much better book on the subject himself. He was also increasingly depressed by Napoleon's antics, and found himself turning inwards as his 'anti-Gallican' feelings grew. The whole French enterprise had been a disaster, and not merely for the French:

They have retarded our progress for a century to come. Literature is suspected & discouraged; Methodism, & the Catholic system of persecution & slavery, gaining ground... Our only hope is from more expeditions, & the duke commander; new disgrace & new taxes may bring the nation to their senses, as bleeding will tame a madman.[56]

There is something of that combination of despair and all-embracing apocalyptic fury which is to surface increasingly in the years ahead.

Southey told Wynn on 24 January that after some time abroad he would live in London, and 'settle to my profession'. Wherever he went, he would take Edith with him; this seems a reasonable enough point, but an odd one to make at all. Out of the various sales of *Joan of Arc* he reckoned he had made £138. 12s. which encouraged him to think he could make a go of the literary life, even though idleness threatened to creep over him.[57] Coleridge 'yearned after' him, and there was more talk of the collaboration on 'Mohammed'.[58] Southey astutely realized that he could well end up doing most of the work; in any case he had his doubts about the project, and was already mulling over other topics, including something on Robin Hood. He was still heavily dependent on stimulants, whether they be porter or the laughing gas: he was 'indeed unable to do without them'.

Coleridge's articles in the *Morning Post* earned his admiration, since they showed a grasp of the political situation which he envied; it occurred to Southey that perhaps he could, after all, write about women and society, and at least produce some 'practical good', ever his chief aim. He felt strongly that too much of his youthful efforts had been no more than unfulfilled dreams, which might help to explain what would otherwise seem a confused and contradictory view of Napoleon: for all his anti-Gallicanism, the British Government's attempts to solve the crisis ('aggrandising' Austria, restoring the Bourbons) struck him as absurd.

I do not justify his assumption of power—let the use he makes of it do that, but in reviewing his past conduct—what I privately know of his youth—what all the world knows of his actions—the rank he holds as a general—the views he entertains as a philosopher—the feelings which made him in the career of victory, the advocate of peace—I do not hesitate in proclaiming him the greatest man that events have called into action since Alexander.[59]

What the thoughts were of his brother Tom—to whom he wrote these words—as he helped the English to wage the naval war, can only be guessed at.

Abroad now meant Lisbon, and he wrote accordingly to his uncle, Herbert Hill. Whilst he waited for a reply, a letter came from Coleridge, saying that Longman was very eager to take on *Thalaba*. Coleridge encouraged him to think he might write a novel: after all, Godwin had got £400 for *St Leon*, which had struck neither of them as particularly good. Other plans included a possible school history of poetry, which would bring in £40. Coleridge was hoping he could prevent Southey's foreign trip; ideally he would get him to come to Alfoxden, which could easily be divided 'for unimpinging Independence'. Coleridge had his virtues, after all. But there was a hidden agenda. As he had foreseen several times before his marriage to Sara Fricker, the union was not the happy one enjoyed by Southey and Edith, and in his marital misery, Coleridge envied his brother-in-law's domestic bliss, perhaps hoping that, if they shared the same house, some of that contentment might rub off on to him. This seems to have have been his first acknowledgement that the marriage to Sara was less than satisfactory—although several people might have noticed his restlessness, his eagerness to leave domesticity behind him. But he had only recently met Sara Hutchinson (Wordsworth's future sister-in-law) at Sockburn in Yorkshire, and very quickly fallen madly in love with her. As things were, he could not hope for happiness himself; in his despair he could only express his envy of Southey in Latin and Greek.[60]

Southey was scarcely much happier himself. He was deeply troubled by the war, felt removed from his brothers because of their lack of moral fibre, was still unwell, and puzzled Coleridge by saying such ill health was 'induced by expectation'. He told Taylor of his seizures in the head, 'a rush thro all my limbs as if the stroke of annihilation were passing thro'.[61] He dreamt that Davy killed himself in an explosion, and awoke in terror. Rickman was coming to Bristol, to keep the idea of the *béguinages* on the

boil, but Coleridge seems not to have understood the underlying egali-
tarian principle; Southey was backtracking on the idea of a history of
poetry, protesting that he did not know enough foreign literature. In reply
to Wynn's question as to his health he replied, with that familiar schoolboy humour, 'How am I? my dear Wynn—sic sum, sum sic'.[62] Wynn
wiped away his tears of mirth, and resolved to come and see him. Whilst
Southey waited for word from Lisbon, he got involved in a slanging match
in the *Gentleman's Magazine* with Sir Herbert Croft, over the subscrip-
tions to the Chatterton volume: Croft had, in his rather bizarre novel,
Love and Madness, of 1778, included some of Chatterton's letters and
poems, without any acknowledgement to the Chatterton family. In 1796
he had been reminded that he had once promised help to the family,
eighteen years previously, but within a year he was in prison for debt.
Southey and Cottle had set to work in 1797 to produce an edition of
Chatterton's works; in the *Monthly Magazine* for November 1799 Southey
had reprimanded Croft for not sticking to his obligations; Croft replied at
length in the *Gentleman's Magazine* in 1800, not attempting to deny his
dirty dealings with the Chatterton papers, but taking the opportunity to
attack Southey, who 'writes prose somewhat like bad poetry, and poetry
somewhat like bad prose'; he got in jibes at Pantisocracy and *Joan of Arc*.
He soon learnt what it was to tangle with Southey in print; and Southey
learnt the pleasure of such entanglements: 'I have set my foot upon the
vipers neck, & tho he may writhe round me it is not in his power to bite.' It
was a small matter; but, once roused, Southey was never afraid to rise to
his own indignation.[63]

     Almost as a reward for such an engagement, he heard a week later that
his uncle would find a house for him in Lisbon near his own, and the plan
was for Southey to set sail from Falmouth in the first week of April. His
mother and aunt would go to Herefordshire, he would take Edith,
Thalaba, and a copying machine promised by the resourceful Wynn.
Southey had a renewed sense of purpose as he envisaged his History of
Portugal: 'no country in her rise ever displayed more splendid actions, or
exhibited a more important lesson in her fall.'[64] For Southey, history was
very much a matter of moral lessons. He was to open his *History of the
Peninsular War* (1823) with this ringing declaration:

The late war in the Peninsula will be memorable above all of modern times. It
stands alone for the perfidiousness with which the French commenced it, and the
atrocious system upon which they carried it on. The circumstances of the resis-
tance are not less extraordinary than those of the aggression, whether we consider
the total disorganization to which the kingdom of Spain was reduced; the inveterate abuses which had been entailed upon it by the imbecility, misrule, and

dotage, of its old despotism; the inexperience, the weakness, and the errors, of the successive governments which grew out of the necessities of the times; or the unexampled patriotism and endurance of the people, which bore them through these complicated disadvantages. There are few portions of history from which lessons of such political importance are to be deduced; none which can more powerfully and permanently excite the sympathy of mankind, because of the mighty interests at stake. For this was no common war, of which a breach of treaty, an extension of frontier, a distant colony, or a disputed succession, serves as the cause or pretext: it was as direct a contest between the principles of good and evil as the elder Persians, or the Manicheans, imagined in their fables: it was for the life or death of national independence, national spirit, and of all those holy feelings which are comprehended in the love of our native land. Nor was it for the Peninsula alone that the war was waged: it was for England and for Europe; for literature and liberty; for domestic morals and domestic happiness; for the vital welfare of the human race...

There was suddenly, because of the impending tour, a lot of domestic activity: books and goods to be packed; arrangements to be made about the subscription (Dyer was being his usual helpful self); the odd small debt to be paid. Peter Elmsley was to give him £100, and May would take the annual £160 from Wynn in quarterly instalments, along with the money due from the *Critical Review*, and the £100 he hoped *Thalaba* would bring in. He left a copy of *Madoc* with Danvers, who, together with Davy, would look after the next *Annual Anthology*; he asked Coleridge, whom he did not, for some reason, want to see before his departure, to be his executor, just in case. He would take *Gebir* and *Lyrical Ballads* with him, as representative of the best of recent literature. This is in itself an important index of his awareness of the two possible ways in which English poetry might move; whether the knowledge would have comforted Wordsworth for the rotten review is another matter.[65]

Southey's eagerness to be in Lisbon was palpable: 'I do not look forward to any circumstance with so much emotion as to hearing again the brook which runs by my uncle's door.' But such expectation was partly in response to his own present world-weariness. 'We are all changing', he told Coleridge; 'one wishes sometimes that God had bestowed upon us something of his immutability. Age, infirmities, blunted feelings, blunted intellect, these are but comfortless expectancies: but we shall be boys again in the next world.'[66] Coleridge replied that, if Southey stayed in Portugal for longer than a year, then he would join him; he reminded him that, whatever his hopes for his History, Southey must 'be ever a Poet in your higher moments'. Coleridge could not, at this apparently crucial juncture, when he perhaps felt he was losing Southey, stop himself from dwelling on the past, on those months when the world had indeed seemed to lie before them:

The time returns upon me, Southey! when we dreamt one Dream, & that a glorious one—when we eat together, & thought each other greater & better than all the World beside, and when we were bed fellows. Those days can never be forgotten, and till they are forgotten, we cannot, if we would, cease to love each other.[67]

After a five-day journey, they were at Falmouth, staying in the room where he had met Lovell on his previous journey. On the way he had met Tom briefly and sadly at Portsmouth, and the combination of these two events made him more conscious than ever of life's uncertainties. He was 'heartily tired, impatient to be gone—half-sick with expectation—& restless enough to require a page of Epictetus'.[68]

On 1 May, after a dreadful voyage that took five and a half days, they arrived in Lisbon.[69]

Southey's immediate aim was to finish *Thalaba*: he had even written half a book at Falmouth, and mapped out the rest during the voyage. He then wanted to pour all his creative energies 'into the great Madoc Mississippi river'; his uncle's library had all the books he needed, 'folio after folio to be gutted, for the immense mass of collateral knowledge which is indispensible—but I have leisure & inclination'.[70] Typically, Southey saw the task as one very largely of amassing material: in other words, *Madoc* was on a par with his own historical researches, and this was how he was eventually to view poetry, and make the logical shift from poetry to history. Lisbon itself he was seeing as if with new eyes: 'So long a time had blunted memory, & every thing seems new to me—new enough to interest—not to depress by a total strangeness. I see much which would else have escaped me, thro Edith's eyes.' Edith was to Southey as Dorothy Wordsworth was to her brother. He was struck by the lack of unpleasant smells in Portugal, and the lack of middle-aged women: Portuguese women were like primrose-tree flowers, blooming and then withering away; married people slept in separate beds. Quite what Southey was implying in these random observations is not clear.[71]

By mid-June he had not only finished Book X of *Thalaba*—leaving only two to be written—but had also gathered a lot of historical material. When he was not writing lovingly detailed letters back home, he took part in the busy social life of the expatriate community. Mary Barker was still there, 'a very clever girl, all good humour, & a head brimful of brains';[72] he met the Koster family, but commented with some disapproval on the son Henry's unbuttoned ways: his opinions 'call forth somewhat more free-

Robert Southey, portrait by Peter Vandyke, 1795

Samuel Taylor Coleridge, portrait by Robert Hancock, 1796.

William Wordsworth, portrait by Robert Hancock, 1798

Greta Hall and Derwentwater, watercolour by William Westall, n.d.

Silhouettes of Robert, Cuthbert, and Bertha Southey.

Edith Southey, portrait by John Downman, n.d.

dom of conversation than I allow myself elsewhere'. In this rather cush-
ioned environment, with money supplied by Herbert Hill, Southey's
spirits settled, and he slept better than he had for some time. At the end
of the month he was rather reluctant to move on to Cintra; but the
demands of the legal part of his history beckoned.

On 23 July he told Wynn that he had finished *Thalaba*, and was already
correcting it. He hoped Wynn would share his enthusiasm for it: 'You will,
I trust, find the Paradise a rich poetical picture, a proof that I can employ
magnificence & luxury of language when I think them in place.' He was
already planning further works, including a 'Hindu Romance, wild as
Thalaba', which would become *The Curse of Kehama*. He hoped that he
would get £100 for a quarto edition of 500 copies, and £140 for a pocket
edition of 1,000. But he did not, at this stage, let such mercenary con-
siderations worry him unduly: there is an almost sybaritic languor about
his state of mind and body.

The spot I am in is the most beautiful I have ever seen or imagined ... I eat oranges,
figs, & delicious pears,—drink Colares wine, a sort of half-way excellence between
port & claret, read all I can lay my hands on,—dream of poem after poem, & play
after play,—take a siesta of two hours, & am as happy as if life were but one
everlasting to-day, & that tomorrow was not to be provided for.[73]

It was so hot that he spent the last ten days of July half-naked, dozing on
the bed in a wet swoon; they all yearned for fog at night.[74]

But sad news interrupted this languid idyll. Joseph Cottle's wife Patty
had died, also Mrs Morgan—another Bristol friend—and Southey's
cousin Margaret was dying of consumption. Politically, things were
potentially anarchic in Portugal, and French affairs were critical. Southey
never the less said he would quite happily settle in Portugal, and 'live like a
bear by sucking my own paws'.[75] He told Wynn in October that 'I like this
country so well that I should be content to exchange the society & the fire
& the fogs & the bread & butter of England for the filth & the fruit & the
sun of Portugal, with no better equipage thro life than a jack-ass.'[76] As it
was, this was unlikely to happen. More probable was a move back to
London; he told his brother Harry that he would be more than welcome
to stay with them there were he to study anatomy at Westminster Hospital
under his old friend Carlisle.[77] Southey had a sense that his family was
rising in the world, and it would be their own fault if they did not 'attain
that station ... to which our intellectual rank entitles us'. Such certainties
were threatened by the pestilence that began to sweep Portugal in late
September; it seemed more important than ever to get *Thalaba* off to
Rickman, with instructions to get the best terms he could. What he did

not want was for the copyright to be sold—in itself a sign of his growing self-confidence: 'my name would carry it through an edition though it were worthless.'[78] He was also thinking of his own career, and asked John May what he thought of the suggestion that he might practise at the East India bar, where success was apparently more or less guaranteed. Writing by itself was still not enough to keep him financially buoyant. As for Harry, the new plan was for William Taylor to look for a place for him in Norwich, at 100 guineas for four to five years. And the more contact Southey had with England, and the longer he stayed in Portugal, the more the novelty wore off. For a man famously sure of his lack of sociability, it is ironic that he should say to Bedford, 'I feel the want of society here—of the free & unrestrained intercourse to which I have been accustomed'.[79]

He heard of the death of Amos Cottle and of Coleridge's friend, Joseph Hucks. As he said to John May at the end of October, 'My acquaintance have been dropping off—not like autumn leaves, but like the blasted spring fruit; & I shall again have the joy of meeting my friends in England poisoned by mourning & recollection.'[80] The news of May's recent parenthood reinforced his sense of growing old, and his enthusiasm for the East Indies waned the more he thought about it. Since his uncle had gone back to England to look at a small living that had fallen vacant, Southey was happy to move into the empty house in Lisbon, and enjoy the library, the fireplace, and the cellar. He continued with his historical work, helped by access to library manuscripts and materials in a nearby convent. Social life was improved by the presence of Barbara Seton, and some pleasant neighbours, the Hammets; Edward du Bois, a friend of the publisher Capel Lofft, was in the vicinity. But Southey was still worried about his finances, the state of which prevented him from dressing quite as he would have liked: detailed sartorial instructions were sent to the obliging Danvers.[81] Southey's cry, 'money, money is my only want', could almost serve as a motto for his whole life: not edifying, but sadly a reflection of his needs. He hoped that *The Curse of Kehama* might help on this front. It was certainly, he thought, going to be better than *Thalaba*, for which his claims were hardly modest: there was nothing between it and *Orlando Furioso*. As Coleridge commented sardonically to Josiah Wedgwood in November 1800, 'a happy age this for tossing off an *Epic* or two!'[82] As for his History, that too more than pleased him: 'You will find my style plain & short, & of condensed meaning,—plain as a Doric building, &, I trust, of eternal durability. The notes will drain off all quaintness. I have no doubt of making a work by which I shall be honorably remembered.'[83]

By the end of March 1801 Southey was talking, rather reluctantly and infuriatingly, of having to return to England. There was the like-

lihood of a French invasion of Portugal, and he could not afford
the risks, certainly so far as Edith was concerned; his own preference,
he claimed, would be to remain, '& witness the whole boderation'.
He would miss the Portuguese climate, and dreaded the general dank-
ness of England: 'I am afraid I shall pine away like a myrtle at a London
parlour window.'[84] Coleridge suggested that the Southeys might like to
join him and Sara up in Keswick, at Greta Hall, where they might still
revive their old ideals: 'I am willing to believe, that the blessed Dreams, we
dreamt some 6 years ago may be auguries of something really noble which
we may yet perform together.' Coleridge added a note about the 'noble
Garden'.[85]

Greta Hall itself was certainly an attractive prospect, and the Coleridges
had settled in there in the summer of 1800 for £42 a year. The house,
perched above Keswick and in the gigantic shadow of Skiddaw, had
wonderful views in all directions; William Jackson, the owner, had rebuilt
what had at one time been an observatory into a large, sprawling, country
house, with rather grandiose curving wings at each side of the imposing
front. He lived at the back of the house, with the housekeeper Mrs Wilson:
the rest, right up to the third storey, was let to the Coleridges. So the offer
to Southey and his family was not unrealistic; furthermore, Coleridge
wanted to share his pleasure:

I see the Sun setting—my God! what a scene—! Right before me is a great *Camp*
of single mountains—each in shape resembles a Giant's Tent! and to the left, but
closer to it far than the Bassenthwaite Water to my right, is the lake of Keswick,
with it's Islands & white sails, & glossy Lights of Evening—*crowned* with green
meadows, but the three remaining sides are encircled by the most fantastic
mountains, that ever Earthquakes made in sport; as fantastic, as if Nature had
laughed herself into the convulsion, in which they were made.—Close behind me
at the foot of Skiddaw flows the Greta, I hear it's murmuring distinctly—then it
curves round almost in a semicircle, & is now catching the purple Lights, of the
scattered Clouds above it directly before me—

As he said to Godwin, 'I question if there be a room in England which
commands a view of Mountains & Lakes & Woods & Vales superior to
that in which I am now sitting.'[86]

This was all very well, but Southey knew he had to make money, not
only for himself, but for the other members of his family. Harry was in
danger of going off the rails: Southey feared, ironically, that he would be
quite ready to sign up for the Church without a shred of belief. But there
was worse: 'to escape the soul & body pollution of Oxford debauchery
requires a stronger moral constitution than his appears to be.' The best
Southey could do, he felt, was to return to Bristol; perhaps in the autumn,

Wales and Cumberland might be able to claim him. His mother's needs were paramount.[87]

After fourteen days at sea, during which he suffered the usual 'tribulation of trullibubs & trouble of tripes', he was only too glad to get within sight of Falmouth, even if the fog prevented him from actually seeing much of it. 'England! England! Oh I do long to stand on firm ground, & eat fresh bread & drink fresh water!' By 6 July he was on dry land, rather surprised to bump into his old Oxford friend 'Horse' Campell in the Post Office, off to Antigua to a comfortable living of £1,000 a year.[88] Southey must have wondered if he had played his cards right.

On his return, Southey seems to have turned, first of all, to Coleridge; his letters of this period convey an intimacy that had been coming to the surface in the last year or so. Southey certainly acknowledges that there is an affinity between them: 'Is it quite clear that you & I were not meant for some better star, & dropped, by mistake, into this world of pounds, shillings, & pence?'[89] Wynn had mentioned the possibility of a secretarial job with the MP Drummond which might take him to Palermo and Constantinople, and Southey toyed with this idea with mock solemnity. What really mattered was his relationship with Coleridge: 'Time & absence make strange work with our affections; but mine are ever returning to rest upon you. I have other & dear friends, but none with whom the whole of my being is intimate—with whom every thought & feeling can amalgamate.' For his part, Coleridge was equally excited at the prospect of a reunion; it was as though those awful quarrels had never been. So much of a 'Fillip' had he received with the news of Southey's return that he would even try to meet him at Liverpool. 'Oh! how I have dreamt about you—Times, that *have been*, & never can return, have been with me on my bed of pain, and how I yearned toward you in those moments, I myself can know only by feeling it over again!'[90] In this intense moment of rapture, Coleridge was even ready to suggest that he, Wordsworth, and Southey should set off for the West Indies. But this seems to have been one of his flights of fancy. Southey, we should emphasize, reciprocated the feelings: if he were to set off abroad again, then Coleridge would be the ideal partner: 'I shall have with me the man, to whom, in all the ups & downs of six years, my heart has clung with most affection, despite even its own efforts.'[91] There is a fascinating combination here of reticence, understatement, and reluctance.

In spite of his sense of not having a home, a place of his own, Southey was proposing to Longman either *Madoc*, or his 'Hindoo romance'. He planned poems on the various mythologies of the world, and thought blithely that within four years he would have them all done. At the same time, he found himself having to admit to some of the failings of *Thalaba*, as pointed out to him by William Taylor—in particular 'a want of sufficient concatenation of events', or as Southey himself was to say to Bedford, 'the miracles like pantomime trials were so rapid as to weary & satiate'. Taylor had harked back to *Joan of Arc* as the real McCoy: 'there is the individual Robert Southey there—& only his imagination in the enchanted fabric'. Taylor was not necessarily right about this. But Southey could see that there were some parallels between *Thalaba* and Beckford's *Vathek* (which could count equally against *Thalaba* as in its favour); *Madoc*, he claimed, would rival Homer in its originality. *The Curse of Kehama* he was less sure about.[92]

By the beginning of August Coleridge was urging Southey to come to the Lakes ('O how you will love Grasmere!'), and to stay there 'till you find the climate injurious'.[93] Southey's climatic doubts seemed to be the main stumbling-block. But he was telling his friend Biddlecombe on 17 August that he and Edith were off to the Lakes, with his mother, in a week's time: quite a lot of furniture had to be sold, except for beds and bedding. He needed money as ever, and *Madoc* was not accepted by Longman on his terms.[94] Coleridge thought this a blessing in disguise, so confident was he of the work's eventual success. Southey still found time to read: *Lyrical Ballads* again, especially 'Michael' and 'The Brothers' ('I have never been so much affected & so *well* as by some passages there'), the Poet Laureate Pye's *Alfred* ('awful'), anything oriental for *The Curse of Kehama*, 'rummaging the dirty dunghill of Irish antiquities for *Madoc*', and Godwin's recent pamphlet on Samuel Parr's Spitalfields sermon. He told Bedford that 'the future wears a better face than it has ever done'.

Godwin and Parr require some comment. Parr had, much to Godwin's dismay and anger, since they had been friends for a long time, spoken out vehemently against what he saw as Godwin's wholly rationalistic philosophy.[95] He had quoted Rousseau, in a manner that might have cut more than just Godwin to the quick: 'Let us beware of those proud cosmopolites who deduce from books the far-fetched obligations of universal benevolence, while they neglect their actual duties to those around them!' Godwin answered with such verve that even Coleridge began to think more kindly of him. Godwin had already made his point in the Preface to his novel *St Leon*, where he acknowledged that there was, after all, a place for the domestic affections; in his *Thoughts* of 1801 (admired by Southey for their 'come kick me' language) he had to admit that 'the mere force of arguments' is seldom enough, and that 'our creed is, ninety nine times in a hundred, the pure growth of our temper and social feelings'. Coleridge had applauded this, even more so when Godwin went on to say that 'the opinion which has its principle in passion [and this was generally the case with the opinions of men on the topic of the French revolution], includes in its essence the cause of its own destruction'. This could be Southey writing thirty years later; but even now, there is something in the political climate that makes Southey more well-disposed towards the very government he has vilified. Henry Addington's administration, which took over after Pitt's resignation in February 1801, was far preferable, especially as it worked towards the Peace of Amiens of 1802.

By September Southey was at Keswick, finding it pleasanter than he had expected, but 'growling at clouds & Cumberland weather',[96] and typically missing Portugal, and dreaming of a consulship at Lisbon that would bring in £1,000 a year, which would at least keep him abreast of 'Horse' Campbell. The cost of wine was dreadfully high, a disadvantage when it was 'almost a sine qua non' of his life. He told Bedford that he 'had lived abroad too long to be contented in England'.[97] The next best thing to a foreign country was Wales, and Wynn obliged with an invitation. Southey set off in mid-September for Llangedwyn, leaving behind in Keswick what must have been a very confused Coleridge (who was to say more than a little ambiguously on 21 October, 'I feel your absence more than I enjoy your society'[98]), and an even more puzzled and exasperated Edith.

Wynn had connections, but so too did Rickman, and it was through him that an offer of a job came, just before Southey was due to return to Keswick after two weeks away. Rickman was in Dublin, as Charles Abbot's (later Lord Colchester) private secretary, and Isaac Corry, the Irish Chancellor, was suggesting there might be a job for Southey for a year, at £200, plus the same amount for travel. Southey was sufficiently keen to tell Bedford that his next letter would probably come from the 'Land of Pistols & Potatoes', but the same letter assured Bedford that Southey had 'no ambition, the paths of privacy are the paths of pleasantness'.[99] But Coleridge saw the chance as more than retreating into a backwater; it could be the first step on a diplomatic career. Things happened quickly. By 14 October Southey, 'the shuttlecock of fortune', was in Dublin, waiting to see Corry, and wondering quite what sort of job was on offer.[100] He was both intrigued and disturbed by Ireland, where the lack of trees suggested 'an instinctive dread of the gallows in the people', where there was so much poverty and 'an innate love of combination', as though everyone was plotting 'against you for more wages', and where the capital city was so beautiful, and set in a magical landscape.[101] But within a week he was telling Bedford that he and Corry were on their way back to London; work was not so strenuous that he had not been able to carry on with *Madoc*. In one of his cheerful moods, bolstered no doubt by the new sense of routine, he announced, 'I am in the road to fortune'.[102]

He travelled to London via Keswick, where he saw a review of *Thalaba* in the *British Critic*: he envisaged a good six months in London, '& God knows how long it is since I have been six months in a place!'[103] Coleridge, who planned to follow him in November, wrote a sad note about his son Hartley (who was fond of Southey): 'If my wife loved me, and I my wife, half as well as we both love our children, I should be the happiest man alive—but this is not—will not be!'[104] Southey's views of personal relationships were just as skewed, in their own way: 'I have a trick of thinking too well of those I love, better than they generally deserve, & better than my cold & containing manners ever let them know'.[105] It is not surprising that there were so many misunderstandings in his life. Southey's own concerns were more to do with the ramifications of his new job, which he saw simply as a means to an end, that end being a 'competence' of about £300 a year. But as usual, things were not that simple. As he told Taylor in November, after his first taste of the public excoriation that was to dog him for the rest of his life:

the civilities which already have been shown me discover how much I have been abhorred for all that is valuable in my nature. Such civilities excite more contempt than anger—but they make me think more despicably of the world than I would wish to do. As if this were a baptism that purified me of all Jacobinical sins—a regeneration—& the one congratulates me, & the other visits me, as if the author of Joan of Arc & of Thalaba were made a great man by scribing for the Irish Chancellor of the Exchequer![106]

The newspapers were already at him, but Southey could not care less: 'I am used to flea bites, & never scratch a pimple to a sore.' This was not entirely true, but at this stage he was more concerned by the reception of *Thalaba*. So far, Longman told him, by mid-November only 300 copies had sold.

The critical tendency has been to dismiss Southey's long poems as over-extended exercises in the exotic. 'Oh Southey! Southey! cease thy varied song!' cried Byron in *English Bards and Scotch Reviewers* (1809), 'A bard may chant too often and too long!' We can, from this distance, enjoy the irony that Byron's own Turkish tales owed some of their popularity to Southey's having helped to set the trend; they also carried their own echoes of Southey's verse: if *The Giaour* opens with a reminiscence of *Thalaba*, then *The Corsair* alludes to *Madoc*. Both echoes help to remind us that neither Southey nor Byron was simply indulging in the exotic or the fanciful: there were political undertones in these poems. On the one hand, the East and the Orient had its own fascination for many Romantic writers, both on the personal and historical levels; on the other hand, the Napoleonic wars and their aftermath led many writers to think of the consequences of a sense of nationhood that was inevitably being redefined. These concerns were sufficiently pressing for Southey to devote much of his energies to long poems that might at times seem remote, certainly when we set them alongside the autobiographical weight of something like Wordsworth's *Prelude*. And yet, as I have suggested, the Turkish tales and *Childe Harold* were amongst Byron's most popular works, not because they were 'escapist' but because they addressed central issues of the day; they were part of a tradition that had its roots in the past of scholarship and literary history, but also in the hurly-burly of the present. Southey might not have achieved Byron's success, but it is important to recognize that he made the attempt.

If Francis Jeffrey scoffed at what he saw as Southey's habit of turning everything in his notebooks into poetry, the question to ask is why Southey found such things so fascinating. One answer would no doubt be psychological: the exotic certainly held its own appeal for a Southey who perversely wanted to deny the very fact. The sheer violence of many of these poems reflects, it is not hard to think, that outburst of feeling against which he felt he had to arm himself. But a more oblique answer might be provided by Shelley's—and Keats's—evident absorption in these poems. *Queen Mab* (1813) and *Alastor* (1816) both owe more than a smidgeon of their power to Southey's influence, and there is no doubt that Keats finds himself building on Southey in his own major attempt at epic, *Endymion* (1818). The very idea of the quest, of the avenging demon, is central to much Romantic poetry, and, as with so much else, Southey is in there at the start. Jeffrey was to say, 'There is nothing so ridiculous (at least for a poet) as to fail in great attempts.'[107] Southey had the courage to take that risk; so, of course, did Keats, who got few thanks for it from Jeffrey.

The risk was the greater in that Southey's view of the East was itself so paradoxical. A large part of him found the whole Muslim tradition absurd, as set against the Judaeo-Christian. And yet, in spite of this apparent absurdity, he devoted three of his longest poems, by each of which he expected posterity to judge him, to stories based on that very tradition. He is simultaneously repelled and fascinated by these people and their beliefs. This accounts for the oddity of *Thalaba*'s opening, where mother and child are set in the solitary splendour of night, exiled and resigned, caught, as the verse and the explanatory notes make perhaps all too plain, between two worlds, hovering between two systems of belief, and perhaps owing allegiance to neither:

How beautiful is night!
A dewy freshness fills the silent air,
  No mist obscures, no little cloud
  Breaks the whole serene of heaven:
In full-orbed glory the majestic moon
    Rolls thro the dark blue depths.
    Beneath her steady ray
    The desert circle spreads,
Like the round ocean, girdled with the sky.
    How beautiful is night!

  Who at this untimely hour
  Wanders o'er the desert sands?
  No station is in view,
No palm-grove islanded amid the waste.
  The mother and her child,
The widow and her orphan at this hour
    Wander o'er the desert sands...

A footnote to the lines 'He gave, he takes away, | The Lord our God is good!' refers to Job, with the comment, 'I have placed a scripture phrase in the mouth of a Mohammedan; but it is a saying of Job, and there can be no impropriety in making a modern Arab speak like an ancient one... I thought it better to express a feeling of religion in that language with which our religious ideas are connected.'

By the same token, Southey launches into one of many lavish descriptions, which is then undercut by a note: 'A waste of ornament and labour characterises all the works of the Orientalists.' An alert reader will remember his preference for the chosen metre of the poem, 'the *Arabesque* ornament of an Arabian tale'. There is little doubt that he is fascinated by ornamentation, just as his own notes spread across far more than the foot of the page, adding their own sense of rich extravagance, curiously supporting the very fabric that he wants to challenge. But it is far more than a poem of mere ornament. Southey confronts, as Byron is to do in *The Prisoner of Chillon* (1816), the dreadful loss of time that goes with loss of freedom: 'Time is not here, nor days, nor months, nor years | An everlasting *now* of misery!' The poem is a study of solitude, solitude that is the consequence of wrongheadedness and, worse, cruelty; it is Thalaba's task to seek redress for the old man's suffering, and by extension for his race. The overweening pride of the King must be challenged: to this extent it is a reworking of the theme of autocratic government that Southey had explored in *Wat Tyler* and *Joan of Arc*.

The narrative can seem absurd, it is true: the same can be said of many Romantic narrative poems. But to some extent the narrative does not really matter; its absurdities, its sudden shifts, its unexplained miracles reflect a bewildering world, bewildering both for us and the poet. It is as though he does not quite know what it is that he has made, rather like Frankenstein; we should remember something of the puzzlement and bafflement that Beckford's *Vathek* evokes, and yet remember too its fascination for Southey and Byron and that whole generation. More important than the narrative is a section in Book II, where one of the evil demons of the drama, Abdaldar, enters the symbolic cavern of the 'eternal flame'. It is a strange experience to read these lines once we have read *Endymion* and 'Kubla Khan':

> A crystal ring Abdaldar bore,
>   The powerful gem condensed
> Primeval dews that upon Caucasus
>   Felt the first winter's frost.
>   Ripening there it lay beneath
> Rock above rock, and mountain ice up-piled
> On mountain, till the incumbent mass assumed,
> So huge its bulk, the Ocean's azure hue.

>   With this he sought the inner den
>   Where burnt the eternal flame.
> Like waters gushing from some channelled rock
> Full thro' a narrow opening, from a chasm
>   The eternal flame streamed up.
>   No eye beheld the fount
>   Of that up-flowing flame,
> That blazed self-nurturd, and for ever, there.
> It was no mortal element: the Abyss
> Supplied it, from the fountains at the first
> Prepared . . .

The strangeness derives from not knowing quite where our sympathies are supposed to lie; Southey cunningly holds the balance, and, in doing so, perhaps helps us to read into Coleridge's reworking of this, in 'Kubla Khan', another, perhaps more disturbing, kind of ambiguity.

There is a rather similar balancing act in Book III, this time centred on the kind of domestic idyll Southey had extolled in *Joan of Arc*, with the storms that threaten from without.

>   Or when the winter torrent rolls
> Down the deep-channelled rain-course, foamingly,
>   Dark with its mountain spoils,
>   With bare feet pressing the wet sand
>   There wanders Thalaba,
>   The rushing flow, the flowing roar,

> Filling his yielded faculties;
> A vague, a dizzy, a tumultuous joy.
> . . Or lingers it a vernal brook
>   Gleaming o'er yellow sands?
>   Beneath the lofty bank reclined,
> With idle eye he views its little waves,
> Quietly listening to the quiet flow;
> While in the breathings of the stirring gale
>   The tall canes bend above,
>   Floating like streamers on the wind
>   Their lank uplifted leaves.

As he gets into his stride, Southey actually quotes, in his lengthy notes, Niebuhr's account of the Arabs with approval: 'The airs of the Orientals are all grave and simple . . . If this music is not greatly to our taste, ours is as little to the taste of the Orientals.'

Significantly, at this point in the poem, there is often only one line of poetry to the page: the rest is given over to the detailed notes which are of no immediate relevance to the narrative but which it is impossible to ignore. The poem almost becomes something of an antiquarian's paradise; when he talks of the 'pearls of poetry' he quotes various authorities in testimony to this 'favourite Oriental figure'. He is struck by the strange coincidence of a sentence 'among the quaintnesses of Fuller. "Benevolence is the silken thread, that should run thro' the pearl chain of our virtues" '. What might have started off as a small note has become a reminder of his philosophical bearings. Once again, the reader could well be confused by such apparent dissimilarities of systems of belief.

Southey spent much of his life contemplating the passage of time; in *Thalaba* he finds a place for this in a poem that is, for much of its length, about change and mortality:

>   but all things feel
> The power of Time and Change! thistles and grass
> Usurp the desolate palace, and the weeds
> Of Falshood root in the aged pile of Truth . . .

It is in this context that Faith becomes so important, and at the end of Book V Thalaba becomes an Adamic figure, whose saving talisman is Faith.

The second part of the poem sees the working-out of this spirit of faith, against all the apparent odds. Laila, the loved one, in her role as bird, guides Thalaba towards the culminating resolution:

> Obedient to the call,
> By the pale moonlight Thalaba pursued
> O'er trackless snows his way;
> Unknowing he what blessed messenger
> Had come to guide his steps,
> That Laila's Spirit went before his path.
> Brought up in darkness and the child of sin,
> Yet as the meed of spotless innocence,
> Just Heaven permitted her by one good deed
> To work her own redemption, after death;
> So till the judgement day
> She might abide in bliss,
> Green warbler of the Bowers of Paradise...

Few of the critics could agree with Southey's own declaration that he knew 'of no other poem which can claim a place between it & the *Orlando*'. The *British Critic* scarcely contained its mirth: 'The process of *writing himself down* is here fully performed by Mr Southey, if it be allowed that he had ever written himself up. A more complete monument of vile and depraved taste no man ever raised.' The *Monthly Mirror* was anxious to be fair, but, acknowledging that 'it is a work of ornament', felt the need to 'preserve a real poet from affectation, puerility, and false English'. More generously, the *Monthly Magazine* saw the connection between Southey's attempts and the elaborate tradition stemming from Pindar; but there was something reluctant about its praise for the poem's variety, which 'shifts, with the camelion capriciousness of lyric inspiration, and with the versatile instantaneity of pantomime scenery, from the blasted wilderness, to caverns of flame'. There was another way of putting this, however: 'Whatever loss of interest the poem may sustain, as a whole, by an apparent driftlessness of the events and characters, is compensated by the busy variety, the picturesque imagery, and striking originality of the parts.'[108]

It was Jeffrey's 'Thalabicide', in the *Edinburgh Review*, which struck home the most, largely because he lumped Southey in with what he called a dissenting '*sect* of poets' (sc. Wordsworth and Coleridge), who aimed at an unholy alliance of originality, 'antisocial principles, and the distempered sensibility of Rousseau', simplicity, and a mixture of homeliness and harshness. All this constituted, for Jeffrey, 'the most formidable conspiracy against sound judgment'. What he could not tolerate was the breaking of all the bounds of decorum: the style was 'feeble, low and disjointed; without elegance, and without dignity; the offspring, we should imagine, of mere indolence and neglect'. Jeffrey displayed his own frustration, in that Southey seemed to be throwing away whatever talents he had; the domestic scenes were truly affecting, there was even some 'very fine poetry' in the last two books, but Southey's 'perverted taste' could not be gainsaid.

Southey felt able to brush Jeffrey's criticisms aside, partly because he was being tarred with the wrong brush: such a 'sect' did not exist, and if it did, he was not part of it. To that extent he was being used as the fall guy for the 'Lake school' of poets. He was content to rest with William Taylor's views in the *Critical Review*, whereby the argument was turned around to Southey's advantage. 'Perhaps no work of art so imperfect ever announced such power in the artist—perhaps no artist so powerful ever rested his fame on such imperfect a production—as *Thalaba*.' In spite of the 'confused and confusing impression' left by the poem (and who could argue with that?), the style has a 'plasticity and variety of which epic poetry offers no other example'. Jeffrey's vices became Taylor's virtues. Southey was happy enough with that.[109]

Southey still hated London, but Coleridge and Dyer were there to make it tolerable. He dined with Lord Holland; he called on Burnett who, he observed to Rickman, 'begins to discover that hackneying authorship is not the way to be great';[110] Rickman, on the other hand, because he 'bends everything to practice' was already 'one of the greatest and most useful men whom our country has produced'. Mary Barker called in, as did Davy, but with the latter there was no longer the old rapport; both Davy and Coleridge insisted on engaging in metaphysics, 'a foul weed that poisons whatever it clings to'. His own mind was of a different cast.[111]

His mother joined them in London, 'far gone in consumption'; with only one sitting-room, and a constant stream of visitors, Southey found it hard to get on with very much. Not that Corry was making many demands; in fact Southey realized by December that the Irish post might just peter out.[112] He was having to go with Corry and his son to a series of lectures, and it gradually dawned on him that what Corry really wanted was for Southey to act as tutor. Just before Christmas he was starting the boy off on a course in Natural Philosophy, but Southey's heart was not in it. His cousin Margaret had died ('I hardly knew how like a sister she was to me before'[113]), and before the end of the year his mother was dead. Coleridge, in response to this, wrote on the last day of 1801, 'Life passes away from us in all modes & ways—in our friends, in ourselves. We all "die daily".' Forty years later Southey's wife was to use the same sad phrase.[114]

Southey's account of his mother's death, in a letter to Wynn, is a poignant document, less metaphysical than Coleridge's view of mortality, and, for that, the more touching:

You will not be surprised to learn that I have lost my Mother. Early on Tuesday morning there came on that difficulty of breathing which betokened death. Till then all had been easy—for the most part she had slept—& when waking underwent no pain but that wretched sense of utter weakness. But then—the struggle & sound in the throat & the deadly appearance of the eyes that had lost all their tranquillity—she asked for laudanum—I dropt some but with so unsteady a hand that I knew not how much—she saw the colour of the water & cried with a stronger voice than I had heard during her illness—thats nothing Robert! thirty drops—six & thirty—it relieved her... 'go down my dear—I shall sleep presently'—she knew & I knew what that sleep would be...

I have now lost all the friends of my infancy & childhood. The whole recollections of my first ten years are connected with the dead. There lives no one who can share them with me. It is losing so much of ones own existence...

When I saw her after death Wynn—the whole appearance was so much that of utter death—that the first feeling was as if there could have been no world for the dead...[115]

Southey and Edith were both made ill by these tragic events.He found some comfort in his historical labours: 'the easy idleness of research suits me well: silk-worm like I prefer eating to spinning.'[116] He hoped that they might go to Norwich soon, to stay with Taylor, but that would not be possible until Edith was a little better. So he made the best he could of London: Charlotte Smith, the writer ('a woman of genius, good sense, & pleasant manners'), Elizabeth Inchbald ('very odd, very clever, very beautiful'), Isaac d'Israeli ('like a Portuguese who being apprehended for an assassin is convicted of being circumcised'), Sharon Turner the historian ('I like the man & only wish there was one spark of genius in that dark warhorse of his'). He met Sir Thomas Lawrence, who was one day to paint his portrait. Although Coleridge talked of taking Southey and Wordsworth, with their families, off to the south of France, Southey was telling Danvers that he and Coleridge were 'not enough alike'.[117] Coleridge reported a dinner he had with Southey: too many greens and too much apple pie led to diarrhoea; he also said that Mary Lovell, Edith and Sara's sister, was going to stay with the Southeys, to help look after the 'exceedingly valetudinarian' Edith.[118]

Although cheered by Rickman's presence in London, and Taylor's too—not to mention the lawyer James Losh, one of Wordsworth's friends from more radical times whom Southey had first met in Bath—Southey really wanted to get away from town. The Chatterton volume had become something of a chore, especially when he found some previously unpublished lines in the British Museum; the History of Portugal still occupied him. But he hoped that by the end of April he could be near

Danvers in Bristol: 'we are the better as well as the happier for local attachments.' He wanted to relive his childhood years, when he walked back from school along the Bristol road ('Eheu fugaces Posthume Posthume—'), whilst at the same time admitting to Mary Barker that 'there are recollections that poison every path which I used to take, with very different feelings'.[119] He was soon renting a house, at a guinea and a half a week, in the same terrace as Danvers on Kingsdown, where he gaily thought he would be able to 'gallop thro a Canto of *Kehama* before breakfast'.

The nomadic life was not yet over. On the one hand, 'I dream of a thousand things which I could do if settled in a house in the country, with a garden'; on the other hand, if he was to pursue a career as a writer—and nothing else had come up—then he would have to be in London.[120] He had still not had a final rejection from Corry, but that could only be a matter of time. As if to prepare himself for the role of 'scribbler', he started on a translation of Vasco de Lobeira's *Amadis the Gaul*, spending two hours a day on it; there was *Madoc* to correct, more work on *Kehama*, and his History of Portugal.[121] 'Necessity', he told Mary Barker in July, 'sends some men to the gallows, some to prison,—me it always sends to the press.' When he finally heard in the same month that his services were no longer needed by Corry, he was not sorry; he did not want to be tutor to the youth who was 'too unmanageable to be kept even at Harrow'. Southey had had his fill, with his younger brothers, of recidivist teenagers. Besides, it was more important than ever to become 'fixed': Edith was expecting their first child.[122]

Coleridge repeated, in July, his invitation to Southey to come and share Greta Hall in Keswick. Southey was certainly tempted, and seems virtually to have asked Coleridge to persuade him. As before, the main objection was the climate, but there might well have been the added difficulty of what he had said about the proposed French plan: he and Coleridge were 'too unlike'. In the summer months he juggled with the two possibilities, Richmond (near John May) or the Lakes. In the mean time he hoped to get some money from his uncle at Taunton. It is curious how determinedly, how pig-headedly, Southey pursues this chimera over the years. He knew he was treading on thin ice, 'but I will see if it will bear'. It did not.[123]

By the end of August, Southey had settled for Keswick, and the offer of half the house for £20 a year. He wrote to Tom, 'Now Tom what say you— with a boat—the Lake—& a fowling piece for idle hours—books—bottle & backgammon for wet weather—& a mountain-pony for the sunny days—what say you to the mountains?"[124] But there was also the sense of an ending. He was going over all his old letters (and anticipating with some glee the sheer scale of the task for any future biographer), and preparing for 'The Whole Works &c, of the late Robert Southey'. As so often, he could use the other side of an image as it suited him: '10 years have materially altered me. The flavour of the liquor is the same—I believe it is still sound—but it has ceasd to froth or to sparkle.—What avails it to discover where & how you lost your way upon a road that is never more to be travelled?"[125] There was the added complication that in August Napoleon had declared himself First Consul for life. Increasingly, albeit with a few hiccups along the way, Southey got caught up in the national mood of anti-Gallicanism. We do well to remember that it was at this juncture that Beethoven, incensed by Napoleon's hubris, scrubbed out his Napoleonic dedication to his *Eroica* symphony; Southey was not alone in his despair.

Margaret Edith was born on 1 September, to universal rejoicing. Southey had begun to fear a childless middle age: 'cats & dogs are not quite enough for me', he told Rickman.[126] John May and Southey's uncle would be godparents. Southey was beside himself in his new role as father: 'what a feeling of awe & adoration is it to see ones own babe for the first time!"[127] But his delight did not prevent his going off with Tom, within a couple of weeks, for a tour of Wales, where they came across a house near Swansea, Maes Gwyn, which would actually be preferable to Greta Hall on several counts, not the least of which was that it would allow him to learn Welsh. They visited their uncle at Taunton, and although he could admit that his motives were entirely mercenary, Southey could also register the sadness of this 'shabby', 'boorish', 'comfortless' old man. 'I heard the click of the clock & the hum of the gnats at evening, & the crumbling of a wood fire, & a man never hears those sounds if he is enjoying himself.' Not that the old man did not put himself out for the visit: his wig was powdered, his Sunday coat proudly worn, a barrel of strong beer broached. Even so, Southey could still express the cynical hope that he remain childless.[128]

Fatherhood brought with it even more financial responsibility. In October Southey was starting to write longish articles for the new *Annual Review*: the first was about the Baptist Missions in Hindustan, a topic close to his heart, for, as he told Wynn, his 'hopes & wishes for the future fate of my fellow kind rests upon the base of Xtianity'.[129] But there was also, and not surprisingly, a sense that this was hack work. Southey was resigned to his fate: 'if I cannot be a great man in the way of the world this generation—why I will be a very great one after my own in the next, & all that are to come in secula seculorum.'[130] The immediate, and ominous price to be paid was severe eye trouble, with inflammation of the lower lids, which put paid to the reading he depended upon; his evenings were spent in darkness. But it was not just his eyes—his whole body seemed to erupt: 'a whole confederacy of evils attacked me immediately: swelled face—to that I applied leeches; toothache—this was cured radically; symptoms of fever—which were driven out at every sally-port...'[131] He took, rather improbably, a potion of cayenne pepper, for the general pain and swelling of his eyes, and claimed to be able to write poetry with his eyes closed.[132]

This was all the more frustrating in that he had been getting into his stride with *The Curse of Kehama*, and also beginning to realize that his gifts lay with history rather than with poetry: for a start, it 'never makes the face burn or the brain throb', he told Wynn. Prose writing also had the advantage that it was more likely to bring home the bacon: he would review whatever books came his way. 'Writing dull comments on dull books' was at least tempered by the pleasure of getting paid for it; and also by the pleasures of fatherhood. Young Margaret was a 'grey-eyed, flat-nosed girl, all life & spirits & good humour, strong as a young savage'; he happily wrote silly verses about her: 'No one can tell how it came about | That instead of a nose, you should have a snout'.[133] Coleridge visited in January 1803; when the topic of where the Southeys were going to live naturally recurred, Coleridge put the claims of Greta Hall, especially since Maes Gwyn had not worked out (because of an unobliging landlord). There were certain delicate problems to be resolved: Southey and Edith would be more than welcome, but Coleridge drew the line at Mary Lovell, and also Tom, who had made a disagreeable impression on Coleridge. The cost would be about £100 a year for them all. Southey was worried less about the cost than about the conditions; Coleridge's defence was that it was Sara who could not face having the others around—it might have been an evil day when he married her, but now he must be her 'Protector & Friend'. Coleridge then lapsed into morbid self-pity, concluding with the startling surmise that he himself might not return to Keswick anyway. Southey must have wondered quite what was going on, and William Taylor's offer of the editorship of a new journal in Norwich must have had some attraction. But Southey knew by now that he was a writer rather than an editor.[134]

Southey was thinking about society in general terms, as in an interesting exchange in April with John May, who had said that he would think as badly of mankind as did Southey. Southey was upset:

I am heartily grieved that the opinion should be purchased so heavily. I would rather you thought as well of man in their *posse* than as badly in their *esse*, in their actual state...everything that I have observed in the history of man & in the nature of the mind of man, has tended to confirm & establish the belief that the inequalities of property are *now* the cause of moral evil & human misery.[135]

Whilst Southey acknowledged that this was Christ's doctrine, he recognized that there was a conflict between religion and society, 'for selfishness & acquisition make the basis of the commercial system'; hence the unprecedented rate of poverty. Here we have Southey beginning to formulate the ideas about social ills in ways that he would develop in his political essays over the next two or three decades. He never shifted from his deep suspicion of the commercial, industrial society that was establishing itself across the country. Interestingly, when he felt that his whole poetic *œuvre*, and not just *Thalaba*, was under attack from Jeffrey the previous year, he had defended his poetry on social, as much as on aesthetic grounds; there was a 'design in the most part of my poems to force into notice the situation of the poor, & to represent them as the victims of the present state of society—the object is to make my readers think & feel—as for the old Antijacobin cry that it is to make the poor rebellious, that is too absurd to require answer'. His own less than satisfactory answer would be that the poor did not read poems, so there was no danger on that front. Never the less he wanted to claim the Jacobin's crown, and thought himself much more deserving of it than Wordsworth or Coleridge; he was certainly pleased when several of his poems ended up (as indeed did some of Wordsworth's ballads) as half-penny broadsheets, hawked around Cumberland ('the highest & most valuable mark of approbation that any of my poems have ever yet received').[136]

Paradoxically, it was partly this concern for the state of the nation that kept Southey's reviewer's nose to the grindstone, for there was an opportunity to pursue some of his favourite themes. John May asked him if he really thought this was the worst of times, and Southey replied in a frustratingly ambiguous fashion: 'on the contrary it appears to me very far the best, as being the most enlightened, it is the best for the best men'. At the same time, for the poor, things were worse than ever. Southey seemed both to be accepting the inevitable trade-off, and to be challenging it: 'The aggregate of human wisdom & human virtue is greater now, but the aggregate of human misery is increased also.'[137] It was left to Dickens to confront this dreadful contradiction with the panache of a novelist; in the mean time Southey did his best.

He was telling his friends that he would, some time in the summer, be going to London, to stay at Rickman's and work in the British Museum. But he was not well, with lime in his kidneys and what he called diabetes; he was prescribed soda and red sulphate of iron. He laughed about it in a letter to Bedford of 9 May: 'I am making history, making verses, making lime & making water, all in very great abundance. I should be worth a King's ransom to a besieged town where the cisterns had failed—or to supply a canal in a hot summer—or to furnish a Spring tide extraordinary for launching an East Indiaman in the middle of the Moon, or to try the effect of irrigation upon the great Zahara.'[138] For all his acknowledged reserve, Southey, like Coleridge, seemed to derive great amusement from his bodily functions. While he was suffering these indignities, he solemnly forged ahead with *The Curse of Kehama*, which he had realized would actually form the foundation stone of his fame; it also had its political significance, as he commented when he sent Book III to Bedford on 20 May: '[it] gives a good sketch of the general state of the Universe in consequence of this Eastern Bonaparte's proceedings.'[139]

By the end of May, war had again been declared on 'that damned Corsican rascal'; because of his History of Portugal, Southey began to think he should go to Portugal to consult the documents whilst he still could. At home, the new Government scarcely impressed him with their talents, but they had at least 'brought back the old temper of Englishness'. He could see no reason why Britain should not support Portugal against the French and Spanish. 'Huzza!' he cried on 27 May, 'God save the King! the Liberty of the Press for ever & no Popery nor Wooden Shoes.'[140] As this suggests, his political affiliations became confused in the summer of 1803, and he was puzzled to find he was closer to the anti-Jacobin William Windham than to William Taylor.[141] He wrote to Wynn in some desperation on 24 June: 'The new militia is indeed stark folly. There seems to be a fatality attending all oppositions in this country. They seem destined to be always in the right, & never to be attended to. God help us! bad weather— the ship heavily laden, & such a pilot!'[142] Three weeks later, contrary to his earlier belief, he fully expected that Britain would be invaded by a Napoleon 'drunk with success'; but he remained confident in the paradox of Britain's defences: 'we have Jacobines enough in England to destroy Bonaparte. The country was never so united & therefore never so strong.'[143] By mid-May, the peace attempt at Amiens had clearly proved a failure, and Southey joined the opposition in its support of the Government's prosecution of the war. With such confusions, no doubt encouraged by a general sense of national alarm, it is perhaps not surprising that by November 1803 Addington was *persona non grata*, just as was Pitt and

the new Government he formed in 1804. Rickman was equally unimpressed, and glad that Pitt and Fox had joined forces to oust 'such
disgracefull & dangerous fools & Court-favourites as we have now been
governed by a long three years'. For Rickman, Pitt's only merit was that he
kept out 'Bonaparte's friend & advocate, C. J. Fox'. Meanwhile, on the
literary front, Southey had settled, with Longman, during a two-week trip
to London, for a 'Bibliotheca Britannica', consisting of 800 pages per
quarto volume, for which he would get £150 per volume: the first part
would be out by Christmas of next year, and Sharon Turner, Carlisle,
Captain Burney, Rickman, and Richard Duppa were already signed up as
contributors.

Mary Lamb told Dorothy Wordsworth in July that Southey was in
town, and he 'seems as proud of his little girl as I suppose your brother is
of his boy, he says his home is now quite a different place to what it used to
be—I was glad to hear him say this—it used to look rather chearless.' The
Lambs took Southey and Rickman and his sister to Sadler's Wells, to see a
programme of Charles Dibdin favourites—Goody Twoshoes, Jack the
Giantkiller, Mary of Buttermere. Charles Lamb and Miss Rickman
laughed their heads off, whilst Rickman and Southey dozed.[144]

John May suggested he could look for a house for the Southeys in
Richmond, and Southey encouraged him to do so. The summer in Bristol
was hot and sultry; Edith grumbled, their daughter's sleep was interrupted by dreams. Even Southey would have been happy to sleep all
day.[145] Coleridge offered his services for the new venture, provided the
remuneration could be bettered: he too was suffering from poor health,
and planned a visit to Scotland with the Wordsworths. Coleridge had also
been the butt of some personal attacks in the press, and Southey readily
leapt to his defence: he was 'ten thousand thousand-fold the mightiest of
his generation!'[146]

A more calamitous form of ill health stole upon the Southeys in Bristol.
Margaret began teething, then to lose weight, then to develop hydro-
cephalus. Southey wrote to Bedford in late August: 'Grosvenor my poor
child is dying—I hope in God she will be dead before you receive this ... It
came on me like a thunderstorm ... Edith is almost heart broken. I am
struggling with my own heart—God only knows with what an effort. I
shall soon be tranquil & contented—but what a happiness have I lost—&
what hopes are all blasted!'[147] They decided to move to Keswick, so that
Edith could be with Sara, and her young child: 'I shall try & graft her into
the wound, while it is yet fresh.' Edith 'is in a deplorable state', Southey
wrote in August, 'of slow silent lasting melancholy. It is the character of
her feelings to be all more chronic than acute ... I think I shall never again

dare to love earthly object so dearly.' Margaret Edith was buried, next to
Mrs Danvers, on 23 August. 'I was fond of her', he told Taylor the next day,
'even to foolishness', and he confessed to Rickman that he had loved her
'better than man ought to love anything of such uncertain existence'.[148]
Whereas Edith was heart-broken, Southey resorted to the suppression
that had become a way of life for him: 'I work double tides, work bodily at
packing—talk—eat—as I should do. I am resigned & shall soon be
contented—chearful—& even joyous—but happy as I have been to that
full extent & with that full knowledge of my own happiness, that cannot
be till I have another child . . .'[149]

They travelled north, spending five days with Mary Barker, and were in
Keswick by the first week in September. Far from being able to graft young
Sara Coleridge into the wound, Southey found her too painful a reminder
of what he and Edith had lost. Much of his sleep passed in nightmares; his
waking hours were devoted, doggedly, to *Madoc* and the Portuguese
history. His desolation was intense. Coleridge wrote from Scotland,
stunned by the news, and promising that 'I will knit myself far closer to
you than I have hitherto done'. He sent his poem, 'Pains of Sleep', in which
he expressed his own anguished torments, 'the self-wreaked Hell within',
and cried out in his despair, 'Change! change! change!—O God of
Eternity! when shall we all be at rest in thee?' He told Sara that he had
spent the whole of that night awake, weeping and vomiting.[150] Coleridge
returned as soon as he could. At the end of the month, Southey told Wynn
that he was no longer the man he was; once *Madoc* and his History were
finished, that could well be that. There was little else to look forward to.

MAN OF LETTERS

1803–1809

SOUTHEY took long walks around Keswick; there was a memorable climb, with Coleridge, to the top of Skiddaw, certainly more rewarding than a production by strolling players of *She Stoops to Conquer*. Coleridge could scarcely say enough in Southey's favour, but Edith and her sister Mary were 'a large, a very large Bolus'.[1] To fight off the demons, Southey kept himself busy; he continued with *Madoc*, and responded to the hanging of the Irish rebel Robert Emmet with a poem that would appear in the *Iris*, and with a comment that got straight to the crux of the matter, even if, fifteen years later, he was to take a rather different view: 'If they mean to extirpate disaffection in Ireland by the gallows, they must sow the whole island with hemp.'[2] Southey took as the starting-point for his poem Emmet's own words, as reported in the press, at his trial for high treason in September 1803, 'Let no man write my epitaph'.

> Emmet, no!
> No withering curse hath dried my spirit up,
> That I should now be silent...
> .   .   .   .
> Here in free England shall an English hand
> Build thy imperishable monument...[3]

Southey enjoyed the paradox, for it was England's 'freedom' that had been responsible with Justice 'Bloody and blind' for Emmet's death. The drift of his poem is very different from Coleridge's comments, because he recognizes the basic rightness of Emmet's idealism, and the folly of such an execution:

> So young, so glowing for the general good,
> Oh what a lovely manhood had been thine,
> When all the violent workings of thy youth
> Had pass'd away, hadst thou been wisely spared,
> Left to the slow and certain influences
> Of silent feeling and maturing thought...

At the same time, as so often with Southey, there is a central contradiction in the poem, in that it ends with the suggestion that Emmet is better dead; to have survived in 'disastrous triumph' would have been to see 'wild Ignorance | Let loose, and frantic Vengeance, and dark Zeal, | And all bad passions tyrannous, and the fires | Of Persecution once again ablaze'. For Southey, Emmet represents something he values, because it was part of his own past; but Emmet had not learned to hold in the reins.

Coleridge was prompted by the same event to mull over his own apparently revolutionary youth, as though he had to exculpate himself. Commenting to Wordsworth's friend Sir George Beaumont, the artist and collector, that Emmet had been only 24, he wrote, 'at that age ... I was retiring from Politics, disgusted beyond measure by the manners & morals of the Democrats, & fully awake to the inconsistency of my practice with my speculative Principles. My speculative Principles were wild as Dreams—they were "Dreams linked to purposes of Reason"; but they were perfectly harmless—a compound of Philosophy & Christianity.' He protested that he and Southey had been but boys, and that the whole episode had been a passing phase, a form of political acne: 'our career of Sedition, our obedience to Sympathy & pride of Talent in opposition to our own—certainly—to *my own*—uniform principles, lasted but 10 months.'[4]

Southey would have found this apology rather distasteful. He was still embroiled in political debate, eager for Rickman to engage with Malthus on the population question (and we can see why it was such a deeply personal matter for him: six years later he was to write, 'very often, when I look at [children], I think what a fit thing it would be that Malthus should be hanged'):[5] 'you ought to set your foot upon such a mischievous reptile & crush him'.[6] Southey would have his own chance to do this ere long. Thomas Malthus's *Essay on the Principle of Population*, which had first appeared anonymously in 1798, under the imprint of the radical (at least in part) Joseph Johnson, had been a retort to Godwin's notions of human perfectibility; for all the apparent aridity of its title, it raised fundamental issues about the philosophy of society. Southey's piece on Malthus's second edition, although following much of what Coleridge had suggested to him, emphasized the point that poverty, vice, and misery were the result not of immutable Laws of Nature, but of a social system that was far from perfect. There is some irony in the fact that it is precisely the argument that Hazlitt was to use much later, and Shelley too; and it was Coleridge's objection to the final line of the final stanza in 'To the Genius of Africa' that led to the stanza's removal in the second edition of *Poems*:

> So perish still the robbers of mankind!
> What tho' from Justice bound and blind
> Inhuman Power has snatch'd the sword!
>   What tho' thro' many an ignominious age
>   That Fiend with desolating rage
> The tide of carnage pour'd!
> Justice shall yet unclose her eyes,
> Terrific yet in wrath arise,
>   And trample on the tyrant's breast,
>   And make Oppresion groan opprest.[7]

Malthus, in Southey's eyes, was destroying any possibility of hope: many have pointed out that Malthus can be seen as a precursor of Darwinian evolutionary theories, a 'struggle for existence' which involved the 'survival of the fittest'. This was not always easy for critics to attack, and there is certainly a tinge of discomfort about some of Southey's responses: Southey, after all, could take a very grim view of human nature. At the same time, he had not forgotten what lay behind his own revolutionary principles, the championing of the oppressed.

Southey had a new project on the stocks, what was to become *Letters from England*, that curiously informative and interesting volume, which at this point he described as 'an omnium-gatherum of the odd things I have seen in England'.[8] It was to be a book in which his eye for detail would be combined with his ability to see things in a generalized perspective, representing the best of his historical kind of political journalism, and preferable, certainly, to the 'Bibliotheca', which Longman was only too happy to set to one side for the time being. Whilst he thought about the new project, Southey revelled in the scenery of the Lakes: it seemed to provide the kind of constancy which life seemed determined to deny him. He thought sadly back to his schooldays, and to friends who had fallen by the wayside; he thanked God that he at least had the safety and seclusion of Keswick. 'Oh that you could at this moment see the moonlight upon Derwentwater—& the cloud in which the moon herself is hidden!' Coleridge, himself more tormented than ever, wrote on the eve of his birthday:

This is Oct. 19. 1803. Wed Morn. tomorrow my Birth Day, 31 years of age!—O me! my very heart dies!—This *year* has been one painful Dream—I have done nothing ... The Lake has been a mirror so very clear, that the water became almost invisible—& now it rolls in white Breakers, like a Sea; & the wind snatches up the water, & drifts it like Snow.—And now the Rain Storm pelts against my Study Window—O Asra Asra [Sara Hutchinson] why am I not happy! ... why for years have I not enjoyed one pure & sincere pleasure—one full Joy! one genuine Delight, that rings sharp to the Beat of the Finger!—all cracked, & dull with base Alloy![9]

For Southey, the demands of day-to-day life reasserted themselves. Harry, whom his recent tutor Dr Martineau of Norwich had thought too idle to bother with any further, was off to Edinburgh to study medicine; John Thelwall, on a lecturing tour of the Lakes, was to visit. Southey thought Thelwall not the man he used to be, more self-centred and rather ridiculous: 'I know not which be the more amusing his marvellous ignorance or his still more marvellous vanity...It would probably have been better for him in the next world had John been hanged in 1794—but not believing in another world John is exceedingly well satisfied to have been left in this'.[10] For his part, Thelwall was struck most of all, as an elocutionist, by what he perceived to be Southey's high-pitched, squeaky voice; but, then, so were others, including Hazlitt. Thelwall went on to lecture in Edinburgh, whilst for Southey writing continued: Myles's *Chronological History of the Methodists* would call forth a warning blast from Southey's trumpet, in the *Annual Review* for 1803, since he saw the Methodists as potentially more corrupting than the Roman Catholics. He started to use Sir Wilfred Lawson's famous library, but rather ungratefully told Wynn that 'our great private libraries put me in mind of a Eunuchs harem'.[11]

Southey saw Methodism as a threat for a variety of reasons: intolerance, superstition, censorship, the notion of eternal damnation. Added to this was the potentially democratic nature of Methodism, whereby people attained positions for which they were unsuited: for Southey the old hierarchical system had its value, even now, and he finds himself proclaiming the Methodists, 'literally and precisely speaking, an Ecclesiastical Corresponding Society—a set of United Methodists'—a jab in passing at the Irish.[12] On the other hand, even Leigh Hunt in the *Examiner* urged, in 1808, the strengthening of the Church establishment against the Methodists and Calvinists, just as Southey later sought in Bishop Richard Watson of Llandaff (to whom Wordsworth had written his unpublished 'Letter' of 1793, aligning himself, as a republican, with the 'Friends of Liberty') an epitome of right-thinking Anglicanism. It was also around this time, partly through meeting the abolitionist Thomas Clarkson in the Lakes, that Southey became interested in the Quakers: George Fox was preferable to John Wesley; the work of Quakers such as William Penn with the American Indians no doubt reminded Southey not only of Pantisocracy but also of his own *Madoc* (in his article in the *Annual Review* for 1806 he did, in fact, as was his wont, quote anonymously from his own poem).[13]

Southey heard that his young whelp of a brother Edward was living on the charity of a Mr Borham at Exeter; worse was to come on that front, but in the mean time some one else would have to pay the bills he was clocking up. Southey dug his heels in, especially when he divined that Edward was in league with his aunt. Nor was he too pleased that Burnett, restless as ever, and of whom Rickman had said in October 1802 that 'it is moral to wish him dead', had applied to John May for £30 to join the militia, and had used Southey's name. He predicted that his other brother Harry would become 'a spendthrift & a coxcomb'. It was a relief to see Hazlitt in December, a 'man of real genius' who had done a fine portrait of Coleridge, a less good one of Wordsworth; this prompted Southey to invite his artist friend Duppa to come up to Keswick. As the year ended, he asked Rickman for information about the slave trade, and seemed to welcome the prospect of invasion: 'it will be a fine thing for the bell-ringers & the tallow-chandlers.'[14]

Coleridge went down to Devon in the New Year, and Southey's neighbours also departed for warmer climes. He was left with Edith and her sisters, his books, Dapper the dog, and the beauty of Skiddaw. He continued his 'clock-work'-like existence, happy that Coleridge's premonitions had proved correct: Edith was indeed pregnant again. Southey wrote to Wynn, to observe that ten years had passed since they were at Oxford: 'I have lived fast, for the wear & tear of mind as well as body must be taken into account, & I am more than ten years older in constitution since you & I used to talk over our claret till midnight in Skeleton Corner.' In this elegiac mood he was happy with his almost total seclusion.[15]

Madoc had been taking up quite a lot of his attention. By November of 1803 he had been envisaging selling it at a guinea per quarto volume, by subscription; according to his calculations, 200 copies would be enough to see him satisfied. But, typically, he felt that in finishing the work he would be losing part of himself, 'as one of the purposes of my existence will then be accomplished'. He felt this the more strongly in that, with the loss of Margaret Edith, he had lost the real reason for living. He consoled himself with the thought that, whatever its immediate reception, it would be followed by a 'fame as lasting as the English language & the passions & affections of man'. But the practicalities of publication worried him, and he went off the idea of a subscription: by mid-January the plan was to get it printed in Edinburgh, and to share the profits with Longman. A month later he was even telling Mary Barker that he could afford 'to lose the sale ... [I] would far rather leave it for publication after my death than lose the pleasurable object of thoughts which it would always be to me so long as it remained my own, & only my own'.[16] If we can understand this possessive attitude, it is also not hard to see that, for an aspiring author, it could prove a handicap.

Malthus was also still bothering him. Coleridge made the interesting observation that Malthus had made the mistake of saying far too much, thereby laying himself open to attack. Southey had the virtues Coleridge admired: 'You possess a real excellence, that of saying what you have to say, *fully, strikingly,* & yet in a nut-shell.—Do take some pains, and exhibit this Talent.' He went on to warn Southey: 'be exceedingly temperate & courteous & guarded in your language.' Once Southey got the bit between his teeth, these were not things he cared much about; Malthus, a favourite of the loathed *British Critic,* was among the 'voiders of menstrual pollution'.[17] So much for restraint.

Another scheme was to be a volume of *Specimens of the Later English Poets,* picking up where Ellis, a previous, anthologizer, had left off in his volumes, but not including living authors. At one time Charles Lamb was going to be involved, as he seemed the man to do it, in Southey's eyes, but nothing came of this. Southey rather unwisely asked Bedford if he would be interested in helping out, since he had the advantage of the London libraries; he would have been much better to keep it to himself, especially as 'the old cerebrum was never in higher activity'.[18] It is significant that he should be looking back to the poets of yesteryear; this was partly a reflection of his increasingly historical bent, partly a reflection of his views of the modern age, and the writers who got the plaudits. He was, for example, unimpressed by Thomas Campbell—'a damnd coxcomb,—& vain of his pretty face'. As he said with some despair, 'The best poet *in season* at present is that lump of lasciviousness little Moore'. As for the wretched Peter Bayley, 'the most rascally of all plagiarists', who had misused both Southey and Wordsworth, scoffing in his *Poems* (1803) at Wordsworth's simplicity, Southey would 'break him upon the wheel'.[19]

He expected to be in London in May, to work on the *Specimens*: since he would leave the copying to a publisher's amanuensis, he thought it would be quite painless, and he would enjoy being in the libraries. He was not perturbed by a brief scare when guns were heard off the Isle of Man: if the French were indeed coming, they had eighteen volunteers in Keswick to take care of them (sure enough, the French backed off; Wordsworth thought they were 'sadly remiss at Keswick' in their 'defence of the Country...At Grasmere, we have turned out almost to a Man').[20] Of more excitement to him was the arrival of a parcel of books. As he wrote to Coleridge, who was about to set off rather mournfully for a government post in Malta, 'In plain truth I exist more among the dead than the living, & think more about them, & perhaps feel more about them'. This foreshadows one of his most famous and revealing lyrics, 'My days among the Dead are past'.

My days among the Dead are past;
  Around me I behold,
Where'er these casual eyes are cast,
  The mighty minds of old;
My never failing friends are they,
With whom I converse day by day...

My hopes are with the dead, anon
  My place with them will be,
And I with them shall travel on
  Through all Futurity:
Yet leaving here a name, I trust,
That will not perish in the dust.[21]

Coleridge told Southey that his 'presence at Keswick is beyond all compare my greatest *Comfort*'. It would be cynical to see this simply as a reference to the fact that Southey could take care of Coleridge's family; it was also an expression of affection. 'O dear dear Southey! old days crowd in upon me—I love & honour you from my soul. —You will go on as you have gone—.' Southey felt deeply for Coleridge's sense of desperation, his realization (and others') that he had not fulfilled his potential: 'his mind is in a perpetual St. Vitus' dance—eternal activity without action.'[22] Coleridge's addiction to opium was destroying his health; his marriage had become a loveless relationship, made the worse by his unrequited passion for Sara Hutchinson. But Southey knew, for all the differences between them, that he and Coleridge had still much in common; more particularly, he was aware that he was settling down, almost into Coleridge's shoes at Greta Hall, whereas Coleridge was as Southey had been when younger. Hence the combination of admiration, sympathy, and sorrow.[23]

Wordsworth was very different, but not necessarily preferable—he will 'leave behind him a name, unique in his way; he will rank among the very finest poets, & probably possess a mass of merits superior to all, except only Shakespear'. Southey saw Wordsworth as being able to harness these virtues because he allowed himself 'plenty of leisure to be a miserable hypochondriac'. The pair never really got on, which helps to explain Southey's reaction to Sir George Beaumont's portrait of his neighbour: 'It looks as if he had been a month in the condemned hole, dieted upon bread & water, debarred the use of soap, water, razor, & combs, then taken out of prison, placed in a cart, carried to the usual place of execution, & had just suffered Jack Ketch to take off his cravat.'[24] There is a certain grim glee in this description. The other thing about Wordsworth was his ability to be idle when he wanted. Southey, even when ill, kept on going as much as he could. As he wrote to Rickman on 9 April,

I have more in hand than Bonaparte or Marquis Wellesley, digesting Gothic Law, gleaning moral history from monkish legends, & conquering India, or rather Asia, with Alberquerque—filling up the chinks of the day by hunting in Jesuit Chronicles, & compiling Collectanea Hispanica & Gothica. Meantime Madoc sleeps—& my Lucre-of-gain Compilation goes on at night when I am fairly obliged to lay history aside, because it perplexes me in my dreams. Tis a vile thing to be pestered in sleep with all the books I have been reading in the day jostled together.[25]

With all this work on his hands he felt justified in being angry at Bedford's procrastination over his part in the *Specimens*: Duty, he reminded him austerely, would make anybody happy. He none the less hoped that the miscreant would look at the first part of *Madoc*, and make any necessary corrections, before it went off to the printer. He felt dissatisfied with the poem, especially its blank verse, and began to think nothing would match the achievement of *Thalaba*.

Southey's punctiliousness drove him, at the end of April, to apologize to Rickman for the delay in coming down to London; his eyes were bad again, which had held things up slightly. But the other reason announced herself on 30 April, 'an Edithling—very fat, large' and with 'no more beauty than a dodo';[26] she was christened Edith May (after John May) in June 1805. He stayed with wife and newly 'hatched' infant for a week, and then set off south, calling in on the Wordsworths at Grasmere; from Kendal he wrote to Edith, telling her with fine tactlessness that he missed the dog. By 10 May he was in London, so dirty that people laughed at him (or so he fondly thought); the coach had taken him through Oxford at 5.00 in the morning, '& I walked through it at that quiet & delightful hour, & thought of the past & present'.[27] He went to the tailors in London, decking himself out in a new set of clothes, which he confessed to Edith were ridiculous (and, therefore, she might have thought, a waste of what little money they had). Whilst his friends made social demands on him—Peter Elmsley pressing him to go to Edinburgh, Wynn to Wales—he wanted to be back home. London made him 'like a bear with a sore head'. As he told Taylor, the new baby had thrown him into some confusion, lest he should lose her too; 'for now I may tell you that the first loss almost broke my heart'.[28] So he was glad to get back to Keswick at the start of June, 'worn to the very bone' and over-anxious about his child: 'when [she] starts at a slight sound, as she frequently does, it gives me an ominous apprehension lest the brain be prematurely susceptible'.[29] He sought some relaxation in the garden, thinning some trees in front of the parlour window; one of the small rooms was painted, and papered with cartridge-paper. William Owen, the Welsh scholar, had lent him the *Mabinogion*, which Southey likened to the Arabian Nights. If a connection could be made, he would make it.

Summer at Keswick, as Southey soon learned, was a busy time; the fine weather brought visitors from all over the country to see the Lakes, and several of them visited Greta Hall. Wordsworth came in June, as did Thelwall and Richard Sharpe, famous for his incessant chatter; Humphry Davy arrived, absurdly clad, and, as ever, 'stark mad for angling' (he later wrote a poem about his passion).[30] *Madoc* was at the printers—Ballantyne's of Edinburgh—and there had been a reasonable critical response to the recently published Chatterton volume and to Southey's translation of *Amadis the Gaul*. Politics continued to absorb Southey, who was now receiving from Rickman regular bundles of parliamentary papers. 'Our home politics are become very interesting', he declared, '& must ultimately lead to the strongest administration ever seen in England. Pitt has played a foolish game in coming in alone; it has exasperated the Prince, who is the rising sun to look to, & is playing for the Regency'.[31] He hoped that if Pitt could be out of office, and Fox in, 'I shall have friends in power able to serve me.'[32] In May, Rickman had been wringing his hands at the state of the Government; he was less of a Foxite than was Southey, but was grateful that the Fox–Pitt coalition had managed to oust 'such disgracefull & dangerous fools. Court-favourites as we have now been governed by a long three years.' Rickman was already voicing opinions that ten years later would be associated with Southey: 'I am sure our country will be ruined before the benefit and indeed present necessity of official government and comprehensive arrangement of our mighty power and capabilities be enforced.' He had no faith in reform or reformers: Wilberforce was 'verminous'. By the end of the year Rickman was talking of a government with 'absolute' power as the only possible defence against the French.[33]

Harry came to stay in August, and seemed much more the responsible citizen; it was 'a delightful summer'. Southey was entering into the spirit of local activities, making arrangements for a subscription ball at Keswick; Wynn came to stay in September, followed by Duppa in October. There was some kind of riot at the local theatre, which helped to liven things up. A jackass was bought for Edith. Then, suddenly, at the end of October, there was panic when he heard that Greta Hall had, unknown to them, been sold and they would have to move out by the coming Whitsuntide. Southey poured out his scorn of the person concerned: 'this moving mass of blubber... is now laying in a stock of suet, which is to rise again with him, & supply fuel for the wick of his soul to all eternity.' It is easy to get the feeling that for a man to be fat was, for Southey, half-way to damnation. However, after a fortnight at Charles Lloyd's at Amble-side (apparently one of the most reliably entertaining social venues in the neighbourhood), he heard that it had all been a false alarm. His relief was offset by news that Edward had left his ship, and spent all his money in a brothel, cheekily running up a debt in his brother's name; Southey wanted to wash his hands of him: 'he is utterly irreclaimable & must be abandoned to his fate.' By December he was convinced that Edward would 'come to the gallows, & I only wish it was over'.[34] Harry, on the other hand, was now President of the Medical Society in Edinburgh: but he, too, was blotting his copybook by expressing a wish to try for Cambridge, much to Southey's irritation: 'I have no tolerance for that vile vanity which would sacrifice everything.'[35] (His own experience at Oxford had not been particularly edifying.) His other brother Tom was also causing a stir, having been dismissed from his ship for insolence to the captain. Just to add to his woes, he persuaded himself that his Edithling was 'too clever to live'. Furthermore, his doubts about *Madoc*, the work he had for so long looked upon as his poetic gift to posterity, preyed upon him. 'You know not, said Horne Tooke, how proud a man feels when he is to be hung upon a charge of high treason.—You know not how consequential a man feels when he is about to send a quarto volume into the world.'[36] It was possible to feel consequential, and to have doubts at the same time.

As winter came on, Southey was partly glad to see the end of the summer rush of visitors; he played whist in the evenings with his neighbour General Peachey. This renewed sense of solitude led him to ask rather anxiously of William Taylor: 'Am I the better or the worse for growing alone like a single oak?—*growing* be sure I am, striking my roots deeper & spreading out wider branches.'[37] There can be little doubt that Southey felt he was in the right place, doing the right thing.

When it became clear that Britain planned an expedition to Portugal, Southey sounded Wynn out about the chances of some kind of appointment, even as he condemned the folly of the enterprise: 'It is as hard to go to war with Spain because she pays tribute to France as it would be to hang a man for having been robbed. The feelings of all Europe were coming round to us before this act of aggression.'[38] He pestered Bedford to get his name mentioned to some relative of General Moore; he thought he might be an Inspector of Accounts—Rickman would be able to offer some advice about this. Southey's desire for a part of the action was thwarted; but there was enough to occupy him anyway. As *Madoc* was stalled at the printers, he carried on with his work for the *Annual Review*, writing about the South African Missions. In spite of all he said about the drudgery of reviewing, he acknowledged the advantages, in that he was forced to clarify his ideas about topics on which he had previously just had 'very vague opinions'. He was, therefore, improving his brainpan as well as his bank balance. The publication by Longman of *Metrical Tales* (a collection of his earlier ballads) would bring in some more money, with 500 copies and sharing the profits; his History of Portugal was still, in many respects, his major task, and he thought he had ready by the end of January all the necessary materials. He made an astute observation to Rickman: 'Nothing provokes me like a waste of words. Me judice I am a good poet— but a better historian, & the better for having been accustomed to feel & think as a poet.'[39] This sums up many of his virtues as a writer.

At the beginning of February the dreadful news came of the sinking of the *Abergavenny*, with great loss of life. Wordsworth's beloved brother John was among the dead. Southey wrote a brief and touching note of condolence, and spent much of February going over to Grasmere to offer what comfort he could: 'nothing which did not immediately come home to me ever affected me so deeply.' There were good reasons for this, including the fact that there had been more than one scare about his brother Tom. When Dorothy Wordsworth wrote to Lady Beaumont, she recalled how, when she had first met Southey, she had not been particularly drawn towards him (any more, apparently, than was Lady Beaumont); Dorothy thought, no doubt with her brother in mind, at work on what was to become *The Prelude*, that Southey did not have 'the dignity or enthusiasm of the Poet's Character'. But she had to change her mind when Southey came over in February: 'he was so tender and kind that I loved him all at once—he wept with us in our sorrow...'[40] There were some alarms over the Edithling, who had blisters in her ears; his old friend Robert Allen had died. As he said to Wynn in March, with deep feeling: 'The sweets & the sorrows of domestic life are mixed like lemon & sugar in punch:—but tho the sweets be improved by the mixture—I wish all the sours were out of the way. Some evils I have endured heretofore,—but there are none that go to the heart like these hopes & fears.'[41] No doubt partly as a response to such fears, he turned to *The Curse of Kehama*, as though he were contemplating his own fate, his own place in posterity. He had been engaged in major alterations to the poem, in particular with the introduction of rhyme, and asked for Wynn's opinion. 'I shall please nobody', he said, conscious of the quaintness but also of the ambitious nature of the work, part of his grand scheme to cover all the world's mythologies, even the 'Catholic in all its glory'.[42] As he worked at *Kehama*, he also started correcting *Joan of Arc*; it was 'a mortifying task', he admitted to Bedford, 'to find how much is incorrigibly bad'. *Madoc*,

although alarmingly priced at two guineas, would stand as his 'monument': there was no doubt that he would be commemorated in marble at
St Paul's. Catching the absurdity of the moment, he declared to Mary
Barker, 'I beg leave to inform posterity that I am at the present dressed in
corduroy pantaloons, a waistcoat after the fashion of the year of our Lord
1804, & a brown jacket which once was a brown coat'.[43] He was, then, only
a year out of date, not bad for a man sometimes scoffed at for his less than
up-to-the-minute sense of fashion.

Even in June, Southey was talking about a possible move to Richmond
in winter, when he could settle; but he also had his eye on a consulship in
Lisbon. He told Rickman:

> I begin to grow impatient of the discomforts of an unsettled life; the want of my
> own books, & of access to others, becomes daily more & more grievous; & it is time
> to have done with procrastination. I am older in habits & in constitution than in
> years, & have enough in hand for a longer life than mine is likely to be.[44]

If necessary, to make money, he would get up two hours earlier each
morning. It did not look as though the just published *Madoc* was going to
make him a fortune.

In *Madoc* Southey reverted to history rather than myth.[45] As several of
the contemporary reviews commented, the fact that the history was
Welsh and Mexican, often involving people with unpronounceable
names, could be a disadvantage. This did not bother Southey, nor would
we expect it to. What is interesting is the purpose to which he puts this
complex tale of conquest, imperialism, and religious belief; if the epigraph proclaims it a Christian poem, telling how Madoc 'quelled Barbar-
ian power, and overthrew | The bloody altars of idolatry', the poem itself,
as long and tortuous as his other romances (it 'assumes not the degraded
title of Epic'), suggests something more complex. The poem is certainly
an attack on the false gods of the native Americans; but it is also an attack
on the English (Saxon) conquest of Wales, the treachery that involves, and
the consequent need for the Welsh Madoc to set sail for the new promised
land of America. The fact that the poem had such a long period of
gestation is of crucial importance here. Southey began it at the very
time that Pantisocracy was in the air, when it seemed a real possibility
that he and Coleridge would indeed be setting off to America, to start a
new life, according to the Rousseauesque principles scoffed at by Jeffrey in
his review of *Thalaba*; nor should we forget that Wales was the second
option, should the American scheme fall through. For Southey, both
America and Wales represented not just escape from the corruption of
Britain fighting its own war against the French; they stood for freedom,

for innocence, for a new start based on equality. Madoc is, in many respects, the author himself. Southey wrote to Wynn in 1806: 'There is neither metre nor politics to offend anybody, & it may pass free for any matter that it contains, unless, indeed, some wiseacres should suspect me of favouring the Roman Catholic religion.' In the same letter Southey speaks of the need to colonize: for Southey, there is some irony in finding himself declaring that the only way to civilize Ireland would be a Catholic establishment.[46]

Madoc has Southey's rectitude: 'Safe is the straight and open way I tread'; but he is not fooled by King David's claim to have 'rooted out rebellion from the land'. The peace that David claims is to Madoc a betrayal, and beneath the hero's calm exterior is the 'quick wrath like lightning' that Carlyle, many years later, was to see flashing across Southey's middle-aged face. Once again, we have a poem in which rage and fury have to be balanced by the control and dignity of reason and belief, and it is from this tension that the poem derives its chief strength. 'I hate the Saxon!' Madoc cries. This might have had more force for Southey in his radical years, but readers in 1805 would have registered the shock of the declaration: a major poem by one of the major poets of the day, directly attacking the Englishness which the nation clung onto in those desperate years of the Napoleonic wars. It is true that all is rotten in Wales, and the King 'the headstrong slave | Of passions unsubdued'; but all is rotten because those passions have led to an unsavoury compact, through marriage, with the hated English.

In such circumstances, it is no surprise that the poem confronts, head-on, the nature of home and exile. Madoc returns, in Book I, anticipating the ambiguities that play around the return of Byron's Corsair ten years later.

> Fair blows the wind, .. the vessel drives along,
> Her streamers fluttering at their length, her sails
> All full, .. she drives along, and round her prow
> Scatters the ocean spray. What feelings then
> Filled every bosom, when the mariners,
> After the peril of that weary way,
> Beheld their own dear country! Here stands one,
> Stretching his sight toward the distant shore,
> And, as to well-known forms his busy joy
> Shapes the dim outline, eagerly he points
> The fancied headland and the cape and bay,
> Till his eyes ache, o'erstraining; this man shakes
> His comrade's hand, and bids him welcome home,
> And blesses God, and then he weeps aloud...

As Southey knew, home was not necessarily the comforting place Bedford imagined it to be. Madoc becomes, perhaps not so strangely, an Ancient Mariner figure, driven ('Not without a pang!') across the ocean:

> The morning cheered our outset; gentle airs
> Curled the blue deep, and bright summer sun
> Played o'er the summer ocean, when our barks
> Began their way...
> Day after day, with one auspicious wind,
> Right to the setting sun we held our way.
> My hope had kindled every heart; they blest
> The unvarying breeze, whose unabating strength
> Still sped us onward; and they said that heaven
> Favoured the bold emprize...

Whatever the historical foundations of the poem, the metaphysical realms are as important: 'almost it seemed | That we had past the mortal bounds of space | And speed was toiling in infinity'. Just as in *Thalaba* the abyss is peered into, so here the sailors feel they are on the 'verge and brink of Chaos'.

When Southey has to return, as it were, to earth, to the natives on the American shore, he finds himself idealizing them in a strangely ambiguous way.

> I see with what enquiring eyes you ask
> What men were they: of dark-brown colour, tinged
> With sunny redness; wild of eye; their brows
> So smooth, as never yet anxiety,
> Nor busy thought, had made a furrow there;
> Beardless, and each to each of lineament
> So like, they seemed but one great family...

But the real virtue of these natives is their potential freedom and innocence, and their tragedy is that conquest has taken its toll, and the savage idolatrous conquerors are as bad as King David in Wales. The poem becomes a struggle between the conflicting religious beliefs, and it is not as simple a task as Madoc thinks. When he tells his people in Wales of the new-found land,

> The multitude, unheeding all beside,
> Of Madoc and his noble enterprize
> Held stirring converse on their homeward way,
> And spread abroad the tidings of the Land,
> Where Plenty dwelt with Liberty and Peace.

There speaks the eager young Pantisocrat. This is fleshed out when the settlers go about their business, sublimely unaware of the surrounding danger, but—more importantly—echoing fairly closely the combination of work and congeniality that Southey had anticipated in his letters to friends about the delights of Pantisocracy:

> Some go fell
> The stately wood; some from the tree low-laid
> Hew the huge boughs; here round the fire they char
> The stake-points; here they level with a line
> The ground-plot, and infix the ready piles,
> Or, interknitting them with osiers, weave
> The wicker wall; others along the lake,
> From its shoal-waters, gather reeds and canes,...
> Light roofing, suited to the genial sky.
> The woodman's measured stroke, the regular saw,
> The winslow-creaking, and the voice of man
> Answering his fellow, or, in single toil,
> Chearing his labour with a chearful song,
> Strange concert made to those fierce Aztecas,
> Who, beast-like, in their silent lurking place
> Couched close and still, observant for their prey.

Southey realized that Madoc was not a sympathetic hero. Even by August he was planning alterations to the poem, especially to the catastrophe. He had only now appreciated the full truth of the poem's climax, that the 'interest is in the last book transferred from Madoc to Yuhid-thiton, a great & grievous fault'.[47] This is, of course, what makes the poem so much more than a straightforward historical narrative: the very subject-matter itself is riven with a central contradiction. When he wrote to Taylor, in connection with *Madoc*, that he had dreamt on the way back from Lisbon of another poem, 'The Deluge', about the corruption of mankind, he said ruefully, 'I could make it jacobinical to my very hearts content'. He was quite happy to concur with Taylor's view that *Madoc* was the best English poem since *Paradise Lost*—after all, thought Southey, 'this is not exaggerated praise, for unfortunately there is no competition'.[48]

Both Wordsworth and his sister Dorothy felt that one of the poem's main defects was the lack of characterization; in other words, there was insufficient reason to feel for Madoc. This was a charge levelled at most of his long poems, and there is some justice in it. Wordsworth put it in terms of a personal criticism: Southey's 'mind does not seem strong enough to draw the picture of a Hero'.[49] But the Wordsworths were still prepared to give Southey some credit; not so John Ferriar, in the *Monthly Review*:

The dull tenor of mediocrity, which characterizes his pages, is totally unsuitable to heroic poetry... Instead of viewing him on a *fiery Pegasus*, and 'snatching a grace beyond the reach of art', we behold the author mounted on a strange animal, something between a rough Welsh poney and a Peruvian sheep, whose utmost capriole only tends to land him in the mud... A greater waste of exertion we have seldom witnessed, and a more severe trial of our patience we have hardly ever sustained.[50]

Southey's retort was to the point: 'It is stupid and blunt ill nature. A bluebottle fly wriggling his tail & fancying he had a sting in it.'[51] He could take more comfort from the *Imperial Review*, who, rather like himself, regarded the poem second only to *Paradise Lost*. As with some of the reviews of *Joan of Arc*, we can sense the reviewer's political affiliations determining the initial response: 'his muse is always devoted to the service of benevolence, justice, and humanity.' But the rather more prim *Eclectic Review* was less persuaded by the 'affectation of simplicity which is so much beneath him'. The very expense of the poem (hardly Southey's fault), its fine pretensions for the library, were used against it, just as Southey had feared: 'We cannot, therefore, advise our readers to expend their two guineas on this volume, notwithstanding its ornamental appearance, its wire-wove hot-pressed paper, and its costly and elegant typography.' Jeffrey's review of *Madoc* was predictably hostile, and drew a spirited defence from Anna Seward (which did not appear until 1808 in the *Gentleman's Magazine*): she declared with some extravagance, 'for one harsh line that occurs in Madoc, we meet with fifty in the Paradise Lost, amid all the glories of its versification.' Sir Walter Scott knew of Anna Seward's anger, and reassured Southey that the poem could not be sunk: 'We know the similar fate of Milton's immortal work in the witty age of Charles II.' The Milton comparisons spring up throughout Southey's life, an index at least of how several of his contemporaries (and himself at times) saw his work. It was less cheering to hear that after a year the poem had only brought in £3. 17s. 1d.[52]

The financial news from Devon was not good: his wealthy uncle had died, but predictably left nothing to his nephews. Southey felt the pain and wrongness of this quite badly, as though he had not foreseen it. But the imminent arrival of Mary Barker in Keswick would take his mind off what seemed like a catastrophe. There was also a possible new poem— 'Pelayo'—which would become *Roderick, The Last of the Goths*, one of Southey's less inspired titles; he even reverted to plans for some kind of play, whilst admitting that 'dramatic composition is not that in which I excel'. His mind was again tempted by *The Doctor*—'Butlerizing' he called it—and he wished that Bedford would come up, 'that we might talk nonsense & eat gooseberry pie together, for which I am as famous as ever'. As he said, 'Nonsense—sublime nonsense is what the book ought to be'. For all his faults, Bedford was the one person Southey felt might actually help him with this book; he had, after all, written some pretty weird and wonderful ballads. 'I am certain', said Southey, 'that it will attract & *hold* more attention than anything has done since Tristram Shandy.' Southey tried to explain the attractions of 'Butlerizing':

Butler denotes the sensual principle which is subject or subordinate to the intellectual part of the internal man; because every thing which serves for drinking, or which is drunk, (as wine, milk, water) hath relation to truth, which is of the intellectual part: thus it hath relation to the intellectual part; & whereas the external sensual principle, or that of the body, is what sub-ministers, therefore by *Butler* is signified that sub-ministring sensual principle, or that which subministers of things sensual.'[53]

It is unlikely that Bedford could make any more sense of this than we are likely to.

Summer was hectic. Danvers came to visit, as did George Koster, Sara Hutchinson, the Peacheys, the Geddings; he dined with Thomas Clarkson at Grasmere; on the way back from Lloyd's, along the top of Helvellyn, he and Harry got wet through. Harry borrowed Wordsworth's shoes, and Southey spent the night at the Wordsworths', 'the skin of all my toes …peeling off'. At the beginning of October he went with Elmsley to Edinburgh, where he met some of the Scottish 'literatuli'. Jeffrey, who had reviewed both *Thalaba* and *Madoc* with less than enthusiasm, was a mere 'homunculus' (Southey made great play out of Jeffrey's lack of height, as well as what he saw as his moral and literary pigmyism); Sir Walter Scott, on the other hand, he warmed to. By and large he thought the Scots a miserable bunch, but he was won over by Edinburgh itself: 'I never saw anything so impressive as the first sight of [Princes Street]: there was a wild red sunset slanting along it.'[54] He also met Henry, Lord Brougham, the Whig politician and abolitionist with whom he was to clash some years later.

The idea of going to Lisbon had been revived, partly by Herbert Hill, but Edith began to put her foot down; she could not face more upheaval, especially since Southey was talking of a stay of three years. He wrote to her from Edinburgh saying he would not go without her. There is something disturbingly stiff about the way he both admits to, and yet refuses to admit to, his dependence upon her: 'though not unhappy (my mind is too active & too well disciplined to yield to any such criminal weakness), still without you I am not happy.'[55] Such a declaration did not prevent him telling Danvers in November that he would go to Portugal in the spring, if

Edith would not come; if she would, then they would go in the autumn for two years. By the end of November she had obligingly agreed to go; his reward would be a release from incessant reviewing.

On 1 January 1806 he was urging his brother Harry, who was trying to get over a disastrous love-affair, to come with them when they went in September. Southey's note of consolation suggests that Harry's failed affair with Emma Noel, whom he had met at Charles Lloyd's house, reflected his own life: 'what has happened to you has happened almost without exception to every body before, one such disappointment being as regular as the smallpox, & as impossible to be suffered a second time. It too has this advantage—that a man marries his second love with sobered expectations & as Goldsmith says not expecting rapture, makes shift to find contentment.'[56] Coleridge had not passed this test, clearly. At least Harry's life had not taken the plunge Edward's had: for Southey of all people, the last straw must have been the news that his young brother had become a Roman Catholic. Nothing could have been more calculated to send him to the verge of apoplexy. 'The best news', he wrote, 'would be that he was fairly & honestly fit for a mad house.' Southey could say this breezily in 1806; thirty years later his beloved Edith was to lose her sanity. Meanwhile, winter gales rocked the house, shook off some tiles, and dragged down a holly tree at the top of the garden; the rats, reminding him of Bishop Hatto, continued to gnaw at the foundations.[57]

Work on the *Espriella* letters continued: although the book was started merely to make money, Southey began to think, quite rightly, that it could have some permanent value; he was helped by Duppa, who managed to provide some sections on art and architecture in a style indistinguishable from Southey's own. At the end of January, Southey told Mary Barker that he would spend another month on the book, and then set off on his travels to London and elsewhere; apart from anything else he wanted to show Mary Barker around Bath: 'At no place have I been so happy, at none so miserable.'[58] Pitt's death in January 1806, and the swearing-in of the Ministry of All the Talents, gave Southey's heart a lift, for there was a hint that he might somehow benefit from this (it is not clear how). But the political future was not bright: if Fox were to come into government now, he would be 'sadly shackled' because of his views on parliamentary reform, and the Grenvilles would stand in his way. 'The truth is, that the diseases of the state are quite incurable, & nothing can be done effectually to relieve the people with such a load of debt, & the power in the hands of a few families.' Rickman, for his part, claimed to be indifferent, but had strong views on reform: it was 'certain ruin to an old shattered edifice very unsafe for its inmates already. By these I do not

mean the House of Commons but the people whom it governs; which is
much worse.' Southey, who despaired at this 'age of credulity', registered
to Danvers his rather bleak assessment of how things would go, drawing
the important comparison with what he had thought when young: 'what I
ardently wished fourteen years ago from feeling, I now think inevitable,
though at greater distance, & desirable, without wishing it. For myself, it
is best that things should last out my time, so I suppose they may...'
When he tried to explain his political views to Nicholas Lightfoot, in
February 1806, he resorted to an image that was to serve him in good stead
when, a decade or so later, he had to face charges of apostasy: 'my views &
hopes are certainly altered tho the heart & soul of my wishes continues the
same. It is the world that has changed, not I. I look the same way in the
afternoon as I did in the morning—but sunset & sunrise make a different
scene.' (Southey had first used this image in a letter to Mary Barker in
1801.)[59] It is sometimes hard to know whether Southey is being naïve,
genuinely innocent, or resorting to sophistry.

Wordsworth came over in early February, with a poem he had written
in response to the death of Nelson at the battle of Trafalgar. Southey
contemplated a similar gesture, but then said he would wait until
Tom became an admiral, and the poem could celebrate his elevation,
thereby killing two birds with one stone. There was also the fact that,
on land, Napoleon had been everywhere triumphant: his victory at
Austerlitz in November 1805 had been particularly glorious. Southey
still intended to go to Lisbon in September, with Harry, but probably
without Edith or Edith May; he hoped to have some kind of post there,
but he would also be able to get on with his History, to finish *The Curse
of Kehama*, and to write some Portuguese eclogues. Of one thing he
was certain: 'never more shall I waste my time in writing upon subjects
not of my own choosing & no farther interesting than according to the
price per sheet. A seven years apprenticeship at reviewing is service
enough.'[60] His immediate plans were to finish off *El Cid* (another translation) and *Espriella*, and then head for London in about three weeks.
He was being increasingly drawn into political debates, no doubt encouraged by his friendship with Wynn and Rickman, even hoping to turn
events to his own advantage: 'The turn which our politics have taken
is very fortunate; it puts me in the road to fortune & makes my prospects very bright, far higher indeed than they ever could have been had
I stuck either to divinity or law.'[61] Southey the pragmatist, with his eye
for the main chance, begins to take over from Southey the man of
principle. At the same time, there are alarming signs of hysteria, as he
contemplates the dangers of Calvinism, 'spread[ing] like a pestilence

among the lower classes'.[62] Some might think that Southey the potentially public man was becoming dangerous; at least in private he was a good family man, playing with his child, and making the animal noises that gave him such simple pleasure.

His trip to London was slightly circuitous. In April he wrote from Thetford, in Norfolk, a nicely pointed letter to Edith.

I never had a warmer welcome. Wilkinsons heart overflows after dinner with the very cream of human kindness. Never did wine make a man happier, nor better pleased with every body around him—his friend the clergyman was in a high state of enjoyment—his whole face perfectly relaxed with animal happiness—the cheeks hanging down, & an under lip—more like a horses than ever Townsends was—stretched up like a purse, covered the upper one, & then turned down with a flap...[63]

He gave a detailed account of his itinerary, including all those little details about places and buildings which so fascinated him. However, once again, whilst away from her, he realized that he could not contemplate travelling to Lisbon without her, which must have been sweet music to her ears; equally, after he continued on via Norwich to London—having his portrait painted by John Opie, in five sittings in a velvet chair—he was only too glad to get back to Keswick at the beginning of May. London, with 'the detestable composition of fog, smoke, & pulverised horse-dung', had scarcely improved. He had spent four days with his uncle, Thomas Southey, at Taunton, and got £25 for his pains; Lord Somerville was selling his estates, but there seemed little likelihood of Southey's benefiting in any way. He had, it is worth remarking, resisted Wynn's advice not to see the radical Horne Tooke, lest this damage his reputation and his chances of getting anything from the family estates. Southey was not going to toe anyone's line. In view of his apparently growing pragmatism, there is something refreshing about his determination to go his own sweet way. As the sun shone on Keswick in May, he wrote jauntily to Wynn, as though there had been no disgreement: 'There is quite a pleasure in being alive at such a season. I am more idle than I ought to be for sheer happiness.'[64]

In August his brothers Tom and Harry both came to Keswick: it was the first time all three of them had been together in fourteen years. Tom was 'looking prematurely old', and soon fell ill.[65] 'Our house is in a very comfortless state', he told Bedford on 15 August; measles was spreading through the family.[66] One of his political heroes, Charles James Fox, died in late September. Southey, unlike Rickman, had invested his hopes for the country in Fox, and there is something both noble and touchingly personal about his lament:

I am grieved at his death,—sorry that he did not die before that wretched Pitt, that he might have been spared the disgrace of pronouncing a panegyric upon such a coxcombly, insolent, empty-headed, long-winded braggadocio,—grieving that he ever came into power, except upon his own terms,—& still more sorry that he has not lived long enough to prove that his intentions were as good & upright, as, in my soul, I believe them to have been.[67]

The fact that Southey seemed to welcome the prospect of Brougham coming in ('he will be a strong man in the house') suggests, in view of his usually hostile attitude to Brougham, at least a certain confusion in his own mind as to what was politically possible or desirable. When his two brothers had gone, a week later, it was as though another chapter had closed; he announced to Mary Barker his recently adopted motto, 'In Labore Quies'.[68]

A new chapter opened on 11 October at 6.00 a.m. when Herbert Southey was born. Like his father he enjoyed making a lot of noise: 'He astonished the hour by his marvellous loud voice, roaring, they say, before he was born: whereby I prognosticate great things & am satisfied that he is lawfully mine; he is a bouncer, as ugly as may be expected with plenty of dark hair, & his name is Herbert.'[69] Like all his children, Herbert had what Southey called 'Tartar-shaped' eyes. Southey was to derive more pride and pleasure from Herbert than from any other human being. At the other extreme was his wretched brother Edward, now 18, dismissed from the Carmarthen militia for stealing from French prisoners under his guard, and now a strolling player going under the name of Smith. As if to celebrate Herbert's birth, Southey toyed with three possible topics for a long poem—the Flood, Pelayo, or the first deliverance of the Portuguese from Castille. His preference was for Pelayo, but ideally he would prefer an English story: it was not until his tale of Robin Hood, paradoxically never finished, that he found an appropriate narrative.

Southey was settling into his life as a writer, and began to think that a special post of historiographer could be created for him, with an adequate salary. But as his family increased and grew up he also felt that they needed somewhere else to live. 'Greta Hall', he told Wynn, 'will no longer hold us.' He was tempted into thinking that his Uncle Thomas, who had given his brothers £40 for clothes, might fulfil his rather vague offer of a house in Taunton. Southey compared himself yet again to Adam and Eve: 'the whole earth was theirs, & I have not a single spot in it.' As he contemplated his winter solitude, even his work on Henry Kirke White, the Nottingham poet who had died before his time, and who seemed to Southey the equal of Chatterton, provided little solace. He reminded Tom, and therefore himself, of the importance of Stoicism, in particular Epictetus, which had always been in his pocket, 'till my heart was ingrained with it, as a pig's bones become red by feeding upon her madder'.[70] Perhaps it was this that enabled him not only to cope with solitude, Christmas, and the young Herbert's flatulence, but actually to contemplate a History of Brazil, the logical extension of his History of Portugal. The Miltonic reference could be reshaped: 'Here is a fine campaign before me—I like the prospect well, & shall begin it cheerfully.'[71]

In this more optimistic mood he was glad that Harry was going to London, where he would meet all Southey's friends, including the excellent Mrs Gonne, a friend from Portuguese days. Tom was now first lieutenant on the frigate *Pallas*, and when Southey registered that Mrs Coleridge and her children were going off to meet her husband in Bristol, he looked forward to having the house more or less to himself: if they left for good, 'greatly should I be tempted to have the study plaistered & here take up my abiding place'.[72] There was another reason for feeling hopeful: his work on the Methodists for *Espriella* had opened up the possibility of writing about them at greater length. In spite of his earlier sense of alarm about Methodism, he was telling Mary Barker on 1 February that 'the Wesleys were a very extraordinary family', and with the chance of peace and quiet, and the 'deep joy' he derived from the landscape, he envisaged another project.[73] He was even telling Wynn two weeks later that Horace Bedford, who was apparently showing signs of incipient madness, should 'drink in Methodism'. For himself, he was more content than for some time: 'what a happy thing it is to love labour! I do not think there is a happier being than myself upon the face of God's earth.'[74]

By the end of the month he had decided to stay put, even though Coleridge was returning: 'I shall be anchord with a mill-stone about my neck.'[75] The parlour could be papered, the 'abominable curtains' dyed deep blue and fringed. He would have a carpet and white curtains for his study, which he would get properly plastered.[76] Sara Coleridge was obligingly on her way to Bristol, with a pattern of the marble paper needed for bordering one of the rooms; he told Biddlecombe to send on his belongings to Rickman, who would forward them all by sea to White-haven. The outside of the house needed doing, and he would regravel the path, and plant trees at the end of the garden, to 'shut out the lower end of the town'. He could also enjoy the countryside—it had been an excep-tionally mild winter—and went for early morning walks in his boots and bottle-green coat. A social life was starting up again: the Lloyds were coming to dinner, and he hoped Rickman and Mary Barker would visit soon. In the evenings he worked on his edition of the sixteenth-century

Portuguese romance, *Palmerin of England*; this would appear, after much trouble, in four volumes, in 1807.

Southey's financial circumstances were much as before, although there was a change in the sources of his funding. Wynn managed to get him a pension that worked out, after deductions, at £144, rather less than the £160 Wynn had been paying him as an annuity. The *Specimens* were at last about to appear from Longman's, but they were hardly likely to boost his income, and gave Southey little joy in any case: 'the printing is beyond anything execrable'.[77] Much of the blame for the errors lay at Bedford's door, and Southey let every one know this. But he had other things on his mind, as the world of politics impinged even on his Lakeland retreat. The Catholic question was once again to the fore, and Southey was in little doubt about the true horrors of the Catholic Church: 'the most monstrous in its pretension, the most impudent in its assertions, & the most fatal in its tendency that ever human craft imposed upon human credulity'.[78] The change of ministry (the Ministry of All the Talents, after the triumph of abolishing the slave trade, fell because of its refusal to back down on its demands for Catholics to be allowed in the armed services) he claimed to care less about, except as a sign of the general corruption of the state. 'O what a damned trade is politicks!'[79] Southey was increasingly convinced that the whole business of government was absurd. As he told Wynn at the end of March: 'What a precedent—a ministry changed without any wish for the change having been expressed either by the parliament or the country, but who on the contrary were strong almost beyond example in both, from the mere exertion of the prerogative, the mere will & pleasure of the Sovereign, who chuses to put in their place men of tried & convicted incapacity, with an old woman at their Head!'[80] None the less, in his equally strong conviction that Wynn and his allies would be back in power ere long, Southey was not averse to hoping he could get the post he prized, that of Historiographer, with a £300 pension—not, of course, that he had any ambition: 'a man who lives so much in the past, & for the future, can have none.' Whilst the political world went through its convulsions, Southey looked forward to having his books sent to him, bought some furniture, and— that most determined act of someone putting down his roots—planted some currant bushes, to be followed by gooseberries, strawberries, and raspberries.[81]

The news from the Coleridge family was not good: Coleridge was about to separate from Sara, and Southey's comment to Rickman reflects his frustrations with his former soul-mate: 'he does nothing which he ought to do, & everything which he ought not.' Nor could Southey draw solace from his near neighbours the Wordsworths: 'Wordsworth and his sister who pride themselves upon having no selfishness, are of all human beings whom I have ever seen the most intensely selfish. The one thing to which Wordsworth would sacrifice all others is his own reputation, concerning which his anxiety is perfectly childish.'[82]

As summer approached, Southey could rejoice in his own activities. *Palmerin* and *Espriella* would appear together, which would allay suspicion—that is, few would guess who lay behind the Spanish book. *Letters from England: by Don Manuel Alvarez Espriella. Translated from the Spanish* (1807) might seem from its title to be another of Southey's curious jokes; it is, in fact, one of his most interesting prose works, not only for the clarity of the writing, but also for the range of its concerns. Under the guise of a Spanish traveller, encountering England for the first time, Southey presents a series of connected observations on the state of the nation at the beginning of the century, and on the character of the English people. By pretending to be this Spanish Don, Southey is aiming at an objectivity which he might have felt would have otherwise eluded him; after all, he had been writing regularly about political matters, even if anonymously, and had established a set of views and values which were, according to his own lights, consistent. One of the advantages of this elaborate charade (foreshadowing *The Doctor* of 1834) was that Southey could stand back, he could comment on things in ways that would otherwise have surprised us: his real ingenuity lies in using the voice of a Roman Catholic Spaniard, for whatever Southey's beliefs, at whatever time of his life, he was never close to embracing the 'whore of Babylon'. But then, the central point of these *Letters* could be said to be his statement in Letter XVI, that the 'spirit of contradiction is the character of the nation'. And, if it is the character of the nation, it is the character, too, of Robert Southey.

The whole system of England, from highest to lowest, is, and has been, one series of antagonisms; struggle—struggle—in every thing. Check and countercheck is the principle of their constitution, which is the result of centuries of contention between the Crown and the People. The struggle between the Clergy and the Lawyers unfettered their lands from feudal tenures. Their Church is a half-and-half mixture of Catholicism and Puritanism. These contests being over, it is now a trial between the Government and the Subject, how the one can lay on taxes, and how the other can elude them ... [The people] boast of the freedom of the press, yet as surely and systematically punish the author who publishes anything obnoxious ... They cry out against intolerance, and burn down the houses of those whom they regard as heretics. They love liberty; go to war with their neighbours, because they chose to become republicans, and insist upon the right of enslaving the negroes ...

This is a good example of Southey's pinpointing the very contradictions which characterize the nation. Unfortunately, the book as a whole does not rise to a sustained critique of English society; his tendency to be fascinated with everything and anything leads him to some strange juxtapositions: within the space of a few pages he can move from the 'irreverence of [the] English towards the Virgin Mary', to the 'Male Tortoise-shell Cat', to the 'Paper Currency'. In other words, his old commonplace book mentality has not left him; indeed, without it, we would be missing more than just his commonplace books. But such serendipity works better in these *Letters* than in many other places, and the over-arching structure, in terms of Don Manuel's consciousness, provides a sense of wholeness to the work, whatever its shortcomings. And whereas in some of his more polemical writings Southey occasionally gets caught in his own argument, here the added distance lends his accounts of, for example, the iniquities of the manufacturing system a directness and an authenticity which would no doubt have offended Macaulay (as the *Colloquies* were later to do, in 1829), but which would have rung true to many contemporary readers. What Southey says of Manchester, for instance, could have come from the pen of Mrs Gaskell:

The dwellings of the labouring manufacturers are in narrow streets and lanes, blocked up from light and air, not as in our country to exclude an insupportable sun, but crowded together because every inch of land is of such value, that room for light and air cannot be afforded them. Here in Manchester a great proportion of the poor lodge in cellars, damp and dark, where every kind of filth is suffered to accumulate, because no exertions of domestic care can ever make such homes decent. These places are so many hotbeds of infection; and the poor in large towns are rarely or never without an infectious fever among them, a plague of their own, which leaves the habitations of the rich, like a Goshen of cleanliness and comfort, unvisited.

There are many such passages, where the directness of the English has its effect precisely because Southey is not striving for effect. At the same time, there is a considered attempt to analyse this strange country, an attempt to make sense of the anomalies, but also of the complexities of the economic system. We would not expect Southey to provide a rigorous view of the nation's affairs: but he provides a persuasive view, based on knowledge as well as impression. Since so much of the material concerns the history of England in its last decade—but set in a much broader historical context—the *Letters* provide us with an invaluable range of insights from one of the writers who, with this work, was trying to establish his credentials as a voice for the age. Southey achieves a considerable measure of success.

El Cid was the next work to be sent to press; a small edition of *Madoc* was about to appear; *The Curse of Kehama* proceeded apace. As he told Rickman, 'You cannot tell with what satisfaction I feel the time so near at hand when I shall have nothing to delay me from what I most delight in.' His historical career was beckoning: 'there is a delight in recording great actions, & (tho of a different kind) in execrating bad ones, beyond anything which poetry can give, when it departs from historical truth. There is also a source of power even beyond what the poet, creator as he is, can exercise...' Not even the domestic complications of Coleridge's life would get in the way: Mrs Coleridge and Sara would stay at Greta Hall, but Derwent was 'being got rid of (who is by no means an amiable child)'; workmen continued to busy themselves about the house; Jackson was to build a boat-house. There was a very strong sense of consolidation, and even the news that Edward had suddenly popped up in Devon, pestering Southey's friend Lightfoot, was not going to dampen his own ardour, in this 'month of blossoms & beauty'.[83]

During that extraordinarily hot summer—the temperature in June rose to 118°F—the usual stream of visitors came, including Sir George and Lady Beaumont, from Coleorton, who lodged with the Jacksons. Southey continued to spend time and energy agonizing over the Catholic question, using his columns in the *Annual Review* to work out his ideas. Not that he was even now altogether clear about what he thought. As he said to Taylor in July, 'I abhor the cry of no Popery with you, but I dissent from relaxing the laws against it with Erskine & with Ellenborough.'[84] The British attack on Copenhagen, when Denmark was neutral, incensed him: the country was, it seemed, no better than Napoleon: on 28 September Southey expostulated to Wynn, 'The damnable doctrine of expediency will never want advocates.'[85] De Quincey was horrifed at the almost treasonable conversation of Wordsworth and Southey; for one strange moment during the May elections for Westminster, Southey had been supporting Cobbett's rejection of all the political parties; a new broom was needed, to sweep away the 'prodigality & peculation' of those in power. But he kept his spirits up, telling Wynn, 'by Gods blessing I trust to carry with me a boys heart & a boys spirit to the grave. I never yet saw any person whose spirits were so uniformly joyous.'[86] His boyishness was no doubt helped by the arrival of more and more of his books, those friends of his who, in the end, mattered more than most people. He wrote to Rickman in September: 'I have been passing something like a grass-hoppers summer—boating & mountaineering with various droppers-in, bathing in the lakes,—painting bookshelves, arranging & rearranging the books upon them, & rather enjoying the sight of them than making much use of them'.[87] There were already over 2,000 volumes to admire.

It was not all fun and games. Southey took his responsibilites as a writer as seriously as ever, perhaps even more so as he acknowledged where his true bent lay. He explained to Walter Scott the full significance of his turn towards history: he was 'more disposed to instruct & admonish mankind than to amuse them'.[88] The Wordsworthian vocabulary might make us think that he was closer, temperamentally, to his neighbour than he was prepared to admit. He wrote to Reginald Heber, Bishop of Calcutta, on the same theme in November, when he assessed his own value as a poet: 'I feel some pride in having done well, but it is more than counterbalanced by the consciousness that I could do better, & yet am never likely to have an opportunity. St Cecilia herself could not have played the organ if there had been nobody to blow the bellows for her'.[89] It was perhaps this belief in the importance of instruction that led him to see the value of educating his beloved Herbert; learning might not bring him a fortune, but it 'will enable him to be very happy without one, which is a much better thing'. In Herbert he invested all his hopes for the future.

But the winter had to be faced. *El Cid* was at the printers, whilst at home Southey's eyes were bad again, and to counteract the November cold he sat at home in the evening wearing a velvet cap. He began to turn his mind to the Quakers, whose ideas he felt increasingly in sympathy with; he told Wynn, rather mysteriously, 'If it weren't for Bonaparte, I'd declare it the "true system of the Gospels"'.[90] His Quakerish sympathies, it has to be said, did not extend to Ireland, whose problems could only be solved by a 'system of Roman conquest & colonization—& shipping off the refractory savages to the colonies'. Methodism, too, fascinated him, particularly Welsey who, he predicted, was 'destined to hold as distinguished a place as Loyola'. When asked to write for a volume of British biography, the figures he chose were George Fox, William Penn, John Wesley, and the evangelical George Whitefield.

He was then approached by the *Edinburgh Review*, who realized that it would be quite a coup if they could get Southey writing for them on a regular basis: he had already established himself as a name to be reckoned with. But he knew that he had had enough of reviewing, and that his opinions were scarcely likely to chime with those of the *Edinburgh*. Scott was brought in as intermediary, but Southey stuck to his guns: 'my moral feelings must not be compromised'. He was anxious to make it clear to Scott that it was not a matter of personalities, although there could be little doubt about the differences between Southey and Francis Jeffrey: as usual he was trying to make a fine distinction. Jeffrey was for peace, 'I am for war as long as Bonaparte lives. He is for Catholic emancipation, I believe that its immediate consequence would be to introduce an Irish Priest into every ship in the navy. My feelings are still less in unison with him than my opinions. On subjects of moral or political importance no man is more apt to speak in the very gall of bitterness than I am...'[91] Scott assured the sceptical Southey that even Jeffrey had 'the most sincere respect for your person and talents'; and surely the extra £100 to £200 per annum would be more than useful. Certainly the financial rewards were tempting: ten guineas per sheet as opposed to £7 per year; but 'of Judge Jeffrey of the Edinburgh Review I must ever think & speak as of a bad politician, a worse moralist, & a critic, in matters of taste, equally incompetent & unjust'. It was painful to have to acknowledge that the wretched Jeffrey got more from reviewing *Madoc* than Southey got from writing it. 'His mildewing breath cannot wither one laurel-leaf of my garland,—but it blasts my harvest of bread.' The profit from *Madoc* had crept up to £25. As if, even so, in some doubt about his decision, he sent a copy of his letter to Coleridge, 'only to you:—not to be shown & talked of'.[92]

As the New Year began, Tom was staying with the Lloyds at Ambleside, suffering from serious piles; Southey would travel with his brother to Staffordshire, and Tom would go on to Bristol for treatment. Southey was optimistic about the immediate future; he would have 'my whole time at my own disposal'.[93] He was also in touch with the writer James Grahame, who was planning to move from Edinburgh to the Lake District, and Southey would look around for a house for him, probably around Cockermouth. He described some of the attractions of Keswick: 'We have more rain than they have at Penrith—but are much warmer; our mountains stop the clouds which come from the coast & manufacture plenty of their own, but they also screen us from bitter East winds, & our side of Skiddaw is green for many weeks before that which looks towards Carlisle has lost its winter covering.'[94] Southey was also thinking increasingly about his religious faith: 'I am what would have been called a Seeker in former times: belonging to no flock, yet not without a Shepherd.' He repeated what he had been saying elsewhere, that the Quakers, apart from their superstitions, had their attractions. It was superstition that made the likes of Joanna Southcott, William Owen, Richard Brothers, and Bunyan strike him with bemusement. But no religious group seemed to him to offer what was really needed, and he made an interesting appeal to Grahame, in that he was consciously suggesting something that was apparently out of step with the times: 'It is time that there should be a sect of moral Oeconomists in the world,—let you & I do our best to establish it.' It was all the more necessary when what seemed to matter to most people was commercial speculation.[95]

Edith gave birth to another daughter, Emma, in February; not for the first time, the birth of a child sent Southey scuttling off to London, almost as though he had to get away from the very thing he most desired; it is perhaps of some significance that after he had read Wordsworth's *White Doe of Rylstone*, at around this time, he told Scott, that 'the story affected me more deeply than I wish to be affected'.[96] The coach took him through snowdrifts to Liverpool where he met William Roscoe and his friends, and then on to London, meeting up with Wynn for a trip to St Mary Cray in Kent, where his old Westminster friend, the classicist Elmsley, was living in a pleasant old house overlooking the river Cray. It was not quite as romantic as it sounded: the river was clogged up with 'the filth of the village.—potsherds, a dead dog or two &c—'.[97] He planned to continue on to Taunton to see John May; with £25 he had received from Longman, for Kirke White's *Remains*, he would buy a dinner service, to match the breakfast cups and saucers they had broken at Keswick.

Whilst his brother's 'emerods' were being successfully treated in Bristol, Southey, in London, packed up twenty-five more cases of his books, for sending up to Keswick.[98] He met, for the first time, Walter Savage Landor, whose *Gebir* had made such an impression on him. Southey was perplexed by the paradox that, though they could scarcely be more unlike each other, they shared many of the same beliefs and feelings: 'He is of an ungoverned, if not ungovernable mind; & I am in all essential points, almost a Quaker.' Southey was both fascinated by this wild poet and slightly alarmed by his ferocity of feeling; Landor's praise of Southey's work was equally disturbing in its way: it reawakened his 'old dreams & hopes . . . a stinging desire to go on'.[99] Against this was Southey's sense that he had been born in the wrong place at the wrong time: not for the first time he was distressed that so few people seemed to agree with his opinions. Too many were ready and willing to see the country succumb to the French, and he found himself in the odd position of having Wordsworth as his only apparent ally. Fortunately, his conviction of his own rightness enabled him to brush aside his anxieties: 'I require, however, no other sanction to convince me that I am right.' That almost enviable lack of self-doubt is to grow in its clamour as the years wear on.

Interestingly, the self-doubts attached themselves to his poetry. In a mood of uncertainty, he sent Landor what he had written of *The Curse of Kehama*, eager to know what he thought of the lack of rhymes: even for Southey, the poem was highly experimental, and he needed someone else's sanction, at least here. If Landor thought it was worth it, then

Southey was willing, in his puritanical way, to get up two hours earlier each morning to finish it; he could then get subscribers for 500 copies, trying as before to become independent of booksellers. But whilst he doubted his own poetic powers, he urged Landor on to produce the great poem that he perhaps realized he would never produce: 'Pour out your mind in a great poem, & you will exercise authority over the feelings & opinions of mankind as long as the language lasts in which you write.'[100] Southey sees Landor in the same light as Coleridge saw Wordsworth, the one man who could do what he felt he could not. None the less, Landor's response to what he saw of *The Curse of Kehama* was to spur Southey on to finish it, but on his own terms.

Landor explained that blank verse, although our 'noblest measure', was unsuitable for the new poem. 'There must be quicker, wilder movements; there must be a gorgeousness of ornament also—eastern gemwork, & sometimes rhyme must be rattled upon rhyme, till the reader is half dizzy with the thundering echo.'[101] But Southey's independence was still there, his determination to go his own sweet way; for all his talk about having to follow, at least to a certain extent, the prevailing tastes of the day, that was not really his belief: 'the beaten road will not take me where I want to go.' And that was very largely Landor's importance, in that he too, in *Gebir*, had cocked a snook at everyone's literary expectations. It is ironic, then, that Southey criticized Scott's *Marmion* for the very things that he himself was to be criticized for, 'want of taste, & of propriety', the losing of the narrative in the detail. 'Scott', he told Anna Seward, without any trace of self-irony, 'is too passionately the Antiquarian'. Any one who has got lost in the narrative thread of one of Southey's long poems might want to apply Scott's own words, 'He never narrates perspicuously'.[102] As Southey was to say of the catastrophe of *The Curse of Kehama*, giving us (and Bedford) an idea of his own methods, 'the *how* will be compleatly mysterious till the very moment when it takes place'.[103]

Southey kept on writing through the summer, getting up early as he had said he would, in spite of a 'bilious fever' that swept through the house in June. He even reverted to his former plan of a poem on Pelayo, which would allow him to write about Spain in verse as well as prose; he felt that he had been a 'true prophet with regard to Spain', and Spain's freedom would be his vindication. But there was the customary round of visitors to contend with, not all of them by any means unwelcome. He was delighted to see the dramatist Joanna Baillie, a 'lively, good-humourd unaffected woman' who loved playing with the children—how much easier to like her than the starchy Mrs Barbauld.[104] He had never forgiven Mrs Barbauld for her 'Rebuke' in the *Gentleman's Magazine* in 1799, in which she picked up his lines from 'Written on Sunday Morning'—'Go thou and seek the House of Prayer. | I to the woodlands wend'—and threw down the gauntlet (perhaps picking up Coleridge's conclusion to 'The Ancient Mariner'): 'Yes, Southey, yes, I to the House of Prayer, | Each Sabbath Day, will duly bend my way, | For GOD himself requires my presence there.'[105] There was Mary Betham, the painter and poet, and 'the largest damsel I have ever seen that is not of the race of the Giants'.[106] Wade Browne, the Ludlow estate agent, brought his two daughters, and an old Westminster friend, Robert Wolseley, climbed Skiddaw with Southey at the end of July: 'A magnificent cloud rose under our feet when we were on the top. It rose from the Dod, filled it compleatly, & cut off our view of Bassenthwaite, but repaid us with something far finer. It was truly a grand sight to behold it rising below like a bright smoke in the sunshine.'[107]

Other visitors included Humphrey Senhouse, who came over from his family seat at Netherhall, near Maryport (where Southey was often to visit in the years to come), to see the famous 'floating island'. Wordsworth visited with a distressingly plump Coleridge ('about half as big as the house'), who announced plans to send his boys to school at Ambleside, and to live himself at Grasmere. Domestic life was added to by a new kitten, Dido, who played with Herbert in the kitchen.[108] On the wider stage, events in Spain were beginning to move fast: at the beginning of August 1807 Britain sent troops under Sir Arthur Wellesley to support the Spanish insurrection. Napoleon's defeat in Spain was cause for rejoicing, and Southey envied Landor's ability to go over there himself. 'One such Englishman we lost in such a cause as this when Sidney fell . . . Such a man cannot fail to distinguish himself, if he be not speedily cut off.' It was as though a new spirit was abroad: 'It is many a long day since the heart of England has beat with so generous a warmth as at this time animates it! Old honour, old generosity, old heroism are appearing again among us—England is herself again, the cause of liberty, disgraced & almost destroyed as it has been by that cursed monkey nation, is once more to be fought for, once more to be triumphant.' Spain and Portugal both represented values he could admire: 'In both countries there is a proud remembrance of their faded greatness, a generous feeling of what their fathers were, an exultation at the mention of old times, accompanied with an expression of regret & shame, yet not without hope—which no person can ever have witnessed without a conviction that the regeneration of those countries was at hand.' As he wrote to Thomas Smith in December, 'Bad as their Government is, it has never *corrupted* the people as our's has done.' Southey's enthusiasm is such that he can even forgive them their Catholicism: 'Never was any idolatry so fitted to the wants & weaknesses & wishes of human nature,—never was any mythology so rivetted & rooted in the hearts of the people.'[109] This is very revealing, in terms of what Southey is prepared to accept; but there is also a sense of his reliving the old days, not just of romance and chivalry, but of those bright hopes at the start of the French Revolution.

William Gifford was quite keen that Southey should himself go to Spain, to report on the war, for a new journal (the *Quarterly*), but for Southey the terms would have to be right, which, as it happened, they were not. In any case, no sooner had he been celebrating the Spanish spirit than he was lamenting the Portuguese and the Convention of Cintra, under the terms of which the French army, defeated in September by the allies at Vimiero, was allowed by the British to return, admittedly with its tail between its legs, to France. Southey was incensed: 'Oh Christ—this England, this noble country—that hands so mighty & a heart so sound should have a face all leprosy, & a head fit for nothing but the vermin that burrow in it!'[110] Southey once again found himself on the side of the opposition; so too did Wordsworth, who poured his wrath (in spite of his patron Lord Lonsdale's demurral) into his *Tract* on the Cintra Convention.[111] Southey wanted to call a meeting, at which Wordsworth and Coleridge would speak, to mark the 'day of national humiliation for this grievous national disgrace'. But he had to keep on writing: there was a new edition of his Spanish and Portuguese letters, which made him think about another *Espriella* volume. 'The evenings close in by tea-time'; he wrote on 13 October, 'fire & candle bring with them close work at the desk, & nothing to take me from it.'[112] He congratulated himself on having produced twenty-two books so far, and he could see no reason why he should not produce a further five a year for as long as he lived. *Thalaba* had sold out, and the publishers were suggesting a reprint. To help things along, he had access to Senhouse's wonderful library at Netherhall, where he spent five days with his wife and children in the middle of October. This also gave him the opportunity to talk to Senhouse about Cintra, and about what could be done: several local people were anxious to make some kind of public stand, but Lord Lonsdale, being of the Government's party and knowing it, was being more circumspect.[113] Almost as a displacement activity he worked away at *The Curse of Kehama*, anticipating the pleasure of the final catastrophe: 'Zounds what a noise will I make there!'[114] Southey was undeterred by the doubts of Taylor, who thought the poem too outlandish; although he acknowledged that it was 'in its nature out of the reach of human sympathies', he would forge ahead with it.[115]

His uncle Herbert Hill announced his marriage in November to Catherine Wither, one of Jane Austen's friends; Southey told his uncle, 'The
morning & the noon may well be past in solitariness, but for the latter part
of the day it is an evil & a sore evil to be alone.'[116] Southey hoped the newly
married couple would come north to see him, before he set off to see
Harry in Durham. There was also the chance of a visit from Scott, who
had left the *Edinburgh Review*, amidst talk that Gifford was planning a
new journal for which Southey, if he contributed, would get paid at least
ten guineas per sheet. What worried him about the new *Quarterly*, which
was to become a very powerful Tory journal, was the extent to which he
would be allowed the freedom to write as and what he wished. He was
certainly tired of what he saw as the *Edinburgh*'s 'cursed, cowardly, peace-
mongering politicks', epitomized at its most glaring by the article by
Jeffrey and Brougham, in which they cunningly argued that British support for the Spanish revolt was an index of British support for democracy:
combined with a suggestion that war with France was not going to last
long, this seemed like a repetition of 1790s Jacobinism. Southey
announced, fairly enough, that 'it is my nature & my principle to speak
& write as earnestly, as plainly, & as straight to the mark as I think & feel'.
Although he was soon to be writing regularly for the *Quarterly*—they
after all agreed on the two main issues of no peace and no Catholic
emancipation—he soon learnt that editors rarely like the kind of plain
speaking he had in mind. But he was also prepared to trim his sails if
necessary: 'as long as their caravan is going my road I am content to travel
with it.' His first article was to be on the Hindu Missionaries, just as his
first article for the *Annual Review* had been on the Baptist Missions.'[117]

Although Southey felt perhaps one of the people best qualified to write
in the *Quarterly* about Spain, he was reluctant to do so, on two grounds:
first, it was a bit too close for comfort; secondly, it would require 'a
method of logical reasoning to which my mind has never been habitu-
ated, & for which it has no natural aptitude'.[118] He had said this kind of
thing before, and he clearly felt that he did not have the right kind of
analytical mind. There was a lot of truth in this, and he convinced himself
that reviewing was a different matter, which meant that he was soon
taking up the drudgery he had willingly relinquished. It was in his reviews
as much as anything that he would pursue his wish for reform: 'because I
cannot but see that all things are tending towards revolution, & nothing
but reform can by any possibility prevent it'. For Southey's sake, it is
important to acknowledge that even in November 1808 he was prepared,
indeed anxious, to take a stand for reform, even if at the same time there
was a degree of confusion; as he said to Bedford, only two days later, 'At

present I am swimming with the stream, but it is the stream that has turned, not I.'[119] There are shades here of his comment of 1806 about the sunrise and the sunset. His letter to his brother Harry on 14 November reveals something of his own consciousness of the strange turn of events, of his hedging his bets: 'my review is not of a pamphleteering turn', he wrote, '& whenever it is necessary to give my opinions, they are usually given in *neat* spirits, without that due dilution which would weaken them down to common palates ... who says I am a Jacobine—except I myself? *Quis Diabolus* would ever have foreseen that I should have a pension, & be applied to from such a quarter as this upon such an occasion?'[120]

He and Coleridge were, at least here, in step. Coleridge wrote in December 1808, 'The Ministers are afraid of Parliament even in it's present venal state—which is a great datum of Hope for a Reform in Parliament, imperfect, and meagre as any Act-of-Parliament Reform would be'.[121] The general move for parliamentary reform was encouraged by outrage at the Convention of Cintra, and then by the scandal of the Duke of York's adulterous affair with a Mrs Clarke (which appealed to a Southey declaring himself, in response to Rickman's protest that the investigation of the Royal scandal 'stirs up the Swinish Multitude to Blasphemy', 'swinishly inclined'; the irony was that it had been Burke who first likened the people to swine): Sir Francis Burdett thought reform a 'necessity'; so too did Wordsworth, as did Southey, who told Bedford in April that 'a constitutional reform would save the country'. But when in May 1809 Curwen, the Whig Member for Cumberland, introduced a bill to prevent electoral bribery, Southey opposed it. The idea of reform was one thing: universal suffrage was quite another; just to complicate things, reformers tended to favour peace, and this is where Southey and they had to part company. The prosecution of the Peninsular War was his first priority. Southey's confusions come out in a letter to Rickman in early summer 1809,[122] in which he sees the present reform movement as nothing more than a matter of 'paltry savings' (perhaps a dig at Rickman); he was sure it would become something more high-minded, but he had no faith in any of the 'Rogues on both sides'. When he wrote about reform in the *Edinburgh Annual Register* for 1809, he insisted that the present system 'has made us the prosperous, the powerful, the free, the happy people that we are'. It was all very well dreaming of a republic (like a sundial when the sun always shines); but he was in no doubt about the consequences of parliamentary reform: it was 'the direct road to anarchy'. Far better, he thought, to concentrate on other, more pressing matters: civilizing Africa, establishing Christianity in the East, doing something about the poor laws.[123]

He persuaded himself, and Bedford, that as soon as he found himself differing from Gifford he would leave the *Quarterly Review*; but he did not want to appear 'troublesome': 'I am a quiet, patient, easy-going hack of the mule breed; regular as clockwork in my pace, sure-footed, bearing the burden which is laid on me, & only obstinate in choosing my own path ... there is not a lighter-hearted nor a happier man upon the face of the wide world ... I wish you could see my beautiful boy!'[124]

In those dark days of November 1808, as he wrote to Landor about Spain and Portugal, he urged him to get married, so that he should have the delights of parenthood. There is no doubt at all that Southey was deeply sustained by his growing family. This sense of security (which had arrived, it seemed to him, fairly late in the day) made him anxious for his single friends, and for those, like his uncle, who tied the knot just in time. But such security also enabled him to concentrate on his reviewing for the *Quarterly*; although he was aware that his first piece might not entirely please the editor, he put a lot of his energy into it. And he was reminded of his own good fortune by the death of Beddoes in December, and by that of Mrs Barbauld (even though she had never been one of his favourite people). His little Edith gave him the kind of simple pleasure only a child could give, and Herbert delighted him, 'the roundest piece of flesh & fat you ever saw'.[125] This is a rare instance of Southey's tolerating 'pinguitude': but then Herbert could do no wrong.

Illness spread through the house over the new year, preventing him from getting on with *The Curse of Kehama*: 'Anxiety unfits me for anything that requires feeling as well as thought. I can labour, I can think;—thought & labour will not produce poetry.'[126] His anxieties were added to when he saw how much Gifford had mutilated his review: he began to think that perhaps there was less difference than he had expected between the *Edinburgh* and the *Quarterly*. But he needed the money. A visit to Durham to see Harry and his prospective bride, Mary Sealy—one of the Lisbon colonials—provided a pleasant distraction: it was a 'place where any person might live contentedly'.[127] He met a number of interesting people, including the educationist Dr Bell, who had a profound influence on several of the Lakers, Dr Zouch, who had written a life of Sidney (something Southey himself had wanted to do), and James Losh, one of his old radical heroes. Such activities made up for what struck him as a rather feeble review, by Scott, of *El Cid*; undaunted, he started the eighteenth book of *The Curse of Kehama* on 14 March. William Jackson had been very unwell, but seemed better by the time Southey returned. There were practical matters to attend to at Greta Hall: matching curtains and bed-spreads in the end room, and 'the next operation will be to build a grand Pavillion at the back of the coalshed, so constructed as that the winds of Heaven may not visit ones rump too roughly!!'. As early as his first trip to Lisbon, he had been taken by Herbert Hill's 'temple to Cloaca', and now he was to have one himself.[128]

Another daughter, Bertha, was born on 27 March, but the pleasure of this was marred for Southey by his getting mumps soon afterwards. His dear Herbert had the croup: six ounces of blood were taken from the jugular vein. He said to Landor, 'there is a love which passeth the love of women', and regretted his extreme, poetical sensibility. For all his reading of Epictetus, he had to confess, 'I am not a Stoic at home: I feel as you do about the fall of an old tree; but, O Christ! what a pang it is to look upon the young shoot & think it will be cut down...' Increasingly, Southey found himself unable to live, simply, in the present: 'my own nature... pants after things unseen, it exists upon the hope of that better futurity which all its aspirations promise & seem to prove.'[129] At the end of April he was even saying to Bedford that he wished the next hundred years were over: 'the instability of human happiness is ever before my eyes.' As if to prove the point, he had to write to Mary Barker on 13 May with the news of Anna Seward's death; worse was the fact that George Burnett was dying. Southey's sense of guilt is striking for its frankness, as he tries to confront the fact that they had grown apart, and that Burnett was now a sad and solitary figure, the very thing he himself dreaded:

He is better dead than living, but it is shocking that I should think so... That so beautiful a flower should have had its fruit so cankered! The question, whether it would have been otherwise if he had never known me will occur to many persons. On that score I have nothing to repent. I set him no example but what was good. As long as he loved me, he loved what was good.[130]

Before May was out, his young daughter Emma, scarcely a year old, was dead. Southey took her death as confirmation of his hardening views towards life's frailty. His comments here help to explain much of his attitude to what were obviously lesser calamities; the snag is, for us, that his stoicism can seem as cold as the exterior he presented to the world.

In fact, God be thanked for it, there never was a man who had more entirely set his heart upon things permanent & eternal than I have done; the transitoriness of everything here is always present to my feeling as well as my understanding... My notions about life are much the same as they are about travelling,—there is a good deal of amusement on the road, but, after all, one wants to be at rest. Evils of this kind soon cure themselves.[131]

As he put it to Danvers on the same day, 'I am more sad than sorrowful, & more thoughtful than sad.'[132]

'THE MORAL ORDER OF THINGS'

1809–1814

SOUTHEY was growing disillusioned with the *Quarterly Review*, and with Gifford as editor; the problem, apart from Gifford's interference, was that the journal 'wanted party politics, & I could only give them principles'. Even at this stage in his career, Southey did not want any part in a journal that labelled itself 'anti-Jacobine'. He was therefore open to the suggestion from Ballantyne, the Edinburgh publisher, for a new journal, The *Rhadamanthus*, as it was provisionally and not enticingly called, which would bring him in £200 as editor, plus ten guineas per sheet: so far as Southey was concerned, a good bargain. Walter Scott was to be involved, and Southey immediately wrote to ask if Rickman would be willing to contribute; other possible contributors were William Taylor, the historian Sharon Turner, and Charles Lamb.[1]

As so often in the past, Southey's response to a death was to travel, this time to Durham, to help out with his brother Harry's new wife, who was to die two years later: Southey's awareness of the transitoriness of life hardly needed confirmation. When he got back home in mid-June, he was delighted to hear that Charles Danvers was coming up to Keswick: the summer season was about to start up again, so he felt less inclined to go to Portugal, especially in view of the political situation there. His own political sympathies came to the fore when he learnt that Coleridge was in the process of denying his youthful French Revolutionary ardour: he was incensed that Coleridge was so anxious to cover his tracks, whereas he, Southey, was proud to declare that he always had been, and always would be, a Jacobin. As he said of his former confederate, 'if he was not a Jacobine, in the common acceptation of the name, I wonder who the Devil was'. Southey could see that there was a difference between declaring oneself a Jacobin, and necessarily being an unquestioning supporter of the French, and he said of Coleridge, perhaps more in sorrow than in anger, that 'I fear he will totally degrade himself before he has done. There is a baseness in talking about himself as he has done for which even all his power of intellect cannot atone.'[2] The irony from Southey's point of view was that it was he himself who would be charged with such 'baseness'; by comparison, Coleridge got off quite lightly.

Coleridge's new journal The *Friend* (not quite the success he had hoped it would be) contained some of his earlier journalism, with revisions, in which he tried to work out some of his own political developments and contradictions. On the one hand, in October 1802 in the *Morning Post* he had taken on Pitt's comment of two years earlier that 'The mind once tainted with Jacobinism can never be wholly free from the taint'. But, on the other, in the previous week's issue he had printed a revised version of his 'recantatory' ode on 'France' and a long excerpt from 'Fears in Solitude'. It was as though he wanted to show that he had shifted his ground, replacing his enthusiasm for Napoleon with that for the Bourbons, for peace with that for war, for Fox with Pitt. For him, Jacobinism meant a government bound by the will of the people; equal rights; no property rights—and, therefore, universal suffrage. Southey no doubt found it strange that the inventor of the word and concept of 'aspheterism' (i.e. no property) should start his argument with the importance of property as the basis of government. Rather similarly, no doubt, Coleridge's account of Pantisocracy hardly chimed with Southey's recollections: 'our little society, in its second generation, was to have combined the innocence of the patriarchal age with the knowledge and genuine refinements of European culture: and where I dreamt that in the sober evening of my life [I should behold] the Cottages of Independence in the undivided Dale of Industry.'[3] Coleridge's defence for his 'strange fancies' was that he was not alone: many at that time thought along similar lines. This was true, of course. But it still leaves several questions unanswered.

Danvers duly came to the Lakes, with his friend David Jardine, and his cousin Louis; when they dined at Iansons, whom should Southey meet but Dickenson, whom he had not seen since his Oxford days; Mary Betham came, to draw Southey and the children, and Thomas Clarkson too. Young Bertha gave him the kind of poignant pleasure all his children did when young; 'the sweetest infant of all our children; at least I never loved so young a one so much before.' But amidst all this summer activity, he still had to attend to political matters at home and abroad: he looked forward to the time when the Austrians would defeat Napoleon, and he fervently hoped that Canning would not lose the Cabinet struggle. Curwen's populism (introducing in May 1809 a bill to prevent electoral bribery) was not something that appealed to Southey. He decided he was happy to continue writing for the *Quarterly Review*, as it gave him a voice, in particular a chance to have another crack at the Methodists. He wanted to be fair and balanced, and, as we have seen, Methodism held some attractions for him; but increasingly a paranoioa begins to creep in: 'there are limits which common sense must appoint to toleration.'[4] His own common sense had him pricking up his ears when the stewardship of the Derwentwater Estates (belonging to Greenwich Hospital) came up, and he asked Humphrey Senhouse if he might put his oar in on his behalf, with a word to Lord Lonsdale. If Senhouse could not do anything, then he wondered if Scott might approach Wordsworth's friend and admirer, Sir George Beaumont. Southey liked the idea, at least in theory, of looking after the woods, and actually having a say in the development of the landscape. The salary would, of course, be useful.[5]

Events in Austria took an unexpected turn, and Southey wrote to his brother Tom of his reactions: 'I do not know which most surprised me; the former victory of the Austrians, or the utter folly & pusillanimity which has now laid them prostrate at Bonaparte's feet. Henceforth there neither can be, nor deserves to be, any redemption for that vile dynasty.'[6] Southey saw that Spain would once again be the focal point of the war. He read Wordsworth's pamphlet on the Convention of Cintra, but thought the prose too difficult for it to be successful. Against the background of these events, he found it hard to proceed far with *The Curse of Kehama*; it was, he confessed to Scott, the 'wildest of all wild poems', and perhaps Scott would be one of the few who would like it. 'I expect to be abused for having given the language the freedom & strength of blank verse, though I pride myself upon the manner in which this is combined with rhyme.'[7] He later told his uncle that the poem would 'not be generally interesting... but it is written, *me judice*, with great power'. He was certainly pleased when Scott told him that Ballantyne would not only print the work, but was prepared to be paid for the printing by copies of the poem: Southey was anxious to keep the copyright. As William Jackson lay dying at Greta Hall, Southey took out a twenty-one year lease on the house—an indication of his sense of stability, but also, of course, of his responsibilities, not just towards Edith and their growing brood, but also to Sara Coleridge and her children, her sister Mary Lovell, and Mrs Wilson, the house-keeper; but his plan was undermined when he learnt that he had not got the stewardship (not that he was in any way qualified for the job, for which they wanted a farmer who could devote eighteen hours a day to running the estate: it was not meant to be a sinecure). Undaunted, Southey turned his hopes back to the possibility of being elected Histori-ographer Royal (a post held by Dutens at £400 a year): he would have a word with Lord Lonsdale when he next saw him.

Southey's Spanish connections were soon to be put to good use. Following on talk of a possible account of the Spanish campaign, which

only partly tempted him in that honesty would compel him to reveal 'its true colour of shame & horror', he was asked (and agreed) to write about Spanish affairs for Ballantyne's new *Edinburgh Annual Register*. This was the outcome of that original proposal for the *Rhadamanthus*, and Southey's part in it grew until he was practically writing the whole of the political commentary in the volume.[8] He was able to transfer the skills he had developed in the *Annual Review*, now defunct, to the new journal; with a salary of £400 that was more than adequate. As he told Bedford, 'having pretty decided opinions there is some pleasure in giving them circulation'.[9] When Miss Betham came, he was able to enjoy the walks they had, secure in the knowledge that he now had a ready source of income. They made an expedition to Buttermere at the beginning of August, partly to get away from 'Mary's bad dinners'.[10] In August they all went up Skiddaw, and Mrs Coleridge got stuck in a bog (the same thing had happened to Southey not long before); he gallantly washed her petticoat in a stream, and carried it home, waving like a banner on his famous walking-stick.[11] But these high spirits were dampened within a month by the death of William Jackson; Mrs Wilson, who had nursed him tenderly through his final illness, was asked to stay on in the house.

Southey soon realized that, although he was happy enough to write about Spain for the *Edinburgh Annual Register*, 'the rest will be heavy work'. Scott tried to calm him by saying that 'the tone of candour and impartiality' in Southey's historical contributions 'struck everyone'. He rather desperately asked Rickman to send whatever parliamentary papers he could: there was not much time, and he was going to be working under pressure. One thing he felt confident of, as he told Scott, was his impartiality: he did not deliberately set himself against public opinion for the simple reason that he did not care enough about public opinion. There had been some criticism of him, as a poet, actually by Scott, in the *Register*, and Southey's reaction was succinct: 'I should as soon think of being measured with Tom Thumb as with Thomas Campbell—but as every dog will have his day, so it seems may every puppy.'[12] What made the comparison worse was that Jeffrey ('Gog') upheld the virtues of Campbell and Crabbe against the vices of Southey. The birth of Katharine Southey in August 1810 provided him with a countervailing source of deep pleasure: it had been a quiet year of regular scribbling. In spite of the pressure from critics, he was working away at the proofs of *The Curse of Kehama*, and told Landor on 27 September that he had dedicated the poem to him; he was, as we might expect, proud of the notes which were 'copious, & sufficiently dull: I give them as specimens of the ore, that the skill of the refiner may be understood'.[13]

Rickman was sending up whatever he thought would be useful for Southey's political commentaries, including the Accounts, which Southey blithely announced he could not begin to understand. However, he was not one to allow lack of understanding to get in the way, and when he noticed that the *Edinburgh Review* was apparently taking up Malthus's cause again, Southey was determined to counterattack, and get a dig in at the poor laws at the same time: 'There cannot be a better opportunity of knocking down two dodos with one stone.'[14] He relished the opportunity of throwing what he thought of as his considerable weight into the attack, just as he told Landor that he would like 'the bitterness with which I speak of the last coalition ministry.—& the undissembled contempt with which all parties are treated in their turn'. Southey's savagery helped to compensate for his sense of despair as Coleridge, by now far gone in his addiction to opium, sought, vainly, medical help in London: 'O Grosvenor what a mind is here over thrown!' The doctors said there was not much that could be done in the face of Coleridge's lack of will-power, and Southey wrote to Coleridge to ask him to come back to Greta Hall, offering himself, rather forbiddingly, as his 'taskmaster for 3 months'.[15] Southey believed, too simply no doubt, that if Coleridge could keep to a routine, then he would sleep normally, and all would be well. Southey's own reliance on routine is well-attested, but it is worth registering the possibility that it provided some kind of defence mechanism against the kind of chaos that was engulfing Coleridge. Southey, meantime, guessed that his letters to Coleridge lay unopened. As he told Bedford on 14 January 1811, 'Never I believe did any other man for the sake of sparing immediate pain to himself inflict so much upon all who were connected with him, & lay up so heavy & unendurable a burthen of self-condemnation.'[16]

For Southey's career as a poet, of more importance was the publication of *The Curse of Kehama*. For all his growing sympathies towards history as opposed to poetry, he knew that this was an important work.[17] He seems to have been even more conscious with *The Curse of Kehama* than with *Thalaba* that he was laying himself open to charges of absurdity. His Preface acknowledges that in tackling one aspect of Hindu mythology he is almost doing the impossible: 'No figures can be imagined more anti-picturesque, and less poetical, than the mythological personages of the Bramins . . . however startling the fictions may appear, they might almost be called credible when compared with the genuine tales of Hindoo mythology.' Only a deeply perverse poet would embark on such a venture; it seems to be a challenge Southey cannot refuse. As it happens, the poem in many respects follows a similar course to that of *Thalaba*, with a curse working itself out in the narrative, and love and family honour surviving, even within this allegedly barbaric environment. Southey makes no attempt to impose a Christian reading on his material. It becomes, as parts of *Thalaba* threatened to become, a celebration of the very things he finds so distasteful.

There is something grand and majestic about the opening scene:

> Midnight, and yet no eye
> Through all the Imperial City clos'd in sleep!
> Behold her streets a-blaze
> With light that seems to kindle the red sky,
> Her myriads swarming thro' the crowded ways!
> Master and slave, old age and infancy,
> All, all abroad to gaze;
> House-top and balcony
> Clustered with women, who throw back their veils,
> With unimpeded and insatiate sight
> To view the funeral pomp which passes by,
> As if the mournful rite
> Were but to them a scene of joyance and delight.
>
> Vainly, ye blessed twinklers of the night,
> Your feeble beams ye shed,
> Quench'd in the unnatural light which might out-stare
> Even the broad eye of day;
> And thou from thy celestial way
> Pourest, O Moon, an ineffectual ray!
> For lo! ten thousand torches flame and flare
> Upon the midnight air,
> Blotting the lights of heaven
> With one portentous glare.
> Behold the fragrant smoke in many a fold,
> Ascending floats along the fiery sky,
> And hangeth visible on high,
> A dark and waving canopy.

This is a poetry of the grand gesture, aiming for effects which it cannot always attain, but none the less achieving a certain resonance and substance: it has a recognizable Southeian ring to it. But against this can be set the celebration of domestic contentment at the start of Book IV.

> Reclin'd beneath a Cocoa's feathery shade
> Ladurlad lies,
> And Kailyal on his lap her head hath laid,
> To hide her streaming eyes.
> The boatman, sailing on his easy way,
> With envious eye beheld them where they lay;

> For every herb and flower
> Was fresh and fragrant with the early dew,
> Sweet sung the birds in that delicious hour,
> And the cool gale of morning as it blew,
> Not yet subdued by days increasing power,
> Ruffling the surface of the silvery stream,
> Swept o'er the moisten'd sand, and rais'd no shower.
> Telling their tale of love,
> The boatman thought they lay
> At that lone hour, and who so blest as they!

Once again, Southey wants to tease out the implications of rebellion, of gods at war with each other. But there is also a greater sense of control, more sense of Southey's curiously anticipating both Byron and Keats.

> The waters of the holy Spring
> About the hand of Kailyal play;
> They rise, they sparkle, and they sing,
> Leaping where languidly she lay,
> As if with that rejoicing stir
> The holy Spring would welcome her.
> The Tree of Life which o'er her spread,
> Benignant bow'd its sacred head,
> And dropt its dews of healing;
> And her heart-blood at every breath,
> Recovering from the strife of death,
> Drew in new strength and feeling.
> Behold her beautiful in her repose,
> A life-bloom reddening now her dark-brown cheek;
> And lo! her eyes unclose,
> Dark as the depth of Ganges' spring profound,
> When night hangs over it,
> Bright as the moon's refulgent beam,
> That quivers on its clear up-sparkling stream.
>
> Soon she let fall her lids,
> As one who from a blissful dream,
> Waking to thoughts of pain,
> Fain would return to sleep, and dream again ...

One passage of the poem became famous as an anthology-piece (rather to Southey's annoyance, because he did not want his grand designs reduced to their separate parts), and it is worth quoting as an instance of Southey's lyric abilities.

> They sin who tell us Love can die.
> With life all other passions fly,
> All others are but vanity.

In Heaven Ambition cannot dwell,
Nor Avarice in the vaults of Hell;
Earthly these passions of the Earth,
They perish where they have their birth;
But Love is indestructible...

One of the problems with the poem is that it has many fine passages, perhaps more than Southey's other long poems. It is rich and rare, sometimes no doubt too much so, and, as with the early Keats, the detail can swamp the overall sense of structure. The Keatsian reference has a further point, in that there can be little doubt about Keats's debt to Southey's poem, in terms of echoes of lines and phrases, but also in terms of a general sensibility, a relish in the outlandish and the strange, in the luxurious indolence of paradise, and in the relationship between art and nature. By the same token, Coleridge's debt is also clear; his 'miracle of rare device' has its origins here, however surprising that might have seemed to their contemporaries. No doubt Southey himself would have been surprised (or perhaps he would not, so sure could he be of his claim on posterity) that John Clare, a poet in many ways far removed from this exotic tradition, should echo, in his own poems—ranging from *The Shepherd's Calendar* (1827) to the verse of the asylum in the 1840s—so much of *The Curse of Kehama*. For all its faults, it is a poem that had a profound influence on later Romantic writers; it is also a poem with intrinsic virtues—which are often denied to Southey—and a sense of purpose and design (reflected in its careful planning and revising).

The reviews on the whole felt that Southey had been wasting his time and efforts yet again. He was distressed that Scott, in the *Quarterly Review*, had not really grasped what lay 'below the surface'. He hoped that his friend Bedford, apart from reviewing it himself, possibly, in the *British Critic*, might be able to add some sort of qualification. It was important, said Southey,

to point out the moral grandeur of the fable, & how it becomes of universal interest & application, founded as it is upon a particular superstition—& also to show the value of works of high imagination, in taking us out of ourselves, & busying the mind about something which is not connected with the ordinary passions & pursuits of life. Sharon Turners wife said of *Kehama* that she 'felt it elevate her conceptions, & occasion an excitement of mind which made her feel superior to herself.' This is precisely what it ought to do.[18]

It was a rare critic who could sense that 'something extraordinary' was happening in this poem: as the *Literary Panorama* put it, 'it contains lines never excelled for vigour, or surpassed in rhythm'. But John Foster, in the *Eclectic Review*, made his point forcefully: 'a strong, an irresistible impression of flagrant absurdity, will . . . be the predominant perception of every reader incapable of a temporary abolition of his reason.' His outrage was increased by the very fact that Southey actually makes these pagan deities appealing. This is what is so strange about this poem, that Southey achieves something that his other long poems had been working towards, a complete fascination with and for a totally alien culture that he professes to despise. We should not be surprised that his contemporaries felt bewildered by such a work, and could only resort to ridicule: 'myriads of years must elapse before his partners in the godhead can reach either the surprizing height of his extravagance, or the terrible profundity of his bathos.'[19] Nor should we be surprized that for Southey, this represented some kind of vindication.

One of the books that Southey reviewed for the *Quarterly* was Captain Charles Pasley's influential book on military policy, which confirmed his belief that European liberty depended upon the sword. He expanded on a related topic in a letter to Tom of 23 January, in which he touched on what had bothered him for a long time, the role of Church and State. His comments help to explain much of his writing at this period in his life:

both with religious & political revolutions, when the age for them is come there is no way but the recourse of the traveller in the savannahs of America—when the grass is on fire behind him to set fire to it before. Kindle the combustible materials yourself & direct them to your own purpose, or you will be consumed by them. I am never weary of repeating that faith is an appetite of the mind: our establishment starves it, the Catholics gorge it even to surfeiting & sickness.

Southey believed the answer to be an Eclectic Church, getting away from the establishment creed:

The story of the Fall, the plenary inspiration of the Scriptures, & the miracles must be given up. Abandon these, insist upon a diseased moral nature, the necessity of all-sufficiency of grace effecting a moral redemption, preach the doctrine of perpetual revelation, appeal to the heart of man for the truth of these doctrines, & Christianity becomes invincible.[20]

This was not some arcane theological debate: like Coleridge, he recognized that Church and State were intimately related.

At the same time, his views are not always easy to unravel. For example, in February he was telling Herbert Hill that the second volume of the *Edinburgh Annual Register* would make

vigorous war upon the Burdettites. I do not apprehend any possible inconvenience to myself from the freedom with which it is written; that which so strenuously supports the Government, both Church & State, may be allowed to censure the Administration; & as for any personal offence which might be taken, if any man were fool enough to challenge me, I should turn over the correspondence to a lawyer.[21]

Here we get that eagerly pugnacious side of Southey, that legalistic and moralistic rectitude which got him such a bad name amongst many of his contemporaries; but we also get that central contradiction as to what he really believed: his ambiguities about the Established Church, expressed in one letter, are easily ironed out in another. It is in the same proud vein that he can declare, in the same letter, about *The Curse of Kehama*, that 'I was perfectly aware that I was planting acorns while my contemporaries were setting Turkey beans'. Such confidence allowed him to forge ahead with 'Pelayo', doing a few lines each day before breakfast, even if he had not yet settled on a metre. Interestingly, the siren song of the hexameter could be heard; although he recognized its unsuitability for present purposes, the thing was, none the less, 'practicable, *Experto crede Roberto*'. *A Vision of Judgement* of 1821 was to provide him, finally, with the opportunity he craved.

During February Southey gave considerable thought to poetry. He was engaged in a spasmodic correspondence with the Corn Law Rhymer, Ebenezer Elliott, and was content to lean on how a belief that it took time 'before the opinion of the few can become the law of the many'. Southey was closer than either might have suspected to Wordsworth's belief that the poet should be at least a step ahead of his readers. Related to this was his defence of his own metrical irregularities, which had struck several readers and critics as too idiosyncratic for his own good: 'I went upon the system of rhyming to the ear regardless of the eye . . . The verse was no bondage to me . . . it unites the advantages of rhyme with the strength & freedom of blank verse in a manner peculiar to itself.'[22] It is this *sui generis* quality of Southey's verse (which he quite often lays claim to) that is both its greatest strength, when it works, and its greatest weakness, when it doesn't. Southey's zest for verse was further increased by his communications with Landor, whose *Count Julian* had just appeared: what Southey admired particularly was the condensing of thought and feeling in a single line, and he was certainly right to say that Landor was exceptional in this. In fact, Landor's poem—which anticipated in theme his own 'Pelayo'— led him to doubt his own success. He admitted that he did two things— often more, actually—at once, 'from weakness, not from strength'. He could not stand the excitement of too much writing of verse, and recalled how, in 1800, he had only recovered from a similar state of over-excitement by travelling to Portugal.[23] However, he was already planning another poem, as a result of having read Holmes's *American Annals,* based on a New England Quaker hero; what was to become *Oliver New-man* occupied him on and off for the rest of his life.

Rickman and Wynn continued to supply him with political materials, more than he could readily cope with, which in turn made him conscious of the limits of what could be said in the *Edinburgh Annual Register*: perhaps a separate pamphlet would be necessary. He even began to wish he had some actual power: if he were in charge, he would get Napoleon out of Spain by landing the army in Biscay and Catalonia. Spencer Perceval, the Prime Minister, struck him as absurd, and the radical Sir Francis Burdett, with his cries for parliamentary reform, as little better. Southey declared himself, alarmingly, convinced of three things: the need for a prime minister, *tout court*, instead of a cabinet; the absurdity of a regular opposition; and the fact that parliamentary representation could only lead to anarchy.[24] When his guard is down, Southey can seem the rampant anti-democrat he was to become within a few years: and yet it was only three years since he had declared himself so firmly a Jacobin. One minute he could be addressing the Irish question, as in a letter to Rickman of 12 March: 'The Emancipators here have made the Catholicks perfectly frantic—& the Irish are such fools as to believe that Ld Grenville [the Whig advocate of Catholic emancipation, and elected in 1809 as Chancellor of the University of Oxford] cares a fig about them, & to forget all the floggings & half-hangings which were sanctioned by the cabinet in which he was a leading member';[25] the next minute he was approving Henry Koster's pamphlet on bullion, in particular his recognition that it was folly to fix a maximum price for gold. Southey was particularly pleased with what he had said in the *Register* about parliamentary reform, the more so because he felt it came from the heart rather than the head—a strange distinction for a political writer to make, but a significant one.

There was a brief interruption to such cogitations at the end of March. George Burnett had died in a workhouse, and though by the end there had been little love lost between them, Southey felt the shock keenly. Burnett had become a pathetic and wayward figure, but Southey had hoped that the army or the navy might have been his salvation; he blamed Coleridge for his reluctance to even open the many letters Southey sent on the subject of what to do with Burnett (no doubt because there was the subtext of what to do with Coleridge), and felt some responsibility for Burnett's miserable end. His verdict on the hapless Burnett was damning: 'his manners towards women were quite insufferable.'[26]

Whilst sickness ran through Greta Hall during the first three months of 1811, meaning that Southey was unlikely to get to London before May at the earliest, the news from abroad was good: Graham had been victorious;

Wellington was sure to defeat Massena in Portugal; and even Lord Grenville had spoken words of wisdom in the House of Lords about Portugal.
Nothing, however, could soften his wrath when he saw just how much
Gifford had tampered with his essay on Pasley in the *Quarterly*: as Southey
quite reasonably pointed out to Rickman, if they did not like his ideas,
they could have said so before. He was determined to ask for the manuscripts back—or, preferably, the printed sheets, so that Longman could
print the whole article in the *British Review*. Southey was kicking himself
for having declined Longman's previous offer to do this. What really
annoyed him was the 'ministerial patronage' that lay behind Gifford's
editorializing, the very thing Southey had anticipated: 'Gifford will not
insert anything that is not to the taste of the men in power—& they never
like to be dictated to.'[27] Southey was deeply conscious of his invidious
position; as he said to Bedford, with reference to Coleridge's latest offering in the *Courier*, 'no doubt it will be said that he is writing *for* a pension,
& I because I have got one'.[28] Southey was not yet willing to be seen as
anyone's poodle, and he rather defiantly announced, when asked to
translate one of Lucien Bonaparte's poems, that he admired him because
he is a 'true republican, & anywhere out of England that is the best thing a
man can be'; he planned to visit this 'true lover of liberty' on the way home
from the south on his next journey. There is an interesting gloss to be put
on this, in a note to Bedford of April 1811: he pointed to his previous article
in the *Edinburgh Annual Register* on Jacobinism, in explaining his views
about the disturbances that were sweeping the country. 'It is many years',
he told Bedford, 'since I saw that a Government which founds its prosper-
ity upon manufacture, sleeps upon gunpowder.'[29] This is an important
comment, in that it not only foreshadows what he was to go on to write, at
some length, about the dangers of manufacturing and industry; it also
indicates, revealingly, the unorthodox and unpredictable nature of his
political views: he is not to be tied down to any one line, whether
government or opposition. This was the advantage of the *Edinburgh
Annual Register*, as opposed to the *Quarterly Review*, in that it allowed
him the freedom to say what he thought, without fear of censure.

News of Landor's marriage gave Southey particular pleasure, and it
prompted him to spell out his own domestic philosophy. Since Edith can
often seem a shadowy presence in his life, it is worth quoting: 'To be at
rest, without either hope, wish, or desire beyond what the passing history
of the human race ought to inspire, is my *summum bonum*, & this, which,
by God's blessing I have enjoyed for many years, I never could have
attained while unmarried.'[30] His own domesticity was due to be disrupted
in June, when he planned to spend three weeks in London, sorting out

publishing arrangements, then on to Bristol, then to Llantony in the Black Mountains, to stay with the newly married Landor, before returning via Ludlow and Liverpool. The *Register* had taken three more months' work than the first volume, which caused Southey some frustration, in that he knew he could have written his projected *Life of Nelson* in that time. Amongst other people he wanted to see John Thelwall, who had been giving lectures on *The Curse of Kehama*; as usual, Southey was in two minds about this former firebrand who had 'narrowly escaped hanging for high treason' in 1794, and who now went round the country, teaching elocution. Southey could not approve the man's former atheism, and thought him 'imprudentissimus homo & the very emperor of coxcombs';[31] he was none the less an honest enough person, with a good heart.

Southey and Edith were in London in July, and as always eager to get out of it as soon as possible. It was on this trip that he met William Blake, who was holding an exhibition of his paintings in Golden Square: according to Southey, Blake was so 'evidently insane, that the predominant feeling in conversing with him, or even looking at him, could only be sorrow & compassion'. It was hardly a meeting of minds, although, as I have suggested earlier, some of Southey's youthful works appear to glance at Blake's *Songs*; nor was Southey alone in thinking Blake mad: it was a common, defensive reaction to art few could comprehend. Southey's old friend Elmsley visited them, and Southey dined with J. W. Croker at the Admiralty. He picked up the political gossip, finding it hard to believe that Perceval would resign in favour of Canning, who in turn would bring in the dreaded Catholic emancipation. These were matters of interest, but also of dread: accordingly, he spoke of the power of smell, particularly that of flowers, which took him back to his childhood: 'Oh what a happy season is childhood, if our modes of life & education will let it be so!'[32] It is almost as though, whenever he was away from his roots and his children, he remembered the joys of childhood; and the prospect of being in Bristol was always calculated to revive these thoughts. He left Edith in Bristol whilst he went on to Taunton; his last surviving uncle on that side of the family had died, and once again no one in the family benefited. Southey consoled himself with a line from Wither, 'nec habeo, nec careo, nec curo'. Another death, more poignant for Southey, was that of his old school-friend Bunbury; Southey confessed to a 'strange & confused feeling'. His journey back from Taunton took in Wynn, at Llangedwyn, and a visit to the famous 'Ladies of Llangollen', Lady Eleanor Butler and the Hon. Sarah Ponsonby, both of whom were celebrated for their eccentric, reclusive way of life at Plas Newydd, where they embraced Rousseau, fostered a literary

coterie, and turned the face of their famed celibacy to a male world that
had let them down. By 4 September the Southeys were back home, after
twelve weeks away and a round trip of 900 miles.

The stream of late summer visitors began with James White, to whom
Southey was anxious to show some of the beauties of the Lakes. But he
also settled down to writing, realising that 'Pelayo' had a direct bearing
upon the present state of affairs in Spain. He was simultaneously pressing
John Murray to take up Landor's *Count Julian* which had been refused by
Longman: Southey would review it. His own political writings were also
occupying him: there was an essay on Dr Bell's system of education (a
system based on monitors, which appealed to Southey, but also to Wordsworth),[33] and he wanted to write something on the 'happiness of Nations'
which was actually to be about the condition of the poor; in connection
with this he was pestering Murray for a copy of Eden's *History of the Poor
Law*. An article duly appeared in the *Quarterly Review* for December
1812.[34] He was also working on a rather desultory volume of *Omniana*,
supposedly in conjunction with Coleridge, consisting of gleanings from
their joint reading, and on the *Life of Nelson*, which he had started before
he had left on his London excursion. As if this were not enough, he was
reading two folios of Dutch each day, so that he could learn the language.

When an offer of a museum job arose, engineered by Sharon Turner
and Rickman, the prospect of cataloguing books for three hours a day in a
city he regarded as 'an evil' merely confirmed him in his belief that he had
to live in the country; besides, he wanted to be 'master of his own actions
at all times'.[35] He also wanted to get his own back at Jeffrey and the
Edinburgh Review: Southey had never forgiven Jeffrey for his reviews of
Thalaba and *The Curse of Kehama*, but this was more than a personal
vendetta, it was a matter of ideological principle. 'I will throw the gaunt-
lett to the Enemy, & if he takes it up, it is at his peril. Jeffrey little knows of
what stuff I am made. If I once grapple with him in controversy it will be
to break every bone in his body.'[36] He told Mary Betham that he would
expose the folly of the *Edinburgh* by revising what he had written in the
Quarterly for a separate pamphlet, meanwhile enjoying the irony of
Jeffrey's saying that he liked the historical parts of the *Edinburgh Annual
Register*, not knowing that Southey was the author. There was the added
irony that Brougham, hardly one of Southey's allies, had recommended
Southey's account of the political year to Parliament, and this could lead
to his being summoned to London, to meet the great and the good,
something he neither relished nor needed: 'solitary habits have incapaci-
tated me for speaking'. Education, of course, had its own importance as
his children were growing up; he told Mary Betham that Bertha 'is now a

great rosy cheeked girl, so plump & square faced as to have got the name of Queen Henry the 8th.—'.[37]

As the new year came round, Southey took stock of himself. He told the poet James Montgomery of his fear of

nervous diseases, from which nothing but perpetual self-management, & the fortunate circumstance of my life & disposition preserve me. Nature gave me an indefatigable activity of mind, & a buoyancy of spirit, which has ever enabled me to think little of difficulties, & to live in the light of hope; these gifts too were accompanied with an hilarity which has enabled me to retain a boy's heart to the age of eight & thirty. But my senses are perilously acute,—impressions sink into me too deeply, & at one time ideas had all the vividness & apparent reality of actual impressions to such a degree, that I believe a speedy removal to a foreign country, bringing with it a total change of all external objects, saved me from imminent danger. The remedy, or at least the preventation of this is variety of employment . . . That I am a very happy man I owe to my early marriage . . . I had done with hope & fear upon the most agitating & most important action of life,—& my heart was at rest.[38]

A visit from the young Percy Bysshe Shelley was a sharp reminder of what he himself had been like in 1794; he was, as it were, seeing the ghost of his former self, which meant that he was confronted by all those agonies of belief and uncertainty, the horrors of atheism but the equal horrors of bigotry. Shelley's expulsion from Oxford was a reminder of his own from Westminster School, and his own revolutionary fervour at Balliol. Southey could see nothing but a bright future ahead for this young tearaway; he would 'become an honour to his name & his country'.[39] Unfortunately, the apparently mutual admiration was not to last. Something of the split in Southey's personality can be seen in the fact that whilst he was celebrating Shelley's youthful ardour he was also coming to an agreement with Murray about yet another massive project, the *Book of the Church*, from which the profits were to be shared equally for the first edition; for subsequent editions, Southey was to get two-thirds. It was for *The Necessity of Atheism* that Shelley had been driven from Oxford.

When Shelley had first arrived in the Lakes in November, he was all eagerness to meet Southey: however magnificent the scenery, 'the object most interesting to my feelings is Southey's habitation'. But within three weeks of having professed that he would 'not be slow to pay homage to a *really* great man' he was in mid-December distinctly cooler, when he realized the changes that Southey had gone through, his 'tergiversation': 'He to whom Bigotry, Tyranny and Law was hateful has become the votary of these Idols, in a form the most disgusting.' Shelley comforted himself with what he saw as Wordsworth's integrity of independence, but as for

Southey, 'I feel a sickening distrust when I see all that I had considered good great and imitable fall around me into the gulph of error'. Shelley acknowleged that in spite of Southey's advocacy for the existing establishment, he was also 'an advocate of liberty and equality', looking 'forward to a state when all shall be perfected, and matter become subjected to the omnipotence of mind'. The two men agreed that 'original sin' did not exist, and 'that which appears to be a taint of our nature is in effect the result of unnatural political institutions'. Shelley saw through Southey's contradictions, and recognized that eloquence was one thing, but the capacity to reason was something else, and not one of Southey's strong suits. Shelley loved the Southey children, but was hard on the women of the household: 'His wife is very stupid. Mrs Coleridge is worse. Mrs Lovell who was once an actress is the best of them.' It was Mrs Lovell whom Coleridge had not wanted to come to Greta Hall; in fact, according to Lamb, Coleridge said once that of all the Fricker sisters, it was only Martha of the 'Brood' he had 'any regard for'.[40]

By the end of the visit, all the charm had gone. Southey argued that whereas expediency could not be tolerated in morals, it could in politics, whereas for Shelley they were inseparable, and Southey would once have said the same (and not so very long ago). 'Ah!' said Southey, 'when you are as old as I am you will think with me.' Southey was not yet 40; not surprisingly, Shelley saw him as 'corrupted by the world, contaminated by Custom . . . the servile champion of every abuse and absurdity'. Having yearned towards Greta Hall in November, he passed it as he left on 3 February 'without *one* sting'; he could not even believe in the amiability of Southey as a private, as opposed to a public, figure, and was alarmed at the 'hateful prostitution of talents'. Prostitution was to be the precise word that Hazlitt would use, for similar reasons, ere long.[41]

As Southey acknowledged, Shelley's visit was unsettling, whether or not the story was true that Shelley had slipped beneath the table, unconscious with boredom, during Southey's rendition of one of his own epics. (The reverse could equally have been true.) Tom came to stay for three weeks, but more worryingly, Coleridge was due to arrive some time in February, after his course of lectures in London. Southey fondly believed that Coleridge might settle down again in Keswick, and even 'become once more a family man as he ought to be'. But Coleridge's sense of domestic duty was less fully developed than Southey's. There were other problems, too, besides visitors welcome or otherwise. Even in the Lake District disturbances were becoming commonplace, and Southey wrote to Bedford, rather desperately asking for a brace of pistols and a watchman's rattle, to scare away the 'ugly fellows' who prowled around the neighbourhood. News from Carlisle and Cockermouth was alarming: 'last night half the people in Keswick sat up, alarmed by two strangers, who, according to all accounts, were certainly "no beauties",—& I was obliged to take down a rusty gun & manfully load it for the satisfaction of the family.' There was even talk of Shelley's having been knocked down on his own doorstep.[42]

Landor's *Count Julian* appeared in February, to Southey's approbation: 'You are the only poet whom it seems to me impossible to imitate.'[43] This was a fair comment, meant as a compliment; but the other side of the coin, as Southey recognized, was that Landor was unlikely to receive much of a response from the critics. He was also relieved that, in spite of the same topic, his and Landor's poems were radically different from each other. He hoped to elaborate on the poem's virtues in a review, especially since he could see that both of them were addressing a political issue, and his own 'Pelayo', whatever its aesthetic merits, might have an effect on public attitudes towards the Spanish war. A defensive war was not enough: what was needed was more pugnacity, with the Portuguese army trained by the British. As if to qualify his enthusiasm for the young Shelley, his own piece on education would attack Lancaster (Andrew Bell's main opponent) as a 'vulgar-minded plagiarist, & a liar of the foulest kind'; the important point was that the duty of the State was to ensure that national education 'be conducted upon the principle of national religion'.[44]

There were pressing personal matters to attend to. A quarrel had erupted between Coleridge, Wordsworth, and Basil Montague, much of it depending on who had said what to whom. Southey's views, as expressed in a letter of April 1812 to Wordsworth, were clear, if hardly complimentary to the parties involved:

My own feeling is that it is absurd to suppose a man is not fully justified in speaking *to* one friend *of* another with perfect freedom, upon every part of his conduct, & everything relating to him except such things as are confidential. But if we were to search the world through we should hardly find two men to whom they could be so unhappily applied—when of the one almost every part of his conduct is matter of grief & shame, & the other is a cracked pitcher, spoiled in the making, & treacherous because of the flaw.[45]

Southey was not one to mince his words.

At about the same time he was beginning, not for the first time, to think back to the past, and forward to the future. He told Wynn that he had insured his life for £1,000, and it was as though this in itself was a statement about his own loose hold on the world. He was even contemplating, in the event of his not lasting much longer, a subscription edition of his works, to be produced by Longman, just in case his pension did not continue, for the support of his family, after his demise. He said, rather sternly and stoically, that 'a less troubled youth would probably have led to a less happy manhood', and repeated to Wynn what he had said, and was to say, both publicly and privately, to others, that 'we have both of us rather grown than changed, & accident has had as little to do with our circumstances as with our character'. In this rather self-important, self-assured mood, Southey planned to write his memoirs: 'they will contain so much of the literary history of the times, as to have a permanent value on that account. This would prove a good post obit, at least to the amount of my life-insurance, for there can be no doubt that I shall be sufficiently talked of whenever I am gone.' Southey seems to have sensed that, were he to survive—and there was no obvious reason why he should not—he was about to reach a plateau in his career. As he said to Wynn in the same letter, 'I am up the hill of difficulty, & shall very soon get rid of the burthen which has impeded me in the ascent.'[46] Quite what he meant by this it is hard to surmise. There was certainly not much comfort to be had from the general state of affairs either in the Lake District or in the country as a whole.

There were riots in Carlisle, due to differences between the colliers and the pit owners; the price of potatoes was rising.[47] Perceval's death seemed a sign of the times: John Bellingham had murdered Spencer Perceval, the Prime Minister, on 12 May 1812, in the lobby of the House of Commons, and immediately became a hero. It was a genuine blow against the establishment and the foundations of society, and caused correspondingly genuine alarm amongst all conservatives. Coleridge reported hearing the jubilation in a public house at the news: 'This is but the beginning...More of these damned scoundrels must go the same way, and then poor people may live ...' Scott agreed with Southey's analysis: 'You are quite right in apprehending a *Jacquerie*; the country is mined below our feet.' The fact that Bellingham went to his execution not merely unrepentant but actively convinced of his role (rather like Thalaba) as a tool of God merely made things worse. Rickman had expected the murder (or said he had), but at the hands of the Burdettites, 'and other vermin poisoned by violent newspapers'.[48]

There had been other murders, most notably by John Williams of a shopkeeper in London, along with his wife and family: this murder, partly because of its extreme brutality, caught the public imagination, and was immortalized in De Quincey's brilliant essay, 'Murder considered as one of the Fine Arts'. The point is that this murder was not seen in isolation: it was a symptom of society's malaise. As De Quincey put it, 'It would be absolutely impossible adequately to describe the frenzy of feelings which, throughout the next fortnight, mustered the popular heart,—the mere delirium of indignant horror in some, the mere delirium of panic in others...' Interestingly, he mentions Southey by name: 'Southey, I may add, entered deeply into the public feeling on this occasion, and said to me, within a week or two of the first murder, that it was a private event of that order which rose to the dignity of a national event.' Just as intriguingly, in describing the mass horror and excitement, De Quincey quotes from Shelley's *Revolt of Islam*, to make the point that there is something 'rapturous' about this 'whirlpool' of revolution, vengeance, and destruction. And once that connection is made, we can easily think of *Thalaba the Destroyer*, with all its connotations of violence and freedom. In his *Apologia*, Newman saw in *Thalaba* a means of deliverance by the few rather than the many: 'I began to think I had a mission.'[49]

Catholicism would bring down the establishment, in Southey's view: 'You know I am neither a bigot, nor a hypocrite', he assured Wynn, who might conceivably have wondered. To Southey it was very much as though the chickens were coming home to roost (ironically, in view of his motto for *The Curse of Kehama*, 'Curses are like young chicken, they always come home to roost'); he had warned in *Espriella*, and in the *Edinburgh Annual Register*, what the consequences would be of the 'sinking-down of Jacobinism from the middle to the lower ranks'. It was only the army that saved the country from 'Jacquerie'. There was no adequate leader left: Lord Liverpool had not 'audacity', Wellesley was too 'sensual', but that was where Southey pinned his hopes, provided Wellesley was supported by Canning, Huskisson, and Mackintosh. Southey's fear of concessions to the Catholics, and to the Irish generally, was stronger than ever; just as bad was the likelihood of the sale of tithes to bring in money for the Government.[50] If he felt able to tell Danvers that he did not think the country was in any real danger, because, although the people might look forward to 'a second reign of Jack Cade',[51] the Government would in fact be strengthened by the more general popular alarm, none the less he was in no doubt about his own preferred remedies: the press must be curbed, and as for the Luddites, 'I would hang about a score...& send off ship loads to Botany Bay'.[52] He would even suspend habeas corpus. The death of Perceval had reduced him to impotent tears, and just as he had lamented the past of his childhood, he now mourned the loss of the country's past, albeit in ambiguous terms: 'The proudest days of England are to come, but her happiest days, in my inmost heart I fear, are over.' Not for the first time in his life, Portugal became a place where he would hope to escape to, if necessary (again, with the ironic qualification that he would have to be a Catholic). His depression increased as he pondered the conundrum at the heart of his beliefs: on the one hand, he had to acknowledge the gulf between himself and the establishment, because he could not believe in the 'plenary inspiration of the Scriptures'; on the other hand, the greatest calamity would be the overthrow of the Church establishment.[53] Furthermore, the repeal of the Test Acts, which he had never been able to subscribe to, would simply let in more Catholics, and invite more Dissenters. As for men like Cobbett and Hunt, who spoke on behalf of the people, they were 'poison'.[54] In the *Quarterly Review* in June 1812 he had talked about the French Revolution, and just as twenty years earlier he had spoken of the need for a 'revolution in mind', so he now spoke of an 'epidemic of the mind as well as of the body; the revolutionary fever of France was a complaint of a violent and deadly type'. The star that had risen over France was not that of liberty; the storm was not yet over, the ship 'still far from port'.[55]

Amidst all this potential turmoil, Southey learnt that, despite the best efforts of Wynn, Lord Lonsdale, Canning, and Sir George Beaumont, the post of Historiographer Royal had gone, on the death of Dutens, to Stanier Clarke, for whom Southey had scant regard. But, as he awaited a revolution in the Church, to be followed by one in the country, and looked on as America began to stir up more trouble across the Atlantic, he turned, as so often in the summer months, to the consolations of family and friends. Greta Hall had been recoated with rough-cast, and a new slate roof had been put on. There was talk of Mary Barker coming to live opposite in an 'ugly house' which might be up for letting; Danvers was to come in mid-June, and the Coleridge boys were on holiday, which was a mixed blessing: 'Hartley is grown a great fellow, all beard & eyes,—as odd & as extraordinary as ever he was, with very good disposition, but with ways & tendencies which will neither be to his own happiness nor to the comfort of anybody connected with him. Derwent, contrary to all former appearance, is much weaker in body; he is very tractable...' Herbert Southey, of course, was as sweet and loveable as ever.[56]

But Southey did not find it easy to throw off his general sense of anxiety, especially when he felt that no one else was fully aware of the dangers. He likened the present situation to the yellow fever that had swept through Portugal when he was last there, and how everyone had blithely gone about their business (a similar conjunction of imagery was to present itself in the 1830s). In such circumstances, when Canning hinted, among other possibilities, that Southey might become Governor of Botany Bay, the author of the Botany Bay Eclogues of the 1790s saw no irony in the suggestion, and only turned it down because Edith was not too keen on such a radical change of scenery. One of his main regrets about not getting the post of Historiographer was that Clarke was a 'most extraordinary blockhead', and therefore unsuited to put the case for the country's calamitous situation in the pages of the *Quarterly Review*;[57] Southey would do what he could, but the official position would have lent weight to his voice. As if further to prove his historical credentials, his *Life of Nelson* would soon be in the press.

In July, after tramping about 400 miles around the countryside, he settled down to write the next volume of the *Edinburgh Annual Register*, which would keep him away from London for the time being. He was cheered by the fact that a third edition of *The Curse of Kehama* might soon be called for: the first two editions would have made him about £260, which was considerably more than *Madoc*. But Gifford was once again at work with the blue pencil, mutilating Southey's essay on the French Revolution in the *Quarterly Review*, and managing to give the impression that Southey had approved of Pitt;[58] the *Edinburgh Annual Register* included part of his 'History of Brazil', consisting of the life of Lope de Aguirre, which became something of a celebrated piece of Southey's biographical prose. He began to think more about writing a *Life of Wesley*; reviewing d'Israeli's *Calamities of Authors* for the September number of the *Quarterly Review* encouraged him to think more of his own possible Memoirs, which would be a sign of his own importance in the world of letters; certainly when Lord Somerville called in October, Southey felt not just the honour, but the underlying justice of it.[59] Although a third edition of *Madoc* had been a sloppy affair, badly printed with worn-out type, he decided to prepare a new edition of *Joan of Arc*, 'weeded' of its grosser errors.[60] He could only defend the poem as the work of a young man: 'to make it what it ought to be would be a labour equivalent to that of writing a new poem.' He was to feel the same when he reissued all his works in 1837–8; but it is interesting that at this particular juncture in his career he felt no qualms about reviving the revolutionary work of his younger days.

As 'Pelayo', now transmogrified into *Roderick*, progressed, Southey felt increasingly pleased with it, convinced that it was 'unlike anything attempted yet in prose or rhyme'.[61] This confidence might seem to us sadly misplaced (although Byron, intriguingly, was not to think so), and we might conjecture that Southey was not able to separate the poem from the historical events which he thought it mirrored. When Bedford suggested that Southey write a history of the Peninsular War, he was more than eager to take up the challenge. He would allow himself another twelve months to finish *Roderick*, but this of course was on the assumption—reasonable enough—that he would be engaged in half a dozen other things at the same time. (He was rather sour to learn that Scott had received an advance of £3,000 for *his* next poem, but Southey was never in that commercial league.[62]) He began an article for Murray on the poor, 'to set off what has been done, & is doing towards the improvement of the lower orders & bettering their condition, against the wretched generalities of the legislators'.[63] Southey's heart, then, was still in the right place. He was by no means the blind supporter of the establishment at home, any more than he could put faith in Wellington's generals. More hope was to be found in the way Russia conducted itself towards Napoleon.

Another daughter, Isabel, was born on 2 November; the next day he wrote to Bedford, asking for money. In spite of the added burden, he was delighted to be a father again: 'the more the merrier', he exclaimed to Wynn, who had recently become a father himself.[64] Southey wrote in high spirits to Mary Barker, saying he wanted more cheese, and more panta-loons.[65] There was talk of introducing Andrew Bell's educational system into every army regiment, and Southey felt able to bask in at least some of the credit for this. Within a couple of days he was celebrating Guy Fawkes night: his two older girls were at a ball, and the nurse was spinning in the room where Edith lay with their new daughter.[66]

Once General Peachey left in mid-November, Southey donned his leather jerkin, and prepared for the winter. There was plenty of work to be done: another article on Malthus for the *Quarterly*, more history, more on Nelson. He turned to his brother Tom for advice on naval details: as he said, frankly enough, 'I walk among sea terms as a cat goes in a china pantry, in bodily fear of doing mischief, & betraying myself; & yet there will come a good book of it, I verily believe.'[67] Southey's confidence, as it turned out, was well placed. And whilst he was writing about England's naval hero, he rejoiced in Napoleon's retreat from Moscow, for he saw in it not just the deliverance of Russia, but the 'probable deliverance of Eur-ope'.[68] But he cursed Wellington's tactics at Burgos, which meant the loss of an obvious opportunity of delivering Spain; it was also a loss of face for Britain, and Southey found this just as hard to take.

But although there was plenty of work to be done, a winter cold followed by sickness held him up over the New Year. He gave John May a report on domestic events, which is both perceptive and touching: Isabel was well, Herbert was precociously pursuing his Greek studies.

No child ever promised better, morally & intellectually. He is very quick of comprehension, retentive, observant, diligent, & as fond of a book & as impatient of idleness as I am. Would that I were as well satisfied with his bodily health; but in spite of activity & bodily hilarity, he is pale & puny: just that kind of child of whom old women would say that he is too clever to live.

Southey's uneasiness about human frailty finds another outlet: for he sees in Herbert what he himself had been, and would be: Herbert was to be his successor. 'I must sow the seed as carefully as if I were sure that the harvest would ripen.' There is something dreadfully premonitory about that conditional. Bertha, on the other hand, 'grows like Jonah's gourd', whilst Katharine remained dwarf-like, 'round as a mushroom-button. Bertha, the bluff Queen, is just as grave as Kate is garrulous; they are inseparable play-fellows, & go about the house hand in hand.'[69]

Southey told Scott on 13 January 1813 that he felt he was dissipating his energies, and that he must get on with his History of Portugal; periodical work was getting in the way. Once again, the brevity of life obsessed him.[70] His attempts to comfort his friend Dr Gooch in the loss of two of his children were in the vein he had developed over the years for his own losses: 'the evening becomes more delightful than the morning, & the sunset offers brighter & lovelier visions than those which we build up in the morning clouds, & which disappear before the strength of the day.'[71] Wordsworth would have been pleased to know his own more complex statement of such a view, in his 'Ode: Intimations of Immortality', could offer the consolation Southey clearly derived from it. But he was also anxious to enjoy the mild winter, taking the exercise he knew, now, to be essential to his well-being; his children would set off with him before breakfast, 'for the sake of getting the first sunshine on the mountains.— which when the snow is on them is more glorious than at any other season'. He wrote to Wynn on 17 January:

Yesterday I think I heard the Wild Swan; & this morning had the finest sight of wild fowl I ever beheld, there was a cloud of them above the lake, at such a height, that frequently they became invisible; then twinkled into sight again, sometimes spreading like smoke as it ascends, then contracting as if performing some military evolution. Once they formed a perfect bow; & thus wheeling & changing, & rising & falling they continued to sport as long as I could watch them. They were probably wild ducks.[72]

This passage reinforces what was becoming increasingly clear to Southey: he needed the landscape of the Lakes as much as did Wordsworth—or perhaps more pertinently, as much as did Dorothy Wordsworth. He had a similar ability to lose himself in what he saw, without feeling any need to point a moral, whilst the wider world spun apparently out of control. As the storms of February gave way to 'the loveliest month of March I ever remember', the whole family began to clatter about the place in Cumberland clogs; quite why it took them ten years to adopt the 'wisest of fashions' is a mystery, as it was indeed to the usually fashion- and weather-conscious Southey.[73]

He was glad to hear that Coleridge's Play *Remorse*, which had opened in January 1813, had had some success: it actually brought in £400. 'Better late than never', said Southey. His own *Roderick* was not likely to achieve such popularity. 'It is in too deep a strain of passion to become popular till the opinion of the few shall become that of the many... Perhaps my marketable reputation even now is high enough for me to write verse with as much emolument as prose.'[74] A week after this he was saying that he only wrote verse for the sake of pleasing a handful of people; and, in any case, 'Composition, where any passion is called forth, excites me more than it is desirable to be excited.' Since passion was the very thing he was claiming for *Roderick*, he found himself having to slow down. As he had said more than once before, he had lost the ardour of his youth: this meant that he should write less poetry, but equally that he must deride those who called for peace: 'Let us remember Utrecht', he cried, '& not suffer the Whigs of this day to outdo the villainy of the Tories of that.'[75] It also meant he was conscious of where the real danger to the country lay: the ignorance of the poor, the manufacturing system, and the Anarchist Journalists, as he called Cobbett and his friends. What he seems to have been unaware of were the contradictions beneath this particular trinity.

As soon as *Nelson* was finished, Southey wanted to start on a work, 'with some such title as the Age of George III', in which he would trace the revolutions of the last half-century, and if comparisons were to be made with Voltaire, so much the better. He would draw on what had already appeared in the *Quarterly*, and easily envisaged three or four octavo volumes.[76] This was certainly work of a different order of magnitude to the *Life of Nelson*, in itself a rather strange piece, in that, whilst being largely derivative, and starting out as a review of the *Life* by James Stanier Clarke and John McArthur, it has attained something of mythic status in the history of English prose. Southey intended it as a 'manual for the young sailor, which he may carry about with him, till he has treasured up the example in his memory and in his heart'. It is, self-confessedly, a 'eulogy', Southey's answer to Wordsworth's poetical paean. There are the famous set pieces, in particular, of course, the death of Nelson, where Southey's clean prose assists the sense of dramatic tragedy. What is of particular interest is Southey's clear identification with his hero: Nelson's last words, repeated until he dies, could almost stand as Southey's own wished-for epitaph: 'Thank God, I have done my duty!' Southey admired Nelson's self-belief, his confidence that, 'though his judgment might be erroneous, under all circumstances he was right in having formed it'. Nelson wrote to Sir Alexander Ball, 'When I call to remembrance all the circumstances, I approve, if nobody else does, of my own conduct.' What might have started out as another piece of task-work, another review for the *Quarterly*, became both a national rallying cry—in itself of some importance—and a portrait of the kind of man he would have liked to be. It is perhaps not surprising that after such an apologia, however disguised, he should want to turn to something more encyclopedic, recalling perhaps the kind of broad sweep he had covered in those Bristol lectures of 1795. Nothing came of this plan, but ten years later his *Colloquies* were to appear, and in 1832 many of his most important contributions to the *Quarterly* would appear in two handsome volumes. Southey was partly dissuaded from the new work by Murray, who proposed at the end of March something more along the lines of 'A View of the World'. But events in Parliament were moving rapidly to convince Southey that revolution was just around the corner: he even chastized Wynn, for contributing to the destruction of the Church of England; the Methodists would undermine the Church, and the loss of liberty could not be long delayed. Southey's own attitude to liberty was scarcely liberal: those who engaged in seditious libel should be transported: there was no other 'effectual cure'.[77]

He corresponded with Rickman about the relationship between manufacturing industries and poverty: Southey had, up until now, promulgated the view that industry directly contributed to poverty, but he now began to harken to Rickman's contrary views. As for the Catholics, he wished, rather perversely, that Perceval had given them what it was 'right & proper they should have'; he certainly did not like seeing the Government capitulating to them now. The more he thought of Murray's suggestion for some grand overview, the more it appealed to him:

No man has ever taken more interest than I have done in looking back into the history of the human race, or in looking forward to their amelioration, & collecting the light of the past as in the focus of a mirror, to fly it before me that I may see into the future . . . what I propose is not the history of the Age, but the philosophy of that history: having all the results of research but none of the form of it— dealing rather with causes & consequences than with events, culling the flowers of events to illustrate, & elucidate, & enliven, & adorn, & extracting their essential spirit to be the life of the book.[78]

Because of these grand plans, he did not think he would get to London before the autumn. He began to sort out his finances, asking Bedford to add another 200 3 per cents to the 100 he already had;[79] but when he asked Ballantyne for £50, saying he was owed another £175 on top of that, Ballantyne wrote back in May to say he owed Southey nothing. Southey wrote a heated letter to Ballantyne's brother, severing his links with the *Register*.[80] This meant, of course, a loss of income, so that the History of

Portugal once again became of major importance, and he would have to go to London earlier than he had planned, in order to look at Walpole's papers. He would even recast the Spanish part of the *Register* into a separate volume about the Peninsular War.

Accordingly, he would travel to London through Leeds and Sheffield (where he wanted to see the poet James Montgomery) and Coleorton, where he would call on Sir George Beaumont. But there was more delay, as his wife's brother, George Fricker, was mortally ill in Greta Hall with consumption. On 27 June his brother-in-law was buried. Rather callously, Southey's main concern was that his History should get off the ground, before his old enemy Stanier Clarke stepped into the breach.[81] It was with some relief that he heard on 23 July that Murray was offering 1,000 guineas for two quartos, to be completed in eighteen months: Southey calculated that he should earn £800 in 1814.[82] *Roderick* immediately seemed less of a burden, especially when Scott cast his eye over it and said that he liked it; there was no doubt about it, it was far better than Scott's rather feeble poem on the same theme. A week before he was finally ready to leave Keswick for London, at the end of August, he wrote to Bedford, reminding him of the Shandean *magnum opus* that would one day appear as *The Doctor*. 'I have great hopes for Dr Daniel Dove... It is to be *The Book*.'[83] What he could scarcely have foreseen was that, before another month was out, Sir Walter Scott would be offering him the Poet Laureateship. Less pleasing news was a sighting by Wynn of his reprobate brother Edward, apparently married and a member of a company of strolling players.[84] As so often with Southey's life, the sublime and the ridiculous were not far apart.

When the Poet Laureate Henry Pye died, Southey fully expected Scott to take on the mantle: 'tho it may not be desirable to have it, it would not be decorous to refuse it.'[85] But Scott was quick to suggest that in fact the post should go to Southey, and Southey confided to Bedford that he had expected such a turn of events. It is also true that Scott made it quite clear that he did not want the job: 'I should make a bad courtier and an ode-maker is described by Pope as a poet out of his way or out of his senses.' When he wrote to Southey, however, he assured him that he did not decline the post out of any sense of its absurdity. 'Long may you live, as Paddy says, to rule over us, and to redeem the crown of Spenser and of Dryden to its pristine dignity.' There seems to have been a certain amount of confusion about the precise chain of events; apparently the Prince Regent was not too pleased to hear that Lord Liverpool had approached Scott in the first instance, and he observed that Southey had written 'some good things in favour of the Spaniards'. Another version of events had

Croker suggesting Southey as a likely candidate. There is no doubt that Scott wrote to Southey in the following terms: 'I am not such an ass as not to know that you are my better in poetry though I have had probably but for a time the tide of popularity in my favour.' His royalties would have borne this out. Southey promptly wrote to Croker, saying he would accept the office, provided he was 'at liberty to write upon great public events or to be silent as the spirit moves,—but not if the regular routine be exacted . . . if it be given me on these terms, whatever ridicule may be directed toward me at present, the office will be redeemed from it for ever more.'[86]

From our perspective, it might now seem odd that Southey was lined up as Pye's successor; it would certainly be unduly cynical to suggest that one nonentity was being replaced by another. There is no doubt at all about the place that Southey held in the poetic galaxy at this particular juncture. Keats, of course, was still to announce himself as a public poet; 1813 saw the publication of Shelley's *Queen Mab*, but all his important work lay in the future; Blake, notoriously, was known to very few (it is always a surprise to be reminded that even Shelley seems not to have read Blake). Wordsworth and Coleridge both occupied slightly odd positions: after *Lyrical Ballads*, Coleridge had not published much poetry, and his public persona was very much as a prose writer; Wordsworth had written a lot, but it was not until the following year that he would announce, with *The Excursion*, the boldness of his poetic ambitions (only his close friends knew of the existence of *The Prelude*). One name on most people's lips was that of Byron: his brilliant satire *English Bards and Scotch Reviewers* of 1809 had been followed in 1812 by the first two cantos of *Childe Harold's Pilgrimage*, a poem that earned him immediate fame; *The Giaour* and *The Bride of Abydos* of the following year (the year the Laureateship became vacant) furthered what was almost a frenzy, a frenzy that continued until 1816, when the third canto of *Childe Harold's Pilgrimage* appeared, but when the tales of scandal that had surrounded him for so long finally drove him out of the country to exile in Italy. For all the popularity and adulation, Byron was not, nor could he ever be, a candidate for the Laureateship; his satire depended on that very aloofness celebrated in the Turkish tales. Critics could be as scornful of his work as they were of Wordsworth's. Other poets of the time were quite popular, but hardly more than that: Erasmus Darwin, Mary Tighe, Mary Robinson, Thomas Moore, Charlotte Smith, Felicia Hemans, Thomas Campbell, Samuel Rogers, Anna Seward, Anna Letitia Barbauld, James Montgomery— none of these could be said then, or now, to have scaled many heights. George Crabbe was an unusual case, in that his *Tales in Verse* (1812) can now be seen as a major volume of the period, and even at the time it earned a fair degree of public acclamation; but he was also seen as something of an anachronism, reworking the Popean heroic couplet when most writers had bade it farewell. Scott and Southey were the two writers who were widely read, were in the public eye, were able to point to substantial poems, and were also—and this is obviously important, irrespective of their other claims—on the side of the Government: they were established and establishment figures. So, if not Scott, then Southey.

Southey began to prepare for the visit to court, where he would have to dress up in all his finery, including a sword and ruffles. This would be the social highlight of a visit to London that was already becoming fairly hectic, with dinners here and there: Herries, the Gonnes, John Stoddart, John May, Neville White, Croker, Longman, John Coleridge (the nephew), Bedford, and Wynn; he even met John Lack, the uncle of Edward's supposed wife, and learnt that she was scarcely better than her 'husband'. He was happy to see Coleridge looking better than he had ever seen him, and apparently no longer taking opium. He met Madame de Staël, even Lord Byron, which turned out to be a pleasant surprise: 'I saw a man whom in voice, manner & countenance I liked very much more than either his character or his writings had given me reason to expect.' May was to help him fix up insurance to the value of £3,000; the prospect of a new printing of *Espriella* and, possibly, a quarto edition of *Roderick* helped to confirm his sense of increasing value. He could see the funny side, but also the potential significance, of the fact that his appointment would date from 12 August—his own birthday, and that of the Prince Regent.

Amidst all this excitement, he heard the story of the 'Three Bears' from George Nicholls (a poor law reformer, a friend of the engineer Telford, and an important figure in Birmingham), for which *The Doctor* was to be famous, if for nothing else; Southey immediately made the connection between the bears and his Hill nephews.[87] Nicholls was, in 1837, to retell the story in verse, making quite clear the connection between his verses and Southey's prose:

> Unknown Author of 'The Doctor,'
> Great, original Concoctor
> Of the rare story of the Bears,
> Their porridge-pots, their beds and chairs,
> Which you with condescending pen,
> To please 'Good little women and men,'
> Have writ—I pray you to excuse
> The freedom of my rhyming muse,

> For having ventured to rehearse
> This tale of yours in jingling verse;
> But fearing in your book it might
> Escape some little people's sight,
> I did not like that one should lose
> What will them all so much amuse.

The initials 'G. N.' not only half-conceal Nicholls's authorship; they also help to explain his anxiety lest the story remain unknown. It was, for a long time, assumed that Southey was the 'onlie begetter' of this tale; but a version exists in manuscript, dated 1831, told by an Eleanor Mure, 'The Story of The Three Bears, metrically related', and described as a 'celebrated nursery tale'. There are variations, as we would expect in any such tale, and the Opies point to German and Norwegian analogues. What seems to have happened is that Southey heard the tale, as he reports, from Nicholls, and produced a version that became so well known that it was thought to be all his own work, as it were. But within twelve years of its publication, his severely moral version, with the intruder an old woman escaped from 'the House of Correction', was softened by Joseph Cundall, in his *Treasury of Pleasure Books for Young Children*: the old woman became a young girl with 'silver hair', and by the end of the century, 'Goldilocks'. There is some irony in the fact that this slight tale should be, for many people, their only acquaintance with the works of Robert Southey.

The Laureateship was not quite so simple a matter as he had expected, and Southey had to exercise his patience whilst the details were sorted out: until there was final confirmation, he could not do much else. Surely the authorities must realize, he told Mary Barker on 8 October, that, 'in accepting the office, I am conferring a favour rather than receiving one'.[88] It is not entirely clear that the authorities saw things in quite this light. However, as he languished in London, missing the family and Keswick, sitting for a bust done by Frederick Smith, he eventually heard from Croker on 16 October that he was to attend a royal levee the following week. He was duly sworn in at the Chamberlain's Office on 4 November. He was moved to write a poem celebrating his elevation, and wrote to Scott to assure him that there should be no rivalry between them as a result of this business: 'There has been no race, we have both got to the top of the hill by different paths, & meet there not as rivals but as friends, each rejoicing in the success of the other!'[89] Scott might have felt Southey protested too much. Hazlitt was less sanguine on 18 September 1813; after giving the details of the political intrigue, as he saw it, behind the appointment, he declared, 'To *have been* the poet of the people, may not render Mr. Southey less a court favourite; and one of his old Sonnets to Liberty must give a peculiar zest to his new Birth-day Odes. His flaming patriotism will easily subside into the gentle flow of grateful loyalty; and the most extravagant of his plans of reform end in building castles in Spain!'[90]

Southey wasted little time: he left the levee at 4.00 p.m., and was booking, at 5.15, his place on the coach for the following evening; he dined that night with his old friend, the doctor Robert Gooch (whom he had first met in Edinburgh in 1805). He was only too glad to be back by his own fireside by mid-November, and tickled pink to have a letter from the composer Sir William Parsons, addressed to him as Poet Laureate, and offering to set his next Laureate Ode to music. Southey set to immediately, with a poem attacking Napoleon and calling for vengeance in his best blood-thirsty manner; he held little store by it, saying that, 'good or bad, it will be but a weeks wonder'. He planned further such pieces, including some inscriptions to commemorate the Peninsular War, and an epistle to the Prince.[91] But whatever his euphoria, he soon confronted the fact that financially he was not as secure as his new position might suggest: the loss of the *Edinburgh Annual Register* income was a blow, and at the end of November he was having to ask Bedford for money. Scott expressed his sympathy that the Laureateship only brought in £26, which was, insultingly, taxable. The problem was that it was not just his own family he was having to support: there were the blind mouths of the Coleridge tribe. Sara Coleridge was trying to support herself and her three children on £75 a year, and her pleas to her husband seemed to fall on deaf ears.[92]

Josiah Wedgwood was stopping his half of the annuity for Coleridge, news which filled Sara with understandable despair. On the other hand, Coleridge was giving a successful series of lectures at the Surrey Institution, and he had sent £100 of the £400 from *Remorse* up to Keswick; unfortunately his Bristol friend John Morgan, who had been helping Coleridge fight his opium addiction, was declared bankrupt, and Coleridge gave the rest of the money to the Morgan family. His plan to return to Keswick disintegrated, and he succumbed in Bristol to opium: he even began to think that his only chance of survival was to be taken into an asylum, and Cottle encouraged him by suggesting a subscription to this end. But Southey would have none of it. 'This, Cottle, is an insanity which none but the Soul's physician can cure.' Sara Coleridge realized how dependent she was on Southey, who was willing to pay the rent and taxes on Greta Hall, but who thereby gained some kind of control over her. What had been her home had become Southey's, as she waited in desperation to hear from her husband. After all, Hartley's future had to be decided; and yet, as she wrote to Poole, 'You will be shocked to hear that I never hear from C.' She turned, reluctantly but with due gratitude, to all the help Wordsworth and Southey could offer. Southey approved of a subscription to help Hartley to go up to Oxford in a year's time.[93]

Peace with France was about to be declared. Southey was in two minds about this, which is not surprising given his fierce opposition to peace unless it was on the right terms, and the recall of the Bourbons did certainly not constitute, for him, the right terms. He had written to Rickman at the end of November, recalling his own earlier championing of the French Revolution: 'I see as you do, & surely have often expressed, that the whirlwind of the Revolution was necessary to clear away the pestilence of the old Governments—& think as you do that in the moral government of the world & of the Universe general results are those which are contemplated;—& that to these individuals, species & nations will sometimes be sacrificed.' There speaks the true revolutionary, which helps to explain his doubts about the prospective peace: as he said two weeks later, whatever the evils of the French revolution, 'the feelings which occasioned their [the Bourbons'] expulsion were far nobler than those which would bring about their restoration'.[94]

Southey's confusions were worse confounded when he realized that his first Laureate Ode might present political problems, and that he might have to suppress anything that was less than flattering to Bonaparte. Sure enough, his poem was duly edited by Croker and Barrow; the *Carmen Triumphale*, he angrily told Bedford, should be renamed the Carmen Castratum or Damnatum, and used for toilet paper.[95] He said he would get the whole poem printed in the *Courier*, 'before it becomes a libellous offence to call murder & tyranny by their proper names'.[96] Much to Hazlitt's amusement, the poem duly appeared in full on 3 February 1814. It included accounts of particular acts of torture and murder allegedly carried out by Napoleon, in connection with which the more cautious and politic Rickman had advised: what if peace were to be made with Napoleon, and he 'becomes a *friendly Power*—can you stay in office, this Carmen remaining on record? . . . I think you should identify yourself very much with the government. Be as ample in praise as you please, but do not treat an enemy as though never to become a friend. If you did not know me for as desperate an antigallican as yourself (I wish the French one neck & a hatchet in my hand) I should not have spoken so freely of official reserve towards this.'[97] Southey was not interested in such wary treading of the diplomatic line: he was outraged that Britain was actually negotiating 'with this Tyrant!', whose proper end should have been at the hands of the French ages ago. But if Burke had not been able to persuade the British to act according to principle, what hope was there? In his despair, Southey wrote, 'everything which is fashionable in England tends to dwarf the intellect, to deaden the feelings & debilitate the race'. He was convinced that Napoleon would soon be back; and all Britain could do was to console itself with classical education, Shakespeare, and the Bible (and even these had all been perverted and distorted). Southey's violence of spirit was mirrored in the violence of his language. So much for the joys of being Poet Laureate; it was more than a matter of being the 'best-drest Poet in Christendom'.[98]

Southey was still having to contend with his wretched brother, whose 'marriage' had turned out to be bogus, and whose plans to join an acting company were therefore abruptly halted. From Southey's point of view, apart from the embarrassment, financial and otherwise, the worst thing about it all was that he had a brother without any conception of the truth. Meanwhile, Coleridge was mooting plans for starting a school, and Southey was trying to dissuade him. Rather like Edward, Coleridge could no longer be trusted. Southey thought it preferable for him to buckle down and get some more money with his pen, thereby earning enough at least to pay Hartley's bills. His own eldest child had had scarlet fever, followed by croup—sufficient to engender further fears in Southey's already nervous mind.[99]

He was also having to cope with Hazlitt's attack, in the *Morning Chronicle*, on his 'thundering' Ode in the *Courier*; as he had predicted, the Laureateship made him an easy target. Hazlitt had written on 8 January 1814 that the Ode was in the ballad style 'peculiar to Mr. Southey and his poetical friends'; it 'exhibits the irregular vigour of Jacobin enthusiasm suffering strange emasculation under the hands of a finical lord-chamberlain. It is romantic without interest, and tame without elegance.'[100] In other words, just what might be expected from Robert Southey; and, it should be said, it is not one of his happier efforts, as he tries out his hand at the public posture:

> In happy hour doth he receive
> The Laurel, meed of famous Bards of yore,
> Which Dryden and diviner Spenser wore
> In happy hour, and well may he rejoice,
> Whose earliest task must be
> To raise the exultant hymn for victory,
> And join a nation's joy with harp and voice,
> Pouring the strain of triumph on the wind,
> Glory to God, his song, Deliverance for Mankind!

At least *The* Times liked it: 'side winds of this kind are very useful.'[101] But in defending himself in a letter to Wynn he did not suppose

that one who has never feared to speak his opinions sincerely, can have any fear of being confronted with his former self? I was a republican; I should be so still, if I thought we were advanced enough in civilization for such a form of society;—the more my feelings, my judgment, my old prejudices might incline me that way, the deeper would necessarily be my hatred of Bonaparte.[102]

He derived both amusement and gratification from the fact that the *Anti-Jacobin* regarded his *Life of Nelson* as 'infected with the leaven of Jacobinism'. For his own sake, it was a pity that he did not spell things out in his own exoneration in public quite as clearly as he did in his private correspondence; he would have been spared much of the hostility he attracted by his apparently haughty indifference to what others thought. Perhaps there was some private significance in the fact that, at the same time, he was writing a chapter for *The Doctor* about the second fall of Eve: she ate of the forbidden vegetable, the potato.[103] This was not just a diversion for the severe winter, when the snow kept him indoors (his newly acquired clogs could cope with dirt but not with snow);[104] to some extent he had indeed fallen himself.

Roderick was in press, but its writing had cost Southey more than he would have wished: he could not write at a young man's pace any more. Although he was pleased with the poem, thinking of it as some kind of cathartic tragedy, and as representing his maturity, he pursued the logic of that to its conclusion: 'in all things the stage next beyond maturity is decay.' It is sometimes hard to believe that Southey was quite the merry fellow he liked to claim. However, now that this poem was out of the way, he looked forward to getting on with his poems about Oliver Goffe (later Newman) and Robin Hood, even with the Persian or Runic romance he had promised himself as part of his grand plan to cover every great mythological tradition in verse. Not even headache or stomach ache— 'Magnesia, heavenly Maid,—is at the moment playing upon my bowels as on a bag-pipe'—could deter him.[105]

The title-page of *Roderick, The Last of the Goths* announced that the author was not only Poet Laureate, but also 'Member of the Royal Spanish Academy'.[106] This emphasizes the political nature of the poem, reminding the reader very forcibly of Scott's *Vision of Don Roderick* (1811), which was dedicated 'To the Committee of subscribers for relief of the Portugueze sufferers'. Both Scott, and after him Landor, with *Count Julian*, were fully conscious that their poems were political statements about Spain over 'the several periods brought upon the stage'. The historical episode on which all these poems are based reaches back into the eighth century, with the defeat of Roderick, last Gothic King of Spain, by the invading Moors. Scott and Southey both resort to the device of visions, comparable in some ways to Blake's extraordinary use of dreams and visions in *Europe*, whereby the whole of the revolutionary upheavals of Europe are foreshadowed by Enitharmon's opening dream, which links the birth of Christ to that of Orc. Neither Scott nor Southey can match Blake, but in Scott's case it could be argued that a not particularly distinguished poem is held together by its ambitious structural device, whereby Roderick foresees the 'unparalleled treachery of B U O N A P A R T E', but also Spain's freedom regained by the 'arrival of the British succours'.

Southey's poem is longer, and harking back to *Madoc*, uses a serviceable blank verse far removed from the highly wrought embellishments of *Thalaba* and *The Curse of Kehama*. It is a strange poem, overlong (like so much of Southey's work); although he could persuade himself that it was the best thing he would ever do, he did not hold out much hope for its success, partly because he felt he did not have enough detailed knowledge of the costume of the age (the typical anxiety of a Southey who could not believe that costumes do not an epic make). But, more importantly, he wanted to achieve a 'mature style' which 'aims at nothing but to express in pure English what I have to say: & I profess nothing but to avoid the barbarisms & nonsense which have so long past current in verse'. He thought that he and Wordsworth were the only two modern writers who actually wrote English, as against Byron, Campbell, and the Scott to whom he was more complimentary when addressing him personally. But after such a claim, he was quite disconcertingly ready to admit to Bedford that 'the sense may be worthless, but it is not *nonsense*'. *Roderick*, he confessed, as a way out of yet another dilemma, was '*sui generis*. Its character deeply tragical,—but every where rather of an elevating than a distressing nature.'[107]

There is certainly an elevated tone about much of the poem, however convoluted the plot (not helped by Southey's own prefatory summary of the story so far, as it were, which borders on the comical); Southey wears his Christian imagery with pride in a poem that has to come to terms with the familiar themes of Vengeance, Treason, and Violence. If it works, it is partly because Southey's verse more often than not rises to the occasion:

> Too soon
> The gales of Spain from that unhappy land
> Wafted, as from an open charnel-house,
> The taint of death; and that bright Sun, from fields

> Of slaughter, with the morning dew drew up
> Corruption through the infected atmosphere.

He can combine an effective 'descriptive' kind of verse with something more like Shelley:

> hope
> Upon the shadow of futurity
> Shone like the sun upon the morning mists,
> When driven before his rising rays they roll,
> And melt and leave the prospect bright and clear.

The poem is about apostasy; more than once he scoffs at 'renegades' who have been responsible for all the poem's havoc; against such tumult is the central point:

> But where the cement of authority
> Is wanting, all things there are dislocate.

However, the 'Mercy' that is so frequently spoken of in the poem turns to savagery; the cry in the final book is 'Roderick and Victory! Roderick and Vengeance!' and the hero, rather like the author, becomes an avenging angel, precisely to reassert that necessary authority. For all the Christian colouring, Roderick is a later manifestation of Thalaba the Destroyer.

On one level, it is understandable that Charles Lamb should have found the poem more 'comfortable' than the wilder *Madoc* or *Curse of Kehama*: 'I have a timid imagination I am afraid. I do not willingly admit of strange beliefs or out of the way creeds or places...'[108] It is true, the poem displays a more timid front to the world. At the same time, it has its underlying political import, allied to Southey's fascination with the very violence he appears to abhor. What this amounts to is that might is right, provided the fight is right.

The proclaimed peace, as Southey had foreseen, proved elusive: Napoleon could not be trusted, and Wellington was insufficiently active. The 'tragedy' was not, after all, in its final act: he lamented to Landor that England had not been firmer in 1808, 'when the Bayonne iniquity was fresh in the feelings of the public'. The Spanish and Portuguese would have sided with the British, and Napoleon would not have survived. Once again, Southey made the connection between the French Revolution and more recent events: 'I used to think that the Revolution would not have done its work, till the Houses of Austria & Bourbon were both destroyed,—a consummation which the history of both Houses has taught me devoutly to wish for.'[109] He could not stomach having to write

a Laureate Ode in celebration of a tenuous peace, and enjoyed himself
with the poem he later prefaced to the *Carmen Nuptiale*, 'a strain of proud
egotism,—putting on the laurel in defiance':[110]

> Praise to that Power who from my earliest days,
>   Thus taught me what to seek and what to shun;
> Who turned my footsteps from the crouded ways,
>   Appointing me my better course to run
> In solitude, with studious leisure blest,
> The mind unfettered, and the heart at rest...
>
> Sometimes I soar where Fancy guides the rein,
>   Beyond this visible diurnal sphere;
> But most with long and self-approving pain,
>   Patient pursue the historian's task severe;
> Thus in the ages which are past I live,
> And those which are to come my sure reward will give...

When the end came—'So it is over,—dating from the destruction of
the Bastille, a tragedy of five & twenty years!'—Southey was scathing
about the way the curtain had finally come down.[111] Bonaparte

ought to have been hunted down & exhibited upon a gibbet dead or alive. Austria
has prevented this, & I dare say the Parisians are even more disappointed than I
am. That amiable people would have delighted in seeing him on the wheel. He will
suffer more in living to hear the execrations of mankind, which will perpetually
keep him in mind of the damnation in store for him. As for the French people—
they have acted up to their character. Frivolity, baseness & unfeeling folly were
never more beautifully exemplified than in the first effusions of the Bourbonized
Monsters. They have found out that B. is a Corsican!... And I dare say that those
Senators who paid their appropriate reverence to the King of Rome are ready to
exclaim what have we kissed his nasty dirty backside & all for nothing![112]

As Southey contemplated a peace that could only be bad—and his son
Herbert wore a white cockade in celebration—he commented, rather
oddly, to May, on the ruin caused by revolution: 'I have derived nothing
but good from it in every thing...'[113] Whatever he meant by this, his
ambiguities were underlined by a pseudonymous letter from Landor to
the *Courier*, in which Landor wrote, and Southey agreed, that this was
now the time to undo all the mischief of the Peace of Utrecht, by stripping
France of Alsace and Lorraine and Franche-Comté. As he said to Scott,
'Much as I had desired this event, & fully as I had expected it, still, when it
came, it brought with it an awful sense of the instability of all earthly
things.'[114] When he saw Byron's 'Ode to Napoleon', published on 16 April
(Byron's complexity of response reflected in a complexity of rhetoric
beyond anything Southey was capable of), he had to acknowledge its

'great life, spirit, & originality'.[115] Credit where credit was due, even for Byron.

Southey's old friend Charles Danvers died on 3 May. As he told Rickman, his death 'will cast a gloom over the recollections of half my life.— The loss of such a man is like an amputation—the wound heals,—but the limb will always be wanting.'[116] A number of Southey's friends had not lived up to their early promise, and they had drifted apart: Coleridge, Collins, Lloyd, Burnett. But Danvers had been a true intimate, someone he had loved and admired unreservedly; the loss was such that he described himself to Cottle as a 'broken reed', and even a year later he found it almost impossible to talk of Danvers. When Bedford's father died in June, Southey turned to his close relationship with Bedford, remembering especially the summer house at Brixton, where he had finished *Joan of Arc* all those years ago: 'If I were to look round the world & ask you what man there is in it whom I should miss the most if he were removed, you would be the man.'[117] Bedford might have read between the lines here: Southey derived some kind of power from people's absence, just as much as from their presence.

Southey wrote odes without rhyme to the Prince Regent, to the Empress and King of Russia; he sent some 'doggerel' to the *Courier* on the 'March to Moscow'. Two of the stanzas of this light piece, written for the entertainment of his children, were suppressed, but he was amused to hear that a few copies of a special edition, 'on white sattin!!', were sent to Russia. He was able to tell Wynn with a certain ambiguous surprise, when he contemplated the amount of verse he was writing, that he was 'almost as desperate a poet as I was twenty years ago'.[118] The 'March to Moscow' recaptures some of that buoyancy associated with his earlier ballads, or his tumbling, headlong poem on the cataract at Lodore.[119]

> The Emperor Nap he would set off
> On a summer excursion to Moscow;
> The fields were green, and the sky was blue,
> Morbleu! Parbleu!
> What a pleasant excursion to Moscow!
>
> Four hundred thousand men and more
> Must go with him to Moscow:
> There were Marshals by the dozen,
> And Dukes by the score;
> Princes a few, and Kings one or two;
> While the fields are so green, and the sky so blue,
> Morbleu! Parbleu!
> What a pleasant excursion to Moscow!

This kind of thing was not, presumably, what Croker and others had had in mind when they decided to offer the Laureateship to Southey.

But to such things he gave little thought, compared to the larger issues that concerned him: as he said to May on 1 July, 'I love to trace the moral order of things in the history of the world.'[120] This sounds well and good, and when he regrets that the British did not insist that the French abolish the slave trade in the Caribbean, he seems to be voicing the enlightened sentiments of his youth. But there is a disturbing shift in his argument, as he turns to the Spanish and Portuguese colonies in South America. In his view, the aborigines of the new world are either like barren fig-trees, to be cut down, or like Canaanites, 'worthy of extermination'.

If the guilt of misery attendant upon such a process be objected, I feel the weight of the objection; but am, at the same time, satisfied that it resolves itself into the great question of the origin of evil; that, comparing it with the good which there is in the world, the evil seems to me as much lost as the filth & impurity of our navigated river is in the sea; that what evil there is is temporary as to individuals, & evanescent as to the species, & that a future state sets all to rights.

Nothing Southey had said, either privately or publicly, had been as shocking as this. Clearly no defence can be offered; as for explanation, one can only assume that the news of incipient revolution in South America, coming so hard on the heels of the end of the tragedy he associated with the French Revolution, filled him with such terror that he was prepared to countenance anything that would prevent another such tragedy: 'if our own Americans were unfit for independence', he argued to Rickman, 'how much more unfit are these!'[121] By a rather similar token, he was about to wash his hands of Coleridge, 'as if he were no longer in existence, or no longer a moral agent'.[122] He had certainly been shocked to read the correspondence between Coleridge and Cottle, especially Coleridge's refusal to acknowledge his dependence on opium. It seems reasonable to suppose that in 1814 the cumulation of events led Southey to an unprecedented intolerance, almost as though he had lost his moral and emotional bearings. Perhaps that is why he spoke of his poetical works of the time as works without passion or pain. When his bust arrived from London, it was smashed to pieces, and would be used as a scarecrow. He gave a pen-portrait of himself in August: 'I am a man of 40; younger in appearance & habits, older in my feelings & frame of mind.'[123]

'BOOKS, CHILDREN, LEISURE'

1814–1819

SOUTHEY's source for Portuguese documents, Manuel Abella, a secret-ary at the Spanish Embassy in London, had dried up (Southey assumed he was in prison), and when George Canning (the Tory who had, in the *Anti-Jacobin* in the 1790s, mercilessly scoffed at Southey and his friends) offered his good offices for similar ends, Southey was delighted: the History was still his main priority, now that the second volume of the *History of Brazil* was ready for the printer, and Koster was at work on a translation into Portuguese of the first volume. He was still perplexed by events in South America, scoffing at the revolutionary government in Buenos Ayres, and the 'wicked conduct of that beast Ferdinand . . . Alas, that the despotism of the old country, & the republicanism (how is that name polluted!) of the new, should be equally blind, equally bloody, & almost equally detestable!'[1] It is as though the whole world had lost its reason: the mad Joanna Southcott had thousands of followers in Britain, the Jesuits had been restored, the Inquisition re-established, whilst the Virgin Mary ruled the roost in France.

Relations with Coleridge hardly reassured him: Southey asked John May to approach Coleridge's brother George. Hartley was getting free schooling in Ambleside, Derwent was having to pay ten guineas; but since they both boarded in the village, Sara's basic allowance was soon whittled away. Lady Beaumont had offered £30 to help Hartley on his way to Oxford; Thomas Poole, Coleridge's friend from the Nether Stowey days, had offered £10.[2] Southey was quite glad to get away from all these worries at the end of September, when he went to spend ten days with Words-worth. On his return he was gratified to hear that he had been elected a member of the Royal Spanish Academy; his *Life of Nelson* was to be translated into Danish, by the very man whose account of the battle of Copenhagen he had heavily drawn on; he started his *Tale of Paraguay*, and there were three volumes of miscellaneous poems in the press. This was all an antidote to his pressing domestic problems, his fears about Coler-idge—'I cannot but apprehend some shameful & dreadful end to this deplorable course'—and his youngest child's sickness.[3] At the start of November he was having to write yet another of his begging letters to Bedford, as Gray's Inn claimed that he still owed them £7. 15s. 8d.[4]

No doubt under the influence of Rickman, Southey started a paper on 'Moral Statistics', to show 'what has been done toward real, practicable radical reform in this country'.[5] Such an essay allowed him to attend to those specific details which the other half of him wanted to avoid by talking in more general, if not theoretical, terms. The more he worked at this theme, the more optimistic he became. Although he felt a growing diminution in his powers—and greying hair and stiffening joints emphasized the point—he seemed, at the end of November, almost bizarrely cheerful. It is hard to see quite where he got his optimism from, in view of what he had been saying not so very long before; nor would it last. But his friend Dr Gooch must have been cheered by Southey's declaration:

I am fully convinced that a gradual improvement is going on in the world, has been going on from its commencement, & will continue till the human race shall attain all the perfection of which it is capable in this mortal state. This belief grows out of knowledge; that is, it is a corollary deduced from the whole history of mankind . . . Oh! if this world of ours were but well cultivated, & weeded well, how like the garden of Eden might it be made![6]

Southey had, at least momentarily, forgotten the number of times he had imagined himself as the fallen Adam, driven from Eden, facing a bleak and pitiless world. Perhaps he thought things were looking up: Hartley Coleridge had got a postmastership at Merton College, Oxford, the *History of Brazil* was nearly off his hands, even Byron said how much he liked *Roderick* (though Southey took the praise with several pinches of salt, in view of his earlier condemnation of *Madoc* and the inapposite comparison with Milton).[7] No wonder Southey could laugh when, having written fifty stanzas of his poem about the forthcoming royal wedding, he heard that the engagement had been called off. His brother Harry, however, was getting married again, this time to Louisa Gonne (he remembered her as a child in arms in Lisbon), whose mother, he confided to Taylor, had been his 'ideal of all that is lovely in female nature'.[8] Presumably Edith was unaware of this.

James Hogg, the Scots poet known as 'The Ettrick Shepherd', friend of Scott and Wordsworth, but best known for his novel *The Confessions of a Justified Sinner*, told Southey towards the end of the year that Jeffrey might be writing about him again in the pages of the *Edinburgh Review*. Hogg was trying to persuade Southey not to rise to the bait, but Southey had never forgiven Jeffrey for his 'Thalabicide', nor for his infamous review of Wordsworth's *Excursion*: 'This will never do!' As Southey put it to Scott, 'He might as well seat himself upon Skiddaw & fancy that he crushed the mountain.' Southey poured out his invective to Bedford: 'The sum of it [is] that I despise Jeffrays commendation, & defy his enmity; that *nettling* is too weak a word for what I have in store for him,—for in due time he shall be scorpioned & rattelsnaked yea served up to the public like a Turkeys gizzard sliced, scored, peppered, salted ... grilled & properly bedevilled.'[9]

Peace with America at the end of the year hardly satisfied a Southey intent on 'honour & vengeance'. His heated rhetoric spilled over from literature to politics and back again; when he bemoaned the lack of a commanding intellect in Britain, he might have been implying he was the man to supply it. But he was disqualified by these sudden rushes to the head, which led him to see things in such apocalyptic terms that reason lost its hold. None the less, his fight against the iniquities of the property tax had been rewarded, even though he regretted that 'it should have been surrendered to a coalition of the mob & the Squirearchy'.[10] This became a recurrent theme, as he dwelt on the idea that 'the fabric of social order in this country is undermined, & we are treading upon gunpowder'. Abroad, things were no better: the talk of possible independence in Italy provoked a brief outburst: 'How admirably the Pope & the French clergy are acting to exemplify the mildness, moderation, & altered principles of the Catholic Church! Oh, these emancipators!'[11] Strangely enough, he was saying a few days later just how quiet life was in Keswick, as though he had not a care in the world: 'The weeks & months pass by as rapidly as an ebb tide.'[12]

Southey's problem was that such placidity was fleeting. Coleridge was still 'the slave of the vilest & most degrading sensuality', and Southey really thought that Coleridge could end up in prison:[13] by this stage, there was little to choose between his erstwhile fellow-Pantisocrat, and his brother Edward. Southey feared that Hartley was likely to turn out too like his father—'he has a disposition to justify whatever he does & whatever he likes to do,—& I fear that metaphysics are bred in the bone in him, like a moral scrofula—'.[14] When he left him off at Merton College, Oxford, he exclaimed to his own brother Harry, 'think of that fish in a Quadrangle', and painted a grotesque picture of the young Hartley running round and round with his head lolling on one side.[15] As he told John Coleridge (Coleridge's nephew), Hartley, 'without being an ugly fellow ... is a marvellously odd one:—he is very short, with remarkably strong features, some of the thickest & blackest eyebrows you ever saw, & a beard which a Turk might envy'.[16] He also had a disturbingly sure sense, not necessarily justified, of his own abilities.

Southey was equally unimpressed by the 'scrape' the Government had
got themselves into over the Corn Bill, which he saw as a likely provocation to the Luddites: 'Was there ever such a blunder as to quarrel with the
people about *Bread*!'[17] After two years' work, a committee of the House of
Commons suggested, in 1815, a sliding scale for the price of corn: a law was
passed prohibiting the import of foreign corn, provided wheat did not
rise above £4 a quarter. Rickman was less sympathetic than Southey to the
plight of the poor, thinking the 'Government too much influenced by the
mob'. In 1832 the Corn Laws, which had provoked such widespread
hostility over the years, were revoked when the first Reform bill was
passed; two years later Southey's last article for the *Quarterly Review*
was to be on 'The Corn Laws', in which he argued for public subsidy for
agriculture, whilst expressing his fears about the consequences for international politics (he was also slightly peeved that his long reference to
Ebenezer Elliott, the Corn Law Rhymer, was deleted). But for the
moment, and not for the first time, he anticipated 'the horrors of a
Jacquerie & Bellum Servile'.[18] The squirearchy were the villains, in that
'they have no right to fix a minimum unless they could consent to a
maximum at the same time'. Sometimes Southey can seem perfectly
reasonable. But, in almost the same breath, he saw events in France as a
reflection of Britain's lack of authority: the whole of the last twenty-five
years would have to be gone through again. 'This comes of *magnanimity
& liberality*. A halter properly applied would have saved all the evil to
come!'[19] Even his old ally Wynn was of the peace party. The final blow in
France, for Southey, had been for the Jacobins to join forces with Bonaparte, 'for I would fain have believed that with all their dreadful errors,
they set out with a noble principle'.[20]

At least his writing was earning him more than it used to: he was paid
£100 for a review of a *Life of Wellington*, and he began to look upon the
Quarterly Review as his 'sheet anchor'; the snag was that the more he was
paid, the more he was prepared to carry on with the reviewing he had
cursed for so many years as a drain on his energies, a distraction from his
true vocation. Rather perversely, in the circumstances, he declined a
legacy left to him by Charles Danvers. And the more he wrote, the worse
his eyes became: 'at times, a speck which floats upon the book before it,
like a mote in the sun beams.' His friends continued to drop off the
branch: James Tobin, Frederick Smith, the man who had made his bust,
George Strachey's sister, James Dusauty, a young writer he had hoped to
champion. It was perhaps partly the accumulation of such woes that led
him to say that his days as a poet might well be over: recognizing the
increasing stature of Wordsworth, he saw that his own talents lay else-

where: 'As an historian I shall come nearer my mark. For thorough research, indeed, & range of materials, I do not believe that the History of Portugal will ever have been surpassed.'[21] It is important that he should acknowledge Wordsworth's powers: 'in the whole compass of poetry, ancient or modern, there is no collection of miscellaneous poems comparable to them, nor any work whatever which discovers greater strength of mind or higher poetical genius.'[22] This is both generous and perceptive; he could deceive himself entirely about his own work, and he was not always right about the work of others. But every now and then he could pronounce a verdict that was true and fair.

On 24 June Southey heard the bells ringing to celebrate victory at Waterloo: at last, he believed, Europe had been delivered from the wiles of Napoleon. 'The cannon should be sent home & formed into a pillar to support a statue of Wellington in the centre of the largest square in London.'[23] He was quite happy to countenance the destruction of Paris: it deserved to suffer. But, keeping to his scruples, when Murray promised him an extra £50 if he were to enlarge his review of the *Life of Wellington* to form a companion volume to the *Life of Nelson*, Southey told him, 'I should feel it very discreditable thus to write & publish for the demand of the day.'[24] He was just as happy to review, for the *Quarterly*, Gregoire's *History of the Sects of the Eighteenth Century*, and Galt's *Travels*, which would lead to a sketch of a history of the Jesuits in Ethiopia. But Waterloo left a lasting impression on Southey, and was to form the basis, within a year, of one of his most popular poems. It drew from him bubbling bloodthirstiness: he relished the prospect of a general public hanging of all counts, dukes, archdukes, and princes, 'for the sake of the *spectacle*'.[25] Ideally, Bonaparte would be executed by Louis XVIII. The celebrations at home were to include a bonfire on Skiddaw, on the Prince Regent's birthday. If only Bedford could be there: 'we would sup together as near the stars as the Olympic gods themselves, & see how the chasms & precipices of old Skiddaw look by firelight.'[26] Sure enough (albeit a week later than planned), on 21 August the celebrations took place.

Whilst Mrs Coleridge sat at home in Greta Hall, with her child, worrying increasingly as the clock ticked on towards midnight, Southey climbed up Skiddaw with Edith, two of his children, the Wordsworths, Mary Barker, various visitors and servants; they all enjoyed themselves with an ample sufficiency of food and drink, and sent balls of fire hurtling from the top of the mountain. It could have been a scene from Hardy's *Return of the Native*: 'we formed a huge circle round the most intense light, & behind us was an immeasurable arch of the most intense darkness, for our bonfire fairly put out the moon.' Mrs Coleridge had to be satisfied with a more sedate celebration the following week, put on by the local gentry, at a lower and less exhausting altitude. Against all this jollification, however, we should set what he told Harry, who had recently got married (again); congratulations would have been in order, he knew, but that was not his way: 'Occasions of joy & festivity seem rather to depress the barometer of my spirits than to raise it.' He even went so far as to say that Christmas and New Year's Day should 'be blotted from my calendar'.[27] So much for the happy, sociable, family man.

In September, Southey set off for Europe, with his wife and daughter, his brother and bride (and her mother and sister), and Henry Koster, another of his old Lisbon friends. From their first port of call, Ostend, where it was raining dismally, they went inland. Typically, Southey was not only writing home—in particular to John May—but keeping one of his journals: 'I minute down short notes in my pencil book with all possible care & hope in the end to lose nothing.'[28] His journals are another side of that trait that found such fascination in footnotes, however obscure. Southey records as much as he can with detailed fascination: Bruges is 'the most striking city that I have ever seen...The poorest people seem to be well lodged, and there is a general air of sufficiency, cleanliness, industry and comfort which I have never seen in any other place.' Nothing else quite matched up to Bruges (which also had the advantage of being the place where he met Edward Nash, the artist who was to become a firm friend). The problem with Brussels, on the other hand, fine though it was, was that 'the modern parts are French, and the city has the credit (which you and I shall agree in thinking the worst possible character) of being a second Paris'. On the other hand, Brussels could boast a wonderful bookshop, run by the famous collector Verbeyst, from whom Southey was to make some of his major purchases of rare books, including the complete, 52-volume set of the *Acta Sanctorum*. They visited the field of battle at Waterloo, about which he would write in *The Poet's Pilgrimage*; here, he simply records, for John May, some of the details and incongruities:

It would surprize you to see how soon Nature has recovered from the injuries of war: the ground is plowed & sown,—& grain & flowers & weeds already growing over the field of battle, which is still strewn with vestiges of the slaughter, caps cartridgeboxes, hats &c. We picked up some French cards, & some bullets, & we purchased a French pistol, & two of the eagles which the infantry wear upon their caps.

The journey onwards was marred by Edith May's falling ill; but even so, it was a busy time, and as they approached Calais, Southey told May, 'On the whole I believe that I have never passed a month of my life to better advantage.'[29]

They were back in London, in time to see the Lord Mayor's show, on 9 November, but as usual Southey was keen to get back home; and he was telling Mary Barker that, once in Keswick, he would need to borrow £100 from her. On the way back, Edith was unwell, which prevented a visit to Wynn; the carriage broke down in Nottingham, where they visited the White family; finally, on 5 December, they spent a night at Wordsworth's, so that they could arrive at Greta Hall in daylight, and thus see the children. His return, he told John May, had 'something of the character of a triumph'.[30] The Proem to *The Poet's Pilgrimage*, which he thought might be 'obnoxious to the charge of egotism', caught his particular mood of domestic contentment.[31]

> Heaven hath with goodly increase blest me here,
>   Where childless and opprest with grief I came;
> With voice of fervent thankfulness sincere
>   Let me the blessings which are mine proclaim:
> Here I possess, . . what more should I require?
> Books, children, leisure, . . all my heart's desire.
>
> O joyful hour, when to our longing home
>   The long-expected wheels at length drew nigh!
> When the first sound went forth, 'they come! they come!'
>   And hope's impatience quickened every eye!
> 'Never had man whom Heaven would heap with bliss
> More glad return, more happy hour than this.'
>
> Aloft on yonder bench, with arms dispread,
>   My boy stood, shouting there his father's name,
> Waving his hat around his happy head;
>   And there, a younger group, his sisters came:
> Smiling they stood with looks of pleased surprize,
> While tears of joy were seen in elder eyes . . .

To Rickman, two days later, he sighed: 'Thank God I am once more by my own fireside, surrounded with books & papers, & at work once again!'[32]

Although there was ill-feeling about the way his piece on Wellington in the *Quarterly* had been tampered with, Southey was beginning to feel more secure. His version of the *Morte d'Arthur* was to be published by Longman in two quarto volumes, for which he would get £200; *Roderick* was already in its fourth edition; *Amadis* brought in £100, and when all copies were sold he would get another £50. As he told Wynn on 15 December, 'I hope & expect . . . that this next year will set me fairly even with the world, & that afterwards I shall be able every year to lay by something.'[33] Never before had he been in such a position. But, against his own sense of growing financial security, was his feeling that the nation was on the verge of ruin: unless the army were strengthened, 'mob revolution' was likely. 'The foundations of Government are undermined. The props may last during your life time & mine, but I cannot conceal from myself a conviction that at no very distant day the whole fabric must fall!' It seemed a very distant day indeed since, as a young man at Oxford, he had rejoiced in the very 'sapping' of the foundations. (This increasingly apocalyptic tone found its public voice in the essays he wrote the following year, when he was hoist on the petard of his own hysteria.) Five days later, Southey wrote to his brother Tom, and, amongst other things, gave a graphic account of a tremendous storm that had swept across the Lakes on 19 December. We might see this as a metaphor for the turbulence he predicted: 'The wind was nearly due south, & it took up the water of the lake, literally like dust: we could see it beginning to rise far up under Brandelow, white as smoke or as a morning mist, gathering & growing all the way to the bottom of the lake, & there dispersed as far as the tempest would carry it.'[34] Storms could, for Southey, be majestic, awesome, even beautiful; they also allowed him to stay inside, and again we might note the metaphor. He told Rickman on 22 December, 'For the last week I have been shut up in the house by the snow,—no evil for one like myself who am as little addicted to dispensible exercise as tho I were a Turk.'[35] He could get on with his writing: reviews, Laureate poems, his journal of the trip to France (to be arranged for posthumous publication: it took rather longer than expected, but was worth the wait). But he felt he was slowing down, or rather that time was speeding up: he certainly did not have the hour-glass regularity he claimed to have had at Oxford, when he rose at 4.00 a.m. '& portioned out my studies by the hour'.

Edith May's health improved over the winter, and Southey too seemed well enough. He began looking for a house for Tom, who was having to move out of his present abode; Koster, his old friend from Portugal, had suffered financial disaster, and his womenfolk moved into a house near Southey.[36] Such concerns got in the way of writing, at least poetry: prose was not a problem, but he said that he could not write verse 'in the presence of any person, except my wife & children'.[37] His own History of Portugal was being helped by the offical correspondence he was getting from the diplomat, Benjamin Frere, about the conduct of Massena's army; Southey fully believed that once his great work was finished, it would 'tend to mitigate the evils of war hereafter'. In the same way, he thought that what he had to say in the *Quarterly* about the poor would actually assist 'real practicable reform', as opposed to the 'reformers'. There is something curiously naïve about his approach here, something innocently muddled: he later openly admitted in March that he did not understand the agricultural question. As he said to Rickman, 'The poor laws I leave alone, respectfully, in ignorance. But when your turn is come to attack them, I will serve a battery for you with all zeal & diligence.'[38]

In February he heard with pleasure that his Aunt Mary Southey was coming up to the Lakes, to seek relief in the mountains from her own financial problems: Southey could understand her plight, whilst recognizing that the solution was only a short-term one. Tom (now out of the navy), had found a house, Wareop Hall, near Appleby, half-furnished, with a pleasant garden and orchard, for just £30 a year; the youngest of Tom's growing brood was at school, Hannah had a 'situation', Elinor sought one. This was certainly better news than that of Koster, whose child was dying, or of Charles Lloyd, who had finally been declared insane, and was to be removed to the York asylum: his boys would remain at school in Ambleside, his wife and daughters were to move to Warwickshire. There was a mournful leave-taking.[39]

His own children were unwell in the first few months of the year, with Herbert especially developing a nasty cough; the weather did not help, with 'perpetual alternations from one kind of discomfort to another, without one interval of genial sunshine'.[40] The clouds were gathering on all sides. At least by the end of March he had finished, 'Laus Deo', *The Poet's Pilgrimage*;[41] but he worried lest he had not made himself sufficiently clear with regard to the importance of devotion and the dangers of bigotry. As he put it to Sharon Turner, nicely capturing not only his own bemusement, but that of others who wondered quite where they stood: 'When Dissenters talk of the Establishment, they make me feel like a high Churchman, & when I get among high Churchmen, I am ready to take shelter in dissent.'[42] He told Mary Betham wryly towards the end of June, 'I suppose I shall be called a Methodist for the proem & for the Pilgrimage.—with just as much propriety as I have formerly been called an Atheist.'[43] He was partly right about this. Hazlitt enjoyed himself at the poem's, and Southey's, expense on 7 July 1816; Southey was 'still the same pragmatical person—every sentiment or feeling that he has is nothing but the effervescence of incorrigible overweening self-opinion', and the poem itself was beneath criticism—'It is the Namby-Pamby of the Tabernacle; a Methodist Sermon turned into doggerel verse.'[44] Hazlitt's criticism was based on the depth of the political differences between them; here was the author of *Joan of Arc* embracing imperial claims based on the notion of 'the divine right' of kings. Hazlitt would never forgive Southey for this; when he came to write the Preface to his own *Life of Napoleon* (1828), he made the point that Napoleon's importance lay in his challenge to those 'who claimed mankind is their inheritance by a divine right' (quoting Pope's *Dunciad* as ample authority, 'The right divine of kings to govern wrong'). *The Poet's Pilgrimage* is, in many respects, and whatever we might think of Southey's politics, an impressive poem, taking a broad, sweeping view of history, and reaching towards affirmation out of the chaos and waste of war. It is certainly one of his best Laureate poems, no doubt because he is able to combine personal, domestic emotions with the details of history; he had, after all, been to the scene of the battles, and was doing much more than simply producing another public poem. One of the most impressive parts of the poem consists of 'The Vision', in which the poet confronts the doubts and uncertainties that we do not normally associate with him:

> I thought upon these things in solitude,
>   And mused upon them in the silent night;
> The open grave, the recent scene of blood,
>   Were present to the soul's creative sight;
> These mournful images my mind possest,
> And mingled with the visions of my rest.
>
> Methought that I was travelling o'er a plain
>   Whose limits, far beyond all reach of sense,
> The aching anxious sight explored in vain.
>   How came I there I could not tell, nor whence;
> Nor where my melancholy journey lay;
> Only that soon the night would close upon my way...
>
> Full fain would I have known what lay before,
>   But lifted there in vain my mortal eye;
> That point with cloud and mist was covered o'er,
>   As tho' the earth were mingled with the sky.
> Yet thither, as some power unseen impelled,
> My blind involuntary way I held.

In this world of the dead, he meets the figure of Wisdom, a curious anticipation of Keats's figure of Moneta in *Hyperion*:

> Art thou then one who would his mind perplex
>   With knowledge bootless even if attained?
> Fond man! he answered;.. wherefore wouldst thou vex
>   Thy heart with seeking what may not be gained!
> Regard not what has been, nor what may be,
> O Child of Earth, this Now is all that toucheth thee!

Of course, the two poets approach this problem from very different angles; whereas Keats acknowledges the poet's limitations, especially his own, Southey will have none of the pessimism which he has himself invoked. But it is an interesting moment in his poetic development, one perhaps lost in the meliorative conclusion of the poem, entitled 'Hopes of Man'. It is almost as though Southey's honesty gets the better of him, creeping upon him unawares in a poem that is supposed to be celebratory. Not for the first time, one of his poems gains its strength almost in spite of himself.

Southey heard from his former landlord, Peacock, who was now in a private madhouse, partly as a result of seeing the horrific wounds of sailors when the fleet docked at Yarmouth, partly as a result of a disastrous marriage: Southey hoped that Wynn and Harry might visit him.[45]

Closer to home, Herbert's health caused some consternation: he was complaining of pains in his chest and back. Southey vainly tried to amuse him by whipping a large top around the room; but the pains continued, and a fever developed. Herbert's stools were an index of his plight: 'he had a still fouler stool in the night, with such white specks in it, looking like cream when it curdles in your tea.'[46] Southey could only wish, like Macbeth, as things got worse, that the next hundred years were over, and that they were all in a better place, where 'happiness is permanent, & there is neither change nor evil'. By 8 April he had lost all hope, and he could only look to his own resignation, and his belief that there was indeed a better place. Edith was bearing up with 'great fortitude', helped by Mary Barker, who sat with the boy day and night.[47] In desperation, Herbert was given wine 'in almost any quantity' as the best medicine. On Easter Monday Southey wrote to Harry: 'I think this event, cutting off as it does the very head & blossom of my earthly happiness—will determine me to leave Keswick when my lease expires.—it has just one year more to run. Composed I shall be anywhere,—but I fear it will be impossible for me ever to feel any enjoyment in this place, where every object both at home & abroad will perpetually remind me of my loss.' The next day was even worse: 'All must very soon be over. I have seen him for the last time,—unless he should call for me.'[48] Herbert called for his father no more.

Southey's grief was greater than anything he had suffered so far. Herbert, only 9 years old when he died, had been his second self, the paragon he would have liked to be; his life had been 'a continued holiday, so much was his disposition to mingle sport with study, to find recreation in all things'.[49] Southey made a bonfire of Herbert's papers, and wept. It made terrible sense for him to think of leaving Keswick, and he immediately began to calculate the costs: £200 for removal, £400 for another house. Richmond would be his first choice, otherwise Streatham (near his uncle), Hastings, or Bath. He no longer trusted his ability to live in solitude: 'there is a danger…in learning to bear it, unfitting myself for any thing else, by contracting habits of settled melancholy.' His wife, he told Bedford, had 'displayed the most exemplary self-control'.[50] Edith May went to stay with the Wordsworths. Southey decided to write his memoirs, which he hoped Bedford would get published, along with a selection of his reviews; at his death, which he clearly anticipated, he would be able to leave about £10,000 for Edith and the children. John May and Neville White would be his executors. It was as though, with Herbert dead, Southey thought of himself as dead: only religion kept him going, but even that was more a matter of stoicism, he had to admit. He would gaze at the portrait that Mary Betham had made in happier times. Whilst his body took its toll, he continued with his constitutionals, insisting that his mind was still strong: 'I never was more capable of mental exertion, nor more disposed to it. Be assured that my mind will never be suffered to prey upon itself.' Rickman's coldness allowed him to offer his friend little comfort: 'we must not think too much on the aggravations which might be enumerated.' At the same time, he touched on a sentiment that must have found some echoes in Southey's emotions: 'men are overset sometimes by the many reasons they have against giving vent to their feelings.' Southey carried on doggedly with the *Carmen Nuptiale*, now that another royal marriage was imminent; but his determination to hide behind hard work was dented when Edith May returned from the Wordsworths after a week, and the family's terrible wound reopened. To play with his surviving children was more than he could bear. He had lost that aspect of his character that has often got overlooked, the 'hilarity which I possessed more uninterruptedly & in a greater degree than any person with whom I was ever acquainted.'[51]

On 1 May, barely two weeks since Herbert's death, he sent Bedford *The Lay of the Laureate: Carmen Nuptiale*, acknowledging his indifference. He would leave the size and print run to Longman, but would prefer something similar in size to *The Poet's Pilgrimage*. 'It will be very thin', he said, truthfully enough, 'but still might be put in boards to give it a local habitation on the shelf.'[52] There were to be two copies specially bound, one for presentation to the royal bride, the other for Edith. And with this piece of task work that had suddenly acquired a desperate poignancy out of the way, he mooted a poem along the lines of Cowper's *Task*, possibly called 'Consolation': it would not, he thought, be appropriate for publication in his own lifetime. He told Bedford, who was the only person to know about it, not to tell any one else: significantly, this final major work was to be as private as possible.

'It will be Herbert's monument & mine.' Some dreadfully painful frag-
ments remain, published after Southey's death in the volume which
contained *Oliver Newman* (1845).[53]

Thy life was a day, and sum it well, life is but a week of such days,—with how much
storm, and cold, and darkness! Thine was a sweet spring holy-day,—a vernal
Sabbath, all sunshine, hope, and promise.

> and that name
> In sacred silence buried, which was still
> At morn and eve the never-wearying theme
> Of dear discourse.

> playful thoughts
> Turn'd now to gall and esel...

Feeling at Westminster, when summer evening sent a sadness to my heart, and I
sate pining for green fields, and banks of flowers, and running streams,—or
dreaming of Avon and her rocks and woods.

No more great attempts, only a few autumnal flowers, like second primroses,
&c....

Henry Koster did what he could to keep Southey from slipping over into
complete despair, taking him out for walks and chatting as they went; but
Southey just wanted to get back to his study and a mournful routine.

Within a month, Southey felt able to address himself to the concerns of
the wider world: the Corn Laws reform, which provided him with an
opportunity to attack the short-sightedness of the landed gentry; the state
of the Poet Laureateship, which he was confident he had redeemed; *The
Poet's Pilgrimage*, complimented rather half-heartedly by Wynn as the
'most correct' poem Southey had published;[54] the French disarray. He
drafted a rather pompous dedication to the Prince Regent, but then told
Bedford to come up with something better.[55] He returned to his theme
that 'anarchists' like Hunt and Hazlitt should be sent to Botany Bay, and
grumbled at the tax on imported books, especially since the fifty-two
folios of the *Acta Sanctorum*, purchased in Belgium a year before, would
cost up to £40. The riots in the East of England caused him more alarm
than they seemed to cause the Government:

They seem never to dream that revolutions in the state are like the eruption in the
small pox—the consequence of the disease pre-existent in the system—the body
politic has been successfully inoculated for it, & the inoculation has taken;—
the disease exists; & if it should not run the same course as in France, it will be
because Government can depend upon the army, & the Gentry of the country,
Whigs & all, would rally round it in danger. But as far depends upon the opinion of
the multitude, the work is done.[56]

He was afraid that attempts to excite a *bellum servile* would end in a military government: there was, in other words, a 'mortal danger of seeing the liberties of the country destroyed by the abuse of them'.

It was perhaps just as well that the summer brought its share of visitors. Edward Nash had made a drawing from the bust, and was 'sketching here in all directions'; he was working on a picture of the three girls. There was the hope that Wynn might come; and Chauncey Hare Townshend, too, a young writer, to whom Southey extended the kind of hospitality he prided himself on: 'You will find a bed, plain fare, & a glad welcome; books for wet weather, a boat on sunny evenings; the loveliest parts of this lovely county within reach & within sight; & myself one of the best guides to all the recesses of the vales & mountains.'[57] He had decided, after all, to stay in Keswick, and there was a sense of relief once this decision had been made. One of his more unusual visitors was Robert Owen of Lanark, who came in mid-August. Owen, an enlightened industrialist, was a curious mixture of a Benthamite Utilitarian, as Southey would discover when he visited his model town in New Lanark, and a Utopian who acknowledged that the economy had not recovered from the cost of the Napoleonic wars. Owen's idealism, married to his faith in agricultural communities as opposed to industrial cities, appealed to a Southey who remembered his own Pantisocratic schemes: both men were fighting the perceived inequality of the time. The ever-cautious Rickman, it should be said, was less impressed. Southey had been thinking about the state of the poor, and the effects of the manufacturing system, and he saw in Owen someone of like mind, though more optimistic than he himself felt. Owen, in fact (rather as Shelley had been), was 'neither more nor less than such a Pantisocrat as I was in the days of my youth. He is as ardent now as I was then, & will soon be cried down as a visionary.'[58] Certainly Southey could see that Owen was right in some of his diagnoses: that the increase in mechanization could lead to greater unemployment; that it was intrinsically wrong to employ children; and that more goods were being produced than could be consumed. Unfortunately, Owen, he thought, wrote like a madman: Southey's ardour had indeed cooled. Owen's *New View of Society* was reviewed by Hazlitt on 4 August 1816; whereas Southey was persuaded at least of Owen's good intentions, Hazlitt thought it all hopelessly muddled, and in any case hardly new; these ideas 'are not only old, they are dead and buried, they are reduced to ruins'. Hazlitt's point was that we had been here before; look what had happened to Godwin. Ironically, Hazlitt envisaged Owen coming under attack from Parr, Malthus, and Southey. Owen's rather easy (shallow, in Hazlitt's eyes) optimism found no echo in Hazlitt: 'As it is, things will most probably go on as they have done, till some comet comes with its tail; and on the eve of some grand and radical reform, puts an end to the question.'[59]

At the beginning of September a rather unusual proposal was put, through Bedford, to Southey: perhaps he could serve the Government in some official capacity, either in some sinecure in London, or as editor of a national newspaper.[60] Southey was flattered and flabbergasted: he had been saying, not long before, that the country needed an intellect to lead it out of trouble—and now here he was, being singled out as that very Messiah. It was not that he doubted his own powers; as he said, 'If they would but act as I will write,—I mean as much in earnest & as fearlessly— the country would be saved.'[61] There was no one the Whigs and Anarchists hated, because they feared, more: he rejoiced that Leigh Hunt, Hazlitt, and the *Champion* all attacked him; he would even write for something like the *Anti-Jacobin* so desperate was the state of the nation, so alarmed was he. But he could not act as editor, and he must not receive any money from the Government: as he observed with naïve percipience to Bedford, 'it would . . . discredit me with the public'.[62] But Southey was on the verge of selling his soul, more than he knew. Rickman must have registered something when Southey told him, 'the best way to keep the poor in obedience is to better their condition'.[63] At about the same time Southey wrote to Bedford, quoting Horace, '*non sum qualis eram.*—nor shall I ever be again'.[64] No doubt he was referring to private griefs as much as any- thing, to his longing for the end, not so much for the evening of life as the night. But politically and ethically he was becoming a different man. He even told Rickman in October that his scruples about Government payment might be waived—'if it were offered in a form that I could accept'. If this seems devious, Southey's honesty still had a foothold. 'By nature I am a poet', he said in the same letter, 'by deliberate choice an historian, & a political writer I know not how; by accident, or the course of events.'[65] Although he thought he might change the course of events, he was refreshingly unsure of his qualifications.

For the first time ever, the balance of his account with Longman was in his favour. The first edition alone of *The Poet's Pilgrimage* (2,000 copies), had brought in £215: 'The tide of my affairs seems thus to have turned . . . I conclude that so much abuse cannot have been without a propor- tionate good effect.'[66] Only Southey could have so contentedly drawn such a conclusion. None the less, he was at work again, with the third volume of the *History of Brazil* on the boil before breakfast, even writing verse (160 lines of *Oliver Newman* were now written). He resumed the *Tale of Paraguay* in mid-October, and felt sufficiently solvent to send a cheque of £100 to May. In November he intended to write about Wesley for Stoddart's *Correspondent*, and this was to form the basis of his *Life of Wesley*.[67] On a much broader canvas, he told Rickman that he would tackle the evils of society, and how they might be ameliorated.[68]

His correspondence with Rickman assumed even greater significance and value for him, because Rickman was such a good source of the basic information and statistics. Southey was still convinced of the evils of poverty: 'the sort of poverty that exists among us will be no more to be borne than slavery would be at this time in any part of Europe.'[69] He began to relish the furore his work would create, so loathed was he by one side, so beloved of the other. But whenever the *Quarterly* 'castrated' one of his articles, he must have realized that it was not quite that simple: it was all very well taking the 'high ground' but there was more than one moral mountain from which to survey the scene.[70] One of his problems was that he increasingly saw himself as lord of all he surveyed. The great work on which he was about to embark was to be called, starkly, 'Observations upon the Moral and Political State of England': for all his doubts about how and why he had become a political commentator, he was ready to banish those doubts in his eagerness for the fray. '*Ni fallor*', he declared to Bedford in December, 'the book must attract notice,—indeed it will be abused into notoriety.'[71] Seldom can '*ni fallor*' have sounded so defiant. Southey really looked forward to making more than a polite splash in the literary pond. But he could also tell Bedford in December that 'there is some truth in Jacobinism, that inequality, in the degree in which it exists, is a real and grievous evil'.[72] If we are surprised by this, then we can imagine the aristocratic Bedford's response; in fact, most people in the English-speaking world might have been taken aback. None the less, Southey could with confidence decide to write for Murray, for 'I have a great deal to say, & shall make a noise in the world'. For Southey, it had been a dreadful, most painful year; he wrote to Josiah Conder in December, 'it has drawn a broad black line between the years which are gone & those which may be before me'.[73] But if he had lost the person dearest in the whole world to him, he would at least not relinquish what he had left without a bitter, desperate struggle.

Although Edith's spirits were still low, and the weather over Christmas and the New Year bad—with severe storms, snow, and rain—at least the children were well, 'happy as skylarks in a fine day'.[74] Brother Tom was coming soon, as his wife was about to give birth, yet again: this made it all the more urgent for Southey to do what he could towards effecting the improvement of Tom's career prospects. Southey was surprised, but pleased, to read in the *Courier* that he himself had been elected a Member of the Royal Institute of Amsterdam, which led him to fret rather about his sartorial lack of elegance: he needed some new 'pantaloons', which duly came from the ever-obliging Bedford, but striking Southey as *uglyissimi coloris*.[75] They were to give him another topic to weave arabesques around in *The Doctor*.

I cannot approve the colour. It hath too much of the purple; not the imperial die by which ranks were discriminated at Constantinople, nor the more sober tint which Episcopacy affecteth. Nor is it the bloom of the plum;—still less can it be said to resemble the purple light of love. No! it is rather a hue brushed from the raven's wing, a black purple; not Night and Aurora meeting, which would make the darkness blush; but Erebus and Ultramarine.[76]

Such apparent frivolities did not distract him from more serious matters, such as his meditative poem, and his article for the *Quarterly Review* on 'The Rise and Progress of Popular Disaffection'. This was one of several major essays he wrote in these years which reflected his anxieties, whilst at the same time he tried to cling on to a sense of hope, in that he was still able to believe that sense—in his terms—would prevail. It makes for an odd brew: even now Southey did not want to be seen as serving any particular party interest. 'I address myself', he told Murray, 'to the good feelings of mankind. I aim at lessening human misery & bettering the condition of all the lower classes.'[77] Hence his scoffing, in a letter to Rickman in January, at the idea that the Government would have thought he would run a political journal for them; but he acknowledged that he was actually serving them 'ten times better' by writing as he did. He told Rickman that the rabble-rousers like Cobbett, and all concerned with the *Examiner*, should not only be silenced but locked up; ominously, he commented that 'this Manchester affair will do some good, & I believe that most persons who have anything to lose are beginning to open their eyes'.[78] (In March 1817 Henry 'Orator' Hunt held a popular meeting at St Peter's Fields in Manchester, where several speakers were arrested; this foreshadowed the more alarming events of two years later, in the same place.) When he explained to Bedford the additions to his article about the poor (additions about the dangers of the Spenceans and Cobbett), he said, 'This head of mine is curiously furnished with some separate assortments of matter.'[79] This was indeed the case. It helps to explain something of what might strike us as the confusion of the *Quarterly Review* articles; it also helps to explain the bizarre chain of events that was soon to make 1817 seem as crucial a year in his life as 1816 had been, but for very different reasons.

By the end of January the weather had changed dramatically: 'the birds are singing as if it were spring,—the polyanthuses are in blossom, & the winter is as unnatural as the summer was. This I fear looks ill for the ensuing season.'[80] His forebodings were not helped by a visit from Owen, like a ghost of his own past. His comment on Owen's 'wildness' might be entertaining, but it also serves as a reminder of Southey's own lack of clarity: 'He lives in a dream, & his complacency is as amusing, as his immoveable gentleness of temper is remarkable. He will insist that you make a silk purse of a sows ear.—& yet I like the man.'[81] He would, ere long, repay the visit on his Scottish tour later in the year. In the mean time he was off to stay with Senhouse at Netherhall for a week—always a comforting and comfortable retreat, taking Southey back, with its noted Roman antiquities, into the safety of the distant, impersonal past. Or so he thought. On his return to Keswick on 14 February he found himself confronted with an aspect of his own past which was to spark off a rather extraordinary row. This revenant could not be brushed aside quite so easily as the amiable Owen of Lanark.

An advertisement in the *Morning Chronicle*, for his own youthful drama *Wat Tyler*, caught his eye. As this was the poem he had given to the radical printer Ridgeway, when he visited him in prison in 1794, and which had never seen the light of day since, Southey must have experienced, at the very least, a gentle shock of mild surprise.[82] He turned first to Wynn, for advice as to what he should do; but his letter to Murray of 14 February betrays little alarm:

God be thanked that the worst which malice can say of me is no more than what I was once proud to say of myself, & never shall be ashamed of saying, that I was a Republican in my youth... I am very little concerned at this dirty transaction. My heart as well as my mind has been well disciplined, & I have not profited so ill by real & severe affliction, as to suffer any thing for trifles.[83]

The complacency he had remarked in Owen's character was very much part of his own. Typically, he was not going to disclaim the work: it was as natural for him to have written it when he did (and this was the crux of his repeated defences) as 'that now, with the same feelings, the same principles, & the same integrity... I should think revolution the greatest of all calamities, & believe that the best way of ameliorating the condition of the people is through the established institutions of the country.'[84]

The firm of Sherwood, Neeley, and Jones—usually, and ironically in the circumstances, associated with polite travel literature or smart editions of legal texts—produced the first edition of *Wat Tyler* on 13 February 1817; the dramatic poem was anonymous, but the subject and the Shakespearian epigraph on the title-page, 'Thus ever did Rebellion find rebuke', suggested something fairly radical. It had been in December 1816 that the radicals had caused considerable disquiet with their polemical meetings, culminating in the Spa-fields meeting at which Henry Hunt addressed a huge crowd, and a breakaway group tried to capture the Tower of London. Both Watson and Preston, among the ringleaders, were happy to claim a connection between their activities and those of the original poll-tax rebel, Wat Tyler, who 'rose for the purpose of putting down an oppressive tax'. Taxation and Reform were the issues of the day; parliamentary committees, as a result of Spa-fields, examined the state of the nation, in near-panic. The *Gentleman's Magazine* had issued a rallying cry midway through 1816, voicing the Government view that to yield to popular demands would be fatal: 'Shall we be so far misled by the clamours of the ignorant, or the fallacious misrepresentations of the seditious, as to forfeit our Character, long and honourably sustained, for loyalty, firmness, and courage?' The problem for the Government and its supporters—including Southey, Coleridge, Wordsworth, and Crabb Robinson—was that this was both more and less than a rhetorical question: the stakes were high. If there was a golden triad, it consisted of respect for government; the dangers of the press; the importance of the Church. 'As the word "Equality" was the howl of the Demagogues of France, so is "Reform" the popular catchword of our Modern Patriots.'[85]

A longer article in the *Quarterly Review*, 'On the State of Public Opinion and the Political Reformers', which had appeared on 11 February 1816, explored the dangers in greater detail, in particular setting the present unreasonable discontent in the context of the recent glorious victory. The argument of the reformers is examined, that the war was the cause of the present distress and was carried on against the wishes of the people. The *Quarterly Review* turns back to the beginning of the French Revolution, since Waterloo was really the culmination of that whole train of events that began in 1789: 'We appeal to every person who remembers the beginning of the French revolution, whether, if the question of peace or war had been referred to the people of England and decided by universal suffrage, Mr. Pitt would have found a dissentient voice in a thousand?' Well, we might think, people like Southey and Wordsworth were opposed to the war. But the *Quarterly Review* writer rejoices in the fact that the opposition was defeated, and Fox's adherents became an extra-parliamentary faction:

The appellations of republican and jacobin were sufficient to mark a man for personal danger, persecution and ruin. The riots at Birmingham, as they proved of what excesses an infuriated rabble are capable, prove also beyond all possibilities of confutation what were the politics of the multitude at that time.

We can see where the argument is leading: the 'ordinary people' do not have, and never have had, any sense of political propriety, and therefore the notion of universal suffrage is absurd. At the same time, a contradiction is emerging, in that it was precisely to that sense of everyone's being opposed to the war that the writer had appealed a few pages earlier. The more we look at this article, the more it becomes a strange mixture of history—an account of Napoleon's crimes (including the curbing of the press!)—and confused polemic, culminating with the argument that the present hard times are the consequences of peace, rather than war. 'We are treading upon gunpowder', the *Quarterly* urges, reminding us that nothing more absurd than the Gunpowder Plot could have been conceived—and yet it happened. Whereas men like Hunt argue that parliamentary reform 'is the only means to *prevent anarchy and civil war*', the *Quarterly* can see that gentle tinkering with the system of representation might be feasible, 'unless the frantic scheme of universal suffrage were adopted, which would inevitably and immediately lead to universal anarchy'. At least the writer can console himself with the thought that Henry Hunt would never end up as an MP. There is an interesting jibe at the Spencean Philanthropists, and their notion that 'the people have only to say, let the land be ours, and it will be so': Thomas Spence had quite rightly been prosecuted for such nonsense, which smacked of the same kind of grand 'constitutions in the air' as Robespierre and Babœuf had toyed with all those years ago (the same kind of nonsense that one Robert Southey had entertained).

A further essay in the *Quarterly*, in January 1817, 'On the Rise and Progress of Popular Disaffection', addressed the same problem, making an important distinction between the Revolution of 1688—which had been necessary, moderate, and beneficial—and the present disturbances (let alone the American and French Revolutions): in 1688 the Church of England had saved the country, whereas now the danger lay in freethinkers who had no sense of true religion, nor of the conjunction between Church and State. One point that is particularly striking about this piece, apart from its general pessimism and its lambasting of popular figures such as Junius—'the most influential and the most pernicious English writer of his age'—Hunt and Wilkes ('one of the greatest profligates of a profligate age'), is that it displays a reluctance to engage with the very issues it finds so disturbing. Wisdom, it appears, would be reflected in a lack of political involvement: it is duty that drives a man to rise to the occasion, especially when so many are denying the spirit of rebellion in the land. 'Let it be remembered, that of all the shocking diseases to which the human frame is liable, the most shocking and the most loathsome is that in which it is devoured by the vermin which its own diseased humours have generated.'

Such echoes of Bishop Hatto and his rats can be easily explained: it was Robert Southey who had written both these articles in the *Quarterly*. They were published anonymously, but most readers could by now tell a piece of Southey's prose at twenty paces; and it was not long before the authorship of *Wat Tyler* was blazoned across the radical press: the *Morning Chronicle*, first of all, in February, and then, later in the month, William Hone in the *Reformists' Register*, offering mock sympathy to the Poet Laureate, 'compelled to sing like a blind linnet by a sly pinch, with every now and then a volume of his old verses flying into his face, and putting him out!' Initially, Southey was not put out at all; even when his arch-enemy Brougham ridiculed him in Parliament, he could simply rest his defence on 'the perpetual fever of faction' of such men who were 'as little capable of disturbing my tranquillity as they are of understanding it.'[86]

Rather more troubling was William Hazlitt, who mischievously began a review of *Wat Tyler*, and the essay on Reform, in the *Examiner* for 9 March, with the Wordsworthian lines celebrating the child as father of the man, and then proceeded:

According to this theory of personal continuity, the author of the Dramatic Poem, to be here noticed, is the father of Parliamentary Reform in the Quarterly Review. It is said to be a wise child that knows its own father: and we understand Mr. Southey (who is in this case reputed father and son) utterly disclaims the union between the Quarterly Reviewer and the Dramatic Poet, and means to enter an injunction against the latter, as a bastard and imposter.[87]

By this remarkable conjunction of events, Southey's enemies were given all the ammunition they needed: here was Southey, the Poet Laureate, declaiming in the *Quarterly* against the very things championed in *Wat Tyler*, of which he was the author. As Hazlitt put it, the 'Ultra-Jacobin' had become the 'Ultra-Royalist'. For Hazlitt, there was no other person 'in whom "fierce extremes" meet with such mutual self-complacence; whose opinions change so much without any change in the author's mind'. Hazlitt, as we have seen, had said such things before, especially when he had written about the donning of the Laureate mantle in September 1813; but he had never had such a chance to scoff.

The most dramatic exposure of Southey's potentially embarrassing conflict of views took place on the floor of the House of Commons and was the more humiliating in that his tormentor, William Smith, the opposition MP for Norwich (that home of radical dissent in the 1790s), had been one of the friends of the 'Lakers'. During the debate on the

Seditious Assemblies Bill on 14 March, Smith produced, theatrically, from either pocket of his coat, a copy of the *Quarterly* and of *Wat Tyler*, and suggested that the *Quarterly* essayist must approve any suppression of *Wat Tyler* as seditious. This was a neat twist of the knife, and although Southey claimed not to be wounded, he did indeed instruct his lawyers, as predicted by Hazlitt, to move that an injunction be granted against further publication. The final irony was that Lord Eldon, the Lord Chancellor, refused the injunction on the grounds that since *Wat Tyler* was seditious, the author could not claim protection under the copyright laws. Once the legal battle was lost, increasingly cheap editions of the play began to appear, including Sherwood and William Hone's famous 3s. 6d. edition with mocking quotations from 'Southey!!!' on the title-page. John Fairburn produced an edition for 2s., William Sherwin a cheap 'Republican' pamphlet, Richard Carlile a similar one. Southey's son Cuthbert recalled that about 60,000 copies were sold, for not one of which Southey could claim a penny.

Something of Southey's confusions can be gauged by his other activities at this time. He was, for example, warning Townshend of the dangers of poetry, in that it could work against the benefits of stoicism, in keeping feeling in check. It was no good, he told him, to regret the loss of a few trees (thereby dismissing some of the most remarkable poems in English); we need fortitude 'in this changeful world, & the tears are running down my cheeks when I tell you so'.[88] Those tears tell us much about Southey, and it was his misfortune that he kept them hidden from the wider world. Whilst being not quite persuasive on the central conflict of emotion and rationality, he was still able to see the wretchedness of the Government; he could also perceive the 'bigotry' of the Quakers evinced in Thomas Clarkson's *Life* of William Penn (1813), even whilst Clarkson was to be valued for his work on the abolition of the slave trade. The fact that there were no neat categories might help to explain how, although he remembered the 'glee' with which he wrote *Wat Tyler* all those years ago, he was more vexed than he would have liked to be by the whole episode: 'an uneasiness like yeast working in my abdomen, & my sleep was disturbed by it for 2 nights.'[89] He would try (we might think surprisingly) to pour oil on troubled waters in an article on political discontent: 'I shall aim at a conciliative & persuasive tone, & avoid all personalities, while I endeavour, *totis viribus*, to attack that spirit of party which is the curse & the opprobrium of England.'[90] But that 'conciliative' tone was not his natural tone. As we have seen, and William Smith was soon to learn, he could lash out violently. When he heard that he had been attacked by Lord Brougham as well, in the House, he could not let it rest.[91]

Although working on Wesley and the Peninsular war, and relaxing back into his old routines—'the kitchen clock is not more regular in its movements than my life, & scarcely more monotonous, yet time never appeared to glide so swiftly'[92]—Southey was soon penning a letter to the editor of the *Courier*, followed the next day by what he thought was an even better open letter to Smith himself, published as a separate pamphlet. So pleased was he with this rather splendid mixture of rhetoric, honesty, self-defence, and shocked rectitude (seasoned with a modest amount of humbug), that he decided not to pursue the injunction: 'I have spoken about it in a way which will be equally proper, whether it be pursued or abandoned.'[93] Southey was certainly pleased to get a letter of support from his new friend William Wilberforce, but a little upset to be charged by Wynn with intolerance. Wynn, of course, had more need to be diplomatic, especially since he had spoken out in Southey's defence when Smith first raised Cain in the Commons. Southey protested: 'Do you not see that the charge of my speaking acrimoniously against persons for thinking as I once thought is ridiculously false?' But he made some alterations in response to Wynn, because 'I would take reproof from you as a dog does blows from his master'.[94] Perhaps Wynn alone could have had such an effect on Southey.

Amidst all this wrangling and vituperation, which he clearly enjoyed, Southey blithely turned down an offer to take over as editor of *The Times*, for £2,000: he was neither to be bought, nor distracted. He felt that the whole *Wat Tyler* episode had been an enormous waste of time and energy: he was glad to get all the anger out of his system, but by the middle of April was telling Bedford, 'I care not the turn of a straw'.[95] Unfortunately for him, the matter was not allowed to die down quite as quickly as that. He was gratified at Mrs Piozzi's pleasure—'Oh how glad I am to see him trample upon his enemies';[96] but the formidable Hazlitt decided to take up the matter in the *Examiner*. Southey satisfied himself that all right-thinking people would see through Hazlitt's 'scurrility', but Keats was not the only young radical to see that, in Hazlitt, Southey had more than met his match.

At least he got a good scrap out of it. (Wordsworth commented ruefully to Samuel Rogers in May, with reference to this whole affair, 'I begin to fear that I should soon be forgotten if it were not for my enemies.'[97]) Coleridge rallied to Southey's defence, but as Dorothy Wordsworth astutely realized, this defence was 'injudicious' in its emphasis on the difference between Southey the man and Southey the boy.[98] Hazlitt, too, saw through Coleridge's logic. But Coleridge had been vexed 'to the quick' by Southey's letter to the *Courier* (he had also thought *Wat Tyler* nothing more than 'pigs-meat'), so he perhaps felt that he was defending something of a lost cause. He had been under attack himself at the beginning of the year, and certainly felt the dangers of change. He would have preferred Southey's defence to rest on the fact that *Wat Tyler* could have been written by anybody forty years ago 'as a *Poem*. For who in the Devil's Name ever thought of reading Poetry for any political or practical purposes till these Devil's Times that *we* live in?'[99] Even if this had been true, change could not be brushed aside so lightly; Byron put it well in a letter to John Murray of 9 May:

Opinions are made to be changed—or how is truth to be got at? we don't arrive at it by standing on one leg, or on the first day of our setting out—but though we may jostle one another on the way that is no reason why we should strike or trample— *elbowing's* enough—I am all for moderation which profession I beg leave to conclude by wishing Mr. Southey damned—not as a poet but as a politician.[100]

Both Byron and Hazlitt resorted to the concept of apostasy, and its accompanying intolerance: it was the persecution of those who now thought as he once did which was so offensive. Hazlitt dismissed Coleridge's apology, point by point: it was no defence to say Southey was only 19 when he wrote the play, and had abandoned those principles, for the simple reason that it was not true—most of Southey's work until 1803 should logically demand the same injunction sought for *Wat Tyler*; further more, 'a person who forgets all the sentiments and principles to which he was most attached at nineteen, can have no sentiments ever after worth being attached to'; Southey, Coleridge, and Wordsworth were all men at the time, not boys, and 'all the authority that they have as poets and men of genius must be thrown into the scale of Revolution and Reform'; Coleridge's argument that it was all dramatic licence, and had no bearing on the real world, was dismissed as shallow, hypocritical nonsense. For good measure, Leigh Hunt weighed in with two droll pieces, also in the *Examiner*, one on the 'Death and Funeral of the Late Mr. Southey' (13 April), the other (11 May) on the 'Extraordinary Case of the Late Mr. Southey'.[101]

Hazlitt had been no more impressed by Southey's self-defence in his *Letter to William Smith*. We have to admit that Southey is no match for Hazlitt, with his rolling periods, his wit, his sardonic realization that Southey is a lost cause; for him, the Letter is 'a concentrated essence of a want of self-knowledge'.[102] There is much truth in this summary of Southey's processes of logic: 'Once admit that Mr. Southey is always in the right, and every one else in the wrong, and all the rest follows.' Hazlitt was rightly outraged at Southey's hiding behind anonymity in the

Quarterly, as though no one had the right to presume he had written what he obviously had. Southey protested that he felt no shame at what he had written; since then, circumstances had led him to change some of his views; but he was anxious to emphasize his benevolence, his concern for the poor. But Hazlitt was not to be persuaded; he could see that Southey's 'passion for despotism [was] greater than his dread of anarchy'. Southey had resorted to the image of the sun, the one he had used in 1809, in defence of his position, or rather change of position. Unfortunately for him this provided Hazlitt with a perfect target: 'It is not always that a simile runs on all-fours; but this does. The sun, indeed, passes from the East to the West, but it rises in the East again; yet Mr. Southey is still looking in the West—for his pension.' In his comments on *The Lay of the Laureate*, in 1816 (only a year before, after all), Hazlitt had made a rather similar point: 'The sun does not turn to the sun-flower; but the sun-flower follows the sun.'[103]

It is important to make the point that this episode is much more than a damning exposure of one man's contradictions. Southey was not alone in his confusions, even if he might seem alone in his self-righteousness. Thomas Love Peacock, in his novel of the same year, *Melincourt*, poked fun at Wordsworth and Southey, almost echoing what Southey had said to the young Shelley in 1812, when he saw, rather patronizingly, the image of himself as he once was, before wisdom had set in: Mr Feathernest is clearly modelled on the Poet Laureate, and he laughs at the jibes of the Shelleyan Mr Forester: 'I acted accordingly the part of a prudent man: I took my station, became my own crier, and vociferated truth and liberty, till the noise I made brought people about me, to bid for me: and to the best bidder I knocked myself down.' Later, in chapter 39, Forester meets Mr Paperstamp (i.e. Wordsworth): 'Mr Paperstamp did not much like Mr Forester's modes of thinking; indeed he disliked them the more, from their having once been his own.' It was a case of the older man saying 'When you are my age...', conservatism of the worst kind. There is no doubt at all but that Southey had Wordsworth's support: they shared similar beliefs about the way the country was going, the danger of 'injurious writings'.[104] Wordsworth told Daniel Stuart on 7 April that 'the suspension of the Habeas Corpus Act is a measure approved by all the well disposed, who are a large majority of the influential part of the Country'. Although he persuaded himself that 'the spirit among the labouring classes... is incomparably better than it was in 1794 and 5', he confessed himself an 'alarmist', largely because the moral basis of the constitution had gone.[105] Hazlitt's attacks on Southey were really, so far as Wordsworth was concerned, attacks on himself and Coleridge too (as indeed they were, especially since Coleridge got himself tangled in knots over his radical past in the *Biographia Literaria*, also of 1817).

'The miscreant Hazlitt', wrote Wordsworth, 'is not a proper person to be admitted into respectable society, being the most perverse and malevolent Creature that ill luck has ever thrown in my way. Avoid him—hic niger est—And this, I understand, is the general opinion wherever he is known in London.'[106] Henry Crabb Robinson had fastidiously avoided shaking hands with Hazlitt in December 1816, and thought Southey's *Letter to William Smith* 'a spirited little pamphlet [in which] Southey vindicates his change of opinion successfully but does not plead to the charge of illiberality in abusing the present race of democrats'.[107] Wordsworth, however, told Crabb Robinson that although he too thought Southey 'completely triumphant' against Smith, he regretted the tone of the piece, the way in which Southey opened himself to the charge of 'being a *Tool of Power*. A most false and foul accusation, for a more disinterested and honourable Man than Robert Southey does not breathe—'. (Even Hazlitt, according to Crabb Robinson, had admitted that 'he believes Southey to be still a perfectly honest man'—but that was before this latest rumpus.[108]) Wordsworth summed up what seemed to him the state of play, in general terms: it can be seen as a statement of the difference between government and opposition, but also between the generations: against Southey, Wordsworth, and Coleridge stand Byron, Shelley, and Hazlitt. 'The Friends of liberty and good order are alarmed at the corruption of opinion among the lower classes, and Reformers and Revolutionists are irritated and provoked that their plans have for the present been defeated.' Admittedly Wordsworth also told Stuart, in June, that although he and Southey agreed (with reference to the 'Rise and Progress of Popular Disaffection'), he thought Southey was not 'sufficiently jealous of the Power whose protection we all feel to be necessary', and quoted from his own pamphlet on the Convention of Cintra (1808), to make his point: 'There is, in fact, an unconquerable tendency in all power save that of knowledge acting by and through knowledge, to *injure the mind* by whom that power is exercized.' At this point we can see Wordsworth and Hazlitt moving at least one step closer to each other— for this is another version of Hazlitt's scorn at Southey's embracing of 'legitimacy'.[109]

Both Wordsworth and Dorothy commented on the toll this episode had taken on Southey's health, but in slightly different ways. For Wordsworth, Southey proceeded on his way, 'Prosperous in his literary undertakings, admired by his friends, in good health, and honoured by a large portion of the Public'. But the effect of the loss of his child, which

Wordsworth acknowledged, was more keenly observed by Dorothy, who wrote, also in April, 'He works so hard, and looks so delicate, that one cannot see him without anxious thoughts; and, resolute as he is, he will for ever feel his bitter loss. It comes on him heavily at times and he has not the boyish glee he used to have.'[110]

Charles Lamb asked after Southey in a letter to Dorothy of September 1816: 'I hope his pen will continue to move many years smoothly and continuously for all the rubs of the rogue Examiner. A pertinacious *foul* weathered villian *it is*!—'[111] He need not have worried unduly. But Coleridge too was having to confront his past, claiming defiantly in April 1817 that 'there is not a single political Opinion, which I held at five and twenty which I do not hold now'.[112] This was clearly meant to be a sideglance at Southey, and at some newspaper reports that Coleridge was as guilty of apostasy as Southey. Much of the *Biographia Literaria* consisted of his complex attempts to make sense of his intellectual development; as we have seen, he had in the *Friend* of 1809 tried to define his position, and the *Biographia* refers more than once to that earlier defence. It is a long, sprawling, work, with prose at times almost as impenetrable as any to be found elsewhere in his works. Many have thought it—and some have called it—dishonest, in that it does its best to cover the tracks of the younger Coleridge: if ever autobiography were to be seen as a manipulation of the past for the benefit of posterity (and, in passing, of course, for the present), this would be it. For example, in chapter x, in which he describes his attempts to get the *Watchman* off the ground in the mid-1790s, he swears that those who signed up as subscribers 'will bear witness for me, how opposite even then my principles were to those of Jacobinism or even of democracy, and can attest the strict *accuracy* of the statement I left on record in the 10th and 11th numbers of the Friend'. Within a couple of years, he claims, he was a 'vehement anti-ministerialist, but after the invasion of Switzerland a more vehement anti-Gallican, and still more intensely an anti-Jacobin'. He had 'retired' to Stowey. The turbulent, radical society in which he moved in those years might never have been. Southey was at least honest enough to admit openly to his past; but his honesty was of a kind so disarming that he was charged with stupidity and worse.

The attacks to which Southey was subject led Coleridge in chapter 111 of the *Biographia* to launch into a lengthy defence of Southey, partly because, as he says, to have been a friend of Wordsworth and Southey was to be tarred with the brush of their critics; to defend Southey was partly to defend himself. But to emphasize this motive would be unfair to Coleridge's extremely generous assessment of Southey's virtues as writer and man: Southey's more youthful claims to the Miltonic crown are given a gravity and seriousness in Coleridge's summary of his virtues:

That scheme of head, heart, and habitual demeanour, which in his early manhood, and first controversial writings, Milton, claiming the privilege of self-defence, asserts of himself, and challenges his calumniators to disprove; this will his schoolmates, his fellow collegians, and his maturer friends, with a confidence proportionate to the intimacy of their knowledge, bear witness to, as again realized in the life of Robert Southey.

There is much more in the same vein, pouring contempt on Southey's enemies, and praise on his industry, his poetic powers, his sheer range and versatility, and his warm humanity. Of course, Coleridge's view was partial, and was unlikely to change the minds of such as Hazlitt. But it is important for a rounded view of this 'episode' to remind ourselves that if Hazlitt seemed to have won the argument, and if Southey appeared to have done himself no real favours by his reply to Smith, there were other powerful voices who could state the case for him with eloquence and influence.[113]

Southey felt utterly vindicated. By the beginning of May, 2,000 copies of what he wryly called his 'Billet Doux' to Smith had been sold. 'Never had any man a compleater triumph,—congratulations have poured in upon me from all quarters, nor could I have wished for a better opportunity of trampling upon my enemies than this Slander-Smith has afforded me.' He enjoyed his visit to London in April and May, meeting and dining with the Royal Academy people, with Frere, with Benjamin Robert Haydon, and yet as always looking forward to getting home. He met Coleridge, too, and was alarmed to learn that he was threatening to return with him to Keswick. There is a certain world-weariness about his comment to his uncle, in which he moves from a statement of fact to a metaphor for life in one sentence: 'the pleasantest part of an excursion is the end of it.—The best hour of the day is when we go to bed,—& I verily believe that it is mans own fault if the day of his death is not the happiest of his life.'[114] And yet, the very next day, he, Nash, and Senhouse set off for a European tour which would keep them away from England until the beginning of August.

This second continental tour was really to keep his mind, so far as possible, off the dreadful loss of Herbert. They spent five days in Paris, where they visited Wordsworth's daughter Caroline, now married to Jean Baudouin; they also met Helen Maria Williams, the writer who had been imprisoned during the Revolution. Southey could not but be struck by Paris: 'as extraordinary a place, as the most extraordinary accounts describe it, a perpetual mixture of Ranelagh & Bartholemew Fair in the streets & public walks, filth & finery... the beauty,—the picturesque beauty of the city—exceeds anything that has been said of it.' If Edith thought that her husband was enjoying the place, she was soon disabused: 'I have seen the face of Paris compleatly, & shall feel heartily glad to leave it.' There was only so much excitement he could take. Off they went to Switzerland and Italy; the Grande Chartreuse was magnificent, but being in Como was as delightful, in that his hero Walter Savage Landor was living there. Mont Blanc reared up its head, night and day, in the bright, clear sky; at Chamonix, Southey saw the Shelleyan inscription, where someone else had called Shelley an atheist. Southey enjoyed the whole tour, for 'we jest, & we eat & we drink, & take things quietly, & extract amusement or enjoyment from everything'. (The only drawback, apparently, was Senhouse's nocturnal sighing.) But, as usual, he was glad to be going home in high summer; they reached Dover on 7 August.[115]

Everyone seemed well at home, and Southey was not too worried that his attempts to buy Greta Hall had failed, as the new landlord seemed a reasonable person, unlikely to bother them. He was amused to be told that he had actually put on some weight on his travels, but if he was unusually out of proportion, the Lakes weren't. Against the sheer scale and grandeur of the Swiss alps he felt the perfect propriety of his home county, and Skiddaw was still the 'most imposing mountain, for its height, that I have yet seen'.[116] Even the Swiss rivers lacked the purity and cleanliness of Lakeland water. So, fatter and back where he belonged, he could turn to the pile of work that beckoned. Dorothy Wordsworth was less sanguine about his prospects: being at home, she thought, was not altogether good for him. 'How can it be otherwise? A man cannot live with such a set of women and approve of them without being the worse for it. How can he be lively when his Wife is always dull and frown[s] at all his little gaieties?'[117] The reviewing started up again: an article on Lope de Vega in the *Quarterly* for October, the chance of a review of Coleridge's *Biographia Literaria*, and the revival of his previously mooted book on the Age of George III. He was even able to believe that things in Britain were better: the harvest had been good, trade was picking up, the poor laws would be tackled in the coming session of Parliament. Friends such as Bedford and Wynn would be visiting in October. In view of all this, it seems mere perversity of him to say to his uncle, 'it is not a pleasant thing to perceive how much better motion agrees with me than rest'.[118]

By the end of October the house was getting quite full: Nash, another artist called Westall who planned to live in the neighbourhood, Dr Bell, Mary Barker, a Mrs Crothers. There was talk of sending Derwent Coleridge off to stay with his father, but Coleridge senior was unwell; by the following April Derwent had become tutor to some boys under a Mr Hapgood, which would earn enough to set him up for Cambridge within a few years. Southey put aside his plans for the George III book, in favour of some *Colloquies*, modelled on Boethius, in which he would draw comparisons between the present and the Reformation (represented by the figure of Sir Thomas More). 'If I do this', he told Wynn, 'I shall not do it heartily'—presumably because the comparisons would be unfavourable to the present:[119] he said to Rickman that the scheme would 'expose the crisis towards which we are heading'. These *Colloquies* were to occupy him for some considerable time.

For the present, his *Life of Wesley* mattered more. He told Wilberforce that he had seen the great man in Bath when he, Southey, was 6 years old. Wesley came out of one of the rooms in the lodging-house, 'was struck with my appearance', and, placing his hands on the young Southey's head, blessed him.[120] This almost Coleridgean moment stayed with Southey all his life: in the new year he declared on a less personal note that Wesley was 'the most influential mind of the last century . . . I admire his tolerant & truly catholic spirit . . . I wish he had been less credulous.'[121] Wesley had become, bizarrely, some kind of role model for Southey: but there was also the historical importance of the man and the movement. To write on Methodism involved 'little less than the religious history of England for the last hundred years'.[122] This might have been a daunting task, but Southey was not one to be daunted. Just to prove the point, he simultaneously had the third volume of the *History of Brazil* in hand, another paper on the state of the poor, and a life of Walpole. We should perhaps feel relieved that even Southey fell at this hurdle, and never finished the life of Walpole. On the other hand, he was also resuming his series of poetical 'Inscriptions', in the belief that 'they will more completely exhibit my skill as an *artist*, than any other of my poems'.[123] For someone who spent so much of his time on long, sprawling epics (whether he liked the term or not), this is an intriguing admission; but there was also a moral motive behind some of this activity, in that he fondly imagined that, if such inscriptions were inscribed on tablets by the roadside, throughout the country, they would have a beneficial effect on 'the people'. If there is something rather pathetic about this, as though Southey were clutching at straws, there is also something typically Southeian about the combination of optimism and naïvety; in addition, there is a reminder of the connection between Southey's life as a poet and as a social reformer, as evidenced in his prose writings. When Westall's brother began to do some drawings based on Southey's poems, he began to think that Longman should publish all his collected works, with prints, to be followed by a cheaper edition, without notes. Twenty years later, such an edition appeared. In the mean time there was his next article for the *Quarterly*, 'On the Means of Improving the People', which would dwell upon the increase of the educated class, and the implications of this phenomenon. Southey was aware that the *Quarterly*, with a print run of 12,000, provided him with a wide audience. Rickman, it should be said, wrote most of this article, as Southey acknowledged: 'Your labours have given me a sort of holiday from the review.'[124]

The tranquillity of winter life in Keswick was rudely disturbed by the local elections in Westmoreland, where Brougham was standing. Violence soon erupted, and Southey was outraged that one of Brougham's 'mob' had nearly killed a prominent member of the community. So much for democracy, was Southey's simple response. He felt old, and unwilling to exert himself, a torpor exacerbated by the awful fact that his eyesight was deteriorating. When he heard that Scott was recovering from some illness, he wrote rather pompously, 'we stand in need sometimes of visitations which may lead us to look towards eternity; & in such cases the stroke is merciful when it falls on the body.'[125] Southey had certainly had his fair share of such visitations. But eternity would have to wait. If elections provoked such violence, then the mobs would certainly come out on the poor-law question, 'which is as perilous in its nature as a corn law bill'. Southey was convinced that with the firm smack of government all would be well: Canning only rarely rose to the occasion, but when he did, Southey was the first to applaud. As for Brougham's chances in the election, only lack of money would prevent his success. It was the immediacy of this electoral background, where principle seemed not to exist, that lent urgency to Southey's correspondence during March with Rickman about the state of the nation. They were planning a joint paper on this particular problem, in relation to poverty. Southey told Rickman, 'You can no longer have contented, unoffending & submissive ignorance—let us therefore take the people in childhood & teach them what to believe.'[126] Southey's work on Wesley, along with his interest in Alexander Bell, no doubt led him in this direction of quasi-religious fervour, this mixture of compassion and *dirigisme*. He was less compassionate towards the political meetings in Palace Yard: the solution, simple really, was to try the culprits for sedition, and pack them off to the colonies (which was also what he would like to do with quite a lot of ordinary, law-abiding citizens). When Murray told him in April that he would rather not have any of Southey's articles on politics and religion in the *Quarterly*, because they were 'certain of offending a great mass of people', Southey was himself offended. After all, he was not fighting a lone battle: even Words-worth, he said, '(*inter nos*), is at this very time preparing a heavy battery against Brougham', who had, according to Dorothy Wordsworth, virtually incited the mob to stone her brother, 'for stoning is the order of the day'.[127]

The first proofs of *Wesley* were on Southey's desk in May: it was to be a two-volume octavo edition. Southey became either resigned or blasé about politics. He told Croker that 'I neither write nor dream of poetry, & think of political events as little as I can help'.[128] In spite of the surrounding election fever, he saw no prospect of the imminent dissolution of Parliament, and felt he could relax: 'Now that there is nothing of importance at stake', he told John May, 'one may look upon politics as upon a game in which we have no interest.'[129] He was content, so long as peace lasted, to watch the two parties blunder their way through. It was true that Spain might recover her colonies unless America engaged in war, but Southey seems to have become more detached, more unfocused. He told his uncle on 15 May, 'My head is like one of these Kaleidoscopes, full of all sorts of facts & notions belonging to them,—when I sit down to any one subject,—it is like turning the glass, off flies one set, & another arranges itself instantly in regular form.'[130] He enjoyed the glorious weather (in spite of hay fever and a swollen upper lip), and wrote on 18 July, 'we are enjoying a real, honest, old fashioned summer, such as summers were forty years ago, when I used to gather grapes from my grandmothers chamber window'.[131] He began to plan a trip to Scotland, with Rickman and Thomas Telford, the engineer of the Caledonian Canal. He was looking for a house for Wilberforce, who wanted to come and stay in August. There was the occasional rude reminder of political realities, as when Wordsworth's 13-year-old daughter was walking out in Kendal with a yellow ribbon, and was smacked across the face by one woman, and pushed out of the street by another shouting, 'Lowther for never, | A knife in his heart, & a fork in his liver'.[132] But such events seemed less important than the news of the death of old friends like Tom Lamb, or Dean of Westminster School (the latter murdered by a Malay boatman). Of Lamb he said rather dismissively and with a sad lack of self-awareness, 'He was an old man at 30', but then continued, 'Scarcely a week passes in which I do not dream of Westminster, so strong a hold have those years upon the mind'. That hold was indeed strong, and yet the old acquaintances were going, and Southey increasingly felt like the sole survivor from a better and a happier age. That he was expelled from that Eden was either something he conveniently forgot, or something that made him remember it all the more regretfully. When he was offered another sinecure, the Librarianship of the Advocates' Library in Edinburgh, at £400 a year, he found no difficulty in turning it down straightaway. The Lake District had become his home, and was now 'in its utmost beauty, & we now have some refreshing rain'.[133] The only real sadness on the domestic front was that Mrs Lovell was 'miserably weak & ill'. Sara Coleridge was still there, sometimes a nuisance, but for much of the time a foil to Southey's banter: when he tells his uncle that boiling is the best solution for rheumatism, he adds, 'if Mrs Coleridge should complain much more of her rheumatism, I will boil her'.[134]

Southey found himself unwittingly dragged back into party politics in June. When Brougham attacked Wordsworth and Southey on the hustings at Appleby, Southey immediately leapt into action with another 'William Smithiad', which he promised would be a 'thunderer', 'a very proper opportunity for chasing a man who has thus slandered me in the face of my neighbours, & exposing him as he deserves to be exposed'.[135] Duty could be highly pleasurable. Brougham had said that the 'apostate poets' had once been poor and radical, but were now rich and conservative. Earlier, Brougham had said in the Commons that Southey's comments on the Whig politician Whitbread were libellous, and there had been talk of Southey's being arraigned at the bar of the Commons. This latest *brouhaha* gave Southey a chance to get his own back on yet another member of the *Edinburgh Review* brigade. In the event, the counsels of Bedford and Rickman prevailed, and the piece, signed 'Samson Agonistes', was not published, except in truncated form as a postscript to the 1821 edition of the *Carmen Triumphale* (with names carefully removed). But Southey drew strength from his allies: 'The worst symptom of the times', he told Rickman, perhaps more ambiguously than he realized, 'is that you & Wordsworth and S. T. C. so entirely agree with one another in your prognosis.'[136]

Having rhapsodized about the warmth of the summer, Southey told Wilberforce at the end of July that he was glad that the heat (literal and political) had abated, 'So I can have my beloved fire!' By the light of the flames he read a recent volume, *Ellen Fitzarthur*, sent him by a young writer from Hampshire called Caroline Bowles. With that admonitory primness that he used for aspiring writers (Ebenezer Elliott earlier, Charlotte Brontë later), he told her that no criticism could be 'too minute nor too rigid', and proceeded to make detailed comments on her work. This was to be the beginning of a crucial friendship, although neither of them could have known what would develop from such an innocent enquiry. At first it was a friendship based on correspondence, but even then it had an urgency that Caroline Bowles acknowledged in a letter of 21 January 1820: 'I have so often been guilty of replying to your letters with

Sara Coleridge and Edith May Southey, portrait by Edward Nash, 1820

View from the south window of the study at Greta Hall by Caroline Bowles, 1841

Caroline Bowles Southey, self-portrait, n.d.

Robert Southey, portrait by John Downman, 1812.

Bust of Robert Southey by Francis Chantrey, 1832

indiscreet haste...' Longman duly published the poem, without the author's name on the title-page, to be followed in 1822 by *The Widow's Tale, and other Poems.*[137]

Tom, meanwhile, was about to rent a house in the Vale of Newlands, about four miles away, for £50, with thirty acres of land on which he could graze his cattle; the local market for dairy produce was good. Southey was pleased that, after so many years separated by the seas, he would have his brother so close. The Beaumonts spent ten days or so with the Southeys in the second half of August; Murray called in; Charles Lloyd and General Peachey would both visit before the end of the month. As the first rain fell since the first week in May, Southey came to the end of Clarendon's *History of the Rebellion*, and had his belief in the 'conservative principles' of society fully confirmed.[138] He then settled down to write about the copyright question for the *Quarterly*, no doubt feeling more strongly about it as a result of the *Wat Tyler* saga.

It was about this time that Southey continued his correspondence with John Coleridge, who was about to get married—something Southey was usually keen to encourage. John Coleridge was useful to Southey in various ways, partly because of his connections: he had sent him some extracts from the Exeter College records about Wesley's father (duly acknowledged in one of Southey's punctilious notes). Southey was able to send good reports of Derwent and Hartley Coleridge, which made a change. Lord Lowther came over with Wordsworth for tea in mid-September; Wilberforce ('such a *straggling* visitor'[139]) arrived in early October, and then took ages to go. Although he was initially irritated by Wilberforce, and irked by what he saw as his chaotic family, Southey grew fond of him: 'there is such a constant hilarity in every look & motion, such a sweetness in all his tones, such a benignity in all his thoughts, words, & actions, that all sense of his grotesque appearance is presently overcome, & you feel nothing but love & admiration for a creature of so happy & blessed a nature.'[140] Many were to talk in rather similar terms of Southey himself; he recognized, whatever the differences, a kindred spirit when he saw one.

Southey was to be a father again. This filled him with a gloom to which he openly admitted: 'it is but too certain that I should neither have life nor heart ever again to perform my duty by another in the same manner'.[141] No child would replace the lost and lovely Herbert. Towards the end of the year, he thought aloud about growing old, which in turn made him look back to the past. As he wrote to John May about the nature of rebellion, he recalled, as he had often done in rather similar circumstances, that momentous first day of March 1792, when the *Flagellant* first appeared:

'if ever my head touched the stars while I walked upon the earth it was then. It seemed as if I had overleapt a barrier, which till then had kept me from the fields of immortality, wherein my career was to be run.' But against such a triumphant and visionary moment, there was the recollection of Edmund Seward, his 'moral father' at Balliol: 'sometimes even now I dream of him, & wake myself by weeping, because even in my dreams I remember that he is dead.'[142]

In a similar retrospective mood, Southey wrote to Wilberforce on Boxing Day, with a confession that might also have stood as a rebuke. 'When I was a young man I was proud, presumptuous & positive. My views were clear because they were confined.—I saw only the single point before me on which my attention was fixed. I had no misgivings, & was so conscious my intentions were right that it never occurred to me even as a possibility that my opinions might be wrong.'[143] One could speculate on the depths of Southey's remorse here, but it would be fruitless; it is sufficient to see him gazing so honestly at the gap between his two selves.

If Southey was getting too morose over the festive season, the news of Hartley Coleridge's second class degree must have gladdened the general atmosphere: a second was enough to get him his Fellowship at Oriel. Even so, Southey was uncomfortably aware how like his father Hartley was, and therefore unable to be too sanguine about the future: 'a perverse love of paradox... never brings forth good fruit'. It would be fair to say that Southey never succumbed to this particular vice, and that perhaps if he had at least leant in that direction occasionally, then more people would have ascribed to him the virtue he associated with its opposite. Derwent was less of a problem: he would leave his present situation next year with about £370, and had started on a translation of Louis Dobrizhoffer's Latin work, the *Account of the Abipones*, which Murray was prepared to print. (In fact, the work appeared in three volumes in 1821, but from the pen of the young and talented Sara Coleridge.) Derwent would be entered at St John's College, Cambridge, the following May. Southey's brother Tom, however, although he was settling nearby with his family and cattle, still worried Southey, who was not persuaded that the cattle would support a wife and six children.[144]

As the previous year, so January 1819 began rather dolefully. Mrs Coleridge, Sara and Edith went off on New Year's Eve to stay with the Wordsworths, and the three younger children were visiting Mrs Calvert; the house was 'dismally silent'.[145] What he really wanted to do was finish the *History of Brazil* and the *Life of Wesley*, then go to London, so that he could get the *History of the Peninsular War* to press. But he was as anxious as ever about the state of the nation and of Europe; wherever one looked, he said to Landor, 'the materials for explosion seem ready: & there is no exhilarating consideration for one who has lived long enough to know that order is the first thing needful in society. Here in England a fair harvest & a flourishing trade give us a surface tranquillity.'[146] Southey knew, partly because of the turbulence so close to home in the previous year, that such tranquillity could be an illusion. But, in spite of everything, his optimism could still shine through. Apart from anything else, it was so warm that he had not yet had to wear his flannel drawers.[147]

'MY PROPER STATION'

1819–1824

SOUTHEY was spurred on by proofs from Rickman, 'every one of which operates upon me like the crack of a whip in the air upon a willing horse'.[1] That curiously masochistic eagerness kept him going. When he heard the news of Scott's baronetcy, his reaction, as with the Laureateship, was very much in comparative terms: Scott's public success was something he clearly envied, and not just for financial reasons. 'He is a good-hearted man, frank, friendly, generous, without a spark of envy in his nature, & not in the slightest degree inflated by his extraordinary success. As for myself, I know that I am in my vocation, & all things considered I believe that I am in my place.' There is a nice twist about that final qualified statement, for Southey's 'place' was not readily defined; what he objected to was precisely the charge of being a 'place man'.[2]

He was now into the third book of *Oliver Newman*, and planned to revive, in the summer, *Espriella*, again for an interesting reason: it provided him with a mask, an advantage when he was so conscious of the accusation of egotism (to which he had admitted in the Proem to the *Lay of the Laureate*). The idea not so much of anonymity as of disguise stayed with him, helping to explain his fascination with *The Doctor*, and the games he was to play, both within that work and with other people, as to who the author might be. At the same time, his work on Brazil and Wesley continued precisely because of his passionate involvement. For a similar reason he kept in touch with Wilberforce, pleased that he was keen to reform the criminal laws; he also confessed to him that although he had refused as a young man to take orders ('I lost my way in early life'), he now depended upon Christianity, and without it 'existence would be a mystery too dreadful to be endured'.[3] This provided another incentive for pressing on with the *Life of Wesley*.

On 24 February, after a difficult labour, Edith gave birth to a boy, Charles Cuthbert, for whom Wynn and Bedford were to act as god-parents. Edith's health, never good at the best of times, worsened after the birth, and she began to suffer lameness. The other children were naturally delighted to have another sibling; three months later Southey was saying that Cuthbert was liable to be torn to pieces by his sisters 'in their outrageous fondness. He is perpetually reminding me of Gulliver in the arms of the monkey.'[4] But Southey was bemused and saddened: he remembered too well how Herbert had been snatched away, and Edith's illness simply reinforced his sense of life's frailty. 'After an interval of nearly seven years, the cry of an infant in the house is a strange sound.'[5] Far from making him feel young again, the new arrival reminded him of his age. Revealingly, in a letter to Scott of 11 March, he writes as if they have both come to the end of their writing lives, and talks dismissively of their 'successors', who are 'overlabouring their productions, & overloading them with ornament, so that all parts are equally prominent, everywhere glare & glitter, & no keeping & no repose'.[6] This was partly aimed at Henry Milman, but similar criticisms were to be made of Keats (and also, of course, of Southey himself). When an American visitor called, and they spoke of Scott, Southey's competitive edge came out once more: Scott might have his 'golden pap-spoon', but 'I, of the wooden spoon, am likely to become popular in New England by my next long poem'.[7]

Southey was not too well during March and April: in spite of Cuthbert's rapid growth, earning him the unceremonious nickname 'Og', it was 'a dismal house'.[8] Edith developed an abscess on her bottom; Tom was fixed at Newlands with six cows and six children, but the house was only half-built, and the farm was a sorry one.[9] The one advantage was that visiting Tom gave Southey a chance to bathe in the 'beck' at Newlands. Rickman sent some oranges to cheer Southey up; his diet was certainly an odd one, judging by a report to Bedford on 5 May that they had had roasted rat for supper, but it was too young to be really tasty, 'more like roasted pig than anything else... but as for Mrs Coleridge, you should have seen her face when we talked of it at breakfast'.[10] Bishop Hatto was getting his revenge. More importantly, the last chapter of the *History of Brazil* was at the printers, 'the fit conclusion of a work upon which my reputation hereafter may safely rest'.[11] He foresaw a time when Brazil would become the greatest of the new states, provided it could counteract the levelling tendency of America: his *History* was therefore to be seen as a major political statement, not just about the past, but about the present and future. In writing this *History*, he was not engaging in some quaint, antiquarian interest; for him it was the focal point of historical change in the world: 'I have an insatiable appetite for contemporary history', he told his uncle in May.[12] Posterity's cruelty has exposed the wrongness of his diagnosis, but there was at least some logic in what he said. His literary judgements have stood the test of time rather more successfully: against the general ridicule that greeted Wordsworth's *Peter Bell*, Southey (to whom it was dedicated) could see its virtues, partly because he and Wordsworth shared a delight in the combination of the grotesque and the sympathetic which their ballads exemplified. That Southey also liked *Benjamin the Waggoner* is further testimony to his ability to go against the current grain.[13]

Edith was out and about again, but, with an infection in one of her breasts, clearly not right; Southey could only hope that 'air, gentle exercise, & cooking fruits' would get her back to normal. He himself would be in London sometime in the summer, hoping to see John May, his uncle at Streatham, and Walpole's papers in the Foreign Office. He heard that Hartley Coleridge had been elected a Fellow at Oriel, but he was advising Nicholas Lightfoot at the end of May to send his son to Balliol rather than Oriel. Balliol was, apparently, a reformed place, 'no longer the seat of drunkenness, oaffery & indiscipline, as it was in our days'. But he was sad to hear his old tutor, Howe, had retired to a country living: better, he thought significantly, to have become a monk.[14]

In fact, the visit to London was deferred until the autumn, when Rickman and his friend Telford, the distinguished engineer, persuaded Southey to go with them to the Highlands, to see the Caledonian Canal, before Rickman drew up his final report on it. Wordsworth had spent three days with the Southeys, and they had done a lot of walking, in strange weather which combined hot sun and cold winds, 'as if ice were floating in that direction'. Tom had lost one of his cows before half the hay was in, when a downpour made things worse. Southey sought advice from his medical brother Harry about various unspecified ailments. The exultation on finishing his *History of Brazil* was accordingly rather muted: he told his uncle on 25 June that he had ten more years' work in him (an underestimate), but 'who can calculate upon ten minutes?'[15] In something of the same spirit, he warned Allan Cunningham, author of the *Maid of Elvar*, not to rely on the pen: 'to trust to it for support is misery & ruin.'[16] That sounds unduly bitter, especially when ten days later he was looking forward to the £400 he hoped to make with *Wesley*. Meanwhile, one of his '*curmudgeons*', Ebenezer Elliott, the 'Corn Law Rhymer', had produced a poem called 'Night', which Southey could not approve. Far better were Crabbe's *Tales*: his poems 'will have a great and lasting value as pictures of domestic life, elucidating the moral history of these times ... He knows his own powers, and never aims above his reach.' Once again, a perfectly fair comment on another poet throws into some relief Southey's own readiness to overreach himself.[17]

When Southey came across part of Byron's latest poem, *Don Juan*, in a newspaper, with its 'absurd rhyme' on his own name, he claimed not to be bothered. 'Attack me as he will, I shall not go out of my course to break a spear with him; but if it comes in my way to give him a passing touch, it will be one that leaves a scar.'[18] Southey had, after all, decided to leave his own, earlier, attack on Byron unpublished. The lines in question, from Canto I, have become part of the tradition of what might be called making fun of Southey:

> Thou shalt believe in Milton, Dryden, Pope;
>   Thou shalt not set up Wordsworth, Coleridge, Southey;
> Because the first is crazed beyond all hope,
>   The second drunk, the third so quaint and mouthey...

The two of them were soon to lock horns again. In the mean time, Southey could derive some pleasure from the fact that the Dedication, in which he was mercilessly pilloried as an 'epic renegade', had been suppressed: if Murray were the publisher of *Don Juan*, he could well suffer 'loss of credit'. Southey was happy to leave it there for the time being. He went off to Scotland in September, admiring the landscape and the formidable feats of engineering, with a sardonic comment that 'if this had been one of Buonaparte's works half the English would have gone to see it'. He envied the apparent simplicity of Telford's 'happy life':

everywhere making roads, building bridges, forming canals, and creating harbours—works of sure, solid, permanent utility; everywhere employing a great number of persons, selecting the most meritorious, and putting them forward in the world, in his own way . The plan upon which he proceeds in road-making is this: first to level and drain; then, like the Romans, to lay a solid pavement of large stones, the round or broad end downwards, as close as they can be set; the points are then broken off, and a layer of stones broken to about the size of walnuts, laid over them, so that the whole are bound together; over all a little gravel if it be at hand, but this is not essential.[19]

The methodical way in which Southey records in his letters and journal what he sees, how things work, seems to reflect his own delight in such mechanical details. There seems, even, to be a touch of the Utilitarian about him, but this could be misleading, as his account of the end of his trip suggests.

At the end of September they visited Owen's New Lanark, about which he had heard when Owen had visited him two years earlier. The great man—and, whatever Hazlitt's qualifications, there can be little doubt about Owen's stature—led them around the mill:

It is needless to say anything more of the Mills than that they are perfect in their kind, according to the present state of mechanical science, and that they appeared to be under admirable management; they are thoroughly clean, and so carefully ventilated, that there was no unpleasant smell in any of the apartments. Everything required for the machinery is made upon the spot, and the expense of wear and tear is estimated at 8000£ annually. There are stores also from which the people are supplied with all the necessaries of life . . .

This all sounds very well. But Southey realizes the Gradgrind-like implications of the scheme: 'his humour, his vanity, his kindliness of nature (all these have their share) lead him to make these *human machines* as he calls them (and too literally believes them to be) as happy as he can, and to make a display of their happiness.' Southey is brought up against his own revulsion at such apparent manipulation, and also against his own past:

Et in Utopia ego. But I never regarded man as a machine; I never believed him to be a merely material being; I never for a moment could listen to the nonsense of Helvetius, nor suppose, as Owen does, that men may be cast in a mould (like the other parts of the mill) and take the impression with perfect certainty. Nor did I ever disguise from myself the difficulties of a system which took for its foundation the principle of a community of goods . . . He keeps out of sight from others, and perhaps from himself, that his system, instead of aiming at perfect freedom, can only be kept in play by absolute power . . .[20]

But Southey's answer to all this is not very constructive: merely to suggest that perhaps Owen's scheme could be tried out on a colony of paupers. 'Such a variety in society would be curious; and might as well be encouraged as Quakerism and Moravianism.' In other words, they would make an entertaining zoo, a mindless set of monkeys. In the mean time, there was one particular pleasure which he treasured above all, when he cut open the leaves of one of his books for the first time. Furthermore, he celebrated his journey with some Inscriptions in honour of Telford: art could still have the final word.[21]

Telford left the other two at Carlisle, and Rickman returned to Keswick with Southey for a couple of weeks. Southey was soon embroiled again in local politics. Brougham's politicking had alarmed Calvert sufficiently for him to suggest an address be sent to the Prince Regent. Southey wrote a draft, which was revised by Lord Lonsdale, and sent off to General Peachey in the hunt for signatures; he was displeased to learn that his own efforts were substituted by something by a certain Wallace, but sent on the revised version, for Rickman to pass on to Lord William Gordon.

It is the direct and undisguised object of those demagogues by whom the multitude are misled, to bring about a revolution by force. For this purpose men are openly trained to arms, and assembled in bodies which bid defiance to the civil power: assassination has been recommended and in more than one instance attempted; and lists are avowedly kept in which the loyal members of the community are marked for proscription. The rights of property are threatened; and the deluded populace are taught to believe that the administration of public affairs ought to be taken from persons who are qualified by their education and station in life, and whose stake in the country is a pledge for their good intentions, and transferred to the ignorant and needy, who are necessarily incompetent, and who have nothing to lose.... however much we regret the lives which were lost at Manchester, we cannot but see that greater and far more extensive evil must arise, if multitudes are allowed to assemble under such circumstances, in contempt of the constituted authorities...[22]

He was gratified that his own version had been 'pronounced to be the best which had yet been sent forth'. Lonsdale encouraged him to write a vindication of his first address, and in the process to give Brougham a good drubbing. It was time, apparently, to resist the Whigs, especially since the Government seemed to be strong: 'They [the Whigs] will be deserted on this occasion by all who have any regard to decency, or any common sense.'[23] Certainly it was a comfort to find Philpotts writing such a good 'Letter to the Freeholders'; Southey grew confident that any insurrection could be nipped in the bud; all it required was faith in Providence.[24]

Murray was eager for Southey to write more regularly for the *Quarterly*, which merely gave Southey a chance to get on his high horse: 'if preventive means had been used when first I pointed out the coming danger in the Q. R. much of the existing evil might have been easily averted.' Furthermore, whatever he might have said about the advantages of the mask of *Espriella*, there was no advantage in anonymity when it came to matters of state: 'I have already as large a portion of critical & Jacobinical abuse as can possibly be bestowed upon me.' In other words, Southey would be recognized as Southey by anyone who knew what was what. Nor did he feel obliged to Murray any more; there was no need to suffer more editorial mutilations. One day, he could say, he would treat the 'Prospects of Society... in my own way, & to my own satisfaction'.[25]

But Southey could not ignore what was happening, whatever he might tell Murray to put in his pipe and smoke: the so-called Peterloo Massacre of August was seen by many as a disaster. A crowd of about 60,000 had gathered in St Peter's Fields, Manchester, on 16 August, to hear 'Orator' Hunt speak (as he had done two years earlier) on behalf of parliamentary reform: this was simply the most serious of many events in which the clamour for reform, for employment, and for lower taxation found voice. 'Peterloo' acquired something of a mythical significance, partly as a result of Shelley's savage poem, 'The Mask of Anarchy', written soon after the event but not published until 1832. The cruel fact was that eleven people were killed, and about 500 injured, in the mayhem that ensued when soldiers were sent in to rescue the Manchester yeomanry, who found themselves cornered by the crowd as they arrested the speakers. This was enough to turn Hunt into a hero and a martyr; the Government's response was to impose the six 'Gagging Acts' of December 1819. For his part Southey shrugged off the episode as a pardonable mistake on the part of the yeomanry; his comments reveal chillingly just how prepared he was to let Providence and the Government take their proper course. 'I look upon it as an unfortunate business, because it has enabled factious & foolish men to raise an outcry, & divert public attention from the great course of events to a mere accidental occurrence. That the meeting was unlawful, & in *terrorem populi* is to me perfectly clear.'[26] Much the same was said after Bloody Sunday, in Londonderry, in 1971. Southey becomes a distinctly unsympathetic figure in these months at the end of 1819: Peterloo is repeatedly referred to as an 'accident (in the school meaning of the term)', and it is as though he feels vindicated by this violent turn of events. There is no sense, now, of despair: he announces all too smugly to John May on 23 November, 'If the cataclasm comes it will find me in my usual occupations'.[27] He was as worried about his finances as much as anything; and there was always his writing. In a letter to Wynn in December, he had recourse to an image that he had used when a much younger man, but this time what disturbs is the self-conceit; as the world, by his own analysis, is on the brink of collapse, and people are being killed by Government troops, he can write, 'I am as busy & as comfortable as a silkworm who is working upon his cone & has just shut himself in from the external world'.[28] Rather typically, when the death of the King seems imminent, he acknowledges that his own Laureate work will lose its appeal, but also that it will provide an occasion for another poem, and he will go ahead and use the hexameters which he knows will bring ridicule upon his unbowed head. We should note, though, his comments to Croker after Hone's acquittal on a charge of blasphemy in December 1819, when he spoke of what he called, interestingly enough, the 'tyranny of the pen'; 'a plague of wild beasts is less dreadful than a plague of insects & reptiles, & we would rather fall under a lions paw than be devoured alive by vermin.'[29] Once again, the ghost of Bishop Hatto rises from his past. On the last day of the year, he talked to his uncle of his plans for *Colloquies*, for the Age of George III, for the *Tale of Paraguay* (slowed down by the difficulties of the Spenserian stanza); *Wesley* would be finished in January. It was indeed as though the world beyond Keswick could go hang.

To put it like that, though, is not quite fair to Southey. His *Colloquies* were to be much more than a piece of nostalgia for the long lost glories of a golden age; the motto, from St Bernard, '*Respice, aspice, prospice!*', was a reflection of his own role in events. By 14 January 1820 he had written the Introduction (thereby breaking the rule budding writers are usually given), and on the same day, appropriately, he received Hone's savage squib, *The Political House that Jack Built*, and heard, just as appropriately, of Wynn's attempts to get Burdett sent to the Tower for his speech on Hobhouse. If he was curling up inside his cocoon, he was also addressing himself to the issues of the day, both in specific ways and in the more general overviews that he favoured, because they allowed him to see a pattern in the affairs of men. He told Rickman, 'I am less afraid of the eruption of the disease, than of the danger there is that we should again suppose ourselves safe because no eruption takes place.'[30] He had said similar things before, and he was to say them again; he knew the disease was there, and it was a mistake to suppose, as the Government did, that the 'Radicals' had been defeated. The press must be curbed. It is interesting that what he felt and thought about the political turmoil of the day was reflected in what he thought about his own *History of Brazil*: he had come across some more manuscript information since he started the work, but there was no occasion on which he had found himself 'erroneous in the views which I had taken or the opinion which I have formed'.[31] Southey had shed the self-doubts of the truly enquiring mind.

He pursued his poem on the king, *A Vision of Judgement*, 'mere task verses' he called them. But he was asserting his own authority here: 'Most persons I know would dissuade me from such an experiment—but I am following my own humour, & writing in English hexameters.'[32] He was curiously determined to produce the poem that was to bring him more obloquy than anything else he ever wrote; his self-righteousness—moral, aesthetic, and political—would get short shrift from a Byron eager to pounce. But who was Byron to Southey?

News of the Cato Street conspiracy, whereby Andrew Thistlewood and his right-hand man Watson planned to blow up the whole cabinet in revenge for the Peterloo Massacre, aroused Southey's wrath, even more so when the jury acquitted the ring-leaders. Furthermore, there were problems with the royal family: the new King had, in 1795, when Prince Regent, married Princess Caroline of Brunswick; but they had lived apart and both pursued their extravagant lives. George's fear was that Caroline would want, none the less, to return and be crowned Queen (which indeed she did); he accordingly had her arraigned on a Bill of Pains and Penalties in Parliament, on the grounds of her adultery. The trial, if that is the right word, was a farce, with a green canvas bag (a commonly used container for legal documents) being used as the vessel from which statements were flourished about chamber pots and bed linen. The bill was dismissed: there was a strong popular feeling behind Caroline, and against the absurdities of the Regent. It was a field-day for the cartoonists. But Southey was not amused, and clung on to the mistaken belief that at least the Cato Street conspirators would get their just desserts: with relish he declared, 'the gallows will now have its due'. Once that had happened, once the 'devils who are got into the swinish multitude can be cast out', then normal service would be resumed. His optimism depended on the defeat of these renegades, and he saw it as part of his role to exorcize the swine; he had conveniently forgotten that he had once, and not so long ago, admitted to his own 'swinish' tendencies. But his optimism could take some strange forms, as in his expectation of a plague from Providence, 'at once to punish us & to preserve us from the only evil that would be greater'. He was to get his wish sooner than he might have expected. At the same time, there is a certain jadedness of mind when he tries to wrap his thoughts around social issues: for example, he tries to suggest to Rickman, in February, that the distress of the farmers is due to the effects of the war, whereas that of the manufacturers is not: 'it would have been thought but by the Steam Engine tho there had been no war...' He then throws up his hands, as though it is all beyond him—which, in many ways, it is: 'But how complicated are all these questions!'[33] Thirty-four years later Dickens was to do something similar with Stephen Blackpool in *Hard Times*: 'it's aw a muddle!'

The beginning of March was deeply saddened by the death of Mrs Wilson, the housekeeper who had lived with the family for years, 'struck down by a fit which left her deaf, blind & senseless to all appearance'.[34] Southey had been extremely fond of her, partly because of her innate goodness, but partly because she had been part of his life for so long, an antidote to the asperities of his Aunt Tyler: 'there never lived a better creature: I never saw anyone with a more generous spirit, or a more affectionate heart.'[35] She touchingly left £20 to Hartley Coleridge, and £5 each to Derwent, Sara, and Robert Lovell; Southey was her executor. This loss was matched by local upheavals: Brougham was denying any previous abuse, Curwen had ousted Lord Morpeth, and young Graham, a radical, was likely to come in for Carlisle. Southey's conviction that all would be well was shaken by this turn of events: the swinish multitude would not be so easily exorcized.

He set off in April on his travels, to visit London, but also Oxford, Cambridge, and Norwich. On 13 May he wrote a touching letter to his daughter Isabel, telling her about his visit to court, which he had clearly enjoyed. He had remained true to his student rejection of wigs or powdered hair, 'but I had a bag, & lace at my shirt, & lace ruffles, & gold buckles on my shoes, & at my knees, & cocked hat in my hand. Think, Isabel, how grand I must have been.'[36] Much grander than the fat woman who sat in front of him at St Paul's, in a service for children of the clergy: 'she sat so that I could see her stumpy grey bristles under a brown wig, & could not help seeing a dirty under petticoat through her pocket hole.'[37] Southey could be both proud and cruel. What his daughters thought of all this, back in Keswick, we can only surmise.

He spent some time at the end of May in Cambridge, meeting Neville White, hearing Dr Clarke preach, dining with Chauncey Townshend. An invitation came from Oxford, to receive an honorary degree, along with Lord Hill and the Duke of Wellington. Whatever his feelings about Oxford, he could hardly (especially since Rickman was obligingly paying for it) refuse an offer that signified public acceptance by the establishment—in many ways more important to him, as writer and historian, than the Poet Laureateship. He certainly enjoyed the occasion. He was met off the coach by Hartley Coleridge, dined with Chantrey and Collins, and stayed in Oriel with William Heathcoat, nephew of Mrs Herbert Hill: Hartley had, due to drunkenness and neglect of his duties, lost his Fellowship (there had been talk of his more than once being 'picked up dead drunk in the streets').[38] On the day of the ceremony he had lunch with the Vice-Chancellor at Brasenose, and dinner at Balliol at 10.00 in the evening, where he claimed that the only person to recognize him was the college porter, who used to cut his hair, and whose wife did his laundry. He told Lightfoot that none of his contemporaries was there after the ceremony, but he did in fact see Ginger Barnes (failing, at first, to recognize him); 'I walked', he told Lightfoot, 'for some hours alone about the walks & gardens, where you & I have so often walked together, thinking of the days that are gone, the friends that are departed . . . time, & change, & mortality.'[39] He was back in London by 16 June, having had breakfast on the way with Charles Lamb and Mary Betham, who was now sadly deranged; but before he got home, he wrote, from Streatham, a comic letter to his daughters, in which he punctuated the pomposity of the whole occasion. He also wrote to Edith, expressing his anxieties about the children, who had measles, and hoping that summer bathing and ripe fruit would sort them out. Cuthbert's bowels were causing problems: Southey urged Edith to 'introduce him to the strawberry bed'.[40] There seems to have been something about soft fruit. His brother Tom was still a problem, and it was clear that taking in a lodger could only be temporary remedy for their financial embarrassment: the only plausible solution, for Southey, was for them to emigrate. Even though Southey's finances were more secure, with his insurance probably worth £6,000 by now, he did not want to take on the burden of Tom's huge family. He wrote to Edith with the slightly unnerving information that his will was in a sealed paper in his desk: Harry, John May, and Neville White were his executors and trustees. But in spite of this rather valedictory tone, he said he would be returning with his aunt and Edward Nash, the artist. Edith had clearly and reasonably grown tired of the constant stream of visitors, and must have expressed a wish to be alone with her husband and children for a while. Charles Lamb had written in 1801 that Southey's wife 'is considerably improved, and will talk if she is talked to, but she bitterly complains that when literary men get together, they never speak to women'.[41] Southey's response to Edith was rather churlish, and not calculated to endear him to the wife who was all but fading from his life; she had become a piece of the furniture. 'Your wish to have me for a few days at least to yourself, I take kindly, as it is meant.' Alas, poor Edith.

Southey had also seen Caroline Bowles in Chelsea, at the beginning of June; the young writer he had encouraged two years earlier was so over-whelmed by the occasion that she became tongue-tied; within six months Southey was writing, 'you & I must be better acquainted personally; you must become acquainted with my wife & daughter.' He was keen for her to come and stay at Greta Hall. This is all innocent enough, but there is no denying that the relationship gathers a momentum of its own; Southey acts initially as mentor, the mature poet offering advice and encourage-ment, whilst she is the eager acolyte, almost crushed by her humility, her sense of inferiority and resignation: 'How I should long for such pleasure [of going to Greta Hall] had I not almost left off longing for anything...' Alas, poor Caroline; and alas, again, poor Edith.[42]

When he got home, after a difficult journey made worse by the heat—they left Bristol at 8.00 p.m., and it was still 85°F—it was the children, and especially Cuthbert, with his newly acquired ability to walk, and his curly hair (just like his father), about whom he wrote to May. He could spend hours, apparently, making bird and animal noises to amuse Cuthbert, or imitating the cries of London (just as his Uncle William had done, all those years ago). He decided he would set down the early years of his life, in a series of letters to John May. These letters contain some of his most revealing and intimate recollections, providing us with most of our information about his early life before his departure to Westminster; it is our loss that he did not continue them, for whatever reason. Perhaps he realized that everything became rather too complicated after that.

Instead, he planned a history of English literature and manners ('things which ought not to be separated'), and Murray would pay him 1,000 guineas per quarto volume. As for Edith, he told Rickman she would write to him, 'but she loves not pen & ink, & at this time household business is thick & throughly'.[43]

Southey's next large project was to be a history of the Quakers (when he wasn't doing all those other things, like the *Book of the Church, Colloquies, Oliver Newman*, his History of English Literature). He had begun, per-force, a correspondence with the minor Quaker poet, Bernard Barton, which had turned into a discussion of the principles of Quakerism. Spurred on by this, he realized he could do for the Quakers what he had done for Methodism with his *Life of Wesley*: it was typical, and coura-geous, of Southey, to write about sects with which he was not in sympathy, but whose importance he could recognize. Of course, people who knew his views merely regarded him as an interloper in their affairs, and he got few thanks for his pains. But even now, the *Life of Wesley* especially has a value for historians of the age; it counts as one of Southey's important contributions to the study of Nonconformism. Southey, however, did not allow all this to get in the way of summer hospitality, whatever Edith's desire for privacy. Mr Earl brought over some of his grouse in mid-August, and there was a neck of Lowther venison to be consumed (presumably preferable to local rat).[44] Aunt Mary came on 14 August.

The infamous row over the Queen, as we have seen, could not be ignored, even in Keswick: it was another symptom of society's disease, and Southey resorted to one of his favourite images: 'My comfort is that as things must be worse before they can get better, the sooner the abscess bursts the more strength there will be in the constitution to turn off & struggle through the disease.'[45] The national disease had its own family echo in the fate of Hartley Coleridge, and Southey's response to Hartley's downfall, his drunkenness, and his loss of his Oriel Fellowship, and to John Coleridge's letter about it, must partly have been due to some sense that he too had been in a rather similar parlous state nearly thirty years earlier. It was all very well to talk of the 'shame & contrition' Hartley would have felt if he had seen how the Wordsworths reacted to the news. But Southey too had been expelled, first from Westminster, then from his aunt's house, and, in effect, from Oxford, by his own actions; he too had chosen the path of love and marriage, against the better judgement of his elders and betters. So when he speculated that Hartley might marry the woman with whom he was infatuated, to cover 'the disgrace of this sort of expulsion... it will do this, but according to all human foresight, it will compleat his ruin', we, at this remove, can hear the pot once again blackening the kettle. Southey seemed surprised, when he saw Hartley a little later, that he was in such good spirits. He had forgotten his own youthful ebullience at kicking over the traces.[46]

A row with Shelley was a further illustration of this. Shelley had been led to believe that a harsh review of his *Revolt of Islam*, in the *Quarterly Review*, had been Southey's work. Southey denied it, and sent a letter which was hardly placatory:

your powers for poetry are of a high order—but the manner in which those powers have been employed is such as to prevent one from feeling any desire to see more of productions so monstrous in their kind & so pernicious in their tendency... I cannot think of you without the deepest compassion... have they [your opinions] not brought immediate misery upon others & guilt—which is all but immediate upon yourself.[47]

A second letter pursued the comparison which Shelley had drawn between the two of them:

Nor were my opinions ever similar to yours in any other point, than that desiring as I still desire, a greater equality in the condition of men, I entertained erroneous notions concerning the making of that improvement in society & the means whereby it was to be promoted... You would have found me as strongly opposed in my youth as I am at this time to Atheism to Immorality of any kind & to that abominable philosophy which teaches self-indulgence rather than self-restraint.[48]

By November, the popular mood over the 'Queen's business' had become volatile: 'the reign of terror had begun', Southey told Wynn.[49] Illuminations were to take place in Keswick, and Southey feared for his windows (as did John Clare, miles away in Helpstone, Northamptonshire).[50] As the bells rang out in favour of the Queen, Southey could only wonder at the popularity of 'this cursed woman', the 'utmost imbecillity in Government, & the utmost audacity in its assailants'.[51] Even though his windows remained unbroken (Scott's house was attacked), he registered the significance of what had happened: he began to date his letters, 'Anno Reimobbicae primo'. 'Never must we laugh again at the credulity & the stultification of other nations! What are any of the Franciscan legends & mysteries to the mystery of our Immaculate Adultery, & the spotlessness of our Carolina purissima—sin pecado concebida!'[52] To Herbert Hill he declared, 'This infernal woman will raise a rebellion if she can', and the 'moral plague' that was scorching the country reminded him of the yellow fever in Lisbon in 1800.[53] He would now even be glad if a *bellum servile* should break out: that was as much as the people deserved. Even the weather seemed to be going haywire: in Paris it was freezing, in Keswick, in December, it was warmer than ever; there was rain and wind, certainly, 'but such tepid gales, that Cuthbert crows for pleasure when he feels them playing about his head'.[54] To Southey, these winds seemed more like the harbingers of the simoom or the sirocco, something out of one of his own poems. What was happening seemed a complete reversal of what he had understood by the necessary relationship between Government and society: 'We live in strange times', he told Rickman on 19 December, 'the use of government is to protect individuals, & a strange revolution must have taken place before it becomes necessary for individuals to combine for the purpose of protecting Government.'[55] The Constitutional Association, proposed by John Reeve and Stoddart for curbing the licentiousness of the press, would allow the Government to shift responsibility, and for that reason Southey had his doubts about supporting it; at least his belief in the importance of firm government would not allow him, as he saw it, to play the same game as its opponents. It was foolish, in his view, to 'protect Government instead of being protected by it'.

Christmas Day was celebrated, by Southey at any rate, by the arrival of the first proofs of the *History of the Peninsular War*. But Southey's pleasure was dashed in January when he heard that Nash had died: Nash had become one of the family, and his loss was commensurate: 'he was so sensible of any kindness, so thoroughly amiable, & bore his cross so meekly... At any time of life new friendships are rarely formed, & the man of middle age who is richest in friends, can ill afford to lose one of them.' Edith might have wished he had felt able to explain himself to her so directly. Meanwhile Aunt Mary enjoyed playing with the thriving Cuthbert, and in the mild winter weather Southey made the journey to fetch Edith May from the Wordsworths, where she had spent the New Year. Bedford had moved north, to run a small shop, and this put a certain strain on domestic arrangements: 'he takes his rides on Sunday, because his shop is shut on that day, & he comes at an unlawful hour to suit his own dinner time.'[56]

Southey was busy on the Preface to the *Vision of Judgement*, which would allow him to hit out at Byron and *Don Juan*; he planned to add his Odes of 1819 and 1820, with the appropriate title of the 'Warning Voice' (in the event, these did not appear). How he enjoyed playing the role of prophet in his own country. *Colloquies*, with six 'admirable drawings' by Westall, would fit into this pattern, as would the *Book of the Church*. *Oliver Newman* had now reached Book 6, but his lessening interest in poetry meant that prose had to come first.[57] His work on the Quakers became public knowledge sooner than he would have wished, and several Quakers wrote to him, expressing their apprehension lest he speak unfavourably of their founders. But Southey was happy to present things as he saw them, warts and all: George Fox, he believed, did not 'know what he meant', nor did his followers. 'They were blasphemers by chance & medley, & not by design.' This was supposed to be some solace to present-day Quakers, but not all of them could be so sanguine. He mischievously moved back to the question of the Catholics, and suggested that this was a good time for them to re-establish themselves in England: if the Queen was acceptable, then so was 'the Whore of Babylon'.[58]

It was in this swashbuckling mood that he waited for the mud to fly over the *Vision of Judgement*: 'Pelt away my boys, pelt away! if you were not busy at that work you would be about something more mischievous. Abusing me is like flogging a whipping-post.'[59] It would be much worse, he went on, perversely, to receive exaggerated praise. He need not have worried (not that he did). He relished the offence the poem seemed to give to all parties, and was prepared for battle: 'they shall find me by far the most formidable of their antagonists.'[60] Bedford wondered whether Southey was wise about the poem's Dedication, but Southey, having got it out of his system, was no longer bothered.

We owe much to the House of Brunswick; but to none of that illustrious House more than to Your Majesty, under whose government the military renown of Great Britain has been carrried to the highest point of glory... The same perfect integrity has been manifested in the whole administration of public affairs... Under Your Majesty's government, the Metropolis is rivalling in beauty those cities which it has long surpassed in greatness... The brightest portion of British history will be that which records the improvements, the works, and the achievements of the Georgian Age.

This, in itself, would be sufficient ammunition for Southey's detractors, before they had got as far as the poem itself; but he was unconcerned. What he did note, rather sadly, was the difference in feeling between now, and that first number of the *Flagellant*, all those years ago. That had been something triumphant, as we have seen, something to hark back to with pride. For all his bravado over the *Vision of Judgement*, he realized that it was not quite the same. Perhaps he realized fully, for the first time, how much not only events but he, too, had changed. Underneath the surface flippancy and lack of interest was a sense of how truly he now represented the forces of reaction. He, the former champion of the rebel and the scourge of tyrants, had become the Poet Laureate who could write a poem celebrating the arrival of the King of Great Britain in Heaven. When the *Evangelical Magazine* reviewed his *Life of Wesley*, he was tarred with the brush with which he had been ready to tar anyone who crossed his path thirty years earlier: 'They set me down for a book-maker, treat me with great contempt for my ignorance of theology & ecclesiastical history, & hint, at the close, that what I must expect for such a book is—*damnation*.' Byron, for different reasons, felt rather the same way.[61]

It is one of Southey's greatest misfortunes that he tangled with Byron; *Don Juan* had mocked him, but at least he was in good company—not only Wordsworth and Coleridge, but most living poets. Southey's *Vision of Judgement* even now seems like a failure of judgement on his part; the hexameter in itself is not the problem (after all, Clough was to show just how well it could be used to reflect the halting thought processes of a Victorian in mid-crisis). The problem was the combination of a hexameter not fully mastered and a subject that seemed so patently absurd. Southey's attempt to use the occasion as a chance to reflect on British history is hardly successful; the poem stands very much as a warning to all Poets Laureate. It is now remembered because of Byron's merciless response in his *Vision of Judgment* (1822), in which he attacks, as only he could, what seemed to him the egregious overreaching of a much less talented writer who had betrayed himself and his age. The effect, curiously, is that Southey is now forever embalmed in Byron's brilliant satire, a helpless figure of fun.

> He said—(I only give the heads)—he said,
>   He meant no harm in scribbling; 'twas his way
> Upon all topics; 'twas, besides, his bread.
>   Of which he butter'd both sides; 'twould delay
> Too long the assembly (he was pleased to dread)
>   And take up rather more time than a day,
> To name his works—he would but cite a few—
> Wat Tyler—Rhymes on Blenheim—Waterloo.
>
> He had written praises of a regicide;
>   He had written praises of all kings whatever;
> He had written for republics far and wide,
>   And then against them bitterer than ever;
> For pantisocracy he once had cried
>   Aloud, a scheme less moral than 'twas clever;
> Then grew a hearty antijacobin—
> Had turn'd his coat—and would have turn'd his skin.
>
> He had sung against all battles, and again
>   In their high praise and glory; he had call'd
> Reviewing 'the ungentle craft,' and then
>   Became as base a critic as ere crawl'd—
> Fed, paid, and pamper'd by the very men
>   By whom his muse and morals had been maul'd:
> He had written much blank verse, and blanker prose,
> And more of both than any body knows.

> He had written Wesley's life:—here, turning round
>   To Satan, 'Sir, I'm ready to write yours,
> In two octavo volumes, nicely bound,
>   With notes and preface, all that most allures
> The pious purchaser; and there's no ground
>   For fear, for I can choose my own reviewers:
> So let me have the proper documents,
>   That I may add you to my other saints.'

Byron's satire cannot be gainsaid, and no extract can do his poem justice: it is a sustained critique, not just of Southey, but of all Byron supposed Southey to stand for. But it is at least worth trying to redeem, modestly enough, Southey's poem, by quoting some of the lines in which he gazes through his study window at his favourite view:

> 'Twas at that sober hour when the light of day is receding,
> And from surrounding things the hues wherewith day has adorn'd them
> Fade, like the hopes of youth, till the beauty of earth is departed:
> Pensive, though not in thought, I stood at the window beholding
> Mountain and lake and vale; the valley disrobed of its verdure;
> Derwent retaining yet from eve a glassy reflection
> Where his expanded breast, then still and smooth as a mirror,
> Under the woods reposed; the hills that, calm and majestic,
> Lifted their heads in the silent sky, from far Glaramara
> Bleacrag and Maidenmawr, to Grizedal and westermost Withop,
> Dark and distinct they rose...
> Pensive I stood and alone, the hour and the scene had subdued me,
> And as I gazed in the west, where Infinity seem'd to be open,
> Yearn'd to be free from time, and felt that this life is a thraldom...[62]

Southey had not lost all his poetic powers, whatever Byron might have thought.

Southey's Aunt Tyler died, in her eighty-second year, at the beginning of March. So far as he was concerned, it was a death both expected and no cause for grief; but even where there was no affection left, he had to admit that the loss 'presses for a while like a weight upon the mind'. Southey continued with his series of autobiographical letters to May, and turned to a Royal Birthday Ode, hoping that he might imitate, if not match, Thomas Warton's earlier effort; there was a certain wistfulness in his talk of Warton as 'happy, easy-minded, idle ... to whom literature in its turn was as much an amusement as rat-hunting'.[63] One of Southey's problems throughout his life was that he never really knew how much importance to attach to his writing, which in turn helps to explain the confrontation with Byron, who was able to get away with a studied indifference, an aristocratic hauteur; Southey's earnestness was always lurking in the background. He was relieved to hear that Wynn disliked the *Vision* less than he had expected, but Southey's comments on Lord Byron, in the same letter, illustrate the yawning gap between the two poets: 'what I have written proceeded from a sense of duty, not from any personal resentment: if any personal feeling existed, it was a latent apprehension that some undeserved censure might attach to me for the scandalous silence of the "Quarterly Review" concerning "Don Juan".' This sense of duty, behind which he was all too ready to hide, had a severity that made him seem to many priggish to the point of absurdity. What is sad about Southey's relations with his public, and with many of his friends, is that they were not often allowed to see that other, tender, side. For example, the day after the *Vision of Judgement* arrived, he had talked to his uncle about his childhood at Bristol, providing a sharply poignant vignette: 'If there be any spot upon this earth that I remember with more feeling than any other, it is Ashton, such as it was forty years ago, when those village lanes of which you speak were in their beauty. The first time I ever rode on horseback was when you carried me thither, before you, from Bedminster.'[64] But even as he recalled this idyll, he was having to confront the likelihood, as he saw it, of a Spanish civil war, the fall of the King of Portugal, and revolution in Brazil. Perhaps these impending catastrophes made the childhood recollections all the more important, but also the more obviously fragile; similarly, the quarrel with Byron—insistently depersonalized, Southey kept claiming, not always convincingly— became a matter of upholding standards (as it was, also, for Byron). Hence Southey's joy not only that the King should approve of the *Vision of Judgement*, but that 'the verdict of my peers is most decidedly in its favour'.[65]

Southey needed this kind of reassurance. He was disturbed to see that even an old friend and idol such as Humphry Davy could fall away into sensuality and vanity: 'old friends are the best of all possessions, & there is nothing in this world which can supply their loss.'[66] This is another cry from the heart of someone who has lost so many of his former friends. In some respects, loss by death could be explained, and hope put in Providence. But the alteration of someone still alive was a more devastating loss, in that it challenged his system of values, his belief in himself, and his trust in others. On a more mundane and domestic level, it was important for him to cling on to his family of cats. Othello died, to be replaced by The Zombi (a present from Mrs Calvert), who then disappeared to be replaced by Prester John.[67]

The sad irony was that Southey himself had changed. Here he is saying how much depends upon Austria: 'A liberal policy might do wonders now, but the race of statesmen is extinct. With evil on all sides, one has nothing to hope for except tranquillity, & that sort of melioration arising from the spirit of the age, which was going on every day till the French Revolution brought in an age of blood.'[68] He seems to have forgotten his own initial reactions to the Revolution; he also seems confused as to what he really thinks. When he heard of Cobbett's recommendation that Southey be executed 'as one of the first acts of the Radical Government', he was not perturbed so much as amused: after all, there were some Owenites quoting from one of his Odes as though it were the Scriptures for the working man. In other words, he would readily elude any neat and dismissive labelling; and there was always the thought that he and Wordsworth would 'go down to posterity in company'.[69]

Posterity was much in his mind in April. He anticipated that his *Colloquies* and the *Book of the Church* would do his posthumous reputation nothing but good, whatever the immediate reaction from 'the bigotted, the irreligious, & the factious'.[70] The present was not something he need necessarily bother about. Although here again there was of course a central contradiction, in that these works—and the other articles he was producing for the *Quarterly*—were immediate responses precisely to the climate of the times, to what, as we have seen, he called 'the spirit of the age'. As he asked rhetorically of Townshend on 6 May, when would things settle down? 'For myself I know not what to wish for, when on the one side the old Governments will not attempt to amend anything, & on the other the Revolutionists are for destroying everything. Spain is in a deplorable state, which must lead to utter anarchy.'[71] There had been no proper statesman for a hundred years: Burke was the closest to his ideal, but he was 'led away by passion & party, & an Irish imagination'. Southey found some comfort in Hobbes's *Leviathan*, and in Hobbes's belief in the need for public opinion to be shaped by the Government. Less comfort, though, was to be found in Portugal and Brazil: they were bound to go their separate ways, and the tragedy of this was that 'the tendency of all commercial colonies is towards republicanism: the foundations upon which monarchy rests are wanting'.[72] He was right; but he was wrong to see this as necessarily a recipe for disaster.

As summer blossomed ('the delight of bathing draws me out of doors when nothing else would') Southey planned to write about Spain and Portugal in the *Quarterly*; he was also reviewing a *Life of Cromwell*, which he hoped would form part of a biographical series for Murray—six octavo volumes at £500 per volume; the *History of the Peninsular War* was still at the printers, and he enjoyed seeing the sheets as they came from the press. He was, as so often, beginning to be proved right in his predictions; at the same time, he could not envisage pursuing the tragedy any further, for the simple reason that he felt he had written all he could on the subject. It is intriguing that when in July he heard of the death of Napoleon, he should confess to Bernard Barton that he 'did not read the tidings of his death without mournful feelings'—this from the man who had wanted him hung, drawn, and quartered.[73] Southey was now anxious to keep aloof, pursuing his exercise, walking up to twenty miles a day. He went, with the two Ediths and Cuthbert, to stay at Netherhall with Senhouse, who celebrated Southey's birthday with a special, old bottle of Tokay, which had been passed down through the Senhouse family from as far back as the Emperor Joseph; 'There is', said the mournful Southey, 'a flavour of melancholy about all this which makes it worth remembering.'[74] When he was elected a member of the Massachusetts Historical Society, he felt the honour of the recognition, and also felt spurred on to further work on *Oliver Newman*, especially when his American friend George Ticknor sent on some books from Boston. He heard from his one-time lawyer friend Combe, and in telling Wynn about their mutual friend he hinted at what he had missed by not going into the Church: 'He is not married, & speaks of himself as leading a life of tranquil enjoyment in the house where he was born, free from fat & the gout, & not more altered than must be expected from the wear & tear of time.'[75] Rather sadly, against this, he was having to revise his views of his other old friend William Taylor, no longer the paragon he had thought him in 1798. It was not just his paradoxical ingenuity of argument that Southey found disturbing, there was a sense of a lack of fulfilment. No doubt Southey saw the shadow of Coleridge: 'His great talents have been sadly wasted; & what is worse, they have been sometimes sadly misemployed.'[76] But in October Southey could employ his time wisely, in the great library at Lowther, even more than usual because he had stubbed his toe, which prevented his taking much exercise. Whilst there, he met the Duchess of Marlborough, the Dean of Carlisle, and Lord Bentink, who offered to get him even more historical materials; Southey felt he had enough, declaring truthfully, 'I have a dangerous love of detail, & a desire for accuracy, which is much more expensive (both in materials & time) than I ought to afford'.[77] What he did not always acknowledge was that it could often lumber his works with a weight they could not bear.

At the end of October he visited the Calverts, after which an odd little incident took place. Raisley Calvert had shot an owl, and Southey brought it home to show young Cuthbert; since Wordsworth and his wife Mary happened to be at Greta Hall, the bird was cooked for supper: 'the meat was more like bad mutton than anything else. Wordsworth was not valiant enough to taste it.' It is not hard to imagine that Southey was quietly pleased at Wordsworth's squeamishness; he wrote to Bedford, suggesting that, should he ever get the chance to cook an owl, he should 'try it boiled, with onion sauce'.[78] What with owls and rats, Southey might have concocted a useful cookery book; instead, he planned with Senhouse a trip to Holland, and looked forward to doing 'good service hereafter as an iconoclast in the temples of Whig idolatry'. 'What a blessing it is', he said, 'to possess a cheerful & hopeful temper!'[79]

Tom's family was about to increase again, and Southey, in less hopeful temper, foresaw at least another eight before they had done: nothing good would come of all this procreation. He himself enjoyed his own children, reading Ovid to Bertha, and being watched as he shaved by a fascinated Cuthbert who told him he was 'almost as *uggy* as a monkey.[80] He was worried about the financial affairs of John May, who had suffered badly as a result of events in Brazil; Southey wanted Bedford to transfer £625 of his savings to May, and urged May to come up to Keswick. May had, after all, been a source of financial support to Southey on many occasions. All this was against the background of further disturbances in Ireland, to which his attention had of course been turned by his recent biographical work on Cromwell: Southey's solution to the Irish question, not surprisingly, was military rule, and he was confirmed in this by what he read of Spenser's *View of the Present State of Ireland*. He was reluctant to write his New Year Ode on 'that miserable country', and planned to trace the 'evils of Ireland to their source'. In a letter to Neville White in December he voiced an ambiguity which provides a central focus for much of his work:

I may safely assert as a general deduction from all that I have learnt in the course of history, that the more we know of preceding & coexisting circumstances & difficulties, the more excuse we shall find for those men & measures which, with little knowledge of those circumstances, we should condemn absolutely.[81]

We are inevitably led to ask whether this is, or is not, a good thing. There was, however, no ambiguity about his defence of the House of Lords, when it put a stop to Catholic emancipation: he foresaw, as a logical consequence of any such move, a religious war in Ireland; in Britain, the repeal of the Test Acts; the sale of the tithes, the growth of dissenters in all walks of life—all this leading to 'general anarchy & spoliation'. Whatever the temptation to make excuses for the past, Southey knew what he thought about the future.[82]

The turn of the year was occupied with the eruption of the quarrel with Byron into open warfare. Wordsworth told him of Byron's charge of slander in the appendix to *The Two Foscari*: Byron had penned a nicely vitriolic piece about Southey as a writer and a man, following up his earlier attacks. 'There is something at once ludicrous and blasphemous in this scribbler of all works sitting down to deal damnation and destruction upon his fellow creatures, with Wat Tyler, the Apotheosis of George the Third, and the Elegy on Martin the regicide, all shuffled together in his writing desk.' Southey's response was a letter to the *Courier*, written, he claimed, without any feeling of irritation, or without any resort to the anger he attributed to Byron. He adopted a tone of amused detachment: how could Byron be so foolish as to engage with him in combat like this? 'The viper, however venomous in purpose, is harmless in effect, while it is biting at the file . . . When the offence and the offender are such as to call for the whip and the branding-iron, it has been both seen and felt that I can inflict them.' Southey gave some hint of the relish he derived from the exercise, and also of the curiously stated dislike of that very exercise, in a letter to May of 26 December: 'It is well for those who assail me that both from principle & disposition I detest controversial writing,—for there is nothing which I compose with so much readiness, nor with such a sense of compleat power.' Nor is there anything which demonstrates so well his own internal contradictions: he goes on to tell his uncle a month later that 'These things in no degree disturb me', revelling in the 'bed of thorns' which Murray has made for himself.[83]

Politics continued to vex Southey; he was glad Wynn was once again in office, but could not approve of the Government alliance with Grenville's party: the only question on which he could agree with Grenville was his treatment of the Radicals. Southey wanted to write another political article for Gifford, but this would require a greater understanding than he yet had of the agricultural question. Once again, Rickman would be the man to turn to for information. He was rather worried that Hartley Coleridge was talking of coming to live at Greta Hall, and to teach at Ambleside. To Southey, this was preposterous: 'what authority can a mother exercise over a man of six & twenty—the very disease of whose nature is an impatience of all ordinary observance, & of the restraints which he owes to himself as well as others!'[84] Southey's solution was rather ironic, in that he thought the best thing would be for Hartley to stay in London and become a writer.

Another old schoolfriend, James Boswell, the editor of Malone's Shakespeare papers, died; they had shared a room when Wynn left

Westminster, and he, Southey, became head of house. Boswell had been, briefly, commissioner of bankrupts, and had visited in 1815, when they had all celebrated victory at Waterloo with that great bonfire on Skiddaw. Thomas Clarkson was to pass a day at Keswick in June, but even that was to be a source of sorrow, in that Clarkson stayed with the Wordsworths when Wordsworth had injured himself after a fall from his horse; more seriously, Southey recalled their previous meeting in Peterdale in 1819, when 'we drank tea in poor Luff's garden. He is gone, & so are both the men who were my companions at that time.'[85] Cuthbert was 'a fine, joyous creature; an object of the greatest hope—if I could look upon him without fear'. That dreadful sense of impermanence was still there, pressing in upon him more insistently than ever; the approach of political dangers seemed to reinforce this, being a 'much more perilous crisis in society than that of the Reformation'. This was why, as he explained to Landor, his own *Colloquies* were to be so central: 'we are beginning now to perceive', he wrote, 'the whole effects of the three great events of his [Thomas More's] age—the invention of printing, the Reformation, & the discovery of America'.[86] The relationship between his own age and More's, then, was not just one of contrast, but also of cause and effect. Nor was Southey alone. Coleridge for his part merely threw up his hands in despair; 'Of Politics who dare now speak at all? It is enough to wonder—Has the World got the *Staggers*?' Southey despaired of democracy: 'everything will be popularized—that is to say, vulgarized & debased'.[87]

In this mood, Southey was tempted by the possibility of taking over from Gifford as the editor of the *Quarterly Review*, but he realized that he would not even be considered. As he said to Wynn, he wished his 'substance was less precarious'. Southey was thinking about his finances, as well as lack of importance in the literary world. In consolation, he pondered a volume of political history, some kind of companion to the *Book of the Church*: 'I may effect some good, by giving young minds a right bias in time.'[88] This echoed his belief that the only way people would think and behave aright (in his eyes) would be as a result of teaching and example from on high—preferably from the Government. The Government had failed, quite clearly, so Southey would supply the deficiency: that might restore his 'substance'.

The pleasures of summer, including the annual hayfever, lightened his mood, and Bedford was nearby to encourage the kind of childish nonsense they had shared when young men. Southey sent a skittish letter to Edith May in Harrogate; he sent, on 8 June, his famous lines on the Cataract of Lodore, 'Described in Rhymes for the Nursery':

The Cataract strong
Then plunges along,
Striking and raging
As if a war waging
Its caverns and rocks among:
Rising and leaping,
Sinking and creeping,
Swelling and weeping,
Showering and springing,
Flying and flinging,
Writhing and ringing,
Eddying and whisking;
Spouting and frisking;
Turning and twisting,
Around and around
With endless rebound;
Smiting and fighting,
A sight to delight in;
Confounding and astounding,
Dizzying and deafening the ear with its sound.

Collecting, projecting,
Receeding and speeding,
And shocking and rocking,
And darting and parting,
And threading and spreading,
And whizzing and hissing,
And dripping and skipping,
And hitting and splitting
And shining and twining,
And rattling and battling...

If we can see why Southey should eventually incorporate these lines (and they hurtle on far beyond this point) under the rubric 'Nondescripts', we should also recognize his sheer delight in the absurdity of the exercise, his acknowledgement of his children's eager response to such high spirits. As he was to say of himself in a rather similar poem, similarly categorized,

A man he is by nature merry,
Somewhat Tom-foolish, and comical, very...[89]

Southey was enjoying, more than he had before, the verses of Charlotte Bowles, sufficiently to recommend them to Mrs Rickman—they provided light relief after Montaigne and the Danish he was teaching himself in his perpetual quest for self-improvement. He told Mrs Rickman that Charlotte Bowles was 'a little timid creature full of all good feelings':[90]

such women seemed to appeal to him. In July of 1822 Caroline Bowles told him in a letter of her illness:

Yes, I have been very ill, with repeated attacks in the head, each succeeding one increasing in seriousness and continuance, and yielding only to such violent remedies as shake almost to dissolution the fragile frame, at least seemingly not built up for duration. This affection of the head is, I am told, more symptomatic of general debility, and consequent derangement of the nervous system, than in itself a primary complaint; but it is not on that account the less terrible to endure . . . It is an almost total loss of memory, a confusion of ideas, a deprivation of all comprehensive power, with such a darkness of spirit as would, indeed, 'turn my day into night', were it not for the one heavenly ray that pierceth all darkness . . . I dare not look forward to better things, lest the anticipation of evil to come should follow in the train of thought, and cloud my little moment of sunshine. I have but too much reason for sad anticipation. My father I recollect to have been affected as I am. . . . I wish there were a chance of your revisiting Hampshire . . . I do not like to think we shall meet no more in this world . . .[91]

Within a year she would make her first visit to Keswick.

Nicholas Lightfoot came to stay in July, the first time they had met in twenty-eight years: interesting that, after such a long gap, Lightfoot should declare Southey 'to be less altered in appearance & manners than any man whom he ever saw'.[92] This no doubt confirmed Southey in his belief that there had been few internal changes either. At long last, John May arrived, with his son, and they all enjoyed the summer air and the long walks. But, as Southey told Wynn on 17 August, 'What a blessing is tranquillity! I am so accustomed to it, that anything which interrupts my ordinary course of life seems a change for the worse . . .' It was all very well having his friends to stay, but there was always relief when they had gone—how much the greater Edith's relief we can only imagine.[93]

There had been visits to Windermere to meet Lord Canning at Bolton's, and Reginald Heber, Bishop of Calcutta, had been there too, before coming back to admire Southey's Portuguese and Spanish books. Dr Bell was at Keswick again. But the trickle of visitors continued for longer than Southey had hoped. General Peachey came over in stormy weather, and tipped himself into the water when he was trying, umbrella in hand, to manoeuvre his skiff. Southey's brother Harry was coming in mid-September. At least these diversions, and the acknowledgement that the exercise was good for him, persuaded him—if persuasion were needed—that any move to London, even to run the *Quarterly*, would be folly. John Coleridge was the likely candidate to take over the editorship, in which case Southey could play as large a part in it as he wished. He was content to stay in Keswick, reading a variety of books, and the papers on European affairs sent from France by Benjamin Frere; he told his uncle that he was 'no longer a poet', and that he spent his evenings with a glass of black-currant rum and Aitzema's enormous volume on the seventeenth century.[94] He did not tell his uncle that John May sent a steady supply of cider and beer, for Southey to collect at Kendal; nor did he confide in his uncle that 'Old friends & old books are the best things that this world affords (I like old wine also), & in these I am richer than most men (the wine excepted)'.[95]

Shelley's death by drowning in July 1822 was an occasion for Southey to recall their bruising encounters of yesteryear. 'His story, taking it alto-gether, is the most flagitious & the most tragic which I have known in real life'; but at least he was not—unlike Byron—'wicked by disposition'. As for Shelley's writings: 'What merit they had was of too high a kind to be attractive, & their obscurity & extravagance served in some degree to sheath the poison which they contained.'[96] What Southey could not bring himself to admit was just how much Shelley had actually learnt from him. As ever, Southey was fascinated by the gruesomeness of death, in parti-cular by the mutilation of Shelley's body: 'The fish had devoured half of it.' At the back of his mind lurked no doubt the fate of Bishop Hatto, and the equally graphic display of God's judgement. This was another reason for Southey to cling on to his trim figure: there would be little spare flesh for any avenging creatures to gnaw at, should he meet an untimely end.

As winter drew in—and the weather was severe—he continued his reading, finding in Isaac d'Israeli's *New Curiosities* 'the strangest mixture of information & ignorance, cleverness & folly'.[97] Again, we can see some similarity between these two men, and the significance of d'Israeli's sincerely felt dedication to Southey of his later volume. There was talk of Southey's being asked to continue Warton's *History of English Poetry*, but he awaited a publisher's proposal. The recurrent financial problems meant he was once again having to ask Bedford for money, and he was regretting the deal he had made with Murray for the *History of the Peninsular War*: 1,500 guineas for three volumes would have been prefer-able to £1,000 for two (length was never a problem for Southey). On 3 January 1823 he wrote to Wynn, quoting an apparently apposite couplet from Samuel Daniel: 'Time hath done to me this wrong, | To make me write too much & live too long'. This bears an uncanny resemblance to Byron's charge in *English Bards*: 'Oh! Southey! Southey! cease thy varied song! | A Bard may chaunt too often and too long'; but having raised the possibility of comparison, Southey is quick to dash it: 'My disposition is too cheerful a one to admit of a fear that I may ever have occasion to apply these melancholy lines to myself.'[98]

Never the less, there was his family to consider. Matters were not improved by the hostility of the reception of the first volume of his *History of the Peninsular War,* when it appeared at the beginning of 1823: the Whigs were 'up in arms'; Sharon Turner told him he should have been more conciliatory. But that was not his way: 'I had but one course to pursue,—the straightforward one of writing honestly. They cannot hate me worse than they do, & they shall not hate me for nothing.'[99] Once again, there is a clash between his need to earn an honest penny, and his need to be honest; very few pennies were honest, and it was Southey's difficulty that he seldom acknowledged this. However, he consoled himself with the thought that most of his friends had risen 'to their proper stations . . . & it is not the less gratifying because I continue at the foot of Skiddaw, for that is my proper station.'[100] The circle he had to square (or one of them) was occupying that station whilst keeping the wolf from the door. Perhaps there is more than coincidence in the fact that it was at this time that he began to address himself to the general problem of poverty.

His acquaintance Thomas Clarkson had provided a practical example of colonization to relieve poverty. He had shipped off two or three families to Canada at the parish's expense, from a little village near Ipswich, and it had been a success. But the Government was thinking along similar lines, with a plan to transport the able-bodied poor, providing grants of 100 acres per family: although he had mixed feelings about this scheme, Southey by and large approved it, and determined to pursue the matter in his *Colloquies.* He resorted to a rather terrible logic, which perhaps should no longer surprise us: 'if the country is compelled to feed able-bodied paupers, it thereby acquires the right of transporting them to any place where that can be done at the easiest rate, or where the necessity for doing it may be removed.' Southey saw it as a solution to the problem of unemployment: 'the breed of paupers is diminished, & more work left for the hands that remain.'[101] Whether Southey saw through his own argument to the underlying Malthusian rhetoric we cannot say: it is unlikely, given his increasingly paranoid statements about the national danger.

The state of the Catholic Church was what he planned to concentrate on next, reviving an old essay from the *Edinburgh Annual Register,* and producing a pamphlet. The repeal of the Test Acts was another sign of danger, for his view was simple: 'Our constitution consists of Church & State, & it is an absurdity in politics to give those persons power in the *State,* whose duty it is to subvert the *Church.*'[102] Whilst he looked forward to some prosecutions against the radical press, he found refuge in his reading. He was elected a member of the Royal Irish Academy, and he

unknown country; I found in you what I had never met with, even in my lost Eden, and while you hold me fast I shall not want courage to go on, nor inclination to tarry yet a little longer should it be God's pleasure. At present I am disposed to be very much in love with life, and very unwilling to leave it before May. I had no idea whatever of moving from home at that time, and I would not for the world receive your visit anywhere else, because your having been here (even for that visit *volant* you prepare me to expect) will leave a brightness over many succeeding months, and I, as well as you, converse with shadows. If it were good and pleasant for yourself to stay some length of time here how hard I would try to keep you! but what is best for yourself, that shall be best for me, so come without fear of persecution.[113]

But this deep emotional bond lay in the future: in the mean time there was much to enjoy around Keswick. One day a party of thirteen scaled the heights of Causey Pike 'like goats' (Cuthbert was left down below with his patient mother).[114] There was another, 21-mile trip, involving nineteen travellers plus five attendants, three cats, five horses: they dined on the pass between Buttermere and Borrowdale. It was quite a life, whatever the state of his funds. It is no surprise, with all this socializing, that Southey did not set off for London until mid-November; besides, he hated the thought of travelling, which gave him 'a sort of *bowel quake*'.[115]

On 21 November he was writing to Edith from his uncle's at Streatham. He was sitting for a portrait by the deaf and dumb painter Samuel Lane, whom Southey referred to as 'Dumbee'; he thought his portrait as good as Phillips's was bad, for Phillips gave his eyes an expression 'which I conceive to be more like two oysters in love than anything else'.[116] Westall called a few days later; Southey dined with Lady Malet (a friend of the Peacheys), and with Wynn, where he met Bedford; he saw May and Rickman, and met Joanna Baillie at Longman's. On 30 November Martha and Elizabeth Fricker came to dine; his uncle the next day; then he went to the high Tory, Sir Robert Inglis, and on Wednesday to Mrs Hughes (a good friend of Caroline Bowles, and also of Walter Scott's), where the Wynns were also guests; there was an invitation from John Charles Herries to Sevenoaks, where all the gentry would be attending a grand ball; he would see Charles Collins's brother Edward at Maize Hill. Immediately after Christmas there was a trip to Devon, eventually to stay with Lightfoot at Crediton, but calling in at Escot on the way to see Sir John Kennaway, and Henry Coleridge (son of Colonel James Coleridge) at Ottery, the Marriotts who were holding court to a crowd of people, and the Bullers, where he met 'the Great World. There was Lady Duckworth, who is herself as big as the World, & as round, & as good-natured as possible. And there was Lady somebody else, and all the grandees of the neighbourhood, the Whatsisnames, the Whatdyecallums, the

Thingambobs.' It was an exhausting schedule—1,500 miles in fifteen weeks—taking him finally through Suffolk, where he particularly liked Bury St Edmunds, and up to Norfolk, where he was greeted warmly by Neville White. He reassured young Cuthbert that he would be soon home; there were three things in the world 'which keep their appointed course, Time, Tide, & your father'. He promised to teach him Greek if he were good, 'that you may be a good scholar, & so become a wise man. The wiser people are, the better they ought to be; & the better they are, the happier they must be.'[117] Whether or not Cuthbert was persuaded of this line of thought, there is no doubt about Southey's simple belief in this progression towards moral happiness. But there is a certain desperation about that 'ought'.

Southey wrote airily to White, on his happy return to Keswick on 19 February, that if he had been prepared to wait another day, he could have had a doctorate at Cambridge—but 'feathers of this kind are not worth having when fees are to be paid for them'.[118] Southey still had some of his priorities right. The regular routine of Greta Hall embraced him to its bosom: he got on with the *History of the Peninsular War* in the morning, the *Tale of Paraguay* after tea, whilst Cuthbert started to learn the Greek alphabet. Tom, in an effort to make some money, was embarking on a *History of the West Indies*, which Longman would print (750 copies), provided 200 subscribers could be found. Southey was ready to help in whatever way he could, and he prodded Bedford over possible subscribers.[119] There was probably a connection between this and his forwarding a petition to Wilberforce from Keswick, 'for the gradual abolition of slavery' on Clarkson's lines. As if to reaffirm his belonging at Greta Hall, after all that travelling, he had more bookshelves fitted.[120] His daughter Bertha was to visit Rickman on her way back from Sussex; he told Rickman in April that 'you will find Bertha very shy, very timid,—& at first a little helpless. But she is a good girl:—apt & handy when she feels herself at home & knows what she is about.—& I think she will ripen well. At present she is just in her most awkward age.'[121] Edith May was also in London, missed by her parents; Southey wrote to her in May, one of his comic letters, to cheer her up. He wished, in this mood, that he and Bedford could be together, if only to revive their 'Butlerian' plans. 'I am at this time brim full of good, genuine, glorious nonsense, worth all the stupid sense in the world, & worthy of living for ever.'[122]

❧ 10 ❧

'THE DREAM OF LIFE'

1824–1843

BYRON's death in April 1824 called forth from Southey merely a snort of derision: 'I am sorry for his death . . . because it comes in aid of a pernicious reputation which was stinking in the snuff.'[1] He would press on regardless, declining the possibility of editing Sir Thomas Browne, and having second thoughts about the Book of the State, for the simple reason that he had enough on his hands: the proof sheets of the second volume of the *Book of the Church* were beginning to arrive, and provided 'one of the pleasures of life'.[2] His *Colloquies* were increasingly his focus of attention: Landor's *Conversations* had made their mark, and Southey was confident that his equivalent would 'command notice, & provoke hostility'.[3] That was quite enough to satisfy him: he still saw himself as the voice of the nation's conscience, particularly when it came to the manufacturing system, 'which breeds yahoos as fast as they can be bred, & invents machines to throw them out of employ'. It is worth remarking that there is a greater degree of humanity about his views here than when he contemplated the exportation of the poor. But he does not lose his hectoring tone: 'I want more order, more discipline', he tells Montgomery in July, '—less liberty to do ill;—more encouragement—more help—to do well . . . I want to impress both upon the Rulers & the People a sense of their respective duties.' Ironically, in view of such apparently clear-cut attitudes, he was still having trouble with his editors: '[Gifford] thinks me too liberal, & Murray thinks me too bigoted. The middle way, whatever it might have been for Phaeton, is not only the most difficult to keep on earth, but the most dangerous, for you have enemies on both sides.'[4] Southey had good reason to feel warmly about this.

In spite of his hay fever, which was now growing into a recurrent cough, and bleeding from the rectum after a mile's walk, he was determined to forge ahead on several fronts, partly because of his sense that he was 'already among the elders of this age', but also because of the need to address the many problems of the time. As he explained to Rickman that September, 'If I have many irons in the fire, one reason . . . is that there is a large pot to boil'.[5] It is rather strange to find him telling Herbert Hill in the same month, that 'No man can be freer from hypochondriacal fancies, or valetudinarian feelings'; if we might question this, we might be equally bemused to hear him say, in the same letter, that he is different from Montaigne in that he 'had much rather read than write'.[6] If this was indeed the case, then he spent much of his life doing that which he would have preferred, like Melville's Bartleby, not to do. He carried on with the third Canto of *A Tale of Paraguay*, hoping it would be ready for next season; he worked more on the Daniel Dove material for *The Doctor*, acknowledging Bedford's fears that the end result might seem too frivolous: 'It is very much like a trifle, where you have whipt cream at the top of sweetmeats below, & a good solid foundation of cake well steeped in ratafia.'[7] Murray was ready to contemplate publication of a planned History of the Monastic Orders in six octavo volumes, for which Southey would get £500 per volume; as he told Bedford, he was the only person qualified to undertake such a task.

Two letters of December 1824 demonstrate Southey's ability to represent two almost contradictory positions at more or less the same time. In the first, to Rickman, of 12 December, he speaks of the Irish question:

The winter I think will hardly pass over without a rebellion in Ireland—which I must say is well deserved by those who proceed upon the vile system of deserting their friends in the hope of conciliating their enemies. It is well that the object of separation & Catholic ascendancy should be broadly avowed.—& as the crisis is inevitable, it cannot come too soon. I only hope the mischief may not extend here;—but certain it is that the English Radicals have had agents in Ireland. The common revolutionary purpose cannot however prove a bond of union, when the rebellion assumes—as it will without delay or disguise, the character of a religious war.[8]

A week later, Southey writes to Croker, subscribing to an optimism we might find surprising were it not for the previous instances of Southey's apparently schizoid state of mind when he relaxed into the position of spectator:

Our own is indeed a marvellous age in whatever light it be regarded; & a pleasanter one there never can have been to have lived in for one, who like myself, has nothing to do in the world but to learn what has been done in former times, to observe what is going on, & to speculate upon what is to come.[9]

Of course, since his correspondent was Croker, he no doubt felt it necessary to put on a brave face; none the less, such contradictions tell us much about this man who was to say to Wilberforce within three months that he abhorred controversy, and who was to decline writing for

The Times because it was 'dying of the incurable disease of dullness'. At least John Coleridge was now in charge of the *Quarterly*, and Southey could scarcely say enough in his favour:

He is a person in character, habits and attainments *omni exceptione major*, a thorough scholar, thoroughly bred, with a high University character, and good connections: a man of business, punctual, honourable, well-principled and high-principled, independent and discreet, and in addition to the security arising from his temper, judgement and discretion, there is that of his professional knowledge. It is absolutely impossible to find a man better qualified for such a responsibility as the Editorship of the *Q. R.* requires.

Southey was, none the less, to complain in January 1825 that the *Quarterly* contained too many statistics (the very things he kept pestering Rickman for), when it needed 'a humaner tone than it has been wont to observe'.[10]

In the new year Southey became once again embroiled in controversy. His *Book of the Church*, as he had rightly predicted, had provoked hostility—in particular from the Roman Catholic Charles Butler—which would require further vindication on his part: this was to come in Southey's *Vindiciae Ecclesiae Anglicanae* (1826). There were other bones of contention: he was tempted to prosecute the *Morning Chronicle* for what he regarded as libellous remarks about his views on Ireland, but was dissuaded by Henry Taylor, an important figure at the Colonial Office, a good friend of Southey's, but more famous as the author of the poetic drama *Philip van Artevelde*, and John Coleridge; he was proud of his second attack on Byron in the *Courier* (prompted by Medwin's publication of some Byronic conversations), whatever people might have said: 'I am never in the habit of diluting my ink. The outcry against it is in the spirit of these *liberal times*.'[11] The vast sales of his *Book of the Church* merely confirmed him in his self-belief, and when the London Catholic Association applauded Milner and Butler for their refutation of Southey's calumnies, he laughed, and continued with his *Vindication*, in which he would 'batter the walls of Babylon about their ears'. He was telling Mrs Hughes in February 1825, with some pleasure, that 'there is as much abuse of me in print as would break the back of an elephant, & as many lies as a brewer's team could draw'. He remembered Mrs Piozzi's praise for his letter to William Smith of eight years before, and 'that was worth all the panegyric in the world'.[12] But whilst he rejoiced in this form of pugilistic journalism, he was also celebrating childish pleasures: gooseberry pie, sweetmeats, fruit, gingerbread, generally 'playing the fool whenever I feel myself sufficiently at home'. On Cuthbert's sixth birthday, 24 February, he finished his *Tale of Paraguay*.

This is a very strange poem, dedicated rather touchingly to his daughter Edith May with some autumnal lines; the narrative, as so often with Southey, is based on fact, which leads him to broach a familiar topic in his Preface: 'One of my friends observed to me in a letter, that many stories which are said to be *founded* on fact, have in reality been *foundered* on it.' He does not add that some of his enemies made the same point. The poem's chief interest, now, lies in its opening paean to the virtues of Edward Jenner; Southey had cause to be grateful for the advances in medicine that had kept the majority of his children alive:

> JENNER! for ever shall thy honour'd name
> Among the children of mankind be blest,
> Who by thy skill hast taught us how to tame
> One dire disease, .. the lamentable pest
> Which Africa sent forth to scourge the West,
> As if in vengeance for her sable brood
> So many an age remorselessly opprest.
> For that most fearful malady subdued
> Receive a poet's praise, a father's gratitude.

However oddly this might be put, it serves as a reminder of Southey's continuing concern with the iniquities of the slave trade.[13]

In early March, Southey set off to Wordsworth's for a few days, where the snow in fact prevented the very exercise he had gone for. Further travels were planned, to London and the West Country, but he was missing Bertha and Edith May, and wanted them home from London before he set off. He sent John Coleridge a paper on the Church Mission Society for the *Quarterly*, along with a review of Joanna Baillie's *Letters from Lisbon*; the first part of his *Vindiciae* had already been sent off to the press. He was pleased to hear from his old friend William Bowles that he, Bowles, had begun to answer Butler's criticisms of Southey, and that Dr Phillpotts was also pitching in, on the theological side of the argument. Southey was not, then, alone. He knew where his own responsibilites in the debate lay: 'My business, of course, must be to attack him along the whole of his line, which I am doing most effectually.'[14] If this meant introducing the personal element, then so be it; he found himself having to defend the first person pronoun to Bedford, and recalled how Gifford had deleted it in one of his reviews. For all his talk of the importance of keeping issues and personalities separate, Southey knew how much personal investment he had in his own arguments and positions. This was partly a reflection of his doubts about his own abilities to speak out, as opposed to write, in public: if he had, as he told Henry Taylor at the end of March, 'none of that readiness which is required for public life', he had sufficient of it when he had the quill in his hand, and he wanted everyone to know who it was who was doing the talking.[15]

Southey was more than ever eager to go abroad, and planned a trip with Neville White and Henry Taylor, who needed some persuading of the virtues of Holland: 'it is a marvellous country in itself, in its history, & in the men & works which it has produced. The very existence of the country is at once a natural & a moral phenomenon.'[16] If this sounds a bit daunting, as though even a holiday had to have a moral purpose, his excitement as expressed to General Peachey sounds more natural: 'if eating pickled herrings & fresh sturgeon, & drinking Rhenish wine, with now & then a small glass either of right Hollands or *kirsch-wasser* to qualify it, be wholesome diet for a moralistic sort of person (who has however a good stomach) I shall come back like a Giant refreshed not with wine only, but with the very best wine in the world, & good spirits to boot.'[17] There was some delay before setting off, because of a visit from Bedford and his sculptor friend Chantrey; this allowed him to rejoice in the fact that the Catholic Bill was thrown out (thanks partly to a powerful speech by Sir Robert Inglis).[18] But by 3 June he was installed in Harley Street, where his prospering doctor brother Harry now lived.

He was immediately thrown into the usual social maelstrom, with dinners here, there, and everywhere: friends such as Bedford, Henry Taylor, Wynn, Rickman, Gooch, and May; relatives such as Herbert Hill, Martha and Elizabeth Fricker; the Beaumonts, Croker, Murray, William Sotheby—all within the space of a week. The trip to Holland and Belgium at the end of May included Neville White, Henry Taylor, and Arthur Malet: they got to Boulogne on 9 June, and then went on to Leiden. Unfortunately, Southey developed an infection as a result of an insect bite on a foot, and he accordingly spent much of the time laid up in the house of a Dutch poet, Willem Bilderdijk; in fact this suited him just as well, as Bilderdijk and his wife (who had translated *Roderick* into Dutch) were just the kind of book-loving, scholarly couple after Southey's own heart. Southey paid the Dutch poet a tribute in his later 'Epistle to Allan Cunningham' (1828):

> Right-minded, happy-minded, righteous man,
> True lover of his country and his kind;
> In knowledge, and in inexhaustive stores
> Of native genius rich; philosopher,
> Poet, and sage.[19]

By the end of August he was back in Keswick, still suffering from a swollen foot, and the inconvenience of erysipelas. In between the summer visitors (including Scott, who thought Southey was not looking too well), he got on with his reading, and finished the seventh book of *Oliver Newman* by 11 September. He began to reconsider the temptations of a continuation of Warton's *History of English Poetry*, at £500 per volume. He still had time, apparently, to read Erasmus's letters after dinner.[20]

Prompted by Henry Taylor's concern, Southey took stock of his position in the literary world. 'Probably not half-a-dozen even of those persons who are most attached to me, ever read all that I have published.' This did not bother him, in that immediate reputation was not his concern (except from the financial point of view). 'I take up a subject because it interests me. I treat it in the manner which seemeth best in my own eyes, & when it has been sent forth to take its chance, the only care which I have concerning it is to correct & improve it in case it should be reprinted.'[21] In other words, the detachment with which he could, at least for much of the time, regard the world from which he felt removed, could be applied to his own writings. Once they were in the public domain, that was that. This was partly a matter of sensible policy, the professional writer who knew the vagaries of taste and fashion, but also a reflection of his own confidence in what he could do. (Shelley, we might remember, aimed at a modest audience of six.) In the mean time, to keep himself above the breadline, he was prepared to write for the *Quarterly*, now in the hands of Lockhart after Murray and John Coleridge had fallen out. His absorption in the various questions of the day would keep him in the public eye and also help to preserve him for posterity. As he told Gooch, just before Christmas, 'The world closes over me as easily as the waters. Not, however, that I shall sink to be forgotten.' He was, after all, a good swimmer.[22]

As the new year began, Southey was conscious that he should be attending to events in Spanish America, but that he was too busy to do so; he could no longer afford to plan too many large projects, until present schemes were out of the way. He knew at least some of his failings: 'It is indeed the besetting sin of my nature, to plan largely, & extend every design in the execution.'[23] So when Lockhart suggested that he write about South America, Southey could only say that Blanco White would be the ideal person to tackle the problem—except that he had already done so. There is a sense of Southey's drawing in his horns, as he continues with his autobiographical letters to May, and mourns the death of Mrs Gonne, 'the standard by whom I measured other women, for all those qualities that win the heart, & keep the hearts which they have won'.[24] Where he felt most at ease, as his *Colloquies* showed, was in his views on the evils of the manufacturing system, which he foresaw producing, within no more than half a century, 'a more tremendous convulsion than these kingdoms have ever yet sustained'.[25] He preferred to concentrate on these more immediate concerns than on what was happening on the other side of the world. At the end of March he asked Rickman, 'Give me a line when you are at leisure—for, I am out of this world, & know nothing of what is going on in it.'[26] A month later, he was declaring, also to Rickman, 'There is not a spark of fanaticism left in my composition: whatever there was of it in youth, spent itself harmlessly in political romance.' Quite how much Southey is washing his hands of his own responsibility is hard to determine, especially when the same letter contained a further jeremiad against the dangers of industrialization and over-production: 'the steam-engine will blow up this whole fabric of society... the Yahoos will break loose...'[27] Once again, Southey is either having his cake and eating it, or being sadly lacking in self-awareness.

Neither state prevented him from setting out in May for another excursion to Holland with Henry Taylor. They went via Buckland, where they visited Caroline Bowles, momentously, for the first time, and from where he wrote home to Edith, making reference to her apparent melancholy, and offering the strangest kind of comfort: 'I neither felt nor fancied any want of affection in your manner when we parted. You know it is not my way either to make or require demonstrations of feeling at such times—or at any time.'[28] She would soon cheer up, he assured her, provided she remembered the consolations of religion. He had the more tangible consolation of a European tour to look forward to. He also had the strange excitement of seeing Caroline Bowles again; there is little doubt that his visit took her as close to heaven as she dared hope. She would ride along on the back of Oberon, her Shetland pony, whilst the tall, lanky Southey walked along beside. As soon as he had gone, she wrote an impassioned note to him:

The author of *Oliver Newman* cannot find it in his heart to condemn me for obeying a first impulse, a blameless one, though none of the wisest perhaps, which irresistibly urges me to say to him before he leaves England—'God bless you for coming to see me.' The words were in my heart, and on my lips when I parted from you, though they found no utterance, so my pen must convey them to you...[29]

Southey's response was almost as warm, although whatever his thoughts he did not allow himself full rein:

Dear Caroline, God bless you. You have no reason to thank me for a visit, from which, short as it necessarily was, and therefore in part painful, I derived as much pleasure as it was possible that I could give. Be assured that whenever I come within the same reach of you, on my annual journeys, it shall not be a light cause which will prevent me from repeating it.[30]

By the time he wrote to May, from Calais, he could say, in his usual robust fashion: 'I lost my breakfast on the passage, but had my revenge upon the fish at dinner.'[31]

When Southey got back to Keswick at the beginning of July after a fairly uneventful trip to Holland, he was mildly surprised to learn that he had been returned, in his absence, as a result of the good intentions of an admirer, the Earl of Radnor, as Member of Parliament for Downton, and not too amused that the local band was drawn up in his honour.[32] But that at least was a practical problem with a practical solution: he would have nothing to do with such nonsense, especially since he had a Crown pension, and in any case did not have the necessary property qualification. Much worse was his daughter Isabel's failing health (she was now 13), which was obviously no mere passing illness. He told Rickman on 16 July, 'After ten days of anxiety—the last a dreadful one, she past away in a swoon—while I was praying in the room below for such a termination, if her recovery was—as it seemed—impossible.'[33] When Cuthbert Southey came to edit his father's correspondence, he recalled the devastation of this event: 'It was the first time I had seen sorrow enter that happy home; and those days of alternate hope and fear, and how he paced the garden in uncontrollable anguish, and gathered around him to prayer when all was over, are vividly impressed on my mind.'[34] Edith never really recovered from this loss, and Southey began to think mournfully of his own end, now that he had lost the 'flower of a fair flock'. In such circumstances, whatever people might think about his declining a seat in Parliament was irrelevant.

He began to correspond with Bedford about the disposal of his papers; he told Taylor that his autobiography would be left in readiness for the press, and that his poems would need to be edited from his own corrected copies.[35] He told Sharon Turner, apropos his declining the parliamentary seat, that 'the world, thank God, has little hold on me. I would fain persuade myself that even the desire of posthumous fame is now only the hope of instilling sound opinions into others, & scattering the seeds of good.'[36] His letters towards the end of 1826 become increasingly valedictory and retrospective. He agreed with Henry Taylor that he would have made a bad statesman because of his lack of decisiveness, and that he should really have entered the Church: he thought the *Edinburgh Annual Register* was perhaps the best thing he had done, because it forced him to examine his own opinions.[37] The poet Samuel Rogers visited, and encouraged Southey to scrub himself vigorously from head to toe, with a hard brush, night and morning. This scarifying had its attractions for Southey, and he declared that after three weeks he felt 'improved in muscular strength'.[38] Such advice was perhaps as beneficial as a visit from the Archbishop of Dublin.[39] He was still enough of this world to rejoice at the offer from Sir George Beaumont of a pony, and to contemplate the prospect of editing, at Colburn's suggestion, the correspondence of Garrick, and supplying a life; even though there were 2,400 letters, for Southey this seemed 'neither... difficult nor unpleasant'.[40] A fee of 1,000 guineas presumably made it that bit less unpleasant, and took his mind off his wretched brother Edward, who had left his wife, spreading false rumour that she was dead, so that he could live with another woman. 'This has been a vile fraud, & when he ventures to apply to me again, I shall for a long time turn a deaf ear to all his applications.'[41]

Just to make matters worse, his old Dutch friends the Bilderdijks were unwell; Edward Williams, the Welsh poet, died in January at the age of 80; a month later Lord Liverpool was dead from a stroke, and the likely successor, Canning, was not to be trusted. Southey wrote to Landor, still abroad, wishing he were back in England to provide him with some sort of ballast in the face of such bewildering events: 'the strange complexity & contrariety of interests, the strange coalitions, the ferment of opinions, & the causes which are at work to bring about greater changes in the constitution of society, than even the last half century has produced.'[42] It is some comfort to see Southey challenging the Utilitarians, showing in a letter to Taylor that his heart was still in the right place, for all his confusions: 'the prime object of our policy should be to provide for the well-being & employment of the people. Whatever lessens wages & throws men out of employ is so far an evil.'[43] This seems the more humane side of his argument for enforced emigration in order to cut down the numbers of the poor. And when he was invited to write for the *Foreign Quarterly* on the problems of Spain, at £100 an article, he took up the challenge to which he had earlier felt unequal. The award of a gold medal from the Royal Society of Literature perhaps acted as some kind of sop, even though he was not going to make the effort to go to London to receive it (when he did eventually get it, it was absurdly large, unsellable, and therefore useless).[44]

He set off for Harrogate at the beginning of June, and his womenfolk followed a week later. They saw a lot of new faces, and the town itself was pleasanter than he expected; for some reason Southey rarely anticipated any pleasure from any English towns. But he was worried about Edith, and hoped that 'change of air & circumstance', and the waters, might have some beneficial effect: sure enough, after the break he was able to claim, certainly for himself, that 'on the whole, tho far from a sound man, I am in a better condition than for some times past'.[45] Edith's health was more fragile.

When they were back home in August, Southey looked forward to what he regarded as another form of vindication, the publication of his *Moral and Political* essays; he was also working on a review of Hallam's *Constitutional History of England*, a work which supported the Whigs and therefore anathema to Southey. As he acknowledged more than once, these reviews allowed him to sort out his opinions without having to embark on vast research of his own. And looking back to the past, as he told Taylor, was always valuable: '*What might have been* is a profitable subject for speculation, because it may be found useful for what yet *may be*.'[46]

His old friend John May had been appointed manager of a branch of the Bank of England in Bristol, and was feeling rather lost in a strange city. Southey was tempted to visit him, and introduce him not only to the scenes of his childhood, but to friends like Cottle and John King the surgeon.[47] But such a visit could not be made immediately, because of his own multiple concerns in Keswick. The house was beginning to fall apart, and when he asked the landlady for £20 to repair some of the timbers, he pointed out that this was a fraction of what would be required to restore Greta Hall to a state where any other tenant would be attracted to it (the lease was to expire in spring 1831, but he did not particularly want to move, so this was a pre-emptive strike).[48] Southey had been presented with another mission: a servant poet, John Jones, was to be published, and Southey was to be instrumental, as he had been with Henry Kirke White, in presenting him to the public. He saw this as a chance to make some general points about education, especially among the lower orders. There was a moral point to be made, as we might expect, but also a social one: 'I want to show how much moral and intellectual improvement is within reach of those who are made more our inferiors, than there is any necessity that they should be, to show that they have souls to be enlarged, and feelings to be gratified, as well as souls to be saved...'[49] Lest we get too carried away by Southey's apparent philanthropy, we should remember that he did not include John Clare in his roll-call of these 'inglorious Miltons', and that Clare had his own views on Southey's approach to the problem. One of Southey's favourite phrases is the 'march of intellect' and it is for him an ambiguous march; he wants to help it on its way, but 'I do not like the tune to which it goes'. This was a typical reaction from the anti-Utilitarian, warily conservative constituency which Southey had come to represent. One of Southey's problems was that this was a political, as much as an intellectual debate, which was to lead to the Reform

Bill: the fact that people like the Whig reformist Lord Brougham were involved was in itself enough for Southey to urge caution.[50]

Southey went with his wife and daughters at the start of November to stay with William Brown at Tallantine Hall, near Cockermouth, then on to Senhouse at Netherhall for a week. But even this could not keep his mind off the dangers of Irish immigration in the neighbourhood, whereby the Irish were bringing down '*our* peasants' to '*their* level'; it was all part of a plot by the Irish priests to increase the number of Catholics in England.[51] The danger was increased by the likelihood of rebellion in Ireland, which would in turn hasten the end of the Government. And yet he had, as he told Bedford on 15 January 1828, declined Lockhart's invitation to write on the 'State of the Country', on the grounds that he knew too little about it. This was not to say that he did not know what he thought: he wanted the Whigs to remain in power, 'that they might be rib-roasted in Parliament as they deserve, & finally be dashed against their own wall by their living wild Irish allies'.[52] He was not surprised that Wynn had lost his place in the Government, even though he had hoped for a different outcome: 'What a series of perplexities & mischiefs have arisen from Canning's restless intrigues & inordinate ambition!'[53] As if to escape from some of these perplexities—and also from his hay fever—he planned to go south, to Taunton and London, picking up Edith May who was with Mary Wordsworth's brother in Herefordshire. Before he left, he put up some more bookshelves, shifted books around, and even considered someone's suggestion that he write a Life of Napoleon.[54] In the end, he left this task to Scott and Hazlitt; but it is curious that at this stage in his life he was still prepared to weigh up the possibilities. There seemed to be nothing that he would not at least entertain.

Southey's visit to London in May was partly to cure the rectal complaint from which he had suffered for more than a year. Dr Copeland performed a successful operation, which presumably made it less painful sitting for a portrait by Sir Thomas Lawrence and a bust by Chantrey: both were thought to be good likenesses. He visited Caroline Bowles in July, and saw his ailing uncle, Herbert Hill, at Streatham, 'in a pitiable state';[55] Hill died on 19 September, aged 79. It was a sad loss; after their initial lack of mutual sympathy in 1795, the two men had become close friends and regular correspondents, especially about matters Spanish and South American. Southey and Hill's widow were to act as joint executors and trustees. Oddly enough, Southey dreamt about him the night before he died, and when he wrote to Rickman about his uncle's death, he resorted to the dream image: 'Just now I feel, upon looking to the years that are past, & to those which are to come, as if life were a dream from which it would be a relief to be awakened.' He wrote to John May, after the funeral: 'My heart is very full: not sorrow, for I am *thankful* for his deliverance,—but of an aweful feeling which you can very well understand.'[56]

One of Southey's summer visitors (he had seen several people in London, including Samuel Rogers, Sir Robert Inglis, Peel, and the Calverts) was a Russian Under-Secretary of State, Tourgeneff, who told him that the 'Old Woman of Berkeley' had been translated into Russian, only to be censored 'lest it should frighten women & children'. Bizarrely, it was altered into the ceremonies of the Greek Orthodox Church, and as a result was more frightening than ever; it circulated in manuscript, one of the most curious early samizdat publications.[57]

The annual statement from Longman at the end of 1828 told him that he had earned the princely sum of £26; there were still 1,500 unsold copies of *A Tale of Paraguay*; the slight poem *All for Love* had not been a great success (he called it a 'sportive exercise of art', which could be applied, in all honesty, to a number of his later poetical productions). At least the *Colloquies* were nearly finished, and he knew how much he had enjoyed writing them, and how important they might be seen in his *œuvre* as a social commentator. As he told Bedford in December, of all 'the opponents of the great & growing party of revolutionists, I am the one whom they hate the most, & of all the supporters of established things the one whom the anti-revolutionists like the least. So that I fight for others against man, but stand alone myself.'[58] This could stand for one of Southey's epitaphs; one in itself would never suffice.

'We have had the most delightful frosty weather I ever remember', Southey wrote at the end of January 1829, '—a clear sky, & no wind, & a warm sun'.[59] But the Government's incompetence led him to draw up in February a petition against the Catholic claims, and then, soon afterwards, another to the King to dissolve Parliament. Both petitions were printed in the *Westmorland Gazette*, earning him attacks from his opponents. Richard Shannon, an Edinburgh Episcopalian and 'a man with a potato in his head',[60] pilloried him for his anti-Irish views, but Southey responded with the retort that he had not changed his views since 1801: 'It is a fair course of argument to assert that the miseries of Ireland were not caused by the laws which exclude the Roman Catholics from legislative powers, & to infer that they cannot be remedied by the repeal of those laws . . .'[61] The problem with this, of course, lies in the initial assumption; but this did not prevent Southey pursuing the matter further in the Preface to his *Colloquies*, where he stated as plainly as he could that whilst he believed that

Catholics could hold any office unconnected with the legislature, they could not be allowed to have any part of the power in a state whose Church they wanted to overthrow. (This did not mean, he added slightly lamely, that he was not conscious of the sufferings of the Irish.) He also had the support of Sir Henry Taylor, once in *The Times*, once in the *Morning Journal*. Southey could, none the less, with such strong feelings, correspond amicably with John May, who disagreed with his anti-Catholic tirades. Scott, too, took exception to Southey's diatribe in the *Quarterly Review*: 'Let him print and be d——d'. There was no point, Scott believed, in resisting the inevitable, and he therefore lent his support to Wellington and Peel, who believed that emancipation was impera-tive.[62] Southey was amused by Murray's reaction to all these arguments: he 'has a notion in his head that I am a most unpopular person, that I make enemies by my writings etc.—this is of course while a shaking fit of *liberalism* is upon him'. If Southey could console himself with this ex-planation, the fact remained that Murray was anxious about the likely reaction to the *Colloquies*, and held back its publication until things were quieter. In a letter to Caroline Bowles of 15 February, in which he announced the completion of his *Colloquies*, he wrote: 'I have neither time nor heart to say anything of State affairs, but you will of course conclude that I do not turn with the wind.' He enclosed some lines to her, which he said would appear in the *Colloquies*; in fact they did not.[63]

Sir Thomas More: or, Colloquies on the Progress and Prospects of Society (1829), as Southey more than once acknowledged, is an autumnal work: the verse dedication, to his late uncle, Herbert Hill, not only spells out the similarities between Hill and Sir Thomas More, but also Southey's own sense of being 'in the sear, the yellow leaf'. Once his History of Portugal is finished, he implies, his work will be done; meanwhile, these two volumes will sum up his views on 'The Progress and Prospects of Society', views that had been forming over the last ten years, in correspondence and in his journalism. Modelling, as he says, the format on Boethius, Southey presents us with a series of dialogues between Sir Thomas More and Montesinos (who is, very largely, Southey in disguise); the result, it has to be said, is a very peculiar performance, and not totally convincing. Because he is trying to re-create the presence of More, bringing the past back to life, Southey frequently indulges in the worst kind of stylistic mannerism, aiming at some sort of mock-Tudor English which can easily make the whole piece seem laboured. The best, most uncluttered writing occurs in those parts where Southey is being most personal, where, in fact, he forgets the whole contrived pretence, and writes about the landscape, as in his account of a family expedition to Walla Crag, or in a briefer reminiscence of a walk with his friends around Derwentwater, or in his loving account, towards the end of the work, of his library. But in terms of its political intent, this is, in some ways, another, later version of the *Espriella* Letters, less persuasive partly because there is so much antiquarianism, and so determined an attempt to present the whole of British history in the context of what the second Colloquy rather grandly calls 'The Improvement of the World'.

That heading is quite revealing; as we have seen, Southey had been addressing that very question of how far hope was possible at such a time, and what form, both practical and theoretical, it might take. Sir Thomas's role is to cast doubt on Montesinos's basic optimism; as early as Colloquy IV, Montesinos is having to admit that 'civilization' is a rarefied concept applicable to very few corners of the globe. As he says, with a reminder of the contemporaneity of the basic problem, 'In this mood how heartily should I have accorded with Owen of Lanark, if I could have agreed with that happiest and most beneficent and most practical of all enthusiasts, as well concerning the remedy as the disease!'

Significantly, much of the talk in the early part of the work focuses on poverty and squalor, and Sir Thomas endorses Montesinos's conclusion, as though if only he could establish this truth amongst his contemporaries, he would 'not have lived in vain!': 'Thus it is that men collectively as well as individually create for themselves so large a part of the evils they endure.' Sir Thomas's subsequent point is one familiar from Southey's other writings: the country has lost the institutions which allowed each person to have his place; once the feudal system declined there arose a 'vagrant and brutalized population', leading to the kind of smouldering volcano represented by London, and thence to the possibility of rebellion. More tells Montesinos that Britons can be aware of the oppressions of 'negro slaves', but not of the 'defective order among yourselves': 'you have spirits among you who are labouring day and night to stir up a *bellum servile*, an insurrection like that of Wat Tyler, of the Jacquerie, and of the peasants in Germany.' At this point, if not already, it becomes clear that, whatever the personal likeness between Sir Thomas and Herbert Hill, More is often Southey's own mouthpiece. This raises an interesting question in itself; for if Sir Thomas is Southey, then who is Montesinos? The answer to that must be that the whole work represents, in fact, an internal dialogue within Southey himself, as he struggles with his conflicting desires to be both optimistic and pessimistic: if Owen, Clarkson, and Bell are the three moral forces of the present age, Montesinos has to acknowledge that Owen's great failing is his lack of religious faith, or, as he puts it, lumberingly, 'A craniologist, I dare say, would pronounce that the organ of theopathy is wanting in Owen's head, that of benevolence being so large as to have left no room for it.' Once again, Southey is voicing in this debate his own anxieties about any system which dispenses with religious belief; it comes, therefore, as something of a surprise to find Montesinos apparently defending the manufacturing system, the very system Southey repeatedly attacks elsewhere. Sir Thomas soon puts an end to such protestations, but Montesinos keeps his end up with his ameliorative approach: 'it will...be seen how all things have been ordered for the best: and the benefit will remain after all the evils of the process shall have past away.'

But the two men end up agreeing that the system itself breeds evil. When Sir Thomas says, 'Montesinos, that reply is a rambling one', the reader might feel that the comment could apply to much that is said by both men. And that is partly the problem with this work, that Southey allows himself to mull over, without necessarily arriving at any truths, the problems he has already addressed in other arenas. Just as he had, in various ways, gone round in circles, so here the two protagonists circle around each other. However, there is also a central fascination to be derived from the fact that, in a work which concerns itself so much with the problems of the Established Church, and the threats posed by Roman Catholicism and Ireland, he should have Sir Thomas More as his main protagonist. Montesinos might have the last word about Catholicism at the end of Part I (and Southey follows this with his own Ode of 1821–2 on Ireland)—and it is a virulent word—but, as Sir Thomas points out in Part II, there is a 'false dilemma, that, in matters of religion, we must either submit absolutely to authority, or reject it altogether'. Southey had also made this point, especially earlier in his life, when he rebelled against the established forms of worship. When Sir Thomas proceeds to argue that the Methodists ought to be embraced by the Established Church, we might legitimately wonder whether there is any overall authorial point of view: there is little doubt but that Montesinos echoes Southey's own feelings of impending catastrophe when he says that we are like a man falling asleep in his cart, and he 'finds himself when he awakens upon the edge of a precipice, towards which the wheels are approaching'. There is a connection here with the point made by Sir Thomas, once again echoing Southey's own views: 'The march of intellect is proceeding at quick time: and if its progress be not accompanied by a corresponding improvement in morals and religion, the faster it proceeds, with the more violence will you be hurried down the road to ruin.' Perhaps there is more than we might think to Sir Thomas's apparently throwaway reproach, at one point, to Montesinos: 'Allow something, my friend, to the contradictious

principle in human nature.' For, in the end, it is precisely those contradictions that make this work have more value than merely that of curiosity: there is, it is true, much that is weird here; the logic of both parties
can seem as waterlogged as Greta Hall's garden in winter; and there is a
determination to talk, almost for the sake of talking, as though we had a
couple of pub bores with nothing better to do, and hours before closing
time. But the fact that Sir Thomas can leave Montesinos, at the end, with
such a note of ambiguity is in itself suggestive of the book's curious
integrity: 'I leave you to your dreams; draw from them what comfort
you can.'

In June, Southey wrote from Netherhall, where he was staying with
Humphrey Senhouse, in answer to Murray's sense of 'doubt, fear &
dissatisfaction'. Southey could have told him that things would come to
this pass; it was certainly not possible for him to leave out of his account of
the 'Progress and Prospects of Society' any talk of politics and religion:
they were not condiments, after all, but the 'solid food itself'. He had the
support, after the publication of *Colloquies*, of men like Isaac d'Israeli
('the most important work of modern times'), the Bishop of Limerick,
and Anthony Ashley Cooper (later Lord Shaftesbury). For his own part,
Southey thought of them as having 'an evening colouring, & whatever
may be their fortune now, will I think, be deemed of some permanent
value, hereafter'. He was right on both counts. He could, he told Mrs
Hodson, remain detached about public events, but his apologia to Murray spells out quite clearly both his intentions and his view of their
successful fulfilment:

My aim has been to deserve well of this age, & of those ages which are to come; to
stand well, not with the public, but with the wise & the good: with posterity; with
my own heart; & with that Almighty Being to whom the thoughts of that heart are
known, & to whom the final account must be rendered of the talents which he has
committed to my charge.[64]

To those who wrote, urging his active participation in some kind of
ideal society, he presented himself as the prophet: 'If the voice of one
crying on the mountain is heard, all that I am capable of doing is done.'[65]
Southey could propose: let others dispose. As he was to tell Mrs Opie in
August, 'my power is in the inkstand'.[66] Robert Gooch told Southey in the
summer of 1829 about the Brighton Co-operative Society; it seemed to be
a version of Owen's ideas put into practice. Even Rickman (sceptical of
Owen) wrote approvingly of the system, especially in terms of its economic advantages; not that he did not have his conservative doubts, as
when he wrote that '*labour in common* produces idleness in all, or

injustice to the industrious, which they will not tolerate'.[67] As Gooch's article in the *Quarterly Review* was to emphasize, the co-operatives would reduce the inequality against which they had all railed, whilst at the same time actively heading off any move towards revolution. Southey, on the contrary, could not fail to see the revolutionary potential of these societies; he could also see an ominous connection with his own revolutionary past, with the levelling principles of Robespierre and Babœuf (those heroes of his lost youth). The co-operative societies were indeed plausible ideas, to be encouraged and written about, but even then there was danger: they could become a 'bonus for idleness';[68] or, and probably worse, the ideas of Owen and John Bright could be taken up by such as Cobbett, and used as 'an engine of mischief'.[69] Once again, Southey was confused. The co-operative movement was 'the most important that has ever yet affected the political world', he wrote, at the end of August;[70] and yet the limits had to be recognized. To Rickman he declared that they were both probably in agreement about 'common labour' and the solutions were drastic: 'its tendency to produce injustice can only be conteracted by strong despotism, or a sense of duty equally compulsive.' In case we think there is a clear pattern to Southey's thinking, we should note that he writes to Gooch in July of this year, 'I look quietly on the course of affairs, pursue my studies, & write playful verses—as if I were grown young again.' As so often, we can wonder who is trying to fool whom. On the practical level, Rickman, Gooch, and Southey were thinking aloud about the co-operative societies, along with the other two aspects of what became some sort of social Holy Trinity—the need for colonization, and the cultivation of waste land which would further this. Gooch died early in 1830, before anything came of these schemes. Southey's hopes had already diminished, when Sara Coleridge married her cousin Henry in September of 1829; even such an ostensibly happy event was for Southey mournful, because 'all change is mournful'.[71] The change was the more dramatic in that Coleridge's wife left Greta Hall at the same time. There were, at least, fewer mouths to feed.

After one of the most hectic summers he had known (thirty Cantabs. visited Keswick), Southey had a brief tour into Yorkshire in October, spending two days with Lord Lonsdale at Lowther Castle, five with Mrs Septimus Hodson (who wrote under her maiden name of Margaret Holford) at Ripon. He joined Henry and Sara at Penrith on their way to London, he called in to see Mr Morritt of Rokeby, and Colonel Howard (an old Westminster acquaintance) at Levens, where he particularly enjoyed the liquor. But he felt unwell, thought he was succumbing to jaundice, and headed for home, to find the writer Robert Grant—who had reviewed Gifford's *Life of Pitt* in the *Quarterly Review* in 1810—and his new bride waiting for him. He could have done without this; even the success of *Colloquies* (1,600 already sold, and a possible profit of £450) seemed a minor triumph. He wrote to Mrs Hodson on his return, 'Here I am again in the society of the dead, & looking back upon the week past in the society of the living almost as upon a dream'.[72] Rather like Keats, Southey was not always sure whether dreams were good or bad. But his work was increasingly to do with the dead: he contemplated a life of Scanderbeg, one of Cromwell, one of the English divines. Lockhart was asking for an essay on Ireland, 'when the time seems fit for one', but Southey was more interested in the Missionaries in the South Sea Islands, since he had been reading Ellis's *Polynesian Researches*; this was 'one of the most curious chapters in the history of mankind'.[73] Anything that was 'curious' was of interest to Robert Southey.

He was also conducting a fairly detailed correspondence with Rickman about education and co-operatives. When he had been in London, he had attended a meeting about the latter, marred by what he called the 'rankest levelling language', which would only serve to put people off; landowners needed to be treated with caution, or else the schemes would not succeed. Rickman agreed, writing a paper which struck just the right note, 'not least in counteracting that sour spirit of independence which is working like leaven in the mass'. Southey still believed in the 'absolute necessity of discipline' at both the personal and national level.[74]

His own discipline was prodigious. In January 1830 he accepted an offer to produce two volumes on the lives of British Admirals, for £750; he was writing reviews for the *Quarterly*, and a life of Bunyan for a new edition of *Pilgrim's Progress*—the latter, he claimed, for love not money: 'I believe few men ever past thro such a fever of enthusiasm without becoming incurably insane: & perhaps there are fewer still whose intellect ever looks thro so thick & coarse a crust of ignorance'.[75] We can see why Bunyan fascinated Southey, and why he would rather write about him than take up Murray's offer of £300 for a history of the Wars of the Roses. Murray and Longman were beginning to fight over him, as the market for biographies grew.

His brother Henry lost his wife Louisa in January, and was left with seven young children. Southey's advice was practical: he should remarry as soon as possible, even though he said that 'I do not think any man was ever more happily mated or lost more in a wife'.[76] The state of the nation was once more alarming, as talk of war spread from conversations overheard on coaches to correspondence with Lord Ashley. What Southey feared was that Irish troubles would explode on the mainland: the

Government might be reasonable enough, but 'what they can do against the combined marches of manufactures, & distress & intellect, & profligacy, is not under my cap'. Increasingly there is a sense of the inevitable disintegration of society; Rickman encouraged such panic, in his denunciation of '*the spirit of the times, the march of intellect, liberal opinions*'. Southey was to cry out in April, Hamlet-like, '*every thing* is out of joint', and as an illustration of this William Hone of all people was writing to him, thanking him for his words about him at the end of his *Life of Bunyan*; Hone could not believe his eyes.[77] In spite of the radical Hone's previous attacks on Southey (including his mischievous reprinting of *Wat Tyler* in 1817), Southey allowed a letter to Hone of April 1830, in which he praised the *Every-Day Book* and *The Table Book*, to be published in *The Times* on 21 May 1830. Hone had fallen on hard times, and needed all the financial help he could get; the two men actually met, amicably enough, later in the year. To keep his spirits up, Southey tried to keep to his strict regimen of exercise, '2 dutiful hours' whenever he could, with Seneca in his pocket: he would read whilst he walked at 3 miles per hour, and then putting the book away, increase his velocity to 4 m.p.h. But such methodical practice did not prevent the rest of the household succumbing to illness in March: Dora, Wordsworth's daughter, came over to help out, and in spite of what he had said earlier, the charms of Harrogate as a place of convalescence were less than attractive. So he would press on with a Life of Sidney, something he had wanted to do for years.

He was delighted when his daughter Edith May became engaged to John Warter, who was serving as Chaplain to the British Embassy in Copenhagen, in the early summer months: this seemed an ideal match. He secured a new lease on Greta Hall for five years, renewable for a further five years, 'so that I consider myself fixed here for life'. There was an immediate flurry of activity about the house, ' a purgatory of plasterers, paperers, & painters'. He confided to Mrs Hodson the importance of his friendship with the writer Caroline Bowles, 'one of the persons in the world whom I most entirely respect & love'.[78] There is no doubt at all at this stage in their lives about the importance to both Southey and Caroline Bowles of their intimate, detailed, and regular correspondence: Southey had told her in 1829 that their correspondence should be published after their deaths (which, eventually, it was); but by April 1830, she was revealing some of her unspoken desires:

You have long ceased to speak of moving southward, and as I was conscious you could not speak of it as a desirable prospect on your own account, I hardly allowed myself to wish you might do so. My disinterestedness was, however, the less meritorious, as I feel my hold of earth too slight to allow me to build castles on it, as I was once prone to do, and perhaps waywardly mourn that I can do so no longer... Is it not sad to look back on such a youth, and to think how late I began to live?[79]

The imminent death of the King was cause for concern, for the Government would most probably resign, and the Whigs come in with Lord Holland, a 'flying squadron of political economists under Huskisson', spelling the end of small tradesmen and manufacturers who had not already been destroyed. It was indeed the Age of Mutability, and he exemplified it, in that he was to say to Rickman in September 1830 that parliamentary reform was no longer a 'doubtful matter... the old ground of defence [which had been his], that the system works well, is no longer tenable'. His solution was to put his faith in Church and State, let reform of Parliament take its course, and he could carry on with his own affairs, as 'people did in the time of Noah'. Did he remember that he had wanted, when young, to write an epic poem about Noah?[80]

His own affairs, in the summer months, included a visit from Edward Hill, who was working hard for a Maths Scholarship to Oxford; Edward's younger brother, however, had been dispatched from Winchester for his idleness. Southey's new hero, Ellis the Polynesian Missionary, came to visit, as the temperature of a previously rather drab summer improved, enabling them to make a lengthy excursion to Causey Pike at the end of July.[81] By August the usual round of Lakers was flocking to see him. He told Henry Taylor that his American visitors 'regard with apprehension & sorrow the growing tendencies towards democracy in this country'.[82] This lent support to his own growing apprehensions. French politics were moving into another potentially revolutionary phase, which caused Southey anxiety but also a *frisson* of excitement: 'war, by putting the stagnant wealth of the country in motion, would remove most of the present distress, whatever the after consequences might be.'[83] If the French resorted to aggression against the British, the British were ready. Not surprisingly, as he told his prospective son-in-law, he was reminded of forty years previously, but he failed to make the personal connection. '*There* they are in the honeymoon of their new revolution, & here they are applauded & admired by persons as rash as those who fraternised with the old French revolutionists, & as ignorant.'[84] Southey had, by this stage, lost all trace of self-irony: all he could see was the folly of others. As he exclaimed to Rickman on 28 August, 'Here is Hone advertising the *Annals* of a Revolution which is not yet a *month* old!'[85] As Southey saw things, war would check both the French and the Catholics: it was a convenient, if costly, solution. But if that was his view, he did not always subscribe to it. Two weeks later he was anticipating Government betrayal and the collapse of Church and Establishment, '& after that cometh anarchy—jacobinism &—an iron despotism at last'. He then added sagely if not altogether convincingly, 'Men are becoming too *knowing* (not too *wise*)'.[86] And yet, two weeks after this, his buoyancy had returned, even if the ship of state was breaking up: he told Scott that 'things are going on merrily to the old tune of ca ira', and he looked forward to another Waterloo, to be celebrated with another midnight bonfire on Skiddaw.[87] Perhaps the real truth of his position is to be found in a letter to Mrs Hodson of 12 October: 'There is no escaping from political anxieties in this disturbed age. No subject can be less congenial to my inclination, & yet I shall probably be much engaged in it this winter.'[88] Murray was certainly anxious for Southey to 'sound an alarm'.

Southey was in London again in November, dining with the Duchess of Kent, where the young Princess Victoria was brought in to say how much she had enjoyed the *Life of Nelson*. He met Prince Leopold, dined with the Wordsworths, Brougham, and Croker.[89] He happily met up with Rickman, and between them they managed to be 'in good spirits on the state of public affairs; we had both looked on to the evil & now look on to the remedy which it is bringing with it'.[90] They were cheerful enough to travel to Chichester and Portsmouth, calling in to see Caroline Bowles, and then on to Crediton to stay with Lightfoot, and then Taunton, before coming back through Bristol, where he observed, 'It is remarkable how much better the state of public opinion is in Bristol than in any other great city'.[91] But, then, he had always had a soft spot for the city of his childhood. He visited his grandmother's house in Bedminster, 'where the happiest days of my early childhood were past', only to find it modernized, and very few of the old familiar trees left standing. He went to his father's old shop in Wine Street, and when he had bought a neckerchief, announced who he was, and asked to have a look around upstairs.[92]

Southey believed that the Whigs, once in power, would become conservative '*ex officio*; & those who have always been so by principle, will come into power again, at no distant day'.[93] His optimism was not mere complacency; he realized that there were still major dangers associated with the parliamentary discussion of the Reform Bill: 'For if any explosion is intended, it is most likely to be attempted when that debate shows how far short of what is demanded by the Radicals that reform must be.'[94] This was, in fact, his chief fear, that the suggested reforms would not go far enough; for him, the widening of the franchise was anathema, so much so that he wanted to take from 'the rabble that power, which wherever it is in their hands, is most mischievously abused'. He said rather airily to Lord Ashley at the end of February, 'The cry which has been raised in favour of the Ballot seems to show that a cry may be raised about anything.' Southey seems not to have had any concept that this was the culmination of a long, slow debate that had begun before he was being naughty at Westminster.[95]

On 2 April Southey wrote to Rickman, who himself foresaw ruin, 'It seems as impossible as ever to see ones way in the stinking fog of our home politics'.[96] The complexities were brought home to him by a speech given by Hunt in Manchester ('one of his wickedest'): 'it must do good because it tells the mob that the Reform Bill is worth nothing.'[97] This is what he had prophesied, and what he had feared; but he could persuade himself to view even this development in an optimistic light: if the Bill was indeed worth nothing, then perhaps it would not be pursued. He put on one side the other possibility, that if it were seen to be worthless, the Radicals might, like Oliver, ask for more, rather than settle for less. On the very same day, in fact, he put a rather different gloss on events, in a letter to Lord Ashley: 'the populace are beginning to find that the reform Bill gives them nothing,—& the yeomanry, that it takes from them a great deal'.[98] Southey's deep confusions are strikingly illustrated by his final cry in this same letter, that the Government should 'better the condition of the people! that *must* be amended—or we perish'. People—rabble: what Southey wanted, in effect, was the reform without the Reform Bill; keep the people happy, but keep them in their place. In the end, with the Government not satisfying anyone, he could only, as he had done before, trust in Providence, and keep away from the madness of ministers. He enjoyed the lovely summer weather, and stole time away from his desk to walk in the woods with a book in his pocket.

One of the authors he was reading in the early summer months was Saint-Simon, who both fascinated and horrified him by the 'audacity' of a scheme that proposed itself as an alternative to Christianity, and—just as bad—'the whole established system of property'.[99] If he heard echoes of the aspheterism of Pantisocracy, he did not say so. His response was sadly alarmist. In July he was telling Mrs Hodson that he wanted to write about 'Utopian schemes of Government', particularly those levelling opinions that were gaining ground in Britain and France.[100] Chaos, as he so often said these days, was come again. It was not altogether much comfort to have to turn his attention to the affairs of his old, and increasingly sick friend, Dr Bell, who had asked him to become an Executor and Trustee. Southey was rather shocked that Bell had given the bulk of his property— £120,000 worth—to his old University of St Andrews; he left Southey and Wordworth £1,000 each, but he also expected them to publish his works. Southey was reluctant to take on such a mammoth task, but went in mid-June to Cheltenham to see what might be arranged. After a few days there, he concluded that Bell's will would cause endless wrangling, and that Bell's sister would dispute it on the grounds of what she thought was his insanity. Bell was certainly infirm, unable to speak, but, said Southey, 'he is perfectly sane'. But Southey had had enough of difficult wills.

In July he heard of the death of his artist friend, Duppa, a 'clever, singular, lively & most agreeable man'.[101] Southey was deeply saddened by such a loss, and remembered their first meeting in the summer of 1793, when Bedford had come to Oxford with John Seward for the installation of the Duke of Portland as Chancellor. Duppa received a warm mention in the *Colloquies*, and when Southey had seen him the previous December, Southey claimed to have seen a family likeness. In the shadow of Duppa's death, Southey had to face the flock of Lakers; if it had not been for the Coronation, he would have had to cope with Princess Victoria and her mother, who had planned to come up. Westall, making sketches for the new *Colloquies* Southey was planning with Rickman, and James White, were more congenial visitors.

Autumn was a strange time. There was a visit with Edith May to Shropshire, to meet the Warter family into which she was to marry; he would return via Manchester, which, being not as bad as he expected, rather confounded his view of the rebels: 'the Radicals, having routed the Whigs to their hearts content spent the evening in jollity instead of mischief'.[102] Perhaps they had their redeeming features after all. He had none the less heard enough about incendiary activities to fear for the safety of his books, and asked Harry to insure them for £4,000 (Harry had taken his brother's advice, and married for a third time); he would also send the manuscripts of *The Doctor*, so that they should not be lost in any conflagration. But the main fear—or hope, depending on his mood— was the spread of cholera. As he wrote to Mrs Hodson on 22 October, 'if we are visited with Pestilence it will be not be more a visitation of justice than of mercy'.[103] There were rumours of the fever spreading from Liverpool to Penrith, and from Sunderland in the east. No precautions seemed effective, which, thought Southey, was a reflection of the state of the nation and the Government. But, he reassured Lord Ashley, 'we shall retake the ruins'. Southey was hardly surprised to hear that Brougham had been drunk when he spoke on the second reading of the Reform Bill: no one could do such a thing sober. Southey gave an interesting pen portrait of his antagonist, whom he could not help but admire on a personal level.

He is reckless & thoroughly unprincipled, has no control over himself, either in his excesses of anger, or of vanity, & cares neither what he says nor what he unsays. There is no truth in him. But he is not without some redeeming qualities. There cannot be a better son, nor a kinder brother. I do not believe that he hates anybody whom he has injured,—except the Lowthers ... He is not, like his friend Jeffrey, a loathsome sensualist.[104]

We can imagine someone—perhaps Brougham—saying much the same about Southey.

'Oh for a Prime Minister with the principle & the intrepidity of Mr Perceval!' So cried Southey that November.[105] But, at the same time, he settled down to incorporate into *The Doctor* the story of the three bears he had heard from his acquaintance George Nicholls nearly twenty years earlier; he prepared a selection of his work for schools, and he gave advice and encouragement to aspiring writers, such as Mary Collings. As the cholera spread, Southey became more actively engaged in local affairs, and was elected a member of the local Board of Health.[106] This was partly a matter of self-interest, in that if he could keep tramps and beggars out of Keswick, then he would. At least Greta Hall, since it was on a hill, felt safe; but as people congregated in towns, he feared a further, nay complete, breakdown in morality, which led him, ironically, to emphasize the importance of bettering the conditions of the lower orders. He could pride himself once again upon being a prophet crying in the wilderness.[107] His 'constitutional hilarity' would allow him the last laugh: since the Government had been as ineffective in the face of disease as it had in the face of everything else, cholera would 'have as free a course as sedition, treason, & blasphemy'. It was all very well, this rubbing his hands in glee at the Government's discomfiture, or at the Chancellor's anxiety at the effect which any extended quarantine would have on the revenue. But in a letter to Neville White, on 3 January 1832, in which he recalled that he had anticipated such a pestilence long before the event, he recognized the complexities of the issues: 'The possibility of such a political crisis as the present was never in my thought. Who, indeed, could have dreamt that we should ever have a Ministry who would call in the mob for the purpose of subverting the constitution! The fearful question which a few months must resolve is, whether pestilence will arrest the progress of revolution, or accelerate it, by making the populace desperate.'[108] Apart from acting on the Board of Health, he would keep quiet in retirement, 'where I can "commune with my own heart, & be still"'.[109]

The Reform Bill was still uppermost in his correspondence with Lord Ashley, and Southey feared the worst, when he heard that there was talk of compromise in the Lords, and a move to tone the Bill down. It was far better that the House 'should be overborne by some act of unconstitutional violence' than commit 'felo de se'.[110] Delay was the only practicable solution, as it would lessen popular expectations whilst exposing the Government's incompetence; he still fancied his own scheme of colonies for the poor, by means of enforced emigration, to be carried out—and how ominous this is, how deeply disturbing—'prudently & quietly,—& not brought forward for public discussion'.[111] It seems appropriate that he was, in the early months of 1832, reading Sharon Turner's *Sacred History of the World from the Creation to the Deluge*: it could be seen as some kind of allegory for present times.[112] By May, the King was no longer 'with the mob', preferring to present himself as 'a victim in the hands of the Whigs'.[113] Lord Grey's resignation was a relief, as was the conjunction of views between Inglis, Wynn, Peel, and himself. Southey summed up the development of his political views in one of his surprisingly intimate letters to Lord Ashley in June, in which he acknowledged that for a long time his political opinions had been feelings, 'rather excited by sympathy or provocation, than taken up upon enquiry & reflection'. The need to think about issues, rather than merely feel, had been harnessed by the need to write about them; but the underlying confusion of thought and feeling helps to explain at least some of the terrible things he says, just as occasionally it explains his paradoxical eagerness to improve the moral and intellectual condition of the poor: 'the tendency of our social system had long been to brutalize the lower classes, & this it is that renders the prospect before us so fearful.'[114]

On 1 April Southey threw up his hands in delight: he had finished his *History of the Peninsular War*. This had been such a huge project that it had become part of his working pattern for years; but it had also become a burden, and the relief in shedding this was enormous. From our perspective we can see the sadness of this whole venture: it is a massive work, diligently put together from a range of materials that would have daunted most people; the writing, for the most part, is crisp and clear; but the narrative is too sprawling, the historical method insufficiently rigorous, and even in Southey's day there was a better book, from Sir William Napier. Those three large volumes now stand on library shelves as a reminder of time that could have been better spent. At least, now that it was off his hands, there was time for more reviewing, and for spending more time with Cuthbert, reading Herodotus and Homer on alternate days (just to leaven the excitement).[115] News came of more deaths: James Mackintosh, Butler, Jeremy Bentham; Scott did not have long to live, and more than one local worthy succumbed to the fever over the summer. He could still be proud of his thick, curly hair, but it was now white at the temples, and grey everywhere else (no longer a lion's mane);[116] Landor returned from Italy, 'grown fatter, looking older, & apparently softened by time'. Edith was 'relapsing into a sad state of spirits', he wrote on 30 May, and this was to be the beginning of a steady decline from which she never recovered.[117] Her lifelong frailty had almost prepared him for such an end; her despondency had more than once seemed more than a mortal frame could bear. Just as the 'moral contagion [was] universal', so he devised a contraption for pumping heated air into the bed, a mixture of steam, nitrous acid, and laudanum.[118] His Health Board were preparing a pest-house, but 'calling it a House of Recovery—because there is much in names'.[119] Yes, we have to acknowledge, Southey was more or less than confused: he was a cynic. Other practical steps included the cancellation of the annual races, which he regarded as a breeding ground of vice.

As he approached his fifty-ninth birthday in August, Southey summed up his life so far to Mrs Hodson:

in many things I am younger than that age usually makes men,—in others I am as much older. I have been eight & thirty years not merely an author, but *known* as one: & I have been married seven & thirty. Few men have had a more troubled youth, none a more quiet middle stage of life. The way has always been uphill,—but always into better air & brighter prospects.[120]

The metaphor might have had a hollow ring, as the cholera edged ever closer; on the other hand, he could compare himself favourably with the ailing Scott, who was four years his senior. As he told Mrs Hughes on 16 August, 'I have not been a rolling stone, though I have gathered no moss'.[121]

Southey was able to see his own development against the background of historical events. He told Lord Ashley in September what he thought the problem had been: 'I believe that that beast the people is always submissive enough to a good rider, & only becomes vicious when it feels a timid & inexpert one in the saddle. If our miserable rulers had not driven us full speed down the hill of Reform, we might very soon have seen Republics as well as Revolutions brought into disgrace.'[122] There speaks the man afraid of a wild horse. But when he wrote more specifically about the French Revolution, he had to admit that it had made him what he was: otherwise he would have become a clergyman, which would not have been as useful 'as that wisdom which error leaves behind,—or rather which is built upon the ruins of error,—enables me to be'.[123] Destruction was necessary before rebuilding could begin. Such arguments could lead him into absurdity, as in his comments on slavery, which, it transpired, was not 'contrary to Christianity'; it was the state of morality produced by slavery that was the evil. But—and this is an odd 'but'—'Slavery would hardly be an evil if this were corrected: alas, I am far from thinking the abolition of slavery would be a cure for the depravity which slavery has produced.'[124] There is something Alice-in-Wonderlandish about this, just as his growing interest in the state of manufacturing allows him to say that 'A sugar plantation compared to one of these Factories is as a Garden of Eden'.[125] Not surprisingly, he confided to Wynn that the problem was beyond solving by 'human legislators'; and scoffed at William Danby's 'Thoughts on various Subjects', in which he talked of a new golden age: 'He may not live to see the catastrophe, & is the happier for not foreseeing it'.[126]

The plan for another volume of *Colloquies* was put aside in October. Murray had published an attack on Southey by Lord Nugent, in the shape of *A Letter to John Murray touching an Article in the last Quarterly Review*, and Southey determined to reply in kind. When challenged by Wynn as to the propriety of replying, Southey said he did so 'from a feeling that it is not becoming in me to receive insults of this kind silently from one of his station'.[127] It is a curiously stilted, and not wholly convincing, defence of his motives. In fact, the whole episode seems oddly contrived. When, after Christmas, he told Mrs Hughes he was still thinking of a public reply, he said, 'the exposure will be such that I am almost sorry for him. Many a man has hanged himself for less'.[128] But Southey, interestingly, found it strangely difficult to work himself up to the right pitch of rage, perhaps because his confusions were running so deep. In a letter to Mrs Bray at around this time, he cries, like another Coleridge or another Keats, 'we are in a mist'.[129] At least he felt vindicated when the Committee on the Factory system focused on the very cruelties he had condemned twenty-five years earlier. Caroline Bowles knew his feelings on the matter, and sent him her 'Tales of the Factories' in the new year. She was rewarded with this accolade: 'No one in any age or country ever wrote with truer feeling than she does'.[130]

The local conservatives did sufficiently well in the local elections for him to enter 1833 relatively cheerful; he held out high hopes for the young Gladstone. He carried on with his Naval History, and started to work on Dr Bell's papers, for a Life (as so often, it was the two hours before breakfast into which he fitted this extra chore). He thought 1833 would be 'The Bloody Year': rebellion in Ireland was inevitable, and everything would flow from that; O'Connell was in charge of events in the South, and once he made a move, things would erupt in Britain. 'How compleatly have the warnings of those who opposed the Roman Catholic Bill been verified by the course of events!' Yet again, however, there was the contradiction of what was happening in Britain: the Bristol riots were a warning of what was to come as a result of the rise of industry, and Southey had Lord Ashley's support here. As Southey spelt it out to John May on 1 March, the logic, for once, seemed impeccable—and yet entirely at odds with other aspects of Southey's creed:

in the manufacturing district when the wages of the adults are at a starvation rate, & their children are—literally—worked to death, murdered by inches,—the competition of the masters being the radical cause of these evils, there is a dreadful reality of oppression,—a dreadful sense of injustice,—of intolerable misery,—of intolerable wrongs,—more formidable than any causes which have ever moved a people to insurrection,—Once more I will cry aloud & spare not,—these are not times to be silent.[131]

It must have been deeply puzzling to his contemporaries, trying to make coherent sense of his views. He wrote to Wynn in June, 'I sent up a petition from this place in favour of our little white slaves, & refused to sign one for the immediate emancipation of the black ones';[132] this from the author of those stirring poems on the slave trade in the 1790s.

At Greta Hall in June, everyone was affected by influenza. Southey was outraged by Murray's publication of Byron's works: 'one of the very worst symptoms of these bad times'.[133] To keep himself calm, he continued with his Naval History; 'Nothing pleases me better than this sort of mosaic work, in which labour & laziness may be said lovingly to meet, & more time is expended in picking out material... than in putting them together.'[134] This had always been one of the attractions for Southey of any kind of historical writing; it was also one of the bases for criticism of his poetry as well as his prose. This magpie aspect was pandered to by a suggestion he made to Moxon that he might combine extracts from the Divines, with Lives, called 'Christian Philosophy', in twelve volumes, at £600 per volume. Moxon did not have that kind of money. More realistic was his hope that his own works might be published after his death in periodical form, running, he thought, to about fifty volumes.[135]

In response to Southey's desire to get his prospective son-in-law a decent living, Mrs Hodson approached the Bishop of Bath and Wells, but the offer of Bath was politely declined as being too expensive. In any case, John Warter really wanted to live in the country. By the end of the year, the Archbishop of Canterbury had found a living for Warter in Sussex, at West Tarring, which would be worth about £300 a year. Once this was settled, the wedding was fixed for 15 January. As when Sara Coleridge had got married, Southey expressed his sense of melancholy; not only would he be losing a daughter, but in the course of the year Cuthbert would go down to join the Warters for coaching prior to the Oxford exams. Southey kept as calm as he could in the face of this, but also in the face of the likely selling of tithes, and the repeal of the Corn Laws. He marked the end of the year with a graphic account of his wife and children getting caught in a storm on the way back from the Words-worths.[136]

As he predicted, the marriage and its aftermath proved a sad affair. He would continue 'living in the past, & conversing with the dead', but Edith had no such recourse;[137] she was deeply shaken by the change, and all too conscious of the distance between Keswick and the Sussex coast. Southey wrote to Mrs Hodson that 'Death has made many breaches in my domestic circle; this is the first that has been made by the course of life.'[138] As if to cheer himself up, he started quizzing people as to who had written that strange book, *The Doctor*, a copy of which he had just received. He enjoyed the mystery of its authorship, and was ready to palm it off on to a range of people: Frere, Sharpe, Croker, Henry Coleridge, Henry Taylor, Bedford (a bit unfair, this). His reasons are interesting: 'I am willing to have my capacity for the lighter parts doubted; & also to have it deemed inconsistent with my gravity & dignityships.'[139]

The anonymous author speaks in his Postscript (typically placed first) of the Greek Pisander, who 'lived in continual fear of his seeing his own ghost. How often have I seen mine while arranging these volumes for publication, and carrying them through the press!' It is certainly the case that, as we have seen, Southey worked at *The Doctor* over many years, accumulating materials like a magpie; and there is something appropriate that it should appear (or at least its first volume—the two final ones of the seven were edited by John Warter after Southey's death) in 1834, at a time when Southey was indeed feeling he was living among ghosts, and confronting his own. But whereas the *Colloquies* had been melancholy in their general colouring, *The Doctor* is an entertaining *jeu d'esprit*. With its short chapters, interchapters, Anti-Prefaces, and so on, it is self-evidently modelling itself on *Tristram Shandy* (as Southey had said more than once when he spoke about the work to Bedford). It does not have the richness of Sterne, the sheer brilliance of invention; but it is that rare thing, a genuinely readable farrago in which little happens, but the reader none the less wants to see what else will not happen. The claim, early on, that it is 'a production the like whereof hath not been, is not, and will not be' is true enough, provided we do not interpret that as a claim to brilliant originality; as he says elsewhere in the first volume, in the contents list, 'The author confesses a disposition to garrulity'. This too is true, but whereas that disposition vitiates much of the *Colloquies*, here the lighter tone transforms it into a kind of lesser virtue. He is not, in spite of that rather solemn opening about the state of national gloom, trying to put us right about the world; he is being playful, as skittish as one of the many cats celebrated at the end of the work.

Southey moves from one topic to another with blithe abandon, as happy in a digression as in anything more direct; in fact, it could be argued that the whole work is a digression. If, in the abstract, we might be surprised by the idea of a work in which the merits or otherwise of philosophy might be discussed in one section, whilst another might dwell at apparently inordinate length on the environs of Doncaster, and another might mull over the calculations required to work out how many languages a male might learn if he were not to shave each day, and another might recount, with bold Gothic type, the story of the three bears, in that severe version (as we have seen, not necessarily Southey's invention, but in keeping with his stern view of the world) where the intruder is an old woman, sent back, for her sins, to the House of Correction—in practice, as we read, we take these bizarre shifts as they come, for Southey manages, with his urbanely relaxed humour (wit is not the word) to create a world in which we accept his own terms. That had not always been the case with some of his more contentious works; but here the general sense of innocence and ease is infectious, and we follow where we are led (quite often, it must be admitted, by the nose).

We might not have expected Southey to write such a self-referential work; the irony of this lies partly in the fact that he has deliberately effaced himself in the act of presenting the work anonymously (anyone who knew Southey would have recognized many of the references to his own attachments to people and places, but that is another matter). The work itself is about writing: as he says in the opening pages:

what can be more emblematic of the work which I am beginning than the splendid instrument wherewith the Preface is traced? What could more happily typify the combination of parts each perfect in itself when separately considered, yet all connected into one harmonious whole; the story running through like the stem or back-bone, which the episodes and digressions fringe like so many featherlets, leading up to that catastrophe, the gem or eye-star, for which the whole was formed, and in which all terminate.

The quill pen provides the focal point, for it is the tool of his trade as a writer; furthermore, the writer has a curious responsibility, in that to be an author is to assume some kind of authority. This had not always worked in Southey's favour; his anonymity as a reviewer was not something he could hide behind in the fuss over *Wat Tyler* (though he tried), particularly since he so wanted to be regarded as the voice of his age. But here he is content to play around with the whole concept of authorship; the work grows into a game, in which we become embroiled, as to who the author is. Clues are given, but these become so absurd as to be meaningless; he resorts to idiosyncrasies of nomenclature which echo the bizarre 'Lingo Grande' in which Coleridge's wife Sara indulged, and in which he played his willing part. He toys with us, saying that 'Names,

Reader, are serious things', and reminds us of the significance to Adam of the process of naming; but his own name is to remain secret: what is extraordinary is that he manages to make us care sufficiently about this. In the process he goes his own sweet way, devoting pages to the different varieties of gooseberry, apples, and pears; he provides a lengthy list of Irishisms, from an Irish Court of Chancery case, dated 18 May 1816. (It comes as something of a shock to remind ourselves that this was a month after the death of his dear Herbert.)

At times, of course, this can become wearing; a joke about identity cannot easily be extended through the length of seven large volumes. But whatever our reservations, it is hard not to admit that Southey justifies himself here, partly because, in retrospect, we have the advantage of knowledge; we know him to be the author, and we can derive that extra pleasure from such comments as this, in the fifth volume:

One of the most distinguished men of the age, who has left a reputation which will be as lasting as it is great, was when a boy in constant fear of a very able but unmerciful schoolmaster; and in the state of mind which that constant fear produced he fixed upon a great Spider for his Fetish, and used every day to pray to it that he might not be flogged.

When he speaks of the delights of domesticity, and of retirement, we can hear the sage of Keswick speaking from the heart; and since rats and vermin generally feature so prominently in his work, there is piquancy in the fact that in the seventh volume he reports on a 'Plan of the Laureate Southey for lessening their number'. There is a sense of his life coming full circle, in a strangely bizarre way. And where the *Colloquies* concluded with the serenity of the Library, *The Doctor* finishes—in so far as it can be said to finish—with 'Memoirs of Cats' Eden': in other words, he goes out, not with a bang, but with a series of whimpers.

The Lives of the Admirals demanded attention; he started work on a Life and Works of Cowper (another mammoth task from which many would have shrunk). The summer months took their toll on Edith, whose moods began to vary alarmingly; there were times when her behaviour could not be explained, except by Southey's word for it: 'disturbed'.[140] Medicine seemed to be of no use; Georgiana Hill, a younger cousin of 18, came to stay, and they had some good walking expeditions, including one to Honiston Crag, which, whatever it did for Edith, reassured Southey of his own good health. But Coleridge died in July at the age of 62, and Southey wrote to Rickman in his cold way: 'It will not intrude much upon my waking thoughts, but I expect to feel it for some time to come in my dreams.'[141] He told Senhouse

that 'the past seems to us always like a dream!' Southey could not bring
himself to say much, even now, in Coleridge's favour: 'All who are of his
blood were in the highest degree proud of his reputation, but this was
their only feeling concerning him ... Perhaps no mans death has ever
occasioned more of what is now called sensation—or less sorrow.'[142] It
seems a desperately sad culmination, not only to Coleridge's life, but to a
friendship that had shaped both their lives since their first rapturous
meeting in 1794.

Edith continued to decline: 'Sleepless nights, sudden agitations which
make the limbs tremulous, want of appetite, & utter prostration of the
spirits, are the symptoms & proofs of a disease for which no name is
assigned, & no remedy can be found.'[143] Southey thought he might take
her to Sussex the following May, and he and Taylor would then go to
France. But this was not to be. William Charles Macready recorded in his
diary the dreadful moment at the end of September when Edith's mind
gave way: 'For a long time [Southey] remained silent—at length told [his
visitor] that he believed he must dismiss him; in fine he disclosed to him
that within the last five minutes, since he rang the bell at the lawn gate,
Mrs. Southey had, without previous indication or symptom, gone raving
mad, and to that hopeless degree that within an hour he must take her to
an asylum.' Southey wrote to Bedford on 2 October 1834, from York,
announcing that he had left Edith in the Quaker Retreat for Lunatics,
with Betty the maid. 'Forty years she has been the light of my life; & I have
left her this day in a lunatic asylum.' There were no financial worries,
mercifully; and there was something else to be thankful for: 'the stroke did
not fall upon me when the printers were expecting the close of my naval
volume, or the Memoir of Dr Watts. To interrupt a periodical publication
is a grievous loss to the publishers, or, at least, a very serious inconvenience.'[144] Edith would not have wanted to be the cause of such an
inconvenience: as Southey was to say, three days later, 'the depth &
sincerity of her affections are known only to myself'.[145] He wondered
whether he should be in York with Edith, but the doctor assured him that
there was no need, and that it was only a matter of time before she
recovered her equilibrium. Mrs Hutchinson stayed with him at Greta
Hall. Edith had to be operated on, to remove a tumour 'as large as the
largest goose-egg' on her back; she could barely express herself, either
orally or on paper.[146] Southey hoped if he got her back to Greta Hall, her
two unmarried sisters, Martha and Eliza, might come over from the Isle of
Man to look after her. Edith May had a miscarriage, which Southey
attributed to the alarm over her mother's condition. At least in the new
year the news was better: Edith had asked the rather stern mistress of the

Retreat if she was improving, and when told that she was, replied, 'I am so afraid I shall go back again'.[147]

Charles Lamb had died: 'never was there a kinder, a more generous, or a more feeling heart than his'.[148] Telford, too, leaving Southey £500 plus a share in his property amounting to £850. Sir Robert Peel was, in February, offering further help, in the form either of a baronetcy, or of a pension; Southey rejected the former, on the grounds that he was not wealthy enough to accept.[149] He went down to Sussex, with Cuthbert, in March; and then on to stay with Caroline Bowles, before picking up Edith from York. When they arrived there on 20 March, she was rambling on, 'with scarcely a gleam of sanity'.[150] His own ill health—psoriasis and rheumatism—was driving him mad with itching, and the salt sea water of Scarborough appeared a seductive prospect; a week there would, he hoped, clear things up. When they got to Scarborough (staying on the South Cliff, at a Mrs Ling's), although Edith was prone to repeat the same thing over and over again, she managed to get some long walks in the clear air, going down the steep terrace of the South Cliff to the sands below.[151] Southey told Wynn that she never spoke two connected sentences all the time they were there. He wrote to Bertha, before they left for Keswick, warning her what to expect: 'Your poor mother's state is that of compleat imbecillity...'[152] Within three or four miles of Keswick, tears welled up in Edith's eyes; in the evening, back home at Greta Hall, she was perfectly lucid.[153] After five weeks at home, she seemed almost her old self, taking an interest in what was going on, and 'answering reasonably when spoken to'. For his part, Southey's psoriasis ominously crept over his body, a manifestation of all the plagues to which he and the world were heir to.[154]

The History of Portugal, Monastic Orders, the Life of Bell, Cowper's Life and Works: all these kept Southey busy. There was some urgency with the Cowper, as a rival edition in eighteen volumes had just appeared from a Reverend T. Grimshawe—'an evangelical clergyman dirty enough to undertake it' (quite what this made Southey is not clear). In spite of his doubts about the project, Southey pressed on, anxious to find some occupation as Edith's condition worsened: she was increasingly melancholic, and had lost all motivation. 'What use is it?' she would say, or 'It's no good!'[155] Southey decided that he could not take her down to Sussex, as Edith May was pregnant again, and he did not want to induce another miscarriage. All he could hope was that Cuthbert's presence later in the summer might rouse her. Sara Hutchinson, Wordsworth's sister-in-law, died at the end of June. 'Our domestic prospects are darkening upon us daily', Southey wrote, 'I know not whether the past or the present seems most like a dream to me, so great & strange is the difference.'[156] He tried to offer consolation to Wordsworth, but even as he wrote, he heard a cry from downstairs telling him that Edith had fainted and fallen: 'I go about my work with the feeling—& something like the alacrity—of a man who is setting his house in order, before he departs for a long journey.'[157] When Cuthbert returned, Edith at first refused to see him, and urged him to go away; but once she had accepted him, she feasted her eyes on him all day long.[158] There was, however, a general wasting away, as she lapsed into silence. Southey could not possibly accept an invitation to Ireland at such a time: but he could tell his Dublin friends that the word of God was the only thing to save Ireland from 'the profligacy of the Whigs, & the indolent wickedness of the Popish Hierarchy'. Perhaps his horoscope had been right, when it spoke of his 'gloomy capability of walking thro desolation'.[159]

Longman wanted to produce a revised edition of the *Life of Wesley*, now that Southey had more material, including Coleridge's marginalia. Southey was willing, in spite of all his other commitments and the string of late summer visitors. Cuthbert left in the second week of October, and Southey felt once more bereft, but prepared to make the best of it: 'the blossoms of my life are shed, & I stand like a tree in winter,—well-rooted, &, as yet, whole at the heart, & with its head unscathed.'[160] Henry Taylor came to lend moral support, and they set off for a good walk each afternoon at 2.00. Edith May's pregnancy ran its course, and on All Saints' Day, Southey became a proud grandfather.[161] When the first volume of his Cowper appeared at the end of the year, it got a drubbing from the *Evangelical Magazine*: 'They say I shall be known to posterity as embalmed in Lord Byron's verse for an incarnate lie.'[162] But he had the stoicism to bear such minor kicks and pricks. As he wrote to John Horseman, his friend from Corpus of forty-one years earlier, 'no man has enjoyed greater blessings, & few have had keener griefs, but these have been medicinal, & so I trust will be the bitters on which I am now dieted.'[163]

Southey felt increasingly lonely. Whilst his daughters began to visit their neighbours in the evenings, he stayed at home, seeing very few people.[164] Typically, he kept on working, as though this were the only remedy for his depressed spirits: his whole life's discipline had been geared to coping with just such a tragedy. To us the motto 'In Labore Quies' might at this point have a hollow ring; but for Southey it still applied. He kept on with the Cowper, using papers sent on by Mrs Unwin's daughter, and sent off the second volume at the end of January. His daughters helped with some of the transcriptions, and also bound some of his books for him—200 volumes of what he called his '*Cottonian*

Library'.[165] He plunged into the fourth volume of the *Lives of the Admirals*, without any zest; as he had hoped, Martha Fricker arrived from the Isle of Man in February. There was something ironic and cruel about the fact that, at this terrible time in his life, he was having to cope with several people, including Cottle and Allsop, producing volumes on Coleridge's life, which inevitably meant reference to himself. He was adamant that his own papers should not be included in Cottle's *Reminiscences*.[166] He was doing what he could to set his own house in order, with the help of young Davies (who had helped with Bell's papers, and who was still living opposite). 'There will not be much of me for worm's meat, but think, what pickings the booksellers will have of my remains!'[167] He was conscious that Coleridge had, in later life, taken every opportunity to speak ill of him: both Southey and Wordsworth thought it a mistake for Coleridge's letters to be published, for this would simply expose his 'duplicity'. For them, on the other hand, 'when our lives come to be written, there will be nothing that needs either concealment, or varnishing'.[168] When Longman proposed the publication of Southey's works in ten volumes, Southey expressed his confidence that , 'die when I may, my memory will be one of those which "smell sweet & blossom in the dust"'.[169]

The summer was enlivened by a visit from the Luscomes from Devon, and from an old schoolfriend, Edward Levett, and his wife. An American, Dr Sprague of Albany, New York, came with an introduction from Mrs Opie. Martha Fricker was returning to the Isle of Man at the end of May, but then another of Edith's sisters, Mrs Lovell, would come back to Greta Hall to help out. Bedford was, finally, coming, with his cousin, and they would lodge at the bottom of the garden, like benevolent fairies. Bedford made some sketches, including the view from Southey's study window, which would form the frontispiece to the fifth volume of his proposed complete works; but Bedford himself was a diminished figure—deaf, arthritic, and with shaking hands.[170] At the end of July Southey heard of the death of William Taylor, another instance of an unhappy man whose talents had, in Southey's view, gone to seed. He left Southey five of his shares in the Huddersfield Canal, which were not apparently worth very much.

In October Southey was satisfied that it was safe to leave Edith with Mrs Lovell; his brother Harry was also offering a doctor's advice to have a break. He set off for Bristol with Cuthbert, to show him the scenes of his own childhood.[171] It was to be a long expedition, a combination of melancholy and almost painful enjoyment. He was certainly glad to see Cottle and his sisters in Bristol after all these years: Mary Cottle was, comfortingly, hardly altered in face or expression, 'one of the sweetest you can imagine'. He took Cuthbert to see his grandmother's old house, 'the very Paradise' of his childhood. They stayed with Mrs Hodson, and then, after seeing the servant-poet John Jones in Bath in November, set off for the Earl of Devon's, and then on to Exeter, to be met by Lightfoot. They met Derwent Coleridge, 'pretty well cured of all coxcombry', and in any case saved by a good woman; near Penzance Southey saw Charks le Grice for the first time since Cambridge in 1793, and at Truro he saw Jeremy Collins. More important, undoubtedly, was a visit to Buckland, to stay with Caroline Bowles, before heading back to Keswick in February, getting home late at night beneath a lovely moon.[172] Caroline Bowles wrote at once, saying how much she missed him: 'I will not agree with you that it may be better never to meet than only meet to part.'[173] Whilst at Buckland Southey had received a 'flighty' letter from a young Charlotte Brontë, asking for his comments on her poetry: he gave the kind of no-nonsense advice to which he was inclined, and prophesied, rightly enough, that 'probably she will think kindly of me as long as she lives'. But his mind was on other things, and it is not surprising if, at this juncture in his life, he should be concerned more with domestic virtues than with the aspirations of an unknown poet.[174] At Greta Hall Bertha had already redecorated a couple of rooms; Edith, alas, was no better, in fact, 'in the same hopeless state as when I left her'.[175] He tried to work on his poems, for the collected edition, but it was difficult, as he continued to be haunted, as he had been in Bristol, by 'recollections . . . like ghosts' that stared him in the face.[176] Victoria came to the throne in June, and as Laureate he tried to write what he knew must be an optimistic poem on her accession. But it was hard to be optimistic as Edith's end drew near: he imagined she would just fall asleep like an infant and never waken: 'no infant was ever more void of offence towards God & man. I never knew her to do an unkind act, nor say an unkind word.'[177] In October, Southey wrote:

Life has been to her for the last three years like an uneasy dream; & it cannot be long before she will wake from it in a better world. Such a release has long been to be wished; & yet it has been dreadful, for she has become as a child to us. We have been married two & forty years; & a more affectionate & devoted helpmate never man was blessed with. There never was a tenderer or more careful mother . . .[178]

Edith died on 16 November 1837: he felt he had lost part of himself.

It was a desolate time. Cuthbert, of whom Southey was proud, was off to Queen's College, Oxford, in January; Southey had told Mrs Hughes that Caroline Bowles, when they visited in February, had said 'she never saw so loveable a creature; & he says of her that he never took so much to anyone in so short a time'. This was to prove a dreadful hostage to fortune, just as was Southey's comment to Mrs Bray, the same month, that Cuthbert never took a 'liking or disliking without just cause'. Kate was off to stay with the Warters at Terring; Bertha would stay with her father, and they would at least keep each other company. 'Never was there a time when we could see so little before us, either at home or abroad', Southey wrote to Rickman in January; when he said 'home' he meant more than 'England'.[179] And then, news came of the death of his brother Tom, in March: there is a breathtaking statement of Southey's reaction to this, 'an event drawing after it such cares & troubles, that it put everything else out of mind for the day'.[180] But then, Tom had been trouble when alive. A swelling in Southey's groin, which he suspected to be a hernia, made him decide to go fairly soon to London for treatment. Wordsworth urged the use of a truss at all times, the best being 'Salmon and Oddys opposite-sided truss'. Edward Quillinan's father had died through not taking his hernia sufficiently seriously.[181] Southey had the novelty of a train ride from Warrington to Birmingham, at the cost of £7. 10s., on his way to London.[182] There he met, for the second time in his life, Thomas Carlyle, who remarked on the evident decline in Southey's health and spirits: he was a very different man even from the person Carlyle had seen three years earlier, when Southey's sudden outburst of anger at mention of De Quincey had alarmed Carlyle to such an extent that he feared for Southey's sanity, and wondered how on earth someone with such turbulence beneath the surface had survived so long. Southey went on to see Neville White, before setting off for another continental jaunt, with Cuthbert, and his friends Kenyon, Jones, and Senhouse.

They travelled from Boulogne through Normandy, Brittany, and Touraine, before heading for Paris. Southey would potter around the hotels, slightly befuddled, unusually quiet, reluctant to engage with the sights and sounds that would normally have given him such pleasure. But he none the less kept a detailed journal, which at times approached a form of imagistic shorthand: 'Flocks of black turkeys in the fields. Fruit trees along the road. Apples which would have been good had they been nearer approaching to ripeness, some bitter sweet which would make good cider, plums also but unripe . . .'[183] He was also writing letters home, to May and Bedford, and some sweetly paternal ones to his daughter Bertha; his last letter from France, to Bedford, dated 7 October from Paris, announced his imminent return. He had to admit that 'home is no longer home to me'. But, in case Bedford had got the wrong idea, or perhaps heard things from any of the others, Southey insisted:

Do not suppose that I am in bad spirits, or any way given to depression, nor that the sense of time & change weighs me down. On the contrary I am in good heart & hope, & look with more confidence to compleating unfinished works, & executing others which have been long projected, than I have done for many years.[184]

Such optimism, however typical, was to prove sadly misplaced.

On their return to England in October, Southey headed straight for Buckland and Caroline Bowles; any doubts anyone might have harboured about the nature of their relationship could be shed when he wrote to Bertha about their intention to get married:

I have known Miss Bowles more than twenty years; & since Miss Hutchinsons death there has been no woman with whom I have been so intimate, or for whom I have entertained so high a regard. For many years I have never travelled to the South without making Buckland one of my resting places, & it was always the place at which I wished to rest longest. No persons could be more prepared for the relation in which we now stand to each other than we have imperceptibly been while it was impossible that either of us could look upon such an event as among the contingencies of fortune. You & Kate both know enough of my long friendship for her & the grounds upon which it has rested, to understand how suited to each other we are in all respects... You will love her the more for having made me myself again which under any other circumstances I never should have been.[185]

Southey's announcement of his engagement to Caroline Bowles shocked his children, according to Wordsworth. Cuthbert, Southey told Bertha, had written 'intemperately', but Southey would ignore this.[186] A letter survives from Cuthbert to Mrs Hughes, dated from the following year, in which he charges Caroline Bowles with deceiving herself about the true state of Southey's health; what had been a happy house was happy no longer. Kate, according to Southey, 'the only one of my daughters who can be affected by it, sees that it will be greatly for her comfort as well as for mine'. Southey wrote to his cousin Herbert Hill in November: 'I have chosen well for myself, upon an intimacy of more than twenty years. If I had not so chosen, my house would have been a chearless one for the remainder of my life. I shall now have a companion to my hearts content, one of suitable age, & whose disposition & habits are perfectly in accord with my own.' In his later letter to Wynn, it is almost as if he thinks he has made, at last, the ideal match—'two people could not be found better adapted to each other'—and yet there was that dreadful fear, no doubt encouraged by his children, that he had done the wrong thing: it was 'either the weakest or the wisest action of my life'.[187] There was, in fact, to be another marriage in the family, between Bertha and her cousin Herbert Hill (who now had a job in the Bodleian Library in Oxford). Southey would go to Buckland in March, and then return with his bride sometime in June. They were married at Boldre Church, on 4 June 1839; Mr Burrard, her uncle, performed the ceremony; Sir Harry Neale gave her away.

They were installed in Greta Hall by September. But Southey was fading faster than either he or his new bride were prepared to admit. His epistle to Wynn of 5 September is a sad affair, written in a cramped hand, the letters falling over themselves, and denying the calm certainties that Southey was trying to proclaim, as he got back to his 'wonted occupation'.[188] He was going to get on with his second version of *Colloquies*, then the History of Portugal, then the book on the Monastic Orders: he had all the necessary materials. He was even writing some poems again. 'You will infer from this that I am in good heart & with a reasonable prospect of getting thro all that I have projected in prose or verse.'

Within a matter of weeks, Southey's mind had given way: there was no apparent bodily suffering, but Caroline suddenly found herself playing the role of nurse rather than wife, as Southey sat quietly in his study, with Caroline as his silent companion; occasionally he uttered pleasantries: 'I shall see Wynn again then ... who could have thought it—then all are *not* gone—'.[189] During these final years, it is hard to know who to believe, in that very quickly family and friends divided into two camps, with the Wordsworths siding with Cuthbert and Kate against Caroline and the Warters. There is no doubt but that, as Wordsworth says, the new Mrs Southey was 'very hot-tempered', but she was also, as he admitted, 'a most excellent person'. She was, however, a 'strange Creature, putting herself upon the sternest abstractions of marriage rights and privileges, as established by Law, and this in a case where the Husband was incapable from failure of mind to fulfill the Contract in the sense which the Law requires. What a sad thing all this is.'[190] One thing that emerges from Wordsworth's account of events is Kate's severe depression even before her father's engagement. Caroline grew increasingly desperate, sensing that nothing could be done, and firmly believing that apart from his books '*everything here has* proved harmful to him'; she felt '*utterly alone here*'. He would say, repeatedly, 'Let us go back to Buckland & be by ourselves'.[191] The anguish of his illness was increased by the torment inflicted on them both by Southey's children, especially Cuthbert and Kate. Caroline had wanted to break off the engagement in the face of Cuthbert's hostility, but Southey had said that 'undutiful & ungrateful Boy' must learn to like her. He did not; still less did Kate. The first night at Greta Hall Caroline had cried her eyes out once her husband was asleep; she did not realize that Southey had noticed all too clearly what was happening, and he could not conceal his wrath for long: but that just made things worse. 'How', Caroline mused later, 'could I have been so credulous as to believe what her father told me . . . that any grown up children could approve of their fathers taking a second wife'; they were not the friends Southey had assured her they would be. She was, she said, from the very beginning '*an object of aversion*' to Kate and Cuthbert and the housekeeper, with her 'rough manners, and . . . unprepossessing appearance'.[192] However, when she wrote to Lord Ashley on 20 June 1840, explaining why there had been no reply to his last letter, she confessed herself gratified that 'in permitting our late union, *He* has provided for my beloved Husband—his friend of two and twenty years, a more fitting companion for the days of his decline, than any other *earthly* friend could be—'.[193] In July of that year, Wordsworth called: 'He did not recognise me till he was told. Then his eyes flashed for a moment with their former brightness, but he sank into the state in which I had found him, patting with both hands his books affectionately, like a child. Having attempted in vain to interest him by a few observations, I took my leave, after five minutes or so.'[194] Cuthbert and Kate both left the house briefly, and then came back, on their own dreadful terms: the dining-room was to be solely for them and Mrs Lovell, Southey and Caroline were to be confined to the upper floor, and there was to be no intercourse between Caroline and them. Southey could do less and less for himself. 'I have in a manner', said Caroline, 'lost *my identity in his.*' Visitors came, but he did not speak to them; she overheard him say to himself one day, 'I wish my head was in the right place'.[195]

In January 1841 Wordsworth explained his role in affairs to Henry Crabb Robinson. He had tried to assure the children of the advantages of the second marriage, and reported that Kate had said that if her father were to remarry then Caroline Bowles was 'of all Persons, from what she had heard, and seen of her in her writings, the one whom she should prefer'. Wordsworth's view was that Caroline might have made more of an effort towards Kate, and he did what he could to reconcile them; in the end, he gave his blessing to the scheme whereby Kate should stay in Greta Hall, but avoid seeing her stepmother, and seeing her father daily 'at any convenient hour'. He told Kate to write her version of events, just as Caroline had done, and to show it to Myers, the curate of St Johns at Keswick.[196]

On 1 May 1841, Caroline took Southey in the garden, the first time he had been outside since October. She had thought about a wheelchair, but such things were hard to get up to Keswick, let alone Greta Hall.[197] There were problems with the house, and Caroline fixed the chimney slates herself, which solved the problem of the intolerable smoke. People were still using the back of the garden as a short cut, in spite of a wall and a locked gate; and she was having to get the fence fixed.[198] In June, the vicar was reporting that Southey once got so confused in church that he went into the wrong pew.[199] Cuthbert was behaving boorishly: he called in briefly that month, glared at Caroline, said 'Well—how are ye father?' and was out of the house.[200] Caroline's dog died, and she just managed to 'keep her head above water'. By August Southey was barely able to feed himself, and by November he was displaying disturbing signs of violence. Wordsworth recorded in October that there was 'no change in dear Southey except that we understand he is occasionally very much more irritable, sometimes violent. Poor Kate's visits are, as stipulated, merely for a few minutes once a week.'[201] Bertha, who was living at Rydal with her husband, the Reverend Herbert Hill, had gone to stay, but never saw Caroline whilst there. There was a brief, 'most halcyon calm' in December.[202]

Caroline decided to make a gesture to the stepchildren, sending some wine to Cuthbert and Kate; it was returned to the wine merchant, unopened. On 12 February 1842 she reported that 'it is almost come to *carrying* now, when he is moved from place to place—and he cannot—when he tries to do it—lift his dear hand to his head'.[203] She too, feeling the strain, was 'sick in *mind & body*'. There were days when Southey would utter a series of disjointed words—'*sometimes one only for hours together*—as fast as he can speak till I find myself sometimes *writing this word instead* of what I would say...'[204] On 6 April 1842 Herbert Hill recorded how he had taken their new baby to show Bertha's father; Caroline Southey brought him downstairs and he said 'The Baby, the Baby, the beautiful Baby' and the tears came into his eyes.[205] Caroline wrote in June that 'our garden is in the prime flush of full blown summer—Glorious now—but already on the wane—from want of rain added to the scorching sun—we must expect a *flowerless* Autumn I fear...'[206] She was relieved when her two cousins, Laura and Fanny, came in July to help her out. Cuthbert meanwhile, about to go into orders, was living in sin with the woman he was supposed to be marrying, 'without the vulgar shackles of "human ties"'.[207] The pair got married in August, and immediately started a round of socializing, Cuthbert and his 'flippant, underbred Wife'; Caroline could not understand how they lived so extravagantly, with Cuthbert splashing out on a horse, and employing the Southey carpenter to make furniture for them. When she made a visit to their house, she was refused admittance. In October Henry came and diagnosed paralysis and epilepsy, but reassured Caroline that there was no suffering. The following day Southey woke up and called out 'Brother! Brother!'; but Henry had already gone.[208] Southey occasionally registered the presence of

Caroline's cousins, and once said, looking keenly into their faces, 'ah home—here—'.

The nights became *'long & fearsome'* for Caroline. At the beginning of February Southey had a seizure, with convulsions at night: 'He seems *to feel* the fatal weight in the head—'.[209] By March he had contracted typhoid; he died on 21 March 1843, 'as gently as a child falling into a slumber'. For Caroline the relief was considerable; she 'closed his eyes for their long sleep', but at that very moment, she felt utterly deserted by God. She proceeded to beat herself with her own dependency; 'this agony is my just punishment—It is not fitting to love created being, as I loved him—'.[210] At the funeral on 24 March, in Crosthwaite Church, where he had long intended to be buried, two birds sang as the rain streamed down: Edward Quillinan, Wordsworth's cousin, wrote some lines about this. John Warter and Caroline's cousin were both at the funeral; Henry Southey arrived a day late. Wordsworth, pointedly not invited, came anyway. Caroline spoke of the kindness of neighbours, but *'the Son and Daughter in no way* altered.'[211] She planned to move back to Buckland. On 10 April she wrote: 'It is almost *too horrible* to tell—but it is generally observed that the gladness & exaltation of the *bereaved children*—is *excessive*—It was shown *in this house at the most awful hour*...I go from this house...as never Wife before left the house of such a Husband—except under circumstances of disgrace.'[212] She then had to deal with her late husband's papers: Taylor was going to edit the letters, with the infamous Cuthbert and Kate. In the event, it was even worse than this, for Cuthbert took over from Taylor, to produce the *Life and Correspondence*. As she took her leave of Greta Hall, Caroline said, as though she had indeed become her husband, '"Is it a dream?"—I sometimes say as I look round—'.[213] But this was no dream; she lay broad waking.

The Warters gave her their support; John was to edit some further letters in a few years' time. But it was the others who seemed to be in charge. Rickman and Landor both refused to let their letters be printed, but Wynn was more complaisant. Caroline believed that Cuthbert and Kate were so convinced that she wanted to cash in on Southey's life and death that they began work 'before the earth had closed over all that was mortal of their father'. Everything, apart from about 1,000 books, went under the hammer, including his watch, seals, and portrait, his desk, and his writing table.[214] It was heartbreaking. There was to be a monumental tablet in Crosthwaite Church, but Caroline was bitter about Wordsworth's lines for it: 'was ever such a miserable failure?—or any thing so utterly heartless & spiritless?'[215]

Ye vales and hills, whose beauty hither drew
The poet's steps and fixed him here, on you
His eyes have closed! and ye, loved books, no more,
Shall Southey feed upon your precious lore,
To works that ne'er shall forfeit their renown
Adding immortal labours of his own...
Wide were his aims, yet in no human breast
Could private feelings find a holier nest.
His joys, his griefs, have vanished like a cloud
From Skiddaw's top; but he to Heaven was vowed
Through a life long and pure; and Christian faith
Calmed in his soul the fear of change and death.[216]

At least Landor provided, in manuscript, something more appropriate and marmoreal:

In maintaining the institutions of his Country
He was constant, zealous and disinterested
In domestic life he was loving and beloved
His friendships were for life & longer
In criticism, in dialogue, in biography, in History
He was the purest & most candid writer of his age
In Thalaba, Kehama and Roderick the most inventive Poet
In lighter compositions the most diversified
Rarely hath any author been so exempt
from the maladies of Emulation;
rarely any studious man so ready to assist the studious
to raise their reputation & to promote their fortunes
Wonder not then O Stranger that our fellow citizen
hath left among us the resolution to commemorate
and under the same good Providence which guided him
the earnest wish to imitate his virtues—[217]

John Warter managed to get back for Caroline most of the relics she wanted, but not the portrait. When Southey's bust arrived, she suffered agonies, and her servant stood behind it, 'with the tears running down her face'.[218]

EPILOGUE

On the dreary day of Southey's funeral, the future Earl of Shaftesbury (formerly the Lord Ashley with whom Southey had corresponded so openly about social and political issues in the 1830s) wrote in his diary:

After three years of mental eclipse Robert Southey has been gathered to his father; I loved and honoured him; that man's noble writings have, more than any other man's, advanced God's glory and the inalienable rights of our race. He was essentially the friend of the poor, the young, and the defenceless—no one so true, so eloquent, and so powerful.[1]

This is a touching tribute, but curiously symptomatic in its rather epitaphic tone, verging on the coldness Caroline Southey had complained about in Wordsworth's epitaph. Many had admired and honoured Southey; many were to speak of him after his death in these terms. To love him was perhaps more difficult (Nathaniel Hawthorne was to make this point in 1855), and it is interesting how Lord Ashley's expression of love quickly shifts into the reasons for admiration. As we have seen, Southey presented a cold and stern face to the world, and it should be no surprise to find it returned in kind. He had become that strange, but increasingly familiar combination, a very private man in a very public position; as he would have wished, it had long been impossible to separate the man from the work, in that, not only were his books his life, and his life his books, but his views as expressed in his prodigious output reflected his own deeply held moral convictions. Whether these were popular, or would make him popular, was of no concern to him: moral rectitude of this order can easily, as Hazlitt had registered, become offensive and self-deluding.

For Ashley the power of Southey's views and their expression was a source of admiration, just as, in very different circumstances, an early reviewer had spoken of the power of genius displayed by Southey's early poems. Powerful figures, whether tyrants or overthrowers of tyrants, stalk the pages of his epics. Some readers recoiled from such displays of power, precisely because they could seem so cold and overwhelming. There is

something intriguing about John Henry Newman's celebration of
Thalaba as the 'most Sublime of English Poems...I mean *morally*
Sublime';[2] intriguing partly because Southey himself would not have
expected praise from such a quarter, partly because the sublimity—
another version of power—is so emphatically qualified as moral. In
other words, Newman is responding to the very impulse admired by
Ashley, and which Southey himself regarded as supreme. If it was Wordsworth who said of himself that he wished to be considered as a teacher or
as nothing, it was Southey who might more obviously have said it of
himself.

Wordsworth, as it happens, was someone who commented on the very
lack in Southey's work of that 'over powering impulse in [a writer's] own
mind, though his duty to himself and others may require it'. A pointed
comparison between Southey and Coleridge would only show 'how
masterly' was Coleridge: as Wordsworth rather cruelly suggested, a mere
year after Southey's death, the result was that Southey's works are 'read
once but how rarely are they recurred to! how seldom quoted, and how
few passages, notwithstanding the great merit of the works in many
respects, are gotten by heart'.[3] Keats had touched on the dangers, in a
letter to Shelley of August 1820, when he told him to 'curb his magnanimity, and to be more of an artist'; as Wordsworth (and many others)
pointed out, Southey was not a dedicated craftsman, still less, 'else sinning
greatly, a dedicated Spirit', as Wordsworth said of himself in *The Prelude*;
Southey could switch from one occupation to another—in fact he sometimes said he had to, and prided himself on the resultant regularity. But all
that work, all that diligent collecting and collating of materials—whether
for poems, reviews, articles, or historical surveys—was no guarantee of
concentration or even quality: on the contrary, the result was often a
damaging diffuseness.

Wordsworth's open hint that Southey was no longer, by his death, a
widely read poet is itself of some historical interest; the world had moved
on, and the bard of Keswick had ceased, seriously, to be a bard, or to
consider himself one. His main thrust, from the early 1820s onwards, was
towards history and politics, and he was quite open about this. This helps
to explain his neglect as a poet: but we need to remind ourselves that the
blanket of indifference was thrown over many of his contemporaries as
well (and, for that matter, the Wordsworth celebrated by the Victor-
ians was not the Wordsworth later generations have appropriated). The
one creative writer to rise to the challenge, as it were, of Southey's
posthumous reputation was Walter Savage Landor, the writer with
whom Southey, mainly as a result of *Gebir* (1798), had most closely

identified himself. Landor, too, has not fared well in the stakes of posterity—and he fared less well than Southey in his own lifetime. What they had in common was a form of self-belief, a determination to strike out on their own, a kind of studied carelessness towards others' views. What is noticeable is that Landor's praise embraces the man as much as the work; the one grows out of the other, and this very blurring helps to account for Landor's placing of Southey above Wordsworth and Coleridge—indeed, above all his contemporaries apart from Byron (Southey would not have been amused by this, for no amount of 'energy' in Byron's verse could atone for what he regarded as his basic immorality). Landor's extravagant praise is worth quoting:

Never in the course of my existence have I known a man so excellent on so many points. What he was as a son, is now remembered by few; what he was as a husband and father, shows it more clearly than the best memory could represent it. The purity of his youth, the integrity of his manhood, the soundness of his judgment, and the tenderness of his heart, they alone who have been blest with the same qualities can appreciate. And who are they? Many with one, some with more than one, nobody with all of them in the like degree. So there are several who possess one quality of his poetry; none who possess the whole variety... Southey could grasp great subjects, and completely master them; Coleridge never attempted it; Wordsworth attempted it, and failed...[4]

Interestingly, Landor's view of his hero ends, as it begins, with the moral tone. For this reason, Southey's prose is as important as the poetry, for it embodies and enunciates those beliefs that lie behind the poetry. Some writers weighed up the relative merits of Southey's verse and prose, when really this was not the point. The critic John Anster, writing in the *North British Review*, stated baldly something that is both startlingly true, and truly startling:

For a period of more than fifty years the writings of Southey were among those which, in England, most contributed to create or to modify public opinion... Through both his poems and his prose works, his individual character so distinctly appears, that it would be scarce possible to mistake a page of his writing for that of any other man... there is everywhere a definiteness and decision of purpose, which is that which constitutes true originality; and *his* thoughts it is which are expressed in a dialect which he feels to be common property, and of which he as little remembers how each particular phrase or cadence has been formed, as we can determine how we have learned the words of the language we speak.[5]

This sense of Southey's importance—independent, ultimately, of any questions of literary value—needs to be registered, especially now when it cannot be easily confirmed, in that there are no texts readily available to which we can turn. Southey might not have been, even at his death, a figure widely read; but he could not be ignored. Even Charlotte Brontë, whose youthful poems he had politely but firmly returned in the 1830s, was struck by the *Life and Correspondence*: Southey presents an exemplum of the literary life—

Some people assert that Genius is inconsistent with domestic happiness, and yet Southey was happy at home and made his home happy; he not only loved his wife and children *though* he was a poet, but he loved them the better *because* he was a poet. He seems to have been without taint of worldliness; London, with its pomp and vanities, learned coteries with their dry pedantry rather scared than attracted him; he found his prime glory in his genius, and his chief felicity in home-affections. I like Southey.[6]

That final sentence is moving in its directness, and its intimation of Southey the man and Southey the writer being one and the same: she can like him because she knows him, and she knows him because of his writing.

In a piece much more equivocal than Charlotte Brontë's private comments, John Gibson Lockhart addressed many of the issues raised by Southey's career. He lamented the detail and diffuseness that so many of Southey's contemporaries had criticized; he praised the 'Doric simplicity', but wished there were more 'Doric strength'. Lockhart found it hard to praise, purely and simply, for he thought there was a failure of nerve in Southey's work, an inability to go to the limits of his art: 'Somebody compared Coleridge to a muddy torrent, sonorous but not transparent; Southey's delight was in clearer and stiller waters.'[7] Many others said something similar. Lockhart further made a point with which Southey himself would not necessarily have disagreed, that he had been born too late: as the *Colloquies* of 1829 had implied, Southey was really happier with an earlier age. Much of his life and work bears this out: Greta Hall became his own version of a remote monastery, in which he could pursue his own contemplations.

Whilst many have seen the virtues of Southey's life, his dedication to his writing life, Walter Bagehot was unsparing in his scorn, in his belief that Southey's existence had been a wasted one, built on a colossal lie:

it is pitiable to think that so meritorious a life was only made endurable by a painful delusion. He thought that day by day, and hour by hour, he was accumulating stores for the instruction and entertainment of a long posterity. His epics were to be in the hands of all men, and his *History of Brazil* the 'Herodotus of the South American Republics.' As if his epics were not already dead, and as if the people who now cheat at Valparaiso care a *real* who it was that cheated those before them. Yet it was only by a conviction like this that an industrious and caligraphic man (for such was Robert Southey), who might have earned money as a clerk, worked all his days for half a clerk's wages, at occupation much duller and more laborious.[8]

But within a few years, Thackeray, whilst acknowledging that very sense of Southey's belonging to a past age, emphasized by Lockhart, could put the case for him with eloquence and force, precisely because of the life Bagehot thought wasted:

I will take another man of letters, whose life I admire even more,—an English worthy, doing his duty for fifty noble years of labour, day by day storing up learning, day by day working for scant wages, most charitable out of his small means, bravely faithful to the calling which he had chosen, refusing to turn from his path for popular praise or princes' favour;—I mean *Robert Southey*...I hope his life will not be forgotten, for it is sublime in its simplicity, its energy, its honour, its affection.[9]

In his *Reminiscences* of 1867 (but not published until 1881), Thomas Carlyle remembered his few meetings with Southey, shedding light not so much on Southey's writings as on Southey's character; but such light illumines both, for Carlyle astutely realized how much Southey was a figure of pent-up emotions:

How has this man contrived, with such a nervous system, to keep alive for nearly sixty years? Now blushing under his grey hairs, rosy like a maiden of fifteen; now slaty almost, like a rattle-snake or a fiery serpent? How has he not been torn to pieces long since, under such furious pulling this way and that? He must have somewhere a great deal of methodic virtue in him...[10]

It is perhaps Carlyle, with his finely modulated rhetoric, who gets as close as anyone to Southey's essential character. He evinces a fine recognition of Southey's achievement, but also the cost of that achievement; Southey's life had been, in many respects, a 'haggard existence', as he admitted to Carlyle, and rather than mock it, with Bagehot, as an example of wasted effort, we might echo Carlyle's warm, understanding sympathy. His final image is moving and appropriately ironic, in that much of Southey's social comment had been directed at the world of industrialized mechanization; it sums up that sense of a life dedicated, industrious, ceaseless in its activity, and yet, ultimately, and dreadfully sadly, wearing itself completely away:

I likened him to one of those huge sandstone grinding cylinders which I had seen at Manchester, turning with inconceivable velocity...screaming harshly, and shooting out each of them its sheet of fire...beautiful sheets of fire, pouring out each as if from the paper cap of its low-stooping-backed grinder, when you look from rearward. For many years these stones grind so, at such a rate; till at last (in some cases) comes a moment when the stone's cohesion is quite worn out, overcome by the stupendous velocity long continued; and while grinding its fastest, it flies off altogether, and settles some yards from you, a grinding-stone no longer, but a cartload of quiet sand."[11]

NOTES

Abbreviations

(Unless otherwise indicated, place of publication is London.)

Berg	Berg Collection, New York Public Library
Bodleian	Bodleian Library, University of Oxford
BPL	Boston Public Library
Brotherton	Brotherton Library, University of Leeds
CBS	Caroline Bowles Southey
CL	Coleridge: *Collected Letters*, ed. Earl Leslie Griggs (6 vols., Oxford, 1956–71)
Cornell	Cornell University Library
CUL	Columbia University Library
CWW	Charles Watkin Wynn
DW	Dorothy Wordsworth
GCB	Grosvenor Charles Bedford
HL	Huntington Library, California
Houghton	Houghton Library, Harvard University
HS	Henry Southey
HWB	Horace Walpole Bedford
JM	John May
JR	John Rickman
Keswick	Keswick Museum and Art Gallery
LC	*Life and Correspondence of Robert Southey*, ed. Cuthbert Southey (6 vols., 1849–50)
Marrs	*Letters of Charles and Mary Lamb*, ed. Edwin W. Marrs, Jr. (3 vols., Ithaca, NY, 1975–)
NL	*New Letters of Robert Southey*, ed. Kenneth Curry (2 vols., New York and London, 1965)
NLS	National Library of Scotland
NLW	National Library of Wales
PML	Pierpont Morgan Library, New York
Poetical Works	*Poetical Works of Robert Southey, collected by himself* (10 vols., 1837–8)
Rochester	University of Rochester Library, New York
RS	Robert Southey
SL	*Selections from the Letters of Robert Southey*, ed. John Wood Warter (4 vols., 1856)
STC	Samuel Taylor Coleridge
Texas	Humanities Research Center, University of Texas at Austin
TS	Thomas Southey
WSL	Walter Savage Landor
WT	William Taylor
WW	William Wordsworth
Yale	Beinecke Library, Yale University

For all quotations from correspondence the appropriate publication reference is given; quotations have been checked against the MS sources and altered accordingly. In quotations from MSS punctuation and RS's capitalization at the beginning of sentences have been regularized.

Chapter 1

1. For Southey's early life the best account remains his own series of auto-biographical letters, written to John May in the 1820s, and published in the first volume of *LC*; most of the material in this chapter is derived from these letters. A much fuller narrative is provided by William Haller, *The Early Life of Robert Southey 1774–1803* (New York, 1917).
2. *LC* i. 20.
3. RS to GCB, 30 Sept. 1797, *LC* i. 23.
4. *The Doctor* (1834–47), ch. LXXIV.
5. *LC* i. 128.
6. *LC* i. 44.
7. *LC* i. 47.
8. *Poetical Works*, ii. 266.
9. RS to GCB, 1 Oct. 1797, MS Bodleian.
10. *Poetical Works*, ii. 274.
11. *LC* i. 59–60.
12. *The Doctor* (1834–47), ch. X.
13. *LC* i. 131.
14. See Molly Lefebure, *The Bondage of Love: A Life of Mrs Samuel Taylor Coleridge* (1986), 26–31.
15. Ibid.
16. *LC* i. 117.
17. Quoted in Geoffrey Carnall, *Robert Southey and his Age: The Development of a Conservative Mind* (Oxford, 1960), 14.
18. See *SL* iii. 351.
19. MS Bodleian.
20. RS to CBS, *The Correspondence of Robert Southey with Caroline Bowles*, ed. Edward Dowden (Dublin, 1881), 52.
21. See esp. Marilyn Butler (ed.), *Burke, Paine, Godwin, and the Revolution Controversy* (Cambridge, 1984).
22. Quoted in Jack Simmons, *Southey* (1945), 26–7. The original notebook for the *Flagellant* (1792) is in MS Houghton.

Chapter 2

1. RS to GCB, 13 Apr. 1792, *NL* i. 4–5.
2. RS to GCB, 16 Apr. 1792, MS Bodleian.
3. Ibid.
4. *Letters written During a Short Residence in Spain and Portugal* (1797), 127.
5. RS to GCB, 22 Apr. 1792, *NL* i. 5–6.
6. RS to T. D. Lamb, 26 Apr. 1792, MS Houghton.
7. RS to GCB, 14 May 1792, MS Bodleian.

8. RS to GCB, [May] 1792, ibid.
9. RS to Edith May Southey, [n.d.], MS Keswick.
10. RS to GCB, [May] 1792, MS Bodleian.
11. RS to GCB, 30 May 1792, *NL* i. 6–8.
12. RS to GCB, 11 June 1792, MS Bodleian.
13. RS to GCB, [June] 1792, ibid.
14. RS to GCB, 21 June 1792, ibid.
15. RS to T. D. Lamb, 31 July 1792, MS Houghton.
16. RS to GCB, 29 Sept. 1792, MS Bodleian.
17. RS to GCB, 6 Oct. 1792, ibid.
18. See G. Carnall, *Robert Southey and his Age: The Development of a Conservative Mind* (Oxford, 1960).
19. RS to T. D. Lamb, 5 Aug. 1792, *SL* i. 13–14.
20. See *Poetical Works*, iii. 73–7.
21. RS to T. D. Lamb, [Oct. 1792], *SL* i. 3–5.
22. Ibid. 5–8.
23. *Gentleman's Magazine*, 63 (1793), Preface.
24. RS to GCB, 21 Oct. 1792, *NL* i. 8–11.
25. RS to GCB, 19 Nov. 1792, *LC* i. 165–9.
26. RS to T. D. Lamb, Dec. 1792, *SL* i. 10–13.
27. RS to GCB, 4 Dec. 1792, MS Bodleian.
28. RS to GCB, 26 Dec. 1792, *NL* i. 12–14.
29. Ibid.
30. RS to GCB, 30 Dec. 1792, MS Bodleian.
31. RS to GCB, 16 Jan. 1793, ibid.
32. RS to GCB, 8 Jan. 1793, ibid; see Nicholas Roe, *The Politics of Nature: Wordsworth and Some Contemporaries* (1992), 42–3.
33. RS to GCB, 25 Jan.–8 Feb. 1793, *NL* i. 15–20; 5 May 1793, *NL* i. 20–3.
34. RS to GCB, 25 Jan.–8 Feb. 1793, *NL* i. 15–20.
35. Ibid.
36. *Poems* (1797), 135–9; there is a slightly different text in *Poetical Works*, ii. 132–4.
37. *Poems* (1797), 55.
38. RS to GCB, 15 Mar. 1793, MS Bodleian.
39. *Poetical Works*, iii. 109.
40. RS to GCB, 15 Mar. 1793, MS Bodleian.
41. RS to Charles Collins, Easter Sunday 1793, *LC* i. 178–80.
42. MS Brotherton Library, University of Leeds.
43. RS to T. D. Lamb, 3 Apr. 1793, *SL* i. 16.
44. RS to GCB, 4 Apr. 1793, MS Bodleian.
45. Ibid.
46. RS to GCB, 5 May 1793, *NL* i. 20–3.
47. RS to T. D. Lamb, 17–29 May 1793, MS Houghton.
48. See Richard Holmes, *Coleridge: Early Visions* (1989), 47.
49. RS to GCB, 31 July 1793, *NL* i. 30–5.
50. RS to GCB, 1 June 1793, *NL* i. 23–7.

51. RS to GCB, 8 June 1793, MS Bodleian.
52. See Molly Lefebure, *The Bondage of Love: A Life of Mrs Samuel Taylor Coleridge* (1986), 26–31.
53. RS to GCB, 14 and 21 July 1793, *NL* i. 27–30.
54. RS to GCB, 31 July 1793, *NL* i. 30–5.
55. *Poetical Works*, ii. 175.
56. RS to GCB, 14 Oct. 1793, MS Bodleian.
57. *An Improbable Tale*, MS Bodleian.
58. RS to GCB, 31 July 1793, *NL* i. 30–5; 14 Oct. 1793, MS Bodleian.
59. RS to HWB, 20 Oct. 1793, MS Houghton.
60. *Poetical Works*, ii. 198.
61. RS to HWB, 11 Dec. 1793, *NL* i. 35–9.
62. RS to HWB, 22 Dec. 1793, MS Bodleian.
63. RS to HWB, 20 Oct. 1793, MS Houghton.
64. RS to GCB, 26 Oct., 29 Oct. 1793, MS Bodleian.
65. RS to GCB, 26 Oct. 1793, MS Bodleian; to HWB, 30 Dec. 1793–3 Jan. 1794, MS Bodleian.
66. RS to HWB, 3 Nov. 1793, *LC* i. 190–1.
67. RS to GCB, 11 Nov. 1793, MS Bodleian; to HWB, 13 Nov. 1793, MS Bodleian.
68. RS to HWB, 13 Nov. 1793, MS Bodleian.
69. RS to GCB, 22 Nov. 1793, MS Bodleian.
70. RS to HWB, 11 Dec. 1793, *NL* i. 35–9.
71. RS to GCB, 22 Nov. 1793, MS Bodleian; see Roe, *Politics of Nature*, 45.
72. RS to HWB, 12 Dec. 1793, *NL* i. 39–43.
73. RS to GCB, 14 Dec. 1793, MS Bodleian.
74. RS to HWB, 22 Dec. 1793, MS Bodleian.
75. RS to GCB, 18 Dec. 1793, MS Bodleian.
76. RS to HWB, 22 Dec. 1793, MS Bodleian.

Chapter 3

1. RS to HWB, 4 Jan.–18 Feb. 1794, *NL* i. 44–7; to GCB, 2 Feb. 1794, *NL* i. 48–51; *Poems* (1797), 99, 83–4.
2. RS to GCB, 2 Feb. 1794, *NL* i. 48–51; to J. Horseman, 3 Feb. 1794, MS NLS.
3. RS to HWB, 4 Apr. 1794, MS Bodleian. 'To the Chapel Bell' appeared in *Poems* (1797), 149–51.
4. RS to GCB, 13 Apr. 1794, *NL* i. 52–3; *The Autobiography of Leigh Hunt* (3 vols., 1850), i. 128–9.
5. RS to J. Horseman, 16 Apr. 1794, MS NLS.
6. RS to GCB, 13 Apr. 1794, *NL* i. 52–3.
7. Southey did not include this poem in *Poetical Works*; it did, however, appear in the Galignani (Paris) edition of 1829, a volume published without Southey's authority, and a source of grievance to an author deprived of copyright.
8. RS to GCB, 11 May 1794, *LC* i. 205–6.
9. RS to GCB, 1 June 1794, *NL* i. 53–6.
10. RS to GCB, 6 June 1794, MS Bodleian.

11. *Poetical Works*, ii. 264.
12. RS to GCB, 12 June 1794, *NL* i. 56–8.
13. See Richard Holmes, *Coleridge: Early Visions* (1989), esp. pp. 59–88.
14. RS to J. Montgomery, 6 May 1811, *Memoirs of James Montgomery*, ed. John Holland and James Everett (7 vols., 1854–6), ii. 296.
15. RS to GCB, 25 June 1794, *NL* i. 58–60.
16. STC to RS, 6 July 1794, *CL* i. 83–4.
17. See J. R. MacGillivray, 'The Pantisocracy Scheme and its Immediate Background', *Studies in English Literature by Members of the University of Toronto* (Toronto, 1931), 131–69; Eugenia Logan, 'Coleridge's Scheme of Pantisocracy and American Travel Accounts', *PMLA* 45 (1930), 1069–84; Nicholas Roe, *The Politics of Nature: Wordsworth and Some Contemporaries* (1992), 36–55; Ian Wylie, *Young Coleridge and the Philosophers of Nature* (Oxford, 1989), 50–6; Holmes, *Coleridge: Early Visions*, 59–88.
18. Mrs Henry Sandford, *Thomas Poole and his Friends* (2 vols., 1888), i. 97–8.
19. Burnett to Lightfoot, 22 Oct. 1974, MS Bodleian; this letter is printed in Roe, *Politics of Nature*, 156–7.
20. Mrs Henry Sandford, *Poole and his Friends*, i. 213.
21. See Nigel Leask, 'Pantisocracy and the politics of the "Preface" to *Lyrical Ballads*', in *Reflections of Revolution: Images of Romanticism*, ed. Alison Yarrington and Kelvin Everest (1993), 39–58.
22. RS to GCB, 22 Nov. 1793, *CL* i. 194.
23. William Godwin, *Enquiry Concerning Political Justice* (2 vols., 1793), i. 316–17.
24. For Coleridge and Hartley, see Nicholas Roe, *Wordsworth and Coleridge: The Radical Years* (Oxford, 1988), 96, 113, 211–16.
25. See Roe, *Politics of Nature*, 17–35.
26. C. Lamb to STC, 26 Aug. 1800, Marrs, i. 235.
27. See Roe, *Politics of Nature*, 21–8.
28. See Holmes, *Coleridge: Early Visions*, 83.
29. See S. T. Coleridge, *Lectures 1795: On Politics and Religion*, ed. Lewis Patton and Peter Mann (Bollingen series, 1971), 126.
30. *Memoir of John Aikin*, ed. Lucy Aikin (1823), ii. 296, quoted in N. Leask, 'Pantisocracy and politics'.
31. See Molly Lefebure, *The Bondage of Love: A Life of Mrs Samuel Taylor Coleridge* (1986), 34–68.
32. W. Taylor to RS, 1803, *Life and Writings of William Taylor of Norwich*, ed. J. W. Robberds (1843), i. 442.
33. STC to RS, 13 July 1794, *CL* i. 85–90.
34. RS to CGB, 20 July 1794, *NL* i. 60–4.
35. Ibid.; see Lefebure, *The Bondage of Love*: 'Mrs Codian' was the pseudonym of Mrs Coleridge, in an unpublished Memoir, MS Texas.
36. RS to HWB, 1 Aug. 1794, *NL* i. 65–6.
37. RS to GCB, 5 Aug. 1794, *NL* i. 66–9.
38. See Mrs Henry Sandford, *Poole and his Friends*, i. 97.
39. RS to HWB, 22 Aug. 1794, *NL* i. 70–4.
40. See Mrs Henry Sandford, *Poole and his Friends*, 101–6.

41. *The Prelude* (1805), x. 539–40, in *The Oxford Authors: William Wordsworth* ed. Stephen Gill (Oxford, 1984).

42. RS to HWB, 22 Aug. 1794, *NL* i. 70–4.

43. STC to RS, 19 Sept. 1794, *CL* i. 106.

44. Quotations are from *Wat Tyler. A Dramatic Poem* (1817); the poem appears in *Poetical Works*, ii. 21–54, unaltered, but with a brief exculpatory Preface.

45. Coleridge, *Poetical Works*, ed. E. H. Coleridge (1912), 71.

46. Quoted in Lionel Madden (ed.), *Robert Southey: The Critical Heritage* (1972), 37.

47. STC to Charles Heath, 29 Aug. 1794; to RS, 1 Sept. 1794, *CL* i. 96, 97.

48. RS to TS, 7 Sept. 1794, *NL* i. 74–6.

49. STC to RS, 11 Sept. 1794, *CL* i. 101; to Edith Fricker, 17 Sept. 1794, *CL* i. 102.

50. STC to RS, 18 Sept. 1794, *CL* i. 103.

51. STC to RS, 19 Sept. 1794, *CL* i. 105.

52. RS to GCB, 10 Sept. 1794, *NL* i. 76–9.

53. RS to GCB, 15 Oct. 1794, MS Bodleian.

54. RS to GCB, 23 Nov. 1794, ibid.

55. RS to TS, 19 Oct. 1794, *LC* i. 222–5.

56. STC to RS, 21 Oct. 1794, *CL* i. 112.

57. STC to RS, *c.*23 Oct. 1794, *CL* i. 118–20.

58. STC to F. Wrangham, 24 Oct. 1794, *CL* i. 121.

59. For example, the Zombi, Hurlyburlybuss, Rumpelstilzchen, Marquis Macbum, Skaratchki.

60. RS to GCB, 24 Oct. 1794, *NL* i. 82–3.

61. RS to Sara Fricker, 25 Oct. 1794, *NL* i. 84–5.

62. STC to RS, 3 Nov. 1794, *CL* i. 121.

63. STC to G. Coleridge, 6 Nov. 1794, *CL* i. 125.

64. STC to Mary Evans, Nov. 1794, *CL* i. 131.

65. RS to TS, 6 Nov. 1794, *NL* i. 85–6.

66. Quoted in Geoffrey Carnall, *Robert Southey and his Age: The Development of a Conservative Mind* (Oxford, 1960), 32.

67. RS to Edith Fricker, 12 Jan. 1795, *NL* i. 90–2.

68. See Chapter 8 below; Southey included the poem in *Poetical Works*, ii. 21–54, unaltered.

69. RS to HWB, 12 Nov. 1794, *NL* i. 86–7.

70. RS to GCB, 23 Nov. 1794, MS Bodleian.

71. RS to GCB, 4 Dec. 1794, ibid.

72. STC to RS, 9 Dec. 1794, *CL* i. 132.

73. STC to RS, 17 Dec. 1794, *CL* i. 139.

74. Ibid.

75. STC to RS, 29 Dec. 1794, *CL* i. 145.

76. STC to RS, [mid-Jan.] 1795, *CL* i. 149.

77. RS to Edith Fricker, 12 Jan. 1795, *NL* i. 90–2.

78. STC to RS, 19 Jan. 1795, *CL* i. 150.

79. RS to GCB, 8 Feb. 1795, MS Bodleian.

80. Ibid.

81. See Coleridge, *Lectures 1795*.
82. STC to G. Dyer, 10 Mar. 1795, *CL* i. 155.
83. See Holmes, *Coleridge: Early Visions*, 157; STC to G. Dyer, late Feb. 1795, *CL* i. 151; RS to HWB, 12 Jun. 1795, MS Bodleian.
84. In the Bodleian Library; quoted in Joseph Cottle's *Reminiscences of Samuel Taylor Coleridge and Robert Southey* (1847).
85. RS to TS, 21 Mar. 1795, *NL* i. 92–3.
86. Quoted in Madden (ed.), *Robert Southey: The Critical Heritage*, 38–9.
87. RS to CWW, 8 Mar. 1798, MS NLW.
88. STC to RS, 17 Dec. 1794, *CL* i. 138.
89. Cottle, *Reminiscences*, 31–5.
90. RS to TS, 9 May 1795, *NL* i. 93–5.
91. The four 'Botany Bay Eclogues', *Poetical Works*, ii. 71–89, are extremely interesting forerunners of Southey's 'English Eclogues' and of *Lyrical Ballads*.
92. RS to GCB, 12 May 1795, *NL* i. 95–6.
93. RS to GCB, 27 May 1795, *LC* i. 236.
94. RS to GCB, 15 June 1795, *LC* i. 240.
95. RS to R. Duppa, [1795], MS PML; to GCB, 13 July 1795, MS Bodleian.
96. RS to GCB, 13 July 1795, MS Bodleian.
97. RS to GCB, 22 Aug. 1795, ibid.
98. STC to RS, early Aug. 1795, *CL* i. 157.
99. WW to W. Mathews, *Letters of William and Dorothy Wordsworth: The Early Years*, ed. Chester L. Shaver (Oxford, 1967), 20–24 Oct. 1795, 153.
100. Lord Carysfort to RS, Sept. 1795, MS NLW.
101. RS to GCB, 1–10 Oct. 1795, MS Bodleian.
102. RS to GCB, 24 Oct. 1795, *LC* i. 251.
103. STC to T. Poole, 7 Oct. 1795, *CL* i. 160; see Lefebure, *The Bondage of Love*, 71.
104. RS to GCB, 17 Nov. 1795, *NL* i. 102–3.
105. RS to GCB, 25 Nov. 1795, *LC* i. 254–7.
106. RS to GCB, 29 Nov. 1795, *LC* i. 258.

Chapter 4

1. RS to CWW, 26 Jan. 1796, *SL* i. 20.
2. Ibid.; RS to GCB, [20 Feb. 1796], *NL* i. 104–7.
3. STC to J. Wade, *c*.10 Feb. 1796, *CL* i. 184.
4. RS to R. Lovell, 19 Feb. 1796, *LC* i. 262–7.
5. *Letters written During a Short Residence in Spain and Portugal* (1797).
6. RS to GCB, 19 Feb. 1796, *NL* i. 104–7.
7. RS to GCB, 24 Feb. 1796, *LC* i. 267–71.
8. *Letters in Spain and Portugal*, 581.
9. RS to GCB, 24 Feb. 1796, *LC* i. 267–71.
10. RS to CWW, 23 Apr. 1796, *SL* i. 25–9.
11. WW to W. Mathews, 21 Mar. 1796, *Letters of William and Dorothy Wordsworth: The Early Years*, ed. Chester L. Shaver (Oxford, 1967), 169.

12. Southey makes a distinction in his 1837 Preface between 'faults of effort' (mostly left unchanged) and 'faults of language'; political prejudices were adjusted accordingly. Quotations in this chapter are from the first edn. (1796).

13. Quoted in Lionel Madden (ed.), *Robert Southey: The Critical Heritage* (1972), 42.

14. STC to J. Thelwall, 31 Dec. 1796, *CL* i. 294.

15. RS to HWB, 13 Oct. 1795, MS Houghton.

16. See Nicholas Roe, *The Politics of Nature: Wordsworth and Some Contemporaries* (1992), 17–35.

17. C. Lamb to STC, 27 May 1796, Marrs, i. 5.

18. RS to GCB, 15 May 1796, *LC* i. 272–3.

19. STC to J. Cottle, 17 May 1796, *CL* i. 217.

20. RS to CWW, 24 May 1796, *SL* i. 29–30; see Richard Holmes, *Coleridge: Early Visions* (1989), 114.

21. RS to GCB, 27 May 1796, *LC* i. 275.

22. RS to CWW, 24 May 1796, *SL* i. 29–30.

23. STC to J. Fellows, 31 May 1796, *CL* i. 219.

24. RS to HWB, 7 June 1796, MS Bodleian.

25. Lamb to RS, 30–31 May 1796, Marrs, i. 10; STC to J. Cottle, 22 Feb. 1796 *CL* i. 185.

26. RS to HWB, 12 June 1796, MS Bodleian.

27. RS to GCB, 12 June 1796, *LC*, i. 277–9; 22 June 1796, *NL* i. 109–10.

28. RS to GCB, 26 June 1796, *LC* i. 279–82; to TS, 25 July 1796, *NL* i. 110–12.

29. RS to GCB, 31 July 1796, MS Bodleian; to HWB 29 Aug. 1796, MS Houghton.

30. RS to GCB, 31 July 1796, MS Bodleian.

31. RS to GCB, 26 July 1796, *NL* i. 112–15.

32. RS to GCB, 31 July 1796, *LC* i. 286–7.

33. Ibid.

34. RS to N. Lightfoot, 28 Aug. 1796, MS Bodleian.

35. Ibid.

36. *Poems* (1797), 209–10.

37. RS to GCB, 29 Aug. 1796, *LC* i. 296.

38. RS to GCB, 17 Nov. 1796, *NL* i. 118.

39. STC to C. Lloyd, sen., 15 Oct. 1796, *CL* i. 240.

40. STC to B. Flower, 2 Nov. 1796, *CL* i. 247.

41. RS to GCB, 1 Jan. 1797, MS Bodleian.

42. STC to J. Thelwall, 19 Nov. 1796, *CL* i. 258.

43. STC to J. Thelwall, 31 Dec. 1796, *CL* i. 294.

44. RS to GCB, 21 Nov. 1796, *LC* i. 295.

45. RS to HWB, 13 Oct. 1796, MS Houghton.

46. RS to GCB, 1–7 Jan. 1797, MS Bodleian.

47. RS to CWW, Jan. 1797, *NL* i. 119–20.

48. MS Cornell.

49. RS to Edith Fricker, 7 Feb. 1797, *LC* i. 301.

50. RS to J. Cottle, Feb. 1797, *LC* i. 303.

51. RS to J. Cottle, Feb. 1797, *LC* i. 303.
52. RS to J. Cottle, 13 Mar. 1797, *LC* i. 305.
53. RS to J. Cottle, 9 Apr. 1797, MS CUL.
54. George Dyer, *The Poet's Fate* (1797).
55. RS to J. Cottle, [May 1797] *NL* i. 129–31.
56. RS to J. Cottle, 26 Apr. 1797, MS Cornell.
57. *See* Don Locke, *A Fantasy of Reason: The Life and Thought of William Godwin* (1980), 136.
58. RS to GCB, 25 May 1797, *LC* i. 312.
59. RS to CWW, 2 June 1797, *SL* i. 30–2.
60. RS to HWB, 11 June 1797, MS Bodleian.
61. RS to JM, 26 June 1797, MS Texas.
62. See Orlo Williams, *Lamb's Friend the Census-Taker: Life and Letters of John Rickman* (1911).
63. RS to W. S. Landor, 9 Feb. 1809, *LC* iii. 216.
64. See Williams, *John Rickman*, 83.
65. C. Lamb to Manning, 3 Nov. 1800, Marrs, i. 243.
66. RS to GCB, 30 June 1797, MS Bodleian; to CWW, 11 July 1797, *NL* i. 132–4.
67. RS to CWW, 11 July 1797, *NL* i. 132–4.
68. STC to RS, 17 July 1797, *CL* i. 332–6.
69. RS to TS, 9 July 1797, *SL* i. 35–7.
70. STC to J. Wade, 1 Aug. 1797, *CL* i. 339–40.
71. RS to CWW, 16 Aug. 1797, *NL* i. 140–2.
72. RS to GCB, 2 Aug. 1797, MS Bodleian; 10 Aug. 1797, ibid.; to CWW, 16 Aug. 1797, *NL* i. 140–2; 24 Aug. 1797, MS NLW.
73. RS to GCB, 3 Sept. 1797, *NL* i. 142–3.
74. RS to CWW, 12 Sept. 1797, *NL* i. 146–7.
75. RS to GCB, 22 Sept. 1797, MS Bodleian.
76. RS to GCB, 30 Sept. 1797, *NL* i. 149–51.
77. RS to W. B. Thomas, 11 Nov. 1797, MS Yale; to GCB, 7 Nov. 1797, MS Bodleian.
78. RS to J. Cottle, 19 Nov. 1797, MS Cornell.
79. RS to GCB, 19 Nov. 1797, *LC* i. 323.
80. RS to GCB, 4 Dec. 1797, MS Bodleian.
81. RS to TS, 3 Dec. 1797, *NL* i. 154–5.
82. Ibid.
83. Ibid.
84. RS to TS, 24 Dec. 1797, *LC* i. 326.
85. RS to J. Cottle, 14 Dec. 1797, MS CUL; the MS 'Proposals' are in Rochester University Library, NY.
86. RS to TS, 15 Jan. 1798, *SL* i. 47–50.
87. C. Lamb to RS, 15 Mar. 1799, Marrs, i. 161–3.
88. *Poetical Works*, ii. 236–8.
89. RS to TS, 24 Jan. 1798, *NL* i. 159–60.
90. RS to TS, 18 Feb. 1798, *SL* i. 50–2; to HHS, 7 Mar. 1798, *NL* i. 161–3.
91. RS to GCB, 9 Mar. 1798, MS Bodleian.
92. Ibid.

93. RS to JM, 10 Mar. 1798, *NL* i. 163–5.
94. RS to GCB, 25 Mar. 1798, MS Bodleian.
95. RS to CWW, 4 Apr. 1798, *LC* i. 329.
96. RS to GCB, 30 Mar. 1798, MS Bodleian; to JM, 6 Apr. 1798, *SL* i. 52–4; to CWW, 10 Apr. 1798, MS NLW.
97. C. Lamb to RS, 20 Mar. 1799, Marrs, i. 164.
98. RS to CWW, 11 May 1798, *SL* i. 54–6.
99. RS to JM, 5 May 1798, MS Texas; to CWW, 5 May 1798, *LC* i. 331.
100. RS to JM, 5 May 1798, MS Texas.
101. RS to Edith Southey, 21 May 1798, MS Yale.
102. RS to JM, 27 May 1798, MS Texas.
103. RS to JM, 28 Mar. 1799, ibid.
104. RS to GCB, 3 June 1798, MS Bodleian.
105. RS to GCB, 27–8 May 1798, *NL* i. 165–6.
106. RS to JM, 6 June 1798, MS Texas.
107. RS to T. Lamb, 13 June 1798, *SL* i. 56–7.
108. RS to CWW, 14 June 1798, MS NLW.
109. RS to TS, 27 June 1798, *LC* i. 340.
110. RS to JM, 23 July 1798, MS Texas.
111. RS to HS, 14 July 1798, *LC* i. 341.
112. RS to CWW, 21 July 1798, *NL* i. 172–4.
113. RS to CWW, 27 June 1798, MS NLW; 15 July 1798, *NL* i. 170–2.
114. RS to CWW, 15 Aug. 1798, *LC* i. 344.
115. RS to GCB, 26 Aug. 1798, *NL* i. 174–6.
116. *Poetical Works*, iii. 3, 16.
117. See Lynda Pratt, 'Coleridge, Wordsworth, and *Joan of Arc*', and 'A Coleridge Borrowing from Southey', *N&Q*, NS 41 (1994), 335–8; Mary Jacobus, 'Southey's Debt to *Lyrical Ballads* (1798), *RES*, NS 22 (1971), 20–36.
118. RS to JM, 2 Sept. 1798, MS Texas.
119. Ibid.
120. See Nicholas Roe, *The Politics of Nature: Wordsworth and Some Contemporaries* (1992), 56–72.
121. RS to JM, 26 Sept. 1798, MS Houghton.
122. WW to J. Cottle, [Summer 1799], *Letters: The Early Years*, 267.
123. RS to W. Taylor, 5 Oct. 1798, MS Huntington.
124. RS to JM, 22 Oct. 1798, MS Texas; to C. Biddlecombe, 6 Nov. 1798, MS CUL.
125. RS to CWW, 29 Oct. 1798, MS NLW.
126. RS to N. Lightfoot, 4 Dec. 1798, MS Bodleian.
127. RS to JM, 14 Dec. 1798, *LC* i. 350; to CWW 14 Dec. 1798, MS NLW.
128. C. Lamb to RS, 27 Dec. 1798, Marrs, i. 154.
129. RS to JM, 2 Jan. 1799, MS Yale.

Chapter 5

1. RS to JM, 22 Jan. 1799, *LC* ii. 10.
2. See *NL* i. 168.
3. RS to CWW, 9 Jan. 1799, *LC* ii. 5.

4. RS to CWW, 15 Jan. 1799, *SL* i. 62–5.
5. RS to TS, 5 Jan. 1799, *LC* ii. 2.
6. RS to GCB, 21 Jan. 1799, *LC* ii. 8; for the ballads, see *Poetical Works*, vi. 151–4, 56–60.
7. RS to JM, 22 Jan. 1799, *LC* ii. 10.
8. RS to GCB, 10 Feb. 1799, MS Bodleian.
9. RS to JM, 26 Feb. 1799, MS Yale.
10. RS to CWW, 13 Mar. 1799, MS NLW.
11. RS to JM, 28 Mar. 1799, MS Texas.
12. RS to C. Biddlecombe, 6 Apr. 1799, MS Berg.
13. RS to WT, 15 Apr. 1799, MS HL.
14. RS to Edith Southey, 3 May 1799, MS J. Wordsworth (*LC* ii. 15).
15. RS to TS, 12 May 1799, *SL* i. 70–2.
16. RS to Edith Southey, 13 May 1799, *NL* i. 183–6.
17. RS to Edith Southey, 15 May 1799, *NL* i. 186–9.
18. RS to Edith Southey, 20 May 1799, MS BPL.
19. RS to Edith Southey, 16 May 1799, *NL* i. 189–91.
20. RS to Edith Southey, 19 May 1799, *NL* i. 192–5.
21. RS to Edith Southey, 16 May 1799, *NL* i. 189–91.
22. Ibid.
23. *The Oxford Authors: Samuel Taylor Coleridge*, ed. H. J. Jackson (Oxford, 1985), 89–98.
24. RS to H. Davy, Oct. 1799, MS Berg.
25. STC to WW, *c.*10 Sept. 1799, *CL* i. 527.
26. RS to Edith Southey, 19 May 1799, *NL* i. 192–5.
27. RS to Edith Southey, 20 May 1799, MS BPL.
28. RS to GCB, 25 June 1799, MS Bodleian.
29. RS to WT, 5 Sept. 1799, MS HL.
30. RS to JM, 29 July 1799, MS Yale.
31. RS to JM, 21 Aug. 1799, MS BPL; STC to T. Poole, 10 Sept. 1799, *CL* i. 526.
32. RS to JM, 21 Aug. 1799, MS BPL.
33. RS to JM, 29 July 1799, MS Yale.
34. 'Mohammed: A Fragment' appears in *Oliver Newman: a New-England Tale (unfinished), with other Poetical Remains* (1845), 113–16.
35. RS to J. Cottle, 22 Sept. 1799, *LC* ii. 24.
36. RS to JM, 20 Oct. 1799, MS Yale.
37. C. Lamb to RS, 31 Oct. 1799, Marrs, i. 172.
38. RS to JM, 10 Oct. 1799, MS Texas; to STC, 11 Oct. 1799, *NL* i. 200.
39. RS to J. Cottle, 12 Oct. 1799, MS Yale.
40. STC to RS, 10 Nov. 1799, *CL* i. 546.
41. RS to STC, [Oct.] 1799, *LC* ii. 29.
42. RS to STC, 11 Oct. 1799, *NL* i. 200–3.
43. RS to JM, 20 Oct. 1799, MS Yale.
44. RS to GCB, mid-Nov. 1799, MS Bodleian.
45. RS to CWW, 9 Dec. 1799, MS NLW.

46. See Hazlitt, 'My First Acquaintance with Poets', *The Complete Works*, ed. P. P Howe (21 vols., 1930–4), xvii. 113.
47. STC to RS, 24 Dec. 1799, *CL* i. 551; 19 Dec. 1799, *CL* i. 547; *Poetical Works*, iii. 87–100.
48. RS to GCB, 21 Dec. 1799, *LC* ii. 33.
49. STC to RS, 24 Dec. 1799, *CL* i. 553; 28 Dec. 1799, *CL* i. 554.
50. RS to JM, 27 Dec. 1799, MS BPL.
51. RS to STC, 23 Dec. 1799, *NL* i. 209–11.
52. RS to GCB, 1 Jan. 1800, *LC* ii. 37.
53. RS to STC, 16 Jan. 1800, *NL* i. 214–17.
54. STC to W. Taylor, 25 Jan. 1800, *CL* i. 565.
55. STC to T. Wedgwood, 2 Jan. 1800, *CL* i. 558.
56. RS to JR, 9 Jan. 1800, *LC* ii. 44; 17 Jan. 1800, *NL* i. 217–19.
57. RS to CWW, 24 Jan. 1800, *SL* i. 88–90.
58. STC to RS, 25 Jan. 1800, *CL* i. 562.
59. RS to TS, 2 Feb. 1800, *NL* i. 220–3.
60. STC to RS, 12 Feb. 1800, *CL* i. 569–71.
61. RS to WT, Feb. 1800, MS HL.
62. RS to CWW, 20 Feb. 1800, *SL* i. 97–9.
63. RS to JM, 12 Mar. 1800, MS Texas; for Croft, see E. H. W. Meyerstein, *A Life of Thomas Chatterton* (1930), 491–8.
64. RS to TS, 23 Mar. 1800, *SL* i. 99–101.
65. RS to STC, 1 Apr. 1800, *LC* ii. 53.
66. Ibid.
67. STC to RS, 10 Apr. 1800, *CL* i. 585–6.
68. RS to JR, 19 Apr. 1800, MS HL.
69. See *Robert Southey: Journals of a Residence in Portugal 1800–1801, and a Visit to France 1838*, ed. A. Cabral (Oxford, 1960).
70. RS to STC, 1 May 1800, *LC* ii. 61.
71. RS to JR, 2 May 1800, *NL* i. 223–7.
72. RS to JM, 23 June 1800, *SL* i. 112–17.
73. RS to CWW, 23 July 1800, *LC* ii. 94–8.
74. RS to C. Danvers, 25 July 1800, *SL* i. 117–22.
75. RS to Margaret Southey, 21 Aug. 1800, *LC* ii. 99.
76. RS to CWW, Oct. 1799, MS NLW.
77. RS to TS, 25 Aug. 1800, *LC* ii. 107.
78. RS to JR, Oct. 1800, *LC* ii. 121.
79. RS to GCB, 23 Sept.–1 Oct. 1800, MS Bodleian.
80. RS to JM, 29 Oct. 1800, *SL* i. 127–32.
81. RS to C. Danvers, 18 Dec. 1800, *NL* i. 230; to JM, 16 Dec. 1800, *SL* i. 132–5.
82. STC to J. Wedgwood, 1 Nov. 1800, *CL* i. 646.
83. RS to CWW, 21 Feb. 1801, *LC* ii. 131.
84. RS to JM, 27 Mar. 1801, *NL* i. 242.
85. STC to RS, 6 May 1801, *CL* ii. 727.
86. STC to S. Purkis, 29 July 1800, *CL* i. 614–15; to W. Godwin, Aug. 1800, *CL* i. 620.

87. RS to JM, 23 May 1801, *SL* i. 157.
88. RS to GCB, June 1801, *SL* i. 161; to CWW, 6 July 1801, MS NLW.
89. RS to STC, 11 July 1801, *LC* ii. 149.
90. STC to RS, 22 July 1801, *CL* ii. 745.
91. RS to WT, 27 July 1801, MS HL.
92. Ibid.
93. STC to RS, 1 Aug. 1801, *CL* ii. 749.
94. RS to C. Biddlecombe, 17 Aug. 1801, *NL* i. 245.
95. See Don Locke, *A Fantasy of Reason: The Life and Thought of William Godwin* (1980), 163–5, 192–204.
96. RS to HS [Sept. 1801], *NL* i. 247–9.
97. RS to GCB, 6 Sept. 1801, *LC* ii. 161–3.
98. STC to RS, 21 Oct. 1801, *CL* ii. 767.
99. RS to GCB, 29 Sept. 1801, MS Bodleian.
100. RS to M. Barker, 10 Oct. 1801, *SL* i. 172.
101. RS to C. Danvers, 15 Oct. 1801, *NL* i. 250–3.
102. RS to GCB, 20 Oct. 1801, *SL* i. 147.
103. RS to GCB, 29 Oct. 1801, MS Bodleian.
104. STC to RS, 9 Nov. 1801, *CL* ii. 774–5.
105. RS to STC, 10 Oct. 1801, *LC* ii. 171.
106. RS to WT, 11 Nov. 1801, MS HL.
107. See Lionel Madden (ed.), *Robert Southey: The Critical Heritage* (1972), 68–90; quotations from *Thalaba the Destroyer* are from the first edn. (1801).
108. *Robert Southey: The Critical Heritage*, 63–7.
109. Ibid. 91–5.
110. RS to JR, 27 Nov. 1801, *SL* i. 181.
111. RS to C. Danvers, 2 Dec. 1801, *NL* i. 259.
112. RS to JR, 11 Dec. 1801, MS HL.
113. RS to CWW, 17 Dec. 1801, MS NLW.
114. STC to RS, 31 Dec. 1801, *CL* ii. 778.
115. RS to CWW, 9 Jan. 1802, *LC* ii. 179.
116. RS to WT, 6 Feb. 1802, MS HL.
117. RS to JR, 6 Feb. 1802, *NL* i. 268–70; to C. Danvers, 6 Feb. 1802, *NL* i. 270–2.
118. STC to Sara Coleridge, 19 Feb. 1802, *CL* ii. 785.
119. RS to GCB, 30 Mar. 1802, *LC* ii. 182; to Mary Barker, 9 July 1802, *SL* i. 200.
120. RS to JR, 2 June 1802, *SL* i. 195.
121. RS to CWW, 21 June 1802, MS NLW.
122. RS to JM, 4 July 1802, MS Texas; to Mary Barker, 9 July 1802, *SL* i. 200.
123. RS to CWW, 8 Aug. 1802, MS NLW.
124. RS to TS, 19 Aug. 1802, *NL* i. 281.
125. RS to CWW, Aug. 1802, *SL* i. 202.
126. RS to JR, 2 Sept. 1802, MS HL.
127. RS to JM, 5 Sept. 1802, MS Texas.
128. RS to CWW, 14 Sept. 1802, *NL* i. 285.
129. *Annual Review*, 1 (1800), 207–18; RS to CWW, 19 Oct. 1802, MS NLW.
130. RS to JM, 26 Oct. 1802, MS Texas.

131. RS to WT, 21 Nov. 1802, MS HL.
132. RS to JM, 23 Nov. 1802, *SL* i. 204; to CWW, 5 Dec. 1802, *NL* i. 296.
133. RS to JR, 12 Jan. 1803, *NL* i. 300; to Mary Barker, 14 Jan. 1803, *SL* i. 209.
134. STC to RS, 15 Feb. 1803, *CL* ii. 923; 17 Feb. 1803, *CL* ii. 928.
135. RS to JM, 19 Apr. 1803, MS Texas.
136. RS to JM, 9 Mar. 1803, MS Rochester.
137. RS to JM, 1 May 1803, MS Texas.
138. RS to GCB, 9 May 1803, MS Houghton.
139. RS to GCB, 20 May 1803, ibid.
140. RS to GCB, 27 May 1803, ibid.
141. RS to WT, 23 June 1803, MS HL.
142. RS to CWW, 24 June 1803, MS NLW.
143. RS to WT, 13 July 1803, MS HL.
144. Mary Lamb to Dorothy Wordsworth, 9 July 1803, Marrs, ii. 117.
145. RS to JM, 20 July 1803, MS Rochester.
146. RS to WT, 23 June 1803, MS HL.
147. RS to GCB, 19 Aug. 1803, MS Bodleian.
148. RS to JR, 24 Aug. 1803, MS HL; to WT, 24 Aug. 1803, MS Berg; to [?GCB], 26 Aug. 1803, MS Bodleian.
149. RS to JR, 24 Aug. 1803, MS HL.
150. STC to RS, 10 Sept. 1803, *CL* ii. 982; to Sara Coleridge, 11 Sept. 1803, *CL* ii. 985.

Chapter 6

1. STC to J. Wedgwood, 16 Sept. 1803, *CL* ii. 992; to T. Poole, 14 Oct. 1803, *CL* ii. 1015; RS to C. Danvers [Oct. 1803], *NL* i. 330.
2. RS to J. King, 28 Sept. 1803, *SL* i. 234.
3. *Poetical Works*, ii. 245–8.
4. STC to the Beaumonts, 1 Oct. 1803, *CL* ii. 999.
5. RS to R. Duppa, 31 Mar. 1809, *LC* iii. 226.
6. RS to JR, 12 Sept. 1803, *NL* i. 326.
7. See Geoffrey Carnall, *Robert Southey and his Age: The Development of a Conservative Mind* (Oxford, 1960), 67.
8. RS to TS, 29 Oct. 1803, *LC* ii. 229.
9. RS to CWW, [Oct. 1803], MS NLW; STC, *Notebooks*, ed. Kathleen Coburn (3 vols., 1957–73), i. 1577.
10. RS to JR, 2 Dec. 1803, *NL* i. 336.
11. RS to HS, 23 Jan. 1804, MS Berg; to CWW, 12 Jan. 1804, MS NLW.
12. RS to CWW, Dec. 1803, *SL* i. 248.
13. Carnall, *Southey and his Age*, 71.
14. RS to JR, 2 Dec. 1803, *NL* i. 336; to Danvers, 9 Dec. 1803, *NL* i. 340; to TS, 31 Dec. 1803, *LC* ii. 244.
15. RS to CWW, 21 Jan. 1804, *NL* i. 348.
16. RS to Mary Barker, 17 Feb. 1804, *SL* i. 259.
17. STC to RS, 11 Jan. 1804, *CL* ii. 1026; 25 Jan. 1804, *CL* ii. 1039; RS to JR, 9 Mar. 1804, *NL* i. 356; see Carnall, *Southey and his Age*, 62–6.
18. RS to STC, 19 Feb. 1804, *LC* ii. 263.

19. RS to CWW, 18 Feb. 1804, MS NLW; to Mary Barker, [1804], *SL* i. 253.

20. RS to GCB, 8 Mar. 1804, *LC* ii. 269.

21. RS to STC, 12 Mar. 1804, *LC* ii. 271; *Poetical Works*, ii. 257–8.

22. STC to RS, 20 Mar. 1804, *CL* ii. 1068.

23. RS to JR, 30 Mar. 1804, *LC* ii. 276.

24. RS to Mary Barker, 3 Apr. 1804, *SL* i. 269.

25. RS to JR, 9 Apr. 1804, MS HL.

26. RS to GCB, 1 May 1804, MS Bodleian; to JR, 1 May, MS HL.

27. RS to Edith Southey, 10 May 1804, *LC* ii. 283.

28. RS to WT, [May 1804], MS HL.

29. RS to JR, [June 1804], MS HL.

30. RS to TS, 30 July 1804, *LC* ii. 259; to JR, 6 Aug. 1804, MS HL.

31. RS to TS, 27 June 1804, *LC* ii. 295.

32. RS to TS, 30 July 1804, *LC* ii. 299.

33. Orlo Williams, *Lamb's Friend the Census-Taker: Life and Letters of John Rickman* (1911), 110.

34. RS to CWW, 25 Nov. 1804, MS NLW; to J. Cottle, 16 Dec. 1804, *NL* i. 366.

35. RS to WT, 6 Jan. 1805, MS HL.

36. RS to CWW, 24 Oct. 1804, MS NLW.

37. RS to WT, 6 Jan. 1805, MS HL.

38. RS to CWW, 12 Jan. 1805, MS NLW.

39. RS to JR, 23 Jan. 1805, *NL* i. 375.

40. DW to Lady Beaumont, 11 Apr. 1805, *The Letters of William and Dorothy Wordsworth: The Early Years*, ed. Chester L. Shaver (Oxford, 1967).

41. RS to CWW, 4 Mar. 1805, MS NLW.

42. RS to CWW, 24 Mar. 1805, *NL* i. 377.

43. RS to Mary Barker, 11 May 1805, *SL* i. 323.

44. RS to JR, 11 June 1805, *SL* i. 325.

45. Quotations are from the first edn. of *Madoc* (1805).

46. RS to CWW, 6 Apr. 1806, *LC* ii. 322; see Nigel Leask, *British Romantic Writers and the East* (Cambridge, 1992), 25–6.

47. RS to TS, 22 Aug. 1805, *NL* i. 391.

48. RS to WT, 2 Sept. 1805, MS HL; to TS, 7 Dec. 1805, *LC* ii. 357.

49. WW to Sir G. Beaumont, *Letters: The Early Years*, 595.

50. Lionel Madden (ed.), *Robert Southey: The Critical Heritage* (1972), 103–4.

51. RS to Richard Duppa, [22 Nov. 1805], *NL* i. 407.

52. Madden (ed.), *Robert Southey: The Critical Heritage*, 104–10.

53. RS to GCB, 6 July 1805, *LC* ii. 336; a quotation from *Butler's Remains* provided an epigraph to *The Doctor*.

54. RS to CWW, 13 Oct. 1805, MS NLW; 20 Oct. 1805, *SL* i. 341; see *Southey's Common-Place Book*, ed. J. W. Warter (4 vols., 1849–50), iv. 526–31.

55. RS to Edith Southey, 14 Oct. 1805, *LC* ii. 348.

56. RS to HS, 1 Jan. 1806, *NL* i. 413.

57. RS to HS, 11 Jan. 1806, *NL* i. 415.

58. RS to Mary Barker, 31 Jan. 1806, *SL* i. 352.

59. RS to N. Lightfoot, 8 Feb. 1806, *LC* iii. 20; to C. Danvers, 3 Feb. 1806, *SL* i. 355; Williams, *Life and Letters of John Rickman*, 138.
60. RS to TS, 5 Mar. 1806, *SL* i. 360.
61. Ibid.
62. RS to JR, 19 Mar. 1806, *SL* i. 368.
63. RS to Edith Southey, 5 Apr. 1806, *NL* i. 419–24.
64. RS to CWW, 18 May 1806, MS NLW; 6 May, *SL* i. 371.
65. RS to R. Duppa, 5 Aug. 1806, MS Rochester.
66. RS to GCB, 15 Aug. 1806, MS Bodleian.
67. RS to GCB, 20 Sept. 1806, *SL* i. 391.
68. RS to Mary Barker, 25 Sept. 1806, *SL* i. 394.
69. RS to CWW, 11 Oct 1806, *SL* i. 395.
70. RS to CWW, 25 Nov. 1806, *NL* i. 429; to TS, 21 Dec. 1806, *SL* i. 398.
71. RS to JR, 28 Dec. 1806, *NL* i. 431.
72. RS to HS, 30 Dec. 1806, *NL* i. 433.
73. RS to Mary Barker, 1 Feb. 1807, *SL* i. 408; to GCB, 2 Feb. 1807, *SL* i. 412.
74. RS to CWW, 15 Feb. 1807, *NL* i. 436; to JR, 13 Feb. 1807, MS HL.
75. RS to JR, 23 Feb. 1807, MS HL.
76. RS to TS, 25 Feb. 1807, *NL* i. 437.
77. RS to C. Danvers, 2 Mar. 1807, *SL* i. 414.
78. RS to C. Biddlecombe, 25 Mar. 1807, MS Berg.
79. RS to GCB, 25 Mar. 1807, MS Bodleian.
80. RS to CWW, 27 Mar. 1807, *NL* i. 441.
81. RS to WT, 13 Apr. 1807, MS HL.
82. RS to JR, [mid-Apr. 1807], *NL* i. 448.
83. RS to JR, 9 May 1807, MS HL; to C. Danvers, 25 May 1807, *NL* i. 450.
84. RS to WT, 31 July 1807, MS HL.
85. RS to CWW, 28 Sept. 1807, *NL* i. 458.
86. RS to CWW, 1 Aug. 1807, MS NLW.
87. RS to JR, 22 Sept. 1807, MS HL.
88. RS to W. Scott, 27 Sept. 1807, *LC* iii. 109.
89. RS to R. Heber, 16 Nov. 1807, *LC* iii. 116.
90. RS to CWW, 3 Dec. 1807, MS NLW.
91. RS to W. Scott, 8 Dec. 1807, MS NLS.
92. RS to STC, 9 Dec. 1807, MS Cornell (facsimile).
93. RS to H. Hill, 2 Jan. 1808, MS Keswick.
94. RS to J. Grahame, 4 Jan. 1808, *NL* i. 467.
95. For RS's other comments on 'moral oeconomy', see the 'Commonplace Book', MS Yale, 124.
96. RS to W. Scott, 11 Feb. 1808, *LC* iii. 131.
97. RS to Edith Southey, 22 Mar. 1808, MS Yale.
98. RS to JR, 15 Apr. 1808, MS HL.
99. RS to A. Seward, 18 Apr. 1808, *NL* i. 469; to GCB, 26 Apr. 1808, *LC* iii. 137; to JR, 29 Apr. 1808, MS HL.
100. RS to WSL, 2 May 1808, *LC* iii. 142.
101. RS to WSL, 20 May 1808, *LC* iii. 145.

102. RS to A. Seward, 28 May 1808, *NL* i. 475.
103. RS to GCB, 5 June 1808, MS Bodleian.
104. RS to H. Hill, 9 July 1808, MS Keswick.
105. *The Poems of Anna Letitia Barbauld*, ed. William McCarthy and Elizabeth Kraft (Athens, Ga. and London, 1994), 194, 333.
106. RS to WT, 11 July 1808, MS HL.
107. RS to TS, 3 Aug. 1808, *NL* i. 477.
108. RS to TS, 16 Aug. 1808, *LC* iii. 162.
109. RS to A. Seward, [Aug. 1808], MS Rochester; to T. Smith, 15 Aug. 1808, MS Cornell; to T. Smith, 5 Dec. 1808, MS Bodleian.
110. RS to J. N. White, 28 Nov. 1808, *SL* ii. 111.
111. See Stephen Gill, *William Wordsworth: A Life* (Oxford, 1989), 274–7.
112. RS to TS, 13 Oct. 1808, *LC* iii. 170.
113. RS to H. Senhouse, 19 Oct. 1808, *NL* i. 483.
114. RS to GCB, [Oct. 1808], *NL* i. 487.
115. RS to WT, 6 Nov. 1808, MS HL.
116. RS to H. Hill, 10 Nov. 1808, *NL* i. 488.
117. RS to JR, 18 Feb. 1809, MS HL.
118. RS to GCB, 9 Nov. 1808, *LC* iii. 182.
119. RS to GCB, 11 Nov. 1808, *NL* i. 490.
120. RS to HS, 14 Nov. 1808, *SL* ii. 109.
121. STC to RS, Dec. 1808, *CL* iii. 129.
122. RS to JR, [early summer 1809], MS HL.
123. *Edinburgh Annual Register*, 1 (1809), 289.
124. RS to GCB, 17 Nov. 1808, *LC* iii. 185.
125. RS to C. Danvers, 4 Jan. 1809, *NL* i. 496.
126. RS to GCB, 12 Feb. 1809, *LC* iii. 218.
127. RS to TS, 14 Mar. 1809, *LC* iii. 223.
128. RS to TS, 14 Mar. 1809, *NL* i. 502.
129. RS to WSL, 23 Apr. 1809, *LC* iii. 228.
130. RS to GCB, 30 Apr. 1809, *LC* iii. 232; to Mary Barker, 13 May 1809, *SL* ii. 137.
131. RS to TS, 22 May 1809, *LC* iii. 233.
132. RS to C. Danvers, 22 May 1809, *SL* ii. 141.

Chapter 7

1. RS to WT, 24 May 1809, MS HL.
2. RS to C. Danvers, 15 June 1809, *NL* i. 509.
3. *The Friend*, ed. Barbara E. Rooke (2 vols., 1969), ii. 146–7.
4. RS to W. Scott, 6 July 1809, *LC* iii. 242; to TS, 6 July 1809, *SL* ii. 147.
5. RS to H. Senhouse, 25 July 1809, MS Rochester.
6. RS to TS, 30 July 1809, *SL* ii. 152.
7. RS to W. Scott, 30 July 1809, *LC* iii. 246.
8. See Kenneth Curry, *Sir Walter Scott's Edinburgh Annual Register* (Knoxville, Tenn., 1977).
9. RS to GCB, 4 Sept. 1809, MS Bodleian.
10. RS to TS, 30 July 1809, *SL* ii. 152.

11. RS to HS, 17 Aug. 1809, *SL* ii. 155.

12. RS to WT, 3 Nov. [?1810], MS HL.

13. RS to WSL, 27 Sept. 1810, *SL* ii. 202.

14. RS to JR, 7 Dec. 1810, MS HL.

15. RS to GCB, 22 Dec. 1810, *NL* i. 547; to WSL, [1809], *SL* ii. 114.

16. RS to GCB, 14 Jan. 1811, *NL* ii. 3–4.

17. Quotations are from the first edn. of *The Curse of Kehama* (1810).

18. RS to GCB, 1 Jan. 1811, *NL* ii. 1.

19. Lionel Madden (ed.), *Robert Southey: The Critical Heritage* (1972), 146, 138–45.

20. RS to TS, 23 Jan 1811, *NL* ii. 5.

21. RS to H. Hill, 5 Feb. 1811, *SL* ii. 211.

22. RS to E. Elliott, 7 Feb. 1811, *LC* iii. 297.

23. RS to WSL, 12 Feb. 1811, *LC* iii. 299.

24. RS to GCB, 16 Feb. 1811, *LC* iii. 302.

25. RS to JR, 12 Mar. 1811, MS HL.

26. RS to C. Danvers, 31 Mar. 1811, *NL* ii. 7.

27. RS to JR, 6 Apr. 1811, MS HL.

28. RS to GCB, 21 Apr. 1811, *LC* iii. 309.

29. RS to GCB, 11 Apr. 1811, MS Bodleian.

30. RS to WSL, 8 May 1811, *SL* ii. 219.

31. RS to GCB, 9 June 1811, *LC* iii. 311.

32. RS to WSL, 15 July 1811, *LC* iii. 312.

33. See Alan Richardson, *Literature, Education, Romanticism* (Oxford, 1994).

34. Repr. in *Essays, Moral and Political* (1832), i. 75–155.

35. RS to JR, 11 Oct. 1811, *SL* ii. 237.

36. RS to J. Murray, 23 Oct. 1811, *NL* ii. 10.

37. RS to M. Betham, 30 Oct. 1811, MS Yale.

38. RS to J. Montgomery, 2 Jan. 1812, MS Yale.

39. RS to JR, 6 Jan. 1812, MS HL.

40. P. B. Shelley to Elizabeth Hitchener, 14 Nov. 1811, 15 Dec., 1811, 2 Jan. 1812, *The Letters of Percy Bysshe Shelley*, ed. Frederick L. Jones (2 vols., Oxford, 1964), i. 183, 208, 218.

41. Ibid. 7 Jan. 1812, 13 Feb. 1812, i. 223, 249.

42. RS to GCB, 17 Jan. 1812, *LC* iii. 326.

43. RS to WSL, 9 Feb. 1812, *SL* ii. 252.

44. RS to J. White, 28 Feb. 1812, *SL* ii. 254.

45. RS to WW, [Apr. 1812], *NL* ii. 32; see Stephen Gill, *William Wordsworth: A Life* (Oxford, 1989), 292.

46. RS to CWW, 15 Apr. 1812, *LC* iii. 330.

47. RS to Mary Barker, 3 May 1812, *SL* ii. 265.

48. Geoffrey Carnall, *Robert Southey and his Age: The Development of a Conservative Mind* (1960), 138–48; Orlo Williams, *Lamb's Friend the Census-Taker: Life and Letters of John Rickman* (1911), 160.

49. Carnall, *Robert Southey and his Age*, 192.

50. RS to CWW, May 1812, MS NLW.

51. RS to C. Danvers, 9 May 1812, *SL* ii. 267.
52. RS to TS, 12 May 1812, *SL* ii. 271.
53. RS to GCB, 16 May 1812, *LC* iii. 338; to JR, 25 May 1812, MS HL.
54. RS to JR, 18 May 1812, *LC* iii. 341.
55. See *Essays, Moral and Political* (2 vols., 1832), i. 75–155; RS to TS, 12 May 1812, *SL* ii. 271.
56. RS to Mary Barker, 9 June 1812, *SL* ii. 278.
57. RS to TS, 17 June 1812, *SL* ii. 281.
58. RS to JM, 14 Aug. 1812, *NL* ii. 37.
59. RS to GCB, 16 Oct. 1812, MS Bodleian.
60. RS to CWW, 16 Sept. 1812, MS NLW.
61. RS to J. White, 27 Sept. 1812, *SL* ii. 292.
62. RS to GCB, 20 Oct. 1812, MS Bodleian.
63. RS to JR, 25 Oct. 1812, MS HL.
64. RS to CWW, 5 Nov. 1812, MS NLW.
65. RS to Mary Barker, 4 Nov. 1812, *SL* ii. 296.
66. RS to W. Browne, 5 Nov. 1812, *SL* ii. 299.
67. RS to TS, 18 Nov. 1812, *SL* ii. 303; 30 Dec. 1812, *SL* ii. 315.
68. RS to TS, 24 Dec. 1812, *SL* ii. 311.
69. RS to JM, 3 Jan. 1813, *LC* iv. 5.
70. RS to W. Scott, 13 Jan 1813, *LC* iv. 8.
71. RS to R. Gooch, 20 Jan 1813, *LC* iv. 13.
72. RS to CWW, 17 Jan. 1813, *LC* iv. 10.
73. RS to JR, 5 Mar. 1813, MS HL.
74. RS to TS, 20 Jan. 1813, *NL* ii. 42.
75. RS to J. White, 25 Jan. 1813, *LC* iv. 14.
76. RS to H. Hill, 1 Feb. 1813, *LC* iv. 17.
77. RS to JR, [Mar. 1813], *LC* iv. 28.
78. RS to J. Murray, 31 Mar. 1813, *NL* ii. 53.
79. RS to GCB, 7 Apr. 1813, MS Bodleian.
80. RS to GCB, 16 May 1813, ibid.
81. RS to J. Murray, 9 July 1813, *NL* ii. 60.
82. RS to GCB, 23 July 1813, MS Bodleian.
83. RS to GCB, 21 Aug. 1813, ibid.
84. RS to JR, Aug. 1813, MS HL.
85. RS to W. Scott, 31 Aug. 1813, *NL* ii. 62.
86. RS to GCB, 4 Sept. 1813, MS Bodleian; to Edith Southey, 5 Sept. 1813, *NL* ii. 64; see Edgar Johnson, *Sir Walter Scott: The Great Unknown* (2 vols., 1970), i. 426–8.
87. RS to Edith Southey, 5 Sept. 1813, *NL* ii. 64; 28 Sept. 1813, *NL* ii. 76; see Iona and Peter Opie, *The Classic Fairy Tales* (1974), 199–200.
88. RS to Mary Barker, 8 Oct. 1813, *SL* ii. 330.
89. RS to W. Scott, 5 Nov. 1813, *LC* iv. 40.
90. *The Complete Works of William Hazlitt*, ed. P. P. Howe (21 vols., 1930–4), vii. 24.
91. RS to GCB, 30 Nov. 1813, MS Bodleian.

92. RS to C. Danvers, 9 Dec. 1813, *NL* ii. 88.
93. RS to J. Cottle, 17 Apr. 1814, *NL* ii. 93.
94. RS to JR, 30 Nov. 1813, *SL* ii. 337; to J. White, 12 Dec. 1813, *SL* ii. 338.
95. RS to GCB, 26 Dec. 1813, MS Bodleian.
96. RS to H. Hill, 28 Dec. 1813, *LC* iv. 53.
97. Williams, *Life and Letters of John Rickman*, 173.
98. RS to GCB, 26 Dec. 1813, MS Bodleian.
99. RS to C. Danvers, 7 Jan. 1814, *NL* ii. 91.
100. Hazlitt, *Complete Works*, vii. 25; the 'Carmen Triumphale' is in *Poetical Works*, iii. 179–90.
101. RS to GCB, 9 Mar. 1814, MS Bodleian.
102. RS to CWW, 15 Jan. 1814, *LC* iv. 56.
103. RS to GCB, 25 Jan. 1814, MS Bodleian.
104. RS to GCB, 26 Jan. 1814, *SL* ii. 341.
105. RS to GCB, 25 Feb. 1814, MS Bodleian.
106. Quotations are from the first edn. of *Roderick, The Last of the Goths* (1814).
107. RS to JR, 2 Aug. 1814, MS HL.
108. C. Lamb to RS, 6 May 1815, Marrs, iii. 154.
109. RS to WSL, 9 Mar. 1814, *LC* iv. 60.
110. RS to GCB, 22 Mar. 1814, MS Bodleian.
111. RS to JR, 11 Apr. 1814, MS HL.
112. RS to GCB, 13 Apr. 1814, MS Bodleian.
113. RS to JM, 25 Apr. 1814, MS Texas.
114. RS to W. Scott, 27 Apr. 1814, *LC* iv. 68.
115. RS to J. White, 29 Apr. 1814, *LC* iv. 71.
116. RS to JR, 9 May 1814, MS HL.
117. RS to GCB, 22 June 1814, *SL* ii. 354.
118. RS to CWW, 21 June 1814, MS NLW.
119. *Poetical Works*, iii. 73–7; vi. 217–22.
120. RS to JM, 1 July 1814, *SL* ii. 356.
121. RS to JR, 3 July 1814, *SL* ii. 359.
122. RS to JM, 15 July 1814, MS Texas.
123. RS to JR, 3 Aug. 1814, *SL* ii. 370.

Chapter 8

1. RS to J. White, 7 Sept. 1814, *SL* ii. 375.
2. RS to JM, 10 Sept. 1814, MS Texas.
3. RS to J. Cottle, 27 Oct. 1814, *NL* ii. 106.
4. RS to GCB, 4 Nov. 1814, *NL* ii. 108.
5. RS to JM, 9 Nov. 1814, MS Texas.
6. RS to R. Gooch, 30 Nov. 1814, *LC* iv. 87.
7. RS to J. King, 12 Dec. 1814, *SL* ii. 383; to CWW, 15 Dec. 1814, *SL* ii. 386.
8. RS to WT, 27 Dec. 1814, MS HL.
9. RS to W. Scott, 24 Dec. 1814, *LC* iv. 94; to GCB, 22 Dec. 1814, MS Bodleian.
10. RS to JR, 3 Mar. 1815, MS HL.
11. RS to JR, 12 Feb. 1815, *SL* ii. 399.

12. RS to J. White, 16 Feb. 1815, *LC* iv. 102.
13. RS to J. Cottle, 2 Mar. 1815, *NL* ii. 16.
14. RS to JM, 20 Mar. 1815, MS Texas.
15. RS to HS, 16 May 1815, *NL* ii. 122.
16. RS to J. Coleridge, 14 Mar. 1815, MS Cornell.
17. RS to JR, 13 Mar. 1815, MS HL.
18. RS to JM, 20 Mar. 1815, MS Texas.
19. RS to JR, 24 Mar. 1815, MS HL.
20. RS to J. Montgomery, 29 May 1815, MS Berg.
21. RS to CWW, 26 May 1815, *LC* iv. 109.
22. RS to J. White, 8 May 1815, *SL* ii. 407.
23. RS to GCB, 24 June 1815, *LC* iv. 117.
24. RS to H. Hill, 27 June 1815, *SL* ii. 411.
25. RS to JR, 10 July 1815, *LC* iv. 119.
26. RS to GCB, 8 Aug. 1815, *SL* ii. 420.
27. RS to HS, 23 Aug. 1815, *LC* iv. 120.
28. RS to JM, 6 Oct. 1815, MS Texas.
29. Ibid.
30. RS to H. Hill, 6 Dec. 1815, *SL* iii. 5; to JM, 6 Dec. 1815, MS Texas.
31. RS to CWW, 15 Dec. 1815, *NL* ii. 124.
32. RS to JR, 8 Dec. 1815, MS HL; *The Poet's Pilgrimage to Waterloo* (1816), 3–4.
33. RS to CWW, 15 Dec. 1815, *NL* ii. 124.
34. RS to TS, 20 Dec. 1815, *SL* iii. 8.
35. RS to JR, 22 Dec. 1815, MS HL.
36. RS to HS, 14 Jan. 1816, MS Bodleian.
37. RS to GCB, 4 Feb. 1816, *LC* iv. 148.
38. RS to JR, 9 Feb. 1816, MS HL.
39. RS to HS, 23 Feb. 1816, MS Bodleian.
40. RS to M. Betham, 19 Mar. 1816, MS Yale.
41. RS to HS, 23 Mar. 1816, MS Bodleian.
42. RS to S. Turner, 2 Apr. 1816, *LC* iv. 154.
43. RS to M. Betham, 24 June 1816, MS Yale.
44. *The Complete Works of William Hazlitt*, ed. P. P. Howe (21 vols., 1930–4) vii. 86–7.
45. RS to CWW, 30 Mar. 1816, *NL* ii. 136.
46. RS to HS, 6 Apr. 1816, MS Bodleian.
47. RS to HS, 8 Apr. 1816, ibid.; to S. Turner, 2 Apr. 1816, *LC* iv. 154.
48. RS to HS, 15 Apr. 1816, MS Bodleian; to GCB, 16 Apr. 1816, MS Bodleian.
49. RS to W. Wilberforce, 25 July 1816, MS Yale.
50. RS to GCB, 18 Apr. 1816, *LC* iv. 161.
51. RS to JM, 17 Apr. 1816, *SL* iii. 21; Orlo Williams, *Lamb's Friend the Census-Taker: Life and Letters of John Rickman* (1911), 179.
52. RS to GCB, 1 May 1816, MS Bodleian.
53. RS to GCB, 10 May 1816, MS Bodleian; 'Fragmentary Thoughts, occasioned by his son's death', in *Oliver Newman* (1845), 93–5.
54. RS to GCB, 18 May 1816, MS Bodleian.

55. RS to GCB, 20 May 1816, ibid.
56. RS to GCB, 22 June 1816, ibid.
57. RS to C. H. Townshend, 22 July 1816, *LC* iv. 190.
58. RS to JR, 25 Aug. 1816, *LC* iv. 195; see Gregory Claeys, *Citizens and Saints* (Cambridge, 1989).
59. Hazlitt, *Complete Works*, vii. 97–103.
60. RS to GCB, 7 Sept. 1816, *SL* iii. 42.
61. RS to JR, 9 Sept. 1816, *LC* iv. 205.
62. RS to GCB, 11 Sept. 1816, *LC* iv. 209.
63. RS to JR, 14 Sept. 1816, *SL* iii. 44.
64. RS to GCB, 19 Sept. 1816, MS Bodleian.
65. RS to JR, 2 Oct. 1816, *LC* iv. 213.
66. RS to GCB, 11 Oct. 1816, MS Bodleian.
67. RS to GCB, 10 Nov. 1816, ibid.
68. RS to JR, 16 Nov. 1816, MS HL.
69. RS to JR, 26 Nov. 1816, *LC* iv. 218.
70. RS to GCB, 29 Nov. 1816, MS Bodleian.
71. RS to GCB, 7 Dec. 1816, ibid.
72. RS to GCB, 13 Dec. 1816, *NL* ii. 114.
73. RS to J. Conder, 10 Dec. 1816, MS Houghton.
74. RS to JM, 1 Jan. 1817, MS Texas.
75. RS to GCB, 4 Jan. 1817, *LC* iv. 232; 20 Jan. 1817, *SL* iii. 51.
76. *The Doctor* (1837), Interchapter xx.
77. RS to J. Murray, 14 Jan. 1817, *NL* ii. 147.
78. RS to JR, Jan. 1817, MS HL.
79. RS to GCB, 20 Jan. 1817, *SL* iii. 51.
80. RS to H. Senhouse, 27 Jan 1817, MS Rochester.
81. RS to JR, 3 Feb. 1817, MS HL.
82. See F. T. Hoadley, 'The Controversy over Southey's *Wat Tyler*', *Studies in Philology*, 38 (1941), 81–96.
83. RS to J. Murray, 14 Feb. 1817, *NL* ii. 149.
84. RS to Longman, 15 Feb. 1817, *LC* iv. 241.
85. *Gentleman's Magazine*, 86/2 (1816), Preface.
86. RS to H. Hill, 28 Feb. 1817, MS Keswick.
87. Hazlitt, *Complete Works*, vii. 167.
88. RS to C. H. Townshend, 16 Feb. 1817, *LC* iv. 242.
89. RS to GCB, 19 Feb. 1817, *LC* iv. 244; 22 Feb. 1817, *SL* iii. 59.
90. RS to CWW, 23 Feb. 1817, *SL* iii. 60.
91. RS to H. Hill, 28 Feb. 1817. MS Keswick.
92. RS to CWW, 10 Mar. 1817, *SL* iii. 63.
93. RS to CWW, 19 Mar. 1817, MS NLW.
94. RS to CWW, 13 Apr. 1817, *LC* iv. 259.
95. RS to GCB, 17 Apr. 1817, *SL* iii. 70.
96. RS to WW, 5–8 May 1817, *NL* ii. 55.
97. WW to S. Rogers, 13 May 1817, *Letters of William and Dorothy Wordsworth: The Middle Years*, ed. Mary Moorman and Alan G. Hill (Oxford, 1970), 382.

98. DW to Catherine Clarkson, 13 Apr. 1817, ibid. 380.
99. STC to T. G. Street, 22 Mar. 1817, *CL* iv. 713.
100. Byron to J. Murray, *Letters and Journals*, ed. Leslie Marchand (12 vols., 1973–82), v. 220.
101. Hazlitt, *Complete Works*, vii. 178–85; *Leigh Hunt's Political and Occasional Essays*, ed. L. H. and C. W. Houtchens (1962), 116–28.
102. Hazlitt, *Complete Works*, vii. 187.
103. Ibid. 203–4.
104. See Howard Mills, *Peacock, his Circle and his Age* (Cambridge, 1968), 115–17.
105. WW to D. Stuart, 7 Apr. 1817, *Letters: The Middle Years*, 375.
106. Ibid. 377.
107. Henry Crabb Robinson, *On Books and their Writers*, ed. Edith J. Morley (3 vols., 1938), i. 201.
108. Ibid.
109. WW to D. Stuart, 22 June 1817, *Letters: The Middle Years*, 387.
110. DW to Catherine Clarkson, 13 Apr. 1817; WW to D. Stuart, 7 Apr. 1817, *Letters: The Middle Years*, 380, 377.
111. C. Lamb to DW, 23 Sept. 1816, Marrs, iii. 226.
112. STC to D. Stuart, 2 Apr. 1817, *CL* iii. 719.
113. *Biographia Literaria* (1817), ch. III; in *The Oxford Authors: Samuel Taylor Coleridge*, ed. H. J. Jackson (Oxford, 1985), 192.
114. RS to H. Hill, 8 May 1817, MS Keswick.
115. RS to JM, 7 Aug. 1817, MS Texas.
116. RS to WW, 23 Aug. 1817, *LC* iv. 276.
117. DW to Catherine Clarkson, 16 Oct. 1817, *Letters: The Middle Years*, 401.
118. RS to H. Hill, 6 Oct. 1817, MS Keswick.
119. RS to CWW, 20 Nov. 1817, *SL* iii. 78.
120. RS to W. Wilberforce, 10 Dec. 1817, MS Berg.
121. RS to W. Wilberforce, 3 Jan. 1818, ibid.
122. RS to JM, 3 Jan. 1818, MS Texas.
123. RS to GCB, 6 Jan. 1818, *SL* iii. 85.
124. Williams, *Life and Letters of John Rickman*, 196–7.
125. RS to W. Scott, 10 Mar. 1818, *LC* iv. 295.
126. RS to JR, 17 Mar. 1818, *NL* ii. 179.
127. RS to JR, 5 Apr. 1818, *LC* iv. 298.
128. RS to J. W. Croker, 11 May 1818, MS PML.
129. RS to JM, 8 May 1818, MS Texas.
130. RS to H. Hill, 15 May 1818, MS Keswick.
131. RS to W. Wilberforce, 18 July 1818, MS Berg.
132. RS to CWW, 7 June 1818, *SL* iii. 90.
133. RS to Gen. Peachey, 20 June, *NL* ii. 184.
134. RS to H. Hill, 10 July 1818, MS Keswick.
135. RS to JM, 13 July 1818, MS Texas.
136. RS to JR, 4 Aug. 1818, MS HL.
137. RS to C. Bowles, 12 Aug. 1818, *NL* ii. 189.
138. RS to JR, 1 Sept. 1818, *SL* iii. 95.

139. RS to JR, 5 Oct. 1818, *SL* iii. 95.
140. RS to CWW, 4 Nov. 1818, *LC* iv. 315.
141. RS to GCB, 26 Oct. 1818, *SL* iii. 102.
142. RS to JM, 16 Nov. 1818, *LC* iv. 318.
143. RS to W. Wilberforce, 26 Dec. 1818, MS Berg.
144. RS to JM, 28 Dec. 1818, MS Texas.
145. RS to GCB, 1 Jan. 1819, *SL* iii. 106.
146. RS to WSL, 3 Jan. 1819, *LC* iv. 108.
147. RS to H. Hill, 6 Jan. 1819, MS Keswick.

Chapter 9

1. RS to JR, 25 Jan. 1819, *SL* iii. 114.
2. RS to H. Hill, 26 Jan. 1819, *SL* iii. 115.
3. RS to W. Wilberforce, 16 Feb. 1819, MS Berg.
4. RS to W. Browne, 14 May 1819, MS Cornell.
5. RS to JM, 14 Mar. 1819, MS Texas.
6. RS to W. Scott, 11 Mar. 1819, *LC* iv. 337.
7. RS to H. Hill, 22 Mar. 1819, *SL* iii. 124.
8. RS to H. Hill, 24 Apr. 1819, MS Keswick.
9. RS to JR, 26 Apr. 1819, MS HL.
10. RS to GCB, 5 May 1819, *SL* iii. 130.
11. RS to Longman and Co., 7 May 1819, *SL* iii. 131.
12. RS to H. Hill, 10 May 1819, MS Keswick.
13. RS to JM, 22 May 1819, MS Texas.
14. RS to N. Lightfoot, 29 May 1819, *LC* iv. 342.
15. RS to H. Hill, 25 June 1819, MS Keswick.
16. RS to A. Cunningham, 10 July 1819, *LC* iv. 349.
17. RS to CWW, 22 July 1819, *LC* iv. 354.
18. RS to C. H. Townshend, 20 July 1819, *LC* iv. 352.
19. *Journal of a Tour in Scotland in 1819*, ed. C. H. Herford (1929), 54.
20. Ibid. 259.
21. *Poetical Works*, iii. 163–7.
22. See RS to General Peachey, *NL* ii. 202.
23. RS to H. Hill, 30 Oct. 1819, *SL* iii. 152.
24. RS to HS, 1 Nov. 1819, *SL* iii. 154.
25. RS to J. Murray, 10 Nov. 1819, *NL* ii. 203.
26. RS to N. White, 20 Nov. 1819, *LC* iv. 359.
27. RS to JM, 23 Nov. 1819, MS Texas.
28. RS to CWW, 11 Dec. 1819, *SL* iii. 162.
29. RS to J. W. Croker, 15 Dec. 1819, *NL* ii. 208.
30. RS to JR, 14 Jan. 1820, *NL* ii. 210.
31. RS to Longman and Co., 21 Jan. 1820, *SL* iii. 172.
32. RS to JR, 7 Feb. 1820, MS HL.
33. RS to JR, 18 Feb. 1820, MS HL; 1 Mar. 1820, *LC* v. 24; to J. Kenyon, 21 Feb. 1820, *SL* iii. 183.
34. RS to JR, 21 Mar. 1820, MS HL.

35. RS to HS, 11 Mar. 1820, *SL* iii. 185.
36. RS to Isabel Southey, 13 May 1820, *NL* ii. 212.
37. RS to Katherine Southey, 28 May 1820, *SL* iii. 195.
38. RS to Edith Southey, 16 June 1820, *NL* ii. 214.
39. RS to N. Lightfoot, 2 June 1821, *LC* v. 82; to WSL, 14 Aug. 1820, *SL* iii. 205.
40. RS to Edith Southey, 25 June 1820, *NL* ii. 215.
41. C. Lamb to JR, early Dec. 1801, Marrs, ii. 40.
42. See *The Correspondence of Robert Southey with Caroline Bowles*, ed. E. Dowden (Dublin, 1881).
43. RS to JR, 7 July 1820, MS HL.
44. RS to JM, 15 Aug. 1820, MS Texas.
45. RS to WSL, 14 Aug. 1820, *SL* iii. 205.
46. RS to J. Coleridge, 20 [? June] 1820, MS Cornell (facsimile).
47. RS to P. B. Shelley, 26 June 1820, MS Cornell (facsmile).
48. RS to P. B. Shelley, 12 Oct. 1820, ibid.
49. RS to CWW, 13 Nov. 1820, *SL* iii. 217.
50. *The Letters of John Clare*, ed. Mark Storey (Oxford, 1985), 110.
51. RS to JR, 22 Nov. 1820, MS HL.
52. RS to JM, 18 Nov. 1820, MS Texas.
53. RS to H. Hill, 29 Nov. 1820, MS Keswick.
54. RS to JR, 8 Dec. 1820, *NL* ii. 218.
55. RS to JR, 19 Dec. 1820, MS HL.
56. RS to H. Hill, 8 Jan. 1821, *SL* iii. 224.
57. RS to HS, 15 Jan. 1821, *SL* iii. 228.
58. RS to Edward Atkins, 16 Jan. 1821, *NL* ii. 222.
59. RS to GCB, 26 Jan. 1821, *LC* v. 59.
60. RS to JR, 27 Jan. 1821, *SL* iii. 231.
61. RS to Longman and Co., 7 Feb. 1821, *SL* iii. 234.
62. 'The Vision of Judgment' in *The Oxford Authors: Byron*, ed. Jerome J. McGann (1986), 966; 'A Vision of Judgement', *Poetical Works*, x. 213.
63. RS to JM, 4 Mar. 1821, *LC* v. 62.
64. RS to H. Hill, 14 Mar. 1821, *SL* iii. 235.
65. RS to GCB, 3 Apr. 1821, *SL* iii. 240.
66. RS to CWW, 4 Apr. 1821, *SL* iii. 244.
67. RS to GCB, 3 Apr. 1821, *SL* iii. 240.
68. RS to CWW, 6 Apr. 1821, *SL* iii. 246.
69. RS to GCB, 15 Apr. 1821, *LC* v. 54; to CWW, 18 Apr. 1821, *NL* ii. 226.
70. RS to N. White, 25 Apr. 1821, *LC* v. 76.
71. RS to C. H. Townshend, 6 May 1821, *LC* v. 78.
72. RS to JM, 15 June 1821, *SL* iii. 254.
73. RS to B. Barton, 9 July 1821, *SL* iii. 262.
74. RS to GCB, 31 Aug. 1821, *SL* iii. 267.
75. RS to CWW, 29 Sept. 1821, *SL* iii. 274.
76. RS to N. White, 20 Oct. 1821, *LC* v. 95.
77. RS to CWW, 5 Nov. 1821, *SL* iii. 280.
78. RS to GCB, 11 Nov. 1821, *LC* v. 98.

79. RS to H. Hill, 23 Oct. 1821, *SL* iii. 277.
80. RS to H. Hill, 8 Dec. 1821, *SL* iii. 287.
81. RS to N. White, 11 Dec. 1821, *LC* v. 103.
82. RS to WSL, 19 Dec. 1821, *NL* ii. 231.
83. See Southey, *Essays, Moral and Political* (2 vols., 1832), ii. 183–205; RS to JM, 26 Dec. 1821, MS Yale; to GCB, 2 Jan. 1822, *NL* ii. 233; to H. Hill, 25 Jan. 1822, *SL* iii. 293.
84. RS to WW, 11 Apr. [1822], *NL* ii. 234.
85. RS to T. Clarkson, 29 May 1822, *NL* ii. 236.
86. RS to WSL, 27 May 1822, *SL* iii. 311.
87. RS to STC, 16 May 1822, MS BPL; to H. Senhouse, 13 May 1822, MS Rochester.
88. RS to CWW, 4 June 1822, *NL* ii. 236.
89. *Poetical Works* (iii), 73–7; 'Robert the Rhymer's True and Particular Account of Himself', *Poetical Works*, iii. 78–9.
90. RS to JR, 7 July 1822, MS HL.
91. CB to RS, July 1822, *Correspondence with Caroline Bowles*, 29–30.
92. RS to GCB, 12 July 1822, *LC* v. 117.
93. RS to CWW, 17 Aug. 1822, *SL* iii. 323.
94. RS to H. Hill, 14 Oct. 1822, *SL* iii. 333.
95. RS to CWW, 14 Dec. 1822, *SL* iii. 351.
96. RS to B. Barton, 26 Nov. 1822, *NL* ii. 239.
97. RS to CWW, 15 Dec. 1822, *SL* iii. 351.
98. RS to CWW, 3 Jan. 1823, *SL* iii. 371.
99. RS to JR, 4 Jan. 1823, MS HL.
100. RS to H. Hill, 26 Jan. 1823, *SL* iii. 375.
101. RS to CWW, 25 Jan. 1823, *SL* iii. 373.
102. RS to GCB, 23 Feb. 1823, *LC* v. 136.
103. RS to GCB, 22 Mar. 1823, *SL* iii. 382.
104. RS to HS, 28 Mar. 1823, *NL* ii. 243; to CWW, 14 Feb. 1823, MS NLW.
105. RS to H. Hill, 27 Apr. 1823, *SL* iii. 387.
106. RS to WSL, 8 May 1823, *SL* iii. 388; and see to John Taylor, 7 June, 6 July, 8 Aug., 24 Oct., 30 Oct., MS Yale.
107. RS to HS, 22 June 1823, MS Berg.
108. RS to JR, [n.d.], MS HL.
109. RS to JM, 2 Aug. 1823, MS Texas.
110. RS to JR, 12 Aug. 1823, MS HL.
111. CB to RS, Feb. 1825, *Correspondence with Caroline Bowles*, 33–4.
112. RS to CB, Feb. 1825, ibid. 42.
113. CB to RS, 27 Feb. 1825, ibid. 79.
114. RS to N. White, 11 Sept. 1823, *SL* iii. 401.
115. RS to H. Hill, 27 Oct. 1823, MS Keswick.
116. RS to Edith Southey, 30 Nov. 1823, *NL* ii. 256.
117. RS to Cuthbert Southey, 9 Feb. 1824, MS Yale.
118. RS to N. White, 19 Feb. 1824, *SL* iii. 409.
119. RS to JR, 28 Feb. 1824, MS HL.
120. RS to Edith May Southey, 12 Mar. 1824, *SL* iii. 412.

121. RS to JR, 21 Apr. 1824, MS HL.
122. RS to GCB, 24 May 1824, *SL* iii. 424.

Chapter 10

1. RS to H. Taylor, 26 May 1824, *LC* v. 178.
2. RS to Mrs Hughes, 12 Aug. 1824, *SL* iii. 433.
3. RS to WSL, 14 Aug. 1824, *SL* iii. 437.
4. RS to J. Montgomery, 21 July 1824, MS Yale.
5. RS to JR, 12 Sept. 1824, *SL* iii. 439.
6. RS to H. Hill, 24 Sept. 1824, MS Keswick.
7. RS to GCB, 12 Oct. 1824, *LC* v. 189.
8. RS to JR, 12 Dec. 1824, MS HL.
9. RS to J. W. Croker, 18 Dec. 1824, *NL* ii. 275.
10. RS to J. Murray, 25 Oct. [1824], *NL* ii. 273; to J. Coleridge, 30 Jan. 1825, *LC* v. 201.
11. RS to H. Taylor, 10 Jan. 1825, *LC* v. 199.
12. RS to Mrs Hughes, 24 Feb. 1825, *SL* iii. 472.
13. *A Tale of Paraguay* (1825), 1 . i.
14. RS to W. Bowles, 19 Mar. 1825, *LC* v. 206.
15. RS to H. Taylor, 28 Mar. 1825, *LC* v. 208.
16. RS to H. Taylor, 2 May 1825, *LC* v. 211.
17. RS to Gen. Peachey, 6 Apr. 1825, *NL* ii. 278.
18. RS to JR, 22 May 1825, MS HL.
19. *Poetical Works*, iii. 312.
20. RS to JM, 11 Sept. 1825, MS Texas.
21. RS to H. Taylor, 22 Oct. 1825, *LC* v. 235.
22. RS to R. Gooch, 18 Dec. 1825, *LC* v. 237.
23. RS to J. G. Lockhart, 2 Jan. 1826, *NL* ii. 297.
24. RS to JM, 7 Jan. 1826, MS Texas.
25. RS to N. White, 11 Feb. 1826, *SL* iii. 525.
26. RS to JR, 30 Mar. 1826, *SL* iii. 536.
27. RS to JR, 30 Apr. 1826, *LC* v. 250.
28. RS to Edith Southey, 25 May 1826, *NL* ii. 302.
29. Caroline Bowles to RS, *Correspondence with Caroline Bowles*, 106.
30. RS to Caroline Bowles, ibid. 107.
31. RS to JM, 3 June 1826, MS Texas.
32. RS to HS, 3 July 1826, *NL* ii. 306.
33. RS to JR, 16 July 1826, MS HL.
34. *LC* v. 252.
35. RS to H. Taylor, 31 Aug. 1826, *LC* v. 265.
36. RS to S. Turner, 12 Nov. 1826, *LC* v. 271.
37. RS to H. Taylor, 13 Nov. 1826, *LC* v. 269.
38. RS to JR, 14 Oct. 1826, MS HL.
39. RS to CWW, 24 Aug. 1826, MS NLW.
40. RS to C. Bowles, 31 Dec. 1826, *NL* ii. 307.
41. RS to GCB, 14 Jan. 1827, *NL* ii. 309.

42. RS to WSL, 21 Feb. 1827, *LC* v. 287.
43. RS to H. Taylor, 12 Apr. 1827, *LC* v. 290.
44. RS to JR, 23 Apr. 1827, *LC* v. 293; to JR, 4 Jan. 1827, MS HL.
45. RS to GCB, 10 June 1827, *LC* v. 300.
46. RS to H. Taylor, 13 Sept. 1827, *LC* v. 307.
47. RS to JM, 15 Sept. 1827, MS Texas.
48. RS to Miss Wood, 22 Oct. 1827, MS Yale.
49. RS to GCB, 31 Oct. 1827, *LC* v. 315.
50. See Marilyn Butler, *Peacock Displayed: A Satirist in his Context* (1979), 183–230.
51. RS to H. Hill, 4 Nov. 1827, *NL* ii. 319.
52. RS to GCB, 15 Jan. 1828, *SL* iv. 82.
53. RS to CWW, 27 Jan. 1828, *SL* iv. 85.
54. RS to W. Ainsworth, 21 Feb. 1828, *NL* ii. 322.
55. RS to JM, 4 Aug. 1828, MS Texas.
56. RS to JM, 22 Sept. 1828, MS Texas; to JR, 23 Sept. 1828, *SL* iv. 115.
57. RS to H. Hill, 18 Aug. 1828, MS Keswick.
58. RS to GCB, 8 Dec. 1828, *LC* v. 334.
59. RS to JR, 24 Jan. 1829, MS HL.
60. RS to JR, 1 Mar. 1829, *SL* iv. 131.
61. RS to R. Shannon, 2 Mar. 1829, *LC* vi. 33.
62. See Edgar Johnson, *Sir Walter Scott: The Great Unknown* (2 vols., 1970), ii. 1101–2.
63. RS to GCB, 28 Mar. 1829, *NL* ii. 333; RS to Caroline Bowles, 15 Feb. 1829, *Correspondence with Caroline Bowles*, 154.
64. RS to J. Murray, 19 June 1829, *NL* ii. 336.
65. RS to N. Lightfoot, 12 July 1829, *LC* vi. 51.
66. RS to Mrs Opie, 30 Aug. 1829, *LC* vi. 62.
67. Orlo Williams, *Lamb's Friend the Census-Taker: Life and Letters of John Rickman* (1911), 246.
68. RS to JR, 6 Aug. 1829, *SL* iv. 144.
69. RS to WSL, 22 Aug. 1829, *SL* iv. 144.
70. RS to Mrs Opie, 30 Aug. 1829, MS Brotherton.
71. RS to JM, 19 Sept. 1829, MS Texas.
72. RS to Mrs Hodson, 27 Oct. 1829, MS HL.
73. RS to J. G. Lockhart, 15 Dec. 1829, MS NLS.
74. RS to JR, 5 Jan. 1830, *LC* vi. 82.
75. RS to CWW, 9 Jan. 1830, *NL* ii. 349.
76. RS to GCB, 3 Mar. 1830, *SL* iv. 168.
77. RS to H. Taylor, 15 Apr. 1830, *LC* vi. 96; to W. Hone, 23 Apr. 1830, MS NLS.
78. RS to Mrs Hodson, 15 May 1830, *LC* vi. 102.
79. Caroline Bowles to RS, Apr. 1830, *Correspondence with Caroline Bowles*, 190.
80. RS to Mrs Hughes, 8 June 1830, *SL* iv. 180; to JR, 11 Sept. 1830, *LC* vi. 117.
81. RS to JR, 10 July 1830, MS HL.
82. RS to H. Taylor, 24 Aug. 1830, *NL* ii. 354.
83. RS to J. G. Lockhart, 24 Aug. 1830, MS NLS.

84. RS to J. Warter, 25 Aug. 1830, *LC* vi. 111.
85. RS to JR, 28 Aug. 1830, MS HL.
86. RS to J. G. Lockhart, 13 Sept. 1830, MS NLS.
87. RS to W. Scott, 26 Sept. 1830, *NL* ii. 356.
88. RS to Mrs Hodson, 12 Oct. 1830, MS HL.
89. RS to A. Bell, 25 Nov. 1830, *LC* vi. 123.
90. RS to Edith May Southey, 10 Dec. 1830, *SL* iv. 203.
91. RS to JR, 22 Jan. 1831, MS HL.
92. RS to Edith Southey, 18 Jan. 1831, MS Berg; to GCB, 29 Jan. 1831, *NL* ii. 360–2.
93. RS to A. Cooper, 12 Feb. 1831, MS Berg.
94. RS to JR, 24 Feb. 1831, MS HL.
95. RS to A. Cooper, 28 Feb. 1831, MS Berg.
96. RS to JR, 2 Apr. 1831, MS HL.
97. RS to JR, 16 Apr. 1831, ibid.
98. RS to A. Cooper, 16 Apr. 1831, MS Berg.
99. RS to J. G. Lockhart, 25 June 1831, MS NLS.
100. RS to Mrs Hodson, 30 July 1831, MS HL; to Mrs Bray, 13 Aug. 1831, *SL* iv. 234.
101. RS to J. Warter, 20 July 1831, *SL* iv. 230.
102. RS to JR, 14 Oct. 1831, *LC* vi. 162.
103. RS to Mrs Hodson, 22 Oct. 1831, MS HL.
104. Ibid.; to A. Cooper, 7 Nov. 1831, MS Berg.
105. RS to A. Cooper, 7 Nov. 1831, MS Berg.
106. RS to Mrs Bray, 24 Nov. 1831, *SL* iv. 248.
107. RS to Mrs Hodson, 23 Dec. 1831, MS HL; to J. Warter, 27 Dec. 1831, *LC* vi. 166.
108. RS to N. White, 3 Jan. 1832, *LC* vi. 174.
109. RS to T. Allison, 17 Jan. 1832, MS Yale.
110. RS to A. Cooper, 18 Feb. 1832, MS Berg.
111. RS to A. Cooper, 30 Jan. 1832, ibid.
112. RS to J. Warter, 7 Mar. 1832, *SL* iv. 261.
113. RS to J. G. Lockhart, 22 May 1832, MS NLS.
114. RS to W. Bowles, 30 July 1832, MS Cornell.
115. RS to GCB, 15 Mar. 1832, *LC* vi. 188.
116. RS to Mrs Bray, 1 May 1832, MS Rochester.
117. RS to JM, 30 May 1832, MS Texas.
118. RS to N. White, 13 July 1832, *SL* iv. 285.
119. RS to A. Cooper, 21 July 1832, MS Berg.
120. RS to Mrs Hodson, 6 Aug. 1832, MS HL.
121. RS to Mrs Hughes, 16 Aug. 1832, *SL* iv. 295.
122. RS to A. Cooper, 11 Sept. 1832, MS Berg.
123. RS to A. Cooper, 17 Sept. 1832, ibid.
124. RS to J. Murray, 25 Aug. 1832, *NL* ii. 300.
125. RS to A. Cooper, 23 Mar. 1832, MS Berg.
126. RS to Mrs Hodson, 24 Oct. 1832, *NL* ii. 384.
127. RS to CWW, 1 Dec. 1832, *SL* iv. 311.
128. RS to Mrs Hughes, 27 Dec. 1832, *SL* iv. 316.
129. RS to Mrs Bray, 16 Dec. 1832, MS Rochester.

130. RS to A. Cooper, 6 Feb. 1833, MS Berg.
131. RS to JM, 1 Mar. 1833, MS Texas.
132. RS to CWW, 4 June 1833, *NL* ii. 399.
133. RS to A. Cunningham, 3 June 1833, *LC* vi. 214.
134. RS to CWW, 4 June 1833, *NL* ii. 399.
135. RS to E. Moxon, 7 Aug. 1833, *SL* iv. 350.
136. RS to JM, 30 Dec. 1833, MS Texas.
137. RS to H. Taylor, 16 Jan. 1834, *LC* vi. 229.
138. RS to Mrs Hodson, 9 Feb. 1834, MS HL.
139. RS to HS, 12 Feb. 1834, MS Berg.
140. RS to JR, 9 June 1834, MS HL.
141. RS to JR, 27 July 1834, ibid.; to Senhouse, 17 July 1834, MS Rochester.
142. RS to JM, 29 Aug. 1834, MS Texas.
143. Ibid.
144. *The Diaries of William Charles Macready*, ed. W. Toynbee (2 vols., 1912), i. 185; RS to GCB, 2 Oct. 1834, *LC* vi. 244.
145. RS to JM, 5 Oct. 1834, MS Texas.
146. RS to JM, 24 Dec. 1834, ibid.
147. RS to JR, 3 Jan. 1835, MS HL.
148. RS to E. Moxon, 10 Dec. 1834, *SL* iv. 394.
149. RS to Mrs Bray, 16 Feb. 1835, MS Rochester.
150. RS to Bertha Southey, 20 Mar. 1835, MS Keswick.
151. RS to Bertha Southey, 24 Mar. 1835, ibid.
152. RS to Bertha Southey, 29 Mar. 1835, ibid.
153. RS to CWW, 2 Apr. 1835, MS NLW.
154. RS to JM, 6 May 1835, MS Texas.
155. RS to CWW, 19 June 1835, MS NLW.
156. RS to Mrs Hughes, 1 July 1835, *SL* iv. 407.
157. RS to WW, 25 June 1835, MS Dove Cottage.
158. RS to CWW, 5 July 1835, MS NLW.
159. RS to WW, 11 June 1835, MS Dove Cottage; RS to H. J. M. Mason, 15 July 1835, MS Yale.
160. RS to J. Warter, 1 Oct. 1835, *LC* vi. 275.
161. RS to CWW, 6 Nov. 1835, *NL* ii. 429.
162. RS to Cuthbert Southey, 16 Dec. 1835, *LC* vi. 280.
163. RS to J. Horseman, 21 Dec. 1835, *NL* ii. 433.
164. RS to Mrs Hodson, 26 Jan. 1836, *NL* ii. 437.
165. RS to JM, 30 Jan. 1836, MS Texas.
166. RS to J. Cottle, 5 Mar. 1836, *NL* ii. 444.
167. RS to Mrs Bray, 11 Apr. 1836, *SL* iv. 447.
168. RS to J. Cottle, 14 Apr. 1836, *NL* ii. 449.
169. RS to Longman and Co., 25 July 1836, *SL* iv. 459.
170. RS to CWW, 17 Aug. 1836, MS NLW.
171. See RS to Bertha Southey, 5 Dec 1836, *NL* ii. 457–62; to Mrs Bray, 6 Nov. 1836, *SL* iv. 472–3; to CWW, 9 Nov. 1836, *SL* iv. 474; to GCB, 10 Nov. 1836, *LC* vi. 311–14.

172. RS to Bertha Southey, 4 Nov., 30 Nov., 26 Dec. 1836, MS Keswick.
173. Caroline Bowles to RS, Feb. 1837, *Correspondence with Caroline Bowles*, 348.
174. RS to Caroline Bowles, Jan. 1837, ibid. 347.
175. RS to Mrs Hodson, 1 Mar. 1837, MS HL.
176. RS to Mrs Bray, 6 Feb. 1837, MS Rochester.
177. RS to Mrs Hodson, 27 Oct. 1837, MS HL.
178. RS to Caroline Bowles, 18 Oct. 1837, *SL* iv. 531.
179. RS to JR, 22 Jan. 1838, MS HL.
180. RS to JR, 11 Mar. 1838, ibid.
181. WW to RS, Mar. 1838, *Letters of William and Dorothy Wordsworth: The Later Years*, ed. Alan G. Hill (4 vols., Oxford, 1978–88), iii. 533.
182. RS to JR, 10 Apr. 1838, MS HL.
183. *Robert Southey: Journals of a Residence in Portugal 1800–1801 and a Visit to France 1838*, ed. Adolfo Cabral (Oxford, 1960), 191.
184. RS to GCB, 7 Oct. 1838, ibid. 245.
185. RS to Bertha Southey, 15 Oct. 1838, *NL* ii. 479.
186. RS to Bertha Southey, 26 Oct. 1838, MS Keswick.
187. RS to CWW, 17 Dec. 1838, MS NLW; Cuthbert Southey to Mrs Hughes, 14 Oct. 1839, MS Houghton; to Mrs Hodson, 18 Feb. 1839, MS HL.
188. RS to CWW, 5 Sept. 1839, MS NLW.
189. CBS to Mrs Hughes, 4 Apr. 1840, MS Houghton.
190. WW to Isabella Fenwick, 23 Nov. 1840, *Letters: The Later Years*, iv. 147.
191. CBS to Mrs Hughes, 16 June 1840, MS Houghton.
192. CBS to Mrs Bray, 1 May 1840, MS Rochester; to Mrs Hughes, 4 Jan. 1841, MS Houghton.
193. CBS to A. Cooper, 20 June 1840, MS Houghton.
194. WW to Lady F. Bentinck, 30 July 1840, *Letters: The Later Years*, iv. 97.
195. CBS to Mrs Hughes, 23 Sept., 24 Oct. 1840, MS Houghton.
196. WW to Henry Crabb Robinson, 26 Jan. 1841, *Letters: The Later Years*, iv. 169–75.
197. CBS to Mrs Hughes, 3 May 1841, MS Houghton.
198. CBS to [landlord], 12 June 1841, MS NLS.
199. J. Bush to Mrs Bray, 29 June 1841, MS Rochester.
200. CBS to Mrs Hughes, 18–19 June 1841, MS Houghton.
201. WW to Henry Crabb Robinson, 14 Oct. 1841, *Letters: The Later Years*, iv. 250.
202. CBS to Mrs Hughes, 18 Dec. 1841, MS Houghton.
203. CBS to Mrs Hughes, 12 Feb. 1842, ibid.
204. CBS to Mrs Hughes, 10 May 1842, ibid.
205. H. Hill, 6 Apr. 1842, MS Cornell.
206. CBS to Mrs Hughes, 11 June 1842, MS Houghton.
207. CBS to Mrs Hughes, 22 Aug. 1842, ibid.
208. CBS to Mrs Hughes, 11 Oct. 1842, ibid.
209. CBS to Mrs Hughes, 9 Feb. 1843, ibid.
210. CBS to Mrs Bray, 22 Mar. 1843, MS Rochester; to Mrs Hughes, 1 Apr. 1843, MS Keswick.
211. Robert Campbell to Mrs Hughes, 29 Mar. 1843, MS Yale.

212. CBS to Mrs Hughes, 10 Apr. 1842, MS Houghton.
213. CBS to Mrs Hughes, 25 Apr. 1843, ibid.
214. CBS to Mrs Hughes, 7 June 1843, ibid.
215. CBS to Mrs Hughes, 18 Dec. 1843, ibid.
216. Inscription on the monument in Crosthwaite Church (quoted in Lionel Madden (ed.), *Robert Southey: The Critical Heritage* (1972), 416).
217. H. Hill Album, MS Cornell (facsimile).
218. CBS to Mrs Hughes, 14 July 1843, MS Houghton.

Epilogue

 1. *The Life and Work of the Seventh Earl of Shattesbury* (3 vols., 1886), i. 262.
 2. *Letters and Diaries of John Henry Newman*, ed. C. S. Dessain and others (London, 1961–), xiii. 449.
 3. *Letters of William and Dorothy Wordsworth: The Later Years*, ed. Alan G. Hill (Oxford, 1988), vii. 614–15.
 4. *Fraser's Magazine*, 42 (Dec. 1850), 647.
 5. *North British Review*, 12 (Feb. 1850) 371–410.
 6. Charlotte Brontë to W. S. Williams, 12 Apr. 1850, MS HL.
 7. *Quarterly Review*, 88 (Dec. 1850), 197–247.
 8. In 'Shakespeare the Man', *Literary Studies* (1879).
 9. *Cornhill Magazine*, 2 (Oct. 1860), 385–406.
10. *Reminiscences*, ed. J. A. Froude (2 vols., 1881), ii. 309–29.
11. Ibid.

SELECT BIBLIOGRAPHY

1. *Manuscript sources*

The bulk of Southey's manuscripts can be found in the following libraries:

Beinecke Rare Book and Manuscipt Library, Yale University, New Haven.
Berg Collection, New York Public Library.
Bodleian Library, Oxford.
Boston Public Library.
Bristol Public Library.
British Library.
Brotherton Library, University of Leeds.
Carl H. Pforzheimer Collection, New York Public Library.
Columbia University Library, New York.
Cornell University Library, Ithaca, New York.
Dr Williams's Library, London.
Duke University Library, North Carolina.
Edinburgh University Library.
Harry Ransom Humanities Research Center, University of Texas at Austin.
Huntington Library, San Marino, California.
John Rylands Library, University of Manchester.
Keswick Museum and Art Gallery.
Library of Congress, Washington, DC.
National Art Library, Victoria and Albert Museum, London.
National Library of Scotland, Edinburgh.
National Library of Wales, Aberystwyth.
Pierpont Morgan Library, New York.
Princeton University Library, New Jersey.
Rochester University Library, New York.
University of Kentucky Library, Lexington, Kentucky.
Victoria University Library, Toronto.
Wellesley College Library, Wellesley, Massachusetts.
Wordsworth Trust, Dove Cottage, Grasmere.

2. *Works by Southey*

There follows a list of Southey's works, published in his lifetime; full bibliographical details can be found in William Haller, *The Early Life of Robert Southey
1774–1803* (New York, 1917), and the *New Cambridge Bibliography of English
Literature*. (Unless otherwise indicated, place of publication is London.)

The Flagellant [anon.] (1792).
The Fall of Robespierre, by S. T. Coleridge [Southey's name not on title-page]
    (Cambridge, 1794).

Poems: containing The Retrospect, Odes, Elegies, Sonnets, &c. by Robert Lovell, and Robert Southey (Bath and London, 1795).

Joan of Arc (Bristol and London, 1796; 2nd edn. Bristol 1798; then 1806, 1812, 1817).

Letters Written During a Short Residence in Spain and Portugal (Bristol and London, 1797; 2nd edn. 1799; then 1808).

On the French Revolution, by Mr. Necker [anon. translation], vol. ii (1797).

Poems by Robert Southey. Second Edition (Bristol and London, 1797; then 1800, 1801, 1808).

Poems by Robert Southey. The Second Volume (Bristol and London, 1799; then 1800, 1801, 1806).

The Annual Anthology [ed. anon.] (2 vols., Bristol and London, 1799, 1800).

Thalaba the Destroyer (Bristol and London, 1801; then 1809, 1814, 1821).

The Works of Thomas Chatterton [ed. anon.] (3 vols., 1803).

Amadis of Gaul, translated by RS (1803).

Madoc (1805; then 1807, 1812, 1815, 1825).

Metrical Tales and Other Poems (1805).

Palmerin of England, translated by RS (4 vols., 1807).

Specimens of the Later English Poets (1807).

The Remains of Henry Kirke White (2 vols., 1807; vol. iii, 1822; also 1819, 1821, 1823).

Letters from England: by Don Manuel Alvarez Espriella [anon.] (3 vols., 1807; then 1808).

The Chronicle of the Cid, translated by RS (1808).

The Curse of Kehama (London and Edinburgh, 1810; then 1811, 1812, 1818).

The History of Brazil (vol. i, 1810; vol. ii, 1817; vol. iii, 1819).

Omniana, or Horae Otiosiores [anon.; ed. R. S. and Coleridge] (1812).

The Life of Nelson (2 vols., 1813; then 1814, 1825, 1827, 1831, 1840).

Roderick, The Last of the Goths (1814; then 1815, 1816, 1818, 1826).

Carmen Triumphale, for the Commencement of the Year 1814 (1814).

Odes to His Royal Highness The Prince Regent, His Imperial Majesty The Emperor of Russia, and His Majesty The King of Prussia (1814; 2nd edn. 1821, with *Carmen Triumphale*).

The Minor Poems of Robert Southey (3 vols., 1815; then 1825).

The Poet's Pilgrimage to Waterloo (1816; 2nd edn. same year).

The Lay of the Laureate. Carmen Nuptiale (1816).

The Byrth, Lyf, and Actes of King Arthur, ed. RS, with notes (1817).

Wat Tyler [anon.] (1817; numerous pirated editions).

A Letter to William Smith, Esq., M.P. (4 edns., 1817).

The Life of Wesley and the Rise and Progress of Methodism (2 vols., 1820; 2nd edn. same year).

The Expedition of Orsua; and the Crimes of Aguirre (1821; reprinted from the *Edinburgh Annual Register*, vol. 3).

A Vision of Judgement (1821; then 1822, 1824 [with Byron's *Vision of Judgment*]).

A History of the Peninsular War (vol. i, 1823; vol. ii, 1827; vol. iii, 1832).

The Book of the Church (2 vols., 1824; then 1824, 1825, 1837, 1841).

A Tale of Paraguay (1825; then 1828).

Vindiciae Ecclesiae Anglicanae (1826).

All for Love; and the Pilgrim to Compostella (1829).

Sir Thomas More: or, Colloquies on the Progress and Prospects of Society (2 vols., 1829; then 1831).

The Poetical Works of Robert Southey, complete in one volume (Paris, 1829; unauthorized).

The Devil's Walk, by RS and Coleridge (1830; originally [anon.], 'The Devil's Thoughts', 1799).

The Pilgrim's Progress, with a Life of John Bunyan (1830; then 1839).

Attempts in Verse, by John Jones, an old Servant: with . . . an introductory Essay on the Lives and Works of our Uneducated Poets (1831; then 1836).

Select Works of the British Poets, from Chaucer to Jonson, with Biographical Sketches (1831).

Essays, Moral and Political (2 vols., 1832).

Lives of the British Admirals (vols. i and ii, 1833; vol. iii, 1834; vol. iv, 1837; vol. v, 1840).

Letter to John Murray, Esq., 'touching' Lord Nugent . . . [anon.] (1833).

The Doctor [anon.] (vols. i and ii, 1834; vol. iii, 1835; vol. iv, 1837; vol. v, 1838; vols. vi and vii, ed. J. W. Warter, 1847; reprinted in one volume, ed. J. W. Warter, 1848).

Horae Lyricae . . . by Isaac Watts . . . With a Memoir of the Author (1834).

Life and Works of William Cowper (vol. i, 1835; vols, ii–ix, 1836; vols. x–xv, 1837).

The Poetical Works of Robert Southey, collected by himself (vols. i–ii, 1837; vols. iii–x, 1838).

The Life of the Rev. Andrew Bell (vol. i, ed. Caroline Southey, 1844; vols. ii and iii ed. Cuthbert Southey, 1844).

Lives of Cromwell and Bunyan (1844).

Oliver Newman: a New-England Tale (Unfinished) (1845).

Robin Hood: a fragment, RS and Caroline Southey (1847).

There is no standard edition of Southey's works. The following are the major printed sources, in order of publication, on which readers have, with considerable circumspection, to rely:

The Poetical Works of Robert Southey, collected by himself (10 vols., 1837–8).

The Life and Correspondence of Robert Southey, ed. Cuthbert C. Southey (6 vols., 1849–50).

Southey's Common-Place Book, ed. John Wood Warter (4 vols., 1849–50).

Selections from the Letters of Robert Southey, ed. John Wood Warter (4 vols., 1856).

The Correspondence of Robert Southey with Caroline Bowles, ed. Edward Dowden (Dublin, 1881).

Journal of a Tour in the Netherlands in the autumn of 1815 by Robert Southey, ed. W. Robertson Nicoll (1903).

Robert Southey: the Poetical Works, ed. M. H. FitzGerald (Oxford, 1909).

Journal of a Tour in Scotland in 1819, by Robert Southey, ed. C. H. Herford (1929).

Robert Southey: Journals of a Residence in Portugal 1800–1801, and a Visit to France 1838, ed. Adolfo Cabral (Oxford, 1960).

New Letters of Robert Southey, ed. Kenneth Curry (2 vols., New York and London, 1965).

Letters of Robert Southey to John May, 1797–1838: edited from the Manuscripts in the University of Texas Library, ed. Charles Ramos (Austin, Texas, 1965).

3. *Secondary works*

AIKIN, JOHN, *Memoir*, ed. Lucy Aikin (2 vols., 1823).

ASPINALL, ARTHUR, *Lord Brougham and the Whig Party* (Manchester, 1927).

—— *Politics and the Press 1780–1850* (1949).

[BAILLIE, JOANNA], *A Series of Plays in which it is attempted to delineate the Stronger Passions* (1798).

BARKER, G. F. R., and STENNING, A. H., *The Record of Old Westminsters* (1928).

BAUGHMAN, ROLAND, 'Southey the Schoolboy', *Huntington Library Quarterly*, 7 (May 1944), 247–80.

BETHAM, ERNEST, *A House of Letters* (1905).

BOULTON, JAMES T., *The Language of Politics in the Age of Wilkes and Burke* (1963).

BROMWICH, DAVID, *Hazlitt: The Mind of a Critic* (New York and Oxford, 1983).

BURKE, EDMUND, *Reflections on the Revolution in France* (1790), ed. Conor Cruise O'Brien (Harmondsworth, 1968).

—— *Three Letters Addressed to a Member of the Present Parliament, on the Proposals for Peace with the Regicide Directory of France* (1796).

BUTLER, MARILYN, *Peacock Displayed: A Satirist in his Context* (1979).

—— *Romantics, Rebels and Reactionaries* (Oxford, 1981).

—— (ed.), *Burke, Paine, Godwin, and the Revolution Controversy* (Cambridge, 1984).

—— *Literature as a Heritage: or Reading Other Ways* (Cambridge, 1988).

BYRON, GEORGE GORDON, LORD, *Complete Poetical Works*, ed. Jerome J. McGann (7 vols., Oxford, 1980–93).

—— *Letters and Journals*, ed. Leslie A. Marchand (12 vols., 1975–82).

—— Oxford Authors vol., ed. Jerome J. McGann (Oxford and New York, 1986).

CAMERON, KENNETH NEIL, *The Young Shelley: Genesis of a Radical* (1952).

CARLYLE, THOMAS, *Reminiscences*, ed. J. A. Froude (2 vols., 1881).

CARNALL, GEOFFREY, *Robert Southey and his Age: The Development of a Conservative Mind* (Oxford, 1960).

CHRISTIE, IAN R., *Myth and Reality in Late Eighteenth-century British Politics* (1970).

CLAEYS, GREGORY, *Citizens and Saints* (Cambridge, 1989).

CLARE, JOHN, *The Letters of John Clare*, ed. Mark Storey (Oxford, 1985).

CLAYDEN, P. W., *Rogers and his Contemporaries* (2 vols., 1889).

CLIVE, JOHN, *Scotch Reviewers: The Edinburgh Review, 1802–1815* (1957).

COBBAN, ALFRED, *The Debate on the French Revolution, 1789–1800* (1950).

COLERIDGE, HARTLEY, *Letters*, ed. Grace Evelyn Griggs and Earl Leslie Griggs (1936).

—— *Poems: With a Memoir of his Life by his Brother* (2 vols., 1851).

COLERIDGE, SAMUEL TAYLOR, *Collected Coleridge* (Bollingen Series 75; Princeton): *The Friend*, ed. Barbara E. Rooke (2 vols., 1969); *Lectures 1795: On Politics and Religion*, ed. Lewis Patton and Peter Mann (1971); *The Watchman*, ed. Lewis Patton (1970); *Essays on his Times*, ed. David V. Erdman (3 vols., 1978); *Biographia Literaria*, ed. James Engell and W. Jackson Bate (2 vols., 1983).

—— *Collected Letters*, ed. Earl Leslie Griggs (6 vols., Oxford, 1956–71).

—— *Notebooks*, ed. Kathleen Coburn (3 vols., 1957–73).

—— Oxford Authors vol., ed. H. J. Jackson (Oxford and new York, 1985).

COLERIDGE, SARA, *Memoir and Letters of Sara Coleridge*, ed. Edith Coleridge (2 vols., 1873).

CONE, CARL B., *The English Jacobins: Reformers in Late Eighteenth Century England* (New York, 1968)

COOPER, THOMAS, *The Life of Thomas Cooper* (1872), ed. John Saville (Leicester, 1971).

CORNWALL, JOHN, *Coleridge: Poet and Revolutionary, 1772–1804* (1973).

COTTLE, AMOS, *Icelandic Poetry, or the Edda of Saemund* (Bristol, 1797).

COTTLE, JOSEPH, *Poems* (Bristol, 1795).

—— *Reminiscences of Samuel Taylor Coleridge and Robert Southey* (1847).

COURTNEY, WINIFRED F., *Young Charles Lamb, 1775–1802* (1982).

CROSS, NIGEL, *The Common Writer: Life in Nineteenth-century Grub Street* (Cambridge, 1985).

CURRY, KENNETH, 'Robert Southey', in *The English Romantic Poets and Essayists; A Review of Research and Criticism* (New York, 1957).

—— *Southey* (1975).

—— *Sir Walter Scott's Edinburgh Annual Register* (Knoxville, Tennessee, 1977).

DE QUINCEY, THOMAS, *Recollections of the Lakes and the Lake Poets*, ed. David Wright (Harmondsworth, 1970).

DYER, GEORGE, *An Inquiry into the Nature of Subscription* (1792).

—— *The Complaints of the Poor People of England* (1793).

—— *A Dissertation on the Theory and Practice of Benevolence* (1795).

—— *The Poet's Fate* (1797).

EMSLEY, CLIVE, *British Society and the French Wars, 1793–1815* (1979).

EVEREST, KELVIN, *Coleridge's Secret Ministry; The Context of the Conversation Poems, 1795–1798* (Hasssocks and New York, 1979).

FOSTER, J., *The Register of Admissions to Gray's Inn 1521–1889* (1889).

FREND, WILLIAM, *Peace and Union* (1792).

GILL, STEPHEN, *William Wordsworth: A Life* (Oxford, 1989).

GODWIN, WILLIAM, *An Enquiry Concerning Political Justice, and its Influence on General Virtue and Happiness* (2 vols., 1793).

—— *Things as They Are; or, The Adventures of Caleb Williams* (3 vols., 1794); ed. David McCracken (Oxford, 1970).

—— *St Leon* (1799).

—— *Thoughts Occasioned by the Perusal of Dr. Parr's Spital Sermon* (1801).

GOODWIN, A. *The French Revolution* (5th edn., 1970).

—— *The Friends of Liberty: The English Democratic Movement in the Age of the French Revolution* (1979).

GREAVES, MARGARET, *Regency Patron: Sir George Beaumont* (1966).

GUNNING, HENRY, *Reminiscences of the University, Town and County of Cambridge, from the Year 1780* (2 vols., 1854).

HALLER, WILLIAM, *The Early Life of Robert Southey 1774–1803* (New York, 1917).

HARTLEY, DAVID, *Observations on Man, his Frame, his Duty, and his Expectations* (1749).

HAYDEN, JOHN O., *The Romantic Reviewers 1802–1824* (1969).

HAZLITT, WILLIAM, *The Complete Works*, ed. P. P. Howe (21 vols., 1930–4).

HOADLEY, F. T., 'The Controversy over Southey's *Wat Tyler*', *Studies in Philology*, 38 (1941), 81–96.

HOLMES, RICHARD, *Shelley: the Pursuit* (1974).

—— *Coleridge: Early Visions* (1989).

HONE, J. ANN, *For the Cause of Truth: Radicalism in London 1796–1821* (Oxford, 1982).

HONE, WILLIAM, *The Three Trials of William Hone* (1818), ed. William Tegg (1876).

—— *The Political House that Jack Built* (1819).

HOPKINS, BROOKE, 'Representing Robespierre', in *History and Myth: Essays on English Romantic Literature*, ed. Stephen Behrendt (Detroit, 1990).

HOPKINS, MARY ALDEN, *Hannah More and her Circle* (New York, 1947).

HOWE, H. W., *Greta Hall: Home of Coleridge and Southey* (rev. Robert Woof, Stoke Ferry, 1977).

HUNT, HENRY, *Memoirs of Henry Hunt, Esq., Written by Himself...* (3 vols., Dolby, 1820).

HUNT, LEIGH, *Autobiography* (3 vols., 1850).

—— *Leigh Hunt's Political and Occasional Essays*, ed. Lawrence H. Houtchens and Carolyn W. Houtchens (1962).

JACOBUS, MARY, *Tradition and Experiment in Wordsworth's Lyrical Ballads (1798)* (Oxford, 1976).

—— 'Southey's Debt to *Lyrical Ballads* (1798)' *RES*, NS 22 (1971), 20–36.

JOHNSON, EDGAR, *Sir Walter Scott: The Great Unknown* (2 vols, 1970).

KAUFMAN, P., 'The Reading of Southey and Coleridge; the Record of Their Borrowings from the Bristol Library, 1793–1798', *Modern Philology* 21 (1924), 317–20.

KEATS, JOHN, *The Letters*, ed. Hyder Edward Rollins (2 vols., Cambridge, Mass., 1958).

KNIGHT, FRIDA, *University Rebel: The Life of William Frend, 1757–1841* (1971).

LAMB, CHARLES and MARY, *Letters*, ed. Edwin W. Marrs, Jr. (3 vols., Ithaca, NY, 1975–).

LANDOR, WALTER SAVAGE, *Poetical Works*, ed. Stephen Wheeler (4 vols., 1933).

LEASK, NIGEL, *The Politics of Imagination in Coleridge's Critical Thought* (1988).

—— 'Pantisocracy and the politics of the "Preface" to *Lyrical Ballads*', *Reflections of Revolution: Images of Romanticism*, ed. Alison Yarrington and Kelvin Everest (1993), 39–58.

LEFEBURE, MOLLY, *The Bondage of Love: A Life of Mrs Samuel Taylor Coleridge* (1986).

LINDOP, GREVEL, *The Opium-eater: A Life of Thomas De Quincey* (1981).

LLOYD, CHARLES, *Edmund Oliver* (1798).

LOCKE, DON, *A Fantasy of Reason: The Life and Thought of William Godwin* (1980).

LOCKHART, J. G., *Memoirs of the Life of Sir Walter Scott, Bart.* (7 vols., Edinburgh and London, 1837–8).

LOGAN, EUGENIA, 'Coleridge's Scheme of Pantisocracy and American Travel Accounts', *PMLA* 45 (1930), 1069–84.

MACGILLIVRAY, J. R., 'The Pantisocracy Scheme and its Immediate Background', *Studies in English Literature by Members of the University of Toronto* (Toronto, 1931), 131–69.

MADDEN, LIONEL (ed.), *Robert Southey: The Critical Heritage* (1972).

MALTHUS, THOMAS R., *Essay on the Principle of Population* (1798; 2nd edn. 1803).

MARSHALL, PETER H., *William Godwin* (New Haven and London, 1984).

MAYO, ROBERT, 'The Contemporaneity of the Lyrical Ballads', *PMLA* 69 (1954), 486–522.

MEYERSTEIN, E. H. W., *A Life of Thomas Chatterton* (1930).

MILLS, HOWARD W., *Peacock, his Circle and his Age* (Cambridge, 1968).

MONTGOMERY, JAMES, *Memoirs*, ed. John Holland and James Everett (7 vols., 1854–6).

[MORE, HANNAH], *Cheap Repository Tracts . . .* (3 vols., 1798).

MORGAN, PETER F., *Literary Critics and Reviewers in Early Nineteenth Century Britain* (1983).

MORLEY, EDITH J., *The Life and Times of Henry Crabb Robinson* (1935).

NEWMAN, JOHN HENRY, *Apologia pro vita sua*, ed. Martin J. Svaglic (Oxford, 1967).

OWEN, ROBERT, *A New View of Society* (1818), ed. V. A. C. Gotrell (1970).

PAINE, THOMAS, *Rights of Man* (1791–2).

—— *The Age of Reason* (1797).

POLLIN, BURTON R., 'Charles Lamb and Charles Lloyd as Jacobins and Anti-Jacobins', *Studies in Romanticism*, 12 (1973), 633–47.

POTTER, STEPHEN (ed.), *Minnow among Tritons: Mrs. S. T. Coleridge's Letters to Thomas Poole* (1934).

QUILLINAN, EDWARD, *Poems* (1853).

RAIMOND, JEAN, *Robert Southey, l'homme et son temps, son œuvre, son role* (Paris, 1968).

—— 'Southey's Early Writings and the Revolution', *Yearbook of English Studies* (1989), 181–96.

RICHARDS, GEORGE, *Aboriginal Britons, a Prize Poem* (Oxford, 1791).

RICHARDSON, ALAN, *Literature, Education, Romanticism* (Oxford, 1994).

ROBINSON, HENRY CRABB, *On Books and their Writers*, ed. Edith J. Morley (3 vols., 1938).

ROE, NICHOLAS, *Wordsworth and Coleridge: The Radical Years* (Oxford, 1988).

—— *The Politics of Nature: Wordsworth and Some Contemporaries* (1992).

ROPER, DEREK, *Reviewing before the Edinburgh, 1788–1802* (1978).

St Clair, William, *The Godwins and the Shelleys: The Biography of a Family* (1989).

Sandford, Mrs Henry, *Thomas Poole and his Friends* (2 vols., 1888).

Scott, Sir Walter, *The Poetical Works*, ed. J. L. Robertson (Oxford, 1894).

—— *The Letters*, ed. H. J. C. Grierson (12 vols., 1932–7).

—— *The Journal*, ed. W. E. K. Anderson (Oxford, 1972).

Seward, Anna, *The Letters... Written between the Years 1784 and 1807* (6 vols., Edinburgh and London, 1811).

Shelley, Percy Bysshe, *Letters*, ed. Frederick L. Jones (2 vols., Oxford, 1964).

Shine, Hill and Chadwick, Helen, *The Quarterly Review Under Gifford* (Chapel Hill, 1949).

Simmons, Jack, *Southey* (1945).

Smith, Olivia, *The Politics of Language 1791–1819* (Oxford, 1984).

Storey, Mark, *'A Hold Upon Posterity': The Strange Case of Robert Southey* (Birmingham, 1993).

Strout, Alan Lang, *The Life and Letters of James Hogg, the Ettrick Shepherd* (Lubbock, Texas, 1946).

Super, R. H., *Walter Savage Landor: A Biography* (1957).

Taylor, Henry, *Autobiography* (2 vols., 1885).

—— *Correspondence*, ed. Edward Dowden (1888).

Taylor, William, *A Memoir of the Life and Writings*, ed. J. W. Robberts (2 vols., 1843).

Thale, Mary (ed.), *Selections from the Papers of the London Corresponding Society 1792–1799* (Cambridge, 1983).

Thelwall, John, *Prospectus of a Course of Lectures* (1796).

—— *Poems, Chiefly Written in Retirement* (Hereford, 1801).

Thompson, E. P., *The Making of the English Working Class* (1963).

—— *Customs in Common* (1991).

Tilney, C., 'An Unpublished Southey Fragment', *National Library of Wales Journal*, 9 (1955), 149–56.

Todd, F. M. *Politics and the Poet: A Study of Wordsworth* (1957).

Tyson, Gerald P., *Joseph Johnson: A Liberal Publisher* (Iowa City, 1979).

Wakefield, Gilbert, *The Defence of Gilbert Wakefield* [1799].

Williams, Helen Maria, *Letters Containing a Sketch of the Politics of France...* (2 vols., 1795).

Williams, Orlo, *Lamb's Friend the Census-Taker: Life and Letters of John Rickman* (1911).

—— 'A Study in Failure', *Blackwood's Edinburgh Magazine*, 189 (1911), 324–33.

Woodring, Carl, *Politics in the Poetry of Coleridge* (Madison, 1961).

—— *Politics in English Romantic Poetry* (Cambridge, Mass., 1970).

Wordsworth, William, *Poetical Works*, The Cornell Wordsworth (Ithaca, NY, 1975–89).

—— Oxford Authors vol., ed. Stephen Gill (Oxford and New York, 1984).

—— *The Prose Works*, ed. W. J. B. Owen and Jane Worthington Smyser (3 vols., Oxford, 1974).

—— *Letters of William and Dorothy Wordsworth*, rev. edn., ed. Chester L. Shaver, Mary Moorman, Alan G. Hill (4 vols., Oxford, 1967–88).

WYLIE, IAN, *Young Coleridge and the Philosophers of Nature* (Oxford, 1989).

YARBOROUGH, MINNIE, *John Horne Tooke* (New York, 1926).

INDEX

on slavery 106, 112–13, 166, 235, 257, 302, 306, 328
on society 103–4, 114, 117, 121, 124, 132, 135–6, 157–8, 185–6, 202, 206, 211, 237, 244, 248, 277
Spain and Portugal 171, 191, 192, 193, 194, 196, 211, 214, 290, 311
writes about Spain and Portugal 95–6, 200–1, 208
and stoicism 19, 24, 46, 108, 247, 257
and swimming 98, 133, 187, 195, 273, 290, 300, 308
love of theatre 3, 6
and The Times 258
and treason trials 64, 66–7
violence of language 229, 231–2, 239, 240, 243, 248, 255, 263, 271, 278, 279, 309, 313, 322
on political violence 64, 111, 117
as voice of his age 186, 188, 222, 238, 250, 251, 285, 294, 303, 318, 326
on women 32, 34, 136, 208
WRITINGS:
All for Love 314
Amadis the Gaul 155, 170, 242
Annual Anthology 122, 131, 132, 139
'The Battle of Blenheim' 123
'Bibliotheca Britannica' 160, 164
The Book of the Church 212, 285, 290, 294, 299, 303, 305
'Botany Bay Eclogues' 43, 89
'Bristol! I did not on thy well-known towers' 100
Carmen Triumphale 228, 233
'The Cataract of Lodore' 17, 234, 294–5
'Christmas Day, 1795' 84
'Consolation' 247
'Corston' 71
The Curse of Kehama 21, 87, 141, 142, 145, 155, 157, 159, 172, 180, 186, 190–1, 193, 196, 200, 201, 202, 207, 216, 218, 231
'The Deluge' 176
'The Destruction of Dom Daniel' 95, 122, 125, 126; see also Thalaba the Destroyer
'The Devil's Thoughts' 133–4
The Doctor 14, 177–8, 185, 223, 225, 230, 252, 272, 299, 302, 304, 325–6, 331

'The Ebb Tide' 123
El Cid 180, 186, 188, 196
'Elinor' 77
'English Eclogues' 43, 89, 118–19
'Epistle to Allan Cunningham' 307
'The Exiled Patriots' 49
'Fair is the rising morn' 77
The Fall of Robespierre 59–63, 67, 68, 69, 70, 71, 87, 98
'The First of June' 31
'For a Monument at Oxford' 27
'God's Judgement on a Wicked Bishop' 123–4
Harold 9
History of Brazil 183, 218, 236, 237, 250, 265, 270, 273, 274, 279
History of the Monastic Orders 304, 335, 341
History of the Peninsular War 138–9, 270, 285, 290, 297, 298, 302, 327
History of Portugal 132, 154, 155, 159, 161, 183, 220, 222, 240, 243
'The Holly Tree' 123
'Horace if ought my verse may boast of truth' 57
'Hymn to the Penates' 5, 97
'An Improbable Tale' 34–5
Joan of Arc 32, 33, 34, 40, 53, 56–7, 58, 76, 77, 79, 86, 90, 92, 97, 98, 101, 106, 109–10, 115, 116, 133, 136, 138, 145, 149, 150, 172, 218, 234, 244
'The Kalendar' 119
The Lay of the Laureate: Carmen Nuptiale 247, 260, 272
'Letter to William Smith' 258
Letters from England 105, 164, 179, 180, 183, 185–6, 216, 225
Letters Written during a Residence in Spain and Portugal 84, 92, 94, 95, 105, 110, 116
Life of John Bunyan 320
Life and Works of William Cowper 333, 335–6
Life of Nelson 211, 218, 221–2, 236, 323
'Life of Sidney' 321
'Life of Wellington' 239, 240
Life of Wesley 218, 251, 258, 265, 267, 269, 270, 272, 278, 283, 336